ALSO BY JOHN EGERTON

A Mind to Stay Here
  (with photographs by Al Clayton)

The Americanization of Dixie

Visions of Utopia

Nashville: The Faces of Two Centuries

Generations: An American Family
  (with photographs by Al Clayton)

SOUTHERN FOOD

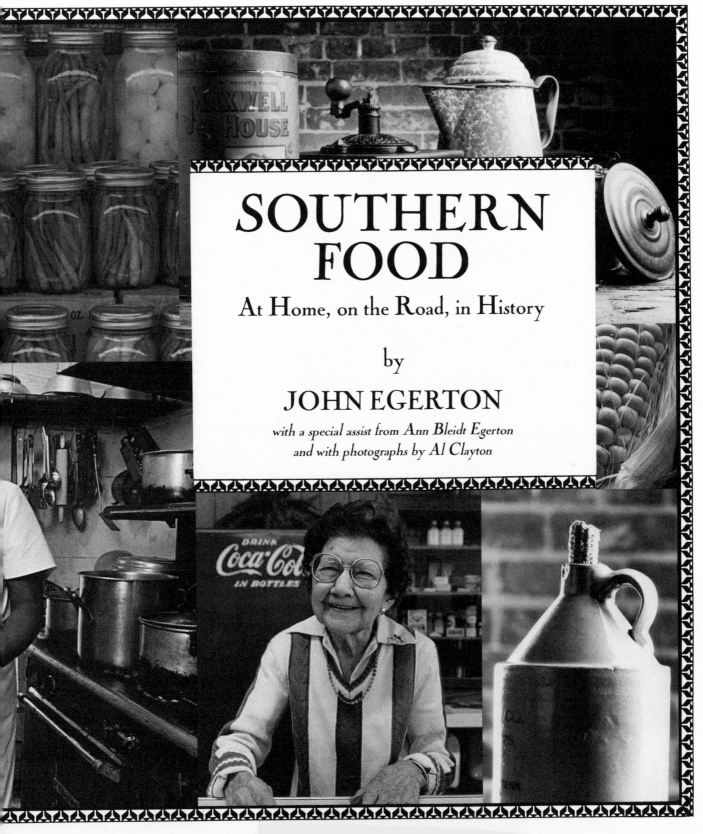

SOUTHERN FOOD

At Home, on the Road, in History

by

JOHN EGERTON

with a special assist from Ann Bleidt Egerton
and with photographs by Al Clayton

This is a Borzoi Book Published by Alfred A. Knopf, Inc.

Grateful acknowledgment is made to the following for permission to reprint previously published material:

American Heritage: Excerpts by Marshall Fishwick from *The American Heritage Cookbook and Illustrated History of American Eating and Drinking* by the editors of *American Heritage.* Copyright © 1964 by American Heritage Inc. *Arkansas Gazette:* Excerpts from the *Arkansas Gazette* by Max Brantley, June 21, 1977; Mike Trimble, April 15, 1979; and Stephen Steed, January 12, 1986. Asheville Citizen-Times Publishing Company: Excerpts from *Mountain Cooking* by John Parris. Copyright © 1978 by John Parris. Colonial Publishers: Poem by Ogden Nash from his Introduction to *The Savannah Cookbook.* Copyright 1933 by Colonial Publishers. Copyright renewed 1960 by Colonial Publishers. Reprinted by permission of Colonial Publishers, P.O. Box 112, Charleston, SC 29402. Dodd, Mead & Company, Inc.: "When De Co'n Pone's Hot" from *The Complete Poems of Paul Laurence Dunbar* by Paul Laurence Dunbar. Reprinted by permission of Dodd, Mead & Company, Inc. Harcourt Brace Jovanovich, Inc. and Harold Matson Co., Inc.: Excerpt from "A Stroke of Good Fortune" from *A Good Man Is Hard to Find* by Flannery O'Connor. Copyright 1953 by Flannery O'Connor. Copyright renewed 1981 by Mrs. Regina O'Connor. Reprinted by permission of Harcourt Brace Jovanovich, Inc. and Harold Matson Co., Inc. Little, Brown and Company and International Creative Management: The poem "Song to Grits" from *One Fell Soup: or, I'm Just a Bug on the Windshield of Life* by Roy Blount, Jr. Copyright © 1975 by Roy Blount, Jr. First appeared in *Eastern Airlines Pastimes.* Reprinted by permission of Little, Brown and Company in association with Atlantic Monthly Press and International Creative Management. *The New York Times:* Excerpts from articles by Turner Catledge, George McMillan, Tom Wicker, William E. Schmidt and Roy Reed. Copyright © 1982, 1983, 1984, 1986 by The New York Times Company. Reprinted by permission of The New York Times Company. William Morrow & Company, Inc.: "Legacies" from *My House* by Nikki Giovanni. Copyright © 1972 by Nikki Giovanni. Excerpt from *Chef Paul Prudhomme's Louisiana Kitchen* by Paul Prudhomme. Copyright © 1984 by Paul Prudhomme. Reprinted by permission of William Morrow & Company, Inc.

Library of Congress Cataloging-in-Publication Data

Egerton, John.
  Southern food.

  Bibliography: p.
  Includes index.
  1. Cookery, American—Southern style.
2. Restaurants, lunch rooms, etc.—Southern
States—Directories. I. Egerton, Ann Bleidt.
II. Clayton, Al, [date]. III. Title.
TX715.E28 1987   641.5975   86-46007
ISBN 0-394-54494-3

Manufactured in the United States of America
First Edition

Composed by Graphic Composition, Athens, Georgia. Printed and bound by Halliday Lithographers, West Hanover, Massachusetts.
Designed by Betty Anderson and Marysarah Quinn

This book is for
Mary Emma and George

and in memory of
Della and Ernest,
Elizabeth and Charles,
Berta and Percy,
and Rebecca and Graham,
who generously and lovingly
gave us our daily bread.

❧

CONTENTS

INTRODUCTION

"Take Out and Help Yourself"

The penetrating eye of the security camera at the Nashville airport revealed five cylindrical objects in my luggage. On the monitor they stood out suspiciously, ominously, like metal explosives.

"What's in the cans?" the wary attendant asked.

"Food," I replied with a casual shrug, trying hard not to seem nervous. "A couple of cans of hominy and three tins of country ham and beaten biscuits."

"Open up and let me see."

The two thirty-ounce cans of white hominy looked innocent enough, if somewhat out of place. The ham and biscuits were more imposing, but they pleaded their own defense: A delicate, unmistakably rich and appealing aroma wafted upward from the opened tin.

"Mmmmmm." The inspector exhaled, smiling.

I relaxed. At last, it was my turn to smile. "They're for some friends of mine," I explained. "I'm going to a covered-dish dinner."

The basement kitchen in Fred and Tabitha Powledge's nineteenth-century Gothic brownstone on Degraw Street in Brooklyn would not have seemed out of place in a French provincial farmhouse, or in a country home in the American South. Brooklyn, of course, is a very long way—in customs and manners and cuisine, as well as in miles—from the rural precincts of the South, not to mention France. But on that day—Tuesday, January 1, 1985—the smells and sights and sounds and tastes were all distinctly Southern. On the first day of every new year for more than a decade, a company of expatriate Southerners and their friends had gathered at the Powledges' to feast upon a communal extravagance of down-home dishes. There, for a little while, they ate and drank and reminisced in a convivial spirit of celebration, and the distances and differences that separated them from their past seemed to diminish into insignificance.

From every Southern state, and from a multiplicity of subregional backgrounds and locales, the hosts and their guests assembled a grand banquet of authentic Southern culinary treasures. There was the traditional New Year's Day good-luck vegetable, black-eyed peas, cooked with hog jowl and served with rice—an ancient dish somehow pegged with the name hoppin John—and

there was another good-luck food, collard greens, their color symbolizing money and promising rising fortunes. With them on the main table and the sideboards were such time-honored favorites as candied yams, fried okra, green beans, stewed tomatoes, cole slaw, congealed salad, ambrosia, pan-fried chicken, barbecued pork shoulder, Brunswick stew, smoked fish, roast venison, corn-bread, and hot biscuits. The drinks ranged from buttermilk to bourbon, and the desserts included pecan and sweet potato and black bottom pies, fudge brownies, and a spectacular snowball icebox cake. From the first nibbles of cheese straws and salted pecans to the last sips of boiled custard, the food was altogether worthy of the rich heritage from which it sprang.

Matalie Grant, an Alabama native who occupied a seat of honor as the senior guest at the party, seemed to speak for the others when she explained why the gathering was significant to her. "When I think of home," she said, "I think of food like this. We were raised on it. Some people say it's too rich or too sweet, but to me it's just mighty good. And I love the company it attracts. Nothing brings Southerners together like a big dinner."

The customs and traditions and impulses that lead Southerners to dine together on special occasions are frequently displayed in towns and cities all across the United States, and sometimes even in other countries. Within the South itself, no other form of cultural expression, not even music, is as distinctively characteristic of the region as the spreading of a feast of native food and drink before a gathering of kin and friends. For as long as there has been a South, and people who think of themselves as Southerners, food has been central to the region's image, its personality, and its character.

Even in the current age of declining regional identity, the food of the South is still an important matter—some would say a consuming passion—to millions of people who have spent enough time in the region to become familiar with its diverse cookery. Accents and attitudes and life-styles may change, but fondness for Southern food persists; for many people, it lingers in the mind and on the tongue as vividly as the tantalizing aroma of barbecue on the pit hangs in the air and penetrates to the core of thought and remembrance.

Edna Lewis, a native Southerner and author of *The Taste of Country Cooking,* no longer lives in rural Virginia, but it still lives in her. "Whenever I go back to visit my sisters and brothers," she wrote, "we relive old times, remembering the past. And when we share again in gathering wild strawberries, canning, rendering lard, finding walnuts, picking persimmons, making fruitcake, I realize how much the bond that held us had to do with food."

Food in the South is more than a social and cultural phenomenon; it has economic and political and religious dimensions as well. Not for cleverness alone are there books with such arresting titles as *Hog Meat and Hoecake,* or

The gathering that New Year's Day was larger than any of its predecessors. The turnout had always been pretty good, but this time the people filled two floors of the old brownstone. It sounded like one of those parties we used to have years ago in Atlanta: the frequent laughter, much of it heavy and hearty and long and obviously sincere; the upraised voices, their volume violating all the rules of polite New York cocktail-party geography and carrying across the rooms and up and down the stairs; and most of all the mellowness of the accents, as out of place in this part of Brooklyn as an Alabama license plate.

It was an annual affair, a ritual consumption of Southern foods by some of us who live in New York and who still call ourselves Southerners. It started some years ago

Hard Tomatoes, Hard Times, or *One Lord, One Faith, One Cornbread.* "High on the hog" is an expression that speaks volumes about economic good fortune, and Southern hymnals are replete with language pertaining to food and drink. Furthermore, such public events as political barbecues, community fish fries, and church dinners on the ground are venerable Southern institutions.

The South, for better or worse, has all but lost its identity as a separate place, and its checkered past now belongs to myth and memory, but its food survives—diminished, perhaps, in availability and quantity, but intact in its essence and authenticity—and at its best, it may be as good as it ever was. In the dark ages before electricity and refrigeration, it took master cooks—culinary magicians—to deliver miracles out of the kitchens of the South; now, with good directions and modern equipment, it is possible for anyone with enough interest to do almost as well, even though the quality of some foodstuffs is not as high as it used to be. When the chemistry is right, a meal in the South can still be an esthetic wonder, a sensory delight, even a mystical experience.

Kentucky historian Thomas D. Clark and Florida novelist Marjorie Kinnan Rawlings, writing from opposite ends of the South in the early 1940s, saw the same social value in the sharing of food. "Eating dinner in Kentucky," Clark wrote in his *Rivers of America* volume on the Kentucky River, "is more than a physiological refueling of the human body, it is a joyous social ritual." Rawlings, in *Cross Creek Cookery,* identified two elements in successful and happy gatherings at the table: "The food, whether simple or elaborate, must be carefully . . . willingly . . . imaginatively prepared. And the guests—friends, family or strangers—must be conscious of their welcome. . . . At the moment of dining, the assembled group stands for a little while as a safe unit, under a safe roof, against the perils and enmities of the world."

Because it is such an integral part of the culture, Southern food provides an excellent entree to the people and their times, whether those times look backward to an Old South since discredited or forward to a New South that always seems to be calling just over the horizon. To learn what has gone on in the kitchen and the dining room—and what still goes on there—is to discover much about a society's physical health, its economic condition, its race relations, its class structure, and the status of its women.

For more than two centuries, a major portion of the hard work associated with food production and preparation in the South was done by slaves. Then, for another century, Southerners black, white, young, old, male, and female often worked side by side in the fields and the kitchens to bring food to the table—but they rarely if ever sat down together to share in the fruits of the harvest. It was not uncommon then, especially in parts of the rural and small-town South, for the white men to eat first, with the women serving and the children in another room and the blacks out back. Fortunately, such divisions

when I, a native Southerner married to a tolerant Chicagoan, and Kitty Terjen, an Atlantan . . . decided to revive for ourselves the Southern tradition of eating hog jowls and black-eyed peas on the first day of the New Year. . . . Gradually, the event and the number of people who were invited to it grew, until by this time, New Year's Day, 1977, it had become something of a feast.

Fred Powledge
Journeys Through the South, 1979

are no longer in force. Not infrequently, Southern food now unlocks the rusty gates of race and class, age and sex. On such occasions, a place at the table is like a ringside seat at the historical and ongoing drama of life in the region.

Curiously, few historians or other professional South-watchers have found this subject worthy of their attention, and most of the cookbook writers have been interested only in recipes and not in the cultural history that surrounds them. There are some notable exceptions. The Time-Life regional cookbooks on Southern and Creole-Acadian cooking, historian Joe Gray Taylor's *Eating, Drinking, and Visiting in the South,* the scholarship of Sam Bowers Hilliard and Thomas D. Clark, the food books of Richard and Rima Collin, and a seventy-five-year-old period piece, Martha McCulloch-Williams' *Dishes and Beverages of the Old South,* all come quickly to mind. So do Edna Lewis' book, mentioned above; *Spoonbread and Strawberry Wine,* by Norma Jean and Carole Darden; and *Kentucky Hospitality,* edited by Dorothea C. Cooper. Some other food writers, notably John and Karen Hess, Waverley Root, Richard J. Hooker, Raymond Sokolov, Evan and Judith Jones, and the editors of *The American Heritage Cookbook,* have made Southern cookery an integral part of broader studies. But by and large, Southern history has seldom held the attention of cookbook writers, and Southern food has been ignored by most historians.

The reasons for these oversights are not clear. Perhaps the historians have been too busy with the larger questions of war and peace and power to give much thought to the dinner table. Perhaps the cookbook writers, so intent on getting the recipes right, haven't had the time or the inclination to determine where the dishes came from or how and why some have gained favor over others. Perhaps the historic and pervasive strain of discrimination against blacks and women in the society ordained that their enormous contributions to American foodways would be neglected and devalued. Or perhaps it is simply too hard to be serious about so joyful a subject as good food—and too hard to be joyful about a subject so fraught with blood, sweat, and ambiguity. Whatever the case, the fact is that relatively little has been written about the importance of food in the social and cultural evolution of the South.

When the school segregation issue was taken up by the federal court in Charlotte, the school board was ordered to give people in the community a chance to have their say. I was involved with a group called the Quality Education Committee, and we decided to contact the various interest groups to see if a consensus could be formed around a workable desegregation plan.

Fools rush in. "The primary requisite for writing well about food is a good appetite," declared A. J. Liebling, who wrote exceedingly well about many things. Seizing upon his remark as an invitation, I have disregarded my lack of formal credentials as either a historian or a cook and entered the arena, armed only with my license as a professional writer and my fifty years of experience as a Southern eater. Taking up pen and fork, I have set about to examine this serious subject in a lighthearted manner, and to explore this most enjoyable activity with the utmost seriousness. If, as the sages have said, we are what we eat, then perhaps there are clues here that can help to explain who and what the people of this region are, as Southerners and as Americans.

There have been books in abundance about the mind of the South, the heart of the South, the soul of the South; perhaps it is time for some lower anatomy, some gastronomical interpretation—such as this layman's journal, a critical, quizzical, occasionally comical look at the stomach of the South.

The familiar staples of Southern cooking—the pork and cornbread, the grits and greens and yams, the cornucopia of sweets—are clearly present in these pages; they are, in fact, prominently displayed. But so are many other elements that give Southern cuisine much more variety than it is commonly thought to have. There are plenty of all-Southern dishes, of course—the book would not be complete without a treatise on fried chicken or an essay on barbecue—but there are numerous subregional specialties here as well.

From the Atlantic Seaboard and the Gulf Coast to the Appalachians and the Ozarks, from the river deltas to the rolling piedmont hills, there is a wealth of gastronomic diversity in the South. The food is not just Southern; in a historical sense, at least, it is also Indian, British, African, Hispanic, Creole, Acadian, French, German, Greek, Italian, even Asian. The South has rich food, poor food, new food, old food, hot food, cold food, fast food, slow food. It has all the main meats that humans eat, a comprehensive abundance of vegetables and fruits, a tantalizing extravagance of sauces and gravies, a rich array of seasoning herbs and spices, the tastiest of hot breads, its own noted beers and wines and whiskeys, and an incurable sweet tooth that is justifiably renowned far beyond the region. Around Southern food there are elaborate rituals, endless stories, and enticing secrets, kept and shared. In sum, there is everything that is needed to turn raw ingredients into a finished creation, whether the end product is intended to be a seven-course dinner, a warmed-over casserole, or a good book. In pursuit of the last, I have organized this offering into three major parts:

❖ Pass and Repast, a historical and contemporary overview of Southern food traditions;
❖ Eating Out, a series of shorter reports on public dining in the South in the mid-1980s;
❖ Eating In, a representative collection of classic Southern recipes, with background information on their origin and evolution in Southern cookery.

In addition, there are more than 200 excerpted quotes and self-contained vignettes on Southern food in the margins throughout the book, as well as an annotated bibliography of more than 250 cookbooks and other resource materials in the back. And, in support of all these elements, there are many distinctive black and white images created by Atlanta photographer Al Clayton.

After exploring the subject of Southern food intensively in kitchens and restaurants and libraries at home and on the road for more than a year and a

There were some very conservative antibusing people, liberal whites, outspoken blacks, and so forth—mortal enemies, you might say—and getting them to associate with one another at all was a big problem. Our idea was to invite representatives of all the groups to a covered-dish dinner, thinking that regardless of race or politics or whatever, Southerners have always been brought up to be nice at the table.

So Betsy Bennett and I wrote letters to the groups, and when the time came we met in the school board conference room. About fifty people showed up, and members of the Quality Education Committee brought the food. I don't remember what we had to eat. I guess I was too nervous to think about that. Everyone was ill at ease at first, but soon after we sat down you could feel the conversation level rising in the room. It was a very pleasant sound, and it told us that our idea was working.

That turned out to be the most close-knit group I've ever been a part of. We don't meet anymore—that was ten years ago—but I think we all must remember that first evening we spent together around the table. Maybe we should have a reunion dinner.

*Maggie Ray,
Charlotte, North Carolina,
in a 1985 interview*

half, I have tried in these pages to fill some of the open space that exists between cookbooks that disregard history and histories that ignore food. The balance point between the two is not easy to find. Twenty months is certainly long enough to gain some insight on Southern food, to locate and catalogue resources pertaining to it, and even to write in a limited way about it—but to master the subject, and to write a comprehensive and authoritative book on food in Southern history, would take much longer. The volume at hand should be understood for what it is: a resident Southerner's moderately well-informed but decidedly nonexpert view of eating in the South.

There are many things the book is *not*. It is not a scholarly history, nor a restaurant guide, nor a cookbook, though it does contain elements of all three. It is not a treatise on dieting, exercise, natural foods, or nutrition. It is simply a book about what the people of the South have eaten down through the years, and how those foods have become a part of the region's character.

The principal essay, Pass and Repast, ranges over four centuries of Southern history to examine both light and serious questions about the role of food in social and cultural life. Race, sex, politics, and religion are part of the picture; pork and corn are too, from Jamestown in 1607 to restaurants and home kitchens throughout the South in 1986.

The Eating Out section is based on eight months of extensive travel through Alabama, Arkansas, Florida, Georgia, Kentucky, Louisiana, Mississippi, North Carolina, South Carolina, Tennessee, and Virginia. (Parts of Texas, Oklahoma, Missouri, West Virginia, and Maryland might well have been included, but the added driving and the limitations of time kept me away.) Sometimes alone, but usually with my wife, Ann Egerton, and frequently with the added benefit of Al Clayton's sharp photographic vision, I accumulated a large body of research materials, ate out more than three hundred times, and wrote these reports on the present state of the ancient art of public dining in the region.

Eating In is about home cooking—some of mine, a little bit of other people's, and a lot of Ann's. From a multitude of sources, we selected the dishes we wanted to consider for inclusion and then, by trial and error and retrial, we finally chose the recipes to present here as a representative sample of traditional Southern cooking at its best. For everything that works, I give Ann full credit. She is an experienced and accomplished cook, and I am a novice; there is hardly a culinary skill short of boiling water that I can truly say I learned without her help. For everything here that falls short of the high quality we strived to attain I accept full responsibility, since the final selections rested with me.

All along the way, there were many hard choices to make. Some were simply matters of taste, others involved complex logistical decisions, still others were a consequence of having far more good material to use than a single noncomprehensive volume could contain. In the end, both the recipes and the restaurants that made it into the book were subjectively chosen on the basis of personal preference, not by any scale or measure of objective worth.

One further choice—between moderation and abstinence—was not hard for me to make. Few of the dishes described in these pages would qualify as health foods; many contain more sugar or salt or cream or butter or grease than most nutritionists would be likely to recommend. But just as there is no diet plan here, neither is the book a trencherman's guide. It should be possible for prudent people who exercise properly to eat moderate amounts of this food and live long and happy lives. For those who eat Southern food with such restraint, long is an expectation; happy is virtually a promise.

Finally, the hardest question of all: Is Southern food, like the South itself, losing its distinctiveness and its identity in the smothering embrace of modern American culture—or could it be that when the last vestiges of Southernness have faded into oblivion, there will still exist somewhere in the region a few more steaming bowls of black-eyed peas and fried okra and turnip greens, a few more cuts of genuine country ham, a few more hot buttered biscuits, a few more slices of pecan pie, and a remnant of surviving Southerners to enjoy them?

You will not find the answer here. I can only tell you what I have seen and experienced in twenty months of immersion, what I have heard from others, what I have eaten, and what I thought of it all.

The signs are mixed. There is some bad food out there—a lot of it, in fact—and there is evidence everywhere that fast is overcoming slow, artificial is overwhelming real, and new is putting old in jeopardy. But in spite of the inroads being made by such pale-imitation substitutes as chicken in a sack, potatoes in a box, and biscuits in a can, there remain many individual cooks, public and private, and many restaurant owners who still believe in taking the time and using the right ingredients and methods to prepare great old Southern dishes the way they were meant to be made. Those foods and the people who create them have stood the test of time; like Faulkner's heroes, they endure.

I have tried here to pay honor to some of the outstanding cooks and recipes and restaurants in Southern history. All of them deserve to be remembered beyond their time, and the best among them have already attained a certain immortality among those whom they have served. Whether the best Southern cooks and Southern foods will still be celebrated beyond our time and that of our children is one of those deep speculations that can only be pondered.

In the meantime, here is my report of what we found in the kitchens and dining rooms and restaurants of the South. There is more than enough to keep prudent eaters busy and happy for a long time to come. So have a seat—and as the mother of one of my boyhood friends in Kentucky used to say whenever I happened to show up at dinnertime, "Take out and help yourself."

We had the first of a very relaxed and informal series of meals with our family. Earlier, when Rosalynn was visiting the White House, some of our staff asked the chef and cooks if they thought that they could prepare the kind of meals which we enjoyed in the South, and the cook said, "Yes, Ma'am, we've been fixing that kind of food for the servants for a long time!"

entry in President Jimmy Carter's White House diary, January 20, 1977

HAMPTON COU
ANNUAL

WATERMEL
FESTIVA

PASS AND REPAST:

A Gastronomical View of the South

When they stepped ashore at the place they named Jamestown on May 14, 1607, after almost twenty-one weeks at sea, Captains Christopher Newport and John Smith and the 118 men who had sailed with them from England came face to face with the local residents, members of the Powhatan tribe of Algonquian Indians. Accounts of their meeting differ, but this much is undisputed: The men from England had with them some domesticated pigs—a boar and a few sows—and the Indians had several kinds of food made from maize, the universal vegetable we now know as corn. There on a riverbank in the wilderness of Virginia, Old World and New World inhabitants thus brought together, perhaps for the first time, two of the oldest, most basic, and most vital food sources ever known in human history.

Pigs and corn. Hog meat and hominy. Pork and pone. Separately, the meat of the hog and the grain of the cornstalk have enriched the diet of people around the world for at least eight thousand years. In combination, they have meant the difference between life and death for individuals, families, even entire communities. In the American South, no other edible substances have meant more to the populace in nearly four centuries of history than pork and corn.

The meeting of English and Indian people at Jamestown and the subsequent intermingling of their foods marked the beginning of American cookery, and more specifically, the regional cookery of the South—although there may be more symbolic mythology than historical accuracy in the suggestion that pork and corn came together for the first time in Virginia. Corn was cultivated in the Americas at least 2500 years before the arrival of Europeans in the fifteenth century; as for pigs, the Spanish explorer Hernando de Soto is said to have had thirteen of them aboard ship when he and a party of men landed near present-day Tampa on the west coast of Florida in 1539, and Hernando Cortez and the conquistadors reportedly took pigs with them when they invaded Mexico earlier in the sixteenth century.

But unprecedented or not, the Jamestown union seems a good and proper beginning for a story about Southern food. Virginia, after all, was the first English colony in what was to become the United States, and the foods of the Algonquians and the British, more than those of the Spanish, were the bases upon which American and Southern cookery was built. And in any case, pork and corn have always been supremely important to the diet of all Americans—and absolutely essential to the diet of Southerners.

The first voyage of Columbus to the Americas was a 115-year-old memory when the Jamestown party reached Virginia in three small ships. Like other colonization attempts before it, the Jamestown venture was a daily struggle on the brink of disaster. There were adventures and excitement in the colony, of course, and there were some vital successes, but the hardships were many, and the company of settlers was seriously diminished by disease, warfare, and "starving times." At one point, the remnant of survivors boarded ship for a desperate attempt to return to England, only to meet an incoming supply fleet in the harbor. The colony endured; England's uninterrupted presence on the continent began there, and its eventual success in the European race for dominion over America finally meant that this new colony and the nation that sprang from it would live under English law, speak the English language, and eat English-style foods.

The settlers brought horses, cattle, goats, sheep, and chickens, as well as pigs; they brought wheat, rye, barley, oats; they brought apples and turnips and cabbage; they brought wine, brandy, rum, and malt brew. They were a meat- and bread-eating, beer-drinking people. The ones who lasted in the harsh and demanding frontier environment tended in the main to be not aristocrats of the leisure class but artisans and merchants and craftsmen who aspired to wealth. They were mostly city people, not farmers; they had a lot to learn about life in the wild.

And it was the Indians who taught them. In spite of periodic hostilities that took many lives on both sides, the Indians adjusted time and time again to the intrusive presence of the whites, and finally they yielded to white power. But first, in a spirit of generosity, they shared the bounty of nature with their white brothers, and taught them how to use it.

The list of native American foods in seventeenth-century Virginia is long and impressive. There were many varieties of beans and peas; there were pumpkins, squash, onions, wild greens; there were blackberries, raspberries, blueberries, and vast quantities of strawberries; plums, cherries, damsons, and fox grapes (also called muscadines and scuppernongs) abounded; and in the woods and waters, the Indians harvested an astonishing array of meat and seafood—turkeys, possums, deer, rabbits, squirrels, ducks, geese, pigeons, turtles, oysters, crabs, shrimp, clams, catfish, trout, herring, mullet, shad—more than two hundred varieties of food from the waters, and nearly as many more from the land.

Corn was first and foremost in this plenteous catalogue of foodstuffs. The Powhatans had been cultivating it for so long (and so had others in widely scattered parts of North and South America) that they had no memory of its origin. They made from it suppone, appone, samp, succotash, rockahominy— forms of bread, porridge, and combination dishes that became fixtures in the diet of the immigrant population and are known now by such names as ashcake, hoecake, corn dodgers, cornpone, cornbread, big hominy, and hominy grits. The Indians also cooked unshucked ears of green corn in hot coals—and these "roasting ears" were an immediate favorite with the newcomers.

Through more than one winter of famine, the white pioneers relied almost entirely on corn from the Indians for their survival. There were times, too—

*A SHORT DESCRIPTION
OF THE VIRGINIA COLONY*

The Situation of Virginia [in the mid-1600s] *is remarkably happy and convenient, having the River* Potowmac *upon the North-east, the Atlantic Ocean on the East, the Province of Carolina on the South, and the Apalachian Mountains on the West, which separate it from* Florida. . . . *As to Animals, there were neither Horses, Cows, Sheep, or Swine before the coming of the English, but they have now plenty of them all.* . . . *As to Birds . . . they have wild Turkies very large, some of them weighing forty Pounds.* . . . *As to Fish, no Country in the World has greater Plenty . . . Trouts . . . Flounders . . . Mullets . . . Oysters, Crabs . . . Shrimps.* . . . *Their Fruits are, Grapes of several Kinds, Cherries of various Sorts, Plumbs from the Bigness of a Damson to that of a Pear; Peaches in such Plenty that in some Places they feed their Hogs with them, Quinces in abundance, and Apples and Pears in as great Plenty as can be wished. Their Corn is of two sorts, English Wheat . . . and Maize, or Indian Corn, which . . . grows in a great Ear or Head as big as the Handle of a large Horse-whip.*

Voyages and Travels,
edited by John Harris, 1748

most notably in 1622—when the persistent raiding of Indian cornfields by the whites led to bloodshed and killing. In the most literal sense, corn was a symbol of both life and death in colonial Virginia.

And then there was pork. As soon as breeding and British supply ships could provide an adequate number of pigs, they were eaten regularly and with pleasure by English and Indians alike. From snout to tail, the pig was a walking meat market. It roamed free, feeding on nuts and roots and scraps, and when slaughtered it yielded enough ham, bacon, lard, and other foods to satisfy a multitude. Pots of beans and peas were flavored with chunks of pork fat. The meat was either eaten fresh—stewed, fried, roasted (barbecued)—or preserved by salting, smoking, or pickling. In whatever form, it was the primary domesticated meat of the colony, and considering its versatility, it was at least as important to daily survival as wild game and seafood.

Most of these gastronomic discoveries and interminglings took place in the first two decades of the Jamestown colony, or so it seems from the various historical accounts. The abundance and diversity of game and fish and other exotic new foods gave great encouragement to the colonists, even causing some of them to portray Virginia as a garden paradise. But as impressive as the botany and zoology were, they could not disguise the harshness and danger of colonial life. By 1625, only about 1500 immigrants could be counted at Jamestown, even though four or five times that many had crossed the Atlantic. All the others had either died of disease, starvation, warfare, or other violent causes, or had returned to England in discouragement.

Furthermore, in the beginning, the great natural wonders of the land and sea and their implications for gastronomy may have been largely lost on the Englishmen, for few of them knew much about cooking. All of those who came to Jamestown in 1607 were Caucasian men and boys, recruited or conscripted agents of a private trading company; a few women came in the next decade, but it was not until 1619 that an appreciable number joined the colony. Curiously enough, the first dozen years of English and Indian sharing of foodstuffs and foodways was essentially an exchange between a small tribe of male and female farmers, fishers, and hunters and an even smaller company of white males.

The year 1619 was also significant for another development at Jamestown. That summer, a Dutch privateer dropped anchor in the harbor, and its captain sold the colonists about fifteen indentured servants from Africa. They were the first blacks to be brought to the North American continent.

European and Indian and African, white and red and black, male and female, free and slave—these were the foundations of early Virginia society established by an English company of free-enterprise traders between 1607 and 1624 and nurtured to a state of virtual self-sufficiency by the British crown over the next quarter century. The arrival of women from England and blacks from Africa changed Jamestown from a commercial trade outpost to a permanent colony committed to both family life and slavery. Having gained at least a measure of control over the native Indian population, the white males of Virginia then brought to the colony some British women, over whom they already claimed authority, and a new class of subjects: the first trickle of what would become a flood of African slaves. For another century and a half—until the American Revolution—these social patterns would remain in place; indeed, they would not be changed substantially until the Civil War.

It was in this crucial first generation of English occupation that the character of the Virginia colony was shaped, and with it the character of its cooking. By 1650, the number of colonists there had reached fifteen thousand, exceeding the population of Indians; of blacks, there were only three hundred. But the English system of stratified social classes was very much in evidence: On the basis of sex, race, religion, occupation, land ownership, or simply the favor of the crown, a few residents held permanent advantage over the many. In the kitchens as in the larger society, social class governed; women of the upper echelon directed the work of white indentured servants or black slaves, and these lower-class workers learned to prepare and serve elegant and elaborate meals that bore no resemblance to the often meager and monotonous diet of the poor. To be sure, there was a small middle class of whites who managed without servants or slaves, but all aspired to wealth and leisure, and the life of the privileged gentry came to personify the "good life" in Virginia and the South.

From Africa with the people in bondage came new foods: okra, black-eyed peas (also called cowpeas), collard greens, yams, benne seed (the mystical and luck-bringing sesame), and watermelons. From Central and South America, meanwhile—sometimes by circuitous routes through Europe and Africa and Asia—came hot and sweet peppers, peanuts, tomatoes, lima beans, chocolate, white potatoes, and sweet potatoes, the latter a look-alike nonrelative of the yam. (Tomatoes would need nearly two centuries to overcome completely the myth that they were poisonous "love apples.") Up from Florida came oranges and peaches, natives of China brought to the New World by the Spanish.

With eggs from the chickens, milk and butter from the cows, honey from native and imported bees ("white man's flies," the Indians called them), native black walnuts and pecans, and syrup extracted by the Indians from the sap of maple trees, colonial cooks enriched and expanded the diet. The food of Virginia gradually took on a distinctive character as English and Indian and African cooks all contributed from their diverse experiences. To the rather dull and plain cookery of sixteenth-century England they added American foodstuffs, Indian harvesting and cooking knowledge, African tastes and seasonings, and

Among the gentry of Virginia, black women slaves traditionally did the cooking. They had brought with them from Africa long familiarity with a number of hitherto little known products whose very use came to characterize southern cookery: gumbo, eggplant, field peas, benne (an African name for sesame), yams (which resemble New World sweet potatoes in culinary use, although not at all related), and possibly tomatoes. Among other products, sorghum and watermelon came from Africa, and bananas were known there.

In addition, many of these black cooks had passed through the way station of the West Indies—or knew those who had—where they picked up a number of dishes . . . and tricks of seasoning from the exuberant Creole cuisines of the islanders. . . .

These Creole cuisines were to color Virginia cookery to an extent which has not been fully appreciated, I think, because in addition to actual borrowings, there is the thumb print that each cook leaves on a recipe.

Karen Hess, in her 1984 Historical Notes and Commentaries on Mary Randolph's The Virginia House-Wife, 1824

such Spanish, French, Dutch, and German touches as managed to penetrate the English circle of colonial power. Within fifty years of the founding of Jamestown, a distinctly American cookery was beginning to emerge, and Virginia's contribution to it was substantial.

Maryland and Delaware were founded in the 1630s and the Carolinas were established by 1670, and all of these new entities developed foodways similar to Virginia's. Most cooking was done in the open fireplace in iron pots and kettles brought from Europe. As life became more settled and the upper class increased its comfort, food took on more of a social function. In the expansion westward and southward, plantations rose to dominate the agricultural economy, and ever-increasing numbers of slaves were imported to do the back-breaking work in the vast fields of cotton, tobacco, rice, and indigo. More slaves filled the kitchens, too, and because of them upper-class white women could devote their time to household planning and management rather than cooking.

The cuisine of the South between 1650 and the time of the Revolution is remembered in the history books and the cookbooks primarily as the cuisine of the upper class. The best food was labor-intensive; home-grown, personally selected for ripeness and freshness, painstakingly prepared, elegantly served, it was more than a meal—it was a show, a performance. Hospitality was the hallmark of every well-to-do household. Guests came by the score, often staying for days, sometimes for weeks. They drank fine wines imported from Europe, ate with imported silver on imported porcelain, and delighted in European and American dishes seasoned with imported spices. Virginia hams, cured and aged at Smithfield and other locations, were already prized delicacies coveted in London. The great bounty of the Southern coastal waters astounded guests and residents alike. English breads and sweets were expertly duplicated, and then augmented with wonderful new hot breads and desserts created in colonial kitchens. It was, in the opinion of some food historians, the golden age of American foodstuffs.

British influence was predominant but not exclusive. At Charleston, French Huguenots made a significant culinary contribution, and at Mobile and New Orleans on the Gulf Coast, French settlers imprinted their native foodways as soon as they arrived early in the eighteenth century. Florida, claimed by the Spanish long before Jamestown, reflected that heritage in its eating habits. But everywhere, it was primarily the presence of slave labor that determined the quality and quantity of fine food. White mistresses may have had favorite recipes they prepared themselves, but wherever there was sumptuous hospitality and elegant service and distinctive cookery, there was almost certain to be a platoon of black cooks and servants to do the lion's share of work.

In the South especially, a home-grown variety of aristocrats had gained power by the middle of the eighteenth century. They were the landed gentry,

All over the Colony, a universal Hospitality reigns; full Tables and open Doors, the kind Salute, the generous Detention, speak somewhat like the old Roast-beef Ages of our Fore-fathers. . . . Strangers are sought after with Greediness, as they pass the Country, to be invited. Their Breakfast Tables have generally the cold Remains of the former Day, hash'd or fricasseed; Coffee, Tea, Chocolate, Venison-pasty, Punch, and Beer, or Cyder, upon one Board; their Dinner, good Beef, Veal, Mutton, Venison, Turkies and Geese, wild and tame, Fowls, boil'd and roasted; and perhaps somewhat more, as Pies, Puddings, &c., for Dessert: Suppers the same, with some small Addition, and a good hearty Cup to precede a Bed of Down: And this is the constant life they lead, and to this Fare every Comer is welcome.

an observing Traveller in Virginia, writing to the London Magazine, *1746*

the planter class, the slave-owning minority, and they effectively controlled the settled areas from Virginia to Louisiana. Their ancestors in Virginia and the Carolinas had come largely from the middle range of English society, or even from the class of indentured servants, rather than from the aristocracy, but these colonial estate holders were the beneficiaries of a century and a half of upward mobility. While democracy and equality were not entirely alien notions in their experience, most of them were far more charmed by the privileges and comforts of wealth. The richest of them lived opulent lives that rivaled those of European nobility. And to support such extravagance, they kept increasing the slave population.

The numbers are dramatic. In the mid-1600s, there were slightly more slaves in the Northern colonies than in the South, but in both areas the total was under a thousand. A century later, fifty thousand Africans lived in slavery in the North, but the numbers were ten times higher in the South. By 1860, on the eve of the Civil War, four million black people lived in bondage in the United States, and almost all of them were in the Southern states.

It was in this same period of explosive growth in the slave population—roughly from 1750 to 1860—that the hospitality and cuisine of the South reached its apex. Throughout the eleven-state region that would eventually become the rebellious Confederacy, and in Kentucky and Maryland and a few other border regions as well, a seemingly endless procession of the finest in native and imported foods and beverages passed before the plantation gentry and their many guests. Here was the very essence of a grand style that came to be renowned as Southern hospitality, a style of gracious and elegant living that up to that time was unmatched in the American nation.

It is difficult to reconcile the glory of the feast with the ignominy of slavery. To praise the food, and then to say that such dining excellence would not have been possible without slave labor, seems almost to amount to an endorsement of slavery itself. But there is another consideration: To throw out the superlative dishes of the colonial and antebellum periods because of their association with slavery would be to ignore the creative genius of generations of black cooks, and thus to discredit one of the truly outstanding achievements in American social history.

In the most desolate and hopeless of circumstances, blacks caught in the grip of slavery often exhibited uncommon wisdom, beauty, strength, and creativity. The kitchen was one of the few places where their imagination and skill could have free rein and full expression, and there they often excelled. From the elegant breads and meats and sweets of plantation cookery to the inventive genius of Creole cuisine, from beaten biscuits to bouillabaisse, their legacy of culinary excellence is all the more impressive, considering the extremely adverse conditions under which it was compiled.

Though you expected nought to eat,
We could have given you some Meat,
Veal that had sucked two well-fed Cows,
Lamb that was fattened in a House,
Bacon well-fed on Indian Corn,
And Chicken crammed both Night & Morn,
Sturgeon likewise adorned the Board,
Of Pears we had a monstrous Hoard.
Half ate, and half untouched remained
For scanty messes we disdained.
Next Strawberries in View appear,
And Apple Tarts bring up the Rear.
These Dainties too were one half left.
Madeira filled each Chink & Cleft.
We ate, we drank, we went to Bed,
And slept as though we all were Dead.

St. George Tucker,
Williamsburg, Virginia, 1781

For many years after slavery began in this country, the contribution of black cooks—indeed, their very presence in the kitchens of the wealthy—was virtually ignored in cookbooks and other places of public record. Much later, in the decades following the Civil War, it became fashionable to regard the new generation of kitchen help with benign indulgence. They were "turbaned mammies" and "voodoo magicians" and "tyrants" who ruled the back rooms with simpleminded power; they could work culinary miracles day in and day out, but couldn't for the life of them tell anyone how they did it. Their most impressive dishes were described as "accidental" rather than planned. Their speech, humorously conveyed in demeaning dialect in many an old cookbook, came across as illiterate folk knowledge, not really funny and not to be taken seriously.

In more recent times these historic injustices have been lessened, though not completely eliminated; blacks, too, write cookbooks now, and have since early in this century, and books about American and Southern food customarily give full credit to its many creators. But the comprehensive history of black achievement in American cookery still waits to be written. From frontier cabins to plantation houses to the White House, from steamboat galleys and Pullman kitchens to public barbecues and fish fries and private homes without number, black chefs and cooks and servants have elevated the art of American cookery and distinguished themselves in the process, and they and all other Americans need to see the story fully told.

Not all blacks have been great cooks, of course, and not all great cooks have been black. Stereotypes die hard, whether they are positive or negative—and both extremes tend to be far removed from the truth. It is worth remembering that most Southern whites did not own slaves in the colonial and antebellum periods and did not have black servants after the Civil War—but almost all of them, regardless of economic status, knew the pleasures of good home cooking, Southern style.

Not all great cooks have been women, either, but until recently, the role of cook was one society expected women to play, whether they wanted to or not. Kitchen work and the other housekeeping and "motherly" chores were generally considered to be *The Whole Duty of a Woman*, as a 1737 book title from London put it. From the earliest colonial times in this country, white women above the poverty level were assumed to have but one "proper place," and that was in the home. They were supposed to marry, to have children, and to take care of the domestic chores, either by their own labor or by planning and managing the work of slaves or servants. The better off they were financially and socially, the less physical labor (other than childbearing) they were supposed to do. One of the most fascinating and ironic indicators of the pervasiveness of this social pattern was the spate of post–Civil War cookbooks aimed at white women who found themselves quite literally help-less after the Civil War.

The close-fisted stinginess that fed the poor slave on coarse cornmeal and tainted meat . . . wholly vanished on approaching the sacred precincts of the Great House itself. . . . Immense wealth and its

The white woman's assigned place, though far more comfortable and less confining than that of the slaves, was nonetheless compulsory. In a sense, white women and blacks were both held captive in the kitchens of early America, especially in the South—blacks by the bonds of slavery and segregation, white women by the social and cultural expectations of the male hierarchy. The kitchen, in fact, was one of the few places where either blacks or women could let their guard down and be themselves. Almost everywhere else, they had to conform to binding roles that stifled expression and killed creativity, but in the kitchen, they could be extravagant, artistic, whimsical, assertive, even sensuous. The proof was in their irresistible cookery. Herein may lie the ultimate explanation for the natural superiority of Southern food.

Cookbooks tend to keep their social and cultural clues discreetly buried between the lines, but when they can be uncovered they may be useful barometers of a society's tastes and priorities and values. The first American and Southern cookbooks are especially revealing of the times and conditions from which they came.

In 1742, a printer in Williamsburg, Virginia, named William Parks issued the first cookbook ever published in America. *The Compleat Housewife; or, Accomplish'd Gentlewoman's Companion*, by E. (Eliza) Smith, had first been published in London in 1727; the American version was an abridgment of the fifth edition of that work. No attempt was made to adapt the recipes to the American kitchen; instead, the book simply provided Virginia readers with an organized collection of foods the way they were prepared in upper-class English homes.

A few years later, in 1747, another cookbook from London reached Virginia, and within a short time it had become the most widely used and influential recipe book in the colonies. *The Art of Cookery, Made Plain and Easy* was written "By a Lady" whose name was Hannah Glasse. (For a long time to come, women often felt compelled to write books anonymously or to disguise their sex by the use of initials or male pseudonyms.) In her introduction, Mrs. Glasse defined her book's purpose as giving simple instructions to servants on the higher art of cooking and serving fine food to the gentry.

Most of the recipe collections of American cooks in the colonies were private manuscripts written with pen and ink. Some have survived as family heirlooms passed down from generation to generation; the best of them, like personal diaries, are valuable profiles of people and their times. Rarely have these artifacts found their way into print. One that has is the receipt book of Harriott Pinckney Horry, a South Carolina plantation lady who began recording cooking and housekeeping notes in 1770, when she was twenty-two years old, and continued the practice until a few years before her death in 1830. (Her mother, Eliza Lucas Pinckney, also kept a collection of recipes and home

lavish expenditures filled the Great House with all that could please the eye or tempt the taste. Fish, flesh, and fowl, were here in profusion. Chickens of all breeds, ducks of all kinds . . . guinea fowls, turkeys, geese, and peafowls . . . partridges, quails, pheasants, pigeons. . . . Beef, veal, mutton, and venison. . . . The teeming riches of the Chesapeake Bay, its rock perch, drums, crocus, trout, oysters, crabs and terrapin, were drawn hither to adorn the glittering table. The dairy, too . . . poured its rich donations of fragrant cheese, golden butter, and delicious cream to heighten the attractions of the gorgeous, unending round of feasting. . . . The tender asparagus, the crispy celery, and the delicate cauliflower, eggplants, beets, lettuce, parsnips, peas, and French beans, early and late; radishes, cantaloupes, melons of all kinds; and the fruits of all climes and of every description, from the hardy apples of the North to the lemon and orange of the South, culminated at this point. Here were gathered figs, raisins, almonds, and grapes from Spain, wines and brandies from France, teas of various flavor from China, and rich, aromatic coffee from Java, all conspiring to swell the tide of high life, where pride and indolence lounged in magnificence and satiety.

Frederick Douglass
Life and Times of Frederick Douglass, 1892

remedies; one of her handwritten books, dated 1756, is now in a museum in Charleston.)

The Horry book, published for the first time in 1984, contains an essay by food historian Richard J. Hooker that skillfully sketches the work's historical context. The manuscript's 124 receipts, as South Carolina women are still fond of calling their recipes, are an interesting blend of English and American tastes, with a bit of French flavor thrown in. As the reigning mistress of Hampton Plantation, a thriving center of rice production some forty miles up the coast from Charleston, Harriott Horry led a busy life as a hostess and manager; though she undoubtedly did little cooking herself, she obviously knew how. The entries in her book were recorded 160 years and more after the settlement of Jamestown, but only a few older collections of Southern recipes can still be found, even in museums and private manuscript repositories.

Mrs. Horry recorded instructions for making butter, vinegar, and yeast, for curing pork and beef, for preserving tomatoes (no fear of "love apples" here), and for pickling a variety of fruits, vegetables, and meats. She gave directions for making spruce beer, cherry brandy, and Duke of Norfolk Punch, a potent concoction containing rum, citrus fruits, sugar, and egg whites. Syllabub, a frothy wine and cream dessert long popular in England, is another of the entries. There is no cornbread, but there are journey cakes (a "pocket" bread served to travelers in England) and rice loaves and unleavened biscuits similar to a kind that would come to be known as beaten biscuits. There is a French *daube* (a covered casserole), a "pidgion" stew, a beef and rice "pye," and a spicy stuffed crab. There are numerous jams and marmalades and preserves, and for dessert there are "mackaroons," gingerbread, cheese cakes, egg pies, a variety of "pudings," and something called Cocoa Nut Puffs, a baked confection made with grated fresh coconut, sugar, butter, and eggs.

All in all, it is an impressive showcase of foods for upper-class South Carolinians—and it seems a very long remove from Jamestown.

Twenty-six years after Harriott Horry started keeping her private book of recipes, a slender volume called *American Cookery* was published in Hartford, Connecticut, by Amelia Simmons, "an American orphan." It is remembered now as the first cookbook to be written by an American for American readers, and it includes a goodly number of early American—and Southern—favorites: roast turkey, chicken pie, Indian pudding, apple pie, bread pudding, rice pudding, hoecake, pound cake, cucumber pickles. What is perhaps most interesting about the Simmons volume is not its contents but the fact that it took almost two centuries for food fanciers on this side of the Atlantic to get some of their own recipes into print. Up to that time, every cookbook that was available in America was English through and through—and there were precious few of them.

YAM PUDING

Take a pound of Yams boil'd dry, beat it fine in a mortar with a pound Butter til it Puffs, take ten eggs, half the whites, beat them with a pound sugar and half a pint of wine with Spice, the juice of a lemon with a little of the rine, and some slices of citron laid on the top.—

Eliza Lucas Pinckney
Rect. Book No. 2
Charleston, South Carolina, 1756

As the United States became accustomed to nationhood in the early decades of the nineteenth century, more cookbooks came along, and among them were several notable volumes from the South. Some of the best of these have been reprinted in facsimile editions in recent years, and they make available to contemporary cooks and students of social history a wealth of information about Southern homes before the Civil War.

Probably the best of these was also the first: *The Virginia House-Wife*, by Mary Randolph, published in Washington, D.C., in 1824. In the introduction to the 1984 facsimile edition, food historian Karen Hess called it "the most influential American cookbook of the nineteenth century," a singular work that was "solidly based on Virginia produce and Virginia practice."

In Mrs. Randolph's book, for the first time, the bounty of American fields and woods and waters and the influences of Indian and African cookery were given some attention. There were recipes for oyster and "ochra" and onion soups; for beef steak, mutton chops, "barbacue shote," fried perch, and (in the third edition, 1828) fried chicken; for briefly boiled asparagus, fried white potatoes (early French fries), field peas cooked with pork fat, broiled sweet potatoes, buttered squash, and "gumbs" (stewed okra). Among the breads were yeast biscuits, buckwheat cakes, cornmeal bread, batter bread, and rice waffles, and the sweets included apple fritters, ice cream, sponge cake, and doughnuts ("a Yankee cake"). There was also lemonade.

Had the term "populist" been in use by 1824, it probably would have been applied to the Randolph collection; it was hardly egalitarian, but it was definitely more of a people's cookbook than anything that had come along before it. The original *Virginia House-Wife*, 225 pages long, contained close to five hundred recipes. It became a model of nineteenth-century American cookery, an example to be followed—literally copied, in fact—for generations to come. Plagiarism—in this case, recipe thievery—has always been a common failing among cookbook writers; the practice may have originated with people who coveted Mary Randolph's eclectic kitchen treasures.

Two later books that borrowed from her title (and possibly from her text) but contained impressive original material were *The Kentucky Housewife*, by Mrs. Lettice Bryan, published in Cincinnati, Ohio, in 1839, and *The Carolina Housewife*, by "a Lady of Charleston"—Sarah Rutledge—published in Charleston in 1847. The Kentucky book, an inclusive 450-page volume, has somehow managed to slip unnoticed past all but a handful of food historians, and a valuable record has thereby been almost lost. Mrs. Rutledge's anonymous work is much more widely known and honored in the Carolinas and elsewhere in the South. Both are sterling examples of the depth and breadth and quality of nineteenth-century Southern cooking.

Another antebellum volume of note that has faded into obscurity is *The*

In 1824 appeared one of the most important cookbooks ever published in America. The Virginia House-Wife or, Methodical Cook, by Mary Randolph (1762–1828), is not only one of the finest; it may also be called the first truly American cookbook in that all the strands of influence in Virginia cookery were beautifully worked into place. . . . Following is [Mary Randolph's] recipe for:

APOQUINIMINC CAKES

Put a little salt, one egg beaten, and four ounces of butter, in a quart of flour—make it into a paste with new milk, beat it for half an hour with a pestle, roll the paste thin, and cut it into round cakes; bake them on a gridiron, and be careful not to burn them.

These are beaten biscuits, and we have not found an earlier version. The Indian name is difficult to account for, because the ingredients are thoroughly English. Since it would have been black women who beat them, it is possibly an African technique for achieving tenderness.

John L. Hess and Karen Hess
The Taste of America, 1977

Southern Gardener and Receipt-Book, by Mary L. Edgeworth, a Georgia lady about whom little is recorded. It was published in Philadelphia in 1859, not long before the Southern states seceded from the union, and it thus offers a final glimpse at the plantation-era dinner table. There are touches of New Orleans and Charleston and Savannah in the book, and flavors from the inland estates that had sprung up in fertile river bottoms from the James to the Mississippi. This was the fabled South of wide renown, the South of spectacular repasts, of unmatched hospitality for those with the means to enjoy it. Mary Edgeworth catalogued the food and drink extensively. Without knowing it, she had written the last word from the kitchen on the art of Southern cooking in the age of slavery.

Two and a half centuries after the Jamestown landing, the South was a study in contrasts. Where only native American Indians had lived, there were now approximately six million whites, four million blacks, and the scattered remnant of a few thousand Indians. There were bustling cities dotted along the coast and vast stretches of wilderness in the interior. A small percentage of the whites lived in ostentatious wealth, while virtually all of the blacks and Indians and a substantial proportion of the whites knew only varying degrees of poverty and need.

Inevitably, food reflected these same social and cultural and economic patterns. In the seaport cities, it tended to be more ethnically diverse and varied; in the plantation dining rooms, it was stylish and sumptuous; among the poor everywhere, it was limited and monotonous, albeit nourishing.

The British remained dominant in the region until the Revolutionary War, but Spanish, French, German, and other immigrants came in ever-increasing numbers, and many of them joined the push from the coastal cities to the interior. Virginia, the Carolinas, Georgia, Kentucky, and Tennessee were established primarily by English and Scotch-Irish settlers, and not only the South's oldest cities (Richmond, Norfolk, Wilmington, Charleston, Savannah) but its deepest interior settlements (Louisville and Nashville) were founded by people of British descent. Spain held the upper hand in Florida (St. Augustine preceded Jamestown by almost fifty years) and vied with France for dominance along the Gulf Coast, where Pensacola, Mobile, Biloxi, and New Orleans all were established before 1720.

Louisiana received an influx of French-speaking Roman Catholics exiled by the British from Acadia in eastern Canada in 1755, and in the swampy backcountry west of New Orleans and above the city along the Mississippi River, they transplanted a culture that would cling to Catholicism, the French tongue, and a distinctive Acadian style of cooking. In New Orleans, meanwhile, Louisiana-born Spanish and French colonists, calling themselves Creoles, were evolv-

[Plantations] were not merely houses, but little planetary systems around which a whole set of people and buildings orbited—schoolhouse, stables, henhouse, dairy, dovecot, smokehouse, springhouse, slave quarters, icehouse, kitchen. Usually a short distance from the manor, the kitchen was full of the cook's wares: pots, kettles, waffle irons, swinging cranes, bake ovens, scales, iron firedogs holding rotating spits. This was the spot in which southern cooking had its inspiration and consummation. The demand was great: often as many as fifty, even seventy, people would be on hand for a meal.

Conjuring up mental pictures of such lordly estates, we inevitably confront the plantation lady—fluttering her fan and filling guests' wineglasses—forgetting that she also managed a huge kitchen and staff with responsibilities that would floor the modern can-opening housewife. The plantation became a kind of matriarchy; the real focus was not the planter but his wife, whose benevolent rule extended over the entire household, white and black. . . . She kept the keys and the recipes.

Marshall Fishwick,
in *The American Heritage Cookbook*, 1964

ing their own distinctive way of cooking and dining. Creole cuisine, a blend of French and Spanish, African and Indian, English and American, Italian and perhaps other elements, was widely admired within a few years after Louisiana was made a state in 1812. By 1840, New Orleans had a number of notable public restaurants—including Antoine's, which prospers even now as one of the oldest restaurants in the United States.

France took America's side in the War of Independence, and from that time on, French cultural influences—including food in particular—fared well against the old and habitual English ways. Benjamin Franklin and Thomas Jefferson served successively as envoys to Paris during and after the war, and both took American foodways with them and brought back many in return from the French. Jefferson especially loved French cuisine; at the White House and at Monticello he embraced the French manner of eating and drinking, to the irritation of some of his associates.

The young United States developed rapidly as a nation in the first half of the nineteenth century, though the pace and the patterns of its growth were spotty and erratic. Steamboats and railroads vastly improved transportation, and even some interior roads were at least minimally satisfactory for wagon, coach, and horseback travel. Hotels and taverns and inns were more and more to be found, and most included public dining places. Imported coffee, tea, and chocolate became popular in all the states, and stronger drinks, from cider and beer to wine and rum and whiskey, were consumed heavily. Trains and steamboats made it possible to transport barrels of oysters to inland cities, and they became instantly prized and coveted everywhere they could be found.

Glass dishes, time-saving kitchen utensils, and even such luxuries as ice slowly came into fairly common use in the South. By 1845, when Florida entered the Union, all of the region west and south from Virginia to Kentucky to Arkansas and Louisiana was in the national fold, sharing in the fruits of the nation.

But for all its cookbook glories, its hospitality, and its culinary reputation, the South still had trouble feeding its own people. Except for the rice that was raised in South Carolina (and later in Louisiana, Arkansas, and Texas), the main agricultural products that brought great wealth to Southern landowners lacked the saving virtue of feeding the multitudes. Tobacco, cotton, indigo, and wood products were not edible, of course; to be "nourished" by these goods, it was necessary to own and market them.

If the South was ever agriculturally self-sufficient, even in its antebellum heyday, it was a spare and repetitive sufficiency. The majority of its people, black and white, sustained themselves primarily on the same basic foods the colonists at Jamestown ate: corn and pork, with an assist from whatever nature provided free of charge. A little game meat, some shellfish or finned fish, and occasionally

In the middle of the 1700's our third President, Thomas Jefferson, brought back from France a Negro as his servant. His name was James Hemming. Hemming was not only a servant, he was a first class chef, schooled in the art of French cuisine. He and Jefferson concocted the great continental cuisine of France and made some of our most glamorous American dishes. At Monticello and the White House, they introduced ice cream, macaroni, spaghetti, savoye, cornbread stuffing, waffles, almonds, raisins, vanilla and many more dishes and foods to America. James Hemming and other of Jefferson's servants from these two great houses handed down to generations of Negro and white families alike the repertory of the American table.

Leonard E. Roberts
The Negro Chef Cookbook, 1960

some fruits and vegetables, cultivated or gathered in the wild, supplemented the basic diet that came from corn in all its many forms and from the hog, which yielded not only hams, shoulders, and bacon, but also lard for shortening and many other delicacies—the head, the organs, the feet.

Cornmeal mixed with water, salt, and a little grease could be fried in a skillet or on a piece of metal (hoecake), roasted in the ashes of the fireplace (ashcake), or baked in a makeshift oven (pone). Pieces of side meat as well as other meats and some vegetables could be rolled in cornmeal and fried in hot grease. Corn could be eaten roasted on the cob, scraped and cooked in a pot or a skillet, or mixed with beans (succotash). When corn grains were soaked in lye water and the hulls removed, they were known as hominy; when the hominy was dried and then coarsely ground, it became grits. Bacon, variously called side meat, salt pork, white meat, fatback, middlings, or simply meat, could be added to pots of vegetables to give them flavor and seasoning. The liquid from these kettles, called pot likker, could be sipped like soup or soaked up in dry pieces of cornbread. Finally, and not least important, corn could be fermented and made into whiskey—and in that form it was, from colonial times onward, a mixed blessing for makers and drinkers alike. More prudent souls drank spring water or homemade cider or perhaps sweet milk or buttermilk, if it was safe.

If this was self-sufficiency, it was nonetheless a hard diet. It was also a common diet across most of the South when the Civil War broke out in 1861. Within a short time, and for a long time to come, there were uncounted thousands of Southerners who would have given almost anything to have enough cornmeal and fatback to feed their families.

With the somber reality of war between the states—and then, in 1865, with the defeat of the Confederacy—there would be a new dispensation in the South, a new social order. Slavery was over, and the plantation culture that had controlled the economic and political and social fortunes of the region since the middle of the 1600s was in shambles. The Old South was formally and effectively ended; a New South would have to be created to replace it, and that massive task would occupy successive national administrations, the governments of the states, and the people of the region for the remainder of the century.

From the war itself through Reconstruction and all that followed it, the South was in many ways truly transformed, pervasively and permanently changed. In other ways, though, it was hardly changed at all, and still would not be altered significantly fifty or even a hundred years later. Likewise the food: It was different, and it was the same.

The war years brought physical devastation to the Southern landscape and desperation to the people. Shortages of such staples as salt, sugar, meat, and

[In the antebellum South] corn was the companion food to pork and in many respects it was more important. . . . During early summer, while still green, it was boiled on-the-cob, cut off the cob and creamed (called "fried corn"), and roasted in the shuck. After the ears had ripened and dried there were many other ways it could be prepared. The most common was to grind it into meal from which an almost endless variety of breads were concocted. Cornbread was the most common which, in its simplest form,

flour were at first an inconvenience—and then alarming, even terrifying. What little meat there was often spoiled for lack of salt to cure it. Corn, too, was scarce, and that limited the bread, without which there was almost nothing. Mass hunger led in some instances to public uprisings; Richmond and Mobile were among the cities where food riots erupted. Things were no better for the army, which often fared worse than the civilian population.

The only cookbook to be published in the Confederacy during the war was the *Confederate Receipt Book,* a compilation of recipes and home remedies aimed at helping people adapt to shortages. In it were instructions for purifying muddy water (with alum) and preserving meat without salt (by drying); there was also a substitute for coffee (acorns), and there were recipes for "artificial oysters" (a fried mixture of corn and egg) and for a mock apple pie made with crackers. For the poor, such resourceful ways of making do were old hat—but for the planter class, poverty was a new experience.

City dwellers suffered the worst from hunger, primarily because they were thrown together in greater numbers and because they could not turn to the land for relief. In the rural areas, whatever could be harvested from the woods, the creeks and rivers, the fields, and the gardens often made the difference between hunger and starvation. Though they had not been accustomed in the past to eating a great diversity of vegetables, Southerners in the war years consumed everything they could find growing—sweet potatoes, cabbage, okra, turnip greens, turnips, collards, pumpkins, squash, cowpeas, field peas, tomatoes, eggplant, pokeweed, walnuts and pecans, berries, and of course corn. In all its wondrous forms, corn was still the staff of life and a shield against starvation, as it had been for more than 250 years.

When the war was over, the differences between the victorious North and the prostrate Confederacy became more pronounced, and the enormous chasm separating the two regions would keep them divided for generations to come. A century after they and the Northern colonies had joined forces to throw off the yoke of British rule, the Southern states found themselves returned to a colonial status, this time under the rule of the North. For another hundred years, the South would languish as a poverty-ridden backwater, an economic dependency of the expanding, industrializing North.

In 1860, Southern plantations had produced virtually all of the nation's rice (along the lower Atlantic coast) and much of its sugar (in the cane fields of Louisiana), not to mention all of its cotton and tobacco. Southern farms also raised close to half of all the nation's pigs and corn on the eve of the war. But in the decades of the sixties and seventies and eighties and on into the twentieth century, Southern food production for domestic consumption would be perpetually insufficient, and food for export would be practically nonexistent.

The plantation society had been laid low, and it would never regain com-

was baked cake or "pone" made from meal, salt, and water. Variations upon this included the addition of milk, buttermilk, shortening, or eggs. After hog-killing, bits of crisp "cracklings" left over from the lard-rendering process were added to make "crackling bread."

In addition to the use of corn as meal, southerners converted it into hominy and grits. Both were made from corn but the grains went through a soaking process which removed the husk (not the shuck) from the grain. Hominy consisted of whole grain corn boiled and eaten as a vegetable. When hominy grains were dried, ground into a coarse meal, and boiled, the dish was called grits. . . . Contrary to popular opinion, neither grits nor hominy ever came close to being universally used in the area prior to the Civil War.

Sam Bowers Hilliard
Hog Meat and Hoecake, 1972

plete dominance in the region, but the planter mentality was not dead. The former slaves were legally free, but most of them were severely handicapped by the economic and social conditions under which they lived. They and the poor whites who made up the laboring under-class of sharecroppers and tenant farmers struggled to eke out a living on the land—and still, all too often, wound up in debt to the plantation commissary. The planters who were able to reopen their estates invariably turned again to the money crops—cotton, tobacco, sugarcane—and there was not enough home-grown pork or corn to supply even a subsistence diet for the poor.

As the trauma of war and defeat gradually began to subside, a minority of white Southerners could see some improvement in their lives. Professional people, the merchant class, some planters, anyone with money or with carry-over status from the prewar years made up this remnant of upwardly mobile citizens. They began to surface in the cities and on some of the large estates, and though their presence did not signal a return of the planter aristocracy, it did sometimes revive a style of living reminiscent of antebellum society, particularly where dining and hospitality were concerned. Whether these postwar activities indicated a measure of returning prosperity or simply served as a genteel mask of poverty, they did occur with increasing frequency. Prosperous or poor, the advantaged white minority sought to recapture its lost glory—and once again, black cooks, maids, and servants did most of the work. The whites were employers now, not masters, and they were obliged to provide some compensation to the blacks, where none had been required before. The blacks were not legally bound to stay, either. Nevertheless, most of the ones who stayed on as domestic employees of the upper-class whites found themselves, like sharecroppers and tenant farmers, as economically dependent as they had been before the war. For paltry wages (supplemented by the leftovers they ate or took home to their families), the cooks gradually restored the celebrated Southern cuisine to a semblance of its former quality.

There was much irony in these postwar relationships between white and black women in Southern kitchens. They had been there together for a long time, mistress and slave, rich and poor, combining their talents to produce an impressive array of culinary masterpieces. Now, their relative status was altered. The white woman lived with the burden of a reality called defeat, the black woman with the disillusionment of an abstraction called freedom. Everything was changed—and yet, nothing was changed. The black woman was still poor; the white woman, more often than not, still had property and status but not much money, and so was poor too. The old domestic and maternal roles to which women of both races had been confined since colonial times remained in force.

With far less money for food and with no access to the expensive imported products they once had used freely, these white homemakers and the black women who cooked for them were thrown back on their own resources. They responded by practicing economy as impressively as they once had practiced extravagance—and this time, the black women were the teachers. They turned pork fat and flour into rich gravies, stale bread and cold rice into sweet puddings, leftover meats and vegetables into soups and stews and baked dishes. Turn-of-the-century Southern cookbooks—aimed, as always, at the social elite of white women—acknowledged for the first time the major contributions of black cooks to the cuisine, describing their kitchen creations as a high form of primitive art.

The cookbooks were mirrors of the times in more ways than one: They also revealed that in some Southern homes and public dining rooms, modern trends were beginning. Books by Mrs. M. E. Porter and Mrs. A. P. Hill typified one kind of offering. Written by Southern women and published in the North, they were directed at "New South" cooks who did their own kitchen work without hired help. *The New Kentucky Home Cook Book* and *Housekeeping in the Bluegrass*, compilations by groups of small-town Kentucky church women, showed surprising sophistication and variety in their offerings, as much so as the *Tested Recipe Cook Book*, an impressive urban collection put together by Mrs. Henry Lumpkin Wilson for the Atlanta Exposition of 1895. *Housekeeping in Old Virginia*, a comprehensive book edited by Marion Cabell Tyree, was published in 1879; its contributions from 250 of "Virginia's noted housewives" represented an advanced system of cookery that Mrs. Tyree called "the very perfection of domestic art."

From New Orleans in 1885 came two important new volumes, the first of many great cookbooks to originate there: *The Creole Cookery Book*, compiled by the Christian Woman's Exchange, and *La Cuisine Creole*, written anonymously by a well-known journalist, Lafcadio Hearn. *The Dixie Cook-Book*, another anonymous work, was published in Atlanta in 1883; it turned out to be one of several related collections issued within a few years of each other in Ohio, Colorado, Minnesota, and Georgia by the same enterprising writer, the mysterious Estelle Woods Wilcox. One edition of the *Dixie* volume contained nearly 1300 pages.

There were other signs of recovery and change. The restaurants of New Orleans already enjoyed a national reputation by the time Lafcadio Hearn got around to putting the city's cooking into print. Creole cuisine was praised by visitors and residents alike. Crayfish bisque, okra gumbo (African style), filé gumbo (made with powdered sassafras leaves, a culinary contribution of the Choctaw Indians), jambalaya, bouillabaisse—these were among the famous dishes of New Orleans before and after the Civil War. In fact, they had already been transplanted to menus in other cities before 1880. Several noted Southern

The majority of southern [white] women convinced themselves that God had ordained that they be deprived of pleasure. . . . These women turned away from the ugliness which they felt powerless to cope with and made for themselves and their families what they called a "normal" life. . . . In these homes, food and flowers were cherished. . . . Out through the back door went the unpleasant and unmentionable; in through the back door came trays laden with food as delicious as can be found in the world. . . . the groaning table was left free.

Lillian Smith
Killers of the Dream, 1949

hotels featured Creole cooking, including the Galt House in Louisville, the Maxwell House in Nashville, and the Peabody in Memphis. The menu at the Maxwell House on Christmas Day, 1879, highlighted no fewer than a dozen classic Creole dishes in an orgiastic offering of fine foods in twenty different categories.

Pullman sleeping and dining cars were introduced on the nation's railroads in the late 1860s, and the food they featured rivaled that of the best hotels, thanks largely to the Southern black men who cooked and served so much of it. People who could afford to travel in such style also had exclusive destinations—seaside resorts in Florida and along the Atlantic and Gulf coasts, mountain retreats in the Appalachians, country inns and health spas in every state. For the small minority of Southerners whose affluence permitted them to move in such company, the Gay Nineties were indeed years of conspicuous consumption.

At the opposite extreme in the postwar South were millions of people for whom "recovery" and "reconstruction" and "new social order" were meaningless terms. Southern historian Thomas D. Clark has etched a vivid picture of the vast multitude of small farmers in the region subsisting mainly on cornmeal, fatback, and cheap molasses, most of which was produced in the Midwest and marketed through Southern crossroads country stores. Life for the hard-pressed Southern poor "was of a marked degree of whiteness," Clark wrote. "There was white meat, white gravy, white bread, and white shortening on the table, white supremacy at the polls and white gloves for the pall bearers at the graveside."

In *Eating, Drinking, and Visiting in the South*, a superlative social study of the region by historian Joe Gray Taylor, the abject poverty that affected so many postwar Southerners is tellingly described. Uncounted thousands of people suffered from rickets, pellagra, worms; many of them ate clay to ward off the pangs of hunger. Even in the best of years, Taylor noted, "scores of thousands of families in the South quite literally lived on the edge of starvation." That would have been tragic enough had it lasted only a generation after the war, but as Taylor points out, the condition of the poor generally did not begin to improve until the New Deal era commenced with the election of Franklin D. Roosevelt in 1932.

It is impossible to be precise about the number and percentage of Southerners who made up this severely deprived under-class, but it seems safe to generalize that a substantial majority of all the black people in the region and close to half of all the whites subsisted on what would be considered by today's standards a hunger diet made up of a few store-bought rations and whatever could be gleaned from the fields and streams and forests. Even by the narrowest definition of poverty, the struggling sharecroppers and tenant farmers in the countryside and the unemployed and landless poor in the cities probably made up a

In Louisville and Natchez and the plantations along the River Road, many of the best of the public cooks by 1850 were black and male and so well trained that those of them who took over the galleys of the luxury steamboats plying the Mississippi and the Ohio were masters of haute cuisine. . . . [But] the percentage of slaves who were taught to cook in a European style is slight in comparison to the number of black women who were forced to make do for their families—especially in the economic debacle that followed the defeat of the Confederacy—with roots, beans, fish, opossums, and other wild animals. Yet the food that was prepared in the fields or in slave quarters, regardless of the raw materials, had its own style and flavor because the same food had been cooked for generations in Africa. . . . The South owes its penchant for hot sauces to the women in its kitchens who retained a memory of African seasoning. . . . Other

majority of the South's population in 1880—and the percentages had not changed dramatically fifty years later when the Great Depression brought still another "starving time" of crisis.

And yet, as bleak as this picture is, there is another dimension to the story of Southern survival in the last third of the nineteenth century. Between the well-off few and the destitute many at opposite ends of the economic pole, a very sizable and significant number of people picked up the shattered pieces of their lives and their land after the war and started over. Here was the nucleus of the middle class—small farmers, storekeepers, schoolteachers, people skilled in crafts and trades. If they owned a little land, they kept a garden and perhaps some chickens, or even a cow and a pig or two. Their aim was independence and self-sufficiency—and with hard work and some luck, they moved in that direction. Most but not all of them were white; the racially divided society dictated that. They began with little in the way of material possessions, but they made the most of what little they had.

And they ate well. They had their own produce, and nature's larder, and cooks who knew how to get full measure from the resources at hand. Food was important to them. They planted and harvested, cooked and baked, canned and preserved in a continuous cycle of utilization and renewal. Most of what they consumed cost them little or no money—just energy, of which they had an abundance. Their lives were plain and simple and hard, leaving little time or resources for leisure or entertainment, but they certainly took satisfaction and pleasure in the fruits of their labors, from smoked hams and rendered lard to dried and canned and preserved vegetables. They spent a lot of time at the table, during and after meals—it was in many ways the focal point of their homes and of their lives as families.

The diet of this middle group of Southerners improved in these postwar decades. Earlier, their vegetable consumption had mainly been limited to corn, sweet potatoes, turnips, and cowpeas; now, the staples included Irish potatoes, green leafy vegetables, and all sorts of beans and peas. The bread got better, too. Commercial development of baking powder and baking soda, two substances that produce a rising effect in baked goods, made flour biscuits a popular item, and with flour from the Midwest affordable for the first time (it fell to around three dollars a barrel in the 1880s), biscuits took their place beside cornbread as a daily favorite among all hot-bread-loving Southerners.

Wheat breads, like the diversity of cornmeal products, had many devotees. Where there were cows and chickens, cooks had milk, butter, and eggs to enrich the bread recipes; the cookbooks included dozens of ways to make such popular specialties as Sally Lunn bread, yeast rolls, and unleavened beaten biscuits.

Flour and lard or butter also made pastry, and that meant pies, cobblers, and other desserts. Flour, butter, sugar, cream, and eggs were the basic ingredi-

documentary examples are not hard to find. Slave cooks adapted the tradition of simmering turnip and other greens with hog jowl, developing variations drawn from their African backgrounds. . . . "A type of cooking made necessary by the environment in which southern blacks lived" is the phrase one soul food restaurateur used to describe his cuisine.

Evan Jones
American Food, 1974

ents of cakes as well as puddings, cookies, and candies, and these delights were also within reach of many households. Southerners of every class and calling seemingly have coveted sweets since the Virginia colony was in its prime, and they have almost always managed to put something sweet on the table, whether it was a fancy layer cake or a plain sweet potato pie or a simple blending of butter with honey or sorghum molasses.

Ice cream was another Southern treat. Since its first reported appearance in colonial Maryland in the 1740s, it had spread to all parts of the country. Ice cream was available commercially in New Orleans in the early 1800s, and it was in that city in 1865 that the first mechanical refrigeration plant for the manufacture of ice was built. Not only homemade ice cream but lemonade and iced tea rose in popularity with the availability of ice. Insulated iceboxes soon appeared in some kitchens, harbingers of the twentieth-century era of battery-powered refrigerator units and plug-in electric refrigerators. (Even after World War II, some Southerners would still call their refrigerators iceboxes.)

At the start of the twentieth century, all but the richest and poorest of Southerners were cooking on cast-iron woodstoves. The poor still cooked before the open fire; the more affluent were being introduced to stoves fueled by coal or coal oil, and it would not be long before they would have gas ranges and even electric cookstoves. Meanwhile, many other innovations and improvements had made kitchen work easier, from meat and coffee grinders to egg beaters and measuring spoons. Window screens also came on the market, improving sanitation.

The South at the turn of the century seemed to fit the symbolism of ending and beginning. There was still the Old South, more myth than reality, and there was a New South rising, more hope than substance. The region had been profoundly changed by the war and its aftermath, but it was also in many ways the same as before—divided from the rest of the country and divided within itself. As the nation entered the twentieth century, and for a long time thereafter, its formerly rebellious Southern states were physically and philosophically isolated, wracked with poverty, and obsessed with the enforcement of legalized racial segregation. Those same conditions—isolation, poverty, and segregation—affected every dimension of life in the region, including the growing, cooking, serving, and eating of Southern food.

Millions of Americans waltzed through the Gay Nineties and on into the new century, and they were still dancing in the Roaring Twenties when the music finally stopped. There followed a decade of crippling economic depression and then a half-decade of world war. Throughout that fifty-five-year period, from 1890 to 1945, the South made little headway in its struggle for parity with the rest of the United States. Neither calls for national reconciliation by a wave of "New South" advocates nor efforts by the Populists and the Progressives to bring about certain social reforms were enough to remove the barriers that divided the region from its sister states in the North, East, and West.

Without money to buy modern goods, Southerners were bound to become more and more isolated from the rest of the country in the new century. By almost every measure of modernity—miles of railroad lines, miles of highways, numbers of automobiles, numbers of telephones, numbers of households with electricity and refrigerators and gas or electric stoves—the South lagged far behind. Without cars to ride in or roads to drive on or money to buy train tickets (if and when there were trains), Southerners stayed isolated not only from non-Southerners but often from one another—mountain people from coastal people, hill folk from delta folk, city residents from country dwellers, Mississippians from Georgians from Virginians. Not until radios began to spread in the 1930s was there any major change in that pattern.

For the vast majority of Southerners, white and black, coping with daily life required imagination, improvisation, sacrifice, and a high degree of self-sufficiency. Food was a constant preoccupation. Some items could be bought from the huckster wagon or the country store or the mom-and-pop grocery in town, but their wares were limited, and they cost money; most families, whether dirt-poor or comfortably fixed, still relied primarily on other resources to feed themselves.

There were fish in the creeks and rivers, ponds and lakes, and small game—squirrels, rabbits, coons, possums, doves, quail—in the woods. (Most of the larger animals and even some small ones had been slaughtered to the point of extinction.) Fruits, nuts, and berries that grew wild could be harvested in the summer and fall—persimmons, blackberries, quince, mulberries, walnuts, pecans, plums, muscadines. A single apple or pear or cherry tree in the yard might yield enough to provide a little flavor and variety at the table for an entire winter. There were edible wild mushrooms, too, and greens in abundance, from pokeweed and dandelion and lamb's quarters to dock and mustard and watercress.

There were ways to preserve food that would spoil before it could be eaten, and some of the methods were ancient: smoking, drying, and salting meat, drying and pickling fruits and vegetables and fish, cooling foods in cellars and springhouses. Modern methods of canning in glass jars had revolutionized food preservation, and so too, eventually, did freezing, which was introduced in the 1930s.

With cornmeal and flour, Southern cooks continued and enlarged the tradition of making and serving hot breads, so much so that most households, rich and poor, followed the practice at least once a day. They might offer the simplest

Until I went away to war in 1942, I ate far more like my ancestors of the 1830s than the way I eat today. If the South was conservative in mores and politics, it was equally conservative in diet. . . . Southerners continued to eat corn bread, and as the years passed, good cooks became more and more sophisticated in their variations on the theme. . . . A southerner who matured in time for World War II could fill many pages with praise of the biscuit. Many families ate them three times a day; everyone of substance that I knew ate them for breakfast. . . . Probably southerners ate a greater proportion of pork to other meats for the eighty years following the Civil War than they had eaten during the preceding century. Those who raised their own hogs probably ate about the same quality of meat that their fathers and grandfathers had eaten; but black and white sharecroppers who depended upon the commissary or the general store, and yeoman farmers and denizens of the small towns who did not cure their own meat, lived on low quality bacon or fatback from the Middle West.

Joe Gray Taylor
Eating, Drinking, and Visiting in the South, 1982

meal-and-water pone or soda biscuit, but it was usually there to sop up the last bit of gravy or pot likker.

Another product of isolation—and of corn—was whiskey. Pennsylvania resisters of a federal excise tax on distilled spirits had fled in 1794 to the territory of Kentucky to escape the tax and to see for themselves if Kentucky corn and limestone water did in fact make a superior liquor, as rumor had it. It must have been true; Kentucky quickly became the principal producer of whiskey in the new nation, and it has remained so ever since. A Baptist preacher named Elijah Craig is remembered in legend as the originator of bourbon whiskey, so named because it was produced in what was then Bourbon County of the Kentucky territory. Craig's 1789 corn liquor almost certainly was not the first—earlier claims are made for many other Scotch-Irish distillers—but in any case, Kentucky was the favored place; property inventories show that there were about two thousand stills in the state by 1811.

Southerners, at least as much as other adult Americans, consumed large quantities of alcoholic beverages from the earliest years of European settlement to the time of the Civil War. There was a large and growing antiliquor movement by 1870, but efforts to prohibit the manufacture and sale of alcohol needed fifty more years to succeed with the ratification of the 18th Amendment to the Constitution in 1919—and it was repealed fourteen years later.

It is interesting to note in the pre-Prohibition-era cookbooks—including some compiled by Southern Methodist and Baptist church women—that drinks and desserts containing rum, brandy, wine, and whiskey remained popular. True to its schizophrenic nature, the South somehow managed to lead the nation in bourbon manufacturing, moonshine making, and temperance fervor; even now, some of the region's most famous whiskeys are legally manufactured in counties where their sale is prohibited by law.

Moonshine making and bootlegging flourished in some sparsely populated regions of the South during the first half of this century, particularly in the Prohibition and Great Depression years. Much has been made of the adventure and romance of such enterprises in the stereotyped image of Southern mountaineers and hill-country folk, but not enough has been said about the economic realities. Backwoods farmers were quick to realize that in hard times, their patches of corn would return much more per acre in liquid than in solid form; furthermore, while the unshelled grain might be exceedingly difficult to transport to market, buyers of the bottled variety would come and get it. Thus, some farmers considered it worth the risk to supply what the market demanded, just as their forebears had done in the 1780s. From a social perspective, the main difference was that preachers and presidents were among the distillers in the eighteenth century, while in the twentieth the practice stigmatized and further isolated those who took part.

In the early days, making or selling whiskey was not considered reprehensible, even when done by government officials or by preachers. In fact, a Baptist preacher is the person most often credited with having discovered by accident in 1789 the process of making bourbon whiskey. The preacher was the Reverend Elijah Craig, one of the two Craig brothers who led their "Travelling Church," singing hymns and preaching along the way, over the mountains and through the wilderness to settle in Kentucky. Elijah Craig, with James and Alexander Parker as partners, ran a grist and fulling mill near Georgetown, and a distillery as well. At the Craig-Parker distillery, according to one legend, Craig happened to store whiskey made from sour mash in charred oak kegs which, it was discovered, mellowed the sharp taste, changed the color to amber, and removed foreign particles. . . . Apparently the whiskey was named for Bourbon County, where at present whiskey can be sold legally only in the town of Paris.

Marie Campbell,
in Kentucky Hospitality, 1976

Isolation also limited the development of hotels and restaurants in the South in the early years of this century. Aside from the noted urban attractions that traveling salesmen and the few tourists frequented, there were scattered here and there some mountain and seaside resorts, a few country inns, some health spas, a number of places near the main railroads and highways, and not much else. The only significant change in the pattern of such public accommodations since the 1870s was that a good many Southern towns could boast of a hotel or a boardinghouse by the early 1900s. These establishments usually served regular meals, but it was exceedingly rare for their food to receive much attention beyond the vicinity. (It did occasionally happen, though; the Sedberry Hotel in McMinnville, Tennessee, and the Purefoy Hotel in Talladega, Alabama, were among the few small-town Southern hotels that diners from around the nation went out of their way to visit long before highway travel was commonplace.)

Where it could be found, good restaurant fare in the South was quite inexpensive prior to World War II; it was not at all uncommon then for dinners to cost less than a dollar. But many people could not afford even that small amount, and since the quality of the food was so uneven and the places were so few and scattered, Southerners generally ate almost all their meals at home until dining patterns changed dramatically during the war. Before that, the most popular public eating places in the region probably were the country stores, where slabs of cheese and bologna on crackers from wooden boxes could be washed down with Southern-made carbonated soft drinks, and the cafes and diners in the cities, where working people could get lunch.

As in previous times, Southern cookbooks of the period were mostly aimed at white women who had help in the kitchen. Some of the books were quite good, and they seemed to increase in number and quality after the Depression. The celebrated *Picayune Creole Cook Book* from New Orleans and Jennie Benedict's *Blue Ribbon Cook Book* from Louisville led the turn-of-the-century parade, establishing Louisiana and Kentucky as the top producers of good books about food. Smaller cities such as Fort Smith, Arkansas, and Laurel, Mississippi, also generated popular collections in the first decade of the century.

Henrietta Stanley Dull of Atlanta wrote her *Southern Cooking* in 1928, and it was still in print and still in demand more than forty years later. *Marion Brown's Southern Cook Book*, published in North Carolina in 1951, gradually took the place of Mrs. Dull's volume at the top of the regional list. *The Savannah Cook Book* and *Two Hundred Years of Charleston Cooking* were the leading offerings from Georgia and South Carolina in the 1930s, and in the same decade there were notable new volumes from New Orleans by three of the city's most respected cooks—Natalie V. Scott, Mary Moore Bremer, and Lena Richard. In Virginia, Helen Bullock compiled an interesting and valuable historical

Southern farmers knew an institution peculiar to their section. During the last third of the nineteenth century and well into the following one, a southern country store was likely to have, in a corner, a long counter equipped with bottles of pepper sauce, catsup, vinegar, well-worn knives and forks, cracked plates, a mechanical cheese cutter, and boxes of crackers. Here many a rural Southerner first met "bought" foods—canned oysters, sardines, salmon, or link sausages from a midwestern packing plant. A particular favorite of the farmers was sardines seasoned with pepper sauce and eaten with salt crackers.

Richard J. Hooker
Food and Drink in America, 1981

collection called *The Williamsburg Art of Cookery* in 1938—almost two hundred years after the first cookbook to be published in America was issued in the same city. A delightful narrative called *Cross Creek Cookery*, by Florida novelist Marjorie Kinnan Rawlings, was published in 1942. Marion Flexner wrote an exceedingly popular volume, *Out of Kentucky Kitchens*, in 1949.

A Southern phenomenon of the same decade that eventually spread across the country was the Junior League cookbook. The women's service organization apparently discovered the fund-raising potential of cookbooks when the Montgomery, Alabama, chapter published a slender volume called *Southern Recipes* in 1941. The chapter in Charlotte, North Carolina, came out the following year with the *Old North State Cook Book*. Then, in 1950, *Charleston Receipts* became an instant best-seller for the Junior League in South Carolina's oldest city, and two years later, *The Memphis Cook Book* was a big commercial success in Tennessee's largest city. Since then, more than 125 American cities have followed the example, if not the success, of the women in those pacesetting Southern communities.

It is rare to find much social or cultural or historical content in these early examples of twentieth-century food books—and even rarer to find in them any recipes for the staple dishes of poor and working-class Southern families. Such foods as collard greens, field peas, white beans, pot likker, sawmill gravy, fried salt pork, and even cornpone seldom got much attention from cookbook writers then, even though most families in the Southern states were well acquainted with those dishes, and many people ate them regularly.

Just as isolation affected the vast majority of Southerners in the first half of this century, so did poverty. Even among the well-to-do, forced austerity that began with the Civil War was still common seventy years later, when the Great Depression arrived. Whether out of necessity or habit, most Southerners of every social class had by then been doing without so much for so long that many of them claimed to notice little change. Hard times to them simply meant more—or rather less—of the same.

In the depths of the Depression, economic crisis stalked not only the masses of unemployed people but also the underpaid employed—cotton pickers in the black belt, mill workers in the textile factories, coal miners in Appalachia, hill farmers in the Ozarks, fishermen along the coasts, and cooks everywhere. What industry there was depended primarily on Northern capital and used cheap Southern labor to extract and export the region's resources. Even the food industry followed that pattern; vegetables and citrus fruits and seafood from Florida were much more likely to end up in New York than in Birmingham or Nashville or Richmond, and as far as the rural South was concerned, the only hope of getting fresh vegetables and fruits was to raise them at home. Cheap cuts of pork from packinghouses in the Midwest remained the principal source of meat for Southerners in the first third of the twentieth century, just as they had been in the last quarter of the nineteenth.

European immigrants who ended up in the South in the half-century or so following the Civil War added some variety to the homogeneous populations of Anglo-Saxons and Afro-Americans, but most of them were as poor as the poorest of Southerners, and they had in addition the disadvantage of not speaking the language. Unlike the French who came to Louisiana in the eighteenth century and the Germans who settled in Louisville, Nashville, and other cities after the Civil War, the twentieth-century immigrants seemed intent only upon blending into the culture of the white South. For those who found entry-level jobs in the food industry—and they were numerous—the model was not the French chef or the German baker or the master cooks of their own countries; it was the free-enterprise American.

Greeks offer an especially interesting example. Between 1865 and 1915, when about a quarter of a million Greek immigrants entered the United States, more than 25,000 of them moved into the South. Aside from a few thousand who congregated in Tarpon Springs, Florida, to develop a sponge-fishing industry, the Greeks tended to scatter across all the states of the region. Many of them found their way into the food business (though their prior experience in that field was limited)—but instead of transplanting Greek food traditions, they sought to cater to Southern tastes. To this day, almost every Southern state has a few Greek-owned restaurants of notable longevity and quality, most of them specializing in seafood, steaks, or even traditional Southern "home cooking." Poor though they were when they arrived, the Greeks found a home in the South—and for many of them, food was the ticket to better times.

Southern poverty was so widespread and crippling by the 1930s that the Roosevelt administration declared it to be the nation's most serious economic problem. The New Deal marked the beginning of a gradual climb toward recovery in the region, but the process was painfully slow, so slow that hunger and malnutrition were still a major concern three decades later. The South's isolation from the rest of the country gradually diminished with the coming of better roads, the interstate highway system, air travel, television, and other modern developments, and significant attacks on poverty were begun in the 1960s, but these chronic problems continued to plague the region. So did the third of the South's major handicaps: racial segregation and discrimination.

From the beginning of slavery in Virginia nearly 370 years ago, the white South clung stubbornly to a way of life that perpetuated color-based inequality. Having fought and lost a civil war at least partly for the legal right to keep slavery,

About 1907, there came to Chattanooga a group of Greeks, who opened the Grand Ocean Cafe, possibly inspired by the grand ocean over which they had but recently passed. It was something new to Chattanooga, walls and floors tiled in beautiful patterns. Those Greeks knew perfectly well how to prepare sea food. For many years they enjoyed a splendid business, and some of them branched out for themselves. One, Gus Tombras, opened the White House Restaurant on East 8th Street. He could prepare the best tenderloin trout that any man ever sank a tooth into. I followed him wherever he went for that delicacy, and when he saw me coming he would shout an order back to the kitchen for tenderloin trout. Later, Gus established [the United States Cafe on Market Street, the Manhattan Cafe at 9th and Broad, the Farmers Market Restaurant on East 11th Street, and the Mount Vernon Restaurant on South Broad]. He bought a farm east of Missionary Ridge and raised his vegetables and hams, and a street in that section is still called Tombras Street for him.

J. P. Brown, Sr.,
in the Chattanooga Times,
circa 1950

the region's political and economic leaders began in the 1890s to write into law a complex scheme designed to serve two basic purposes: first, to keep the black population (approximately one third of the total) available as a source of cheap labor and, second, to prohibit their intermingling socially with the white majority. The concept was called, ironically, "separate but equal development." It was a contradiction in terms and, in fact, a subterfuge to get around the equal-justice requirements of the U.S. Constitution, but the Supreme Court nonetheless upheld the laws in 1896, and they remained in force until the court reversed its position in 1954.

A classic illustration of the illogical and essentially unfair ways in which the racial contradiction was played out in the daily lives of black and white Southerners during those years can be found in the realm of food. From the fields in which it was grown to the kitchens in which it was prepared to the dining tables where it was eaten, Southern food in the first half of the twentieth century revealed a society living blindly and destructively with institutionalized racism.

Segregation dictated a welter of gross inconsistencies and inequities. Blacks who were employed by whites and cooks worked long hours for low pay, creating culinary masterpieces that they could test-taste in the kitchen but never eat in the dining room. They were the principal cooks and waiters in restaurants where they were not allowed to eat, on trains and boats where they were not allowed to ride as passengers, and in churches and clubs where they were not allowed to hold membership. Blacks invented new dishes, taught whites how to cook, and even on occasion wrote cookbooks (as two barrier-breaking food specialists, Mrs. W. T. Hayes and S. Thomas Bivins, did in 1912), but they seldom received credit for their accomplishments.

And yet, somehow, in a society of such commonplace discrimination and inequality, the food of the twentieth-century South sprouted and flowered like daisies blooming in a rocky field. Segregation may have kept black and white Southerners from eating together, but it could not keep them from eating the same things, and for the most part they did—pork and chicken, cornbread and biscuits, the whole range of vegetables and fruits, and a multitude of pies and cakes and other desserts straight out of their common heritage. Whether they called it Southern food or soul food, country cooking or home cooking, it all sprang from the same basic traditions established by generations of imaginative Southern cooks, black and white, and enforced segregation was powerless to alter that fact.

Out of its complex and troubled history, the South has evolved a curious and fascinating mélange of food customs and traditions, as well as a bulging catalogue of distinctive recipes. Many of the foodways reach far back into the region's past; most were firmly established by the time the Depression had run its course and World War II had brought the nation to the threshold of the

I remember how startled I was to discover, as I got older, that my mother really couldn't cook at all. Whenever I came home from camp, college, or the Navy, Zola would fix up a brisket, or some crisp roast chicken, or a perfect corned beef; her matzo-ball soup was as deep a Sabbath tradition in our home as the Friday night candles and the kiddush. Zola would also cook up Southern dishes like squash casserole, fried okra, butter beans, and she rolled her fried chicken in matzo meal. (Because my mother never served pork at the table, Zola would pretend to cook bacon for herself when I wanted some.)

Eli N. Evans
The Provincials, 1973

contemporary era. At their best, these customs and traditions cut across the dividing lines of race and class, age and sex, politics and religion and geography. They are worth considering here, both as a culmination of three and a half centuries of regional history up to the middle of the twentieth century and as a prelude to the enormous changes that would ensue in the decades to follow.

The South's food heritage is filled with clues to the character and personality of the region itself.

The heritage originated in nature, in sun and earth and water. From early in its history, the South seemed made to be a food-conscious culture: It had the necessary range of altitudes and temperatures, the proper levels of rainfall and humidity, the right kinds of soil, and the wild habitats to create a strong balance of resources and to allow for optimum growth. Even when these gifts were abused by careless or greedy stewards, the potential was still there, waiting for wiser hands to prevail.

From the beginning, Southerners, like most Americans, were close to the soil. Their lives revolved around the seasons, around sowing and cultivating and harvesting. They were never a monolithic community of interdependent people, but they did always have some common interests, and foremost among them was a primary concern for food—where to get it, how to prepare it, when to eat it. Most of them grew food, either as their principal occupation or as a supplementary activity, and at various times in their history, they experienced the terrible fear of not having enough to go around. In every generation prior to World War II, the vast majority of all Southerners spent most of their waking hours in direct or indirect association with the broad subject of food.

In the fields, work went on from dawn to dusk. In the kitchens, the cooking and serving, canning and preserving, making ready and cleaning up were virtually unending. Families commonly numbered six to twelve or more people, and often included others besides parents and children. They sat down together to three meals a day when there was food enough to serve: breakfast early, dinner at noon (lunch was a seldom-used term), and supper by early evening. Regularity was important, even essential, to cooks and field hands alike, and the clanging of the dinner bell in the yard always brought a prompt response.

If the fare was repetitive, it could also be inventive; there were many ways to make cornbread, to cook pork, to fix a skillet of gravy. As times and fortunes improved, so did the menu: chicken to go with the pork (and even beef and turkey on special occasions), fresh vegetables from the garden or the pantry, pies and cakes that used farm-fresh eggs and butter. Fresh food was always the best, but women who became proficient at canning and preserving— and most did—could almost duplicate the best of July dinners in January.

Family life often revolved around the kitchen and the dining table. Birthdays, anniversaries, weddings, and reunions were celebrated there with food and drink prepared especially for the occasion. Prayers were said at the table, important decisions were made there, and the principle of family unity was repeatedly reinforced there. Holidays brought command appearances by sons and daughters who had moved away.

Sunday dinner became an institution unto itself. It typically began with the ceremonial dispatch of a chicken or two in the backyard, their heads suddenly wrung from their bodies or chopped off with a hatchet by a family member designated to be the executioner. Young roosters and pullets were fried in lard; hens were baked in the oven, often with cornbread dressing. There would be gravy in either case, and it would usually run out before all the biscuits and mashed potatoes or rice could be covered. Green beans and limas, turnip greens and sweet potatoes, corn and squash, sliced tomatoes and cucumbers and onions, cabbage and okra and fried apples would circulate continuously, and there would be frosty pitchers of iced tea and buttermilk to accompany them. Lively conversation also lubricated the palates. As soon as the table was cleared, the pies and cakes were brought in, and finally, the diners struggled to their feet and retired to the porch or the parlor—"tight as a tick," someone invariably complained—and talked or napped while they waited for ease from the agony of overstuffing. The preachers who rotated among their flock for such Sunday spectaculars often had the girth to prove how well-regarded they were.

It was not just the happy occasions that brought food into the center of family life; mourning, too, had a gastronomical dimension. A death in the family always brought a steady procession of kin and neighbors to the door with food to feed the funeral guests. Before the days of funeral homes, death was a domestic experience; the undertaker came to lay the corpse out in the bedroom or the parlor, and burial might take place in a family cemetery nearby. Houses commonly were built with parlor doors wide enough to allow caskets to pass. People who came from afar to participate in the ritual of death and burial sometimes stayed for days, and together with the local mourners, they presented the survivors with logistical problems, not least of which was feeding the assemblage.

When the departed loved one had been widely known and liked, the funeral crowd was apt to be large—but so was the offering of sympathy, help, and food. A caller who wished simply to be polite might bring a routine offering, even something with a name to fit the occasion, like "funeral pie." Deeply grieving mourners, on the other hand, might present several dishes, including one or more of their most prized and elaborate creations. Thus, in many a family, regardless of its wealth or stature, a rough measure of the esteem in which the deceased was held could be taken by observing the number and kind of gift

I will draw you a gastronomic profile of a white family in the rural South during the Great Depression. We were yeoman farmers, the impoverished gentry. We owned two hundred acres on a dirt road five miles out of Elberton, Georgia. The family's cash income was less than one thousand dollars a year, and that supported us and two black tenant families.

We had a wood stove, no running water in the house, no refrigeration

dishes in the kitchen and on the serving tables.

No matter what the occasion, Southern cooks took pride in their ability to bring joy to a crowd of hungry people. They had their subregional or local or individual specialties, things like hickory-bark syrup in the mountains of North Carolina and chocolate gravy in the Arkansas Ozarks and smoked mullet on the Florida Gulf Coast, and they had their universal favorites too: boiled custard, ambrosia, hush puppies, fried chicken, chess pie. Sweets were a particular delight; it was a rare cook who could not whip up a quick batch of cookies or egg kisses or pastries—or something heavier, such as a blackberry cobbler or a banana pudding. It was not at all unusual to find sacrifices to the legendary Southern sweet tooth taking up at least half the pages in a cookbook.

There was a period after the Civil War when cookbook writers and other food specialists in the South emphasized eating to live rather than living to eat. They focused on health, nutrition, economy of time and money, and serious utilitarian purpose; they disdained those who sought to please the palate, to stimulate the appetite, to elevate the experience of dining. Cooking as a sensuous art was criticized and discredited. But it was in this same period that many Southern women, white and black alike, found what little freedom and pleasure life offered them in the kitchen—and little though it was, it was better than nothing. The utilitarian movement never had a chance against the cooks and eaters who looked upon food as the primary source of joy and satisfaction in their lives.

Though they were securely based in the home, Southern food customs and traditions also reached into the larger community. The church was one locus; in both symbolic and literal ways, food played an important role there. It was in the sacrament of communion (bread and wine), in the life of Jesus (the Last Supper), and in the hymnals: "Dwelling in Beulah Land," a popular hymn in the nineteenth century, extolled the virtues of "drinking at the fountain that never shall run dry . . . feasting on the manna from a bountiful supply." In more concrete terms, Southern churchgoers long ago incorporated the brotherhood dinner and the Sunday afternoon picnic into their activities, and few traditions were more basic to a Southern country church than an all-day singing and dinner on the ground.

Schools and political parties also used food to attract a large public following. The harvest festival and the pie supper are examples. So is the political barbecue, an outdoor cookout for a multitude; it was a fixture in the South before the turn of the century—in fact, before the Civil War. The public fish fry and the oyster roast are similarly of long duration and popularity. In Virginia, the Carolinas, and Georgia, throngs have flocked to steaming kettles of Brunswick stew for so long that no one can prove which Brunswick—the city in Georgia or the county in Virginia—is the true originator (history favors

or electricity. Practically everything we ate was produced there on the place. A meal without meat, without some kind of flesh, was somehow lacking—even if it was nothing but fried fatback, which it frequently was. We always had bread, too— cornbread or cornpone or biscuits. Dinner, the midday meal, was the main meal. Besides meat and bread, there were lots of vegetables— beans boiled forever with fatback, greens, potatoes, corn, field peas, turnips, squash, cabbage. It was field-hand food, what the poor ate; I happened to think it was both good and filling. The leftovers went into the oven warmer or were covered over with a cloth, and we ate them cold for supper.

Desserts were big, too, especially on Sunday or whenever the preacher was coming. On those occasions there seemed to be five kinds of everything. Sunday dinner was a major event, a ceremonial affair. In fact, you might say that every day, food was the big central preoccupation of all people in similar circumstances. Anyone who grew up in the South in those years can identify with this description.

a reminiscence by Harold Fleming, Washington, D.C., 1985

I had visions of another meal in the greasy restaurant of the day before. [But] when I saw the neat appearance of the cottage we entered, my fears vanished, and when I saw the woman who kept it, my doubts followed the same course. Scrupulously clean, in a spotless white apron and coloured head-handkerchief, her round face beaming with motherly kindness, she was picturesquely beautiful. She impressed me as one broad expanse of happiness and good nature. In a few minutes she was addressing me as "chile" and "honey." She made me feel as though I should like to lay my head on her capacious bosom and go to sleep.

And the breakfast, simple as it was, I could not have had at any restaurant in Atlanta at any price. There was fried chicken, as it is fried only in the South, hominy boiled to the consistency where it could be eaten with a fork, and biscuits so light and flaky that a fellow with any appetite at all would have no difficulty in disposing of eight or ten. When I had finished, I felt that I had experienced the realization of, at least, one of my dreams of Southern life.

James Weldon Johnson
The Autobiography
of an Ex-Coloured Man, 1912

Virginia). In Kentucky, a stew of the same basic contents (and also of uncertain origin) was attracting hordes of people to public feasts well over a century ago. It is called burgoo—and no one knows where that name came from, either.

Southern restaurants developed some traditions of their own. In New Orleans before the Civil War, some men's bars served free lunches to attract drinking customers—and in parts of south Louisiana today, the "free lunch" sign can still be seen. Tearooms owned and operated by women and catering to a female clientele were present in some Southern cities around the turn of the century, and a few, such as the Satsuma Tea Room in Nashville and the Chesterfield Tea Room in Richmond, are still in business, serving lunch to downtown crowds of men and women. Small country hotels such as the Wayside Inn in Middletown, Virginia, and the Nu Wray Inn in Burnsville, North Carolina, pride themselves on their longevity and the quality of their food.

Whether in the home or in public places, the food traditions that had become a part of Southern culture by the 1940s could be summarized under a single descriptive heading: hospitality. As overworked and ambiguous as the word may have been to many, it had meaning to most Southerners. It was not a myth, nor was it a hallmark of the rich alone; it was simply the way people were. Twice in their history since the Revolutionary War—in the aftermath of the Civil War and in the depths of the Great Depression—Southerners had known hunger, even starvation, and that knowledge had taught them to enjoy the moment, to feast when food was available, and to keep a wary eye on the future. Among all classes—those who had plenty and those who had nothing and all the others in between—food was a blessing, a pleasure, a cause for celebration. The tradition of hospitality, of serving large quantities of good things to eat to large numbers of hungry people, of sharing food and drink with family and friends and even strangers, proved to be a durable tradition in the South, outliving war and depression and hunger. Hospitality could be extended over an elegant and sumptuous dinner, an intimate private party, a picnic for the multitude, or a simple meal of cornbread and beans. It had as much to do with table talk as it did with food, though the talk would often be about the food itself, or about great meals of the past, or great ones still to come. Southerners delighted in what George Bleidt, a veteran eater and talker and for many years the postmaster of Golden Pond, Kentucky, called "a coming together to pass and repast"—a gathering of relatives and old friends to exchange greetings and to dine together on their assembled culinary specialties.

The South was not the only region in the country with an abiding interest in food-related activities, nor was it necessarily the first to develop such an interest. But as the first half of the twentieth century came to a close, it seemed fair to say that no other region had been more obsessively preoccupied with food throughout its history, and none had made it more a part of its culture and traditions. In every generation, in every social and economic group, and in every locale, Southerners had made food a central focus of their lives. In different ways and for different reasons, they had all come to the same conclusion about food: Fix plenty, make it irresistibly good, and share it around.

By the time World War II was over, the South had begun to assimilate many modern American foodways, and to originate still more of its own. Recovery from the Depression, stimulated by the war economy, accelerated the pace of change. The war years brought food rationing and victory gardens—nothing new to most Southerners—and stimulated the development of public eateries where people could get food in a hurry. Hurrying was not a strong Southern trait, but it eventually caught on anyway.

J. A. Morrison and G. C. Outlaw had opened a cafeteria in Mobile, Alabama, in 1920, a quarter of a century after the concept was introduced in Chicago, and Morrison's Cafeterias went on to become the largest chain in the country. Robertson's, a cafeteria in Charleston, South Carolina, also opened for business in 1920, and others, such as Bryce's in Texarkana, Arkansas, and Wise's in New Orleans, were started in the early 1930s. Cafeterias proved to be popular in the South, and also durable: Morrison's still leads the chains, and Robertson's, Bryce's, and Wise's still thrive as nonchain enterprises.

Chains also were the wave of the future in the grocery business. Chains that originated in the South in the twentieth century included Winn-Dixie, Publix, and Piggly Wiggly. Clarence Saunders, who founded the Piggly Wiggly stores in Memphis in 1916, also introduced the supermarket concept to America by equipping shoppers with baskets and letting them, rather than clerks, select food from the shelves.

The hamburger restaurant, harbinger of the fast-food industry, started in Wichita, Kansas, when the first White Castle opened in 1921, and eleven years later, the South introduced its version of the same when Krystal opened in Chattanooga, Tennessee. Another famous sandwich, the poor boy, originated in New Orleans in 1929, but nobody perfected a way to franchise such a juicy combination: roast beef, gravy, mayonnaise, lettuce, tomato, pickle, and mustard on an individual loaf of French bread. It has also proved to be exceedingly difficult to apply the chain-store concept to barbecue sandwiches, though some determined entrepreneurs continue to try. Barbecue sandwiches are as old as sliced bread, and the meat, of course, goes back much farther than that. Only when the sandwiches are made from meat fresh from the pit, where it has cooked slowly over hardwood coals, can they truly be worthy of the name barbecue.

The South had its own beers in the nineteenth century, most of them de-

Travelers in the South who have heard of the delights of Southern cuisine are about as likely to find them as they are to be hit by a meteor—unless they have some Southern cousins or belong to a Southern country Sunday school.

This explains why tourists get a shock when they cross the Mason-Dixon line and gleefully enter a café rubbing their hands and licking their chops with the thought: "Now for some real Southern fried chicken!" Just why they think they will find that rara avis in a restaurant, of all places, is still a mystery to Southerners who have been trained to look for it only at home.

As they travel over the South their disappointment increases. . . . But there are notable exceptions. There are oases in the Sahara of Cuisine.

There are people in the South who know how to baste bluefish with butter . . . who know how to cure hams over hickory smoke . . . who can do things with shrimps and crabs . . . and who can prepare barbecue (if given twenty-four hours) that bears the same resemblance to the wayside Bar-B-Q product that a Beethoven violin concerto does to a Crosby croon.

William T. Polk
Southern Accent, 1953

veloped by German immigrants in such river cities as Louisville, Nashville, and New Orleans. Winemaking was popular, too; for example, in the Arkansas hamlets of Tontitown and Altus, Italian and German immigrants were fermenting the juice of the grape before 1900, and the tradition continues to this day. Most of the leading soft drinks also came from the region, including Coca-Cola, which was created by John S. Pemberton, an Atlanta pharmacist, in 1886. Originally a patent medicine, a remedy for headaches and hangovers, the drink was made from extracts of the cola nut and the leaf of the coca plant. Cocaine is also a product of the coca leaf, and before 1900, Coca-Cola contained an infinitesimal trace of cocaine, but Asa G. Candler, the man who bought the rights to the soda syrup and turned it into a refreshment, took pains to make sure that all traces of the drug were removed. It seems a reasonable supposition that the drink's nickname, Coke, and another term for soft drinks widely used in the South in earlier years—namely, "dope"—were oblique references to the narcotic. But Coke and its principal Southern rivals, Pepsi Cola and Dr Pepper and Royal Crown Cola, were innocent pleasures destined for a wider market.

Other snack foods also grew increasingly popular: peanut butter and crackers, salted peanuts, candy bars such as the Goo Goo Cluster from Nashville, snack cakes such as the Moon Pie from Chattanooga. An RC Cola and a Moon Pie was an often-called-for quick lunch or snack, and kids loved to pour peanuts into their Cokes and Pepsis.

When the Tennessee Valley Authority and other utilities began to make electricity more widely available to homes across the South in the 1930s, a revolutionary change reached into the kitchen: the electric refrigerator-freezer. Only twenty thousand such units were in American homes in 1923, but by 1941 the number had soared to three and a half million, and many of them were in the South. Refrigerated trucks were on the roads, too, and that meant that such perishable delicacies as shrimp could be transported from Southern ports to distant locations inland. Shrimp abounded in Southern waters many centuries ago, but it was not until the 1930s that they began to appear in cookbooks and on restaurant menus in the nation's interior. Without modern technology, they simply could not be made available far from the coast.

Other contemporary Southern favorites thought to be eternal were also latecomers to the region's cookbooks and restaurants, among them such famous desserts as pecan and chess and black bottom pies.

Another phenomenon of the 1930s, made popular by the proliferation of automobiles, was the drive-in restaurant. By 1950, virtually every town of any size had at least one such establishment—although thirty years later almost all of them were gone, replaced by the eat-in or takeout chains of the fast-food era. Drive-ins added greatly to the popularity of sandwiches, hamburgers, and soft drinks, but they were not "fast"; on the contrary, they invited patrons to park and stay a while.

Finally, a Southerner by the name of Duncan Hines used his car to help knit the separate pieces of America together, and he remains a symbol for the entry of the South and the nation into the modern age. His main contribution was a little red book called *Adventures in Good Eating.*

Duncan Hines grew up on his grandmother's Southern country cooking near Bowling Green, Kentucky. In 1898, when he was eighteen years old, he went to work for Wells Fargo in Arizona, and eventually he made his way back to the Midwest. In Chicago in the 1930s, he gained a reputation as a discriminating eater with a keen homing sense for good restaurants. As his job took him around the country, he began to keep notes on places he had eaten, and in 1935 he printed a little Christmas booklet for his friends, giving them tips on restaurants and their specialties and prices. So well received was it that Hines decided to expand the booklet into a softcover directory of restaurants in cities and towns and along the highways of all the states. The first edition of *Adventures in Good Eating* was published in 1936.

That was the beginning of a phenomenal conglomerate of food-related enterprises: semi-annual and annual restaurant guidebooks, hotel and motel guides, cookbooks, travel books, packaged food products ranging from country hams to cake mixes, a cooking school, a food institute. For a number of years after he returned to Bowling Green in 1939, Hines operated his lucrative businesses from his hometown with the creative aid of his collaborator, Roy H. Park, a native North Carolinian. Procter & Gamble bought out the entire operation in 1957 and Hines died two years later, but he had lived to see his name become a household word throughout the nation. Building on his native food heritage as a Kentuckian and a Southerner, he had produced the nation's first restaurant guide and elevated the stature of regional food in the process.

It is interesting to note in passing that more than a dozen of the Southern restaurants that Duncan Hines recommended in his first guidebook fifty years ago are still in operation. Among them are Columbia Restaurant in Tampa, Florida; Antoine's and Arnaud's in New Orleans; Weidmann's in Meridian, Mississippi; the Peabody Hotel in Memphis; the Smithfield and Williamsburg inns in Virginia; the Jarrett House and High Hampton Inn in the mountains of North Carolina; and four Kentucky inns—Boone Tavern in Berea, Beaumont Inn in Harrodsburg, the Shaker Village Inn at Pleasant Hill, and the Old Stone Inn at Simpsonville.

A strong argument can be made that the South has experienced more fundamental change in the four decades since the end of World War II than in all the three and a half centuries of its history before that. This argument will not be

Many Southern ladies had Negro cooks to help them; and just how much we owe to their skill I have no way of knowing except that almost all of the finest Southern dishes are of their creating or at least bear their special touch, and everyone who loves good cookery should thank them from the bottom of his heart. They cooked by instinct, these artists of the saucepan and skillet, like a musician who plays by ear, and measured everything as "a smidgin of this and pinch of that"; and their educated hands could tell when bread or pie crust felt just right. But what is a smidgin? Or a pinch? I don't know, and I'm sure the cooks didn't either; or if they knew, it was their way of keeping secret their own recipes. I've spent hours in Southern kitchens watching these cooks and trying to learn from them just how much of what went into a dish that I particularly enjoyed.

Duncan Hines
Food Odyssey, 1955

pursued here, except as it relates to the growing, cooking, and eating of Southern food. In that realm, the transformation has truly been enormous—and as change usually is, it has been for better and worse.

Dinner bells bring big prices in antique shops now. There is no more dinner at midday; there is only lunch. Dinner took the place of supper in the evening. For a significant and growing number of Americans, none of the meals they used to sit down and eat at home three times a day are now taken in that fashion. Breakfast comes in a cereal box or a juice can or a Styrofoam coffee cup from the takeout counter; lunch is in a brown bag, a snack-pak, a diet drink, a quarter-pounder; dinner is microwaved chicken or grilled steak or broiled fish, and it comes with baked potato or French fries and the soup and salad bar, all you can eat. People aren't eating the way they used to—not at home, not together, often not sitting down, and never three times a day.

This is mostly good news for women, particularly those who used to spend the bulk of their hours and days and years in one phase or another of the food game. The rules of that game have changed, and that, too, is a good thing. It is no longer considered to be the sole responsibility of females to shop, cook, serve, and clean up the kitchen. That carry-over from the time when men spent all their waking hours raising the food is an anachronism now for the vast majority of American males who grow nothing but beards, and maybe a little crabgrass.

About half of women now work outside the home, and most of those who don't have paying jobs pursue other responsibilities and other interests that take them away from the house during the day. Few of them have the time or the desire to fix food in the old manner—and on the rare occasions when they do, they can expect dinner to compete and conflict with other attractions.

Supermarkets still do a booming business, of course, but their heaviest volume is not in the made-from-scratch department—it is in processed foods: canned, frozen, concentrated, precooked, artificially flavored, shrink-wrapped, plasticized, new-and-improved, ready-to-eat foods.

Curiously, cookbook sales seem not to have diminished at all in the midst of this whirl of changes; on the contrary, there are now more cookbooks than ever, and they sell briskly. Cookbooks are like Bibles in the South: There is no end to them, and every version seems to find a market. *Southern Living* magazine, the glamorous daughter of the plain old *Progressive Farmer* in Birmingham, Alabama, has more than two million subscribers to its monthly compendium of recipes and other home features, and the cookbooks that roll from its presses are so numerous and so similar in content and appearance that it is hard to tell them apart. Countless other commercial and not-for-profit organizations have tried to emulate the phenomenal success of *Southern Living* with

My mother died when I was eleven, and that's when I started to work—washing dishes, cleaning, learning how to cook. That was in Georgia and Florida, back before World War I. I made two or three dollars a week back then.

By the time I got to Nashville in about 1932, I had learned how to cook by experience, by just doing

cookbooks of their own, and though they cannot catch the leader, they usually succeed on a smaller scale.

In many of the modern volumes, signs of the momentous changes that are taking place may be subtle and muted, but they are there: no-fat versions of rich desserts, salt-free and sugar-free recipes, steamed or quick-cooked vegetables, recipes that call for packaged mixes or artificial topping, decaffeinated coffee and tea crystals, meat substitutes, microwave and food-processor quickies, even such strange-sounding new foodstuffs as tofu, bulghur, tabouli.

Another measure of the accelerating shifts in Southern social and cultural patterns can also be found in the cookbooks, and the Junior League library covers the entire evolution. In the 1950s, the young white woman whose recipes appeared there was "Mrs. John Smith"; in the 1960s, she was "Mrs. John Smith (Betty)"; in the 1970s, she was "Betty Smith (Mrs. John)"; in the 1980s, she is "Betty Jones Smith."

For black women and men, there has been a revolution on the surface of Southern social and cultural life in the past forty years, and however deep it has penetrated in other areas, it has certainly reached the kitchen. There are black cooks still living who can remember working seven days a week for "a couple of dollars and some leftovers," and who finally got two dollars a day from a white employer who grumbled that the raise amounted to a 700 percent increase. Far fewer black cooks now live in or travel daily to the homes of white Southerners, and those who do make considerably more than two dollars a day (though still not as much as other skilled professionals, whether they be doctors or plumbers or restaurant chefs).

In the public arena, the end of segregation opened restaurants and other facilities to blacks, and they have made their presence felt as both patrons and proprietors. They have also continued in large numbers to work in restaurant kitchens. Their accomplishments there have never been fully appreciated, as Nathaniel Burton and Rudy Lombard persuasively contend in *Creole Feast*, their book about fifteen master chefs of New Orleans, but the picture has improved substantially in many places. In other places, unfortunately, there has been hardly any change at all—in clientele, in kitchen help, or in the attitudes of white owners and patrons.

But just as whites are no longer the only customers in restaurants, blacks are no longer the only cooks and kitchen workers. The segregated South of isolation and poverty, of white Anglo-Saxon Protestants and black descendants of former slaves, is a more open and prosperous and diverse region now, and its foods have been expanded accordingly.

The people may have been all Indians and British and Africans at first, but they didn't stay that way long—and in Florida, where the initial immigrants

it—and I was good at it, too. I could fix any kind of dinner. If you wanted plain, down-to-earth home cooking, Southern food, I could do that, and if you wanted real fancy dishes, I could do that too. You know, some people can learn to cook and some can't, and some just know how right from the start. I was that way—just a natural-born cook.

I'm eighty years old now, and I'm not able to cook anymore, but I cooked and catered with the best of them here in Nashville for over forty years. I've been on TV and in the papers, and back when I worked for the Hank Williams family I went to California with Hank Jr. while he was making a movie, and stories about my cooking got in the paper out there too. I was the first black person to write a cookbook in Tennessee, and one of the finest food markets here in Nashville used to carry some of my packaged food products. Yes, I've done it all. I have a lot of good memories about food and people.

Flossie Morris,
Nashville, Tennessee,
in a 1985 interview

were Spaniards, the strongest ethnic influences have always been Hispanic. Many millions of "new" Americans have come to the South from Spain and Minorca, from Mexico, from Cuba and Puerto Rico, from all over Central and South America, and they continue to arrive in large numbers.

There were French Catholic Acadians in Louisiana and French Protestant Huguenots in South Carolina by the middle of the eighteenth century, and now there are newly arrived French-speaking Haitians in Florida. Jews of many nationalities arrived early in the Atlantic Seaboard states, and so did the Moravians (German Protestants) in North Carolina, the Shakers in Kentucky, and the Amish and Mennonites in Tennessee. Italian and Greek and Lebanese immigrants became Southerners in the nineteenth century. There are Chinese-Americans in Mississippi now whose ancestors settled there more than a century ago, and there are people of Japanese descent in Arkansas whose parents and grandparents were brought there to be housed in internment camps during World War II. More recently, Southeast Asian refugees have settled in various parts of the South, and immigrants from India have become active in the motel and restaurant business in the region.

And then there are the Yankees, who have been arriving from the East and the Midwest and the West right along, in good times and bad. Altogether, the "non-Southern" Southerners are numerous enough to shatter the myth of a monolithic region closed to outsiders. If it was ever that, it is no longer. The immigrants have brought their own national and regional food specialties with them, and in greater and lesser degrees these comestibles have strengthened and enriched the treasury of Southern foods.

The diversity of recipes and restaurants that newcomers have brought to the South is one of the most significant trends of the postwar era, but a countertrend of even greater importance has been the proliferation of chain restaurants and franchise food shops that are distinguished by the uniformity of their offerings and their decor.

It was in the 1950s that McDonald's and its string of fast-food hamburger-outlet imitators began their takeover of the turf staked out by Krystal and White Castle a generation earlier. It was also in the fifties that Harland Sanders, the goateed "colonel" with a gift for gab and a knack for cooking chicken, opened his first Kentucky Fried Chicken place in Corbin, Kentucky. In just thirty years, these fast-food pioneers have become global giants—and they have revolutionized the eating habits of countless millions of people. The thoroughfares of cities and towns everywhere are lined with legions of food shops, and their wares are hawked on television and in every other medium of advertising. The South is at least as fully loaded with these outlets as any other section of the country; in fact, several of the chains originated in the South and maintain

I had a couple of friends in from the country where I used to live, ten miles out of Charlotte. I prepared some refreshments—some anchovies, good Liederkranz cheese, a piece of Stilton aged in port wine, and some black olives. With crackers and beer it made a respectable snack. The folks dipped into this and that, and finally the lady, showing great surprise, said, "You all don't eat like we do, do you?"

Harry Golden
Only in America, 1958

their headquarters in the region. (Kentucky Fried Chicken is one of these, in a roundabout way; its main offices are in Louisville, but it was owned until 1986 by a Connecticut-based beverage company, which in turn was owned by a North Carolina–based tobacco company. Now the brainchild of the late Colonel Sanders belongs to Pepsi Cola, a Southern-born soft drink that long ago moved north.)

Among the most interesting food chains with headquarters in the South are three Tennessee companies that base their appeal on a nostalgic restaging of the "down-home" country dinner. The most successful of the three, Shoney's, is the least "Southern"; it calls itself "America's dinner table," and its menu and appearance are regionally neutral. The Cracker Barrel, a chain of "old country store" restaurants, is decidedly Southern in its makeup and its menu: breakfasts featuring ham and biscuits and gravy, meat-and-vegetable dinners, cobblers for dessert, and an array of Southern-style foods and gifts for sale in the adjacent shop. The food is similar at Po Folks, the third of the chains, but the menu takes "Southern" to its ultimate extreme, enthroning the stereotype of the dumb hillbilly who can't spell, count, or think.

Considering how much of the food in these restaurants is processed rather than fresh, it is surprisingly good. That it is now the best Southern food available in many locations is a clear measure of how much the traditional cookery of the region has changed and how many of the fine old cafes and diners have disappeared.

If the restaurant scene has changed dramatically, the home front has been just as completely affected. Space-age technology has delivered new tools—the microwave oven, the food processor—and television shows these wonders to rich and poor alike, urging them to buy. Cookbooks and food magazines sing the praises of a dizzying array of dishes, too many to grasp. There is confusing and sometimes conflicting news about nutrition, about harmful chemicals in foods, about what is good for you and bad for you. The processed foods from the grocery are often bland and unappetizing, and the fresh fruits and vegetables may have been sprayed with harmful insecticides or injected with artificial coloring or just picked green, before the flavor was set. Even if everyone showed up for dinner, the obstacles to putting a tasty meal on the table are high, and climbing higher.

Out in the fields, there are new crops in the South. The nonedibles, cotton and tobacco, seem to be fading, but their replacement is soybeans, which are not much help at the dinner table. Peanuts are big in Virginia and Georgia, and sugarcane is a major crop in Louisiana and Florida, but you can't make a meal of them. Arkansas grows a lot of rice (Louisiana and Texas do too), but most of it is exported, and even the school cafeterias don't use much of it. Florida's

He spent a lot of time thinking about his plan. What should he call his chicken . . . lip-smacking, crispy, juicy, down-home, kitchen-fresh, tooth-tender? How about Colonel Sanders' Fried Chicken? With his picture as the Kentucky colonel? Maybe he ought to bring in the name of Kentucky. How about Colonel Sanders' Kentucky Fried Chicken? Was that better than Southern Fried? Farm Fried? Home Fried? Yeah, he decided, it was. Kentucky had a good ring to it—rolling bluegrass meadows, white fences, pillared old mansions, smells of cooking wafting out of the old kitchen. And after all, he was a genuine Kentucky colonel. . . . Colonel Sanders' Kentucky Fried Chicken. That would do it. He decided to incorporate as soon as he got home. Thought maybe he'd better copyright the name, too, and his picture, with the white suit, goatee, and all.

John Ed Pearce
The Colonel, 1982

winter vegetables are in grocery displays everywhere, but the flavor of such items as hothouse tomatoes leaves much to be desired.

Two of the most important crops in the South now are chickens and catfish. Georgia, Alabama, Mississippi, North Carolina, and Arkansas are prime producers. The chickens are fat caricatures of the slender little "frying-size" pullets that used to scratch for feed in Southern barnyards, but they are trucked out by the millions to supermarket meat counters and fast-food cookers all over the country. The catfish are an anomaly: one of the few artificially produced foods that may be better than the original. River catfish have almost succumbed to pollution.

Gardens are still popular in some parts of the South, but they are like any other activity: They take time, and time is the one thing that few people seem to have enough of. Many a well-intentioned gardener, tired of battling floods, drought, insects, rodents, birds, and mysterious plant maladies, finally gives up the fight and goes to the grocery or the farmers' market, if such a useful institution still exists in his community.

By any measure, it is a new and different South in the world of food, a South that has gained much in the postwar age, but also lost much. In both directions, it would be beyond the recognition of Captain John Smith or President Thomas Jefferson or General Robert E. Lee. When change finally came to the South, it came with a mighty rush.

What remains of the South that now seems worth protecting and preserving? What is left that is authentic and valuable and representative of the best that Southerners could do? It is a short list: some of the literature and music and the arts, the oral tradition, the speech patterns, some of the traits of character and personality—and some of the food. There probably is very little that anyone can do to assure that these dwindling treasures will keep their vitality and usefulness. As long as enough people value them, they will last. How many is enough, and what constitutes value? No one can say. You can only do your part and hope for the best.

With food as with the other remaining assets, the problems are many. Take breakfast: From the earliest years on the Virginia frontier, it was an important meal, probably the most important of the day. It was a heavy meal then—pork and beef, fowl and fish, game meats, hot breads, cheese, eggs, fruit, ale and other drinks, cakes and pies. It made sense nutritionally, providing as it did the body fuel for long days of hard physical labor. Such heartiness was also hospitable to the guests who often came and went in the wilderness and stayed overnight. When inns and taverns were established to accommodate travelers such as these, they too featured large early-morning meals.

The tradition carried over into the eighteenth and nineteenth centuries,

The Virginia middle class on the Piedmont during the Revolution, after getting up around six and having an eye opener of strong toddy, went out and worked or supervised till ten o'clock, and then sat down to cold meats, cold turkey, fried hominy, toast and "cyder," ham, bread and butter, tea, coffee, and chocolate. The Cumberland farmer [in Kentucky and Tennessee] soon was having most of this, especially the ham, toddy, bread and butter, but more coffee than chocolate or tea. . . . Many Cumberlanders preferred such a breakfast to anything else—good fresh eggs, home-cured bacon, hot cornbread with plenty of good butter, gravy, or honey in the comb, all with good coffee and good whiskey, the whole flavored slightly with wood smoke from hardwood embers, was not bad eating.

Harriette Simpson Arnow
Seedtime on the Cumberland, 1960

and while the fare grew lighter (more bacon and eggs instead of venison or goose), it remained plentiful. From this period in every Southern state, there are stories of fabled breakfast feasts—for social occasions such as fox hunts and horse races, for the benefit of houseguests who happened through, and even for families preparing for a long day in the fields. Even now in the rural South, it is possible to experience such a meal.

But the tradition is fading. The food is said to be too heavy, and unhealthy as well: too much sugar in the pancakes and syrup and jam, too much fat in the bacon and sausage, too much cholesterol in the eggs, too much salt in the ham, too many calories in the biscuits and butter. The preparation time is also a problem; it simply takes too long to deliver an elaborate breakfast of fresh and homemade foods to the table—and when it has been eaten, more time is needed to clean up the dishes and put away the leftovers. The cost is a factor too; a big breakfast for six or eight or a dozen people is not cheap.

So breakfast has been transformed—speeded up, trimmed down, liquefied, purified, packaged. If you miss it at home, you can grab it at a fast-food outlet on the way to work, or even from a coin-operated machine. A large and varied and delicious morning repast to be shared in good company, or even lingered over alone with an extra cup of coffee and the morning paper, has become a pleasure more to be remembered wistfully than experienced. Some restaurants still work at it, and some have instituted a weekend brunch that is reminiscent of a first-rate breakfast, but the real thing is hard to find, whether you're eating out or at home.

Or, to illustrate the problem further, take barbecue, one of the most distinctly and representatively Southern of all foods. Midwesterners may have raised most of the pigs since the Civil War, but they have never mastered the art of roasting them slowly over hardwood coals, an art the Indians of the Caribbean and the Southeast reportedly had perfected with other meats long before the first Europeans arrived, and that Southerners of all races have excelled at ever since.

Classic Southern barbecue is the antithesis of fast food; it is slow food, requiring hours of patient preparation. But technology has introduced shortcuts to cooking barbecue, and they are spreading like an insidious disease. In some places, gas flames have replaced hickory fires, and liquid smoke is being applied to simulate the smell and taste of wood smoke. Controlled temperatures in air-tight ovens have speeded up the cooking time, and pressure cooking with steam is now practiced by some barbecuers. Warming ovens and microwaves are used to approximate the effect of straight-from-the-pit freshness. The spicy sauces that once added zest to real pit barbecue may now be nothing more than shortcut combinations of catsup, vinegar, and liquid smoke. And perhaps inevitably, products labeled barbecue can be found canned and frozen in supermarkets. In the meantime, a genuine barbecue sandwich made from slowly cooked, hickory-smoked pork shoulder (or beef or mutton, if you prefer) and served fresh from the pit is a rare commodity in the South—and virtually nonexistent anywhere else.

Time and cost and changing habits are the primary factors in the disappearance of traditional Southern food—and as Raymond Sokolov discovered and skillfully reported in his book *Fading Feast,* the phenomenon is by no means limited to the South. It is especially noticeable here, however, because food has always played such an important role in the region's social and cultural history. Southern food by whatever name—home cooking, country cooking, Creole, Cajun, seafood, soul food, cracker cooking, low-country/hill-country/ mountain food, field-hand food, tearoom food, slow food—is in danger of disappearing. There may be plenty of places that advertise the native fare on interstate highway billboards and dish up facsimiles of it in plain and fancy establishments dotted across the landscape, but only a small and diminishing number of them are reliable sources of authentic and traditional Southern food.

Almost every restaurant owner and home cook who does still specialize in the preparation of such food will acknowledge that the future of this rich and diverse cuisine is in jeopardy. The quality and availability of many foodstuffs is declining, they will tell you; the cost of good ingredients is becoming prohibitive; more and more people prefer speed, convenience, and ready availability over quality, and are losing the ability to distinguish real food of high value from its artificial substitutes. In restaurants, the profit margin is low, and the chains are cutting costs and driving the independents out of business; the pay for good cooks and other food workers is too low to keep reliable hands in charge; and the eating public doesn't appreciate good food enough to pay higher prices for it. With so many problems, the wonder is that Southern food has not already disappeared.

But it has not. Surprisingly, amazingly, there are still places in the region where people congregate to "pass and repast," to talk and eat in the time-honored fashion. There are restaurants in every Southern state where these pleasures are repeated daily, places where regulars and newcomers keep on stopping for a taste of their past, a sample of something familiar and comforting. There are public occasions, too—barbecues, fish fries, pie suppers, picnics— where the same familiarity can be felt, and there are of course some home breakfasts and lunches and dinners at which the food and the conversation capture and embrace the same spirit. In the right circumstances, nothing that remains of the Southern past—not even its language and songs, its words and music—can be more strongly reminiscent of the best the region has to offer

Then far down at the corner I saw an old man warming his hands against the sides of an odd-looking wagon, from which a stove pipe reeled off a thin spiral of smoke that drifted the odor of baking yams slowly to me, bringing a stab of swift nostalgia. I stopped as though struck by a shot, deeply inhaling, remembering, my mind surging back, back. At home we'd bake them in the hot coals of the fireplace, had carried them cold to school for lunch; munched them secretly, squeezing the sweet pulp from the soft peel. . . . Yes, and we'd loved them candied, or baked in a cobbler, deep-fat fried in a pocket of dough, or roasted with pork and glazed with the well-browned fat; had chewed them raw—yams and years ago. . . .

"Get yo' hot, baked Car'lina yam," he called. . . .

"How much are your yams?" I said, suddenly hungry.

"They ten cents and they sweet," he said, his voice quavering with age. . . .

I took a bite, finding it as sweet and hot as any I'd ever had, and was overcome with such a surge of homesickness that I turned away to keep my control.

Ralph Ellison
Invisible Man, 1947

than a good meal carefully prepared from fresh native foodstuffs for a company of kin and friends. The hospitality of the Southern table still can be summoned on occasion to create a memorable dining experience.

Food is the only element in our culture that reaches our consciousness through all five of the senses: We can feel its smooth or rough texture, see its diverse colors and shapes, hear it boil or sizzle in preparation for the table, smell its sweet or pungent aroma, and finally taste its wonders—and savor every moment of the experience. Such a powerful force is bound to linger in the memory. Food in the South has symbolized pleasure even in times of sadness and trouble. It has given strength to the weak and hope to the discouraged. It has offered relief from discrimination and poverty and hunger. It has animated the conversations and stimulated the memories of Southerners far and near since time immemorial. Little wonder that it should be among the last vestiges of a "Good South" we all like to remember.

By the broadest definition, Southern food is anything that the people of the region have eaten and enjoyed for a long time. Where can such food still be found? Who cooks it, serves it, knows its mysteries and wonders? Why are the good restaurants still good? How have they managed to stay in business? What are their prospects for the future? And what about the future of home cooking? These are some of the questions that surround the art and science of Southern food. An enjoyable and rewarding search for answers must be focused on two fronts: the road, where the public examples of the cuisine are located, and the kitchen, where those who value the food can experiment extensively in the preparation of it.

In neither place is there an intention to "bring back" Southern food to the center of contemporary life. Practically speaking, it *is* too time-consuming, too costly, too complex, too rich for the blood and the body, to be seriously advocated as the principal diet of modern Americans. But as a part of our heritage and as a source of abiding pleasure, there is ample reason to bring the best of Southern cooking to the table occasionally, and to enjoy it to the fullest. As anyone who grew up on the food can attest, life without a little South in your mouth at least once in a while is a bland and dreary prospect.

And so the car is packed, and the table is set. It is time to hit the road, to go in pursuit of the perfect barbecue sandwich or seafood gumbo or sweet potato pie, or to get into the kitchen and have a go at making scratch biscuits or hoppin John or peach cobbler. The search will not be without some frustration, even failure, but it will have its rewards, and they will make the effort seem worthwhile. Eating out or eating in, Southern food at its best is one of the enduring pleasures of life.

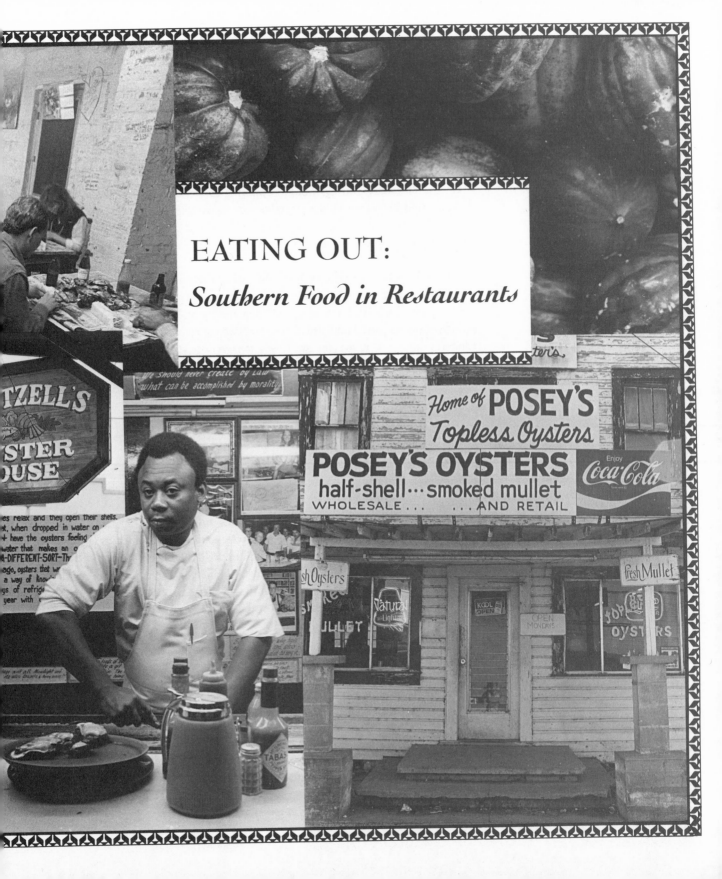

EATING OUT:

Southern Food in Restaurants

Rolling through the south Georgia countryside on a sun-splashed November morning, I counted the miles to Savannah and thought about Sema Wilkes. In another hour, her boardinghouse dinner tables would be spread with starched white linens, set with heavy china and flatware, and laden with the fare of the day: pickles and preserves and gravies, hot biscuits and corn muffins, coffee and iced tea, five kinds of meats, a dozen hot vegetables and cold salads. The cakes and pies and puddings would be waiting in the kitchen. The first wave of diners would be seated at the six tables for eight, happily serving themselves and passing around the bowls and platters. I glanced at my watch. If we were lucky, we would get there before the food was gone and Mrs. Wilkes had to close.

It was Day 3 in Georgia, early in the second month of our quest for restaurants serving traditional Southern foods—an interesting and enjoyable assignment, to say the least, but a physically demanding one too. In fact, in the first month of the venture I had already learned two valuable but conflicting lessons. One was that we were moving too slowly to cover the vast territory from northern Virginia to southwest Louisiana in the time I had thought it would take; the other was that we were moving too swiftly to absorb the facts, let alone the meaning, of the experiences we were having.

"If General Sherman had kept a pace like this," I mused aloud as we zipped past the Statesboro-Claxton exit on Interstate 16, "the war probably would have ended a lot sooner."

Ann thought about that for a minute and replied, "If he had stopped for barbecue and catfish as often as we have, he never would have made it to the coast."

Big projects always seem easier in the talking and planning stage than in the doing. I had begun this one logically and systematically by compiling a list of criteria to help me identify the restaurants I hoped to find, and then circulating the list to a hundred or so friends and acquaintances who were present or former residents of the South. I asked them to write to me about any eating places they knew of that met more than half of these criteria:

❖ The restaurants, cafes, diners, and other eateries should be known in their circles as favorite places specializing in native or adopted Southern dishes.

❖ The regional specialties on their menus should be derived from old and authentic Southern recipes and made, whenever possible, with fresh ingredients, not with frozen or canned or otherwise prepackaged foods.

❖ Each restaurant should be one of a kind, not one of a chain; it may be small or large, but it should be locally owned and operated and highly individualized—imitated by others, perhaps, but duplicated by none.

Commercialized "Southern cooking," the kind advertised by gaudy signs along thousands of highways in the Deep South, has almost spoiled the reputation of real Southern food. Real Southern food, despite what its crass promoters and its bigoted detractors say, is not always fried, nor is it typically greasy or heavy or monotonous. And the notion that it must have its taste disguised by heavy slatherings of catsup is blasphemous. Southern food is as delightful and as varied and as interesting as the region from which it comes.

Kathryn Tucker Windham
Southern Cooking to Remember, 1978

❖ They should have been in existence long enough to have stable and firmly established local (and perhaps regional) reputations; ten years would be a reasonable minimum, but more would be better.

❖ They should avoid advertising, particularly large-scale, high-visibility exposure such as that offered by television, interstate highway billboards, and major regional or national magazines.

❖ They should be accessible without reservations, although it might be necessary to wait for a table.

❖ They should avoid phony touches, such as fake Southern or country or "hillbilly" decor, phonetically misspelled menus, formal dress codes, and waiters and waitresses who are required to introduce themselves ("Hi, my name is Jerry and I'll be serving you tonight").

❖ They would more likely be found on city side streets, in small towns, or even in remote country locations than in large hotels and motels, high-rise office buildings, or shopping malls.

❖ They should accept cash or even personal checks more readily than credit cards, the plastic money being a telltale sign of too much organization.

❖ Finally, the meals in these restaurants should be priced in the low to moderate range—say, around five dollars or less for breakfast or lunch and ten dollars or under for dinner.

Restaurants that met all ten of the criteria would be prime candidates for inclusion in the book, of course, but it was not my intention to rank the eating places in any order, or to compile a state-by-state guide to them. Those functions, first assumed by Duncan Hines fifty years ago, are now handled quite thoroughly and skillfully by Jane and Michael Stern and a host of other food critics and guidebook writers. I was not looking for "the best" or "the most" or "the only" Southern restaurants, but simply for a variety of good places to eat in the South—authentic and representative examples of the Southern food heritage. Furthermore, it was not just the food that interested me, but also the cooks and servers, the owners and managers, the clientele, the setting, the atmosphere, the table talk, the history. I wanted to take a close look at the public art of Southern cooking and to write about the traditions of hospitality and service and fine food that are exemplified in the region's restaurants.

Soon after I sent out copies of the list of restaurant criteria, suggestions began to pour in. "Let me tell you about some truly peerless catfish," a letter would urge, or "This is quite simply the best barbecue between here and China," or "Forget what you think you know about real fried chicken and listen care-

It was not only the private homes but many of the taverns which served—as Savoyard said of the old Allen Tavern at Munfordville—"as good old Kentucky cookery as you ever flung your tongue over." The early innkeepers had a heavy but wonderful list to choose from—venison, bear, wild turkey (not yet surpassed by the tame variety), squirrel, rabbit, grouse, quail, wild pigeon, and many other things which Nature provided, free of charge.

As the years went on, their menus became less sylvan, more elaborate, more refined in cookery. But true to the nature of Kentuckians, they retained certain individualisms, which sometimes became famous. At Whaley Pedigo's tavern at Edmonton, in Metcalfe County, in the 1870's, a remarkable dessert was a stack of custard pies (meringueless, of course), one on top of another, a foot high—one old-timer even swears to fifteen inches; and when you wanted pie, you just cut a thin wedge down through the rick from top to bottom.

Alvin F. Harlow
"Weep No More, My Lady," 1942

"It should come as no surprise that from the very beginning [in 1908], dinner at [Mrs. Mary Bobo's Boarding House in Lynchburg, Tennessee] was a gastronomic treat. The noon-hour meal was dished up "family style." Guests sat down together, and platter upon platter of food was brought to the table. The dishes varied from day to day, depending both on Miss Mary's mood of the morning and on the season—what was fresh and available. But it was always Southern fare at its peak. Classic dishes, like fried chicken dipped in a rich egg batter, golden biscuits, or cheese grits, appeared often and were always accompanied by plenty of fresh vegetables. Desserts were almost always pies—fruit pies, custard pies, rolled-up pies—just about any kind of pie one could imagine. This was typical Southern cooking a hundred years ago . . . and it is still the food to be found in Lynchburg today.

Diana Dalsass
Miss Mary's Down-Home Cooking, 1984

fully to me." I was astonished by the energy, the spirit, the depth of feeling in these letters. My inquiry had sprung the latch on a storehouse of happy memories.

I was also surprised by the diversity of suggested restaurants and food styles: plate-lunch places, meat-and-three diners, tearooms, barbecue pits, catfish shanties, soul food cottages, drive-ins, truck stops, boardinghouses, mountain cabins, cafes, seafood shacks, country inns, taverns, oyster bars, plantations, manor houses, grills, dockside kitchens, cafeterias, bakeries, fish camps, lodges. Terms such as "native dishes" and "regional specialties"—in fact, the very idea of Southern food itself—took on broader meaning. The range of regional foods was so broad that inclusion of all the different varieties and styles in our travels would be difficult at best. We would have to follow our own preferences to reach a shorter and more manageable list of restaurants to visit.

Having thus defined the region to be covered and the restaurants to be sought, and having received from our correspondents dozens of specific suggestions of places to eat, we next compiled separate lists for each state and began to plan the series of trips we would make to them. It takes a certain naive innocence, a blind enthusiasm, to look at a project of this magnitude and see only the pleasure in it. I seem to have that capacity.

"You're perfect for this," Ann said. "You're the type who can look at a dish like spoonbread or lemon chiffon pie or custard and whipped cream and convince yourself that because it's light and fluffy, it must be low in calories."

And so, on the first day of October 1984, Ann and I set out for the coast of South Carolina on the first leg of our travels. With Nashville as our base and with Tennessee and Kentucky as our larger patch of home turf, we proceeded in systematic fashion to eat our way across the South. Usually with Ann, sometimes with Al Clayton, once in a while with other companions, and occasionally alone, I piled up the days and weeks of time on the road.

Eight months and more than 27,000 miles later, I had a box full of notes, clippings, menus, and assorted artifacts from 335 restaurants in eleven Southern states. I had interviewed cooks, waiters and waitresses, managers, owners, customers; combed through newspaper files and library cookbook collections; and sought out as many of the eating places on my list as time would allow. It was in no sense a canvass of the field, not a comprehensive examination of the region's restaurants. We had missed a lot, of course, and a hefty percentage of the places we visited gave me nothing distinctive or even interesting to write about. But there remained about two hundred places, give or take a few, that provided a wealth of material on the current state of Southern cooking away from home. These places are mentioned briefly or discussed at some length in the essays that follow here. As incomplete as the sample is, it is nonetheless large enough to suggest some trends and patterns and to yield some informed impressions and tentative conclusions about what is becoming of Southern food.

Two points should be repeated before we move on. First, this is not a guide; no specific information is included here on the exact locations of restaurants, their hours of operation, phone numbers, menus, prices, and such. There are local, state, regional, and national guidebooks, magazines, and directories that can be consulted for these facts.

And second, this is not a rating or rank-ordering of restaurants; the opinions expressed are my own subjective views, and not even Ann and Al and the others who occasionally dined with me necessarily concur in them. The food itself was not my only concern. There were other attractions—people, atmosphere, history—that made me think of these places as typical and representative parts of the Southern whole.

In the end, I have written about the places that were the most interesting to me, the ones that I would visit again with pleasure any time I had the chance. Seeking them out was a great adventure. Keep in mind that I am describing here the collective experiences that made up that adventure in 1984 and 1985. I make no stated or implied suggestion that the reader should find these restaurants as appealing as I did, nor that they are better than other dining places not mentioned, or even that they are still in operation. I am simply reporting the strongest impressions I gained from my Southern journey. The accounts are all about eating out . . . for breakfast, for lunch, family-style, for dinner, in Louisiana, by the waters, on the barbecue circuit, and all over the South.

Breakfast

On May 2, 1936, Kentucky Governor A. B. "Happy" Chandler and his wife invited a few of their friends to breakfast at the chief executive's mansion in Frankfort. It was a small and rather elegant but informal affair, a convivial prelude to that afternoon's sixty-second running of the Kentucky Derby. The menu was made up of traditional "company" fare, the food of many a special morning occasion in the Bluegrass state: two-year-old country ham and red-eye gravy, eggs, grits, coffee, homemade jams and jellies, hot biscuits.

Without knowing it, Happy Chandler had started something special. His successors in office, responding to popular demand, made the Derby breakfast an annual tradition, one more example of Kentucky's celebrated Southern hospitality.

On May 4, 1985, Governor Martha Layne Collins hosted the fiftieth Kentucky Derby breakfast on the capitol grounds. A crowd of thousands—by some estimates, as many as ten thousand—passed through the serving lines to receive generous portions of ham, sausage, bacon, scrambled eggs with mushrooms, cheese grits, country fried apples, biscuits, blueberry muffins, Danish pastries, juice, coffee, and fruit.

The ham was quick-cured, too tough, too salty. The eggs were tasteless, the grits bland, the biscuits a doughy disappointment. The "china" and "silver" and "crystal" were disposable plastic. It's hard to do anything special with a mess-tent meal for ten thousand people. But no one seemed to mind. Almost everyone was dressed to the nines in spring finery, and a spirit of gaiety and cheerfulness suffused the crowd. The Derby breakfast fare is now only a pale facsimile of what Happy put before his friends, but the tradition continues, so popular as to be almost beyond control.

In countless homes around the Bluegrass that same morning, Kentuckians and their guests sat down to private versions of the governor's spread. The Derby Day breakfast is now almost as firmly entrenched as the Derby itself. There are formal repasts for a few seated guests and elaborate buffets for multitudes; there are early and late breakfasts, midday brunches, early and late lunches; some cleave to the traditional fare, others feature such Kentucky spring delicacies as strawberries, Bibb lettuce, and asparagus spears, still others swing to the modern and exotic with all manner of hot casserole combinations and delicate finger foods. In whatever form, these banquets are ubiquitous events that command the presence of many thousands of Kentuckians on the first Saturday morning of every May.

Like the hunt breakfast that preceded it in Kentucky and Virginia, the

In the morning they rose in a house pungent with breakfast cookery and they sat at a smoking table loaded with brains and eggs, ham, hot biscuits, fried apples seething in their gummed syrups, honey, golden butter, fried steaks, scalding coffee. Or there were stacked butter-cakes, rum-colored molasses, fragrant brown sausages, a bowl of wet cherries, plums, fat, juicy bacon, jam. At the midday meal they ate heavily: a huge, hot roast of beef, fat, buttered lima beans, tender corn smoking on the cob, thick red slabs of sliced tomatoes, rough savory spinach, hot yellow corn bread, flaky biscuits, deep-dished peach and apple cobbler spiced with cinnamon, tender cabbage, deep glass dishes piled with preserved fruits—cherries, pears, peaches. At night they might eat fried steak, hot squares of grits fried in egg and butter, pork chops, fish, young fried chicken.

Thomas Wolfe
Look Homeward, Angel, 1929

Derby breakfast harks back to the sumptuous plantation hospitality of colonial times. For the leisure and laboring classes alike, the first meal of the day in those days was often extensive and substantial, if not elaborate. Ever since, breakfast has been a major repast in the South, and people of all classes have often made of it an occasion for heavy consumption. The nature of Southern breakfasts certainly has changed in the food revolution of the past forty years, but there remains a large percentage of people in the region who prefer this meal above all others.

Pork probably has a lot to do with that—hickory-smoked ham, sausage, and bacon. So does Florida citrus, oranges and grapefruit in particular. And so does hot bread—especially biscuits, but also pancakes, waffles, French toast, and even some forms of cornbread. And of course eggs are important, and grits, and a variety of fried dishes—fish, tomatoes, apples, potatoes. To be sure, most of these items can be found on some breakfast menus outside the South, but many of them are directly and specifically tied to Southern cooking, and have maintained a highly visible and abundant presence on morning tables in the region for a very long time. The Southern breakfast is symbolic of much that is distinctive and exemplary about food in the South.

In the past decade or so, the fast-food chains and franchise restaurants have entered the Southern breakfast trade, and the trend has now spread across the country. All of the major hamburger and chicken chains started serving breakfast after Jack Z. Fulk of Charlotte, North Carolina, a franchisee in the Hardee's hamburger business, started making passably decent biscuits in the early 1970s. In 1977, after he had fine-tuned his biscuit recipe, Fulk parlayed it and a Cajunstyle formula for spicy fried chicken into a successful new chain called Bojangles'. Fast-food biscuits swiftly became a permanent fixture in the chains. They are now so common and pervasive that in many communities they are the new standard of what a biscuit is—the best (and sometimes the only) restaurant biscuits in town. Some of them are quite good, but they all tend to be as big (not to say as hard and heavy) as hockey pucks. Made-from-scratch Southern biscuits that are smaller, lighter, flakier, and more delicate than these lumberjack versions are rarely found in restaurants today.

Shoney's, the Southern-based chain of nearly five hundred company-owned and franchised family restaurants, introduced a breakfast bar in the early 1980s, and customers flocked to it immediately. The extensive buffet of hot and cold items offers a blend of juices and fresh fruits with breakfast meats, eggs, grits, potatoes, and hot breads. (The biscuits are unexceptional, but the overall offering is usually quite good.) Both people in a hurry who want speedy service and less rushed customers who want a leisurely morning meal are attracted to it. On weekends, the Shoney breakfast buffet is an economical brunch that keeps customers coming all morning.

Virgil paid him no mind. Almost breathless he called out: "Mamma's fixing a new breakfast. I told her you was coming, Mr. Beckwith. She throwed everything out and started all over again. New biscuits even. She's cooking them on hickory wood. And we're going to have ham! Just for you! Ham and red-eye gravy and apple stew. We're going to have ourselves a breakfast!"

And now Brian laughed again. "So what if God Almighty was to come down to have breakfast? What more would his mamma do? What more could she do?"

Sam flushed. "I didn't even mean to eat."

"You better brace yourself then. It looks like to me that you're going to be eating."

Richard Marius
The Coming of Rain, 1969

The credit for introducing the idea of brunch into the standard Southern dining pattern probably belongs to Elizabeth Kettenring Dutrey Bégué of New Orleans. In 1863, she and her first husband, Louis Dutrey, opened a dining place and bar—a coffeehouse, they called it—near the open-air market in the French Quarter. After Dutrey's death, his widow married another Frenchman, a butcher named Hypolite Bégué, and in 1880 they changed the name of their coffeehouse to Bégué's. The German-born Madame Bégué was justly famed as a cook in the best Creole tradition, and merchants from the market were particularly attracted to her "second breakfast," a splendid repast she served regularly for them at 11 a.m., after the morning rush of shopping was over. Promptly on the hour, the butchers and bakers and produce merchants paraded into Madame Bégué's second-story dining room for a multi-course epicurean feast that began with boiled crawfish and ended an hour later with coffee and brandy.

The tradition continued for twenty-five years, and it became a New Orleans dining experience of the first order for local patrons and food-loving visitors alike. By the time Madame Bégué died in 1906, her "second breakfasts" were renowned far beyond New Orleans. Hypolite Bégué kept up the morning repast until his death in 1917, and the memory lingers to this day among New Orleanians of that generation. Far more than the usual breakfast fare graced Madame Bégué's table, for the meal was as much an early lunch or dinner as it was a late breakfast, but the Bégués and their patrons always referred to it as breakfast, and the dishes did include some that are now morning standards in New Orleans and elsewhere. There was an egg course, usually omelets of all sorts, and there was also pain perdu, or "lost bread"—otherwise known as French toast. Crawfish bisque and Creole gumbo and jambalaya were among the more substantial and celebrated regular dishes. Nobody serves breakfasts like that anymore, not even in New Orleans.

The closest to it may be Brennan's, a forty-year-old French Quarter restaurant founded by Irishman Owen Brennan and maintained since the 1950s by various members of his extended family. It was not the breakfast tradition of Madame Bégué that attracted the Brennans, though; it was rather a novel about the century-old Antoine's, the oldest and most famous restaurant in New Orleans.

Brennan's was a new enterprise when novelist Frances Parkinson Keyes wrote *Dinner at Antoine's* in 1948 and brought added visibility to that already renowned and venerable French Quarter restaurant. The Brennans, led by Owen's brother Dick and sister Ella, were inspired by the Keyes novel to create a showcase of their own: a platonic forenoon feast called Breakfast at Brennan's. It was an immediate success, and it remains a celebrated New Orleans institution; not even long lines, jaded waiters, and prices in the twenty-five-dollars-per-person range seem to discourage the hordes of tourists who arrive early and wait patiently on the street to try the Ramos gin fizzes, eggs Hussarde and other sauce-rich poached egg dishes, grilled grapefruit, bananas Foster and other flaming desserts, café brûlot, and fine wines. The house on Royal Street is packed almost every morning, and others pay Brennan's the ultimate compliment by imitating the grand dishes wherever lavish breakfasts and brunches are served.

On the other side of Jackson Square from Brennan's—and at the opposite extreme from its Creole elegance—is the Café du Monde, where the main feature is café au lait (savory New Orleans chicory coffee with hot milk) and beignets (piping hot and puffy squares of doughnutlike deep-fried pastry). For a dollar or two at any hour of the day or night, you can enjoy these two treats at an outdoor table while watching the human comedy in perpetual parade on Decatur Street.

Pain perdu to rival Madame Bégué's can be found reasonably priced at such places as Mena's Palace, an old and respected Italian restaurant that caters to a diverse clientele in the Quarter. The bread comes fried to perfection, having been dipped in a batter of milk, egg, and vanilla and then sprinkled with cinnamon and powdered sugar as soon as it leaves the grill. With a cup of the house coffee, it's both a bargain and a pleasure—as well as a little slice of New Orleans history.

For many Americans on the run, coffee with a doughnut or pastry and a glass of orange juice has become a standard breakfast. That wouldn't be a bad idea at all, occasionally, if you could get the real thing—but all too often the coffee is instant, the doughnuts are stale or frozen, and the juice is canned or concentrated. Coffee is at best a hit-or-miss proposition, and the South is not as noted for its doughnuts and pastries as some other bakery-rich regions, but all the oranges and grapefruits grown east of the Mississippi River are Florida products, and that ought to make those fruits available fresh in hundreds of Southern restaurants. Alas, it isn't so. Not even in Florida is it the least bit common to find fresh-squeezed orange juice or tree-ripened grapefruit on breakfast menus.

At Pahokee, in the sugarcane and winter vegetable belt of south Florida around Lake Okeechobee, we found fresh fruit at Maxine's, a country-style restaurant owned by John and Maxine Lane, and the breakfast we had there on a Sunday morning in November was noticeably enriched by that freshness. Starting at five o'clock every morning, the Lanes serve three meals a day to a mixed trade of field hands and fishermen, tourists and local regulars. "Everything we serve is fresh," John Lane said. "It's a lot harder that way, but it's the only way to do it right."

At Pensacola, in the Florida panhandle, Earline and Fred Cleaveland have built a twenty-five-year reputation for breakfast excellence at the Coffee Cup, a restaurant that had been a local favorite for fifteen years when they bought

The good old Southern breakfast of grits, country ham, biscuits and red-eye gravy is a thing of the past.

At least that's the word from anthropologists at the University of North Carolina, who recently did a survey of the eating habits of the residents of a small Southern town. They found that the typical breakfast is now cold cereal, milk, toast, coffee and juice, and that anyone who did have biscuits used refrigerated dough or a mix. . . .

This is all very depressing. For years, I've heard that the South will rise again, but nobody told me it would rise to a breakfast of cold cereal. . . .

I am alarmed over the grits situation. . . . You have to ask the waitress to bring you grits. Previously, you only had to ask the waitress not to bring you grits.

More recently, there has been an even more alarming trend in this regard. At some restaurants, you not only have to ask for grits, but have to pay for them as well. I consider this a sacrilege, as I am quite sure that the Lord never intended for grits to be sold.

*Charlie Robins,
in the Tampa Times,
September 26, 1980*

it in 1960. Their specialties are omelets of all kinds and Nassau grits—regular grits fortified with a minced and sautéed mixture of tomatoes, green peppers, onions, bacon, and sausage. A three-to-one mix of regulars and passers-through makes up the clientele, and many of them are there when the Cleavelands open at 6 a.m.

There is another Coffee Cup in Charlotte, North Carolina, and many local diners swear by it. Tucked away in the warehouse district near the downtown area, the small building boasts a big sign: a steaming coffee cup, 1940s-style. Inside, a bar with eight stools and tables for about thirty are clustered in cozy proximity. A jukebox near the door offers soul and country in roughly equal proportions, and the customers are of a similar mix, black and white. The coffee, true to its billing, is first-rate—rich, aromatic, and steaming hot in thick white china cups.

Between Chris Crowder and Mary Lou Maynor, who owned the Coffee Cup when I stopped by, and Myrtle Heath, from whom they bought it, the restaurant has a twenty-year history of fine food. But, said Crowder, "It was here before that—it's *always* been here." Lunch is the main meal, but breakfast is the attraction for many daily patrons. In addition to the standard breakfast fare, they like the fried pork skins, the salmon croquettes, the liver mush. Dot Jackson, a food-wise and otherwise knowledgeable North Carolinian, once described the Coffee Cup as "the sublime of black diners." To the east, in Chapel Hill, a cafe of similar style and quality is Dip's Country Kitchen, where the breakfast menu includes chicken and gravy, salmon cakes, and pork tenderloin.

Unusual breakfast dishes like these show up in lots of places besides Pensacola and Charlotte and Chapel Hill. B.J.'s Restaurant in Benton, Arkansas, has fried bologna and pork chops among its morning meats. At McLean's Restaurant in Richmond, Virginia, we found salt herring, brains and eggs, and fish roe on the menu, along with buckwheat cakes. (Salt herring is among the oldest of commercial fish offerings, but it seldom shows up in modern restaurants.) At Mabry Mill on the Blue Ridge Parkway near Meadows of Dan, Virginia, the specialties are cornmeal griddle cakes and buckwheat cakes made from old-fashioned bolted meal and flour ground on the premises. And at Pat's in Aiken, South Carolina, I encountered salmon and grits on the breakfast menu, along with corned beef hash, apple pancakes, homemade loaf bread, and quail with eggs.

Stan's Restaurant and Country Store near Columbia, Tennessee, has been in business since 1947, and the "hillbilly" breakfast seems like a relic of those postwar times. Included are such rarities as brains and eggs, poke sallet, and pork chops. The menu is ham shaped and written in hillbilly phonetics. The owners, W. W. Daniel and W. O. Stanfill, take note of the fact that Po Folks, a highly successful new chain of restaurants, has adopted an exaggerated country

This restaurant I favor is the country farm kitchen come to town and gone commercial. Prices are cheap, people are friendly, and they let you alone if you want to read the paper. They keep about 12 waiters and waitresses hustling, but somehow all of them seem to enjoy their work and have honed the art of public service to a fine edge. . . .

Sit-down, simple-fare, low-cost restaurants are important to building community spirit. They are the common man's country clubs, where the affairs of the town get discussed and chewed over.

They are, of course, among the many non-chain small businesses which are being pressed into oblivion in our society.

> Larry McGehee,
> in his syndicated column,
> "Southern Seen," 1984

bumpkin style strikingly similar to Stan's. Home-cured ham and red-eye gravy with biscuits, grits, eggs, sorghum molasses, honey, jams and jellies, and coffee constitute the mainline breakfast at the restaurant, which draws its customers from both the local area and the adjacent interstate highway.

Country ham is also the main feature in the dining room at the Nu-Wray Inn in Burnsville, North Carolina, one of many summer hotels in the Blue Ridge and Smoky Mountain region. Four generations of the Wray family have owned the inn since 1870, and it was in business for more than thirty-five years before that. There are thirty-one guest rooms in the rambling, three-story structure, and when the guests come to the dining room, they eat family-style at long tables spread with white linens. Twenty-two oak chairs surround the biggest table. A large cut-glass bowl of mountain honey and another of homemade apple butter are kept moving and kept filled, complementing the breakfast bowls and platters of grits, scrambled eggs, spiced applesauce, hot biscuits, red-eye gravy, and Rush Wray's widely praised country ham. Eating at the big table now is probably much like it was a century ago.

In Williamsburg, Virginia, history is the primary tourist attraction, and there are many restaurants that attempt to reproduce antiquity in authentic ways. One of the more successful of these is the Old Chickahominy House, a twenty-five-year-old reproduction of a two-hundred-year-old plantation house. Breakfast there is also a reproduction of sorts, featuring old-style Virginia ham, bacon, and sausage with the usual accompaniments. The most successful bit of culinary history made new on the morning we were there was the venerable standby: a good cup of hot coffee in a large heavy restaurant-china cup. The ham and biscuits fell short of reproduction quality.

For most people, breakfast is more repetitive than other meals, and some creatures of habit eat the same thing every morning. It may also be the most sociable repast, as witness the many places where regular customers gather at the same time each morning to eat, linger over coffee, and talk. We ran into that practice in numerous places. At The Palace, a block or so from the state capitol in downtown Columbia, South Carolina, the conversation was lively and uninhibited (and the grits, incidentally, were as hot and tasty as any could be). At the Merry Acres Restaurant in Albany, Georgia, nearly a hundred patrons were gathered when we stopped by, and most of them seemed to know one another. At least they stayed a long time to read the morning paper, tell some animated tales, and eat the good basic breakfast. And at the Southern Grill in Knoxville, Tennessee, breakfast is such a major offering throughout the day that the waitress pours you a cup of coffee automatically, even at one o'clock in the afternoon, unless you stay her hand.

Another restaurant that specializes in breakfast is Skin Head's in Paducah, Kentucky. Owner Jim Skaggs, a Yul Brynner look-alike, calls the place "the

Everything is on the table in the Nu-Wray Hotel at Burnsville [in North Carolina]. Nobody waits to give an order. They bring it in, three or four kinds of meat, all the vegetables of the whole mountain countryside. There are dishes of homemade jellies and preserves. The country ham is excellent. The stout tables do not groan but the stuffed guest rising sometimes does. Not often does the traveler come on such plenty in North Carolina. It is country plenty, country cooked and country served, but in proof that the persisting homesickness for country eating is not entirely based on legend. I think that even Thomas L. Clingman, whose name is on the biggest mountain in the Great Smoky National Park, would approve of the biscuits and the other hot breads, as well.

Clingman, who was . . . a general in war and a Congressman in peace . . . was a man of both ideas and indignations. In . . . 1875 . . . he had zeal left over for the denunciation of "something called biscuits which was in fact rather warm dough with much grease in it."

"Within ten years," he said, "as many people have died prematurely in this State from bad cookery as were slain in the war."

Jonathan Daniels
Tar Heels, 1941

Breakfast House of the South," and if that seems overstated for a dumpy-looking concrete block building that used to be a drive-in restaurant, the menu reprints articles from *Newsweek* and *Esquire* in support of the claim. Breakfast is the all-hours headliner, and it runs the gamut of traditional Southern dishes prepared in the usual ways, but nothing I tasted there would place Skin Head's above the best of the South's breakfast restaurants. It's an interesting and entertaining little place, though, even if it's not the breakfast house of the South. There may not be such a place.

Nevertheless, there are some warm and inviting spots to observe the Southern breakfast tradition in fine style, as the examples already cited here indicate, and there are others of equal or greater merit. To underscore the point, consider these brief sketches of a half-dozen widely scattered restaurants where breakfast, among other meals, is a matter of pride for staff and patrons alike:

❖ Mom's, in Port Royal, South Carolina, puts the lie to the old admonition that you should never eat at a place called Mom's. This one is a plain and cozy little cafeteria-style establishment that serves home cooking three meals a day. Rosa Lee Scott, who is Mom, has been in the business for over twenty-five years, and like all mothers, she's much more than a cook. While Mrs. Scott was in the kitchen making a fresh batch of breakfast biscuits, we fell into conversation with a regular customer named Florence. "Coming here," she said, "is just like eating at home, like sitting at your own table, drinking your own coffee—only none of us can fix food the way Mom can. She's got a lot of 'children' like me. Nobody cooks at home anymore—we're all too busy. So we lean on Mom, and she never lets us down."

She didn't let us down either. The biscuits were flaky, roll-like, and slightly sweet, almost as rich as pie crust. When actor Robert Duvall was filming *The Great Santini* in the Port Royal area a few years ago, he often ate twice a day at Mom's, and he has been back a couple of times since then. He obviously knows a good cook—and a good friend—when he meets one.

❖ Jones Cafe, in Noble Lake, Arkansas, is a little roadside restaurant on a straight stretch of highway near Pine Bluff that could easily be missed if you weren't looking for it. Ruby Jones and her son W. R. run the place, she in the kitchen and he out front, and the truck drivers and local people who eat there regularly praise the food as home cooking at its finest. Mrs. Jones has been a restaurant cook for over forty years, but only since about 1980 has she been "discovered" by Arkansas food critics. *Arkansas Times* magazine gave the cafe its "Best Plate Lunch" award in 1984, and a writer for that magazine called her "the Renoir of Arkansas piemaking."

Nobody is keeping up with the Joneses at breakfast, either. The morning we ate with them, the biscuits, bacon, eggs, grits, and coffee were of genuine home-

As I drove in she was walking into the house with eggs for breakfast and homemade biscuits ready for baking. Somehow in rural Southern culture, food is always the first thought of neighbors when there is trouble. That is something they can do and not feel uncomfortable. It is something they do not have to explain or discuss or feel self-conscious about. "Here, I brought you some fresh eggs for your breakfast. And here's a cake. And some potato salad." It means, "I love you. And I am sorry for what you are going through and I will share as much of your burden as I can." And maybe potato salad is a better way of saying it.

Will D. Campbell
Brother to a Dragonfly, 1977

cooking quality. Mrs. Jones and two kitchen helpers were busy preparing lunch, and when she took a fresh coconut pie out of the oven, the sweet aroma was overpowering. It was the only time I can ever recall having pie for breakfast.

✤ The Waysider, in Tuscaloosa, Alabama, is in an old house in which Archie Farr and his parents before him have served two meals a day for over twenty-five years. Elizabeth Snow Farr was "the one who made it go," her son says. She also is the one who taught Archie to make biscuits, yeast rolls, cornbread, pies, and cobblers, and to serve up a breakfast that local folks consider the best in north Alabama.

"Places like this are getting hard to find," Farr said, "and they're even harder to keep going. The chains are undercutting us on price—they're winning the fight. But they don't have the pride that we do, and their mass production can't match our freshness and quality. All that plastic food in a plastic environment won't last. Southern food will eventually come back."

✤ Smitty's Cafe, in Oxford, Mississippi, is one of the places where a comeback won't be necessary. William Faulkner, who used to live a few blocks from Smitty's, once remarked, "In the South, the past is not dead. It's not even past." He could well have been talking about Louise Smith's restaurant, where traditional Southern cooking is all they've ever done—and the townspeople and University of Mississippi students who make up most of its customers wouldn't want it any other way. The counter stools, booths, and tables at Smitty's get plenty of wear three times a day, pretty much the same as they have since Louise Smith opened her first Oxford restaurant in 1955.

"I don't think this kind of food is dying out at all," she said, "at least not here. We're getting new customers all the time. The secret to our success is four great cooks. Nettie Gordon, Pearline Thomas, Rudell Carrothers, and Ruthie Howell are the best Southern cooks you could ever hope to find. They've all been with me for a long time—from about twelve years to thirty." Among their many accomplishments are muscadine preserves and other homemade jams and jellies to accompany the morning biscuits. Breakfast is traditional fare expertly prepared. The regulars tend to linger over it, sipping the good coffee, discussing the day's news and gossip, and eyeing with small-town curiosity the occasional strangers who happen to drop in.

✤ Chase Street Cafe, in Athens, Georgia, is a nondescript little cracker-box of a place with lots of late-model cars parked around it. The drivers can be found inside, vying for the twenty stools around the horseshoe-shaped counter. Mark Hansford, the owner, is on a first-name basis with most of his customers. He has been there for seventeen years, his parents were there for fourteen years before that, and others preceded them back to 1947, when the cafe opened. It

Southern cooking is not one thing for rich people and another thing for poor people. It has its roots in war-torn soil. In the couple of hundred years during which our ways of cooking evolved, a calamitous war was fought and lost on the land; and then the Great Depression deepened the poverty in a region without much industry. Of course there were always pockets of wealth, and of course there are many proud and well-off city Southerners. But true Southern cooking has its foundations in the country kitchen. It is characterized by the gracious willingness to share a meal with strangers as well as loved ones, which is something you will find everywhere people have known hard times.

Nathalie Dupree
Cooking of the South, 1982

has the look and feel of that era—lots of shiny stainless steel on the walls and counters, an overhead fan whirling quietly, the inviting smells and sounds of breakfast rising from the grill. Mark's mother, seventy-four-year-old Sarah Hansford, still works inside the horseshoe, arriving in the early morning hours to make ready for the 6 a.m. opening. She and two other women spend most of their time preparing lunch, while Mark works the counter at breakfast.

He is a big, friendly, garrulous fellow, a native of Athens and a former cop who prides himself on his knowledge of the town and its people and all the latest scuttlebutt. He keeps charge tabs on some of his customers—especially students from the nearby University of Georgia—and they settle up with him on a weekly or monthly basis. Others in the regular crowd—lawyers, doctors, business people, clerks—find the cafe a preferable alternative to eating at home, and many of them are there every day. At lunch they get hearts of Southern: black-eyed peas, okra and tomatoes, beets, mashed potatoes and gravy, country fried steak, fried chicken, chicken mull (a hot and spicy stew), biscuits, and cornbread.

Breakfast is especially inviting. It comes hot and fresh, straight from the grill. I ordered scrambled eggs, grits, sausage, biscuits, and coffee, and every bit of it tasted as fresh and delicious as the best homemade fare. The sausage, made daily at a local packing house, was spicy hot with red pepper and sage, the way farm sausage used to taste. Sitting there in the cozy little cafe on a brisk November morning, sipping on my second cup of coffee and listening to the cheerful banter of Mark Hansford and his friends, I thought about how much good luck and good timing have to do with finding good food on the road.

❖ Bailey's Restaurant, in Hazard, Kentucky, is one of those improbable successes that breaks all the rules of marketing. Perched on the outer lip of a sharp curve on a narrow road at the edge of Hazard, the restaurant is too small, too old-fashioned, too hard to get to—and there's nowhere to park. (The half-dozen or so spaces are completely inadequate for a drive-in—which, among other things, Bailey's is.) There's a tire store and service station adjacent to the place, and on the face of it, tires and food don't seem to go together very well.

If there had been a marketing specialist around to advise James and Pauline Bailey when they opened the restaurant in 1954, he surely would have told them their venture was bound to fail—and he would have been dead wrong. Bailey's is very much alive and thriving, thanks to three-meals-a-day delivery of first-rate Southern food. The customers get there somehow—and once they've tried it, they keep coming back. Lunch and dinner menus run the gamut of old standards, from meat loaf and fried chicken to the full range of vegetables, hot breads, and homemade pies. Breakfast covers the usual items too, but there's a difference—the fried potatoes are freshly peeled and cut up, there's a bowl of delicious cream gravy on the side, and the biscuits are absolutely unexcelled. Laverna Hughes and Lou Hurt and Evelyn Ritchie are mainly responsible for the cooking, and they have mastered the craft admirably.

"We don't cut any corners," Pauline Bailey said. "Everything is fresh and homemade. I just wouldn't have it any other way. But this kind of country cooking is on the way out. We're the last ones left in Hazard, and I don't know of any other restaurants like this in eastern Kentucky. We've got loyal customers, though, I'll say that, and they bring us new ones all the time. You can't beat the mouth for advertising."

Some people along the coast of South Carolina, Georgia, and Florida are fond of fish and grits as a breakfast combination, but we rarely found the two paired on a breakfast menu. We didn't find many fresh fried apples in the high country of Virginia and North Carolina, either (though the canned ones weren't bad stewed). Another old and familiar Southern favorite—green or pink tomato slices coated with cornmeal and fried in bacon fat—never appeared on any breakfast menu that we saw during our travels.

Breakfast is a highly perishable meal. Eggs don't keep well after they have been cooked, and neither do hot breads or fried dishes such as fish, potatoes, and tomatoes. Orange juice and coffee must be at the peak of freshness to be superior. Surely all that has something to do with the small and diminishing number of first-class, full-scale restaurant breakfasts to be found in the region. For freshness and immediacy, not to mention quality and variety, few restaurants can deliver breakfast dishes to match the ones you can prepare at home.

But there are some good breakfast places left, as we found out, and some of them feature dishes at least as good as—if not better than—anything we can fix at home. Everyone needs an occasional break from the home routine, too, and it's nice to have places to go on those mornings when you're not in a hurry and you want to take your time and enjoy a fine breakfast made to order in a cheerful and inviting atmosphere. We're fortunate to have a few such places within driving distance, one of which is the Loveless Motel & Cafe on the outskirts of Nashville.

The name was never meant to express humor or forlorn hope; it was simply what Lou Loveless thought he ought to call his little twelve-room tourist court when he built it in the 1950s. It was located on the old state road to Memphis, and the increasing mobility of Americans in the postwar years suggested to Loveless that a few rooms and a good cafe would make him a nice business. The survival of the cafe and even a few of the motel rooms under just three owners since then seems to have borne out his belief.

Little about the cafe has changed in that time. It is primarily a dinner place, even though the country ham and eggs and biscuits that head the menu are

Caviar may be the most famous type of fish roe, but it is not the only one. As a native Tar Heel, I grew up breakfasting on herring roe and feasting on shad roe. Overnight guests at my house are likely to be subjected to a Chowan County breakfast of fish roe, grits and bacon. My mother grew up in Edenton, on the Albemarle Sound in Chowan County. She remembers the fantastic herring runs every spring, when the fisheries would operate all night to process the catch. The runs have since all but vanished, but you can still buy cans of Chowan County herring roe if you know where to look. When I struck out for extended stays in Latin America and Europe, I took with me cases of herring roe straight from the cannery, the shiny tin cans still unlabeled, along with an ample supply of grits. This meant that whenever homesickness overwhelmed me, I could assuage it with a breakfast (or often a supper) that was, to me, the pure essence of home.

*Anna Hayes,
Raleigh, North Carolina,
in Spectator, April 24, 1986*

more closely associated with breakfast. The dinner entrees are limited to ham, fried chicken, chicken livers and gizzards, and a couple of steak specialties. On the weekends, the little cottage with seats for seventy-five people is crowded with customers from open to close. The wood floors creak under so many feet, and the red-and-white-checkered tablecloths may support as many as 350 meals on a busy day.

On weekday mornings the pace is much less hectic. Donna McCabe is usually there—she's the owner now—and Elizabeth Roberts or Mary Lou Perry is in the kitchen, and Sherry Downing or Lisa Carter is waiting tables. The coffee is fresh and hot, the biscuits are homemade and right out of the oven, the peach and blackberry preserves are also cooked on the premises, and there's sorghum molasses and honey, butter and cream, eggs fixed any way you like them, bacon and sausage, and of course the country ham for which Loveless has long been known.

People who know country ham understand that its proper curing is at best an inexact science. The old-fashioned way involves covering fresh pork hindquarters in salt for a period of time during cold weather, then smoking and aging the resurrected hams through a subsequent period that must include hot weather. We'll get into all that a little more deeply in the Eating In section on pork (see page 256); suffice it to say here that the old-fashioned way of preparing country hams has all but vanished, and it is a rare restaurant or market that offers genuine slow-cured country ham for sale.

The Loveless gets about as close to that standard as anyone. Donna McCabe buys as many as three thousand hams a year from a single Tennessee supplier who adheres to the dry-salt curing method and ages the meat for a minimum of six months. I have on occasion encountered a slice of Loveless country ham that was too salty or too tough for my taste (curing, as I said, is an inexact science), but most of the time it's just right—rich, tender, aromatic, and delicious, with an elixir of precious red-eye gravy on the side.

On cold winter days, the morning sun streams through the front window of the Loveless Cafe and bathes the table there in light and warmth. That's my favorite table, and my favorite time of day to eat. With a hot platter of choice ham and custom-cooked eggs, a pan of Elizabeth Roberts' made-from-scratch biscuits, some gravy, a little butter and jam, plenty of coffee, a good newspaper, and some time to tarry, I'm about as close to home as I can get—and as close to Southern comfort as a breakfast can be.

Lunch

James B. "Hap" Townes once stood smiling behind the steam table, greeting each customer like an old friend, giving each a running commentary on the day's menu features. "How's it going, brother? Haven't seen you in a long time. We've got some good country fried steak today, and pork tenderloin, and some good old roast beef. Got some white beans, turnip greens, baked squash. Or how about some stewed tomatoes, or some good old stewed raisins? Got mashed potatoes, too. Steak and potatoes? All right, sir, coming right up. You want a little touch of gravy on those potatoes? And here's your turnip greens, and your tomatoes, and here's a nice hot corn cake, right off the griddle. Good to see you, brother. Hope you enjoy your lunch."

In pretty much the same manner for almost sixty-five years, the two Hap Towneses of Nashville, father and son, served up Southern home cooking to a long line of faithful and appreciative customers. Hap the elder started the tradition in 1921 with a curbside eatery on wheels, literally a movable feast. Hap the younger took up the spoon and spatula when he returned from the war in 1946. Together they built a new cafe, a little stone diner with forty-nine seats, on a quiet back street in south Nashville and made it into a lunchtime institution. The father kept an active interest in the business until shortly before he died at the age of ninety. The son sold out and retired in 1985. But the "Hap Townes" sign still hangs over the front door, and the new owner has vowed to keep things just the way they were. Scores of anxious patrons have found relief and reassurance in that promise. Said one of them: "We've never known a time when we didn't have the option of lunch at Hap's."

The genesis of plate-lunch dining in America can be traced to such public eateries as Hap's. Back in the days when lunch was dinner and dinner was supper, the midday meal generally was the main repast for people of all classes. The food was hearty and substantial, and for good reason; the time to eat heavily, most people agreed, was not in the evening before bedtime but early in the day, when energy was needed for the hard work at hand. As dinner for working people gradually moved from home kitchens to the cafes and restaurants of cities and towns, the pattern of heavy dining at noon was continued.

The plate lunch, a singularly American invention, became firmly fixed in the restaurant trade early in this century. Before long, there was even a custom-made plate for it: a large, heavy, china plate in the popular and familiar blue willow pattern, with compartments to divide the meat or other main dish from the vegetables. The blue-plate special (or lunch, or supper, or dinner) was a quickly understood term for a generously large and inexpensive meal that commonly consisted of a main dish, three or four vegetables, some kind of bread, and a drink.

Southern cooking, with its emphasis on meats and gravies, vegetables, hot breads, and desserts, was especially well suited to plate-lunch dining. Restaurants featuring blue-plate specials came early to the region, and many of the best of them have survived to this day, withstanding the fast-food revolution and other modern gastronomic upheavals. Hap Townes is such a place. In history, style, and quality, the little cafe is a good and typical example of the traditions associated with eating out for lunch in the South.

"I used to get in here at four o'clock every morning," said the junior Hap Townes shortly before he retired, "and my father did the same before me. We always cooked the same kind of food, just regular Southern food. Everybody used to do it like this—in every restaurant, every house. This is what all the people that I knew ate every day. I never thought of it as having a name—it was just the plain, everyday food of the South: white beans, pintos, black-eyed peas, crowders, butter beans, green beans, hominy, fried apples, cabbage, turnip greens, white potatoes, stewed tomatoes, candied yams."

The litany of vegetables led him into descriptions of other specialties of the house—skillet-fried chicken and various cuts of pork, cornbread, fruit cobblers. "We used to serve three meals a day, seven days a week," he said, "but in recent years we've been primarily a lunch place. I generally had seven people working for me, and on a good day we'd serve as many as 250 lunches a day. You've got to have good help to do that, and we've had some fine ones, people like Veora Chatman and Ruth Maxwell and Erfie Williams. Veora's the one who came up with the recipe for stewed raisins, and that's one of the most popular side dishes on the menu. We've had some very faithful customers down through the years, too, people from all walks of life. I've loved this place, and I'm going to miss it. I always enjoyed coming in and preparing the food for these good folks, just cooking the food and meeting the people. It was a joy, a real joy."

If there is a common denominator to the plate-lunch palaces of the South, it probably has something to do with that Hap Townes notion of the joy of cooking. We ate in close to fifty such restaurants in our travels around the region, and many more than that are still in business. There are some obvious differences among them—in ownership, history, clientele, cuisine—but in the best of them there is a universal pride of mission and reputation, a celebration of longevity, a joy of service. It is these qualities that make owners go whistling off to work at four in the morning, and employees serve faithfully for years on end, and patrons return time and time again with enthusiasm, and restaurants survive and prosper for decades. Whether good food produces these qualities or the qualities determine the caliber of the food is a chicken-and-egg question that has no clear answer. In any case, traditional Southern food is still available

BIRMINGHAM, Ala.—For years this has been a city of heavy industry and even heavier lunches: groaning noonday meals of fried chicken or country ham, tall tumblers of sweetened ice tea, plates of steaming cornbread and three side orders of vegetables, seasoned with bacon drippings.

It is an event of such proportion that a lot of people here have traditionally referred to it as dinner. But like Alabama's steel industry, the Southern lunch may have seen its better days.

"People these days just don't have the time to eat such large lunches, not to mention what it does to anyone on a diet," said James Salem, a professor of American Studies at the University of Alabama in nearby Tuscaloosa. "The traditional Southern lunch is fading away because the

in a large number of plate-lunch cafes and diners and restaurants around the region, and much of it is quite good.

A couple of Louisville-area establishments underscore both the similarities and differences of lunch places on the list. The Melrose Inn in Prospect, Kentucky, has a look and feel of the fifties about it. There are starched cloths and fresh flowers on each table, and the waitresses seem to know most of the diners. Country ham and fried chicken are standard features on the menu, but the restaurant's chief claim to fame is Derby Pie, a chocolate dessert with a name that is a registered trademark and a recipe that is under lock and key. The restaurant is open daily for breakfast and dinner as well as lunch, and at every meal the food resembles in style and quality what you would have expected to find there thirty years ago.

In Middletown, not far away, a favorite spot for lunch and dinner and weekend brunch is Down Home, a contemporary version of what the menu calls "a good old days restaurant." The menu features soups and sandwiches and salads as well as plate lunches. Most items are homemade, including the yeast rolls and cornbread, and the desserts are especially impressive: pies, dumplings, cobblers, and even such made-from-scratch rarities as fresh coconut cake. Down Home is a family enterprise of the 1980s that features timeless Southern food.

Virginia has its share of standard plate-lunch establishments, places like Brooks Restaurant in Verona and Durham's Restaurant in Wytheville—but for out-of-the-ordinary eateries, it would be hard to imagine two more dissimilar places than the Chesterfield Tea Room in Richmond and Knox's Cafe in Big Stone Gap. The Chesterfield ("Old Virginia Cooking Since 1903") serves light luncheons—salads, sandwiches, hot plates, and desserts—to an interesting mix of elderly people, business executives, service workers, and college students. There is a look of tattered gentility to the century-old dining room on the main floor of an inner-city apartment building. "I've eaten lunch here for forty years," said Creston Farrow, a cheerful gentleman who sat at the table next to ours. "It hasn't changed much in all that time. You can always depend on the Chesterfield."

Knox's, in a mountain town far across the state, is a combination bar/ motel/restaurant/grocery and community gathering place. Knox Leggs built it in 1947 as an all-purpose institution for blacks in a mostly white and segregated coalfield town. Desegregation and the fast-food chains have brought substantial changes since then, but the Leggs family has adapted, and their place of business now blends the best of old and new. The menu includes pigs' feet, pickled eggs, chitterlings, barbecued ribs, and steak. Knox Leggs, an ex-coalminer, and his wife, Fannie, an able cook, are striving to preserve some old Southern food traditions in the new age of processed and standardized fast food. They face an uphill fight, but they are holding on.

pace of life has changed throughout the South. Those big lunches date from another time." . . .

Even so, there are others who are not as persuaded by the evidence.

At the University of Mississippi's Center for Southern Culture in Oxford, scholars who follow such regional trends argue that the South's affection for large noonday meals and its own heavy cuisine remains unchecked.

William E. Schmidt,
in The New York Times,
May 11, 1984

People like Knox and Fannie Leggs seem to show up frequently in the Southern food business. Proud, independent, hardworking, expressive people, they are just as compelling as individuals—as indomitable characters—as they are as cooks or restaurateurs. It's not that their food is lacking, but rather that personality and place overpower it and crowd it from memory. I can think of a good many places on our itinerary that I would eagerly return to for the conversation and the personal encounter, as much as for the food itself.

Effie Lord's Cafe in Clayton, Georgia, is such a place. The front window is a showcase for her collection of potted plants and pretty rocks and bottles. The painted letters on the glass read LORD'S CAFE, and "HOME COOKED" MEALS. When I peered in early on a crisp fall morning, I saw a small woman wearing a smock and a blue bandana moving slowly about the kitchen, stirring pots and lifting black iron skillets on a gas stove. No one else was there.

Effie Lord glanced up briefly when I walked in, and then turned her attention back to the stove. No, she said, in response to my question, she didn't serve breakfast, but I could help myself to a cup of coffee. I did, and looked around as I sipped it. Stools and a counter ran along one wall, and a half-dozen tables and about twenty-five chairs sat on the dusty tile floor. Stylized prints of Spanish bullfighters and Rocky Mountain vistas hung on the concrete block walls. The kitchen was a chaotic jumble of pots and pans and cooking equipment. The calm, patient, placid little woman moved unhurriedly from one task to the next, as if everything was in order and under control. She looked considerably younger than her eighty-three years.

We chatted casually for several minutes, and when she saw that I was interested in the food she served, she talked slowly and with deepening interest about her life in the restaurant business:

When I first married, I couldn't cook a lick—just had to learn by myself. My husband was an Irish Catholic, a second-generation Georgian, and we had six children, so I *had* to learn to cook. We lived in Athens then. My husband died there, and then I married a second time, and we moved up here to Clayton and opened a cafe in about 1945. I've run this place myself since my second husband died in 1960.

All it is is just plain old Southern cooking, or mountain cooking, or home cooking, or whatever you want to call it. I don't go for anything fancy. I just take my time, and cook fresh things whenever I can get them—string beans, mashed potatoes, sweet potatoes, rutabaga turnips, okra and tomatoes, soup beans, pintos. I fry my chicken in lard or shortening in these big black skillets, and I make meat loaf, fix liver, pork chops—two meats and five vegetables every day, and cornbread and biscuits, and a cobbler. In the winter I'll serve lunch to twenty or twenty-five people—twice that many

Mountain food and how it is cooked is very much a part of this sense of place. Ask any displaced Appalachian what he misses most about being away from the mountains and he will probably talk about soup beans, cornbread, sallet greens, fresh milk and butter, eggs, country ham, "and homemade biscuits every morning of the world." Some will speak of the joys of hunting wild game and birds. The women talk of missing homey things; sitting on the front porch or in the yard after all the chores are done and listening to the night sounds, watching the moon come up, or going to a church supper. They may also talk about the kitchens back home, the feeling of warmth from wood-burning stoves, the smell of coffee simmering on the back and biscuits baking in the oven, and the family gathered around the kitchen table to eat and talk.

Sidney Saylor Farr
More Than Moonshine, 1983

in the summer—and I come in about five-thirty every morning to get things started.

Nobody works here but me. I do everything—the shopping, the cooking, the cleaning up. I don't wait tables, though. My customers come in the kitchen, get a plate, and serve themselves off the stove. They can come back for seconds, too, if they want, and I stay open until the food gives out, which is usually around two o'clock in the afternoon. Then I clean up, go shopping for the next day's lunch, and get home about five-thirty. So I spend half my time here and half at home. It's a hard life for an old woman. My children have been after me to retire for a long time, but I'm better off working. I like to cook, and I want to be my own boss. And besides, I've got several old people I look after. They depend on me for this one hot meal every day, and they need me. I just hate to give up, I guess. My mother's still living—she's 104. She was a York, a cousin to Alvin York, the war hero. That old York blood is powerful.

Not many places have this kind of food anymore—fresh vegetables like that good old mountain cabbage; you just can't beat it for taste or nutrition. It's mighty good, but it's going out, and it won't be long before it's gone. Folks are going to live on hamburgers, hot dogs, French fries. Fast food is taking the day. I can't eat those hamburgers myself. That smell just penetrates your clothing. People don't realize it's ruining their stomach—but everybody to their own notion, I reckon. I can't keep things as neat here as I could when I was younger, but my customers don't complain. The way I see it, I'm meeting a need. Some take advantage of me and don't pay, but I'm no money lover. Just so I can keep my debts paid, I don't care. I think I'll just keep on cooking until I give out. Maybe me and this old slow-cooked food will give out about the same time.

A personality of a different sort presides at Bonner's Cafe in Crawfordville, Georgia. Seventy-nine-year-old Annie Lou Bonner has been in the business for sixty years. For more than half that time, she has depended on Sarah Dozier to wait tables and Mary Thomas to do most of the cooking. The little restaurant on the town square in Crawfordville has always offered home cooking in the old Southern style, and the desserts are especially fine; people have been known to drive long distances just for a slice of sweet potato pie.

But the interstate highway passes nearby, and it has left Crawfordville dozing in the shade, and the freeway food chains likewise have cut deeply into the trade at Bonner's Cafe. "I may have to sell out or close up," said Mrs. Bonner. "This food we serve costs so much and takes so long, people won't keep eating it. We tried to economize by going to a cafeteria style, but these ladies that's got on pretty dresses, they didn't like it. You've got to tote the food to them.

Then we cut out Sunday dinner, just to save on expenses. I'd rather close than take shortcuts on the food, though. If we can't make things the old way, like they're supposed to be, I'd rather not make them at all."

As I waited for a second slice of sweet potato pie, I nodded in total agreement with that philosophy.

Down the road in Madison, Georgia, Jimmy Cunningham runs Ye Olde Colonial Restaurant on the square pretty much the way his parents did when they started it in 1954. A mercantile company and a bank used to occupy the space; now, instead of dry goods and crop loans, Southern food can be found there for breakfast, lunch, and dinner six days a week. Lunch on the day I stopped in could be chosen from a selection of three meats, eight vegetables, two hot breads, and two fruit cobblers. The vegetables were outstanding—turnip greens cooked with seasoning bacon, a squash casserole made with cheese and eggs, fried okra, black-eyed peas, and world-class sweet potatoes, mashed and fluffy, seasoned with milk, butter, eggs, and spices.

"People have given Southern food a bad name." Jimmy Cunningham said. "There are so many bad places out there that I've almost come to the point of calling our food something else. We serve all the fresh food we can get, and nothing but the highest quality. You just can't offer people poor food and hope to get them back. When my father opened this place, there were three restaurants in Madison; now there are fifteen or twenty. But our business has always been good, and it's because of the consistent high quality of our food. Word of mouth is our best advertising. If we can get you in here once, you'll come back. If our experience is a fair indication, I'd say this kind of food is going to survive for a long time to come. We may have to quit calling it Southern food, but it'll be just the same as it's always been here—fresh, homemade, slowly cooked, well seasoned. People who eat here have learned to expect that quality."

East into the Carolinas, we found more Southern lunch tables featuring foods of a similar style and quality, and both the settings and the people in them were diverse and interesting. To illustrate, here are three choice spots in South Carolina.

Mrs. Frances Kitchen at Prince's Place traces its roots in Myrtle Beach back to the late forties, when Frances Iwilla Gainey Bowens, a native Floridian, first opened for business. Until she died in 1983, Mrs. Bowens enjoyed a sterling reputation as a Southern cook, and her restaurant was generally regarded as the best source of such food in the area.

Prince Bowens III, her son, has taken her place—not filled it, he is quick to say, but taken it. He and his wife, Queen, do most of the cooking. "When I went away to college and the service, I really missed this food—Mom's cooking," Prince Bowens said. "She was a wonderful cook. She and my dad and my wife taught me everything I know about Southern food."

Quite often when confronted with still another restaurant menu that includes the likes of an elaborate seafood terrine with a delicate

What he knows is a lot. The food at Prince's Place is fresh, varied, well-seasoned, and attractively presented. Most of the standard Southern meats and vegetables are on the menu, along with hot breads and desserts. There are some uncommon dishes, too; chicken bog, shad roe, barbecued coon, fried chitlins. "The cuisine here is superb," says a sign on the wall, "and the food ain't bad either!" Indeed it is not. Mrs. Bowens would be proud to see that the quality is still quite high.

The same sort of continuity also pertains to the Central Coffee Shop in Manning, a town in the South Carolina midlands. George "Papa Jack" Metropol, a Greek immigrant, opened it in 1909; now his son Jimmy and daughter Helen carry on at the same location, serving a compatible blend of Southern and Greek foods to patrons whose families have been regular customers for three or four generations.

"When my father died," said Jimmy Metropol, "the legislature passed a resolution in his honor. He was just a poor boy who spoke no English when he came here in 1900, but he made this place a favorite of hundreds of visitors as well as residents. Lots of big-league baseball players used to stop here on their way north from spring training—Ted Williams, Roger Maris, Whitey Ford—and Jimmy Cagney used to come in too. We built our reputation on extra good coffee with real cream, but our food is fine too—Greek and Southern, white and black, the best of both worlds for over seventy-five years."

Agatha Burgess makes no such claim of longevity for her little home dining room in Buffalo, South Carolina, but in personal terms she certainly qualifies as an elder. She is past eighty, and for more than sixteen years she has served lunch in her home five days a week to friends and strangers. She refers to her customers as "the boys," though all of them are adults and some are women.

"I'm just cooking food like my mother cooked, the same old-fashioned way," she said. "The boys don't go for fancy dishes—they just want Southern food, home cooking." The truck drivers and bankers and store clerks all love it, and so do the elderly shut-ins for whom she prepares takeout lunches in a "meals on wheels" program. And so too do the employees of a nearby textile mill, where Mrs. Burgess herself worked for thirty-four years.

"My son was working down there after I retired," she said, "and I used to fix his lunch for him, and when other people saw what he was having, they wanted it too. So I started fixing these dinners for plant workers, and now I serve as many as a hundred a day, either carry-out or to eat here."

Two or three meat dishes, about five vegetables, two hot breads, at least two desserts, and coffee or tea are available every day. Those who eat in with her go to the kitchen and help themselves to such specialties as fried chicken, meat loaf, country fried steak, macaroni and cheese, corn, potatoes, beans, greens, cornbread and biscuits, and delicious pies and cakes.

sauce, a sautéed fresh duck foie gras and a couple of pristine veal medallions perfumed with exotic wild mushrooms, my thoughts drift to crisp southern fried chicken, short ribs of beef falling off the bone, baked cheese grits, Greek-style lamb stew with lots of garlic and briny black olives, and Swedish meatballs redolent of fresh dill. I gaze at the innocuous, dried-out fancy roll on the china plate and dream of oven-warm puffy biscuits or crusty country yeast bread. I try to negotiate the perfectly sculptured, undercooked, tasteless vegetables while entertaining visions of unctuous, flavor-packed Kentucky Wonder green beans that have simmered for hours with pork fat. . . .

Don't get me wrong. There's nobody on earth who appreciates fresh caviar, paper-thin carpaccio sprinkled with grated Parmesan and virgin olive oil, or truffled roast chicken more than I do. I eat Chinese sea slugs, stuffed goose neck, tiny fragile game birds you pop in your mouth, eyeballs and all, and, when forced, I'll even consent to an occasional nouvelle dish—of French or American persuasion. But the food I respect, the food that sustains me, the food I truly love on a regular basis is the honest, wonderful, home-cooked fare I knew as a child.

James Villas,
in Food & Wine, February 1986

"She's like a mother to everybody," said one of her regular customers. Agatha Burgess made me think of Effie Lord, her octogenarian counterpart in Georgia.

North Carolina's plate-lunch eateries eluded us somehow; except for Bullock's, a Durham institution for more than thirty years (and some family-style places to be reported on later), we missed the meat-and-vegetable emporiums entirely. Bullock's specializes in barbecue, but its menu contains no fewer than thirty main-dish items and half as many more side dishes from which combination hot plates can be assembled. With seats for three hundred people, it's a big-volume operation.

Another state where we almost missed out on the standard meat-and-three-vegetables plate lunch is Alabama (the good lunches we had there fit better into other categories). But we did stop at Twix 'n' Tween, an all-hours cafe and truck stop in Centerville, and found there both plate-lunch specials and good barbecue, as well as homemade pies. In almost forty years of existence, the Twix 'n' Tween has earned a well-deserved name for itself as a good place to eat.

Ruth and Jimmie Davis of Abbeville, Mississippi, have had a lunch counter in the back of their country store since 1973. Oxford, the university town just up the road, had just one fast-food place at that time, and the people who couldn't get into Smitty's and the handful of other local restaurants for lunch started driving to Ruth and Jimmie's. "We've got twelve stools in here," said Jimmie Davis, "but I remember one day when we served two hundred fifty-seven lunches, including carry-outs." Now there are about three dozen quick-eat places in Oxford, and the Abbeville trade is down to fifty or seventy-five a day—not bad, even so, for an out-of-the-way country store.

The Davises are transplanted Tennesseans, farming people who grew up on country cooking and enjoy it still. The fare at their lunch counter is standard Southern: three meats and a dozen vegetables every day, plus rolls and corn-bread and a couple of desserts. Farming remains a part of the Davis family's life (among other things, they cure their own hams), but storekeeping and food service are also important to them. In addition to the lunch counter, they own and operate a catfish restaurant, Hurricane Landing, on nearby Lake Sardis.

Across the Mississippi River in Arkansas, lunch comes in a variety of Southern styles, from Earl's Hot Biscuits Restaurant (formerly Earl's Truck Stop) in West Memphis to Bryce's Cafeteria in Texarkana. The middle-of-the-road standard, Jones Cafe in Noble Lake, falls geographically and gastronomically between those two, and so does the Club Cafe in Hot Springs. The Jones place has already been noted in Eating Out for Breakfast, and Bryce's will be included in Eating Out Family-Style; Earl's and the Club Cafe need a few more words of description here.

When it started as a truck stop across the Mississippi from Memphis in the

When people ask me about soul food, I tell them that I have been cooking "soul" for over forty years—only we did not call it that back home. We just called it real good cooking, southern style. However, if you want to be real technical on the subject, while all soul food is southern food, not all southern food is "soul." . . . Soul food cooking is an example of how really good southern Negro cooks cooked with what they had available to them, such as chickens from their own back yard and collard greens they grew themselves, as well as home-cured ham, and baking powder biscuits, chitlins, and dubie [berry cobbler].

Bob Jeffries
Soul Food Cookbook, 1970

1940s, Earl's was widely known and praised both for its automotive services and its food. In its newest form it's a much tonier place, clean and carpeted and decorated in a modern style. The food has survived these changes. It's still quite good—by some accounts, even better than it used to be. If the white beans and cornbread and the bread pudding we enjoyed are a fair indication, the plate lunches certainly should be up to par.

The Club Cafe opened for business in downtown Hot Springs more than forty years ago, and a sure sign of its continuing popularity is the fact that regular customers usually outnumber tourists in this resort-town eating place. Plate lunches share the menu with steaks and chops, seafood, sandwiches, and the like, but the main attraction at the Club is desserts—pies, to be specific, more than a dozen different kinds, all on display on a long counter in the center of the restaurant. Billowy clouds of meringue and flaky strips of crust crown this impressive assemblage of sweets. Arkansas has gained an outstanding reputation as a pie state, and places like the Club Cafe help to explain why.

Skipping across the region to Florida, a traditional plate-lunch restaurant of solid reputation can be found at the State Farmers Market in Fort Myers. The big eighteen-wheelers that haul winter vegetables to the rest of the eastern United States make regular stops here, and their drivers are the principal clientele at this restaurant, which was opened after the war nearly forty years ago. Local customers and winter tourists also go there regularly. Karan Roach and her brother, Bill Barnwell, natives of the region, own the restaurant now, and they offer a wide range of meat and vegetable dishes. In addition to the meat-and-two combination plates (three on Sunday), there are à la carte items, short orders, standard breakfasts, and desserts.

Two soul-food diners in north Florida stand out in our remembrance as excellent lunch places. One of them is Mama Cole's in Panama City, started in the midfifties by Lucille "Mama" Cole and her husband, Leo. "It was May 5, 1955, to be exact," said Leo Cole, who is seventy-six years old. Mrs. Cole and her daughter Mercy do most of the work on a six-burner gas stove in the tiny kitchen, and they serve a diverse mix of customers at the five tables crowded into the main room.

Mama Cole's has survived, said its namesake, simply by delivering good and dependable food day in and day out. "Soul food, Southern food, call it what you want," she said. "It's all the same: beans and greens, yams and chicken—it's what a mother cooks at home for her family. They don't have this food up North. What makes it different is two things: quality ingredients and seasoning. You've got to put something into it to get something out of it. It may cost more to do that, but it's the only way."

In Gainesville, a few blocks away from the University of Florida, Lorene Alexander has operated Mama Lo's for eighteen years in a little eatery not much bigger than Mama Cole's, and her reputation has reached heroic dimensions among the faithful. There is a room to one side that contains a pool table, a video game, and a jukebox, but most of the significant action takes place at a dozen tables in the dining room and in the small kitchen behind it. To a steady stream of midday diners (and others early and late), Mrs. Alexander and a few helpers offer an amazing array of freshly prepared meat-and-three combinations. A dozen or more main dishes may be offered on any given day, including chicken four or five ways (fried, baked, with dumplings, with rice). On the day we were there, eighteen vegetables were featured, including mustard greens, eggplant casserole, succotash, fried corn, buttered carrots, baby limas, and steamed yellow squash. There are homemade desserts, too.

"I have fresh vegetables every day," Mama Lo said as she prepared huge bunches of collard greens for the pot. "That's what home cooking is, and it's better than any other kind. I'm afraid this kind of food will be over with in another ten or fifteen years, though. It's hard work, and it takes time, and fewer and fewer people are willing to give it what it takes. But as long as we can put it out here, people will come to eat it. My customers love it, and I don't ever worry about them losing their taste for it."

It is that abiding affection for Southern home cooking that has prompted several chain-food entrepreneurs to package some of the tastes and a lot of nostalgia in the look-alike strings of new restaurants that are spreading across the region and beyond. Almost all of the food they serve is canned or frozen or otherwise processed to meet the standardized requirements of high-volume food service; even so, some of the dishes are quite good, and many knowledgeable customers consider the overall result an acceptable facsimile of the home cooking they used to enjoy.

Already, there are a good many Southern communities where the best home (country, soul) cooking available to the general public is in a Cracker Barrel or Po Folks restaurant. "It may not be as good as my mother used to serve," a Cracker Barrel customer in North Carolina said to me as he lounged in a rocking chair on the restaurant's front porch, "but it's a damn sight better than nothing." Many others clearly agree; there are now forty-nine Cracker Barrels in eight states and 167 Po Folks in twenty-four states, and more are on the way.

It may be more than a mere coincidence that the two most successful country-cooking chains are Tennessee enterprises. For reasons that are unclear, Tennessee is the leading Southern state in both the number and the quality of cafes, diners, and restaurants featuring traditional down-home cooking for lunch (and many of them also serve other meals). More than a dozen fine independent establishments show up on our lunch list in Tennessee, far more than in any other state. With due allowances for any unintended bias in favor of our home state, and with allowances too for better knowledge of the terri-

Collards, collards, collards,
Boiling in the pot,
With backbone, ham or fat back,
And pepper red and hot.
Of all the vegetables, leafy and
* green,*
Collards are definitely the queen.
Some say collards don't smell so
* nice,*
But eat them once, and you'll eat
* them twice.*
The collard is a beautiful thing,
It's nutritious for the human being.
Some worms like collards, and that
* is true,*
When they nibble my collards, I get
* blue.*
The worms that raid my collard
* patch*
Are destroyed before I cook my
* batch.*
Collards taste fine with cornbread
* and sweet taters,*
That combination will satisfy the
* best of debaters.*
Raising, cooking and eating collards
* is fun.*
Excuse me now! The collards are
* done.*

Colleen Bunting,
Scotland Neck, North Carolina,
in Leaves of Green: The Collard Poems, 1985

tory, that is still a remarkable disparity. Most of the Tennessee establishments are at least twenty-five years old, and some of them have been around for more than fifty years. They tend to be located off the beaten path, yet they thrive on dependable regular customers and a steady flow of new ones drawn by word of mouth. Their reputations are based on consistent delivery of the plate lunches their customers clamor for—traditionally prepared meat and vegetable combinations with hot bread and homemade desserts.

A partial listing of these older Tennessee restaurants in the Hap Townes tradition inevitably risks exclusion of some outstanding places—but not to mention a dozen or so would be a worse mistake. Here, briefly, are a few:

* The City Cafe in Murfreesboro, a downtown dispensary of plate lunches and pies for decades;

* East Hills Restaurant, a family-owned cafe in Dickson, where the vegetables, tea, and pie are always fresh;

* Breece's in Centerville, where a Tennessee governor recently took several of his visiting counterparts from other states to sample the home cooking;

* Dotson's Restaurant, which has delivered good quality consistently to three generations of Franklin customers;

* The Mark Twain Motel & Restaurant in Jamestown, where the food is as highly regarded as the establishment's namesake (John Clemens and his pregnant wife, Jane, moved from Jamestown to Missouri in 1835, shortly before their son Samuel—Mark Twain—was born);

* The White Cottage in Nashville, a tiny gem of a dining room that has attracted a loyal following for decades;

* Swett's Dinette, a first-rate Nashville eatery serving plate lunches cafeteria-style since 1954;

* Mack's Country Cooking, an all-night diner in Nashville that serves what food critic Joan Dew once called "comfort food that takes me back to my roots";

* The Elliston Place Soda Shop, which started out as a drugstore soda fountain in Nashville more than fifty years ago and became a plate-lunch restaurant when present owner Lynn Chandler bought it in 1939;

* The Satsuma Tea Room, started by two young home economics teachers in downtown Nashville in 1918, which still features such rare Southern delights as spoonbread, corn light bread, blueberry muffins, and caramel pie.

It is time to eat. Here is supper. Black-Eyed Peas with Ham Hock. . . . Fried Okra. . . . Country Cornbread. . . . Sweet Potato Pie. . . . You talk of supping with the gods. You've just done it, for who but a god could have come up with the divine fact of okra?

James Dickey
Jericho, 1974

Notwithstanding this substantial group of plate-lunch places in Tennessee, we have four more to cite—four of the best, by almost any measure. They are final proof, if more proof were needed, that Tennessee is the fertile heartland of Southern plate lunches.

The FourWay Grill in Memphis features, among other things, what a local food critic has called "the best fried chicken I have ever eaten in a restaurant." That would be enough to make it special, but there is more. Irene Cleaves, who started the place with her late husband in 1947, is still in charge. Seven days a week, from morning until night, the restaurant maintains a standard of cookery that would be the envy of most cafes. The front room is a noisy area of booths and counter stools, and the adjacent kitchen is a chaotic control center around which more than twenty employees move in haste. Some customers go through the kitchen to a dining room in the rear, or knock on the locked outside door there and wait to be let in. That dining room, in contrast to the front, is a neat, quiet space where the tables are covered with white cloths and a frosty pitcher of ice water is brought by the waitress with the menus.

In this peaceful little sanctuary, a wonderful array of classic Southern dishes is available—salmon croquettes, beef hash, turkey and dressing, pork in every form from chitlins to tenderloin, and of course chicken; yams, corn, cabbage, greens, carrots, green beans, potatoes, beets, rice, limas; steaming hot and delectable cornbread muffins; peach cobbler, rice pudding, and all manner of pies. "Every meal is supervised by top professionals," says the menu, and who could doubt it?

Mrs. Cleaves, a pleasant and placid lady with a motherly demeanor, moves about the busy kitchen with easy grace. She has gradually shifted from cooking to supervising since she turned seventy-five a few years ago, but she is still definitely in charge, and the quality of the food shows it. The FourWay Grill is one of those surviving Southern diners that give eternal hope to lovers of the cuisine.

Duncan's Diner in Gallatin, a middle Tennessee community, is in a small, pink concrete-block building on a back street off the main highway. It has been there for twenty-five years, a family enterprise owned by Baxter and Carrie Duncan and catering to the Southern tastes of its regular clientele. Four or five main dishes, twice as many vegetables, a couple of salads, a dessert, and delicious, deep-fried, hot-water corn pones are the standard menu features. Whenever the restaurant is open (for lunch six days a week, for dinner three days), the sixty-seven table places are apt to be occupied. Regular customers know to get there early, before the food runs out.

At Duncan's, food comes to the table attractively prepared by Mrs. Duncan and her assistants in the kitchen. Freshness is the hallmark, and peak flavor is the standard; hot dishes are steaming hot, cold ones crisply chilled, and every-

The fact that snow is important to Eskimos is supposedly indicated by the seven or twelve or however many different words they have for it. What, then, are we to make of the hundred-plus expressions for cornbread of various kinds that one folklorist uncovered in South Carolina alone? Obviously, food is and has been important to southerners—in part, perhaps, because some have never had enough, and there have been times when no one had enough.

*John Shelton Reed, in the
Georgia Historical Quarterly, 1982*

thing is seasoned just the way it's supposed to be. Baxter Duncan, a quietly friendly man, has the easiest job in the house; he greets the satisfied customers at the cash register on their way out.

Of all the good Tennessee plate-lunch diners in out-of-the-way places, none is more remote than the Hilltop Cafe—but at noon on any given day, its parking lot is apt to be crowded with cars, some of them from far away. The Hilltop is perched on a winding razorback ridge a few miles north of Celina in the Cumberland Plateau region. Strung out along the ridge flanking the restaurant is the community of Free Hill, so named because it was settled by ex-slaves after the Civil War. Upward of fifty families, most of them descendants of the founders, live on the ridge now. Clorina and George Andrews, owners of the Hilltop, are among them.

George Andrews and his father before him have long been well-regarded locally as barbecue makers and short-order cooks, and the Hilltop's reputation has continued to spread since Clorina Andrews turned her attention to it in the late 1960s; now, throughout the hills that stretch along the Tennessee-Kentucky border, people who love good Southern food regularly come to dine at the cafe on the ridge. Though it seats only fifty people, it's not unusual for three or four times that many to show up for lunch on a busy day.

It is a well-appointed country cafe with polished wood floors, Formica-top tables, and an array of pictures, calendars, clocks, thermometers, and assorted bric-a-brac on the walls. A color TV set behind the counter plays the afternoon soap operas, and a jukebox in one corner is full of black and white artists ranging from James Brown to James Taylor. Mrs. Andrews or one of her helpers serves plates from a steam table. Two meats and at least a half-dozen vegetables are available every day. Chicken and dumplings is the headliner every Tuesday, and on other days the main dishes include fried chicken, meat loaf, catfish, pork chops, and more.

"I always have mashed potatoes, slaw, and cornbread on the menu," Mrs. Andrews said, "and I serve yeast rolls twice a week, and my special dessert is caramel pie—I make it almost every day." Many customers call ahead to reserve a slice of this old Southern favorite.

Clorina Andrews belongs to that small and select class of experts known as natural-born cooks. She grew up cooking at her mother's elbow, and both the acquired wisdom and her own instinctive skills are now deeply ingrained. "I never use recipes," she said. "I just throw in. I still love to cook as much as I ever did, and that's got a lot to do with it—you've got to love what you do. This is the same food we have always eaten—just regular food, home cooking. If you're from the South, you know what I mean."

Finally, one more natural-born cook: Charlesetta Hughes at Sylvan Park Restaurant in Nashville. She started cooking at home when she was eleven years

In reading lots and lots of cookbooks written by white folks it occurred to me that people very casually say Spanish rice, French fries, Italian spaghetti, Chinese cabbage, Mexican beans, Swedish meatballs, Danish pastry, English muffins and Swiss cheese. And with the exception of black bottom pie and niggertoes, there is no reference to black people's contribution to the culinary arts. White folks act like they invented food and like there is some weird mystique surrounding it—something that only Julia and Jim can get to. There is no mystique. Food is food. Everybody eats! . . . I never measure or weigh anything. I cook by vibration. . . . It don't matter if it's Dakar or Savannah, you can cook exotic food any time you want. Just turn on the imagination, be willing to change your style and let a little soul food in. . . . People who eat food with pleasure and get pleasure from the different stirring of the senses that a well-prepared food experience can bring are my kind of people.

Vertamae Grosvenor
Vibration Cooking, 1970

old and had her first job in a school cafeteria when she was just fourteen; she has been a restaurant cook for more than thirty years, twenty of them at Sylvan Park. Born and raised in a Tennessee country town, she is heart and soul a Southern cook, and quietly proud of her accomplishments. "Cooking is an art," she says. "It's imbedded in you from birth. I love to do it, and love to see people enjoy it. I come to work at five o'clock in the morning—and I come in happy."

Sylvan Park's customers come in happy too. The little restaurant is precariously placed on a sharp curve, and there's not much parking space, but at noon and six in the evening, all fifty of the seats inside are likely to be taken, and a line of waiting people may stretch out the front door. Almost every morning, at least a couple of cars pull up at ten o'clock, a half-hour before the restaurant opens. One of them is driven by eighty-year-old Charlie Horton. "I've been eating here at least three days a week for twenty-five years," he told me one day. "I get here early so I can be first and not have to rush. This place has got it all—good service, friendly people, and the best food in town."

Another regular, octogenarian Wentworth Caldwell, comes in for lunch five days a week, arriving by taxicab from his nearby office. "He always has a vegetable plate," explains waitress Betty Roberts, "and he doesn't even look at the menu. As soon as he sits down, I just bring him a plate with a selection from whatever we have."

That's not always an easy choice. Each day there are twelve to fifteen fresh vegetables and salads on the menu, plus about eight main-dish entrees, biscuits and cornbread, three or four kinds of pie, and a fruit cobbler. "Almost everything we serve is fresh," Charlesetta Hughes said. "There's so much work involved in peeling a bushel of potatoes or snapping beans or shucking corn or cleaning turnip greens, but we do it every day. I bake between forty and fifty pies every day—make the crust and everything. That's the sort of thing that takes time, but you can't have real home cooking any other way. There are eight people working in the kitchen and five or six more working out in the dining room, and sometimes we feed five hundred people a day. You've really got to work at it to make the last meal taste just as good and fresh as the first."

A Nashville couple, Jetty and Lura Mai Robertson, started the Sylvan Park as a little luncheonette nearly fifty years ago. It is owned now by Lynn Chandler, who also operates three other Nashville lunchrooms. "All of his places have a good reputation," said Betty Roberts, who has worked at Sylvan Park for more than fifteen years, "but naturally we think we're the best. We've got Charlesetta. When you've got a cook as good as she is, nobody can beat you."

Family-Style

The Jarrett House in Dillsboro, North Carolina, celebrated its hundredth anniversary as a lodging and dining establishment in 1984. Like the more venerable Nu-Wray Inn in Burnsville and numerous other rustic retreats in the Southern mountains, the Jarrett House is a throwback to the nineteenth century. Guests in its dining room in the 1980s eat the same style of food in much the same manner as their predecessors did a century ago. The style is strictly down-home Southern; the manner is communal, with each diner serving himself or herself from bowls and platters passed around the table.

Far to the west, in Texarkana, Arkansas, a popular tradition of a similar sort has flourished for more than fifty years at Bryce's Cafeteria. The food, like that at the Jarrett House, is distinctly Southern, but the service is typical cafeteria style, and has been since the restaurant first opened in 1931.

Dining in both of these places during our 1984–85 travels through the South, it occurred to me that they represented two different kinds of family-style dining. The Jarrett House and other serve-and-pass restaurants present their fare much the way families do at home. Bryce's Cafeteria and places like it, on the other hand, qualify as so-called family-style restaurants because their relatively inexpensive food is meant to look and taste like home cooking and is often an attractive choice for family groups dining together.

It is a fine line—and perhaps an arbitrary one as well—that separates plate-lunch eateries from old-fashioned hotel dinner tables, cafeterias, boardinghouses, and other similar dining halls. In the South, all such establishments have served similar cuisine from one generation to the next, and some of them go far back into the region's history. Cafeteria-style service found its way into the South in 1920, but long before that there were public tables at which people regularly gathered and passed around dishes of food straight from the kitchen.

Family-style dining was the common means by which food was served to the public in the nineteenth century, and even though much has changed since then, family-style restaurants and cafeterias are still quite popular in the South. We sampled the food in more than thirty such places as we made our way around the region. A majority of them are included in the descriptions that follow.

First, a few cafeterias:

Technically speaking, Bryce's is not in Arkansas but Texas, standing as it does on the west side of State Line Street in Texarkana. It attracts diners from one state as much as the other, though, and it's not unusual for people to drive from neighboring Oklahoma and Louisiana to share in the regional cuisine.

⊰ Menu ⊱

BANQUET TO

Gen. U.S. Grant

Consomme, a la Reine,

Lake Salmon, Baked.
Potato Croquettes.
'Yquem.

Boiled Supreme of Turkey.
Asparagus. Potatoes in Cream.
Poulet Canet.

Filet of Beef, Larded. Richelieu.
Cauliflower. French Peas.
Roederer Carte Blanc.

Roman Punch.

Broiled Spring Chicken, on Toast.
Potatoes, Saratoga.
G.H. Mumm & Co.

Beef Tongue. Veal Pate Truffee.
Chicken Salad.

English Plum Pudding, Cognac Sauce.

Assorted Cakes. Champagne Jelly.
Ice Cream, Strawberries.
Pineapple Cheese. Edam Cheese.

Fruits. Coffee. Cigars.

PEABODY HOTEL
Memphis, April 13, 1880.

Bryce's has never moved from its downtown location, but it has expanded several times. Its dining room now seats 330 people, and it is often crowded.

Bryce Lawrence started the cafeteria during the Great Depression. His two sons run it now. "Everything we serve is fresh and homemade," said Bryce Jr. "It can't just be good-tasting, either—it's got to be attractive, well-arranged, well-presented. We're a large-volume operation, but our food looks and tastes like it was prepared to order just for you. It's Southern food, traditional home-style cooking, expertly prepared by Southern cooks—black women, mostly, and some men. Many of our employees have been here for twenty-five years or more. We all take pride in the quality of our food and service."

The night we ate at Bryce's, I chose creamed chicken on cornbread, Brussels sprouts with cream sauce, speckled butter beans, and coconut pie. Ann had trout amandine, stewed okra, squash casserole, tomato aspic, corn muffins, and egg custard pie. The combination of familiar and uncommon dishes was uniformly well-seasoned, properly cooked, and delicious. Bryce's reputation for quality is secure.

The South has more than its share of cafeterias—good little ones in small towns, like Stone's in Christiansburg, Virginia, and Stewart's in Americus, Georgia, and Miles & Crenshaw's in Pendleton, South Carolina, and good big ones in cities, like the Blue Boar in Louisville, Kentucky, the Picadilly chain based in Baton Rouge, Louisiana, and the region's oldest and largest chain, Morrison's, headquartered in Mobile, Alabama. Family ownership seems to be as much a part of the cafeteria business as family-style food service. Wise Cafeteria in New Orleans fits the pattern. It was started by Herbert M. Wise in 1930 and is owned now by Milton Wise, his son, who describes the food as being essentially unchanged from what his father served: "well-seasoned, down-home, stick-to-your-ribs good eating." In a word, wholesome.

The same can be said of John and Eunice McDonald's busy cafeteria in Charlotte, North Carolina. John McDonald, a Carolina native, spent twenty years in the restaurant business in New York and returned home to retire in 1969, only to find himself cooking again within a year. "I've been cooking all my life," he explained. "This is my talent, and I finally decided it was also my destiny. I'm still active in the kitchen, although now I'm mostly teaching others to cook."

McDonald's bears no resemblance whatsoever to the hamburger chain of the same name. Its dining room seats two hundred, there are banquet rooms for four hundred more, and large crowds are the rule. They come for the unbeatable combination of traditional and unusual Southern foods, all expertly cooked and seasoned—chicken and turkey, pork and beef, but also lamb and veal and duck, and a wonderful array of vegetables and hot breads and desserts on the side.

I descended to the passage, and found a crowd of expectants before a closed door. Another bell rang out loudly and rapidly from a belfry on the roof of the hotel. The door was unlocked, and we all rushed into a long hall, like a squadron of Hulans charging the enemy, and found tables covered with meat, vegetables, preserved fruit, tea, coffee and bread, both of maize and wheat, and soft hoe and waffle cakes. Down the company sat in a hurry—noses were blown to one side—cotton handkerchiefs were spread on the knees—cuffs were turned back, and then commenced "the crash of the crockery and the clash of the steel!" No ceremony was used; each man helped himself with his own knife and fork, and reached across his neighbor to secure a fancied morceau. Bones were picked with both hands; knives were drawn through the teeth with the edge to the lips; the scalding mocha and souchong were poured into saucers to expedite the cooling,

"It's nothing in the world but what we were raised on," said John McDonald. "What Grandma used to cook—soul food, straight from the heart, typical American home cooking, all the way back to Indian times." In his view, good Southern food knows no racial or ethnic boundaries: "If it's good, everybody loves it." McDonald's Cafeteria easily qualifies as a favorite place to eat in Charlotte.

Davis Bros., a small chain of eighteen cafeterias in Georgia and Florida, makes a public pledge "to offer you the widest selection of farm-fresh fruits, vegetables and other foods found anywhere at any time." That's a tall order— but at the company's restaurant at the State Farmers' Market in Atlanta, the Davis brothers deliver impressively on that pledge. I stopped there at eleven one morning, and stood first in the serving line. The vegetables had just come to the steam table from the kitchen, and I ordered separate servings of green beans, creamed corn, collard greens, cabbage, and black-eyed peas, with a corn muffin and a glass of iced tea. Every dish was at peak flavor—perfectly cooked and seasoned, steaming hot, full of freshness. I felt as if I had heard the peal of the dinner bell and hurried to the farm-kitchen table, there to be richly rewarded for a hard morning's work in the fields.

With food as with so many things, nothing is more important than good timing. Perfect timing at the Davis Bros. Cafeteria in Atlanta had rewarded me with a meal to remember.

The oldest cafeteria in the South, beating Morrison's by a few months, is Robertson's in Charleston, South Carolina. When it opened in 1920, founder E. H. Robertson promised to "keep high standards and serve dishes the patrons want," especially the native low-country food that Charlestonians had prized for generations. True to their forebear's words, the Robertson family is still featuring dishes right out of *Charleston Receipts,* a local cookbook of great renown. Hoppin John, deviled crab, shrimp and oyster and flounder dishes, red rice, sweet potato pie, and Huguenot tortes are among the features, and the dining room, which seats nearly three hundred people, is often packed.

Turkey with cornbread dressing, fried oysters, macaroni pie, okra gumbo, collard greens, and green beans cooked with side meat were on the menu when I was there. So was Lucille's chocolate pie, an icebox pie combining chocolate, pecans, and cream cheese in a pecan butter-nut crust. Without exception, the customers I talked to had nothing but praise for the day-to-day quality of the food.

Manager Danny Du Ross said Robertson's originally was a soda fountain in downtown Charleston. The founder turned it into a cafeteria, and his son and successor, A. H. Robertson, later moved it to its present location in a suburban shopping center. The third generation is in charge now, but the restaurant's traditions are intact. "We make all our own cornbread, rolls, and biscuits," Du

and the cup deposited in a saucerette on the right. Beefsteaks, apple tart and fish were seen on the same plate the one moment, and had disappeared the next! The black domestics bustled about in breathless haste. Mr. Edmondson, the respectable landlord, stood at the end of one of the tables, serving out meat and seeing that his guests wanted nothing.

I was rather bewildered, and could not eat for some minutes.

from "An Englishman's Visit to Nashville," by Capt. J. E. Alexander, in the Nashville Republican, June 20, 1835

Ross said, "and all our desserts too. In fact, the only things we serve that aren't fresh or homemade are soft drinks and saltine crackers."

Cafeterias tend not to have great reputations as places to dine. Perhaps it is their low-budget image that is responsible, or the self-serve dimension, or the undeniable fact that cafeteria cookery sometimes fails to rise above the mediocrity of institutional food. But the examples given here should be sufficient to underscore an important point: Good cooks and good managers can produce good food, regardless of the style of service, the setting, the price, or any other factor. Excellent Southern food can certainly be found in some of the region's cafeterias.

In some family-style restaurants, diners choose from a selection of entrees and everything else is served automatically; in others, all of the food, including the main dishes, is brought to the table and passed around for everyone to share. A third option is the buffet (originally a French sideboard), or what the Scandinavians call a smorgasbord: long tables of displayed foods from which diners make their own selections. By whatever name, these all-you-can-eat banquets are very popular in the South.

There are some interesting social and historical explanations for this popularity. One is the ancient tradition of Southern hospitality, which originally was associated with the lavish feasts that were a hallmark of plantation society. Another originated at the opposite end of the economic spectrum. It holds that the traumatic experiences of extreme hunger that marked the eras of the Civil War and the Great Depression caused many Southerners to develop a cultural mindset or philosophy about food. In essence, it was an attitude of indulgence in the bounty of the table, whatever it offered, for leaner times were apt to lie ahead.

For these and other reasons, people in the South have long attached importance to such public occasions as food festivals, church dinners on the ground, school and community suppers, barbecues, fish fries, and oyster roasts. Indeed, any repast that promises diners all the food they can eat is likely to attract a sizable crowd. When the food is not only plentiful but good, it assures longevity and a favorable reputation for those who cook it and serve it. Thus, the Jarrett House and several other inns in the mountains of North Carolina continue to prosper.

At Belhaven, in the coastal region of North Carolina, the River Forest Manor is a classic example of the buffet style of Southern dining. For three decades, the late Axson Smith, his wife, Melba, and their two sons have taken turns as hosts at a lavish evening repast in an ornate Victorian mansion. More than five dozen dishes regularly fill the tables. "Eat, drink and be merry," a revised proverb on the menu reads, "for tomorrow you may diet."

The Purefoy Hotel opened at its present location [in Talladega, Alabama, on May 17, 1920]. . . . As time passed, the fame of the Purefoy spread far beyond the bounds of Alabama. . . . From Waco, Texas, a cotton merchant broke into print in his enthusiasm about the Purefoy dining room, saying he had at last "found the perfect restaurant with the meal spread on snowy linen, family style, consisting of about 40 dishes with exceptionally fine cooking, with hot dishes piping hot, with cold dishes well chilled, and all served by waiters in spotless white uniforms." . . . thru all the labor and servant problems, the Purefoy has maintained its high standards of service: it continues to advertise Talladega to the world.

Eva B. Purefoy
Purefoy Hotel Cook Book, 1941

Diners come every day from the local area, and a few travelers stay overnight in the mansion's guest rooms, but most of the River Forest Manor trade arrives by boat on the Intracoastal Waterway, docking within a stone's throw of the big house. When they arrive for dinner, they are apt to find such Southern delicacies as fresh yellow baby squash with onions, corn pudding "by our own Southern cook," speckled butter beans, sweet potato fluff, collard greens with ham and cornmeal dumplings, creamed rutabagas, oyster fritters, crab meat casserole, biscuits and hush puppies, and a half-dozen homemade pies and cakes.

The River Forest shuts down for three months in the winter, and it happened to be closed when I stopped by. But Melba Smith and two other women were there, busy with some off-season redecorating, and when I told her my reason for visiting, she graciously invited me to join them for an informal midday meal—"just a little lunch of leftovers," she called it.

A garrulous mynah bird chattered away while we dined on field peas and cornmeal dumplings, string beans and ham, stewed potatoes, chicken salad, iced tea, and chocolate cream pie. They asked me all about my travels, and Mrs. Smith told me the history of River Forest Manor and its dining tradition. I felt more like a friend who had dropped in than a stranger. It was a quintessentially Southern experience.

Two Mississippi restaurants offer an interesting variation on the theme of family-style dining. The Dinner Bell in McComb and the Mendenhall Hotel in Mendenhall feature round-table or revolving-table service. As many as eighteen guests sit at circular tables and rotate enormous center-section lazy susans loaded with about twenty-five different main dishes, vegetables, fruit dishes, salads, hot breads, and desserts.

The Dinner Bell was started in the 1940s and moved to its present location in 1981. John and Carolyn Lopinto, the current owners, came to McComb from New Orleans in 1980 to try to save what Mrs. Lopinto, a local native, remembered from her youth as "a wonderful place to eat." The restaurant had fallen on hard times, but it still had Elise Crosley as its chief cook (she has been there since 1960), and because of her it held on to a reputation for fine Southern cooking.

"The first thing we did before we decided to come here was to secure the services of Mrs. Crosley," said Carolyn Lopinto. "She was essential to our recovery plan. Without her and the other long-time employees, it would simply have been too hard—maybe impossible—to make a go of it."

Elise Crosley was in the kitchen when we sat down to dinner, and her chicken and dumplings, catfish, turnip greens, fried okra, and sweet potato casserole were outstanding dishes. After a period of uncertainty, the Dinner Bell is calling hungry guests to the round table once again.

The Mendenhall Hotel was the originator of the revolving-table style of service in Mississippi. The hotel opened in 1915 and has had just four owners since then, all of them from the same family. Fred and Natalie Morgan own it now, and they and the veteran cooks and waitresses offer Southern cooking family-style, just as the hotel did seventy years ago. I counted five meats, ten vegetables, five salads, biscuits and cornbread, and two desserts on the lazy susan. The hotel still has a few rooms to rent, but most of its business is handled in the dining room, where local people and travelers gather twice a day—at dinner and supper—to enjoy the good taste of traditional Southern food.

There is another Dinner Bell, a "smorgasbord of home-style cooking," near Aurora, Kentucky, and the 4 a.m. to 9 p.m. service makes it a fisherman's haven in a region of lakes and rivers. There is menu service until the evening smorgasbord is set out on antique wood-burning cookstoves, but at all hours the food is typically Southern, from the turnip greens and hog jowl and cornbread to the homemade desserts.

Another Kentucky family-style place is the Lone Oak Restaurant near Bowling Green. Since the mid-1960s it has been serving dinner in an old service station on a narrow country road, but pleased patrons have kept returning, and their trade has kept the light burning in the Lone Oak kitchen. Mrs. Forest Stice and one or two helpers do all the work, from cooking and waiting tables to cleaning up—no small task on a busy night, when a hundred or more people may come to dinner.

"We like for people to call and make reservations," said Mrs. Stice. "That way, we can fix for a set number, just as we would do if they were coming to our house to eat." The chocolate and pecan and "meal" pies—the last a local name for chess pie made with cornmeal—are definitely of home-kitchen caliber.

Boardinghouses once were commonplace institutions in the South. Every little town seemed to have one or more of them—big, rambling houses, typically, serving daily meals to a regular clientele and an occasional visitor, and sometimes renting out a few rooms upstairs. Highway motels and restaurants finally put most of the boardinghouses out of business, and today it is rare to find one that operates in the old manner.

But there are a few left. One of them is Arkie Dell "Ma" Hopkins' place on a residential street in Pensacola, Florida. She got into the business in 1948, just when the death knell was beginning to sound for boardinghouses, and now her business is booming, thanks to a combination of customers: room-and-board regulars, local townspeople, and tourists.

At breakfast around the fourteen-seat main table, eighty-two-year-old Jack Howes was chatting with regulars Pete and Bob, and waitress Betty Norris joined in. Back in the kitchen, Lucille Turner, the senior cook, was working on the noon meal, and Judy Veycock, a niece of Mrs. Hopkins who grew up in the old house, was in the front room snapping beans.

The smells from the Beula Villa met us as we made the turn toward the grand hotel in Sulphur Well [Kentucky]. This was the one Sunday ritual I looked forward to as a child. We got out of our car and headed for the enormous porch which semicircled the hotel, and each adult and child found a high-backed, flat-armed rocking chair in which to rock and talk for at least 30 minutes before dinner.

At the stroke of noon, King Crenshaw would come out on the porch and ring the biggest brass bell I've ever seen. He then led us through the parlor, with its Gone With the Wind lamps and their awesome prisms, to the dining room. There, round tables to seat 12 were ready with starched linens, heavy flatware, and the precious cargo of Sunday dinner: fried country ham still steaming with the smell of coffee in the red-eye gravy, mashed potatoes with butter melting from the peaks, fried chicken and accompanying bowls of cream gravy, green beans visibly bolstered with ham chunks, and those silver dollar biscuits that would fog your glasses when you pulled them apart. How could they

"I love the people here, and the food too," said Howes, a retired merchant who has lived and eaten in the Hopkins household for more than three decades. "You don't get quail under glass or asparagus on toast—just good, delicious food. I attribute my good health to the variety and quality of this food."

At dinner I came back for a home-cooked meal served family-style, and great was my reward: pot roast with carrots and potatoes, chicken and dumplings, turkey and cornbread dressing, sweet peas, Waldorf salad, fried eggplant, rutabagas, green beans cooked with seasoning meat, stewed apples, cornbread muffins, yeast rolls, peach cobbler.

"It hasn't changed a bit in all these years," Jack Howes declared, and those in earshot of his assessment nodded in agreement.

A boardinghouse tradition of much longer duration continues in Lynchburg, Tennessee, in the maple-shaded, two-story frame house of the late "Miss Mary" Bobo. At 1 p.m. six days a week, forty-four people farsighted enough to call ahead and reserve a place are summoned to the four tables for twelve by the ringing of a dinner bell. A hometown hostess presides at each table with eleven guests. "Pass to the left," explained our hostess, retired schoolteacher Elizabeth Cobble, when the steaming bowls and platters arrived. It has been done in very much the same way since Miss Mary opened for business in 1908.

Whiskey maker Jack Daniel and his nephew Lem Motlow used to stroll down the dusty road to eat dinner at Miss Mary's as often as they could. Miss Mary outlasted them—proving, some would argue, that Southern cooking yields a greater life expectancy to teetotalers than tipplers. (She was 102 when she died in 1983, apparently unaffected by pork and sugar.)

Miss Mary's now belongs to the Jack Daniel Distillery, and Lynne Tolley, a Lynchburg native, is the resident hostess. Back in the kitchen, Louise Gregory and Helen Daniel and Barbara McGowan cook garden-fresh vegetables and other Southern specialties the same way they did when Miss Mary was there. Especially in the summer months, when the garden out back is at its peak, midday dinner at Miss Mary's is probably as close as you can get to the taste and feel of a Southern country meal as it must have been in its natural setting about a century ago.

One more Tennessee family-style dining room should be mentioned, for longevity as well as Southern cookery: the Donoho Hotel in Red Boiling Springs. When it first opened in 1914, the sulphur springs that bubbled out of the earth nearby made the town a prime summer resort. It's a quiet village off the beaten path now, but the Donoho, a two-story frame structure with a wraparound porch and guest rooms that open to the outside, still serves meals that make country-raised Southerners wish they were back on the farm.

When Louise Flatt or Esto Whitley is cooking, and when the year-old cured hams are pushing two years and the summer produce is at its peak, you can sit

keep everything so hot! I don't remember salads, except maybe cole slaw, but dessert! I can still taste the mixture of hot apple cobbler and cold ice cream coming together in my mouth.

a reminiscence by Martha Neal Cooke, Louisville, Kentucky, 1986

There is . . . something about the foodways of the mountains . . . that is undeniably compelling, even graceful. Perhaps it has to do with the power of the experience, for older mountain women . . . as a rite of passage in their lives. . . . Perhaps that compelling quality has something to do with the fact that food . . . became somehow a metaphor for the generosity and interdependence of life here that transcended the food itself. . . . Or perhaps [it has to do with the fact that there are] times when a meal, like a friendship quilt, is designed to mark an event in some memorable way. . . . Or perhaps . . . for many residents of the area, the preparation of food . . . or the canning of it, was traditionally a means of engaging everyone's energies around a common task, passing time productively, and cementing friendships permanently. At Aunt Arie Carpenter's, cooking became an event, as opposed to a utilitarian task. . . . there was not a single instance when she did not ask us, with more than a little . . . anticipation in her voice, "Now will you'uns stay and eat with me?"

Eliot Wigginton,
in his introduction to
The Foxfire Book of Appalachian Cookery, 1984

down to a Donoho dinner and know you're in for a treat: fried ham and red-eye gravy, mashed potatoes, fried corn, green beans, sliced tomatoes, fried apples, hot biscuits, honey and butter, iced tea or coffee, and a wedge of pie.

"It's the old-timey way," Mrs. Whitley explained, "from scratch. That's the only kind of cooking there is, as far as I'm concerned."

Our family-style eating odyssey ends in Georgia, with three mountain-area dining rooms of note and with the legendary Mrs. Wilkes in Savannah.

The north Georgia mountains are crowded with tourists and vacationers during the warm months, and many small towns in the region have developed into resort communities along the lines of their older counterparts in North Carolina. Wherever hotels, inns, lodges, cabins, and other retreat housing have developed, there the restaurants have come too, and more often than not, they have turned out to be family-style dining halls of the buffet, cafeteria, or serve-and-pass type. Three of the oldest and best-known are Smith House in Dahlonega, Dillard House in Dillard, and LaPrade's on Lake Burton north of Clarkesville.

Smith House is a small mountain inn with a large dining room, reflecting the popularity of its self-described "Southern hospitality and traditional mountain cooking." It opened in 1922. More than one thousand people a day eat there during the summer months. Four or five main dishes, a dozen or more vegetables, cornbread muffins, yeast rolls, angel biscuits, and an array of cobblers, puddings, and other sweets are on the daily bill of fare. Dahlonega, a gold-mining town before the Civil War, is mining tourist gold now, and Smith House is one of its main attractions.

Dillard House traces its origin to 1915, when ancestors of the present owners started a room and board service in their home. Now, thousands of summer tourists crowd into the dining room for family-service meals that feature locally cured ham, home-baked breads, apple butter and other preserves, fresh vegetables, and fruit cobblers.

LaPrade's is a family-owned fish camp turned rustic mountain resort. Since 1925, its dining room, cabins, and marina have served generations of fishermen and vacationers. Country food is served family-style at four long tables seating thirty-six people each. Locally raised pork and chickens and garden-fresh vegetables are featured.

By comparison with these north Georgia landmarks, Sema Wilkes' Boarding House in Savannah is younger, smaller, perhaps harder to find—and better, if published testimonials are a fair measure. Mrs. Wilkes has been in the food business for forty years. Since 1965, she has operated a small dining room in the basement of a house on Jones Street in Savannah's historic district. The restaurant has no sign, no telephone directory listing, no advertising. But in late morning or early afternoon of any given weekday, a telltale aroma of fine food hangs in the air along Jones Street, and a line is formed along the sidewalk in the 100 block. These are the unmistakable signs leading to a dining experience that has been praised in *Esquire, The New York Times, Town and Country,* and *The Stars and Stripes.*

"Nobody ever taught me to cook," Mrs. Wilkes said. "I just learned as I went along—it just came natural. I always loved to do it for my family, and I never have tired of meeting people and serving them good food." She is in her mid-seventies now, and her grandson manages the restaurant. "I still come in every day, but I'm just a fixture now."

The first wave of forty-eight midday diners fills the chairs at the six cloth-covered tables and waits for L. H. Wilkes, the leading lady's husband, to say grace. Then they begin serving and passing the five meats, ten vegetables, and two hot breads on the table. There are four desserts to choose from later. When places clear at the tables, a waitress resets them with clean china and accessories, and new diners come from the waiting line to have their turn.

The food is classic Southern: fried chicken, roast beef and gravy, chicken and dumplings, smoked sausage, ham, beans, greens, sweet and white potatoes, rice, biscuits, cornbread muffins, big pitchers of iced tea, sweet puddings and pies and cobblers. When the diners have had their fill, they take their dishes to the kitchen and pay the bill (five dollars per person, up from a dollar fifty in 1972). It is a small price to pay for such a feast.

"The cost of everything in the food business kept going right on up," Sema Wilkes said, "and it's harder and harder to get good quality food and dependable help. I've been lucky, and people have been very supportive of our restaurant, but I wonder sometimes if this kind of old-time food has a future. I'm afraid Southern cooking is going the way of the family farm, and in a few years it'll be gone."

Dinner

Jocelyn Mayfield of Ocean Springs, Mississippi, was born into cooking. Her father and uncle were hotel chefs along the Gulf Coast and in New Orleans, her mother was an accomplished cook, and she herself has spent more than thirty-five years mastering the techniques of Creole, Cajun, and indigenous Southern cookery that have dominated the kitchens of the region for nearly three centuries. She has cooked for a private family from Cajun country, worked her way up to manager of a Creole-Southern restaurant, and catered the traditional foods of the coastal South. Now she is the owner, hostess, and head chef of Jocelyn's, an orange-sherbet-colored cottage with white gingerbread trim and lacy curtains at the windows in her moss-draped hometown of Ocean Springs.

The Canadian-born Le Moyne brothers, Pierre d'Iberville and Jean Baptiste de Bienville, placed their first settlement at the present site of Ocean Springs when they began to colonize the lower Mississippi River basin for France in 1699. Bienville later founded Mobile, New Orleans, and Biloxi, all in the vast watershed the French called Louisiana, and the distinctive cookery that has evolved there got its French accent from the Le Moynes and those who followed them. Jocelyn Mayfield is one of the contemporary beneficiaries of that tradition. *Acune place, comme ça,* says a sign outside her restaurant: like this, no place. With allowances for the natural hyperbole of slogans, there is an element of truth to the claim. Jocelyn's *is* an uncommonly good restaurant, and the larger place—the Cajun-Creole coastal strip that extends for a hundred miles or so east and west of New Orleans—is like no other Southern precinct as a purveyor of fine foods.

The western part of that great dinner belt is featured in the following section, Eating Out in Louisiana. But first, we will begin at Jocelyn's and describe some of our evening dining experiences in about forty of the South's established houses of regional cuisine.

There are no hard and fast rules for designating these as dinner places. Some are fancier and more formal—and also more expensive—than the plate-lunch cafes and family-style dining halls on our itinerary, but not all of them are. Some are open for dinner only, and others ended up on this list simply because dinner was the meal we happened to eat there. All of them are restaurants where diners sit down and order from a menu. Beyond that, they are a diverse collection of establishments that offer numerous choices to people who enjoy having dinner out in the South.

Jocelyn Mayfield and her husband, Harold, both worked for many years at Trilby's, the queen mother of Ocean Springs restaurants. "I started there when

I was twenty years old, and I'm fifty-three now," she said. "Trilby Steimer died in 1960 and Teddy, her husband, sold the place a couple of years later, but Harold and I stayed on, and I was the manager for eighteen years. It was and is a fine restaurant, and we had a lot of very loyal customers. One of them was a doctor from Pascagoula. He told me one time, 'Anybody who works as hard as you do ought to be in business for themselves.' He offered to help me if I ever decided to go out on my own. So as soon as our six kids were out of school I went to him, and he was as good as his word. Now we've got a restaurant and catering business that employs about fifteen members of our family—children, brothers and sisters, in-laws. Thanks to our hard work and our guardian angel's backing, we're building a good reputation in the food business."

The reputation is anchored by Jocelyn Mayfield's skill as a creative cook. "I always wondered what my talents were," she said. "Finally I realized that I have a feel and touch and taste for food. Over the years I have learned the traditional styles of the South, but also how to be inventive and flexible, how to do Mexican and Chinese as well as Creole and Cajun. I especially love to make pastries and other desserts—pies, puddings, trifles, five-layer tortes, you name it."

The menu features a variety of shrimp, oyster, crab, and other seafood dishes, beef and chicken specialties, vegetables and casseroles, salads and homemade breads, and the impressive desserts. Our choices included cream of broccoli soup with a sprinkle of nutmeg, an artistically arranged fresh garden salad with homemade French dressing, two very distinctive shrimp and crabmeat casseroles, broiled tomatoes, Creole bread pudding with whiskey sauce, and the best piece of pecan pie I have ever eaten in a restaurant. All of it came with an individual touch from the tiny and immaculate kitchen where Jocelyn and her son Michael do most of the cooking. It was the sort of dinner you might expect to find—for twice the price—in a good New Orleans restaurant, or in a Southern home where cooking is still a cultivated and highly valued art.

Elsewhere in Mississippi, we found some delightful surprises in several restaurants of vastly different ethnic origin—not just black and white Southern, but also Swiss-German, Greek, Italian, and even Chinese Southern.

In Meridian, for example, there is Weidmann's, founded by Swiss-born Felix Weidmann and his German wife, Clara, in 1870 and now so much a fixture in the city that many people refer to it simply as "the Restaurant." Meridian was a muddy little country hamlet, its name only recently changed from Sowashee Junction, when Weidmann arrived. His fourth- and fifth-generation descendants run the restaurant now, and it thrives as a twenty-four-hour-a-day institution that some say is synonymous with Meridian itself.

The front room at Weidmann's, with its old counter top and stools, brass rail, mounted game trophies, celebrity photographs, and other antique touches, is almost like a living museum. The menu has an old-fashioned air about it

François Mignon died a few years ago. He wrote that book about Melrose Plantation, and put some of my recipes in it. I cooked at Melrose for a long time—30 or 40 years. I didn't use any written-down recipes, though—I just cooked from memory, from what my mama taught me and what I learned by myself. The things I fixed back then were Louisiana Creole, I guess you could say. I'm not able to cook any more—my daughter Mary does the cooking for us now. She fixes me what I like best, just good old food, Southern food: greens, peas, turnips, cornbread. Plain, simple—and good.

105-year-old Clementine Hunter, Melrose, Louisiana, in a 1985 interview

too—it's an oversized foldout crammed with a busy jumble of à la carte offerings, house specialties, side-dish listings, recommendations of the chef, and stapled-on daily features. Seafood and freshwater fish are prominent, but there is also plenty of beef and chicken. The vegetables are bona fide Southern (field peas, okra, turnip greens) and the desserts include some classic down-home pies: lemon, almond, egg custard, bourbon, black bottom.

Weidmann's is the same nineteenth-century restaurant it always was, only larger (its rambling network of dining rooms can now accommodate four hundred people). It is one of the oldest such establishments in the South, and one of a very few in the country to last more than a century under single-family ownership. Never Swiss or German in character, it was and is Southern and American to the core, and it seems to go on now almost like a perpetual-motion machine, running on its own self-generated energy.

Babe Ruth ate here, he and Dizzy Dean and Jack Dempsey and hundreds of other stars, and they all left autographed pictures behind to adorn the walls. Dining in the old front room surrounded by their smiling faces, I could easily have imagined that they had been there only yesterday.

In Jackson, the Mississippi capital city, a downtown institution of a similar kind can be found at the Mayflower Cafe. Launched by Greek immigrants in the 1920s, it has survived and prospered as a seafood-oriented restaurant catering to the Southern tastes of its regular clientele, whose Cadillacs and compacts and pickup trucks are parked out on the street.

Unlike Weidmann's, the Mayflower bears at least a few traces of its national origin. You can hear some of it in the voice of Theo Gouras, one of the present owners, as he talks on the phone at the cash register, and you can certainly taste it in the Greek salad and some of the other house specialties. For the most part, though, the Mayflower is a proudly eccentric old cafe where some Southern characters congregate regularly to eat well-seasoned food and swap tales among themselves, with the Gouras clan, or with waitresses like Bertie, a red-haired veteran of booth and table service whose tenure at the restaurant stretches back to 1943.

"One thing's for sure, it never gets dull around here," Bertie said after she had brought us our broiled redfish and red snapper dinners. It was ten o'clock on a midweek evening and the place was crowded with customers. "It goes on like this seven nights a week until midnight or even later, and sometimes it gets so loud you can't hear yourself think."

But compared to Doe's Eat Place in Greenville, the Mayflower seems as peaceful as a prayer meeting. The shotgun-style frame building that houses the restaurant in a black neighborhood near the Mississippi River levee was opened as a grocery by the Italian immigrant parents of Dominic "Doe" Signa in 1903. Signa, who was born in Vicksburg in 1899, followed his father into the business,

Bad dinners go hand in hand with total depravity, while a well-fed man is already half saved.

The New Kentucky Home Cook Book, 1884

but hard times in the twenties and thirties compelled him to pursue other ventures, including bootlegging. The front room of the store became a neighborhood honky-tonk that featured, among other things, Mexican-style hot tamales. By the time World War II was over, some white customers were tiptoeing through the back door to enjoy the food and drink, and eventually Signa converted the place from a black hangout to an all-white eatery featuring tamales and broiled steaks. (It remained segregated until federal law prohibited racial exclusion in public accommodations in 1964.)

Doe's still looks like a run-down old mom-and-pop grocery. Inside, it stirs conflicting images of Depression-era soup kitchens and Roaring Twenties speakeasies. In the front room of the old building, customers waiting for tables stand shoulder to shoulder, some of them sipping drinks from their bring-your-own-bottle bags; against one wall, two black women work serenely to make tossed salads from a huge mound of lettuce, and on the opposite side, Charles and Dominic "Little Doe" Signa take turns broiling inch-thick T-bones and sirloins in a bank of wall ovens and shuttling the finished steaks to waiting diners in the rear.

The second room, directly behind the first, is even more of a three-ring circus. Some women cook on big black gas stoves, others buzz around a long table where orders are assembled, still others mill about with clean or dirty dishes; more customers stand and watch the spectacle or sit at tables nearby. There is another room behind that, and another off to one side. From front to rear, Doe's Eat Place is a sight that defies description. "Even the regulars can't explain it," one of their number told us. "There's no way you can understand this place. What you have to do is just relax and take in the experience."

Doe's is a meat-and-potatoes kind of place serving mostly steaks, French fries, and bread—no desserts. It is possible to order shrimp, spaghetti and meatballs, gumbo, tamales, or chili, if you happen to know they're available, but no one volunteers that information, and there is no menu for guidance.

None of this food except the shrimp and gumbo could be called Southern, but the forty-year presence of such an unusual restaurant in the Mississippi Delta would be hard to ignore. Besides, there is something about the entire adventure of eating at Doe's that probably couldn't be duplicated outside the South. Whatever it is—the determined avoidance of any modern touches, the incongruous blend of steak and tamales, the delicious taste of the food, the white-black-Italian triangle—it is somehow as quirkily Southern as a Eudora Welty short story.

In another part of Greenville, a strikingly different ethnic dining experience is offered at Henry Wong's How Joy ("Good Luck") Restaurant. Authentic Cantonese cuisine is the standard fare, but a special Southern touch is added. How Joy is the oldest and largest Oriental dining place in the city, and perhaps in the

A few miles southwest of Garfield is a grape-growing village called Tonti-town, the oldest Italian settlement in the Ozarks. One night a few years ago I was eating spaghetti and fried chicken at Mary Maestri's, the oldest restaurant in Tontitown and one of the best in Arkansas. Mrs. Maestri, who was about ninety, was sitting at the back. Her son Ed was standing at my table.

"We sure need that four-lane highway," Ed said.

"You'd feel different if they were trying to build it through your kitchen instead of my farm," I said.

He went back to the cash register and pouted, and I ate my spaghetti and sulked. Both Ed and his mother are dead now. The Chambers of Commerce are still trying to build a freeway through the Ozarks, and I am still sore about it. A new generation of Maestris is in charge of the oldest restaurant in Tontitown. Their food is still excellent; I eat there every chance I get. A quarrel is one thing, but good spaghetti is something else.

Roy Reed
Looking for Hogeye, 1986

When I was seven or eight years old, my family took me to Birmingham to visit an aunt. I was born and raised in Mississippi during the Depression, and in that time and place anyone's idea of excitement or genuine adventure was a trip to a big town like Birmingham or Memphis. I remember—to tell the truth, it is the only thing I do remember about that trip—being taken to a Chinese restaurant. There were hanging Chinese lanterns and foreign waiters and real Chinese china and chopsticks and very hot and exotic tea. I cannot recall the menu in precise detail, but I did eat won ton soup and a dish that contained bean sprouts. I marveled over those bean sprouts. What an odd, enticing-looking vegetable! To this day I have not got over an inordinate fondness for won ton soup, and I have retained an all but insatiable appetite for any dish—even a mediocre dish—made with bean sprouts. It is reasonable to suppose that the food I ate then was quite spurious, adapted to the Southern palate, and dreadful. But it kindled a flame.

Craig Claiborne, in his introduction to The Chinese Cookbook, 1972

entire state, having been founded in 1968 and claiming now a capacity of four hundred persons. It is also a direct outgrowth of the initial arrival of Chinese immigrants in the Mississippi Delta more than a century ago.

The first of them came after the Civil War as indentured servants recruited to work on the plantations and railroads and riverboats in the aftermath of slavery. Henry Wong was a latter-day arrival, following relatives into the Delta in the mid-1940s. He was in the grocery business at first, and then he opened How Joy. Like all Oriental restaurants, its cookery is true to its origins—but there are a few exceptions.

"Not everyone who comes here is fond of Chinese food," Henry Wong explained, "so we have a buffet with some American alternatives, such as fried chicken and catfish—good Southern food. I like to eat Southern myself, and at home I have turnip greens, cornbread, grits. But I can't serve those things. I can have the best Chinese restaurant, but not the best Southern one. So I stay with what I know how to do, and leave the other things to someone else."

If you want fine old Southern food of the traditional kind in Mississippi, you need to go to someplace like Mrs. Isaiah's Busy Bee Cafe in Oxford—but first you've got to find it. There is no listing in the phone book, no sign out front, no advertising anywhere—nothing but a faded painting of a buzzing bee above the porch of the ramshackle two-room building where Georgia Lee Isaiah works her culinary wonders. Since 1971, Mrs. Isaiah has served dinner five nights a week at the four tables in the front room. She also cooks and cleans up, sometimes with a little help from her customers.

Now sixty-five and widowed, Mrs. Isaiah is retired from her job as a cook for the chancellor of the University of Mississippi. For the last eleven of her twenty-nine years at the university, she "moonlighted" at her restaurant; now she works six to nine hours a day there to deliver a classic dinner of Southern home cooking consisting of a main dish, two vegetables, a salad, hot bread, a drink, and a dessert. Lemon meringue, chess, and pecan pies and various kinds of pound cakes are among her dessert specialties, and they alone are worth a visit to the Busy Bee.

The little restaurant is neat and tidy, and Mrs. Isaiah moves about in the small rooms with a serene manner that makes her customers feel at ease. A cardboard church fan picturing "Freedom Fighters" John and Robert Kennedy and Martin Luther King, Jr., is mounted on the wall next to a caricature of the Ole Miss mascot, a goateed plantation "colonel." GO-GO-REBELS! says the rallying call beneath. In the rear, a blackboard is posted with the evening's menu.

On our visit, we were served oven-baked chicken, baby lima beans, stewed corn, garden salad, hot biscuits, iced tea, and sour cream pound cake. From start to finish it was an excellent dinner, and Mrs. Isaiah was a gracious and charming hostess. After a raucous evening at Doe's, dinner at the Busy Bee was a welcome and soothing change of pace.

Moving east into Alabama, we came upon some good places to eat barbecue and seafood, and they will be noted subsequently. First, though, this section seems the proper place to mention three notable restaurants in the interior cities of Birmingham, Bessemer, and Montgomery. Seafood is a major emphasis for all three, but not exclusively so. They are long-established institutions, between forty and eighty years old, and all of them are owned by Greek-American families. In addition, they are generally regarded as three of the best all-around restaurants in Alabama. They can't be called native or traditional, but considering their longevity and their popularity, they certainly can properly be called regional and Southern.

The Elite Cafe in downtown Montgomery, a proud possession of the Xides family, has been in its present location since it opened in 1911. Seafood and beef are its specialties, but Greek baklava and other pastries are featured, and the numerous Southern touches include fresh vegetables and corn muffins, gumbo, and two Alabama crab dishes—West Indies salad and deep-fried claws.

The Elite is a prime lunch spot for people who work downtown in the Alabama capital city, and at dinner it attracts patrons from all over the Montgomery area. A large and pleasantly decorated restaurant, it seems less Greek or Southern than international. Like Weidmann's in Meridian, the Elite has been a fixture for so long it is hard to imagine downtown Montgomery without it.

Birmingham's answer to the Elite is John's, thirty years younger and a little less formal but every bit its match for quality. Proprietor Phil Hontzas, a nephew of the original owners, proudly notes that the menu has not changed since the restaurant opened in 1944. Red snapper and flounder are the most popular main dishes, but shrimp, oysters, trout, scallops, lobster, and crab are also featured, and the meats are headed by beef and lamb. Southern corn sticks, fresh vegetables, cole slaw, okra gumbo, and cinnamon muffins are among the regional items, and the hospitality and service are a Southern trademark. "Please report any inattention to the manager," reads a notice on the menu. Inattention is one of the few things you can't get at John's.

The third, the oldest, and in some ways the most impressive of Alabama's Greek jewels is the Bright Star in Bessemer, an industrial city near Birmingham. It was started as a small cafe in 1907 by Tom Bonduris, a Greek immigrant. By 1915 it had outgrown three sites and found its permanent home in the heart of Bessemer. Soon after that, one of Bonduris' relatives, Bill Koikos, arrived from Greece to work in the kitchen. From his start as a non-English-speaking busboy, Koikos moved up to part owner of the business in five years. Now past ninety, he still takes an active interest in the place, although his sons Jimmy and Nick are the general managers.

Since its latest expansion in 1978, the Bright Star can accommodate two hundred diners. In its essential appearance and character, though, it is very much like it was when it moved to its present location seventy years ago. Tile floors and ceiling fans, mirrors and marble, wood paneling, and murals painted by a European artist all suggest the turn-of-the-century period of the restaurant's birth. The food, too, has stood the test of time; by popular demand, the menu seldom varies.

The Bright Star, much like John's, has struck a balance with three basic styles of cuisine: seafood, Greek, and traditional Southern. The seafood specialties include broiled snapper, stuffed shrimp, lobster and crabmeat casserole, and a variety of other baked, broiled, and fried dishes, all made with fresh fish brought daily from the Gulf Coast. The Greek flavor is supplied by spicy lamb and beef dishes, rice dishes, and pastries, and the Southern contributions are gumbo and other Creole offerings, some desserts, and a distinctively Southern lineup of fresh vegetables that includes collard greens, pole beans, squash, yams, and fried green tomatoes.

Florida has some good Greek restaurants, too, the best known being the Louis Pappas emporium in Tarpon Springs, where the Greek salads are peerless works of gastronomic art. But Florida's Spanish heritage provides the dominant ethnic dimension to the food there, whether the focus is on Miami and its burgeoning Cuban population or Tampa and its century-old Hispanic quarter. Tampa's Columbia, founded in 1905, is the oldest and largest Spanish restaurant in the state—in fact, it's the oldest restaurant of any type in Florida, and the largest Spanish-style eatery in the world, with eleven dining rooms seating 1660 people. Its classic specialties—such dishes as Spanish (garbanzo) bean soup, chicken and yellow rice, paella, bolichi, and flan—are worthy of their fine reputation. The same great dishes can also be found in many of the small and relatively inexpensive Spanish restaurants in the city—neighborhood and family-owned cafes such as Alvarez and Latam, and larger places such as Pepe's. Tampa is richly endowed with authentic Spanish restaurants.

Aside from its diverse multitude of ethnic restaurants and its native seafood houses (to be noted later), Florida boasts some other places that offer an altogether different kind of dining experience. Some of these highly individualistic establishments defy classification. Here are three examples:

✤ The Yearling, a backwoods game and fish restaurant, is located at Cross Creek in north Florida, where novelist Marjorie Kinnan Rawlings lived and worked (and where she wrote, among other books, *The Yearling* and *Cross Creek Cookery*). You might call its decor refined rustic and its cuisine wild gourmet; by whatever descriptions, the restaurant has definitely taken on a fancier appearance since its beginnings as a fish camp some twenty-five years

My father was a wonderful man. John Kalogeros was his name. He emigrated to this country from Greece in about 1900, and worked as a laborer, laying railroad tracks, making axe handles, digging coal. He couldn't speak English when he arrived, but he made up for it by working very hard. He married a coal miner's daughter in southwest Virginia, and I was the oldest of their seven children. Then, right in the middle of the Depression, my mother died, and my father had to depend on me to look after the younger children.

I'll never forget a fateful night in Greenville, South Carolina. It was

ago. Herb and Pat Herman bought the place in 1972, gave it more of a club than a camp atmosphere, and spiced up the dining room with an array of specialties from the local woods and waters: cooter (soft-shell turtle), frog legs, catfish, alligator tail, quail, grouper. The dishes are individually prepared to order and served with side dishes that include hush puppies, cheese grits, rice and gravy, and fried potatoes. Lemon, lime, and pecan pies are also on the menu. The Yearling has won several regional dining awards since the Hermans took over. Mrs. Rawlings might not recognize such a place in her old neighborhood—but I venture to say she would love the hush puppies.

✤ Allen's Cafe in Auburndale is a twenty-five-year-old monument to the bygone days of central Florida's range-riding cracker cowboys. Sixty-six-year-old Carl Allen, the proprietor, was born a short distance from his roadside restaurant in the heyday of the crackers, so named because of their whip-cracking method of rounding up scrub cattle in the sparsely populated Florida interior in the period between the end of the Civil War and the beginning of World War II. (The term "cracker" is also used to designate a person born and raised in Florida.) Carl Allen opened his restaurant in 1960, and from the beginning it has been both a museum of early Florida history and a place to sample some of the native foods of that period. The place is filled with thousands of artifacts and antiques he has acquired over the years. Featured on the menu are such exotic dishes as rattlesnake, cooter, armadillo, and swamp cabbage, the last a vegetable delicacy made from the tender heart of the cabbage palm, Florida's official state tree.

"The first crackers survived on things like swamp cabbage," Carl Allen explained. "They learned from the Indians how to live off the land. My grandmother was one of the people that came in here and settled back in the 1880s. This was true frontier country in those days, and it was still very isolated as recently as forty or fifty years ago. My mama used to cook gator and gopher and turtle meat a lot, and we ate salt mullet and Nile perch. Now it's all vanishing—the food, the way of life, everything. I want to keep the memory of all these things alive so people in the next generation will know what the real Florida was like." Allen's Historical Cafe, as its owner prefers to call it, is a little piece of the past captured in antiques and cookery.

✤ Flora and Ella's Restaurant has occupied the same corner in the town of LaBelle since 1943, but it had its beginnings in the 1920s in a grocery and meat market owned by the parents of sisters Flora and Ella Forrey. Fires and hurricanes and other disasters, natural and man-made, have stalked the little town near Lake Okeechobee periodically since the mid-1800s, but Flora Hampton and Ella Burchard symbolize the spirit of survival that seems to prevail there. They opened a short-order restaurant in a log cabin after their parents' store

1932, and there were no jobs. I was fourteen years old. My father said, "Helen, tomorrow we're going up North—I have no idea where." Even now, the memory of that frightening night still brings tears to my eyes.

This is as far as we got. My father got a job here as a restaurant cook—twelve hours a day, seven days a week, for twenty-five dollars. But within six years he had saved enough to open his own restaurant, and he named it the Peerless. It was an English word he loved—the sound of it, and the meaning too. When he died in 1947 my brother Jim took over, and now we have been in this location for thirty-three years, and our restaurant is one of the most popular dining places anywhere around here. So we came through hard times, but we found a happy home here in the mountains of Tennessee. We were lucky, weren't we?

a reminiscence by
Helen Kalogeros,
Johnson City, Tennessee, 1985

was burned out. By the time they moved to the present location during World War II, the enterprising sisters not only ran a restaurant but also a drugstore, the post office, the bus depot, the freight station, and the Western Union office.

The other members of her family have died or moved away now, and seventy-two-year-old Ella Burchard is alone in the enterprise that still is called Flora and Ella's. In appearance the place is a quaint relic of yesteryear, with its old soda-fountain counter and stools, its bus-station and telegraph services, a wooden telephone booth still in use, and drugstore sundries for sale in glass cases. The menu is old-fashioned too, featuring what Ella calls "just plain Southern food, soul food"—greens and beans and peas cooked with seasoning pork, swamp cabbage, cornbread and biscuits and hush puppies, chicken and dumplings, and trademark pies with meringue piled high upon them.

"I'm just an old cracker girl," said Mrs. Burchard, "and this is the food I grew up on right here in LaBelle. I'm as Southern as a bowl of grits. It grieves me to get out on the road and see what's happening to this food. I'm afraid it's going to pass. Fast food is taking over because people don't want to spend this long in the kitchen." They serve nothing but slow food at Flora and Ella's.

Among our evening dining experiences in South Carolina were visits to Henry's in Charleston, The Market in Columbia, and The Old House in Walhalla. Henry's is a fine old low-country Carolina restaurant across from the open-air city market in the historic district of Charleston. It was started there in 1932 by a German immigrant, Henry Hasselmeyer, and in appearance and quality it is not unlike a good Creole-style seafood restaurant in New Orleans. Charleston's reputation for fine cookery derives mainly from its private homes, not its restaurants and cafes, but Henry's is exceptional.

The Market is another of the Greek-owned, seafood-oriented restaurants in the tradition of the Bright Star in Bessemer. It has been a favorite gathering spot of politicians and other downtown Columbia congregants since it first opened there in 1930. John Capilos and two of his brothers started it; John and Dina Stambolitis own it now. It's a large place, spacious enough to accommodate close to five hundred diners—quite a change from the early days, when it was mostly a seafood and vegetable market. The menu still emphasizes fish and shellfish, but there are also beef and pork dishes and Greek souvlaki (marinated lamb), and the vegetables are mostly Southern staples.

It is the desserts, though, that achieve the perfect union of Greek and Southern cookery. For a quarter of a century, Rose Ella Mitchem has drawn upon her black heritage as a Southerner and her acquired Greek pastry expertise to create daily the baklava, galaktoboureko (egg custard), pecan and chess pies, cheesecakes, and other sweet dreams that are the Market's pride and joy.

When H. F. "Red" Harris and his wife, Gerrie, opened a rustic country restaurant in a hard-to-find farmhouse near the upland South Carolina town of Walhalla in 1967, their friends and neighbors were surprised and skeptical. "Nobody thought we would make it," Harris recalled, "but pretty soon it just flambeaued into such a big thing that we didn't hardly know what to do with it." In those days, the Harrises served country ham, fried chicken, catfish, and steaks with a few old-standby support dishes (grits, cole slaw, French fries, hush puppies) and occasionally some fresh vegetables. On busy weekends when football crowds gathered at nearby Clemson University, the Old House sometimes accommodated over three hundred evening diners.

"There weren't any restaurants to speak of anywhere close to us when we started," Harris said, "but now there's lots of them out on the highway. There's a Po Folks, that country-looking chain—it's hard for us to compete with a big outfit like that. To my way of thinking, they sort of patterned their style after ours. If we were just starting out now, we couldn't survive, and even as it is, the competition is cutting into our business. The day of little restaurants like this one may be just about over."

North Carolina's notable dining places range from mountain inns deep in the Smokies to seaside fish houses on the Atlantic. One of the most interesting, historically and gastronomically, is the Old Salem Tavern in the historic district of Winston-Salem. The Moravians, a pious sect of Germanic Protestants, founded Salem in 1766 as a planned congregational community, and though it ceased to function as a church-owned town about a century after that, it has survived as an outstanding example of eighteenth-century German architecture and culture in the South. Salem Tavern, built in 1784, was long noted for its fine food and hospitality as well as a place of lodging. Now, as part of the restoration of Old Salem, it serves lunch and dinner in an atmosphere and style suggestive of the early 1800s.

Facsimile silver, pewter, crystal, china, and furniture are used in the dining rooms of the fine old brick tavern. The night I ate there, Suzanne Lewis, dressed in a period costume, served me cream of broccoli soup, a fresh garden salad, boiled new potatoes, a casserole of squash and carrots and onions, an excellent wiener schnitzel, bran muffins, fine coffee, and a most delicious lemon trifle. Few of the dishes served at the tavern are authentic creations from the Moravian period, but the trifle was a prized eighteenth-century recipe—sponge cake, raspberries, tart lemon custard, and whipped cream, chilled in a wineglass. All by itself, it was more than enough to make me remember Salem Tavern fondly. In our limited dining experiences at Virginia's renowned Colonial Williamsburg, we were not fortunate enough to taste anything as memorable as the Salem lemon trifle.

Elsewhere in Virginia, we stopped for dinner (and sometimes stayed over-

In looking over the older receipts, one is struck by the time consumed in the making as well as the blithe way in which old-timers toss about a dozen eggs, a pound of butter or a quart of cream. But it would not be old-fashioned Southern cooking if time were an object, or substitutes used. As well expect to create a successful French concoction without its attendant sauce or herbs as a Southern dish without its cream or butter.

Harriet Ross Colquitt
The Savannah Cook Book, 1933

night) at five inns of the most diverse character, cost, and quality, and found in them diminishing traces of the great Southern repasts of old.

The Colonial Inn of Smithfield, with a colorful history dating to 1752, is the choice dining place in a picturesque town made famous by country hams (see Eating In, page 256). The menu at the inn highlights Smithfield hams (though seafood, fried chicken, turkey, and pork tenderloin are among the other entrees), and we ordered the house specialty. It was an impressive sight on the plate, a rich red color rimmed with fat, and it was also tender and not too salty, but the flavor lacked genuine distinction of the sort that any devoted traveler to this mecca of country hams would expect to find. The truly great country hams of the past are now almost impossible to find in the restaurants of the South—or anywhere else.

At the Laurel Brigade Inn in Leesburg, a family-owned and -operated enterprise for the past forty years and a sturdy stone presence in the town for more than two centuries, we hoped to find a taste of old Virginia. The fried chicken and homemade pickle relish were worthy offerings, but the vegetables and bread and desserts were less commendable. Overall, it was an uninspired and uninspiring repast, leading me to wonder, as I had in Smithfield, if we had happened by on an off night. I prefer to think so; the Laurel Brigade and the Smithfield Inn belong to the best of Virginia culinary tradition, and it would be sad to find that their best years are behind them.

Two mountain inns attempting to recapture the best of their past are the Highland Inn at Monterey and The Inn at Wise. The Highland, built in 1904, is a three-story frame structure that owner Sue Hereen and a small staff operate energetically following a 1981 restoration. The dining room features mountain trout, pork, homemade breads and desserts, and fresh vegetables in season.

The Inn at Wise, a century-old Victorian structure, is filled with a menagerie of antiques. Its dining room advertises home cooking, and the delivery is close to the promise, but it's not yet on a par with the food Nell Elliott served for thirty-four years at Glenn's Cafe across the street from the inn. Before she retired, patrons came from miles around to enjoy her fresh meats and vegetables, cornbread muffins, potato icebox rolls, pies, and cobblers. Cooks at the inn are trying to emulate her style and her success. "I hope they can do it," said Nell Elliott. "Good country food is hard to find."

Light-years from Wise, in a citadel of the "new American cuisine," is The Inn at Little Washington, an old country store transformed into an elegant and expensive dining place by Patrick O'Connell and Reinhardt Lynch. We went dutch with friends in a dinner party for five, and the tip alone was more than any other dinner tab I paid in our year of eating out in the South. It was, to say the least, an experience.

Esther Mitchell of Lacey Springs, Virginia, supplies the delicious smoked

WELCOME TO WASHINGTON, VA., FOUNDED 1749 reads the sign on the narrow road leading into Little Washington, population one hundred fifty, just ninety miles from the nation's capital. Until five years ago, this was a quaint, virtually unheard-of village in the foothills of the Blue Ridge Mountains. Now it is talked

trout (an appetizer), Virginia wineries provide some of the libations, and local vendors are the source for morel mushrooms and fresh vegetables in season. Beyond that, the only Southern contribution to dinner at the inn is a basket of little yellow cornmeal muffins that could easily be mistaken for a Yankee import. O'Connell and Lynch are not devoted to Southern or American cookery; they are paying homage, as the menu puts it, "to the lawmakers of Classical French Cuisine," and they have done it in a most impressive way. The dinner was truly outstanding, the service was matchless, the desserts spectacular. Not even in the French precincts of Louisiana did we find such a display of what O'Connell of the Little Washington calls "the most complete and satisfying form of theater."

At Wytheville in southwest Virginia, a restaurant called the Log House is one of the area's most original and popular dining places. The two-story structure of oak and cedar timbers was built as a wayside inn on the Wilderness Road in 1776, and stopping there now to dine at tables lit by oil wick lanterns is a way of glimpsing, however briefly, the hard demands of frontier life. Owner Virginia Slotter has taken pains to make the cookery compatible with the setting, and the result is a very satisfying evening of historical dining. The fare was hearty and substantial on the night we were there. Country ham, fried chicken, calf liver, stuffed tenderloin, and stuffed breast of chicken were among the main dishes, complemented by a half-dozen vegetables, homemade rolls, and good hot coffee. The desserts included dumplings and cobblers, four kinds of pie, and carrot cake. Like the inns of old on the Wilderness Road, the Log House once again beckons travelers to the table. It is good to see such ventures in historic restoration succeed.

Another return of sorts—a return to the basic components of Southern cookery in the twentieth century—took place for us at a southwest Virginia cafe called Rosalie's Soul Kitchen in Christiansburg. Rosalie Redman, a widowed mother of seven children, had converted an old store into a small restaurant and bar, and we were treated there to a fine dinner chosen from a menu that included fried chicken, catfish, barbecued ribs, fresh vegetables, potato salad, and cornbread. The chicken was excellent—very dry, crisp, crunchy, tender, and not the least bit greasy—and the other main dishes, though not superior, were certainly adequate. We ate with friends to the jukebox music of Bruce Springsteen, Prince, Willie Nelson, and Roberta Flack, and Mrs. Redman filled in the quiet interludes with some observations on the hazards of the restaurant business. "I may not be able to keep this place going much longer," she concluded. "It takes so much time and effort to do things right, and I've got too much pride to do them any other way."

Out on the four-lane, the fast-food prefabs keep popping up like mushrooms. We may have made it to Rosalie's Soul Kitchen not a minute too soon.

❖ ❖ ❖

about in national newspapers and magazines for its first-class restaurant, the Inn at Little Washington.

As well known in Rappahannock County as the Inn is ninety-six-year-old Mattie Ball Fletcher. A direct descendant of George Washington's brother Charles, Mattie Ball . . . as everyone calls her, resides in the eighteenth-century Peyton House, not far from the Inn. . . .

At Christmas 1971, when Mattie Ball was eighty-three, two granddaughters . . . assembled a pamphlet of her recipes. In the preface they wrote, "She reached out with plates carrying the food of her own childhood . . . and of the childhood of her grandmother. . . . Recipes . . . that when passed through enough generations of memories, become a part of the food of a region." . . .

Mattie Ball has dined at the Inn several times. "Food's quite pretty, but it's not cooked long enough, don't you think? They call it French. It's good, but I like mine better."

Joan Nathan
An American Folklife Cookbook, 1984

In the Ouachita Mountains of west Arkansas, a restaurant named Sam-Ann's has proved that a remote location is no impediment to good business. When the word spreads that dependably fine food is available, customers tend to find their way to it. The word is out on Sam-Ann's. Sam and Anna Herbert started the place in 1951 at Hollis, a wide spot in the road between Hot Springs and Russellville. It was closed for a time after their retirement in the 1970s, but Sharon Nugent and Tony Montgomery reopened it with the old name and the same purpose: "continuing Miss Anna's tradition of excellence."

Sam-Ann's calls itself the "premier country restaurant" in Arkansas. Its features include large breakfasts, soup and sandwich lunches, and dinners built around Arkansas catfish, chicken, pork chops, and fried steak with gravy. Fresh vegetables grown on the place or procured from local farmers are served when available, and the iced tea is freshly brewed. The greatest asset, however, is Sharon Nugent's bakery. It provides the whole-wheat dinner rolls, the breakfast cinnamon rolls and pancakes, the brownies and cookies, and the delicious cream and fruit pies. Many of Sam-Ann's patrons drive from Little Rock—a three-hour round trip—and the baked goods are a major motivation.

In Tennessee, places where traditional Southern foods are served for dinner take a variety of forms. In Chattanooga, for example, there is the Mount Vernon Restaurant, a highly successful family dining place opened by Greek native Gus Tombras, his wife, Myrtle, and their two daughters in 1955. (It was the fifth Chattanooga cafe for Tombras since his migration there in 1905.)

In Nashville, owner-hostess Daisy King sets a pretty table at Miss Daisy's, a small-town tearoom transplanted to a suburban shopping center. The food is mainstream Southern with a modern touch, in the style and spirit of a *Southern Living* magazine feature.

Thirty miles west of Nashville, in the wooded hills of middle Tennessee, Norma and Johnny Crow have restored a frontier-era log cabin and turned it into the Silver Leaf 1815, a country dining inn. Norma Crow is the principal cook, and the food is down-home Southern, from the country ham and fried chicken to the buttermilk biscuits and homemade preserves. Like the Log House in Wytheville, the Silver Leaf fits compatibly into its physical and historical setting.

Buntyn, a Memphis neighborhood restaurant, also has a sense of belonging. Its patrons come mostly from the area around it, and they are a grass-roots mix of students, the elderly, working-class families, business men and women, white and black. Eight regular entrees and a daily special, a dozen vegetables and salads, hot breads, and homemade desserts are the components from which the regulars select their "meat-and-three" plate lunches and dinners. Milton and Betty Wiggins, the owners, advertise "old-fashioned goodness in a home-like

The first and only time the United Nations General Assembly met outside of New York was on June 7, 1976, on the grounds of the Parthenon in Nashville. The delegates and guests, some 1200 people, were served a Southern-style luncheon prepared by Phila Hach, a noted hostess and caterer from Clarksville,

atmosphere," and that says it in a nutshell. Where else but home can you get the likes of Spanish rice, turnips, hominy, and lady peas, with yeast biscuits and triangle-shaped cornbread muffins, a cold glass of buttermilk, and a generous serving of banana pudding? And, Buntyn is a friendly place. Blanche Anita Stone, our waitress and a ten-year employee there, seemed to know most of the customers, and so did the other servers.

A classic and traditional Southern dinner in Tennessee is served at Hachland Hill, a "country dining inn" in Clarksville. Phila Rawlings Hach and her late husband, Adolph, began catering dinner in 1957 and opened their inn in 1963. Old South hospitality and dining elegance characterize the repasts, whether the service is a banquet for three hundred or a private dinner for two. Phila Hach grew up in her parents' restaurant in Nashville and has spent her entire life around food, and the experience shows in her culinary skills. Dinner at the inn is by reservation only, with the entrees ordered in advance and everything else from soup to nuts chosen by Mrs. Hach. The food is impressive—thoughtfully planned, individually prepared, appealingly presented, and usually delicious. The cuisine often transcends the region, but the style and service are distinctly Southern.

Georgia has its share of classic old Southern restaurants, too, ranging from the stereotypical to the prototypical. Aunt Fanny's Cabin in Smyrna is one of the former. Expanded from the plantation slave cabin where Fanny Williams once lived, the restaurant presents a romanticized picture of life in the Old South. Aunt Fanny's life spanned a century that included slavery, war, Reconstruction, and numerous revivals of the elusive New South. As a cook, servant, and resident sage, she attained legendary stature before her death in 1949, and when the restaurant first opened in 1941, she was its main attraction. Now, five hundred or more people come for dinner almost every night, and both food and atmosphere are unchanged from the time when Aunt Fanny sat in her rocking chair and offered her recollections of Sherman's march through Georgia.

Less of a stereotype than the cabin but no less traditional in its cookery is the New Perry Hotel in Perry. A few blocks from the neon jungle at an interstate highway exit, the New Perry (there was never an Old Perry) is a quiet hotel that began in the 1920s as a modern inn on the major north-south highway through the center of town. The interstate bypassed the town and the hotel, but a reputation for good food and good service has kept regular customers on the guest list and in the dining room. Starched cloths and napkins and fresh flowers are on the tables there, and on the night we stopped for dinner, we found lamb chops and chicken livers and Spanish mackerel among the entrees. Candied yams, green beans, squash Lorraine, and cucumber pickles were also served, and the desserts included peach pan pie, pecan pie, and lemon chess pie. The New Perry is Old Southern.

Tennessee. Here is Mrs. Hach's menu:

Mint julep frappé
Orange juice frappé

Baked Tennessee country ham
Fried catfish and hush puppies
Southern fried chicken
Sliced breast of turkey with dill sauce
Hickory smoked beef tenderloin with horseradish

Green beans cooked with ham hock
Sweet boiled corn on the cob with chive butter
Sour cream potato salad
Raw vegetable slaw with spring onions
Sliced, peeled, sun-ripened tomatoes

Iced watermelon, honeydew and cantaloupe
Cottage cheese with homemade mayonnaise
Deviled eggs
Bread and butter pickles

Beaten biscuit
Corn light bread
Yeast rolls

Fudge pie
Black walnut pie
Pecan pie
Chess pie

Ice tea with mint
Sweet milk and buttermilk

So is Lankford Manor in Tifton, but with a twist. Billy Lankford, the proprietor, was ten years old when his father's bank closed in the Great Depression. The family moved into a rambling old frame house on the main highway through Tifton and began renting rooms and serving meals to tourists. That was the start of Lankford Manor. The town and the old highway are two more casualties to the age of the interstate, and the manor now attracts mostly local room and board trade. But dinner there still has its moments, and we got a taste of some of the house favorites when we stopped on a fall evening.

Only two other customers were there, and Lankford was doing double duty as the waiter and cashier. He and a cook were the only two people working. The menu included fresh trout, quail on toast, yeast rolls, and white-acre peas, and there was homemade pie for dessert. "We've always had good desserts," Lankford said. "Key lime and coconut and peanut pies, with real homemade crusts, and cakes too—ginger and apple and devil's food—and all our own home-baked breads. This place has survived for fifty-two years. It put me and two of my kids through school. We've had it all, the good and the bad. Now there's the interstate and big motels and chain restaurants. No telling what will become of this place." And what will become of Southern cooking? "I don't know. I worry about that."

Margaret Lupo doesn't seem so concerned. She is the owner and general manager of Mary Mac's, once a dainty Atlanta tearoom and now a huge, rambling Southern food emporium serving what may be the most comprehensive array of home-style cookery in the region. Mary MacKenzie started Mary Mac's as a small cafe about forty years ago, and Mrs. Lupo and her late husband took it over in 1956. Now the sprawling restaurant serves lunch and dinner to about two thousand people a day, and in spite of the volume, the variety and quality are consistently high.

From start to finish—from turnip green pot likker as a savory appetizer to boiled custard as a crowning touch—the menu choices at Mary Mac's are wide-ranging and delicious. Among the available entrees are baked chicken and dressing, country fried steak, chicken pan pie, fried chicken, roast beef with gravy, rainbow trout, red snapper, shad roe, quail on rice, filet mignon, country ham, calf liver, pork tenderloin, and fried shrimp. Two dozen side dishes are listed, including collard greens, candied yams, squash soufflé, pickled beets, macaroni and cheese, stewed corn, green beans, and lady peas. The hot breads include a rarity: cracklin cornbread. One other Mary Mac's feature seldom found in traditional Southern dining rooms is a bar serving wine, beer, and mixed drinks. And in addition to the heavy volume of food served on the premises, the restaurant also maintains an extensive carry-out trade.

Margaret Lupo presides over this whirlwind of culinary activity with calm self-assurance and good humor. She has 126 employees, including thirteen

Potlikker is the juice that remains in a pot after certain vegetables and their greens are boiled. Huey began to extol the concoction in 1930, and . . . he talked so much about it that he received national attention. . . . Mocking his critics, he called his creation "potlikker à le dictator" and described it as "the noblest dish the mind of man has yet conceived." . . . There should be "plenty of cornpone cooked in a greasy skillet [until] hard enough to knock down a yearling." The diner must hold the cornpone in the left hand and a soup spoon in the right, take a sip of the soup and then dunk the cornpone in the juice and bite off a piece. The real potlikker devotee always dunked, Huey insisted; he never committed the crudity of crumbling the pone in the soup. . . .

cooks, and two of her six children are also involved in the business. "I learned about food from my mother," she said, "and I've been in food service myself since 1945. My aim here has always been to serve the kind of cooking my mother and grandmother did so well. There are two essentials in Southern cooking—or any cooking, for that matter: fresh ingredients, and skillful cooks. That's our formula. My husband was in the produce business, and he supplied the fresh vegetables. I hired him to come to work for me for a dollar a year, a new Cadillac, all the clothes he wanted, room and board, and sleeping privileges. It was a good deal for both of us."

Mary Mac's does not accept reservations or credit cards, but will take personal checks. Most dinners are in the five- to eight-dollar range, and no one has ever been known to leave the place hungry. "Diet at home," says Mrs. Lupo, slim and attractive at sixty-five, "not here." Southern cooking is alive and well at Mary Mac's, and nothing in the operation of the enormously popular restaurant suggests anything but happy days ahead.

Finally, the tour of Southern dinner tables ends in Kentucky, where glorious repasts have been a thriving tradition for more than two hundred years. No Southern state except Louisiana has a more vibrant and ongoing food history than the Bluegrass state; its cookbooks, famous cooks, distinctive dishes, and culinary lore combine to make a rich heritage that Kentuckians proudly claim as their own.

The historic old Talbott Tavern, which opened in Bardstown in 1779, is still functioning as an inn and dining place (though not one of Kentucky's finest), and it is still possible to arrange a special-occasion catered meal at the Duncan Tavern in Paris, built in 1788. Inns and taverns have always been prominent institutions in Kentucky, and the state's continuing reputation as a good place to eat derives in large measure from its famous old inns. Here, briefly, are five where outstanding food is still the main attraction:

❧ Doe Run Inn in Brandenburg, a massive fortress of native limestone and hand-hewn timbers, was first used in about 1818 as a woolen mill, thirty years after Daniel Boone's brother Squire gave the name Doe Run to the stream that rushes close by. The building was first used as a summer resort in about 1900, and has been an inn and dining place since 1927. The most appealing thing about eating at Doe Run now is its large screened porch jutting into the woods near the stream. There on a late summer afternoon, with mist rising on the creek after a rain and the song of the water echoing soothingly, a dinner of ham or chicken with fresh garden vegetables and hot biscuits can be a memorable experience—and a cup of coffee with a slice of lemon pie at dusk can seal the bargain.

Julian Harris, the witty and cultured editor of the influential Atlanta Constitution, devoted a lead editorial to Huey's recipe. The governor of Louisiana might know how to prepare potlikker, Harris said, but he certainly did not know how to eat it: anybody who appreciated this delectable dish crumbled the cornpone. . . . Harris [charged] that Huey crumbled in private. Huey replied in a letter . . . that Harris . . . had gone beyond the limits of respectable journalism with the charge. . . . He [said he had] merely crumbled before a few friends to demonstrate the faults of the technique.

T. Harry Williams

❧ The Old Stone Inn in Simpsonville was a stagecoach stop on the Lexington-to-Louisville road when it was built in the 1790s. It has been an inn and dining room since 1924, and its personality has hardly changed at all since then. The tablecloths and napkins and the old silver and china suggest a distant time of understated elegance, a time remembered but not remarked upon by some of the older diners and the white-jacketed waiters who serve them. The food also belongs to that former time. It is the traditional fare that has distinguished the display of Kentucky hospitality since the first inns and manor houses appeared: old country ham, fried or baked chicken, sweetbreads, roast turkey and dressing, corn fritters, stuffed eggplant, green beans, corn pudding, parslied new potatoes, yeast rolls, a richness of soups and gravies and relishes, iced tea and coffee, hot cobblers, boiled custard, coconut and jam cakes, meringue pies. The Old Stone Inn still serves most of those dishes, but not all. You order only the entree; the rest is served continuously by the waiter. It is a ritual feast that has faded from the scene in most places.

❧ The Shaker Village of Pleasant Hill serves history of a quite different sort—and the food is somewhat different too. When the society of Shakers, a remarkable group of religious zealots, decided at the beginning of the nineteenth century to extend their twenty-five-year experience in colony building from New England and New York into the nation's interior, one of the places their missionaries went was to Kentucky, where religious camp meetings were highly popular. In the first decade of the 1800s, the Shakers started villages at Pleasant Hill near Harrodsburg and at South Union in western Kentucky. Both communities lasted more than a century. In 1961, a group of private citizens set about to preserve and restore the twenty-seven remaining Shaker buildings at Pleasant Hill, and in the late 1960s they opened the village to the public as a living museum. One of its features is a dining room that draws its inspiration and many recipes from the abundantly equipped Shaker cookbooks of old.

The Shakers were a pastoral people with simple tastes, but they ate well. They brought with them from the East a style of cooking that favored hearty, rich, filling foods, and over the decades of their presence in Kentucky they added regional and local touches that their forebears in New England probably would have considered strange, but altogether satisfying: numerous varieties of cornbread, vegetables seasoned with cured pork, country ham, pecan and chess and peach pies. Shaker lemon pie and sugar pie were among the desserts the missionaries brought with them to Kentucky, and they continue to delight visitors at Pleasant Hill. An evening in the dining room there is a wonderful introduction to Shaker cooking with a Southern accent.

❧ Boone Tavern, a hotel and dining room in Berea, was built in 1908 to accommodate visitors to Berea College and mountain travelers on the dirt road

If, beyond the pearly gates, I am permitted to select my place at the table, it will be among Kentuckians, and the food, I hope, will be Kentucky style. Eating dinner in Kentucky is more than a physiological refueling of the human body, it is a joyous social ritual. The table is the great yarning place for the state. Gossip, tall yarns, and laughter punctuate the business at hand of consuming victuals. This, to the Kentuckian, is his great "recalling ground." He drags out his salty little family secrets and laughs about them. A warning to all strangers, however; the family secrets are never quite so secretive or so outrageous as they appear on the surface. There is something about a Kentucky dinner that stretches a yarn or puts spirit into a bit of gossip.

Thomas D. Clark
The Kentucky, 1942

at its front door. Over the years the inn acquired a good reputation for its Southern-style food. But ironically, it was a Northern-born professor of hotel management, Richard T. Hougen, who came in 1940 and elevated Boone Tavern's cuisine from the everyday to the extraordinary. He did it with subtle touches of European and cosmopolitan fare and greatly strengthened local and regional contributions. In thirty-five years as the director of a staff made up primarily of Berea College students, Hougen established the tavern as an outstanding restaurant with a far-reaching reputation. The style of cooking that evolved there (and made its way into three Hougen cookbooks) could be described as modified or stylized Southern. It is served in a somewhat formal setting by students, and it features, among other things, Southern spoonbread, homemade relishes, yeast rolls, chowders and consommés, fresh fruit salad, fresh garden vegetables, and combination casserole dishes. The entrees almost always include country ham and fried chicken, and often include brook trout, leg of lamb, baked pork chops, and chicken pie. Desserts are a tour de force of a half-dozen or more delectables, from old standards like pecan pie to rare specialties such as German lemon rolls and Jefferson Davis pie. Boone Tavern is an unusual Kentucky inn with a unique history and a long tradition of fine dining. The spoonbread alone is enough to justify a visit.

♣ Beaumont Inn in Harrodsburg was the last restaurant on record to serve genuine Kentucky beaten biscuits (until the 1970s), and it may be the last still to serve salt-cured, hickory-smoked, fully aged country hams that have hung in a smokehouse for at least a year. T. C. Dedman, Jr., presides at the white-columned brick mansion where his grandmother, Annie Bell Goddard, established an inn and dining room in 1918. "She had a black cook and maid and companion named Hat Crutcher who urged her to rent rooms and serve meals in this old mansion," Dedman said. "It had been a girls' college, and my grandmother was the dean. She and Hat turned it into an inn and dining room, and it's been going ever since."

Dinner at the Beaumont is a throwback to the glory days of traditional Kentucky hospitality and cookery. There are starched cloths on the tables, the sugar is in bowls (not packets), the cream is in pitchers (not plastic thimbles), and the butter is on plates. Chandeliers, carpet, wallpaper, and ceiling fans attract the eye. The fixed-price menu features two entrees—aged Kentucky country ham and fried chicken—preceded by an appetizer and followed by parslied potatoes, green beans, corn pudding (a specialty of the inn), yeast rolls and corn muffins, and the cake or pie of the day. On the day I ate there, it was Robert E. Lee cake, a spectacular four-layer white cake with orange icing. The ham, cured by a central Kentucky farmer and prepared for the table by boiling and baking, was the only country ham I ate in a restaurant in a year of searching

By 1875 Kentucky manners and accommodations had improved considerably, and hotels offered bills of fare comparable to the best in the nation. In that year a visitor to the Louisville Hotel on Christmas Day could choose from dozens of familiar and exotic dishes, ranging from Boned Capon à la Français and Stuffed Goose with Chestnuts à la Savoyarde to Loin of Kansas Buffalo, Haunch of Rocky Mountain Black Bear and Kentucky Opossum with Sweet Potatoes. The 95 libations on the wine list extended from champagne to Kentucky crab cider. The menu a few blocks away at the Galt House was no less varied and featured such regional entrees as Jambon, decorated à la Galt House, and Kentucky Shoat on His Way to Ohio. Game dishes included venison, wild turkey, antelope, wild goose, duck, bear, grouse, partridge and buffalo.

Wade Hall,
in Kentucky Dossier, 1984

that was worthy of the name and the tradition. The Beaumont Inn may be the last bastion of greatness in hams—among restaurants, at least.

The Whistle Stop Restaurant in Glendale comes fairly close to the Beaumont ham standard—and excels in so many other ways—that no account of Kentucky dining places would be complete without it. If proof were needed that not all of the state's fine restaurants are old inns, the Whistle Stop supplies ample evidence. It is not old, having been started in 1975, and though it sticks to a railroad motif that suggests antiquity, it is much more of a modern than traditional restaurant. It is simply a fine little cafe in a small town off the main road to anywhere, and quality alone has filled it up nightly with appreciative and faithful customers.

James and Idell Sego started the Whistle Stop with seven tables in a single room next to their hardware store a decade or so ago. L&N Railroad freight trains regularly thunder over the crossing just outside, and they were the inspiration for the name and the train-station and boxcar decor. Idell Sego was the cook. "It was just country cooking," she said, "just good homemade food, what you learn from your mother. It hasn't changed since we started. We just have to fix more of it. We bake all our own bread—even the hamburger buns—and make all the desserts, and we use the freshest produce and meats we can get. The only way to make a business like this last is to love it. It takes time and effort, but it pays off."

Does it ever. The Whistle Stop doesn't advertise, doesn't take reservations or accept credit cards, but it has quadrupled its size (to eighty-five seats), and the average wait for a table on Friday or Saturday night is an hour and a half. Thirty people, including three more cooks and three Sego daughters, now work there, and they serve over three hundred dinners on a busy night. Since Glendale is a town of only a few hundred people, the customers must come from afar, and they do—from Louisville (fifty miles), Bowling Green (seventy), and even Lexington (ninety).

What attracts them, most of all, is a modern menu full of timeless treasures—soups, salads and sandwiches for kids and short-order addicts, seafood and steaks for the nontraditionalists, country ham and fried chicken for old-fashioned Kentucky regulars. In addition there are such delectable dishes as white beans and cornbread batter cakes, meat-and-three plate dinners, and Kentucky hot Browns (broiled ham or turkey sandwiches with cheese and tomato). The ultimate attraction is the pies—chocolate, banana, coconut, sugar cream, lemon, and others made daily by one of the cooks, Norma Sue Franklin. They come to the table in wide-load wedges supporting meringue mountains, and they are sublime. The Whistle Stop is a main-track Southern restaurant with a winning combination of traditional and modern elements.

The last stop on our Kentucky dinner-table circuit is at Colonel Hawk's, the Bardstown restaurant of Louis "Hawk" Rogers. When he was commissioned a Kentucky Colonel by Governor "Happy" Chandler fifty years ago, Louis Rogers had not yet opened the restaurant for which he is now famed in the Bluegrass. That phase of his interesting career began in 1941 when Rogers, returning from a stint in Washington as a cook, butler, chauffeur, caterer, and manager of residences for politicians, built a small concrete-block dinner club on a narrow back street in his native Bardstown. For almost twenty-five years, the restaurant was prohibited by law from serving both white and black customers, and during that time it stood as a classic example of the nonsensical contradictions of segregation. It was a black-owned public accommodation with an all-white clientele, and the ultimate irony was that America Rogers, Hawk's wife, could cook on the wood stove in the kitchen and Hawk could wait tables, but they could not legally sit down in their own dining room and eat.

"I never said we didn't want blacks and whites in here together," Hawk explained. "The law said that. Segregation was foolish." For more than twenty years now, the artificial barriers have been removed, and Colonel Hawk's has continued to gain stature as a Kentucky institution. Hawk is in his eighties now, and America has passed on, and their son and daughter-in-law, Newman and May Rogers, own and operate the restaurant. But the colonel is there every evening to greet the customers, most of whom have been coming in regularly for years, and the menu is practically the same as it was back in the early 1940s.

It is essentially a supper-club menu with a Southern accent. The entrees are mostly steak and seafood, but country ham, fried chicken, frog legs, and lamb fries are also featured. (Historian Thomas D. Clark once declared that lamb fries are confined almost solely to the Bluegrass region of Kentucky. "Many a modest hostess has blushed deeply" at the question of what lamb fries are, Clark wrote. "In short, lamb fries are lamb testicles cut in thin sections, breaded and fried in deep fat, and served with a thick cream gravy. Many an individual has rebelled at the idea of eating such a thing, only to wind up being fond of this dish.") The standard side dishes at Colonel Hawk's are stuffed baked potatoes, green beans cooked with ham drippings, and delicious biscuits about as big around as a silver dollar and hot enough to melt butter. There are no desserts.

Colonel Hawk believes that if people like what you have to offer and keep coming back to get it, you must be doing something right. "You don't want to always be changing your menu," he said. "We've got our leaders—steak and potatoes, ham and green beans, hot biscuits and good coffee—and we stick to them. When you've got a good combination working together, you can add to it, but don't ever break it up." The good combination of food, management, customers, atmosphere, and history keeps on working at Colonel Hawk's, almost fifty years after it started.

Louisiana

New Orleans was almost a hundred years old when General Andrew Jackson masterminded the decisive U.S. military victory over British troops there in 1815. Settled by the French and ruled for a time by the Spanish, New Orleans and the whole of Louisiana were securely bonded to the new American nation by that victory, and the city's overjoyed residents celebrated the occasion with a round of banquets, balls, and parties that went on for weeks.

"To give you a description is beyond the power of my pen," wrote Jackson's wife, Rachel, to a friend back home in Tennessee after one particularly lavish event. "Suffice it to say nothing could excel the ornaments and supper.... I have seen more already than in all my past life. It is the finest country to the eye of a stranger, but a little while tires one of the dissipations of this place."

Another 170 years of Louisiana history have not diminished "the dissipations of this place," and many a contemporary Mardi Gras reveler has sent home postcards filled with the same sentiments that animated Rachel Jackson. The disposition of New Orleanians to eat, drink, and be merry was firmly established by 1815, and neither war nor depression nor natural disaster has extinguished the celebratory spirit.

There is not a more food-conscious and cuisine-rich jurisdiction in the nation than Louisiana, and no other state has a better documented, more interesting, or more diverse food history. Virginia and the Carolinas and Florida may have a longer chronology, but theirs is nowhere near as full or as varied. New York and California probably come closest to the Louisiana standards of substance and quality, but they pale by comparison. In a gastronomic sense, there is only one Louisiana, and it is filled with Creole and Acadian and Southern delights that have inspired chefs, cookbook writers, and literary artists for generations.

Louisiana was explored by LaSalle in the 1680s and colonized by the le Moyne brothers and others before 1720; it had been ruled by France for eighty years when four decades of Spanish control commenced in the 1760s. More French immigrants entered the Louisiana backcountry, meanwhile, when the British exiled them from the Canadian province of Acadia. Then, beginning in 1803, Louisiana was first a territory and then a state of the United States for more than a half-century before joining the Confederate rebellion in the Civil War. By 1880, when it had returned to the Union, Louisiana could look back on two centuries of political history that set it apart from all its sister states.

Consider how diverse its ethnic character was. To begin, there were French explorers and colonizers from the mother country and from Canada, and then

You ask about New Orleans of today, and if the cooking here is different from the cooking in other places, and if it is all it is cocked up to be. Without hesitation I say yes. It has all that other places have, and then some. . . . The cooking here, to speak sententiously, is grandchild to France, descendant to Spain, cousin to Italy, and also it is full fledged Southern. The pioneer French woman used what she found here: the fruits, herbs, vegetables, fish, game and meat. The negro woman, who reigned in the kitchen, had inherited from her ancestors in Africa, as well as in America, a knowledge of herbs that made her skill look like magic; and the new women of today, who find themselves in large homes, or in apartments, still have the knowledge and the knack, handed down, of making delectable dishes out of anything that finds its way into their kitchen.

> Mary Moore Bremer
> New Orleans Creole Recipes, 1932

French exiles from Acadia and from outposts in the Caribbean, and then Louisiana-born descendants of the French, who came to be known as Creoles. There were Spaniards from the far-flung Hispanic empire, and then there were also Spanish Creoles. There were blacks, both slave and free, from Africa and the Caribbean, and in time there were black Creoles as well. After statehood in 1812, Louisiana absorbed many English, Irish, and Scotch settlers. The presence of native Americans, principally Choctaw and Natchez Indians, was evident throughout much of the early history. German and Italian and Greek immigrants came in large numbers after the Civil War. And throughout, traders from the American interior and from the ports of the world came to New Orleans via the Mississippi River and the Gulf of Mexico.

Certainly no other Southern state had such cosmopolitan infusions of people, and none except Florida had the combination of coastal and subtropical geography to produce the raw materials for a diversified cuisine. Out of New Orleans came the distinctive cookery of the Creole culture, and out of the rural swamplands and bayous of south Louisiana came the food style now known as Cajun cooking. These two cooking styles transcended the traditional boundaries of Southern food, and yet they were unmistakably and inseparably bound to Southern gastronomic history. Even now, leaving Louisiana out of a study of Southern food would be like leaving the Yankees out of a history of baseball, or skipping over Baptists in a treatise on religion.

If there is a single dimension of Louisiana food that sets it apart from cooking elsewhere in the South, it is without a doubt the French connection. The first eighty years of French control set the pattern, and all the subsequent influences were additions, not replacements. Other Southern states manifest the historical presence of English, Scotch-Irish, or Spanish cultures; only Louisiana is clearly a child of France—and nowhere is that parentage more evident than in the kitchen.

It would be overstating the case to equate Creole cooking with French *haute cuisine* and Cajun cooking with the country food of the French provinces, but there are enough similarities to think of them as cousins. New Orleans–born descendants of French and Spanish colonists contributed inherited ideas to the eighteenth-century evolution of Creole cooking; black cooks drew from their own heritage to add African spices and seasonings; native foodstuffs from the waters and lands of Louisiana completed the triangle. By the time of Andrew Jackson's triumph in 1815 and the return to New Orleans of the Marquis de Lafayette, French hero of the American Revolution, in 1825, the city's reputation for fine and distinctive food was already chiseled in stone.

It was a reputation based primarily on Creole cuisine in the homes of the well-to-do. But unlike such Southern cities as Charleston and Savannah, New Orleans also delighted in lavish public displays of its culinary skills, so much so

The Creoles of New Orleans, those who settled here before the Louisiana Purchase, comprised a mixed group, economically and socially. Some of them were wealthy; many were poor. All of them considered themselves the "natives"—as opposed to the "Americans," the new arrivals who settled "uptown," on the other side of Canal Street from the French Quarter. Creole culture had many of its roots in French culture, but it developed on New World soil. New Orleans food as we know it today originated with the Creoles, who combined French cooking traditions and techniques with seasonings and new ingredients introduced to them by the Spanish, the Indians, and the many blacks who lived in the old part of the city. . . .

In wealthy New Orleans homes most of the older cooks were blacks, whose ancestors had contributed some of the earliest important Creole dishes, such as gumbo. Those black cooks had inherited a love of spicy food and were adept at preparing the old dishes; now [in the 1880s] they were encouraged by their employers to follow the "new" fashion . . . their skill was the most important thread of continuity in the fabric of Creole cuisine.

Rima Collin and Richard Collin
The New Orleans Cookbook, 1975

that travelers and visiting dignitaries such as the Jacksons and Lafayette expected fine dining in the banquet halls, inns, and saloons of the city—and their expectations were fully met. Cajun food would remain an essentially private rural cuisine until improved transportation and communications ushered in the restaurant age after World War II, but eating in New Orleans was both a private and a public luxury before 1800, and it has remained a consuming interest of residents and visitors alike down through the years.

When President Thomas Jefferson purchased Louisiana from Napoleon in 1803 (paying about three cents an acre for what turned out to be virtually all the land between the Mississippi River and the Rocky Mountains), New Orleans entered a golden age that lasted until the Civil War. It was the Queen City of the Mississippi, an international port and market known for its glamour, gaiety, elegance, and wickedness. French and Spanish Creoles dominated the merchant-planter class that effectively ruled the city and the sprawling plantations upriver. They lived in the grand manner of European aristocrats, and they dined on the finest native and imported foods. In the French Quarter of the city, the language, laws, customs, and cuisine of Mother France lingered, but other influences constantly modified the public character.

Food illustrates the point especially well. What came to be known as Creole cuisine was rooted in the soups and sauces and sweet confections of French cooking, but grafted with all manner of supplementary tastes, Spanish and American and Indian and African. Gumbo—the word and the dish—is an African contribution to Louisiana cookery, both the okra (also African) and filé versions, the latter flavored with powdered sassafras leaves, a gift of the Choctaw Indians. Spanish dishes utilizing cooked onions, green peppers, tomatoes, and garlic as a base are prominent in Creole cookery. Grits, pork, and cornmeal, all staples of Southern cooking, are also important in New Orleans kitchens. And an abundance of native foodstuffs, from crawfish, shrimp, oysters, and crabs to hot peppers, rice, cane syrup, and pecans, can be found in every Creole cookbook.

What emerged was not modified French cookery but a distinctly separate and indigenous cuisine, unique to its place. Upcountry travelers moving in and out of New Orleans on the river and the Natchez Trace spread the word about the city's excellent food. By 1830, some steamboats on the Mississippi were elaborate floating palaces featuring food and drink as rich and elegant as the best plantation fare, and New Orleans was the home port for these shipboard feasts. In the same decade, the St. Louis Hotel in the French Quarter and the St. Charles in the nearby central business district added more luster to New Orleans' growing reputation for superlative dining and hospitality. Restaurants, coffeehouses, and taverns complemented this showcase image, and by midcentury New Orleans was second to no American city in its culinary renown.

Roy Alciatore had entered the room and was greeting the guests while his assistants kindled the flames beneath two chafing dishes. Over one of these, the breast filets of the ducks, which had been roasted and carved in the kitchen, were now set simmering. Over the other, a shallow copper skillet, silver-lined, was carefully heated while a lump of

Antoine's, one of the oldest and most famous of all restaurants in the United States, has been owned and operated by the same family in the French Quarter since 1840. Antoine Alciatore, a native of France, was sixteen years old when he opened a small boardinghouse on St. Louis Street; now his great-great-grandson Bernard Guste presides over the Antoine's tradition at another address on the same street. Such longevity is rare, even in New Orleans, but there are many fine restaurants in the city that have been operating for forty years or more—and like Antoine's, they pride themselves on their history as well as their cuisine.

In its nineteenth-century glory years, New Orleans was a boom town on the rural frontier, a metropolis open to the river and the gulf but isolated from the nation's great urban centers in the North and East. The Civil War not only increased that isolation but brought impoverishment too. When recovery finally began in the postwar years, food and hospitality were in the forefront of the revival. A long, anonymously written article in *Scribner's Monthly* in the fall of 1873 described New Orleans as a vibrant city, and food figured prominently in the description. There were the charming little cafes in the French Quarter, where passersby might see "a long and well-spread table surrounded by twenty Frenchmen and Frenchwomen, all talking at once over their eleven o'clock breakfast." And elsewhere in the Quarter, there were "aristocratic restaurants where the immaculate floors are only surpassed in cleanliness by the immaculate linen of the tables, where a solemn dignity . . . prevails, and where the waiter gives you the names of the dishes in both languages, and bestows on you a napkin large enough to serve you as a shroud, if the strange melange of French and Southern cooking gives you fatal indigestion."

By 1885, New Orleans was once again a national attraction. Its recovery from the Civil War had been hastened by the coming of the railroads, which greatly reduced the city's physical isolation from the rest of the country. The World's Industrial and Cotton Exposition in 1884–85 brought a rush of visitors, including many representatives of the nation's press, and most of them found Creole cuisine to be foremost among the charms of New Orleans. Those who dined at the St. Louis and St. Charles, at Antoine's, and at Madame Bégué's helped to spread the popularity of Creole cooking far beyond the borders of Louisiana.

Ironically, this culinary revival came at a time when Creole wealth and influence had entered a permanent state of decline, and the growing dominance of "outsiders" over "natives" was diminishing the social and economic importance of the Creole tradition. The strongest remaining element of that culture was its celebrated cuisine, and its survival became a matter of surpassing importance to many people in New Orleans.

Judging from the gastronomic history and the many fine cookbooks of New

butter softened and melted. The gleaming silver device, part of which resembled a letter press, was now moved forward on the sideboard, and as the screw was turned to put more and more pressure on the chopped duck carcasses in its silver cylinder, the expressed juices were caught in a porcelain bowl. Roy skillfully blended these with various wines and spices over the flickering alcohol flame of his burner. Then he added cream and brandy, almost drop by drop; from a tiny pepper mill he dusted a few grains of freshly ground white pepper into the chocolate-colored sauce, just before this was decanted over the filets.

During the ritual, the guests had left the table and crowded about the masterpiece-in-preparation. Now they returned to their places, murmuring their appreciation as the dish was served and the Château Nénin was poured.

"Uncle, it's scrumptious!" Ruth exclaimed.

Frances Parkinson Keyes
Dinner at Antoine's, 1948

Orleans, it is surprising to discover that none of the surviving recipe collections
from the city was published prior to 1885. Virginia and South Carolina and
Kentucky had excellent cookbooks in print long before that, but New Orleans,
for all its culinary renown, had none. Then, within months of each other, two
volumes appeared: *The Creole Cookery Book*, edited by the Christian Woman's
Exchange of New Orleans, and *La Cuisine Creole*, written anonymously by Lafcadio Hearn, an up-and-coming journalist and author in the city. A primary
purpose of the two books was to record, and thus preserve, the long-established
style and substance of Creole cooking. Now, a hundred years later, many of the
same foods and dishes and recipes that were featured then are still essential:
jambalaya, court bouillon, bouillabaisse, sauce piquante, turtle soup, trout,
flounder, red snapper, redfish, oysters, shrimp, crabs, duck, veal, crawfish bisque,
all manner of sauces and gravies, bread pudding, molasses pie (forerunner of
pecan), strong coffee laced with milk or brandy, and of course the inimitable
Creole gumbos.

Fifteen years later, *The Picayune*, a leading New Orleans newspaper, welcomed the new century with publication of the *Picayune Creole Cook Book*, a
definitive work aimed at preserving the kitchen artistry of "the Creole negro
cooks of nearly two hundred years ago, carefully instructed and directed by
their white Creole mistresses." The newspaper's editor feared that the "vast
upheavels [sic] of social conditions" (by which they apparently meant emanci-
pation and Reconstruction) would eventually bring about the demise of Creole
cooking. On the contrary, however, social conditions had changed little when
the book was published, and for a long time to come, Creole cooking remained
essentially a creation of skilled black cooks and chefs employed by whites. To
the French, Spanish, African, and native Southern dimensions of the cuisine
were eventually added new tastes brought by German, Italian, and Greek immigrants. Far from becoming extinct, Creole cookery continued to flourish.

Further additions to the cookbook treasury followed in the 1930s with
outstanding collections from Natalie V. Scott (*200 Years of New Orleans Cooking*), Mary Moore Bremer (*New Orleans Creole Recipes*), and Lena Richard
(*New Orleans Cook Book*). Pain perdu, pecan pralines, sauce remoulade, red
beans and rice, grillades, beignets, and flan were among the entries. By then,
the Creole revival launched by the Christian Woman's Exchange and Lafcadio
Hearn a half-century earlier had become a thoroughly institutionalized part of
New Orleans culture and a permanent fixture in Southern gastronomic history.
There was no longer any consensus on what it meant to be a Creole, but the
distinctive character of Creole cookery was widely recognized, understood, and
appreciated, and cooks around the South and the nation tried eagerly to reproduce it.

Another fifty years have passed since then, and food remains a paramount element in the allure of New Orleans. The "dissipations" of the city that struck Rachel Jackson with such force in 1815 are now, if anything, more pronounced than ever. The pre-Lenten Mardi Gras Festival is a people's zoo without cages; there is a fun palace called the Superdome that cost ten times more than the Louisiana Purchase; palm readers and fortune-tellers accept MasterCard and VISA; and the ancient French Quarter reeks perpetually with excess and decay. But through it all, New Orleans has never relinquished its reputation as a mecca for fine food and drink. It probably still has more good places to eat than any city in America.

I made it to New Orleans twice in 1985, once with Ann and another time alone, staying a total of five nights and six days. In the context of a South-wide schedule of mostly one-night stands, six days seems like an extended period, but in New Orleans it's barely enough time to get started. There is a limit to how much any person can eat, and whenever I go to New Orleans I learn anew where the boundary is for me. Fortunately for us, our purpose was not to rate the city's restaurants or to include them in a comprehensive guidebook, but simply to give an account of some of our experiences eating out there. With critics and guides and resident historians as good as the likes of Richard and Rima Collin and Tom Fitzmorris, New Orleans needs no outside help. On the contrary, it is the city's wealth of guidebooks, cookbooks, magazines, tabloids, radio and television food programs, archival collections, food festivals, historians, and critics that elevates and enriches the dining experiences of outsiders and gives them, like so many New Orleanians, an almost obsessive interest in food.

Good food is everywhere in New Orleans—in restaurants, cafes, hotels, chain outlets, trains, boats, bars, street stands, groceries, even service stations and liquor stores. A few years ago, a local woman received favorable notice for a portable food shop she operated from the trunk of her car. It was dubbed Mama's Cadillac, and its success prompted her son to open a branch enterprise named—inevitably—Junior's Pontiac. At any hour of the day or night, knowledgeable food hounds can find plenty of good places to eat scattered about the French Quarter and the rest of the city.

Some of the New Orleans breakfast opportunities were cited earlier. Our coverage here begins with lunch, highlighted by three locally created and very original sandwiches: roast beef poor boys, oyster loaves, and muffulettas.

But first, a few appetizing taste whetters—like a steaming plate of red beans and rice. Louis Armstrong, a New Orleans native, relished this dish at the cafe of his friend Buster Holmes in the French Quarter (Satchmo often signed his letters "Red beans and ricely yours"), and there are Creole recipes for the combination dating back to the turn of the century. They still serve it at Buster's, and at many other places around town. The old recipes begin with dried kidney

Even more characteristic than the relaxed manner of eating in New Orleans is the universality of good food, in poor boy places, in lunch rooms, in family restaurants, and in the indispensable and plain-looking seafood places where the greatest sound is the cracking of a crab's claw and the sole decoration a sink in the middle of the dining room for washing one's hands. New Orleanians eat exuberantly. Our great roast beef poor boy sandwiches at their best leak all over everything. Beignets in the French Market or Fat City demand the use of powdered sugar that gets on the beignet, the eater, and the entire surrounding party. Seafood eaten with one's hands or the minimum utensil, a single knife, is part of the basic earthiness and goodness of a cuisine that is vigorous, honest, and fun. Eating is a way of life in New Orleans. All our restaurants are noisy. Frequently the conversations revolve about yesterday's meal and tomorrow's. We love to talk about restaurants and about food, and we eat out much more than people in other cities.

Richard and Rima Collin
The New Orleans Restaurant Guide, 1976

beans soaked overnight and then cooked slowly for several hours with a ham bone and a complement of onions, peppers, garlic, and seasonings, served over rice. Because it is inexpensive and filling as well as delicious, the dish has long been a favorite among all segments of the New Orleans population.

Oysters, the most plentiful and thus the least expensive of the local seafoods, are another standard favorite, and there is not a more basic way to eat them—or a better place—than freshly shucked at the Acme Oyster House, a classic raw bar in the French Quarter. If you love raw oysters, you can stand at the Acme's long marble bar on a humid fall afternoon and let a shucker set you up with a dozen salty bivalves on the half-shell and a frosty mug of draft beer, and you will think you have attained a state of nirvana.

Gumbo—thick and spicy, filled with chunks of seafood or sausage or some other mainstay, founded upon a roux base and made with either okra or filé powder, is on everybody's menu. Any New Orleans Creole restaurant that can't serve a superlative gumbo has a serious credibility problem; dozens of establishments more than meet the test. One of them is Chez Helene, a classic dispensary of soul and Creole cooking. Named for Helene Howard, who started it in 1942, the restaurant has belonged since 1964 to her nephew, Austin Leslie, a master chef whose kitchen artistry runs the gamut from stuffed pork chops and candied yams to crawfish bisque, jambalaya, and bread pudding. A bowl of Leslie's gumbo, full of sausage, shrimp, and crabs and hot with fire and spice, is a dish to remember.

As an appetizing introduction to a larger meal or as meals in themselves, these three great New Orleans specialties have the history, the broad acceptance, and the distinctive taste to qualify as Creole hall-of-famers. For lunch or dinner or in between, it would be hard to beat red beans and rice, raw oysters, or gumbo. Buster Holmes and the Acme Oyster House and Chez Helene typify the many New Orleans restaurants that feature these specialties.

Now to the sandwiches. At Central Grocery, an honest-to-goodness grocery store across from the French Market, the feature is the muffuletta, an Italian creation peculiar to New Orleans. It begins with a round sesame seed loaf, eight or nine inches in diameter. When it has been split in half, it is loaded with Italian ham, salami, provolone and mozzarella cheese, and a dressing called olive salad (mostly lettuce, tomato, garlic, and olives). The top is replaced and the giant sandwich is quartered for easier handling. For size and flavor, a Central Grocery muffuletta is hard to match.

But not impossible. Its peer is the poor boy (po boy, if you prefer), a long loaf of freshly baked French bread loaded with roast beef, or fried oysters, or ham, or some other main item and dressed with gravy or sauce, shredded lettuce, tomato, mayonnaise or mustard, and pickles. Mother's Restaurant, a little eatery tucked among the skyscrapers on a busy downtown corner, has been

In New Orleans they eat oysters all year around, but in fairness to the oysters they shouldn't—they are much better in winter. The Louisiana oyster in winter is still a solace to the man of moderate means, sold across the counter, opened, at sixty-five cents a dozen, and therefore usually eaten a couple of dozen at a time. (I prefer three dozen to any other number of dozen before a meal.) They are wilder and freer than the oysters of Maryland and Long Island and frequently come two or three in a cluster. . . . The patrons mix their own dope from a variety of condiments oysters do not have to contend with in the North— hot-pepper sauce and olive oil as well as catsup, horse-radish and straight Tabasco. Mixing oyster dope is done as solemnly as the Japanese tea rite.

A. J. Liebling
The Earl of Louisiana, 1961

serving them since the late 1930s, when Simon Landry and his wife opened shop. Ed and Jack Landry, their sons, now run the place with Marine Corps precision and typical Louisiana frenzy. It was in downtown New Orleans that the poor boy was created and named during a streetcar strike in 1929. Since then, similar sandwiches have gained fame elsewhere (submarine, hoagie, hero, Cuban, grinder) but the poor boy still reigns in New Orleans, and Mother's is one of its oldest and finest producers. The roast beef poor boy, drenched as it is with rich gravy, is a drippy, messy delight.

The third great New Orleans sandwich is the oyster loaf, another gargantuan combination of locally baked bread stuffed with a main item (in this case, fried oysters) and a generous dollop of dressing. At Casamento's, a popular oyster bar and seafood house in uptown New Orleans, the unsliced loaf of white pan bread is simply split open, toasted and buttered, and stuffed with fried oysters (or soft shell crabs). In Jefferson Parish, west of the city, a neighborhood bar and restaurant named Alonso and Son calls its combination an oyster loaf or a sandwich (a half-loaf), and it comes dressed with lettuce, tomato, and mayonnaise. Three generations of Alonsos, beginning with Albert, a Spanish immigrant, have been in the restaurant business in New Orleans for forty-four years. Raymond, the second-generation Alonso, has a three-point formula for a good oyster loaf—and a successful restaurant. "It's just this simple," he said. "Fresh seafood, a good cook, and clean grease."

There are many more elegant and expensive places to get a fine lunch in New Orleans, of course, but the half-dozen or so mentioned here, and the numerous others where good and simple fare is served, prove the point that the culinary traditions of the city are not all priced beyond the reach of the average diner. By and large, it *has* become quite expensive to eat out in New Orleans; in most of the better-known restaurants, dinner for two can seldom be had for less than fifty dollars, and it is not uncommon for the bill to reach twice that sum. Even so, dozens of small cafes and neighborhood restaurants still manage to serve excellent Creole and other traditional foods at reasonable prices for breakfast, lunch, and dinner, and those who seek them out can readily understand why New Orleans remains head and shoulders above the other cities of the South as a place to dine.

The same pressures that are causing such upheavals in the restaurant business elsewhere in the country naturally are being felt in New Orleans too. Eating habits are changing, costs are rising, skilled employees are harder to find and keep; big chain operations and fast-food outlets are giving a cookie-cutter sameness to the appearance and the fare of many restaurants; processed and prepackaged foods are more and more in use, while fresh foodstuffs are ever more scarce and expensive. Such pressures are particularly hard on the small independents; their struggle to remain competitive can be seriously affected by the loss of one good cook or by a single corner-cutting economy measure. Often the most mediocre chains at least have the virtue of consistency (even if they are only consistently mediocre). The independents, however, can't disguise uneven quality, or overcome its negative consequences with heavy advertising.

Thus, it is possible to go for dinner to a place like Eddie's, a Creole soul cafe north of the French Quarter, where Eddie Baquet, Sr., has built a forty-year reputation for fine food, and get an uneven meal—an unexcelled gumbo, for example, side by side with a highly touted oyster dressing that is simply below par. Or at Mandina's, a comfortable old cafe on Canal Street since the 1930s, the trout amandine may be as good as Antoine's for one third the cost, but the turtle soup with sherry may be far too salty, or the shrimp and oyster loaf may consist of too much loaf and not enough shrimp and oysters. Such shortcomings can be just as common in the big-name restaurants, of course, and they are all the more galling there because they cost more. But the large and well-known places have more resources for combatting such lapses of quality and consistency; they can survive sub-par performances that the smaller restaurants may ultimately find fatal.

All the more reason, then, for fans of traditional New Orleans food to seek out models of consistent quality in the neighborhood and back-street cafes, and to give more than one chance to those whose earnest efforts sometimes yield less than superior results. Otherwise, the little independent restaurants that are the backbone of New Orleans cuisine will fall by the wayside, and only the chains and the prohibitively expensive dining places will remain.

Even on special occasions when a costlier and more elaborate dinner is called for, there are choices to be made. New Orleans has many well-known and highly visible restaurants that differ greatly among themselves, and since one diner's feasting house is another's tourist trap, there is no way to produce a consensus list of the ones that best measure up to any set of standards. Sometimes, customers can have sharply contrasting experiences under the same roof. At Antoine's, for example, a preferred patron who calls ahead to his personal waiter and then enters through a private side door can expect the most attentive and solicitous service, while a first-time visitor through the main entrance may be brusquely or even rudely treated. Considering all the elements that go into a definition of dining quality—the food, the service, the atmosphere, the price, the day-to-day consistency—there are simply too many variables for objective agreement on which are the best of the New Orleans restaurants.

Like all short-term visitors to the city, we have struggled with the problem of having to select a few choice dinner spots from the imposing list of attractive possibilities. Our tendency is to gravitate toward restaurants with a good track record of customer satisfaction, places where the service is at least competent and civil, if not friendly, and where an approximate correlation exists between

To return to my trip to New Orleans with Peter [Feibleman]. The most pleasant part of it happened on the morning we were to leave. I was closing my valises. A tall, young, handsome black man was waiting for me in the lobby of the hotel.

He immediately put out his hand and said, "You are Miss Hellman. I recognize you. My name is Carl."

I said, "Hello, Carl."

He said, "You knew my grandmother. She used to cook in your aunt's boardinghouse and she has nice memories of you as a little girl."

I reached up to kiss him. He was such a pleasant memory of his grandmother.

He looked rather embarrassed in the lobby, but he said, "Miss Hellman, I

the cost of an evening and the value of it. We look for places where the owners are on the premises—and more apt to be in the kitchen than at the cash register. We look for pride of craft in the chefs and servers, and pride of longevity in the staff and the regular customers. And most of all, we look for dependably delicious food.

By these measures, it would be hard to exclude from any list of New Orleans favorites two family-owned Creole restaurants of long tenure and high esteem: Dooky Chase and Galatoire's.

Dooky Chase is the classiest black-owned restaurant in the city. Edgar "Dooky" Chase, Sr., and his wife, Emily, established it in 1941, and though Mrs. Chase is still around to keep a benevolent eye on the place, her son Edgar "Dooky" Jr. and his wife, Leah, are now the principal operators. Located in an unpretentious-looking one-story brick building on Orleans Avenue, across the street from a public housing project, Dooky's is a quiet oasis of comfort and good taste. Its elegantly appointed dining room is decorated in warm shades of wine and mauve, accented with several works of Afro-American art. For more than forty years, the Chases—father and son, mother and daughter-in-law—have focused their considerable talents on developing a first-class restaurant. The personal attention clearly shows; from the front entrance to the kitchen and the rest rooms, Dooky's sparkles with cleanliness and pride. The last time we were there, Leah Chase, an attractive and cheerful lady wearing a starched white smock, was busy directing the preparation and service of Sunday lunch.

"You have to work very hard to keep on top of the restaurant business," she said, "especially in this town. New Orleans has such a great food tradition, so many fine restaurants. We're happy to be one of them. It takes a lot of effort, though. We're here practically all the time."

The cuisine at Dooky Chase is an authentic blend of Louisiana Creole elements—African, French, Spanish, Southern. One of the highlights is a spicy seafood and sausage gumbo that is simply unbeatable. Shrimp Creole, crawfish bisque, smoked sausage, stuffed shrimp, and an array of other classic dishes from the sea and the soil are on the menu, and all are skillfully prepared and artfully presented. The desserts are also a delight to the eye and the palate. Among them is a wonderfully rich and delicious praline pudding topped with whipped cream. Black-tied waiters give pleasant and professional service, and the prices are in line with the value. All in all, Dooky Chase is a New Orleans gem.

Galatoire's, located in an old opera house in the French Quarter, is a reassuring symbol of endurance and quality in the restaurants of New Orleans. It has been more than eighty years since Jean Galatoire, a native of France, attached his name to a cafe on Bourbon Street, then a gaslit avenue of theaters and hotels and fancy residences. The Jazz Age, the Roaring Twenties, and the Great Depression have come and gone since then, and there have been inter-

have brought you something from my grandmother and I hope it's no trouble for you to take on the plane."

He had two very large plastic containers of gumbo, all taped and ready for me to carry on the plane, surrounded by ice. It was just as good a gumbo as I remembered from my childhood.

Lillian Hellman
Eating Together, 1984

mittent periods of war and peace, and Bourbon Street has taken on the look and smell of a Parisian pissoir, but Galatoire's sails serenely on, seemingly unchanged and unaffected by the turmoil around it.

Descendants of Jean Galatoire still own and operate the restaurant at the same address, and it looks as it has for decades. You enter a single large room directly from the street. Heavy green drapes cover the windows. About forty tables spread with white linen are crowded into the space, which is made to seem both larger and fuller by two dozen mirrors lining the side walls. Propeller-blade fans and clusters of light globes hang from the high ceiling. Waiters in formal black scurry about in the narrow aisles, balancing plates of food on their arms. A noisy din of conversation and laughter and clinking china fills the room. Instinctively you may look around, half expecting to see a familiar face or two smiling back at you. Galatoire's is an inviting place.

The attraction is not due to any modern touches. The restaurant doesn't advertise, and no one, however famous or powerful, can make a reservation there; they can wait in line like everyone else, or come at odd hours when the crowd has thinned out. Regular customers can open charge accounts, but credit cards are not accepted. The menu, like the decor, has not changed noticeably in years. It features French Creole cuisine highlighted by seafood dishes, including some shrimp, oyster, and trout specialties that are said to be as fresh, as skillfully prepared, and as attractively presented as they were a half-century ago, when Jean Galatoire's nephews, Justin, Léon, and Gabriel, were in command.

Among the appetizers are a very tangy shrimp remoulade and oysters Rockefeller—not as old as the Antoine's recipe, but arguably as good. Creole gumbo is the class of the soups. With these early courses, your waiter will begin supplying crusty loaves of freshly baked French bread and big squares of butter. Next, there are more than a dozen salads and an even greater number of vegetable side dishes, including potatoes au gratin, fried eggplant, and broccoli with hollandaise sauce. There are chicken and red meat and omelet entrees on the menu, but they are secondary to such Creole seafood classics as trout amandine, pompano meunière, shrimp marguery, oysters en brochette, redfish court bouillon, and bouillabaisse. Delicately broiled or baked or fried seafoods topped with rich butter or cream sauces are mainstays of Creole cuisine, and the chefs at Galatoire's prepare these dishes to perfection. The coffee is rich and aromatic, and the wine list contains about fifty choices in a wide range of prices. The dessert and after-dinner selection includes café brûlot and several fine crepes.

From start to finish, it is a gastronomic tour de force. Every dish on the menu is prepared fresh daily with locally obtained foodstuffs. There are no new twists, no fancy touches, no surprises—just the same tried and proven applications of culinary technique that have worked for generations. It is precisely this consistency, this dependable continuity, that gives Galatoire's its appeal. The local cognoscenti and a steady stream of visitors who gather there each day are united in their praise of the food, the service, the setting. For all of them, nothing seems quite as reminiscent of the past glories of New Orleans— or as representative of its continuing vitality—as an evening at Galatoire's.

Such stability is rare in any setting, but it is especially remarkable in New Orleans, where food is a subject of the most intense and obsessive scrutiny and restaurants are launched and closed with great regularity. On any list of a dozen of the city's best-known restaurants—for example, Antoine's and Arnaud's, Brennan's and Broussard's, Commander's Palace and Corinne Dunbar's, Galatoire's and K-Paul's, Le Ruth's and Mosca's, Pascal's Manale and Tujague's, to name the first twelve that come to mind—there will inevitably be more rising stars and over-the-hill fadeouts than steady cruisers. There will also be plenty of argument about which is which.

We won't enter into that debate here. The larger point is that a dozen well-known restaurants can be named and still not exhaust the list. No other city in the South—and few in the country—comes close to having a comparable group of "name" eateries.

But what finally impresses most about New Orleans is not the excellence of individual restaurants, though they would stand out on almost any list of the South's top twenty-five; rather, it is the number and variety of above-average eating places. Any city with five to ten such places is fortunate; New Orleans probably has fifty to a hundred.

And yet, all the while, the great traditions of Creole cuisine on which New Orleans has built its gastronomic reputation are being transformed by time and circumstances. The strongest European influences on Creole food customs in the past fifty years have not come from the French and Spanish, but from the Italians. The generations of black men and women who have served as private cooks and restaurant chefs in New Orleans since the eighteenth century, and whose culinary skills are primarily responsible for the superiority of Creole cooking, are slowly dying out, and fewer of their descendants are entering the profession. No one wants to spend the time it takes to make real Creole food from scratch. All of the shortcuts to dining that fast-food restaurants and supermarkets now make possible are so many nails in the coffin of any cuisine that is based on fresh foodstuffs slowly and individually prepared for maximum enjoyment.

So Creole food is getting harder to find, both in restaurants and in private homes—and the less there is of it, the less it can be explained, defined, and passed on. It may take another Creole kitchen revival such as Lafcadio Hearn and the Christian Woman's Exchange launched a hundred years ago to keep the cuisine from dying.

The crowning of a grand dinner is a brûlé. It is the *pièce de résistance*, the grandest *pousse café* of all. After the coffee has been served, the lights are turned down or extinguished, brûlé is brought in and placed in the centre of the table upon a pedestal surrounded by flowers. A match is lighted, and after allowing the sulphur to burn entirely off is applied to the brandy, and as it burns it sheds its weird light upon the faces of the company, making them appear like ghouls in striking contrast to the gay surroundings. The stillness that follows gives an opportunity for thoughts that break out in ripples of laughter which pave the way for the exhilaration that ensues.

Lafcadio Hearn
La Cuisine Creole, 1885

In the meantime, one of the "hot" food styles of the mid-1980s is Creole's country cousin: Cajun cooking. Suddenly, it is everywhere—onstage with the trendy offerings of the much-ballyhooed "new American cuisine," uptown with the restaurant groupies of New York and the West Coast, on television and in print with chefs, critics, and cookbook writers. And, of course, it is also in the south Louisiana countryside, where it originated. But before we look in on it there, we need to glance briefly at two purveyors of Cajun influence in New Orleans.

One of them is Paul Prudhomme, a rotund young Cajun chef from a tiny community near Opelousas, where as the last of thirteen children he got personal attention from his mother-mentor, a gifted country cook. Since he opened K-Paul's Louisiana Kitchen in the French Quarter in 1982, the Cajun craze has swept the country, and Prudhomme himself has been proclaimed "a world authority" on the cuisine by none other than Craig Claiborne, food guru of *The New York Times.*

Prudhomme characterizes his offerings as Louisiana cooking, not Cajun. (His most famous entree, blackened redfish, was unheard of in south Louisiana until he invented it, but now the dish is so popular nationwide that it has made redfish an endangered species.) His ambition is to unite Cajun and Creole traditions in an all-embracing Louisiana cuisine that will be both permanent and transportable to other places. Meanwhile, his original cafe in New Orleans looks more like a soup kitchen than a restaurant. Huge throngs of eager diners endure long waits in line to share tables with strangers and be rushed through twenty-five-dollar entrees and five-dollar desserts by curt and harried waiters. Such is the consequence of fame.

The other Cajun entrepreneur in New Orleans is not a Cajun at all but a local native in his early forties who created Popeyes Famous Fried Chicken in 1972 and now presides over a fast-food empire with close to five hundred outlets in thirty-five states. Al Copeland, a tenth-grade dropout from a broken home in a housing project full of low-income whites, appealed to the south Louisiana appetite for spicy hot food with highly seasoned fried chicken, red beans and rice, dirty rice, and other Cajun dishes, and the response was immediate, phenomenal, and continuous. There are about forty Popeyes outlets in the New Orleans area alone.

Convinced that Cajun food is about to become a commercial category as fixed and identifiable as Chinese or Mexican, Copeland is now investing heavily in a new chain of Cajun-American cafes called Copeland's. These fancy fern bars with the brass and stained glass trappings that have become so familiar in new restaurants offer a number of stylized Cajun specialties, including gumbo, jambalaya, and Cajun popcorn (deep-fried crawfish tails).

Whether the new waves of gastronomic energy generated by Paul Prud-

---

A friend of ours once went to a famous restaurant in New Orleans and asked the waiter to suggest a meal that was new and different.

"Ah!" he smiled, "Madame should try the most delicious Le Filet De Pompano En Papillote, a delicate fish baked in a paper bag."

"Oh, we have that at home," replied the customer. "What else would you suggest?"

"Then, perhaps Madame would like Le Filet De Truite Amandine, an elegant combination of trout with an almond sauce."

"We have that at home," said Madame.

"Le Coeur De Filet De Boeuf Marchand De Vin?"

"That too."

"Langouste Thermidor?"

"Also."

With an incredulous air the waiter regarded his customer. "But, Madame," he cried, "where are you from?"

"Tampa, Florida," replied our friend and settled for a savory bowl of gumbo, one dish she could not get at home.

> Patricia Morgan,
> in her introduction to
> *The Gasparilla Cookbook,* 1961

homme and Al Copeland and their colleagues and competitors will prolong the life of authentic Louisiana Cajun and Creole food or hasten its demise is a question that no one can answer now. But this much is certain: A tremendous wellspring of gastronomic creativity still exists in New Orleans, as it has for nearly three centuries—and the same vitality is also apparent when you venture out into the south Louisiana country.

Similarities and differences abound in any historical or gastronomic comparison of Cajun and Creole cultures; like siblings, they are in some ways almost identical—and in others, polar opposites. The French-Canadian exiles who filtered into the Louisiana backcountry in the last half of the eighteenth century were the principal ancestors of Cajun society, and many of their descendants still think of themselves as country sons and daughters of an essentially non-American heritage. Still mostly Catholic, still speaking a French-rooted patois, they stand out from the majority of country folk in the South more distinctly than any other group. Other influences have been there all along, of course, from the black, Indian, and English-speaking people who began arriving in south Louisiana generations ago to the Italian, Mexican, and Asian immigrants of more recent times, but Acadiana, as the low-country region is called, has remained predominantly French in its basic character and personality. It has also remained primarily a rural and small-town culture—and that, more than anything else, may account for the differences that exist between Cajun and Creole cooking.

The absence of an extensive written record of Louisiana food history prior to the 1880s makes direct and specific comparisons difficult. Did rice attain prominence as a staple in New Orleans before it did in Acadiana, or vice versa? Could it be that okra gumbo originated in the city, where black cooks were more numerous, and filé gumbo was created in the country, where native American Indian influence was greatest? Is crawfish bisque a Cajun dish, or was it first made in New Orleans (where in 1819 a noted architect from the East, Benjamin Latrobe, praised it as "an excellent and handsome soup")? Who made the first roux in Louisiana? The first jambalaya? There are claims and counterclaims, but not much clear proof.

In a general way, though, the two cultures—and their cuisines—have developed quite separately and differently. Think of old New Orleans as urban, cosmopolitan, race- and class-oriented, preoccupied with wealth, leisure, and refinement. Its founding fathers brought fine wines and brandies from France and rum from the Caribbean; one of its adopted sons invented cocktails almost two centuries ago. The city's foodstuffs were purchased fresh daily at the dockside and streetside markets—shrimp and crabs and oysters and worlds of produce, soon to be transformed by gifted cooks into delicate, fancy, complex

Creole dishes. Only the finest ingredients—butter, eggs, cream, sugar, lemons, spices, and such—went into these elaborate creations. The result was a plenteous array of beautiful and delectable culinary masterpieces as impressive as any American kitchen could produce.

Now think of the Acadian culture and its foods between, say, the American Revolution and World War II. A small and scattered population of farmers, fishers, hunters, and trappers lived in a sprawling region of swamps, marshlands, bayous, and coastal islands, isolated not only from inland communities but from one another. Short of both money and tillable land, they ate largely what they could grow, catch, or forage—a make-do diet built around game meat (deer, duck, alligator, turtle, and the like), shellfish and finned fish, rice, beans, yams, spicy hot peppers, and sweet cane syrup. They drank wine (and later beer), and they probably ate less cornbread and fewer biscuits than anyone else in the South, there being only limited supplies of cornmeal and wheat available. It was a plain and simple diet, heavier and spicier and more robust than what the Creoles ate, and no doubt greasier. Among the distinctive foods the Cajuns prepared were andouille (a smoked pork sausage), tasso (spicy smoked ham), boudin (peppery-hot link sausages), various gumbo and jambalaya combinations, coush-coush (cornbread and clabber), and several blends of beans or meat or seafood with rice, often smothered with a thickened gravy or sauce (étouffée). All of these are still popular favorites.

Crawfish, the little freshwater crustaceans that proliferate in Louisiana, are celebrated in legend as Nova Scotia lobsters that followed the Acadians south when they were cast out of Canada in the 1700s; the long journey and the increasing heat and humidity diminished them from giant superclawed monsters to little mudbugs only four or five inches long, but they stayed with the Cajuns all the way, and now they are a highly visible symbol of the regional cuisine, available in seemingly endless supply to be served boiled, fried, in étouffées and bisques and pies. Until about twenty-five years ago, crawfish were mainly used as fish bait, simply because it was considered too much trouble to peel and pick enough tail meat to make a meal. Now, though, people in Louisiana eat about fifty million pounds of the delicacy every year, and its popularity is spreading with the rage for Cajun food in other parts of the country.

It is probably inevitable—and certainly ironic—that the very act of extending a style of cooking into a larger circle adulterates it. Commercialized Cajun food can't be the same as when it was essentially a private, home-style cookery. As all sorts of modern influences creep into Acadiana and its kitchens, the traditional and authentic essence of the food slowly leaks out. But the process has not yet gone so far that Cajun cooking has lost its vigor and originality. Like New Orleans, the country district is immersed in a food-oriented culture; it is, if anything, even more preoccupied with the subject than the city

There are crawfish (or crayfish, or crawdads) all over the country, but outside of Louisiana they are all but ignored—lumps of clay lacking a sculptor. People outside of Louisiana, in fact, often scoff when they hear of people eating crawfish—the way an old farmer in Pennsylvania might scoff at the New York antique dealer who paid fourteen dollars for a quilt that must be at least a hundred years old and doesn't even look very warm. A New York crawfish craver who couldn't make it to the Atchafalaya Basin would have to settle for Paris, where crawfish are called écrevisses, except by people from Louisiana, who always call them inferior.

Calvin Trillin
American Fried, 1974

is. Food is in its history, its legends, its music; it is in restaurants and cafes, markets and bakeries, bars and taverns, groceries and service stations; it is in such basic manufactures as sugar and salt and rice, and in such enduring commercial enterprises as McIlhenny, making Tabasco Sauce since the late 1860s, and Trappey's, packing hot peppers and other native foodstuffs since 1898; it is in the industries that harvest and process crawfish, crabs, oysters, shrimp, and other seafoods; it is in the scores of fairs and festivals held annually in communities all over the region to celebrate one kind of food or another; and finally, it is still simmering on Cajun cookstoves in tens of thousands of homes, where the tradition began. Cajun food may eventually blend into the gastronomic mainstream—but as of now, it remains a distinctive cookery, much closer to its origins than Creole cuisine is, and thus much more accurately reflective of the culture from which it came.

The geographical and cultural center of Acadiana is Lafayette, a city of about eighty-five thousand people located twenty miles west of the Atchafalaya River and 135 miles west of New Orleans. On the way there from any direction, you can stop to sample an impressive variety of Louisiana foods. Here are a few random examples—representative, perhaps, but in no sense inclusive:

Between Shreveport and Alexandria in the northern part of the state is Natchitoches, the oldest permanent settlement in Louisiana, predating New Orleans by four years. History lives on in the well-preserved architecture of the town and in several old plantation houses nearby, but the best-known restaurant has been in business under twenty years. Lasyone's Meat Pie Kitchen and Restaurant grew out of James and Jo Ann Lasyone's butcher shop in 1968. Remembering the delicious meat pies he used to buy from vendors on the street when he was a boy growing up in Natchitoches, James Lasyone decided to experiment with some recipes. He ended up with a highly seasoned beef and pork hash deep-fried in a half-moon pastry, and the combination was so well received that it became the feature of a new restaurant. Jo Ann Lasyone added a creation of her own—a rich chocolate and custard filling in a gingerbreadlike cake—and this Cane River Cream Pie, along with a meat pie, proved to be a perfect lunch. The rest of the menu, consisting of a variety of Southern meat and vegetable combinations, has fallen into place around the two specialties, and Lasyone's is now as much a fixture in Natchitoches as the historic old buildings that surround it.

Passing through Alexandria, we stopped to inquire about local dining arenas of note. "Good places to eat?" our informant said, repeating the question. "Oh, yeah, there's lots of them around here. McDonald's, Hardee's, Western Sizzlin—name-brand places." It was too early for dinner anyway, so we kept moving south toward Cajun country.

The road took us first to Lake Charles, and then east toward Lafayette. At

When he returned to Spain from the West Indies in 1493, Columbus brought the first hot peppers ever seen in Europe. . . . The speed with which hot peppers spread around the globe is unequalled in the annals of food. Never have so many different cultures embraced a food so rapidly. . . . Capsicum frutescens, which is the hottest pepper grown in the United States . . . will only grow in a handful of North American locales and it grows best in the area around Iberia Parish. . . . The people of Southern Louisiana call it a tabasco pepper.

Richard Schweid
Hot Peppers, 1980

Jennings, Ellis Cormier's Boudin King Restaurant featured a spicy-hot blend of ground pork, rice, and seasonings stuffed into link sausage casings. Like a multitude of little shops scattered throughout the region, from Mama Mia's Grocery in Opelousas to Baudin's in Breaux Bridge to Robichaux's in New Iberia, Cormier's Boudin King declares its boudin to be "the best in the world." The annual Boudin Festival in Broussard crowns a new "Boudin King" each year, and every one has a different recipe. Dudley Hebert, the 1985 king, stuffed his casings with pork shoulder, heart or kidneys, liver, onions, celery, bell pepper, rice, and lots of Cajun hot stuff. Back at Cormier's place in Jennings, meanwhile, you can get a half-pound of boudin, a cup of red beans and rice with sausage, or a cup of chicken and sausage gumbo—any one of the three—for less than a dollar, and they're all very tasty. New Orleans, take note.

There are two main routes to Lafayette from New Orleans. One is Interstate 10 through Baton Rouge; the other is U.S. Highway 90, an older and more southerly road through Houma, Morgan City, Franklin, and about two dozen other small towns in the vast Atchafalaya Basin that runs through the middle of Cajun country. At Thibodaux, a few miles off Highway 90, Sam Bilello opened a restaurant in 1950 that is now highly regarded as a prime dispenser of Cajun-Italian food. Bilello's father, "an immigrant straight off the Italy boat" when he arrived in south Louisiana at the turn of the century, once operated a bar and club in Thibodaux that featured poor boy sandwiches. Sam Bilello realized his father's bigger dream when he opened the restaurant, and now *his* son Donald is in charge—but Sam is still there every day, working in the kitchen. Their menu includes such items as "Wop" salad, stuffed mirliton (a squash-like vegetable pear filled with shrimp and crabmeat), fried crawfish tails, crawfish étouffée, and broiled oysters with bacon. The cooking style is lighter and more delicate than mainline Cajun—and surprisingly, there is no Louisiana hot-pepper sauce on the table to boost the octane. Bilello's is a reminder that food doesn't have to be fiery hot to be good.

Middendorf's, a catfish and seafood restaurant at Pass Manchac on Interstate 55 northwest of New Orleans, is not so much a Cajun or Creole dining place as it is simply a seafood house—with freshwater catfish as the specialty. There's enough good gumbo and raw oysters on hand to remind you that you're still in south Louisiana, but the Mississippi pond-raised catfish, with an occasional supplement of river cat, is what most people go to Middendorf's for. It's one more example of the broad-based excellence of Louisiana cookery.

And then, in Baton Rouge, an unexpected surprise and a delight: Juban's, an old-looking but quite new gourmet restaurant that has a very comfortable and individual style of its own with both Creole and Cajun touches. It is tucked away in the back corner of a shopping center, but on the inside it looks like a restored New Orleans residence. In this quiet and pleasant setting, Glynn Juban,

When the outside world thinks of Cajun food, it thinks of crawfish, shrimp, oysters, jambalaya and gumbo. You learn of other, more primitive, foods as you penetrate the Acadian Coast and the bayous. . . . One of the least known and perhaps the most addictive of the Cajun dishes is boudin. Boudin (the last syllable rhymes with can, nasally) is a sausage containing rice, pork and pork liver. Cajun children eat it like ice cream in a cone.

I have a friend in New Orleans who knows food, as well as politics, law and other Louisiana weaknesses. He had told me, with some show of confidentiality, where to find the world's best boudin. It was in the town of Jennings at a cafe named the Boudin King. . . .

I drove on to Eunice to spend the night and that evening . . . I visited

a Baton Rouge native who once lived on the shopping-center property, has assembled a professional staff of chefs and servers and put together a menu that any classy New Orleans or south Louisiana restaurant would be proud to claim. Ann had stuffed soft-shell crabs so delicately sculpted and beautiful that she hated to disturb them—until the first bite spurred her on. Her side dish was a potato carved like a mushroom. I had a bowl of duck and sausage gumbo, and it was so rich and spicy and delicious that I couldn't manage a Creole dessert with my dark-roast coffee. Juban's had the decor, the service, the artistically presented and uniformly excellent food, and the reasonable prices to make us think of it as one of the absolute highlights of our Louisiana journey.

Later, on another trip, I found a somewhat similar place called Patout's in an old house in New Iberia, south of Lafayette. Alex Patout and his sister Gigi started it in 1979, following a family tradition of restaurant management. Patout's, like Juban's, seems more like a French Creole place in New Orleans than a Cajun country cafe, and its menu has touches of both: Creole baked redfish stuffed with shrimp and crab dressing, for example, and Cajun crawfish prepared in a variety of ways. Enjoying my redfish with a bowl of authoritative gumbo and a hot loaf of French bread with butter, I found myself thinking what a sensation it would cause if a restaurant like Patout's or Juban's suddenly appeared in, say, Knoxville or Richmond or Raleigh.

At Abbeville, a small and picturesque town in the Cajun orbit of Lafayette, we came upon two very basic dispensaries of local shellfish. One of them, Richard's, is a no-frills crawfish shack owned and operated by Calvin Richard, whose father, Ovey, better known as Red, started it about thirty years ago. The featured food is boiled crawfish, served in a three-pound mound for six dollars. You can get boiled potatoes or onions or corn on the side, and a beer or a soft drink, and that's about it. (Boiled shrimp and crabs are also on the menu, but Richard's is primarily a crawfish place.) Catsup, mayonnaise, lemon juice, horseradish, and mustard are available for you to make your own sauce, and of course there's plenty of commercial hot-pepper sauce. The popularity of Richard's underscores the point that peeling and eating boiled crawfish tails is one of the favorite pastimes of people in south Louisiana.

The other Abbeville shellfish palace is Depuy's Oyster Shop, a little terrazzo-floored cafe that Joseph Depuy opened before 1900. His son Ferdnand, with help from his wife, Loretta, took over in 1929. Now Jack and Diane Phares manage the place, and Ferdnand Depuy comes by every day or so to chat. Depuy's has changed little over the years. The house specialty is still oysters, fried or on the half-shell, and we found them to be first-rate both ways. Shrimp, crabs, catfish, gumbo, and a few other items are on the menu. In an oyster shop, though, you should try the oysters—and at Depuy's, that's definitely the way to go.

a bar called the Blue Goose. . . . The conversation turned to food. . . . "Ah, now, Cher," [the barmaid] said, "the best boudin is made here in Eunice. You go try the boudin at Johnson's Grocery."

The next morning . . . I drove 10 miles north to Mamou. . . . [The barmaid at Fred's Lounge said,] "Listen, Cher, the best boudin in the world is made at the grocery store right here in Mamou, down the street here."

Roy Reed,
in The New York Times Magazine,
October 9, 1983

On Louisiana 14, a narrow state highway that winds from Lake Charles through Abbeville to New Iberia, one bar, tavern, club, service station, and country store after another advertises freshly prepared Cajun food. Some even offer free supper to customers who come in for an evening of drinking and dancing—calling to mind the free-lunch promotion that began in some New Orleans hotels 150 years ago and became a popular and long-lived tradition.

In Lafayette proper, two of the favorite haunts of local people are Don's, the flagship of a Cajun seafood chain, and Dwyer's Cafe, a downtown diner. Several members of the Landry family independently own and manage the half-dozen or so Don's restaurants around the state, as well as a place called Landry's in Henderson, but the original eatery in Lafayette is considered the best of them. It has, among other things, a couple of fine gumbos and a very good crawfish bisque. Dwyer's, a homey little corner cafe, occupies a long, narrow room with a tile floor and lots of windows facing the street, and it echoes all day with Cajun camaraderie. When we stopped in for breakfast, the waitress greeted us like regulars, transmitted our orders verbally, and gave us no check. When we were ready to leave, we simply told the cashier what we had had, and she rang it up. Such casual informality is rare—and refreshing.

Good-natured informality seems to be a common Cajun trait, and it fits right in with some others—talking and storytelling, hunting and fishing, singing and dancing, eating and drinking. All of the above except hunting and fishing are indulged in at Mulate's, a Cajun restaurant at Breaux Bridge, just east of Lafayette. Edwin "Mulate" Guidry had a popular eating, drinking, and dancing place there back in the 1940s, and the memory of it inspired Kerry Boutte to open the new Mulate's in 1980. Now the large, rustic dining room and dancehall is a favorite of both travelers and Acadiana residents. A good Cajun band is there almost every night to play energetic two-step dance music. The menu, printed in English and French, includes stuffed crabs (delicious) and broiled or fried frog legs in addition to the familiar litany of gumbo, crawfish, catfish, shrimp, and oyster dishes. The checkered oilcloth on the tables is staked down with giant twelve-ounce bottles of Tabasco Sauce. Mulate's is a proud conservator of Cajun food and music traditions.

Five miles up the road, on the edge of the Atchafalaya Basin, another Guidry, Henry, opened a cafe and dancehall on a dirt road near the levee in 1934. That was the beginning of Henderson, Louisiana, now a small town of homes, shops, waterfront businesses—and three or four of the finest Cajun restaurants to be found anywhere. Henderson is a narrow, two-mile-long community wedged between sugarcane fields and Interstate 10 on a state highway that dead-ends at the levee. It's the sort of place that freeway travelers tend to speed past without noticing, unless they are armed with some inside knowledge of the treasures it holds. Ann and I, following some sage advice, stopped there

People often ask me what's the difference between Cajun and Creole cooking. . . . Both are Louisiana born, with French roots. But Cajun is very old, French country cooking—a simple, hearty fare. Cajun food began in Southern France, moved on to Nova Scotia and then came to Louisiana. The Acadians adapted their dishes to use ingredients that grew wild in the area—bay leaves from the laurel tree, filé powder from the sassafras tree and an abundance of different peppers such as cayenne, Tabasco peppers, banana peppers and bird's eye peppers that grow wild in South Louisiana—learning their uses from the native Indians. . . .

But Creole food, unlike Cajun, began in New Orleans and is a mixture of the traditions of French, Spanish,

for lunch at Robin's Restaurant on our journey through Louisiana early in 1985, and we were rewarded with a crawfish bisque so superior that we talked about it for weeks. Months later, I returned to Henderson with a friend and fellow scrivener named Dave to visit Greg and Bubbles Guirard at their farm a few miles down the levee, and in our short stay in the area I got a first-hand account of some of the evolutionary history of Cajun cookery.

Over a mound of boiled crawfish on their kitchen table, Greg and Bubbles talked about food and customs in their native St. Martin Parish. They trace their ancestry to Canada and France, and they think of Cajun culture as still being much more French than Southern. They spoke of men learning to cook at hunting camps deep in the swamps, and of Pie Day, a Good Friday pastry feast that originated in Normandy centuries ago.

"The food we ate at home when we were growing up was in many ways very different from contemporary Cajun restaurant cooking," Bubbles said. "We didn't eat much crawfish then, but we ate plenty of game—squirrel, rabbit, frogs, turtles, venison, duck—and we ate pork and beef and lots of fried catfish. People didn't have big gardens the way they did in other parts of the South, so our vegetables were mainly such staples as rice, red beans, white beans, sweet corn, and sweet potatoes—we called them *bon bon du close,* candy from the field. We often had coush-coush at breakfast or supper, and our main breads were French loaves and biscuits, with cane syrup to pour over them."

The Guirards still enjoy preparing many of those foods, as well as such traditional specialties as gumbo and jambalaya. Both are skilled cooks whose repertoire also includes boudin, étouffée, bisque, and alligator sauce piquante. They like to eat out, too, especially at the good Cajun restaurants in the area.

Dave and I had time for a couple of meals in Henderson, and we chose well. We had lunch with Pat Huval, the first and only mayor of the town and the owner of Pat's Fisherman's Wharf Cafe on Bayou Amy in the shadow of the levee. "I'm the original," he said. "I bought Henry Guidry's old cafe and dance-hall in 1954 and put crawfish on the menu—and I put Henderson on the map, too. We've got several good restaurants here now, but they all learned from me."

Actually, Pat's Water Front Restaurant, directly across the canal from Fisherman's Wharf, is the original Huval place. The mayor's former wife, Agnes "Vieille" Huval, retained it in their divorce settlement, and because of the obvious advantage of name recognition in a well-regarded restaurant, she also retained the right to call the place Pat's. Thus, confusingly, Henderson has two fine Cajun restaurants named Pat's—the new one belonging to Pat himself, and the old one owned by his ex-wife. There is also Las's, which belongs to Pat's brother. The complex genealogy aside, all three are highly rated dining places.

At the mayor's table, I ordered a house specialty called Jambalaya, Crawfish Pie and Filé Gumbo—the name borrowed from the classic old Hank Williams

Italian, American Indian, African and other ethnic groups. Seven flags flew over New Orleans in the early days, and each time a new nation took over . . . most of their cooks and other servants stayed behind. The position of cook was highly esteemed and the best paid position in the household. Those cooks, most of whom were black, would be hired by other families, often of a different nationality. . . . Over a period of time, they learned how to cook for a variety of nationalities, and they incorporated their own spicy, home-style way of cooking into the different cuisines of their employers. . . . Creole cooking is more sophisticated and complex than Cajun cooking— it's city cooking.

Today, in homes, there is still a distinction between Cajun and Creole cooking; in restaurants, little distinction remains. That's why I've begun referring to the two together as one—Louisiana cooking.

Paul Prudhomme
*Chef Paul Prudhomme's
Louisiana Kitchen, 1984*

song—and every dish in the combination was cooked to perfection. In addition to the three named items, the dinner included fried crawfish tails and a small serving of étouffée, as well as a pineapple-and-Cheddar cheese salad on lettuce.

"I was the first man to design a crawfish dinner like that," Pat Huval said proudly. "They all have a tough time beating me. I'm deep-down Cajun, and I can cook with anybody."

For lunch the next day, we met Greg and Bubbles Guirard at Robin's, and it was a perfect conclusion to a short but satisfying Louisiana restaurant safari. Lionel and Peggy Robin, the owners and principal chefs, joined us at the table for part of our two-hour course of food and conversation; so did Aristile Robin, Lionel's father, and George Depuis, a family friend from Lafayette who happened by. We made our way through servings of boiled crawfish, bisque, boulettes (ground crawfish rolled into balls, floured, and deep-fried), crawfish gumbo, fried crawfish, and crawfish pie (étouffée baked on a very light and flaky round of pie crust). The various dishes of crabmeat, frog legs, catfish, red snapper, shrimp, and oysters we reluctantly but necessarily left for another time; this was the occasion for a crawfish feast, and it would be impossible to imagine a more sumptuous one.

"My father and mother worked in Henry Guidry's cafe, the first one here," Lionel Robin said, "and then they started their own place, Robin's Seafood, in 1947. I grew up around that place, so I've got it in my blood. Peggy and I built this restaurant in 1974. She's a master chef, the very best. We do almost all the cooking, the two of us."

The conversation turned to Paul Prudhomme and to the Cajun craze that had swept the country. (In the first week of 1986, a food writer for *Time* magazine reported that Cajun fare was in eclipse. "Small wonder," she wrote, "when the gumbos, jambalayas and red beans of Louisiana became overworked into clichés.")

"Prudhomme has done more for Cajun food than Muhammad Ali did for boxing," Lionel Robin said. "His particular style of cooking is not Cajun—it's just his own—but it has put this region and its food in the national spotlight, and we're all grateful to him for that. It may be that the best Cajun restaurant food can't be duplicated outside this region. Time will tell. But I know this: Consistency is what makes a great restaurant. We stay in our league, in our ballpark. We do what we do best—and only that—and we stake our reputation on it."

When the "new American cuisine" versions of Cajun cookery have faded from sight and memory in Manhattan and California and the French Quarter and new culinary fads have taken their place, chances are better than even that you'll still be able to get a superlative Cajun meal in places like Henderson, Louisiana.

By the Waters

The mention of Southern food commonly brings to mind certain dishes steeped in tradition and history: pork and corn, grits and greens, black-eyed peas, country ham, fried chicken, barbecue, cornbread and biscuits, chess pie, peach cobbler. But as Louisiana's rich gastronomic heritage clearly shows, there is much more to the foods of the South than these features, extraordinary as they are. The creatures of fin and shell are far more important than pigs and chickens to the cooks of Louisiana, and yet the essence of Creole and Cajun cookery is as inseparably Southern as ribs and roasting ears and hoecake.

It is the same with Southern cooking elsewhere along the coast. From Louisiana around the Gulf crescent to the tip of Florida and up the Eastern Seaboard to Virginia and beyond, the sea has always been dominant in the diet of the people, yielding up to them an unending abundance of oysters, shrimp, crabs, and fish of all kinds. This saltwater harvest is the heart and soul of coastal cookery. In the interior regions, food from freshwater sources also plays an important part in defining what people eat. Among the more appreciated delicacies are frog legs and turtle meat and alligator tail. Mountain brook trout and numerous other kinds of fish are plentiful in some places, and the once-lowly catfish has made it into the chain-restaurant kitchens and is fast becoming a national favorite. Louisiana crawfish are another freshwater resource, of course. All in all, the products of Southern rivers, lakes, and seas make up a substantial and indispensable part of the region's total menu.

This water-based dimension of Southern food is no recent addition to the diet, either; in fact, the Indians who were here when the first Europeans arrived had long since mastered the art of shucking oysters, both raw ones straight from the water and those they roasted in the fire, and they ate shrimp and crabs and fish more frequently than Southerners do now. Seafood is not in any sense an exclusively Southern comestible, but it has been a primary component of the regional diet for all the four hundred years of its recorded history. Now, the trend away from heavy consumption of red meat is making fish and shellfish more important than ever in the cookery of the South.

Oysters are a prime example of a universal seafood with a particular link to the South. The ancient Greeks and Romans devoured oysters, harvesting them in the bays and channels where they grew wild and learning early to cultivate them, so that by the sixteenth century they were as common as cabbages all over Europe. So plentiful and cheap were they, in fact, that they were not only a delight of kings and gourmets but a staple in the diet of many poor people as well. Then as now, they were both coveted and shunned by large numbers of

The lands are laden with large tall oaks, walnut and bayes, excepting facing the sea, it is most pines tall and good. Good soyl . . . and we think may produce any thing as well as most part of the Indies that we have seen . . . Plenty of corn, pompions (squash), water-mellons, musk-mellons . . . The countrey abounds with grapes, large figs and peaches; the woods with deer, conies, turkeys, quails, curlues, plovers, teile, herons . . . and innumerable of other water-fowls whose names we know not, which lie in the rivers, marshes, and on the sands; oysters in abundance, with a great store of muscles; a sort of fair crabs and a round shelfish called horse-feet. The rivers are stored plentifully with fish that we saw play and leap.

William Hilton
Voyage to the Carolina Coast, 1664

people, there being no apparent middle ground in the love-hate business of oyster eating.

The species *Crassostrea virginica,* so named because biologists first identified it on the Virginia shore, was thriving all along the Atlantic coast when the explorers arrived from Europe. In the bays and estuaries where salt water and fresh water come together, they were astonished to find oysters as big as pies, weighing a pound or more, and those whose taste ran to such behemoths delighted in them. Even the more squeamish eventually ate them, more out of necessity than choice. The remnant of Jamestown colonists who survived the threat of starvation in the winter of 1609 probably would not have made it without *C. virginica.*

By the time of the Revolution, Americans from New England to Louisiana were rapidly developing a robust appetite for these native American oysters, and in the nineteenth century they spread like the wind across the continent. Enterprising merchants on the coast discovered that in the colder months from September to April, oysters could be kept in their shells for weeks without spoiling. Soon they were packing them in barrels or under damp straw and ice and sending large quantities in wagon trains and steamboats to distant outposts of the nation's interior. Canned and pickled oysters also became popular. It seemed that virtually all who so desired could have their fill of oysters for a pittance, and such a plentiful "food of the people" meshed easily with America's expansive and democratic image of itself. Kentucky native Abraham Lincoln embellished that image by hosting all-you-can-eat oyster parties in Springfield, Illinois, hundreds of miles from the nearest coast. At that time, plump bivalves as big as goose eggs could be had in the oyster houses of New Orleans and Charleston for a dime a dozen.

The golden age of oysters reached its peak in about 1850, and since then they have grown smaller, less plentiful, and more expensive. Hurricanes, pollution, coastal encroachment by developers, and the insatiable gluttony of oyster lovers have combined to deplete the great spawning beds along the Atlantic and Gulf coasts, lowering the quality and driving up the price. Even so, such names as Bon Secour and Apalachicola and Chesapeake still stand for the best, and a few fine old oyster bars in New Orleans and a handful of other ports continue to offer eye-catching and palate-pleasing quality on the half shell.

Oystermen in the Chesapeake Bay, where competitors from Virginia and Maryland have carried on an intermittent war for more than three centuries, are still intensely vying for the dwindling harvest. In the shallow coastal waters of the Carolinas, along the Atlantic and Gulf costs of Florida, in the waters off Alabama and Mississippi, and along the shores of Louisiana and Texas, a similar competition is staged daily. This vast expanse of Southern coastline, zigzagging for thousands of miles from Baltimore and the Eastern Shore to Port Arthur

MR. LONG. Mr. President, people up in this part of the country never have learned to fry oysters as well as we have done down our way. . . . I had a bucket of oysters sent to me from Louisiana the other night, and I was asked by a very fine bunch of my friends if I would not drop around with the New Orleans oysters and fry some of them for them in good Louisiana style and way. So, Mr. President, I bought a frying pan about 8 inches deep . . . and about 17 inches in diameter . . . and I bought a 10-pound bucket of

and the southern rim of Texas, is the principal oyster-producing region of the United States, now as ever.

The same waters also yield an abundance of shrimp. Like oysters, shrimp are found in many parts of the world, and no region can claim them as an original or exclusive delicacy. The South, though, has supplied the lion's share of all the shrimp eaten in the United States since pre-Columbian times, and as supplies of the ten-legged crustaceans have diminished, Southern fishermen have led the fleets farther out to sea in search of them.

Shrimp are the most popular shellfish in the United States, more so than lobsters or crabs or crawfish (oysters, though they live in shells, are not classified as shellfish). Indians and Europeans in the seventeenth century considered shrimp a great delicacy, but until about 1920 they could be enjoyed only by people living on or near the coast, simply because they were so quickly perishable out of the water. Combustion engines gave offshore trawlers mechanized nets and a wider range, and refrigeration allowed them to harvest on a commercial scale and transport the catch to distant markets. Freezing added further to the shrimper's capability. By the mid-1930s, the shellfish could be found as an expensive "cocktail" treat on some menus in Chicago and other inland cities. Only since the 1950s, though, have shrimp become commonplace in cookbooks and restaurants around the nation.

The Gulf of Mexico is the richest shrimping bed in the world, and the Atlantic offshore from Florida and the Carolinas is also a fertile harvesting area. Thus, ports between Norfolk and New Orleans commonly offer live shrimp in abundance, and restaurants along the coast serve them up fried, boiled, broiled, grilled, smoked, baked, and barbecued, as well as combined with other seafoods in a variety of rich dishes. Cities within a few hours' drive of the coast also serve fresh shrimp trucked daily from dockside sources. The seafood specialties that modern methods of preservation now make available to everyone used to be an exclusive privilege of coastal Southerners, and they incorporated shrimp into their cooking long before cookbooks in other parts of the country even mentioned them. Harriott Horry's eighteenth-century recipe collection in South Carolina indicates that she often served shrimp, oysters, and crabs at her table.

Crabs are another of the South's crustacean specialties (a Pacific and North Atlantic favorite too), and the sweet white meat shows up in all sorts of savory stews, soups, and baked dishes. Stuffed crab, deviled crab, crab cakes, she-crab soup, soft-shelled crab, and deep-fried crab claws are among the most familiar and cherished preparations of the shellfish in Southern kitchens. With oysters, shrimp, and crawfish, crabs make up a favorite foursome in the parade of shell-dwelling seafoods that Southerners have harvested from saltwater and fresh-water sources for centuries.

Snapper, flounder, grouper, mullet, shad, trout, and bass are among the

cottonseed-oil lard . . . and when I got to the place to fry the oysters I had everything there except the meal and the strainer. . . . I took the oysters, Mr. President, the way they should be taken, and laid them out on a muslin cloth, about 12 of them. . . . You dry them, you see, first with a muslin cloth, and then you take the oysters . . . and you roll them into a meal which is salted. . . . Then, let the grease get boiling hot. You want the grease about 6 inches deep. Then you take the oysters and you place the oysters in the strainer, and you put the strainer in the grease. . . . Then, you fry those oysters in boiling grease until they turn a gold-copper color and rise to the top, and then, you take them out and let them cool just a little bit before you eat them.

MR. TYDINGS. Does the Senator realize when he describes how these oysters are cooked and how appetizing they seem to be, that those of us who are listening are being inhumanly punished? [Laughter.]

MR. LONG. I had forgotten that.

Senator Huey Long of Louisiana, in a filibuster oration, June 12, 1935

finned fish that enjoy wide appeal in the region. But the newest star in Southern waters is the whiskered, scaleless catfish, a rags-to-riches swimmer in rivers and ponds everywhere.

Time was when the channel catfish, an omnivorous scavenger and bottom feeder in American waters, could get no respect from fish eaters outside the South. Matters worsened in the years after World War II as pollution ruined both the taste and the nutritious qualities of river cats. "It may be suspected that a sort of catfish cult which leads Southerners to speak sentimentally of this fish and class it with 'soul food' comes under the heading of local pride," wrote food historian Waverley Root disdainfully. "True, catfish flesh is fine-grained, there are not many bones, and it has a sweet taste, but it lacks character."

Deservedly or not (and many Southerners thought not), the much-abused catfish appeared doomed to permanent status as a lowly trash food eaten mainly by the poor. But then, in the mid-1960s, farmers in Mississippi and elsewhere in the South began to experiment with the raising of catfish as a systematically planned farm crop. In just twenty years, they have increased the harvest to nearly 200 million pounds a year, and in Mississippi alone, there are now about 75,000 acres of catfish ponds—three fourths of the total acreage nationwide. Most of the rest are in Arkansas, Alabama, and Louisiana. Mississippi farmers facing the worst depression since the 1930s began to turn their fortunes around by plowing up their cotton and soybean fields and digging catfish ponds instead. For some, the turnaround has been profoundly dramatic.

Belzoni, Mississippi, in Humphreys County, calls itself the "Catfish Capital of the World" and celebrates the claim each spring by staging the "World Catfish Festival." The county has a right to crow; its nearly 25,000 acres of custombuilt fish ponds make up one third of the state total and equal the combined acreage of all other states except Mississippi. (As far as festivals go, however, the catfish bash in Paris, Tennessee, has a leg up on Belzoni. They bill theirs as "The World's Biggest Fish Fry." It's been held each April since 1954, and in 1986 the town served up ten thousand pounds of catfish to 75,000 people during the week-long celebration.)

From the digging of the ponds to the stocking, feeding, harvesting, and processing of the fish, the catfish industry in the South is becoming a model of quality control and efficiency. More to the point, the end product is a rare anomaly in the food world: an artificially developed and mass-processed package food that tastes better than its "natural" predecessor. It's also cleaner, healthier, and more appealing to the eye.

The Church's Fried Chicken chain based in San Antonio, Texas, gave the catfish industry a tremendous boost in 1985 when it added pond-raised cats to its fast-food menu. Church's ordered 54 million pounds of the fish—one fourth of the industry's total annual output—and found to its delight that the tasty and nutritious fried fillets were an immediate success, not just in the South but all over the country.

More and more Deep South farmers now dream of reversing their downward slide with this new cash crop, King Catfish. It can be grown continuously, harvested the year around, and restocked perpetually. At the table, it is high in protein, low in fat and cholesterol, versatile as a single dish or in combination with others, and pleasing to the taste in almost any form. Waverley Root to the contrary, catfish *does* have character, and there are restaurants in almost every Southern state where the cooking of it has been elevated to a fine art. If Mississippi and the other states where catfish farming has caught on should find themselves on the leading edge of a new culinary wave, there are legions of catfish lovers across the South who would observe the phenomenon with a sense of vindication and pride.

Seafood and freshwater cookery in the South is as ancient as the Indians' roast oysters and as contemporary as the Mississippians' pond-raised and deep-fried catfish. We offered a sample of the Louisiana fare along with the Creole and Cajun dishes in the previous chapter; now it's time to look in on about twenty-five representative places in other Southern states where food from the waters dominates the menu.

On a rainy winter day, Al Clayton and I drove seven hundred miles across Georgia and Alabama in a rush to reach Mary's Place for supper. It was pouring when we slipped past Mobile in the dark, but Bayou La Batre and Coden were just a little farther on, nestled against the Gulf, and I had my mouth set on the delicious baked stuffed crabs that the late Mary Branch bequeathed to her family as a culinary heirloom. Her restaurant had been a fixture in Coden since about 1940, and I was urged on by the prospect of settling in for an evening of seafood feasting there.

It was closed. Perhaps the weather was the cause. No one we could find to ask seemed to know when it would reopen. "This is bad news," I said to Al. "It used to be that two of the greatest assets of the Alabama coast were Meme's in Bon Secour, on the east side of Mobile Bay, and Mary's Place here in Coden— two of the finest seafood restaurants you could ever hope to find anywhere. Now Meme's is gone, and Mary's may be too. What is this world coming to?"

Al was glassy-eyed. "I'm hungry," he muttered. "Where are we going to eat?" Fortunately, I still had at least two good answers.

Wintzell's Oyster House in Mobile is remembered for two things: great seafood for lunch and dinner, and ten thousand signs of political commentary, personal philosophy, and cornball humor on the walls. J. Oliver Wintzell, a pudgy, cigar-chewing Mobilian with a quick wit and a keen business eye, opened the place in 1938. Now it sprawls through several rooms, seats 350 people, and

SUNFLOWER, Miss.—Turner Arant wasn't exactly there at the creation, but he was close enough to be called a pioneer, and he gets a visionary gleam in his eye when he starts talking about the ponds.

They stretch for miles across the flat Mississippi River Delta, squarish breaks among the cotton, soybeans and rice, and they hide one of the best kept secrets in American agriculture.

The secret is the catfish. Plain old channel catfish.

Turner Arant, of course, is in on the secret. He's been raising catfish in his ponds for 20 years and is a messianic promoter of the glory of these farm-grown, grain-fed fish that provide income for hundreds of farmers. . . . These fish, fed a sophisticated mix of grains just as a farmer would feed hogs or cattle, produce a flaky, delicate meat that is rapidly finding its way to American dinner tables. . . . It doesn't take much leap of fancy to see the low-fat, high-protein catfish one day becoming as basic to the American diet as beef, pork and poultry.

Ward Sinclair,
in the Washington Post,
April 4, 1983

bustles with an active and lively trade. You can entertain yourself reading the signs, or you can sit down at the counter in front of someone like Willie Brown, an employee there for twenty years, and get into some serious eating while he shucks twenty-five to thirty dozen oysters in an hour. We chose eating.

"Oysters fried . . . stewed . . . & nude," said the menu. "We sell fresh seafoods, nothing prebreaded, so it takes a little longer." The choices included seafood gumbo, stuffed flounder, catfish and hush puppies, stuffed crab, crabmeat omelet, broiled snapper, stuffed shrimp. Two south Alabama regional favorites were also featured: West Indies salad and deep-fried crab claws. William Bayley, founder of another popular Mobile restaurant, brought the salad recipe from the Caribbean in the 1940s. Its essence is crabmeat marinated in a vinegar and oil dressing seasoned with onions and spices. The crab claws are claimed by several area restaurateurs.

J. Oliver Wintzell died in 1980, but the present owners have kept the place in the founder's style. "He used to shuck oysters with a cigar in his mouth, and he couldn't shuck and talk too, so he put up the signs," explained Tom Burke, Jr., the manager. "He was a phenomenal character. It wouldn't be the same place without his signs."

It wouldn't be the same place without people like Willie Brown, either, he and the forty or fifty cooks and table servers who make Wintzell's a prime place for seafood. I had a cup of gumbo, a West Indies salad, and an oyster loaf, and every bite was a delight. Al ordered oyster stew and a dozen on the half-shell. "They're as fine as I've ever eaten," he said when he had finished. "Fresh, salty, plump—just precisely the oyster flavor you always hope for but seldom get."

A plaque on the wall behind Willie Brown named Jimmy Langford as the all-time oyster-eating champion at Wintzell's—he downed 247 in twenty-five minutes back in 1975. I found him in the local phone book and gave him a call. "The rules allowed an hour," he explained modestly, "but I quit a lot sooner because I didn't want to put the record out of reach."

When we finally located Wolf Bay Lodge on the east side of Mobile Bay the next day, owners Charlie and Sandy Wrape were enjoying a mid-afternoon break between lunch and dinner crowds. The restaurant is not easy to find. For mail delivery purposes it's at Miflin, but actually it sits beyond a grove of pines at the end of an unmarked sandy lane. Wolf Bay doesn't advertise or take reservations, but almost every night several hundred people show up at its door.

Alabama native Frye Gaillard, a *Charlotte Observer* writer, is one of the occasional Wolf Bay visitors. "As a lover of truth and a reporter thoroughly schooled in the principles of objectivity," he once wrote, "I am here to testify that [Wolf Bay cuisine] is the finest food ever cooked."

What drove Gaillard to such a reckless assertion was Sandy Wrape's fried crab claws. The boiled claws, about three or four inches long, are lightly breaded and deep-fried to a golden brown in pure vegetable shortening. They look like miniature chicken drumsticks loaded with tender white meat. Dipped in a cocktail sauce or a butter and lemon sauce, they are simply delicious. It might be closer to true objectivity to say that several Alabama Gulf Coast restaurants excel at these morsels, but none outshines Wolf Bay Lodge.

It is from places like Miflin, Coden, Bayou La Batre, and Bon Secour that the fine upstate Alabama seafood restaurants get their fresh catches daily via refrigerated trucks. The Elite in Montgomery, John's in Birmingham, and the Bright Star in Bessemer are foremost among them. Another is Walt's Seafood in Opelika. Owners Walt and Margaret Williford opened the place in 1972, and word-of-mouth praise soon brought a steady stream of seafood-hungry diners to their door. At first, he drove the truck on the four-hundred-mile round-trip route to the coast and she did the cooking; now they're doing well enough to have plenty of help at both ends. "We prepare every order individually," Walt Williford said. "It takes a lot of time, but that's the only way to treat fresh seafood."

Florida is synonymous with seafood. It is also a deceptively large state (nearly a thousand miles from Pensacola to Key West), and I didn't begin to touch all its bases. In two forays there, circumstances kept me from reaching Key West and the lower east coast, where a substantial part of Florida's culinary reputation resides. But we did sample some fine seafood from the Panhandle to Fort Myers and in the northeast coastal counties—and almost every stop turned out to be a winner.

At the Oaks Motel and Restaurant beside the Ochlockonee River in Panacea, for example, we encountered some very spicy shrimp, oyster, and okra gumbo, an artistically designed cold shrimp plate with Greek salad, and the standard array of flounder, snapper, grouper, and mullet dishes for which Florida is famous. Alton and Ora Oaks founded the place in 1953, and it has since built a loyal clientele by delivering consistent quality from the kitchen.

At St. Marks, where the Panhandle coastline begins to bend toward the south, T. J. Posey built a restaurant in the 1930s, and the sea-weathered old building is still headquarters for two of the Gulf Coast's culinary treasures: smoked mullet and hush puppies. Posey has passed on and Bill Helson now owns the place, but nothing appears to have changed since the long-ago days when Posey was the local mayor and the restaurant was called City Hall Cafe. Whether or not Posey's is the true home of the hush puppy, as the menu claims, it is indisputably one of the prime makers of that cornmeal delicacy, and the smoked mullet is delicious too—one-pound fish about eight inches long, cooked to a deep brown over a slow fire. The meat is smoky-rich but mild, and tender enough to fall from the bones.

Far to the south on Captiva Island, where the romance of Spanish exploration and piracy linger in the intermingling of history and legend, Ann and I stopped for lunch at Timmy's Nook, a restaurant and marina, and co-owner Charlotta Carper gave me a capsule version of her family's odyssey. "My grandmother migrated here from Canada in the 1890s," she said. "Homesteaded on Buck Key, and then moved here to Captiva in 1903. She was a real frontier woman, twice-married and very independent. I thought the world of her. My mother was one of her daughters. She married my father, Thomas Mahlon, a farmer from Griffin, Georgia. They had seven daughters. Finally, my father built this restaurant to escape female domination at home. His nickname was Timmy."

Timmy's Nook thrives on seafood—oysters on the half-shell, boiled shrimp, stone crab claws, broiled grouper and snapper and flounder, and sometimes a pleasant surprise: deep-fried barracuda fillets. There's an excellent shrimp scampi dish, too—jumbo shrimp sautéed in butter, garlic, oregano, and white wine. And on the day we stopped, another treat came in the form of a lime pie made with real Key limes. "It's rare to get these anymore," said Charlotta Carper. "They don't keep well, and you seldom see them growing." A barracuda for lunch and a slice of genuine Key lime pie gave us a south Florida dining experience to remember.

On the east coast, we found a late-night catch of fresh seafood at Oyster Island, a restaurant near Cape Canaveral that boasted "the world's longest raw bar." The raw and steamed oysters, boiled shrimp, and smoked mullet were served at their peak, and the bar did indeed seem long enough to qualify for some sort of record. And at Whitey's Fish Camp on a tributary of the majestic Johns River near Orange Park, we ate a sampling of catfish, oysters, frog legs, quail, and turtle with puffy, golf-ball-sized hush puppies, all of it cooked to order and served with crisp and crunchy fresh cole slaw.

Seafood restaurants are everywhere now, of course, but there is something about the cookery and the character of many Southern seaside places that sets them apart. Some of the difference is in the menu, in such local and regional specialties as smoked mullet, she-crab soup, creek shrimp, roasted oysters, deep-fried crab claws. Part of it may also be in the air of informality and familiarity that seems to surround cooks, cashiers, waitresses, fishermen, patrons, and even strangers passing through. No matter how universal the fare becomes, seafood remains an integral part of restaurant and home cooking in the South, and dining on fresh seafood in Florida and the Carolinas and other coastal states is almost always a delightful experience.

Georgia's hundred-mile strip of Atlantic coastline is dotted with cities, towns, and end-of-the-road villages with seashore names: Pine Harbor, Sea Island, Shellman Bluff. Savannah is the last and largest stop on the northbound

A local fish dish that residents of the Carolina Sea Islands have been enjoying for more years than anybody can trace has become a current favorite at some fancy restaurants in Charleston and some of the resorts along the Carolina coast. Called Frogmore stew, it is what the natives of the coast, many of whom are shrimp fishermen, eat on the sort of ritual occasion that their inland neighbors might celebrate with a barbecue. This folk dish is a highly

road into South Carolina. There are too many promising seafood houses in Savannah to make a passing visitor's choice easy. Going as much on the sound of the name as anything else, we picked Teeple Seafood Restaurant in Thunderbolt, a venerable town in the metropolitan area that historians say is "older than Oglethorpe," the founder of Georgia. Indians reportedly named Thunderbolt after they saw lightning strike there and bring forth a spring of water.

Charlie Teeple was born and raised in Thunderbolt. "I sold boiled crabs on the street corner in Savannah when I was a kid," he said. He still sells crabs—and oysters, hard-shelled rock shrimp, clams, scallops, flounder, and even conch chowder, a delicacy seldom found north of the Florida Keys. The restaurant is a no-frills model of utilitarian simplicity: concrete floors, gunny-sack wall coverings, tables with eight-inch-square holes in the center and plastic-lined garbage cans beneath to receive discarded shells. Newspapers serve as placemats, and there is a roll of paper towels on each table.

Steamed oysters arrive in the shell and by the bucketful to be opened with knives by each diner. Shellfish also come wearing their natural armor. (The hard-shelled rock shrimp are especially interesting—and delicious.) Drawn butter and cocktail sauce are available, and cold drinks, and not much else. This is major-league seafood eating, serious and sustained, albeit friendly and cheerful. The customers are an uncommon mix of white and black, working-class and professional. They bend to the task, and the clash of steel and shell echoes from table to table like epées in a fencing class. Affable, easy-going Charlie Teeple contentedly observes the proceedings from behind the cash register. The knives and shells are playing his tune.

Just across the Savannah River lies South Carolina, and the low-country expanse of creeks and rivers, salt marshes, and sea islands that extends for almost two hundred miles to the North Carolina border is a haven of seafood cookery and history. From Beaufort to Myrtle Beach, the South Carolina coast presents many contrasts: cities and towns and unpopulated pine forests, exclusive new resorts and weather-beaten old vacation cottages, row-crop agriculture and heavy industry, eighteenth-century plantation splendor and twentieth-century urban blight. Charleston, the dowager queen of Southern cities, is itself a study in contrasts. In all of these places, no common denominator is stronger than the pull of the ever-present sea, and no common interest is greater than the seafoods that have sustained Carolinians for centuries.

The restaurants reflect this admixture of unity and diversity. Some aspire to a modern style of dining elegance, others cling to a familiar pattern of coastal traditions, still others follow a path of functional simplicity, yet all of them draw both inspiration and nourishment from the harvest of the sea. Regardless of style or station, nothing is more basic and essential to cooks in the Carolina low country than local fresh oysters, crabs, shrimp, and fish.

seasoned stew of such improbably combined ingredients as sausage and shrimp and crabs plus some other things like corn on the cob. The people who make the stew often boil the ingredients in beer.

The dish gets its name from a place that has only a post office on one side of the road and a two-story white country store on the other. Frogmore is the mailing address . . . for the residents of St. Helena Island. . . . Frogmore stew is only one of many examples of Gullah life surviving on St. Helena. . . .

When it comes to Frogmore stew, every man is his own best chef. But all recipes have hot sausage, corn and shrimp in whatever amounts the cook chooses, and it doesn't seem to matter to those who eat it. The common denominator of Frogmore stew seems to be: "There's never any left."

*George McMillan,
in The New York Times,
February 2, 1986*

There are many fine seafood restaurants on the South Carolina coast—fancy ones in the resort communities, traditional ones in places like Mt. Pleasant and Murrells Inlet, newer ones from Beaufort to Charleston to Myrtle Beach. And then there is Bowen's Island Seafood Restaurant, a forty-year-old establishment on a seventeen-acre island in the salt marshes south of Charleston. A *Vanity Fair* writer once showed up there in a chauffeured limousine and went away later trailing words of wonder and praise. His subsequent article on Charleston was about "the juxtaposition of grace and decay." Such imagery has been applied before to Charleston and the greater South. It could also be said of Bowen's Island itself. "It'll never win the Good Housekeeping award," a Carolina friend told us, "but it's special, it truly is. Bowen's Island is one of a kind."

On our first search for it, we drove three times past the narrow, rutted lane of packed sand that knifes through the salt marsh from Folly Road. Taking the right turn finally, we bounced past a couple of mobile homes in the dark, followed the wrong path to the water's edge at high tide, corrected course into a thicket of pines and palmetto clumps, and ended up in front of a squat, square, concrete-block building that looked as if it were propped up and held in place by the dense undergrowth and pyramids of oyster shells around it.

Several cats lounged lazily amid the clutter on the screened front porch. Inside, a single large booth and a dozen rickety tables with unmatched chairs awaited the evening trade. In one corner, echoes of another era drifted up from an antique Seeburg jukebox—Tommy Dorsey and Benny Goodman and Bing Crosby at a bargain tariff of five plays for a quarter. Next to the juke, heaped upon a table, were dozens of spiral notebooks filled with the poetic and confessional ramblings of four decades of patrons. "Dear whoever takes the time to read this," began a 1969 entry in one of the books, "I came here alone tonight. . . . This place holds a lot of memories. . . ."

The walls were a solid thicket of carved and painted graffiti, partially covered with dime-store prints and original works of amateur artists. Also hanging there was the establishment's only menu: shrimp dinner $3, seafood platter $4, steamed oysters $7. There were some laudatory press clippings, too, and old photographs, and beer signs. In the kitchen, Jimmy Bowen sat serenely in a battered easy chair surrounded by dusty heaps of old books and unassorted odds and ends. May Bowen, his wife, a diminutive woman with an alert and unblinking gaze, watched us from behind the counter. John Sanka, the cook, busied himself around the gas stove in the back.

We ordered the shrimp and seafood platters and watched as Sanka pan-fried all the fish and the hush puppies in black iron skillets. Mrs. Bowen served the meal straight from the stove with a few condiments on paper plates. The fish and shrimp were lightly battered and tasty, the pups crunchy and piping hot. It was a slow night, and May Bowen was in a talkative mood.

My father, Alexander McIntosh Durant, got into the commercial shrimping business in about 1930. Up until then, there wasn't much shrimp harvesting done except in the bays and inlets, and the only market for them was for home eating along the coast. Restaurants didn't serve much shrimp, and nobody ate them inland. Most people thought of them as sea worms, if they thought of them at all.

But then the internal combustion engine and the diesel engine came

"My family goes back a long way in Charleston County," she said. "My parents were raised on the Edisto River, and I grew up here too. I've lived outside—Philadelphia and around—but I'm always glad to get back home. I never liked it inland, never liked the hills and mountains. You can never see what's on the other side. Here, you can see forever, just like the song says."

Jimmy Bowen migrated south from Baltimore in the 1920s. An ex-marine, a prizefighter, a semipro baseball player, he was at heart a survivor, and he stayed, working as a printer and playing trombone in a dance band. "I met him at a dance in Savannah," May Bowen recalled. "We got married in 1935." Several years later, at a U.S.O. dance, they became friends with John Sanka, a navy cook from Pennsylvania, and when he left the service he joined the Bowens in pursuit of May's dream: to build a boating club and fishing haven on a little salt-marsh island she had bought for a song near the road to Folly Beach.

At high tide it was accessible only by boat, so they built a causeway. The dock and the clubhouse followed, but that's as far as the money and the dream would reach. There were not enough members, and better-financed enterprises soon passed them by. "I was looking forward to no more cooking," said Mrs. Bowen, "but the restaurant turned out to be all we had, and down through the years we've had a lot of very satisfied and faithful customers. People come here from all over the world, but most folks around Charleston don't even know about us. All they've got to do is drive out here. We're open from eight in the morning until ten in the evening, three hundred sixty-five days a year."

Four decades after they started their ambitious project, the aging trio remained in residence on the island. Nothing had changed, not even the menu. In a long, narrow room off the main dining room, John Sanka prepared the house specialty, roast oysters. A quiet, bookish man, he looked older than his seventy-three years, and a young assistant was taking over the strenuous task from him. Jimmy Bowen was eighty-six and in poor health. May Bowen, seventy-five, was the strongest of the three, a feisty scrapper, proud and stubborn. "We'll never leave," she said defiantly, with the slightest trace of a smile. "Why should we? We have everything right here."

Of all the intriguing dimensions to Bowen's Island, it is the oyster roast that lingers in my memory, not because the oysters were superior (they were good, not great), but because the ritual of their preparation is older than the South itself. "The Indians used to do it like this," John Sanka said. In fact, it was at Port Royal, just a short distance down from the Carolina coast, that native hosts first served Spanish explorers roast oysters from the open fire in 1566, or so the story goes.

At Bowen's Island, the process begins each day when local fishermen harvest the oysters from the surrounding creekbeds and shorelines and bring them in bushel baskets to the restaurant. When I returned on another evening to enjoy

into general use, and that made it possible for the boats to go out farther in the ocean, and to harvest large quantities of shrimp in big mechanically operated nets. And then refrigeration and freezing came along, and that meant this highly perishable food could be kept fresh longer. After World War II, shrimp started showing up on restaurant menus and in cookbooks—and now, of course, they're popular everywhere.

Over fifty years ago, before all that happened, my father and his brother were driving to the Fulton Fish Market in New York almost every week—that's a round trip of over 1,600 miles—with several hundred pounds of green [fresh] shrimp iced down in the back end of their Model T truck. New York had a European population that was used to eating all kinds of seafood, from snails to squid, so there was a market for shrimp up there.

Charles Durant,
of Darien, Georgia,
in a 1985 interview

the experience, Sanka's understudy, Doug Mahan, built a roaring blaze in the fireplace at one end of the oyster room. As the guests began to arrive and take seats at newspaper-covered tables, Mahan heaped bushels of oysters in the shell onto a heavy metal plate suspended over the fire. He poured a pitcher of sea water over the shells and covered the mound with a wet burlap sack. Billows of steam rolled forth and mingled with the wood smoke. In a few minutes, the intense heat and steam began to crack the shells open. Mahan scooped them up in a wide-blade shovel and deposited them in front of a party of waiting eaters who began shucking them with oyster knives, devouring the juicy mollusks with a touch of seasoning as they went. The procedure was repeated for each table of diners, and it continued until they could eat no more.

Long after May and Jimmy Bowen and John Sanka are gone and their island retreat has disappeared, memories of the atmosphere they created there will remain—the plaintive messages in the notebooks, the strains of Benny Goodman's clarinet, the crisp and tangy flavor of Sanka's pan-fried shrimp, the faces of the aged trio, the pungent odor of steaming oysters and salt water and smoke. The Indians and Spaniards who met at Port Royal 420 years ago would no doubt recognize and appreciate the Bowen's Island enactment of their ancient ritual.

The seafood tradition continues in North Carolina, starting at Calabash, an inlet fishing village just across the state line from the Myrtle Beach area. From there to Virginia by way of the Outer Banks is a three-hundred-mile journey, part of it by ferry boat, and almost every mile of it is an intimate encounter with the Atlantic. In this context, Southern food means, first and foremost, seafood.

"Calabash-style" seafood is advertised up and down the North Carolina coast, and inland too. The meaning of the term is elusive. Does it have to do with a particular style of cooking? If so, no one seems to know what it is. In Calabash, restaurant owners told *New York Times* reporter Steven Roberts a few years ago that Calabash-style meant (a) generous portions, (b) reasonable prices, (c) fresh-caught seafood, (d) a relaxed and homey atmosphere, or (e) what one-time customer Jimmy Durante meant when he closed his broadcasts with the words, "Good night, Mrs. Calabash, wherever you are." The Calabash mystique lives on.

Far up the coast at Nags Head, sisters Judy and Jakey Waits bought a ramshackle, weather-beaten cottage in 1972 where Sam and Omie Tillett, father and son, had started a rustic haven for fishing parties in 1947. "There was nothing out here then," Judy Waits said. "Tom McKimmey bought the place from the Tilletts, and we bought from Tom, and it's never been called anything but Sam and Omie's."

The Waits sisters remodeled. They put checkered oilcloth on the tables, paneling on the walls, curtains at the windows. There is a bar, a jukebox, a pool table, a video game. Fresh flowers grace the tables, but seafood still heads the menu. Some things never change. Clams, crabs, oysters, scallops, and shrimp are cooked to order. "If I wouldn't eat it, I won't let it go out of the kitchen," Judy Waits said. "It fits my definition of Southern, which is as close to fresh and homemade as we can get it." Sam and Omie's has become a forty-year-old Outer Banks tradition.

At Williamston, a hundred miles inland, C. T. Roberson continues an even older tradition: the Sunny Side Oyster Bar, started by his father in 1930. It is a sight to behold. The floor inside the horseshoe bar is covered with sawdust. Naked lightbulbs dangle overhead. There are twenty-two stools around the bar, and every night from October through March they stay filled, while expectant late-comers wait patiently in another room. Behind the bar, a half-dozen young black men are in charge. They wield oyster knives expertly, shucking to keep pace with the eaters, moving with quiet assurance, setting up vessels of drawn butter and cocktail sauce on the side, the latter poured from stainless-steel pitchers, hot both to the touch and the taste. There are fresh steamed shrimp too, and like the oysters they come from the steam room in the back, where C. T. Roberson and his son Charles are the sole conductors. The high-temperature process allows prime oysters from Stumpy Point and Albemarle and elsewhere to simmer in their own salty juices to the stage their customers order, from barely warmed to well-done. They go then in half-peck buckets (15 to 25 oysters, depending on the size) to the shuckers, who deftly place the mollusks one by one in a shallow white dish. As soon as as the diner spears one with his fork and spirits it away, the shucker replaces it with another, hot and juicy, redolent of the sea from which it came.

"I could have made a few improvements over the years, but maybe it's best that I didn't," C. T. Roberson said. "People seem to like the place just the way it is. The millionaire will come in and sit down beside the ditch digger, and they're both content." The Sunny Side is the very essence of what an oyster bar should be.

Our last stop on the Atlantic coast was at Yorktown, Virginia, at the southern end of Chesapeake Bay. Nick and Mary Mathews, immigrants from Greece in the 1920s, built a twenty-four-seat lunch counter there that grew into Nick's Seafood Pavilion, a sprawling, four-hundred-seat restaurant that serves a thousand or more people a night. Their success filled them with a patriotic and philanthropic zeal which inspired them to sponsor and promote *The American Dream,* a permanent exhibit at the Yorktown Victory Center. Nick Mathews died en route to a Mississippi shipyard and the christening of the U.S.S. *Yorktown* in 1983. His wife carries on the philanthropy and the restaurant, where

"Oystering as it is now practiced on the rivers and islands of South Carolina's low country is done in virtually the same manner as it was practiced by the first settlers who carved dugouts from the huge cypress logs and gathered the oysters by hand. The oysterman's boat is a rough-hewn, flat-bottomed vessel known as a bateau. Rugged and river-worthy, these boats, with their long, wide shape, fit perfectly the nature of their function: to receive enormous loads of oysters. They must be loaded with skill and precision; an improperly balanced boat might tip and sink in the choppy water of the incoming tide. . . .

It is a tradition of pride and hard work, and a tradition cloaked in secrecy. A lone oysterman searches not just for any oyster, but for the best oyster, and in places known only to him. Most oystermen work alone, the only sound being the cast-iron claw-tongs crunching into the oysters and the thud as the oysters are slung in one graceful movement into the bateau. "The salt air brings me back in the fall," one man says. "The river is my blood."

Jack Leigh
Oystering, 1983

Chesapeake Bay seafood—fried, baked, and broiled—flows from the gigantic kitchen like produce from a cornucopia.

The nineteenth-century oyster craze that propelled wagonloads of the shelled bivalves far inland established some lasting traditions. One is in Louisville, Kentucky, where Italian immigrant Philip Mazzoni started a bar in 1884. He served oysters raw, stewed, and pan-fried, and he also created the rolled oyster special, a cluster of three or four oysters heavily battered with crumbs and deep-fried into a hand-sized snack. Mazzoni served them free with a mug of beer. Later, he charged a nickel. When the bar celebrated its centennial in 1984, owner Kenny Haner, who is married to a fourth-generation Mazzoni, had a two-for-one rolled oyster special. At ninety-five cents, Philip Mazzoni's creation is still a bargain.

Exceptions like Mazzoni's notwithstanding, strong seafood traditions seldom take hold in cities far distant from the coast. In spite of improved freezing techniques and even the same-day delivery of fresh seafood by air, it is rare for an outstanding restaurant to thrive inland in competition with other more established food styles. Fast-food chains featuring seafood do well in the South and elsewhere, and sit-down chains such as Red Lobster, based in Orlando, Florida, are also popular. By and large, though, when most noncoastal Southerners think of food from the waters, they think of freshwater fish—and in particular, they think of catfish.

One of the curious things about catfish restaurants is how so many good ones are tucked away in small towns off the main highways, or even hidden in backwoods locations far from the nearest paved road. Among Tennessee's most popular places, for example, are Brantley's in Ashland City, Catfish Kitchen near Burns, Pickwick Catfish in Counce, and Catfish Hotel in Shiloh—all small towns, most of them not even on a blue highway. (Shiloh is also known for its Civil War battlefield and for a hush puppy factory that turns out one and a half *million* spicy little cornmeal doughballs every day.) Another Tennessee catfish emporium of some renown, Fuchs' Restaurant near Milan, is hidden from view beside a pond on the back side of a pasture at the end of a winding gravel road.

The same pattern can be found elsewhere in the South. Near Athens, Georgia, Charlie Williams' Pinecrest Lodge and the Swamp Guinea come to mind; near Griffin, Georgia, it's the Lighthouse. Ralph and Mary's, near Forest City, North Carolina, calls itself a fish camp; so does Boyette's near Meridian, Mississippi. Sue & Charlie's has been drawing fish lovers to little Aurora, Kentucky, for over thirty years, and Catfish'N is a popular riverbank restaurant on a back street in Dardanelle, Arkansas. Malone's Fish and Steak House near Tupelo, Mississippi, is another country-lane enterprise, and its reputation in the vicinity

We lived in a section of the Appalachian highlands known as "the goiter belt" because many people suffered in this way due to a lack of iodine in the diet. My own great-grandmother had one of those ugly thyroid growths bulging from her neck. She often was used as an object lesson to exhort the younger generations to "eat right." Fish, we learned early, was good for us.

Our Friday fish meals came mostly from cans, however: salmon patties, tuna casseroles, or sardines on toast. The company-owned meat market in our little coal-mining town almost always had glistening sea bass or rockfish laid out on beds of crushed ice. And they had oysters in season, of course, big vats of them which were dipped out for customers into pint containers made of waxed paper. Fresh seafood was expensive, however, and usually re-

is unassailable. "Is Malone's the best place to eat catfish around here?" I asked a clerk in a convenience store out on the highway. "Around here," he replied, "or anywhere else."

In the tiny village of Taylor, Mississippi, Mary Hudson operates the Taylor Grocery and Restaurant—a genuine country store with a tin roof and a wooden sidewalk and gas pumps out front. The restaurant consists of a few tables in the back end of the store. *Sanctuary,* William Faulkner's novel set in Taylor, is summarized in fifty-eight words penned on the wall by Willie Morris, one of the patron saint's veteran disciples. The big story, though, is the catfish, fried whole or filleted in peanut oil. It is light, moist, tender, flaky, sweet. Slaw, hush puppies, good coffee, and homemade pie round out a fine meal.

Taylor Grocery is yet another in the pattern of country catfish houses. Back in the days when most or all of the fish came from local ponds and rivers, the restaurants tended to spring up close to the favorite haunts of the fishermen, the better to be assured of steady supplies of fresh fish. Now most of it comes cut up and packaged from the plants that process pond-raised cats, and although that has made it possible for restaurants to locate virtually anywhere, a disproportionate number still seem to remain in out-of-the-way locations. What is more, they seldom advertise, and many of them don't even put up signs to guide customers to them.

Riverbend Restaurant, between Thomaston and Woodland, Georgia, is a good example. When I was led there in the dark of night by area residents Andy and Jane Lipscomb, I thought we had come upon a crap game or a cock fight. The building sits on a wooded cliff above rapids of the Flint River, and the dirt road leading to it was lined with parked cars. The decor inside is a sort of rustic modern. There are seats for two hundred people, and on a busy night, three times that many come to eat. J. B. and Celia Berryhill opened the place in 1970, and they have expanded it twice. No crap shooters or cock fighters in this crowd—just serious catfish eaters.

"No need to advertise," said J. B. Berryhill. "We've got all the business we can handle. We buy pond-raised catfish from Alabama, cook it in peanut oil, and change the oil very frequently. That's what makes it good—fresh fish, real potatoes, and homemade hush puppies, all cooked in clean oil and served hot with good slaw and pickles. People just like that combination, and they know they can depend on it to be good, so they keep coming back."

As usual, there are exceptions to the "rural isolation" rule. Cock of the Walk, a "city" fish house born on the east bank of the Mississippi River at Natchez, is now a chain of Cajun-like catfish restaurants springing up in urban areas across the South. Nevertheless, out-of-the-way independents still seem to have the lion's share of character, charm—and good fish.

served in our household for special occasions.

I've often wondered if the idea of fish as "brain food" could have originated with mountain people, who severed their ties with the sea generations ago. Our diet was so rich in animal fats. Pork chops, fried chicken, steak, and wild game were common even for breakfast. Perhaps some instinctive folk wisdom finally surfaced to remind us that fish in the diet would help keep the mind alert and the memory sharp.

Reita Rivers
"Seafood Is Special,"
University of Georgia, 1979

IN THE MISSISSIPPI DELTA

*Suddenly a wagon rumbles up out
of the darkness, dripping water. The
driver jumps down from his seat,
lights two or three lanterns, and in a
loud sing-song cries his wares:*

*"De catfish man is here. De catfish
man is here. Bolivar Lake catfish.
Bolivar Lake catfish. Spoonbill cats
from Bolivar Lake. An' channels fum
de river."*

*At the sound of his voice he is sur-
rounded by a crowd. The catfish
man brings out his scales and does a
flourishing business. A mass of
people press closely around him,
clamoring to be served, fearful that
all the fish will be sold before their
turn comes. Negroes and discerning
whites know that the catfish is one
of the most delicious of God's gifts
to man. The fish-seller, busied with
making change, weighing fish, and
putting strings through their gills so
that they can be dragged along by
his customers, bursts into song:*

*"I got yellow cat and the white cat,
Got everything but the tom cat,
And he's on the inside.
If you believe I'm lying
Buy one and try him.
Take him home
And then you fry him."*

> David L. Cohn
> *God Shakes Creation*, 1935

Our catfish finale was on a side street in the little town of DeValls Bluff, Arkansas, where we stopped, as Mike Trimble wrote in the *Arkansas Gazette*, "at what appears at first glance to be a minor train derailment." Actually, it is Murry's Cafe, a rambling catacomb of interconnected coaches, trailers, and pre-fabricated rooms. Olden Murry has been frying fish for the faithful there for about twenty years, before which he was a riverboat cook on the Mississippi. On the wall inside the cafe is a photograph of U.S. Senator Dale Bumpers. It is autographed to Olden Murry, "the best cook in Arkansas." With generous allowances for political overstatement, Bumpers may have been right on target.

Here is a man with forty-five years of cooking experience whose reputation is secure, not only for the catfish he prepares but for the steaks, chicken, quail, frog legs, barbecue, shrimp, oysters, and veal. He makes his own meal-based and flour-based batters and breading to dredge his seafoods and meats in, and he keeps the formulas to himself. He buys catfish both from fishermen on the nearby White River and from commercial processors. He completely empties and refills his deep-fat fryers with fresh cooking oil at least twice a week—a sure sign of devotion to quality—and he cooks his fish quickly at high temperature, the better to seal in flavor and produce a crisp, crunchy crust. "I go by looking at the fish and listening to the grease to tell when it's done," Murry said. "Every batch is different, so you have to pay attention." No automatic timers or fixed temperature controls for him.

There is no sign of any kind outside Murry's Cafe, and there are none out on the highway, but it is not at all unusual for two hundred or more people to show up there on any given night, many of them having driven sixty miles from Little Rock. Most of the people who work at Murry's are members of his family, including a majority of his seven children. Murry's is a home-folks kind of place—the same staff serving consistently fine food to mostly regular customers in plain and unpretentious surroundings. Its seems to be an invincible combination.

The day Ann and I stopped there, it was four o'clock in the afternoon, and Olden Murry was just about to open for business. A fisherman who called himself Catfish John was there with a hundred pounds of dressed fresh White River catfish, and soon he and Murry consummated a deal for them. Then the veteran chef heated his fresh oil to just the right temperature, rolled some of Catfish John's finest fillets in the secret batter, and fried them for us. The plates he brought to our table were like advertising pictures—the crisp golden fish, long slivers of French fries, a mound of creamy cole slaw, a ring of fresh onion, a length of dill pickle, a pepperoncini pepper, a wedge of lemon, a smoking-hot corn cake that looked and tasted like a hush puppy's rich first cousin. Everything was artistically arranged, prepared to perfection, and delicious. Olden Murry, a Rembrandt of the kitchen, had just completed another masterpiece.

On the Barbecue Circuit

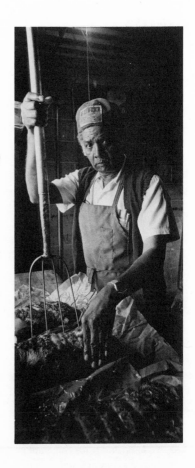

On a back road in, say, eastern Arkansas, or maybe north Alabama, or any one of several other states, a vagabond Southerner returning after a long absence to the land of his youth is brought to a halt by an evocative aroma that subtly invades his senses. The air is perfumed with a mingled fragrance of smoldering hickory and slowly roasting pork. It entices him forward, and it also draws him back in time to carefree summer days when pits glowed with hardwood coals, and racks suspended above them sagged with whole hogs, pork shoulders, beef, mutton, or goat, and tenders of the fire and the meat sipped short drinks and spun long tales, and these all-night rituals yielded up meat too tender for words and memories so vivid that they became permanent and indelible.

A telltale billow of gray-white smoke rolls up into view from atop a square cinder-block building painted two shades of green. The back portion of the tin-roofed structure is screened on three sides, and smoke sifts through the screen like sunlight through fog. A stack of hickory slabs is piled against the building. There is a Coca-Cola sign above the front door (or is it Pepsi, or RC?). Painted on it in large block letters is something like BUCK'S B-B-Q or HOG HEAVEN or PIG CITY. Surveying the parking lot, the traveler counts seven late-model sedans, a tractor-trailer rig, two police cars, two import compacts, two motorcycles, a bread truck, six pickup trucks, and three cars with government license plates. Seized by a long-buried yearning and spurred on by an acute sense of impending joy, he pushes open the front door and walks in.

The aroma is overpowering now, sweet and smoky and pungent. He straddles a stool at the counter and stares up at the menu on the wall. All around him, men and women are lost in concentration over their plates, oblivious to him. A waitress arrives with a glass of ice water in one hand and a ticket pad in the other. She is about his age—middle age—and vaguely familiar, a cheerful, outgoing woman with deep brown eyes and curly black hair flecked with gray. On her apron is pinned a button that reads NATIONAL PIG IMPROVE-MENT ASSOCIATION.

"Howdy do," she chirps. "What you gonna have today?"

The vagabond returns her greeting and then answers her question with one of his own. It seems to form itself independently in some subconscious reservoir of his mind, and it pops easily to the surface, like a cork in water.

"Is it chopped or sliced?" he asks.

The friendly waitress plants a set of knuckles on one hip, shifts her weight to the other, and smiles reassuringly. "Neither one, hon," she replies. "It's pulled."

Is it a dream, a figment of the imagination—or is it reality? The ultimate barbecue discovery lives in the minds of countless thousands of Southerners as a seamless blend of wishful fantasy and actual experience. They see it shining graillike in the distance, shimmering with all the intensity of summer heat on south Georgia asphalt: a simple shelter under a tin roof and a creosote-blackened chimney—and inside, waiting on the pit, is an utterly perfect slab of smoked meat that has just at that very moment reached the pinnacle of readiness.

It comes minced, chopped, sliced, pulled, or clinging to the ribs; on light bread, buns, cornbread, or as an entree; with sweet, tangy, thick, thin, mild, medium, or hot sauce; topped with cole slaw, onions, pickles, or nothing; accompanied by baked beans, potato salad, sliced tomatoes, corn on the cob, French fries, potato chips, hush puppies, Brunswick stew, burgoo, or hash on rice. In all its myriad combinations, shapes, and tastes, it's a many-splendored comestible with a single name: barbecue (barbeque, Bar-B-Q, B-B-Q), the smoky, roasted, sauce-doused meat that is second to none as a mouth-watering favorite of Southern eaters. There may be religious, political, athletic, or sexual images that stir deeper emotions—*may* be—but nothing in the realm of Southern food is regarded with more passionate enthusiasm by the faithful than a perfectly cooked and seasoned pork shoulder or slab of ribs.

How did this devotion to barbecue become so deeply ingrained in the South? Why isn't the best such meat found in the Midwest, where most of the hogs are? What is there about the South that caused outdoor cooks to start earlier and persist longer in their attempts to perfect the methods of roasting pork and other meats, and to invent sauces that could best bring out their rich flavor? These are deep mysteries, all of a piece with the secret recipes and special pit techniques and other forms of unrevealed wisdom that comprise the essence of the Southern barbecue mystique.

In any discourse on this complex and sometimes controversial subject, it helps to identify some ground rules and boundaries to be followed, and it seems only fair, too, for the writer to disclose his or her natural biases at the outset. These things I gladly do. First, we are discussing mostly pork here, because (a) beef barbecue is principally a Texas product, and Texas is outside our area of coverage; (b) chicken is more common (and, in my opinion, better) as a backyard barbecue meat; (c) goat, game, sausage, and other meats, while delicious as barbecue, are rarely found in commercial pits. (We will consider mutton—mature sheep—because of its historical significance in a small area of Kentucky.)

Second, our focus is on the heart of the Southern barbecue belt, which we define here as including all or part of seven states: Alabama, Arkansas, Georgia, South Carolina, North Carolina, Kentucky, and Tennessee. In spite of a few

Barbeque is serious business in the South. . . . In many respects, barbeque is taken as seriously as religion. . . . The Barbeque Eucharist serves as the perfect metaphor for understanding contemporary Southern society. The catechism contains a reverence for tradition and the heritage of the past, the vestiges of rural camp meetings, a chorus of regional chauvinism, a pulpit for oratory, an opportunity for community participation, appreciation for the vernacular, equality of opportunity, and subtle interracial respect. . . . The community values represented by the high priest cooks and the dedication of their congregations suggests that the rhetorical ritual of barbeque, characterized by hyperbole and boastful humor among friends, may also serve to further human understanding and humanitarian values among the faithful.

> Stephen A. Smith
> "The Rhetoric of Barbeque:
> A Southern Rite and Ritual,"
> in Studies in
> Popular Culture, 1985

anomalous exceptions spotted here and there in our travels, we were unable to find a strong and continuing commercial barbecue history and tradition in Virginia, Florida, Louisiana, and Mississippi—at least not enough to put them in the same class with the districts noted above.

Third, having eaten barbecue in more than sixty restaurants in eleven Southern states and in Texas in 1985 alone, and having consumed it in countless other locations in and out of the South in my adult lifetime, I feel compelled to state candidly my personal preferences in the matter. Though I sincerely believe that good barbecue comes in many types and styles, the kind I like best is pit-cooked pork shoulder, pulled from the bone and chopped slightly, mixing the crusty outside meat with the moist and tender inside. Piled on a warm bun, it may need no sauce at all, and certainly does not need any other dressing or condiment. If sauce is called for, I prefer it to be medium-hot and fairly thick and tangy, with tomato and vinegar as its base flavors.

Having said all this—and mindful that I may have alienated some loyalists of other stripes in the process—I hasten to add in my defense that I do not cling to my views with the blind certitude of a religious zealot. I may have personal preferences, but I don't believe there is One True Barbecue. I am an ecumenical pit follower who on occasion has found ecstasy in ribs, whole hog, beef brisket, chicken, mutton, goat—and I am as able as any person to describe fairly and objectively what I perceive to be the current state of the art and trends in barbecue production in the South. So here goes.

Barbecue is as old as fire. The cave dwellers started it when they discovered that meat tastes better cooked than raw. Spanish explorers in the New World found Indians in the Caribbean roasting meat over open fires on frames made of green wood, and they gave a name—barbacoa—to this framework. In time, barbecue came to mean a way of cooking, the meat thus cooked, and the social event that often surrounded the serving of it. The name and the meanings have stuck. (The popular belief that *barbecue* is from the French *barbe à queue*—beard to tail—meaning whole-hog cooking, is dismissed by the *Oxford English Dictionary* as "an absurd conjecture.")

Barbecue made its way into Southern cooking and culture very early in the region's history. Native Americans were practicing the art when the first Europeans arrived. Before the 1600s ended, Virginia had enacted a law prohibiting the shooting of firearms at barbecues, and Carolinians incorporated the word into their common language before the colonial period was over. Soon after 1800, when Kentucky was a young state, barbecues there were a primary form of summer social entertainment, and by the end of that century, the same could be said for every state in the region. The practice was not confined to the South, of course, but it took root there when slavery was practiced, and black

A REMEMBRANCE OF CHRISTOPHER GRAHAM, A GUEST AT THE WEDDING DINNER OF THOMAS LINCOLN AND NANCY HANKS IN WASHINGTON COUNTY, KENTUCKY, JUNE 12, 1806

We had bear meat, venison, wild turkey and ducks, eggs wild and tame, maple sugar lumps tied on a string to bite off for coffee or whisky, syrup in big gourds, peach and honey, a sheep barbecued whole over coals of wood burned in a pit, and covered with green boughs to keep the juices in; and a race for the whisky bottle.

quoted by Carl Sandburg,
in Lincoln: The Prairie Years, 1926

men were the ones who did the hot and difficult work that was and is a necessary part of good barbecue making. To this day, a high percentage of the South's master pit men are black.

Brunswick stew has a long history as a hearty, souplike dish accompanying barbecue, particularly in the coastal regions of Virginia, North Carolina, and Georgia. Burgoo, a close cousin of Brunswick stew, originated in Kentucky and still shows up at barbecues there. In South Carolina, it has long been popular to serve a hot pork hash over rice with barbecue.

In the early 1900s, when restaurants were gaining popularity, barbecue slowly crossed over from the church picnic and political rally to the commercial arena. Hamburger buns and sandwich bread were generally available by 1920, and within a few years there were pit barbecue stands scattered around the South dispensing prime pork sandwiches on light bread. It is still a common practice in some places to serve barbecue heaped on a plate with two or more slices of plain bread on the side.

Sauces also came into their own when the sandwich trade picked up, and for some, the sauce became more important than the meat itself in defining the individuality of a given cook. The meat, after all, could only be prepared in so many ways, but the sauce could be made in infinite varieties. Each one could be touted as the chef's secret treasure, and the sauces could not only accent good meat but also hide a multitude of sins. Styles of sauce attached themselves to particular areas—vinegar here and tomato there and mustard somewhere else, sweet or tangy or tart, thick or thin, mild or hot. Some used it sparingly, others with abandon.

Until the end of World War II, pit barbecue was probably the most popular short-order item in Southern restaurants. Most pits had risen above the ground by then, elevated to waist level in brick or concrete-block firebeds that made the backbreaking work a little easier, but the basic method of cooking was unchanged. The meat was placed on a metal rack about two feet above a bed of slow-burning coals. The heat was maintained at this low level of intensity—a "cool" fire, never flaming—and the meat, loosely covered, cooked slowly through and through. Turned infrequently and basted sparingly, it was transformed by the heat and the smoke into a moist, tender, delicious, and distinctively original delicacy. It took all night—eight to twelve hours, depending on size—to cook a pork shoulder to perfection. Many a first-rate pit in an otherwise undistinguished restaurant or cafe or shack performed the miracle daily.

A lot has changed since then. Speed has become a chief characteristic of most food-dispensing enterprises. Barbecue, like so many other time-consuming culinary activities, is no longer practical or profitable for most restaurants. Some have tried other methods: gas or electric heat, liquid smoke, pressure cookers,

Beargrass Creek, which is one of the many beautiful streams of the highly cultivated and happy State of Kentucky, meanders through a deeply shaded growth of majestic beech woods, in which are interspersed various species of walnut, oak, elm, ash, and other trees, extending on either side of its course. The spot on which I witnessed the celebration of

air-tight ovens with thermostats and timers, even microwaves. Canned, refrigerated, or frozen meat is sometimes warmed over and served. Store-bought sauces have replaced many old "secret" recipes. Those who cling to the tried and true methods of old must contend with many problems. Skilled pit men willing and able to do the strenuous and demanding labor are hard to find; hickory and other hardwoods are scarce; health departments can be rigid in their disapproval of certain pit conditions (even though, as one victimized defendant complained to an Arkansas writer, "anyone with a lick of sense knows that you can't make good barbecue and comply with a health code").

With so many obstacles to its survival, the wonder is that old-fashioned pit barbecue has not been completely ruined, or eliminated altogether. But somehow, in a few places, the tradition has remained so strong and the demand so great that the genuine article not only survives—it thrives. We didn't find all of the best places on what remains of the old Southern barbecue circuit, but we did locate quite a few, and the following state-by-state review describes about four dozen of them briefly.

Most of the best barbecue in Alabama can be found in the northern half of the state, but a notable exception is Cromwell's Bar-B-Que, a back-street pit in Phenix City that was known far and wide as Chicken Comer's until Comer died a few years ago. (Actually, the change in names has gone unnoticed by many people, since there is no sign on the premises.) The feature there is sliced pork shoulder cooked on the brick pit that Comer built out back. It's served warm on a paper plate in a pool of red-hot sauce, with enough light bread on the side to sop up the fiery liquid, and legions of old customers still troop in regularly for a fix. The sauce and the style are just as Comer left them, but the meat sometimes lacks his master touch.

In the Tuscaloosa area across the state, two small and long-established pits—Archibald's in Northport and the Dreamland Drive-Inn on a country road south of Tuscaloosa—are held in the highest esteem by knowledgeable consumers of Alabama barbecue. Like Cromwell's, they are unadorned pork pits of the most basic sort, dispensing their prize products without benefit of flatware or china—and proving in the process that good barbecue needs no amenities to make a favorable and lasting impression.

Archibald's operates out of a tiny cinder-block building with a creosote-encrusted chimney. There is just enough space inside for a counter and five stools. George Archibald has presided there for twenty-five years (and James Morris cooked before him), serving directly from a waist-high warming rack that is part of his pit. He cooks pork shoulders for about ten hours and ribs for about five on an enclosed roasting rack three feet above smoldering hickory coals, basting the meat sparingly with a little water if necessary and then dousing it

an anniversary of the glorious Proclamation of our Independence is situated on its banks, near the city of Louisville. . . . For a whole week or more, many servants and some masters had been busily engaged in clearing an area. . . . Columns of smoke from the newly kindled fires rose above the trees; fifty cooks or more moved to and fro as they plied their trade. . . . As the youth of Kentucky lightly and gaily advanced towards the Barbecue, they resembled a procession of nymphs and disguised divinities. . . . Now the stewards invited the assembled throng to the feast. . . . How the viands diminished under the action of so many agents of destruction I need not say. . . . Kentuckians are neither slow nor long at their meals. . . . With me the time sped like an arrow in its flight, and although more than twenty years have elapsed since I joined a Kentucky Barbecue, my spirit is refreshed every 4th of July by the recollection of that day's merriment.

John James Audubon
"Delineations of American Scenery and Character," 1834

with a mild red sauce at the end. Meat, sauce, light bread, potato chips, and a soft drink constitute the full menu, and it is a coveted offering.

Dreamland is a rib joint owned and operated by John Bishop and his wife, Lillie (now joined by their son John Jr.), since 1958. Four booths, eight tables, and a nine-stool bar take care of the seating, and the menu is strictly pork ribs, served by the sandwich, the plate, or the slab. A spicy tomato-based sauce covers the meat, which comes on a paper plate with the obligatory white bread. Beer and soft drinks are available, and packaged chips, and that's it—and it's plenty, in terms of both quantity and quality. The volume of Dreamland's business is a clear barometer of customer satisfaction. "On busy weekends, I get calluses from forking up so many of these ribs off the pit," said John Bishop, Sr., with a smile.

Cromwell's, Archibald's, and Dreamland are all black-owned businesses with a substantial mix of black and white customers—three of many such places to be found in every barbecue state in the region. Their lengthy and continuing presence as highly regarded community institutions supports an interesting sociological observation: Long before schools, churches, sports teams, and even other restaurants in the South got around to lowering the barriers of racial segregation, many of the region's best barbecue pits maintained a thriving interracial trade.

Barbecue enjoyed a resurgence in the postwar decade of the 1950s, when drive-in restaurants were in vogue and carry-out service presaged the start of the fast-food revolution. A number of good Alabama pits started in those years are still in business, including Old Plantation Bar-B-Q, one of several pork palaces in Birmingham. In business since 1950, it has maintained the look and feel of a neighborhood tavern—and also the taste of smoky pork straight from the pit.

In Bessemer, Bob Sykes has gone in thirty years from one pit to fourteen and back down to one, but it's a good one, serving pork shoulder sandwiches and ribs, and even some beef. Poor health, not bad barbecue, caused Sykes to cut back; his wife, son, and daughter run the home pit now. The pork sandwiches are made with either tender inside meat or the crusty outside, or a combination of the two, and the ribs are especially crisp and juicy. The red sauce is rather bland, but the meat holds up quite well without it.

Finally, in Huntsville, David Gibson's Bar-B-Q # 2, a local fixture since 1956, is a legacy of the late "Big Bob" Gibson, whose tenure as king of the north Alabama pits began in Decatur in 1939. The original place is owned now by the elder Gibson's sister, and two of his nephews also have a pit in Huntsville, but it is his son David who sticks closest to the cooking methods that made Bob Gibson's name synonymous with fine pit barbecue in upstate Alabama.

"We still do it the old-fashioned way," said David Gibson. "We use only hardwood coals—no gas—and we cook on the old pits in the slow manner, the way you have to do it if you want the real thing. You can't hurry good barbecue." Shoulder, ribs, and beef are the featured meats, and the menu also includes barbecued chicken and Brunswick stew. The table sauce for the meat is thin and vinegary, and not very hot.

Arkansas counts among its barbecue traditions the generosity of a black octogenarian from the Pine Bluff area named "Daddy Bruce" Randolph. Gratified by the success of his barbecue restaurant in Denver, Colorado, he returns to Pine Bluff around his birthday every February to serve as underwriter and host of an outdoor barbecue party for the general public, and thousands of local residents from all walks of life turn out for a taste of his ribs, his beans and slaw, and his infectious good humor.

The commercial barbecue traditions in Arkansas are also well established. Our sample includes two pits in Hot Springs, two in Little Rock, and two in the northeast corner of the state.

Hot Springs is on the Texas side of Arkansas, and that may explain why beef outsells pork in the barbecue restaurants there. At Stubby's, a cafeteria-style hickory pit in business since 1951, three fourths of the meat sold is beef, either ribs or brisket. Baked beans, slaw, potatoes, and pickles are among the side dishes, and the barbecue sauce is tomato based and very sweet; a little of it goes a long way on the ribs.

Across town, McClard's Barbecue dates to 1928, when Alex McClard and his wife, operators of a tourist court, accepted a recipe for "the best barbecue hot sauce in the world" from a man who couldn't come up with the money to pay for his room. They started a restaurant with the sauce and a new pit, and now their son, J. D. McClard, presides over a thriving enterprise that Little Rock newspaperman Max Brantley a few years ago called "the single best restaurant in Arkansas." Not just the best barbecue pit—the best restaurant.

It was a drive-in with carhops in the forties and fifties; now its booths and tables are crowded with people who like to linger inside, and there is a brisk carry-out business too. McClard's smokes upward of four thousand pounds of beef and pork a week over his hickory fires. It also serves, among other things, beans, slaw, French fries, hot tamales, milk shakes, and cold beer. The sauce recipe that started it all is still a well-guarded secret, but J. D. McClard, an affable and outgoing man, has been known to list the ingredients as tomato purée, vinegar, black pepper, red pepper, salt, lemon juice, onions, sugar, and water (about quantities, he is not so specific). The sauce is a nicely balanced blend of thickness, hotness, sweetness, and tartness. "We ship it out all over," McClard said. "Some people even put it on their tuna fish." Both the beef and the pork at McClard's are delightfully moist and smoky, and with the sauce they make an impressive eating experience.

Yes, I love barbecue, even to the point of going to ridiculous lengths to try a new variety. But surely there are very few other zealots like me lurking around Arkansas.

That's what I thought before articles I wrote about my favorite barbecue spots appeared in these pages a few weeks ago.

Boy, was I wrong.

You think crime, pollution, bigotry and official abuse of power are raging concerns of the day. Think again. Judging from the response to my articles, the next presidential candidate better have a barbecue plank in his platform.

I received eight letters, dozens of phone calls and a disturbing late-night visit from an irate barbecue man. Little of the response was even partially complimentary.

Max Brantley,
in the Arkansas Gazette,
June 21, 1977

In the metropolitan area of Little Rock and North Little Rock, two of the oldest and best barbecue restaurants offer a study in contrasts. One, started in about 1950 by Allen Sims and managed now by two of his nephews, is a neighborhood beer joint and pork pit featuring coarsely chopped shoulder sandwiches and ribs with the basics: light bread, potato chips, and two kinds of sauce, one mild and innocuous, the other full of fire. Once, when a shooting took place in the dining room, Sims was quoted as saying, "I didn't see nothing. I was just basting my ribs." Such single-minded devotion apparently makes for good customer relations—and certainly produces excellent ribs.

The other place is Lindsey's Barbecue, started by Church of God in Christ Bishop D. L. Lindsey in 1955 and owned now by his nephew, Richard Lindsey. It is a teetotaling house of barbecue exotica—not just beef and pork, but duck, turkey, goat, rabbit, deer, beaver, coon, and whatever else local hunters and others bring in to be custom-cooked. Aside from the barbecue, which is generally if not uniformly good, Lindsey's has an enviable reputation for making outstanding apple and peach fried pies.

At two locations in Jonesboro, a city of some 30,000 people in northeast Arkansas, Couch's Bar-B-Q features hickory-smoked beef and pork, both enhanced by a spicy hot, smoky sauce with a tomato base and heavy infusions of vinegar and black pepper. Couch's, too, is big on fried pies, and it also serves something called barbecue salad—a mound of barbecue on a bed of lettuce, topped with your choice of sauce or dressing. The combination didn't appeal to me—but the pork ribs were fine.

They don't do ribs at the Dixie Pig in Blytheville, up near the borders of Tennessee and Missouri—because, said owner Buddy Halsell, "it's hard to keep them fresh, and ribs aren't good if they're not fresh." His father started the business in 1923. Halsell concentrates now on hickory-smoked pork shoulders, which he chops and serves with slaw on a hot bun. His sauce is pepper-hot and vinegary, and quite good, a fitting complement to the meat. The Dixie Pig may be the oldest barbecue restaurant in Arkansas, and it still puts out a tasty and satisfying sandwich.

There are some well-regarded barbecue pits elsewhere in the state, particularly in the northwest region around Fayetteville. The six places noted here are just a sample of the variety to be found in Arkansas barbecue.

(A short distance beyond the southwest corner of Arkansas—thirty-eight miles as the crow flies, to be exact—a courageous porker has stood firm against the beef people for sixty years. Neely's Brown Pig, a little sandwich shop and hickory pit in Marshall, Texas, was a drive-in until it lost the younger set to the fast-food trade. But James and Frances Neely and their small staff continue there much as Neely's father did when he opened a place in Marshall in 1927. The slow-cooked pork and tomato-based sauce are good enough to be remembered by Bill Moyers of New York, who grew up in Marshall, as "the best bar-becue sandwich between here and China . . . an original, the only one of its kind in America." Strong words, and reminiscent of North Carolina barbecue boast-ing—but the Brown Pig *is* good, and the Neelys are storytellers in the best Southern tradition.)

Georgia is another state with a diversity of pits. Most of the ones we found were within fifty miles or so of Atlanta, the two exceptions being Walter's, a smoky pork shop in Athens, and Country's Barbecue, a somewhat trendy place done up in barnboard and old signs in Columbus. Jim Morpeth opened Coun-try's in 1975 as a combination barbecue and country cooking restaurant, and both its pit meat and its plate lunches are very popular.

"I grew up on Chicken Comer's shoulder sandwiches in Phenix City, across the river from here," Morpeth said. "There are some good barbecue places in this area, but they're more carry-out shops than sit-down restaurants. What I've tried to do with Country's is develop a good place to go out and eat bar-becue for dinner."

In Fayetteville and Newnan, two small towns south of Atlanta, pit-cooked pork is big business, primarily because of Kenneth Melear and the Sprayberry family. Melear has been operating his Fayetteville restaurant and catering ser-vice for almost thirty years, and three generations of Sprayberrys have directed their Newnan pit since the mid-1920s.

Virgil Melear, Kenneth's father, first entered the barbecue business in Union City, Georgia, in about 1935, and his father before him was also drawn to the art and science of pit cooking. Quite naturally, then, Kenneth grew up with "barbecue sauce in my veins." He opened his Fayetteville place in 1957, and it has since become a big-volume operation. On the evening we stopped in, Me-lear's chief pit man, Willie Hugh Thompson, and Thompson's wife, Gussie, had just finished supervising the preparation of eight thousand pounds of pork and beef and three hundred gallons of Brunswick stew, most of it for a gigantic catered spread for four thousand people in Atlanta. "Not every day is *this* busy," our weary waitress said, "but we do sell a lot of barbecue around here."

What they sell is mainly pork shoulders and hams, with beef brisket in a supporting role. The Brunswick stew, thick and smoky and very flavorful, is a popular item, and so are the homemade pies and the quart-sized glasses of iced tea. It is primarily the pork, though, that accounts for Melear's solid reputation. The meat is pulled, chopped a little, and served with light bread, potato chips, sweet pickles, and your choice of sauces: mild and sweet and tomatoey, or thin and orange and fire-breathing hot.

A handsome statue of a hog, cast in heroic dimensions, stands watch over the front entrance to Melear's. The boss obviously knows and appreciates the source of his good fortune.

No one who has had the good for-tune to attend a barbecue will ever forget it. The smell of it all, the meat slowly roasting to a delicious brown over smoking fires, the hungry and happy crowds. . . .

"Cue" is what they call it in Georgia, where it has been famous for many, many years. England has its roast beef and plum-pudding dinners, Rhode Island its clambakes, Boston its pork and beans, but Georgia has its barbecue which beats them all. So famous is it, in fact, that it has become a social and political force, and as a political entertainment has been duplicated in many States of the Union. . . . It is no exaggeration to say that many a gubernatorial election in Georgia has been carried by means of votes gained at barbe-cues, and no campaign for Governor is complete without a series of such popular feasts.

John R. Watkins,
in The Strand Magazine,
London, October 1898

At Sprayberry's, a family restaurant with lots of long-time regular customers, the brick open pit is right outside next to the parking lot, and there is almost always something cooking. Pork shoulders are the main meat, and they roast for about ten hours over a low fire of hickory and oak wood. The pulled and chopped barbecue makes a fine sandwich, especially when the moist and tender inside is combined with crispy chunks of outside meat. The sauces and the Brunswick stew lean to the mild side, but can be doctored for greater potency. One other Sprayberry feature is fried peach pies; they're delicious.

Atlanta is a pretty good barbecue town, with more than two dozen thriving pits to choose from. In suburban Mableton, on the old highway to Gadsden and Birmingham, Pete McKelvey has a large and faithful following at Old Hickory Barbecue, a traditional dispensary of hickory-smoked ribs and shoulder. The chopped shoulder plates and sandwiches are plenty good, but the ribs are the real feature—wet, messy, and wonderful, bathed in a tangy tomato and vinegar hot sauce. There is a chain of ten Old Hickory House barbecue places in Atlanta, but this is not one of them; McKelvey's pit stands on its own.

In the heart of the city, ribs of a somewhat different style—but just as impressive—are the main attraction at the Auburn Rib Shack on Auburn Avenue, not far from the Ebenezer Baptist Church where the Reverends Martin Luther King, father and son, used to preach. Dorothy Clements, the owner and manager of the Rib Shack, is a soft-spoken master practitioner of the fine art of rib cooking. The tiny shop has a thriving carry-out trade, but there are a few counter stools and booths to accommodate those who want to sit and eat ribs or plate lunches. The vegetables and other meats represent a high class of soul food, but nothing can beat the ribs, which are neither wet nor dry but middle-of-the-road: tender, meaty, moist, and enhanced by just the right amount of tangy red hot sauce with a faint hint of chili powder in it. A rib sandwich—three long ribs, two slices of light bread, and as much sauce as you want, served on a paper plate—makes a perfect light lunch. When a pit makes ribs as good as those at the Auburn Rib Shack, there's no need for shoulders. However you prefer your pork, though, Georgia has some fine pits.

In South Carolina, the most popular side dish with barbecue is hash, called liver hash by some and pork hash by others but served by all as a sort of thick meat gravy spooned over rice. The dish apparently was created to utilize liver and other organ meats not included in chopped whole-hog barbecue.

Hash is one of the few subjects about which South Carolina barbecue people seem to agree, that and the use of pork as the meat of choice; just about everything else related to the pits is subject to loud and sometimes angry argument and dispute. Some places swear by whole-hog cookery, others go for shoulder, still others lean to ribs. An interminable intrastate battle rages over the right way to make sauce (there are three base camps—tomato, vinegar, and

Barbecue lovers will excuse almost anything once a restaurant's product earns their loyalty. In fact, some say the best barbecue is found in cafes belonging to an architectural classification we shall call Barbecue Primitive Style. These are often older barbecue eateries, identified by torn screen doors, scratched and dented furniture, cough syrup calendars, potato chip racks, sometimes a juke-

mustard). And many traditionalists consider it an unthinkable travesty that some establishments have abandoned wood fires for gas or electricity. In South Carolina, they do not take their barbecue lightly.

One of the converts to gas is Shealy's Bar-B-Que House in Leesville, a popular midlands eatery established by Victor and Sarah Shealy in the late 1960s and operated now by their son Tommy and his wife, Cheryl. They cook whole hogs slowly over charcoal in a gas-fired pit and serve the meat chopped or minced with a mild and somewhat sour mustard-based sauce. From the size of the crowds there, it is obvious that the Shealy style of South Carolina barbecue meets with much favor. Coming as I do from a very different tradition, I found it to be lacking in smokiness, tang, texture, and overall flavor. For comparative purposes, though, it certainly offers an interesting contrast.

In Spartanburg, the Beacon, a drive-in, includes pork sandwiches among an incredibly diverse array of short-order specialties, but it's as much fun to go and marvel at the Beacon itself as it is to eat there. The place has hardly changed at all since John White opened it in 1947; you can still get curb service, or you can go inside and watch J. C. Strobel run the serving line with all the skill of a master logician and the facile charm of a vaudeville trouper. The barbecue, once you get your mind on it, is sliced inside or outside meat, and the sauce is a spicy vinegar and tomato blend. Like many of the other features at the Beacon, it has a nice hint of the fifties about it. (As a drive-in, the Beacon is a classic—but for sheer size, it yields the title to the Varsity in Atlanta, a sprawling short-order dispensary that was founded in the 1930s. The Varsity sometimes serves over 17,000 customers *a day*, and no challengers have disputed its claim as "the world's largest drive-in.")

South Carolina has managed somehow to save a few of its old drive-ins from extinction. Another good one is Maurice's Piggy Park in Columbia—and its main attraction is barbecue. Maurice Bessinger got into the pit business with his brother Melvin in the early 1950s, and his Piggy Park is now the leading pork dispensary in the state's largest city. (Members of the family also operate Bessinger's Barbecue in Charleston.) Maurice's sandwiches, ribs, and pork plates lean to the firm and crusty side, having cooked long and slowly over hickory coals. His "million dollar secret sauce" is yellow with mustard and very popular locally, though I liked the meat better without it. Maurice's latest entrepreneurial achievement is "fresh frozen" barbecue, freeze-dried straight off the pit and packaged for shipping across the state or around the world. The jury is still out on this radical disposition of freshly cooked meat, but the method is yet another source of controversy for South Carolina's battle-scarred barbecue troops.

Around Orangeburg, Earl Duke's name is synonymous with barbecue—so well-known, in fact, that when you ask directions to Duke's, you could end up in three or four different places. The original pit, in business for more than

box, and always the counter, producing an ambience similar to a county-line beer joint.

The other classification is the Neo-Primitive Revival Barbecue Style— the more urbane establishments that hang old tin signs, plowshares, and singletrees on the walls and dress their help in calicos and denims in an attempt to look country.

The barbecue addict who is also a seasoned traveler looks only at the parking lot to pre-judge a restaurant's product. If pickup trucks are parked beside expensive imports, he knows the barbecue is good because everyone in town eats there. More than any other cuisine, barbecue draws the whole of Southern society, from down the street and from miles around.

Gary D. Ford,
in Southern Living, May 1982

thirty years, was sold by Duke a few years back, but then he went over into a neighboring county and opened another place at Cameron. Others in and out of the family operate Duke's Bar-B-Q places elsewhere in the state. Regardless of the confusion, the fare at all the pits is quite similar: chopped pork on light bread, ribs, pork hash, and a tomato-based sauce that is closer to sweet and sour than hot and spicy.

Sweatman's Bar-B-Que near Holly Hill is a distinctive-looking place—an old, unpainted, weather-worn frame farmhouse built on brick pilings under a canopy of pecan trees. Like many Carolina pits, it is open for business only on the weekends, and during those days a motley assortment of vehicles fills the parking area. H. O. "Bub" Sweatman and his wife Margie bought the house in about 1970. Their pit men cook whole hogs in a concrete block building with a vented tin roof in the backyard. I preferred it before the mustardy sauce went on, when you could appreciate fully the meat's smoky flavor.

Our last stop for pit pork in South Carolina was at Yum Young & Sons Barbecue Place on the coastal highway near Pawleys Island. George "Yum" Young, a retired former valet for railroad tycoon George Vanderbilt, opened for business in 1978. His unpainted cinder-block building sits off the highway in a pine thicket. There are no tables inside—just the pit and a counter and Young's overstuffed easy chair. He cooks pork shoulders, ribs, chicken, and other meats every weekend, and also makes a pot of pork hash. His sauce is a distinctive combination of the tomato, vinegar, and mustard flavors other South Carolinians fight over. "I integrated my sauce," he said with a smile. "It's got a different taste from any of the others." Young's old-fashioned slow-fire cooking with hickory has twice won him the top prize at the World International Barbecue Championship in nearby Georgetown, South Carolina. Whether or not it is the best in the world, it is certainly a worthy example of finely wrought pork.

The claim is often made by North Carolinians that their state produces the best barbecue in the South, which means the best in the world. It is a serious and substantial assertion that might be assumed to have some basis in fact, were it not for one thing: There are two basic styles of North Carolina barbecue, and proponents of each are so disdainful of the other that doubt is cast on both. West of Raleigh, at places like Stamey's Old Fashioned Barbecue in Greensboro, an order for a sandwich will get you chopped pork shoulder on a bun, with vinegary slaw and a medium-hot catsup-and-vinegar sauce added. East of Raleigh, in places like Wilber's Barbecue in Goldsboro, sandwiches are made with whole-hog meat that has been finely chopped, seasoned with a sharp vinegar and pepper sauce, and served with slaw on top or on the side. To outsiders, the differences may seem insignificant, but to the faithful on both sides, they loom as a yawning chasm never to be bridged.

Southern pork barbecue will make its debut in Times Square next week.

Performing the introduction will be Barry Farber, talk-show host for Radio Station WMCA, who grew up in Greensboro, N.C.

Except for one or two haute cuisine restaurants in Washington, D.C., barbecue has yet to make its way north. This baffles Farber.

"New York is the second largest Southern city in America," he said. "First is Chicago. There are more

North Carolinians who live "down east," as they call the region east of Raleigh, have long had a distinct preference for whole-hog cooking. Occasions referred to as pig pickings—spreads at which roast suckling pig is the main feature—are held frequently in the region, and these public and private gatherings are always well-attended. Young pigs weighing sixty to ninety pounds are split in half, eviscerated, and spread out on grills over slow-burning hickory and other hardwood coals to cook for ten hours or more. Most pit watchers prefer to baste the pig occasionally with the universal sauce of the region (vinegar seasoned with pepper and not much else). When the meat is ready, diners can look it over and pick the morsels they want to make their own sandwiches and plates; that, in essence, is what a pig picking is.

Restaurants in the region follow the same method, more or less. At Wilber's, for example, the split halves of ninety-pound hogs cook ten to twelve hours over oak coals, after which the meat is chopped with cleavers, seasoned with hot sauce, and served with slaw, hush puppies, and potato salad. "That's the way we've done it here ever since Wilber Shirley opened the place in 1962," said manager Charlie Watson, "and most of the barbecue you'll find in eastern North Carolina is served pretty much the same way."

At the Skylight Inn in Ayden, Pete Jones and members of his family serve pork, slaw, and cornbread the same way they always have, going back to 1948, when Jones opened the restaurant—and he says some of his forebears there were selling barbecue more than a century before that. Keeping up with the Joneses is no easy task; they have Oscar-like trophies to show for their triumphs in regional barbecue cooking contests, and the taste of their chopped and seasoned whole-hog meat is prima facie evidence of their skill.

Another eastern North Carolina tradition lives on at Melton's Barbecue in Rocky Mount, where the late Bob Melton's thriving business has been passed on to some of his disciples. The large, rambling block and frame building is hidden away at the end of a narrow street on the edge of town, but customers have no trouble finding it. The meat is minced and pulverized almost to a hash, heavily seasoned with vinegar sauce, and topped with slaw. The flavor is not bad, but it's not as good as it used to be and the main reason apparently is that what Bob Melton started in the 1930s over hickory coals is carried on now with gas and hickory chips. As a civil libertarian, North Carolina native Tom Wicker has defended such practices. "But to anyone deeply into barbecue," he added in his *New York Times* column, "the idea of cooking it any way but over live coals is repugnant."

Another North Carolinian turned New Yorker tried in the late 1970s to introduce real pit barbecue to the Manhattan commercial trade. Barry Farber, a radio talk-show host and unsuccessful candidate for mayor of New York City in 1977, formed a partnership with a Times Square restaurateur to serve gen-

Southerners here than there are in Atlanta."

But nobody thought to bring any barbecue along. You can't even get BAD barbecue in New York, he said.

. . . . .

For years he has been trying to persuade someone to steal his idea. "My only vested interest has been to be able to buy some barbecue when I wanted it," he said.

Finally, he realized that the only solution was to open a stand himself, and he broached the plan with Alex Parker, a New York realtor who owns . . . a bagel shop. . . . Barbecue will be put on the menu.

Guy Friddell,
in the Roanoke *Times & World-News*,
April 8, 1978

uine North Carolina pork sandwiches, with the meat to be flown in fresh daily. The ultimate failure of the effort apparently stemmed from three basic causes: the lack of a barbecue tradition in New York, Farber's own difficulty in choosing between eastern and western Carolina pork, and the fundamental fact that real barbecue loses its unique powers in direct correlation with its distance from the pit.

Stamey's in Greensboro is a monument to that last truism. Warner Stamey started it in 1930, and with it he apparently founded the western North Carolina tradition: shoulders instead of whole hogs, and tomato added to the sauce. His sons Keith and Charles Stamey and his daughter Sara Hodgin own the restaurant now, and they have kept it the way it was, serving chopped or sliced sandwiches and plates with slaw, hush puppies, and baked beans on the side. They still cook with wood—and they haven't opened branches in New York, or even in New Bern.

On the old Asheboro highway out of Charlotte, the Old Hickory House Restaurant is another pit in the Stamey's tradition. It serves the same sort of slow-cooked pork shoulders, sliced or chopped, and the same kind of red sauce. It also offers a very thick and spicy bowl of Brunswick stew packed with long-simmered vegetables and chunks of meat.

One of the best-known pits in western North Carolina is Lexington Barbecue # 1 in Lexington, where Wayne Monk, a disciple of Warner Stamey, has been in business for over twenty years. (His brother owns Lexington # 2, but they operate independently.) Monk is a shoulder cook all the way. On his slow hickory fires, the meat holds its moisture without basting (it cooks for about ten hours), and then it is chopped and sliced to order and served on a bun with slaw and a mild red sauce unless you specify otherwise. Some people like their slaw on the side, slathered with the same sauce. Hush puppies are a crossover item from east to west, and the ones at Monk's place are especially good. Outside the Carolinas, few cooks would dream of serving hush puppies with anything but fish. But that's the way it is with barbecue; quirky little local touches are viewed locally as the normal and natural order of things, while outsiders see them with humor or horror as aberrations.

Kentucky, a prime district of the barbecue belt, has several such peculiarities in its pits. Instead of getting slaw on your sandwich, you're liable to get a slice of dill pickle or onion, or both; in place of a bun, you might get your pork on a delicious cornbread batter cake; rather than pork, you could get mutton; and instead of Brunswick stew, you might get a wonderfully rich and peppery dish of a similar sort called burgoo.

Kentucky's barbecue traditions are heavily concentrated in the western end of the state, in places like Mayfield, where Keith Weaks and his son David operate Fat Boy's Bar-B-Q, a pit dispensing pulled pork shoulder meat slowly cooked over hickory coals and augmented with a fine red sauce that the elder Weaks "paid big money for." The ribs there are also delicious.

Just up the road in Paducah, an Ohio River city of 30,000 people, there are more than twenty barbecue places in the Yellow Pages. One of the oldest and most popular is Starnes Barbecue, where the hickory-fired pits have been burning for more than forty years. Custom cooking of shoulders, hams, ribs, beef brisket, and other meats is a Starnes service that many customers like; in fact, about half of its business involves this carry-out commerce, rather than sandwiches and plates. Either way, Starnes is one of the temples of western Kentucky barbecue lovers. One unusual feature at Starnes is that toasted light bread is used instead of buns.

West of Paducah, near the little town of Heath, a superlative pit called Leigh's Barbecue has graced the countryside since the late 1940s. Leonard Leigh started it; his wife, Becky, took over when he died; and their son Eddie Ray now manages the pit, which opens directly into the kitchen area of the small, square cinder-block building where customers sit on stools around a horseshoe counter. The shoulders cook so slowly for so long that they seem to fall apart at the sight of a knife. Customers order light, medium, or heavy sandwiches— local terminology which means a little, a bit more, or a lot of the warm and peppery-hot tomato and vinegar sauce that accents the meat. You can also specify inside or outside pieces. The meat is not pulled from the shoulder until your sandwich is ordered—which means that what you get at Leigh's is pit pork shoulder at the very peak of its flavor.

Owensboro, 150 miles upriver on the Ohio from Paducah but still in western Kentucky, is a major-league pit city that unabashedly calls itself the "Bar-B-Q Capital of the World." Here are found the pickle and onion, the mutton, the burgoo; more impressively, here is a nineteenth-century barbecue heritage that is as clear and continuous and as well-documented as any in the South.

As far back as the 1830s, churches in the vicinity of Owensboro were having barbecues as a social adjunct to their religious activities, and since farmers in the area raised a lot of sheep, mutton was the primary meat to be cooked. The first recorded account of such an affair was at a Baptist church in 1834, but it was Catholic parishes that turned the casual practice into a continuing tradition, and it is largely Catholic fundraisers that keep the barbecue torch burning today. ("It takes teamwork to make good barbecue," the whimsical explanation goes, "and there's too much free will among Protestants to do it right.")

Religious, patriotic, political, and fraternal organizations staged summer barbecues so frequently by the late 1800s that Owensboro and its sister communities nearby were renowned for the quality of the celebrations—and the pit-cooked meat. In 1890, a black man named Harry Green opened the first

The early regional differences in food consumption [between the South and the rest of the country] reflected differing conditions of soil, climate and culture, but the continuing modern differences, in view of the vast improvements in preservation and transportation, must be seen as being more the result of distinct social and cultural factors. One example which highlights these contemporary differences can be found in searching the cuisine guides in the Yellow Pages of telephone directories. The Atlanta directory boasts 28 barbecue locations, 7 southern style restaurants and 5 soul food listings. By contrast, the Boston Area Yellow Pages has 26 pages of restaurant listings, but not a single entry in these three categories—and not a single advertisement pictures a smiling pig or a walking catfish. The Manhattan Consumer Yellow Pages has 29 pages of restaurant listings, but the cuisine guide doesn't even have a barbecue heading. The single entry under soul food is Jack's Nest, which claims "Bar-B-Q Ribs and Chitterlings Our Specialty," but it is an obvious fraud since "chittlins" is misspelled.

Stephen A. Smith,
in American Material Culture, 1984

commercial barbecue stand in Owensboro. Burgoo was a part of the tradition by then, and while everyone seemed to love the spicy stew, no one knew where either the dish or its name came from, or how it found its way to western Kentucky (the similarity to Brunswick stew is obvious—but nobody west of the Appalachian chain was accustomed to eating Brunswick stew).

Charles Foreman, an Owensboro blacksmith, began barbecuing mutton in 1918, and the family has continued the tradition into the fifth generation at Old Hickory Bar-B-Q. "About seventy-five percent of what we sell is chopped or sliced mutton," said Harl Foreman, the present owner, "and most of the rest is pork." Whole sheep are quartered and cooked about sixteen hours over a cool fire of hickory coals. They are turned once and basted sparingly, then sliced and served with a distinctive tomato and vinegar sauce. "We serve onion and pickle slices with our sandwiches," Foreman added. "Not slaw—I never did understand what slaw had to do with barbecue."

Shady Rest Barbecue, another Owensboro institution, was started by Dick and Louise Griffith in the 1940s, and like Old Hickory, it is a mutton pit with pork shoulder, ribs, chicken, and burgoo as backups. "Little Mary had some lamb," the menu says. "Won't you have some too?" A steady stream of customers has been saying yes to the Shady Rest invitation for four decades.

There are other long-established pits in and around Owensboro. But for sheer magnitude, not to mention quality, none of them can hold a candle to a relative newcomer: Moonlite Bar-B-Q Inn, established by Hugh Bosley, Sr., in 1963. In under twenty-five years, Bosley and his children and grandchildren have ballooned a roadside stand into a sprawling enterprise that employs a hundred people, feeds a thousand or more a day in its three-hundred-seat dining room (and untold hundreds more through catering and carry-outs), and disposes of about two tons of meat and two hundred gallons of burgoo a day during the busy summer months. Since nobody raises sheep around Owensboro anymore, the Bosleys buy them in refrigerated car lots from the upper Midwest—as many as six hundred dressed carcasses a week.

They serve other things besides barbecue at the Moonlite—country ham, catfish, shrimp—but the house feature is a barbecue buffet that defies the imagination. Mutton, pork, beef, and chicken in nine different barbecue styles form the centerpiece, and they range from above average to outstanding. One or two other kinds of meat, half a dozen fresh vegetables, three or four kinds of hot breads, a salad bar, burgoo and soup, tea and coffee and soft drinks (beer and wine are also available), and an utterly superfluous but delightful array of homemade desserts round out the feast. The cost for that in 1985 was $7.25 (a little higher on weekend evenings). That's about like paying a couple of bucks for a World Series box seat. The Moonlite is a Kentucky wonder of a barbecue palace.

Both casual backyard cookers and serious pit crews vie for prizes and prestige at the International Bar-B-Q Festival in downtown Owensboro each summer, and upward of fifty thousand people turn out for the event, which supporters have dubbed "the burning of Owensboro." The success of the festival is a tribute to the city's long history of pit cooking and its continuing devotion to those traditions. It may not truly be the "Bar-B-Q Capital of the World," but it certainly deserves to be recognized as one of the primary centers.

At first glance, it would seem that Memphis boosters are more modest; they merely call their city the "Pork Barbecue Capital of the World." Actually, though, the west Tennessee metropolis on the Mississippi River can make a strong and convincing case for total supremacy. In 1984, reporters for a local newspaper compiled a list of eighty-four active commercial pits in the city—far more than any other community can boast—and the annual International Barbecue Cooking Contest there has become such an attraction that an estimated 300,000 people crowded into the festival's riverfront site in 1985. We conclude our barbecue safari with a visit to some Tennessee pits and a lingering look at Memphis, the fabled mecca of pork.

The story of Bobby Hendricks, a.k.a. Bobby Que, is illustrative of the magnetic pull and potency of the pit culture in Tennessee. A native of Texas, Hendricks migrated to Memphis in 1970, hoping to make a name for himself as a rhythm and blues and gospel singer. But it was the gospel of barbecue that fired his soul and his imagination, and after seven years of experimental cooking he published a book, *Mr. Bobby Que*, that included testimony on his secret sauces. At last report, the self-styled "barbecue research scientist" had moved to the West Coast, hoping to evangelize the heathen masses into the pork kingdom.

And so it goes in the Volunteer State, particularly in its western reaches. For the better part of a century, pork barbecue has inspired cooks and eaters, poets and novelists, painters and photographers, politicians and bureaucrats, in such legendary and charmingly named Tennessee pits as Bozo's, Buck's, The Nice Pig, Goat City, Hog Heaven, Pic-A-Rib, Porky's, and The Tail of the Pig. And that's just in the commercial realm; at other levels of Tennessee society, barbecue has been cooked and served with deep pride and consummate skill since early in the nineteenth century.

Together with country ham and smoked sausage, two more prized products derived from the hog, barbecue has given pork a lofty status as an object of value in Tennessee. In Memphis and a few other towns, a six-pack is as apt to mean six barbecue sandwiches to go as it is a carton of beer. For more than 125 years, Tennessee law has fixed the maximum penalty for stealing a hog at fifteen years in prison—three times greater than the penalty for involuntary manslaughter. No other element in the society more effectively bridges the gaps of

WHEN DE CO'N PONE'S HOT

When de cabbage pot is steamin'
An' de bacon good an' fat,
When de chittlins is a-sputter'n'
So's to show you whah dey's at;
Tek away yo' sody biscuit,
Tek away yo' cake an' pie,
Fu' de glory time is comin',
An' it's 'proachin' mighty nigh,
An' you want to jump an' hollah,
Dough you know you'd bettah not,
When yo mammy says de blessin'
An' de co'n pone's hot.

The Complete Poems
of Paul Laurence Dunbar, 1935

race, sex, age, socioeconomic status, religious belief, and political philosophy than barbecue. David Dawson, writing about pit power in Memphis, called it "that element which binds us into a community. Barbecue is a social cause, something which gives meaning to our existence." It is also a family affair, a church function, a party ice breaker, a political wheel greaser, a beer drinker's chateaubriand. In Memphis and west Tennessee, barbecue sometimes seems to take on the trappings of a state religion.

The pit tradition is far less powerful in east Tennessee. Chattanooga does have a few good places, and there are a couple in Knoxville, and occasionally in the smaller towns and along the back roads you may happen upon a nice little smoky spot, but by and large, those are not what a dedicated pork scout would call good hunting woods. One notable and unusual place in the east is near Bluff City. Ridgewood Restaurant, owned and operated since 1948 by Grace Proffitt, serves a barbecue sandwich that people in the flatlands five hundred miles to the west wouldn't recognize. It's certainly different—and it's also very good.

Ridgewood starts with fresh hams, not shoulders. The meat cooks and smokes for about ten hours over hickory coals. Then it is chilled in a cooler, sliced cold, and reheated on a hamburger grill at high temperature. While it sizzles, it is doused generously with a spicy-sweet and mildly hot tomato-based sauce. The mound of moist and piping-hot meat is then troweled onto a toasted bun and served with slaw and French fries, both freshly made and of the highest quality. They've been doing it that way for nearly forty years, and customers eagerly wait in line every day for the Ridgewood to open.

You have to get all the way out of the mountains and into the rolling hills of middle Tennessee before the traditional smoking pit becomes a familiar sight—and even there, it's not all that common anymore. Murfreesboro, Columbia, Franklin, Dickson, and Springfield, small towns in the Nashville orbit, all boast one or more hickory pits of good caliber, and Nashville itself has about twenty-five commercial pork parlors, the best of which are carry-out shops such as Mary's Old Fashion Barbecue Pit and R & R Pit Bar-B-Q. But Nashville has lost some of its better places in recent years, and many of the survivors have converted to kitchen cooking with gas or electricity. The barbecue tradition is waning in Nashville.

It sparkles a little farther west in Clarksville, though, at a place called Pic-A-Rib, where good pulled shoulder and ribs share the menu spotlight with excellent home-style plate lunches and homemade pies. Edna Law has owned the place for more than twenty years, and it's been there since the early 1950s, maintaining all the while a sterling reputation for turning out smoky, saucy, falling-apart tender ribs and crusty pork shoulder on cornbread battercakes.

Beyond the Tennessee River and into the farmlands of the weststate you finally begin to find more prime pits of the sort that Memphis is famous for. (It is at the river, too, that dill pickle slices disappear and little mounds of cole slaw take their place atop pork sandwiches.) In a town like Dyersburg, for example, you will find several barbecue spots, including The Hut, a rustic-looking dinner restaurant built in 1937 and noted both for its steaks and its genuine pit barbecue. The pulled chunks of outside meat are especially fine.

And then there is Goat City Bar-B-Q, a little roadside stand on the highway south of Milan. J. R. Bettie and his brother Jack before him have been cooking shoulders on a brick pit there for about twenty years. "I keep them for twelve hours or more over a cool hickory fire," J. R. said. "No basting, no turning—and I go easy on the sauce. Lots of people come in here from out of state, and when they stop once, they generally keep coming. It's strictly pork, though, not goat. Goat City's the name of this little community around here—but you know, I was born and raised near here over sixty years ago, and I don't have any idea how that name got started." His pork knowledge, however, is vast.

The final stop before we reach Memphis is in the little town of Mason, home of Bozo's Pit Bar-B-Q Restaurant. Thomas J. "Bozo" Williams began this legendary place in 1923, and his daughter, Helen Williams, carries it on now. The wisest pit heads in Memphis consider Bozo's a shrine; these "Pilgrims of Pork," as magazine writer Mark J. Davis called them, "turn their eyes to the East and follow the road to Bozo's."

There's nothing special about the unpretentious block building that houses the restaurant. What distinguishes the place is the succulent pork shoulders that pit man Shorty Maclin sends to the kitchen. They have been cooked to tender perfection in about ten hours over hickory coals, and they are pulled or chopped to make prime sandwiches and plates of inside (white) or outside (brown) meat. "Give me a white-pull pig plate," the waitress will call back to the kitchen, or "Let me have two brown pigs"—and if the latter is your order, you'll get crusty pulled chunks of meat on lightly toasted buns with a mound of slaw (unless you have it sidetracked). The sauces, hot and mild, are not as great as the meat, but they're not needed. There are other things on the menu, but the crowd wants pork. Helen Williams surveys the Bozo phenomenon with tranquil grace. "Daddy always loved this business, and he loved the people around it," she said. "I know it would please him a lot to see so many people still coming here and enjoying it, because we still do everything exactly the same way we always did."

And then Memphis: three quarters of a million people served by at least eighty-four smoking commercial pits, plus the more than two hundred fires at the annual cooking contest and the uncounted tens of thousands more in back-yards across the city. Pork barbecue so thoroughly dominates the gastronomic image of Memphis that little else manages to shine through the smoke. The

ODE TO PORK

Crisply braised,
A paragon of fat and lean
Drips juicily upon the pit.
Sustainer of the South,
The Pig doth yearn to sacrifice
And serve.
I eat it lustily,
Sauce-stained and smiling.

Anonymous

cooking contest has exploded from a parking-lot assembly of dedicated souls roasting shoulders to perfection under sheets of tin to a legion of uniformed teams with corporate sponsors operating computer-designed ovens mounted on flatbed tractor-trailer rigs. As Southerners are prone to do (witness the Mardi Gras, the Kentucky Derby), the pit freaks of Memphis have just about over-cooked their golden goose. Calvin Trillin of *The New Yorker*, who need bow to no one as an authority on barbecue eating (or as a writer on the subject), seemed to suggest after visiting the 1985 contest that Memphis was making too big a deal of it. "It would hurt to see barbecue go the way of chili—cross over what I now think of as the Chili Line," he wrote, and he went on to explain that a food was in serious trouble when it was "labelled and packaged and relentlessly organized and fitted out with promotional T-shirts," and "surrounded with enough self-conscious boasting and slick packaging to impair the appetite."

That may well be the fate of the city's international contest; but it is hard to imagine that even a total collapse of the promotional event would have much effect on the commercial pits or the thousands of customers who frequent them habitually. It is not just quantity and hype that make Memphis barbecue great; it is quality. Without belaboring the point, let me mention just a few of the many prime pits:

✤ *Gridley's*, a family-owned enterprise that opened in 1975, now has four locations with seating for nearly 1200 diners, and is far and away the largest barbecue operation in the city. Shoulders, ribs, beef, chicken, and even shrimp get the pit treatment. The ribs are a delight to those who like them wet, messy, and glazed with a baked-on sweet sauce. Gridley's is the General Motors of the Memphis pits, the leading mass producer of competitive barbecue.

✤ *Charlie Vergos' Rendezvous* is a cavernous rib cellar in downtown Memphis where on any given night you can expect to find the four hundred seats taken and people waiting on the stairs. Since 1948, Greek immigrant Vergos—now aided by his son Nick—has won thousands of converts to his specialty: charcoal-broiled ribs coated with a powdery dry seasoning of various herbs and spices. The taste is very different, but quite good.

✤ *Payne's*, a rib and shoulder pit in a converted service station, keeps its fresh-cooked meat on the pit until you order. Emily Payne is in charge, and members of her family have two other pork places in town. In the highly competitive Memphis rib trade, Payne's offers moist and tender ones smothered in hot or mild vinegar and tomato sauce, and they are equal to the competition.

✤ *John Wills* won the coveted grand championship of the city's cooking contest in 1980 and again in 1981, and the young businessman promptly opened a commercial pit to capitalize on his visibility. It's now in the top ten based on volume, and its many fans give it equally high marks for taste and overall quality. Ribs and shoulders are the headliners, and the red sauce is good.

✤ *Tops* is a chain of eleven Memphis barbecue shops, each with its own pit on the premises. Shoulder sandwiches are the mainstay, and have been since the first Tops opened in 1952. There's a fast-food character to the places, but the barbecue is fresh and tasty.

✤ *Leonard's* is the granddaddy of all the Memphis pits. The first outlet (there are now three in the city) was opened in 1922 by Leonard Heuberger; it was a seven-stool sandwich stand that made deliveries by bicycle. Later, Leonard's grew to become one of the largest drive-in restaurants in the nation, but always, its emphasis has been on barbecue. Almost from the first, Heuberger operated a serious pit for two-fisted eaters, and he is reputed to be the originator of the classic Memphis pork barbecue sandwich: pulled or chopped shoulder meat on a bun with a little tomato-based sauce and a bit of creamy cole slaw. Everyone else followed suit, and the standard has not changed in more than sixty years.

A small group of Memphis business partners owns Leonard's now, but most of the employees go back a long way. Dan Brown, the general manager, started work there when he was thirteen, more than twenty-five years ago. James Willis and Milton Smith, the principal pit men at the main location, have been on the payroll for more than forty years each; Willis, the senior cook, started as a helper around the pits in 1938. His mastery of rib and shoulder cooking is complete, and the effortless manner in which he handles the fires and the meat disguises what a hot and heavy job it is. "This is a slow operation," he said, as he checked a rack laden with dark brown shoulders. "You can't rush it. You have to know how to wait, and when to act—and when the time comes, you have to move fast and then wait some more. It's too tedious for most young people— they don't have the patience for it. But lots of folks do love this meat, so somebody will keep on cooking it, and that means there'll be good barbecue around here right along. People are always gonna be coming to Memphis looking for barbecue."

All Over the South

When the 27,000-mile odyssey was behind us and I had finished writing about eating out in the restaurants and cafes and fish houses and barbecue pits of the South, I found myself not only savoring the highlights of the journey but also lamenting all the good places we had missed. I knew of some great restaurants that had been down-graded or closed before we got to them, and others that our poor timing or bad scheduling had kept us from enjoying, and still others that we simply hadn't learned of until it was too late to go back and visit them. No doubt there are many more places still unknown to us that are serving good Southern food to appreciative customers even as I write.

Change is inevitable, and not always for the best. Pearl Jordan is gone from the barbecue pit at Pete Light Spring Cafe near Cadiz, Kentucky (she was a rarity, a white woman whose barbecue skills were equal to those of the best black pit men). Mary Majors has departed from the Tiny Castle near Kuttawa, Kentucky, and Mary Branch no longer presides at Mary's Place in Coden, Alabama—two among a multitude of anonymous black women whose culinary achievements deserved far more notice and reward than they ever received.

Meme's, a wonderful seafood shack at Bon Secour, Alabama, is closed, and so is Mohler's Restaurant near Lexington, Virginia, where country ham and beaten biscuits used to be on the menu, and so is Buck's, a classic barbecue pit in Clarksville, Tennessee—all symbolic of the erosion of quality and individuality in Southern eateries. Likewise departed and lamented are Fancy Hill Restaurant near Natural Bridge, Virginia, the Lunch Box in Darlington, South Carolina, and the Old Mill Restaurant at Cumberland Gap, where Virginia and Kentucky and Tennessee are joined. It's a sad experience to find a once-great dining spot padlocked and shuttered.

Not all of our failures were a consequence of arriving after the funeral. For a variety of good and bad reasons, we missed eating at a number of places that ranked high on our list of recommended restaurants—Williams Seafood in Savannah, Georgia; Mrs. Speed's Kitchen in Shellman Bluff, Georgia; the Old South Tea Room in Vicksburg, Mississippi; the Shatley Springs Inn at Shatley Springs, North Carolina; the Tale of the Trout in Rogers, Arkansas; and Mosca's and Le Ruth's in New Orleans, to name a few. Perhaps worst of all, we missed the entire southern tip of Florida, including Miami and Key West, as well as the Gulf Coast village of Cedar Key—all prime destinations in our initial plans. Who knows what other treasures escaped us as we went about compiling our random sample of Southern eateries.

But there was a lot we didn't miss. Stopping at 335 restaurants for compar-

Oxford, Mississippi
December 13, 1950

King Gustav VI of Sweden
Stockholm, Sweden

Your Majesty:

I saw a picture of you giving William Faulkner a prize last Monday, and I'll bet William didn't tell you what a big coon and collards eater he is. Now, I told William to carry some delicious

ative purposes in a period of about eight months is an unusual experience, and it taught us some valuable lessons. For example, we disagreed with other people's judgments and with each other enough to learn that what is outstanding to one may be mediocre or even terrible to another, and what is good or authentic or even here today may be bad or phony or gone tomorrow. The lesson: Other people's opinions, subjective as they are, can never predict reliably what your own will be. We found plenty of surprises, too—some unsettling, some puzzling, some whimsical and delightful. They run together in the memory like a jumble of unconnected thoughts:

In C. S.'s Bar in Jackson, Mississippi, one of the featured appetizers looks like fried oysters but turns out to be deep-fried dill pickles—and they're delicious. At the Dixie Kitchen in Berea, Kentucky, and at Hall's on Main, a seafood restaurant in nearby Lexington, there is a similar snack on the menu: fried banana peppers. At Scott's, a ticket-booth-sized street dispensary in Greenville, Mississippi, and at Charlie Greene's rib shop in Knoxville, Tennessee, you can get first-rate Chicano-class hot tamales wrapped in cornshucks or papers. One of the oldest restaurants in or near Little Rock, Arkansas, and one of the most popular eateries in that state, is Mexico Chiquito, a south-of-the-border cafe started in 1935 by a gringo Irishman named W. F. "Blackie" Donnelly. Muscadine wine, first made on these shores by French Huguenot immigrants in the seventeenth century (if, in fact, the Indians didn't beat them to it), is now a viable commercial product in at least eight Southern states. One of the most impressive pie bakeries anywhere in the South is the Family Pie Shop in DeValls Bluff, Arkansas (population 738), where Mary Thomas, working alone in a converted tool shed, turns out diverse dozens of pies daily, and customers come in from all around to snap them up. Two of the four fried-chicken places chosen by diners as the best in Arkansas (the leading poultry-producing state in the United States) are Kentucky Fried Chicken fast-food outlets. Almost half of the restaurant display ads in the Richmond, Virginia, Yellow Pages are for Oriental restaurants, while the colonial and Southern heritage of Richmond is hardly represented there at all. There may be more soul food restaurants in Kentucky, which has the lowest black population in the region, than in Mississippi, which has the highest. Librarians in the South and elsewhere report that books on cooking and books on sex are the most likely to be stolen or checked out and never returned. (This bit of information caused one colleague of mine to remark: "Of course. After all, the two arts have many things in common. One seldom finds full satisfaction in either on a first try, no matter how carefully the recipes are followed—and in both, individual initiative makes a vast difference.") Librarians, incidentally, rank with courthouse workers and traveling sales representatives as the best people to ask for restaurant advice in a strange town.

This stewpot of profundity and trivia is infinitely expandable, like a sim-

coon and collards to you. If he had I am sure you would have given him a larger prize.

In spite of William's dereliction in this respect, I am sure you liked him, because he is the kindest and most courteous person I ever knew. Knowing this, I am sure he treated you with royal respect and courtesy.

．　．　．　．　．

Since you have been so nice to our friend, Mr. Ike Roberts and I and all the rest of the boys invite you to our camp next Fall for a coon and collard dinner, for if you are a friend of William Faulkner's you are a friend of ours. This includes the cooks, the horses and the hounds.

Now, King, I want you to be sure to come to our camp next Fall because I am sure that when you leave you will say you never had a better time and never was in better company.

Please be assured that we Mississippians, and particularly we Lafayette Countians, are deeply grateful to Your Majesty for the courtesies extended our great fellow-citizen.

Sincerely yours,
John B. Cullen
Old Times in the Faulkner Country,
1961

mering kettle of gumbo or burgoo. I'll cut it off arbitrarily after mentioning one more pleasant surprise we found in our travels: The ethnic dimension of Southern food is far more extensive and varied than I had realized. The traditional cuisines of the region embrace all of the foods we identify as soul, country, Creole, Cajun, coastal, mountain, Southern, and just plain home cooking. And beyond these, there are substantial and continuing influences from French, Greek, Spanish, Cuban, Mexican, German, Italian, and Oriental cooking. Add to these such elements as the Shakers in Kentucky, the Moravians in North Carolina, and the Indians in every Southern state, and you have an international and intercultural harvest of gastronomic history that reaches back through four centuries. It is a heritage to be enjoyed and appreciated and cultivated, lest it be swept away in the fast-food tides of packaged uniformity or the deeper undercurrents of perpetual novelty.

With all the changes for better and worse that have come along since World War II, eating out in the South can still be a distinct pleasure, and it is certainly one of the most common of all public activities. At the beginning of this century, restaurant dining in the region was a luxury primarily reserved for wealthy people and certain travelers; now, eating out is as common as eating in for a major segment of the population, and by the start of the next century, it could be that home cooking and dining as we have known them will be largely consigned to history.

Before the curtain is drawn on those private traditions and rituals and daily habits, a lingering look at them is in order, and that is the purpose of the next section, Eating In. Our transition from the public to the private realm of Southern food leads us past three stops in our travels that involved no restaurants or other commercial activity. They were experiences in which we encountered the kitchen wisdom and culinary handiwork of private cooks, all generously offered for the enjoyment of family, friends, and even strangers. These, too, are a rich and valuable part of the tradition of eating out all over the South.

The first belongs to the category of family homecomings, wedding feasts, church dinners on the ground, community food festivals, brotherhood and sisterhood dinners, pie suppers, and other collective repasts that bring private cooking together with public eating. One such feast I attended in 1985 stands out in my memory as an individual feat of impressive dimensions. It was Visiting Friends Day at Mount Pisgah United Methodist Church in the rural countryside of Davidson County, Tennessee. Sister Maggie Dunlap, a professional cook and a lifelong member of the church, has prepared Sunday dinner for the congregation and invited friends once each summer for the past fifteen years or so. "It's a way of saying thanks to the people I love," she said, and her style of expression, like her personality, is generous and overflowing.

In the age of air conditioning, dinner on the ground now means dinner in

A good-sized crowd of farmers was still gathered around the homestead of Harvey and Neal Holzhauer of Gillett [Arkansas] early Thursday afternoon, putting the finishing touches on . . . preparations for the town's 43rd annual Coon Supper Friday night.

A few hours before, the farmers—all members of the event's sponsor, the

the fellowship hall at most churches, and Mount Pisgah is no exception. It was there that Mrs. Dunlap, with others serving but with a minimum of cooking help, assembled a banquet one June day after church. There was baked ham, fried chicken, meat loaf, cornbread dressing, and gravy; congealed salads, deviled eggs, potato salad, sliced tomatoes, marinated onions and cucumbers, chowchow; turnip greens, pinto beans, corn, sweet potatoes, broccoli casserole; cornbread, rolls, coffee, mint tea, chess and pecan pies, chocolate brownies, and four kinds of baked-from-scratch cakes. About a hundred people partook of these thoroughly Southern blessings, and Maggie Dunlap smiled with pleasure and pride as the feast filled the appetites and the hearts of her gathered friends.

The second transitional experience between the public restaurant and the private kitchen has to do with wild game. For as long as human beings have walked the lands of the South, they have hunted animals for food—and for almost that long, they have celebrated the success of the hunt with sumptuous spreads of native food and drink. In every Southern state, all manner of special occasions—coon suppers, rabbit and squirrel dinners, duck and goose banquets, venison feasts—are widely enjoyed as seasonal or annual events. I attended one such affair, a "critter supper," at a rural retreat in southern Kentucky in the spring of 1985, and it was a memorable evening of music, conversation, and fine food.

James E. Gillenwater, an attorney and former county judge, is the chief convenor of the suppers, which have been taking place in various backwoods cabins and lakeside fishing shacks off and on since 1955. Upward of three dozen diners may attend, and they are an interesting mix of farmers and lawyers, fishers and hunters, musicians and storytellers, cooks and eaters. Most of the cooking is done by Layton Harrison or Depp Wheat and his sister Minnie. The night I attended with three Tennessee friends, the menu included groundhog, raccoon, bear, goat, venison, pasture oysters (beef testicles), rabbit, squirrel, chicken, possum, catfish, crappie, bluegill, cole slaw, sweet potatoes, sawmill gravy, and soul bread. A few of the meats were fried, but most were baked or roasted; the sweet potatoes were baked with the coon and possum.

The soul bread was prepared by Tom Hall, one of the Tennesseans, as a gesture of our appreciation for the hosts' hospitality. Drawing upon a recipe entrusted to him by Maggie Dunlap—the same Mrs. Dunlap whose Mount Pisgah feast we have already described—Hall ceremoniously rinsed his hands in a little aged bourbon and then fashioned pones out of a batter made with stone-ground cornmeal and hot water. These were dropped directly into hot lard in a large black cast-iron skillet and fried to a crisp golden brown.

Judge Gillenwater, a blue-eyed, silver-haired Scotsman with a courtly manner, welcomed us cordially before the feast. "We are just simple country people," he said, "but we are rich with the blessings of nature, and we gladly share our

115-member Gillett Farmers' and Businessmen's Club—had removed 2,012 pounds of raccoon from large vats of boiling water spiced with celery and other vegetables "to take out the wild taste," one member said.

The coon was then stored in a refrigerated truck until Friday morning, when the meat was spread over a fire of hickory and oak logs and doused with barbecue sauce.

Across town, at the high school cafeteria, the women of Gillett were cooking 10 bushels of sweet potatoes, 100 pounds of barbecued rice, 14 large hams (for those who decline to eat coon), about 2,000 rolls and numerous cakes.

And by Friday night, most of the coon had been eaten by the 1,200 or so people from five states and about 60 Arkansas towns able to [buy tickets at $11 each] and crowd into the Gillett High School gymnasium.

Stephen Steed,
in the Arkansas Gazette,
January 12, 1986

bounty with our guests from Tennessee, who have come as strangers—but will leave, I trust, as friends." Then, seated in folding chairs around a long wooden table in a plain and spartan tin-roofed shack, we commenced to consume a banquet worthy of the gods. Had a party of early Americans from seventeenth-century Virginia happened upon the scene, they surely would have found the food—and the company—most inviting.

And finally, one more remembrance of eating out in a private, noncommercial Southern setting: on Sapelo Island, a seashore fastness in the labyrinth of salty creeks and marshes on the coast of Georgia.

Sapelo had been known for centuries by Indian, Spanish, and British sojourners (its name is from a Spaniard) when it was bought by a British land speculator in 1760. An agricultural estate for the next thirty years, it was then bought by Frenchmen. In 1802, Thomas Spalding, a Scotsman, came to develop a sprawling cotton and sugar plantation there, and he and his heirs remained for 110 years (excepting the period of the Civil War and its aftermath). Howard Coffin, a founder of the Hudson Motor Company, bought the island in 1912 and kept it for over twenty years, and Richard J. Reynolds, a Reynolds tobacco fortune heir, then held it until midcentury, when an agricultural research foundation took control of the property. The University of Georgia has a marine biology research laboratory that is the principal activity on the island now.

The main house on Sapelo, a mansion begun by Thomas Spalding 175 years ago, is now used primarily as a conference center. We were invited there in the fall of 1984 to learn about the island's foodways. Our hosts included two people with more than a passing interest in the social and cultural dimensions of Southern food: Reita Rivers of the University of Georgia, who, drawing on her family roots in the mountains of Kentucky and Virginia, wanted to work with people in the small, long-established community of black residents on the island to develop a book of recipes and local food history; and Charles Durant, a resident administrator, who had grown up in a coastal family of fishermen—his father was a pioneer in the commercial shrimping business on the East Coast, trucking iced shellfish to the Fulton Fish Market in New York back in the 1930s.

In the main dining room of the old house, about a dozen people gathered for a dinner that included such local dishes of special note as shrimp pilau, smoked mullet, and sweet potatoes. Later, in the kitchen, I learned from thirty-five-year-old Lula Walker, the cook, that the people who lived on Sapelo "still try to keep some of the traditions we were raised by." The examples she mentioned all had to do with food: "Yard chickens, home-grown vegetables, lots of fish, collard greens, sweet potatoes—it's just plain cooking, Southern cooking, whatever you want to call it. I use more seasoning in the food I cook at home than we do in this kitchen. We serve some fancy dishes here, and some things that aren't Southern, but what I fix at home is the kind of food that people on

Sapelo have been eating for a long, long time—hoppin John, red beans, dried limas, cornbread, pork roast, possum and sweet potatoes, raccoon and rice, and of course all the seafood we get around here. We don't have lard the way we used to, or crackling to make crackling bread, and I don't make cakes with grated citrus rind and real butter the way my great-granny did, but I'd say most of our food hasn't changed."

Some of Lula Walker's older kin remembered earlier times. Hicks Walker, eighty-one years of age, could name more than a dozen kinds of fish his grand-mother used to cook in the open fireplace—and his mother cooked them too, on her woodstove. "We killed our own hogs back then," he recalled, "and salted and smoked the meat. We made our own sugar and syrup from cane, and our tea from sassafras roots, and wine from muscadines, and my grandmother wrapped ashcakes in pumpkin leaves and baked them in the fire. We still eat some of those old dishes, like smoked mullet and hominy grits, but a lot of that food has left here. The new ones, they don't cook like the old-time people. One of my grandsons cooks in a restaurant in New York, and he says people like what he fixes—but of course it's not the same as here."

The oldest resident of Sapelo Island, Annie Walker, remembered too, and she spoke with expressiveness and clarity from her perspective of more than ninety years. She recalled the cotton and rice fields, the pecan groves, the abun-dant wild grapes, and "working in the fields and in the kitchen from the time I was eight years old." The staples in her family's diet were fish, chicken, and pork, beans and greens, rice and potatoes, cornbread—the foods she still prefers:

"I like bass, croaker, trout, yellowtail. And stewed oysters, now that's a good dish—a little bacon, a little flour, then your oysters, maybe some water, then season it with salt and red pepper. You need grits with fish—I don't ever cook a fish if I got no grits to go with it. Did you ever have punkin grits? Now that's a dish. You peel your punkin, cut it up, cook it, mash it. Then you cut up some bacon—side meat—and you cook it, and throw off some of the grease. Then you put the bacon in the pot with the punkin, put in your grits, cover the pot and cook it, and you got something good. Black-eyed peas, red peas, corn-bread—that's my kind of food. And collard greens—you're supposed to eat them without fail on New Year's Day, because they're green like money, and they bring you good luck."

Annie Walker's favorite foods have come from long ago and far away and near at hand, from subtropical climates, from dark woods and fertile soils and warm coastal waters. They echo Africa, as surely as France resonates in the cuisines of Louisiana, and like those Creole and Cajun foods, the cookery of Sapelo Island is fundamentally Southern in its heart and soul. It is one more example, original and yet familiar, of food as a defining element in the history and culture of the region.

I was then able to show my guests a Savannah picnic, which is an institu-tion peculiar to the place. Leaving the city in a river steamer our party consisting of one hundred people, after a little over an hour's sail we reached an island in the Atlantic Ocean, known as Dawfuskie, a beautiful spot on which stood a charming residence, with five acres of roses surrounding the house. The heads of families carried, each of them, huge baskets containing their dinner, and a full table service, wine, etc., for say, ten or a dozen people. On our arrival, all formed into groups under the trees, a cloth was laid on the ground, dishes, plates and glasses arranged on it, and the champagne at once frapped in small hand pails. There was then a dance in the open air, on a platform, and in the afternoon, with cushions as seats for the ladies, these impro-vised dinner-tables were filled. Each had its separate hostess; all was har-mony and pleasure. As night ap-proached, the people re-embarked on the steamer and returned home by moonlight.

Ward McAllister
Society As I Have Found It, 1890

EATING IN:

Southern Food at Home

Sometimes the nicest thing about traveling is getting home. Too many miles and too many meals can finally dull the senses; the states and cities and towns begin to blur and run together at the edges, the restaurants and their menus take on a predictable veneer of sameness, and finally a yearning vaguely akin to homesickness sets in, a longing for nothing more than a cup of tea and a piece of dry toast and a good night's sleep in your own bed.

Our journeys in search of Southern food through the winter and spring of 1985 often lasted a week or more, and they seemed to come up with increasing frequency as the months wore on. They were in a sense only preliminary, however, to a longer and more complex undertaking that lay ahead: researching and writing the home-cooking phase of the book.

Periodically through the fall and winter and spring, and then more intensively from June 1985 until the following spring, we worked our way through consideration of several hundred recipes and the stories behind them. All in all, we actually prepared and sampled about four hundred recipes, and finally settled on approximately 160 as a broadly representative sample of Southern cookery at its diverse and delicious best. These are the recipes we present in the pages that follow. All of them have been tested by us, and some have also been tried by others who volunteered for the enjoyable task, or whom we enlisted for that purpose. Whenever necessary, old recipes have been adapted to modern methods and materials in order to make them functional.

All of the foods in this collection have had a long identification with the South. They include native and original foods, local creations, and dishes adapted from other places and other cultures. Regardless of their origins, they have enjoyed great and lasting popularity in the Southern states; in fact, their longevity and their place in the social and cultural history of the region may have as much to do with their inclusion in these pages as their culinary qualities. It bears repeating that the recipes in these pages were chosen for their historical interest and their narrative qualities as well as for their appearance and taste. They are *broadly representative* of Southern cookery at its best, not necessarily *the best Southern recipes* by any meaningful standard of judgment.

With allowances for some notable exceptions, it seems fair to say that the best Southern food now available is just where it has always been: at home. As much as home cooking has changed, it is still the most reliable source of the best Southern hot breads and vegetables and the widest range of choice desserts. To be sure, these dishes are not as easily found as they once were, because not as many home cooks still prepare them. The art of Southern cookery requires time, skill, and experience, as well as fresh foodstuffs of the highest quality, and a declining number of people seem willing or able to bring these elements to the task. But the foodstuffs can be found, the skill can be mastered, the experience can be gained, and the time spent can be satisfying and enjoy-

Yes, you're cooking on the Dixie Range
even though you've had to change
two electric eyes gone bad
and lay the deep well to rest. But you're glad
the Dixie Range keeps on cooking,
looking good in white enamel and chrome, booking
meal after meal into History digested.
Here the South was never bested!
Supper's ready. Now bow your head,
say a quick "A-men!" then pass the cornbread.
A knock on the door . . . There's plenty in the pot
to share with a friend. Come on, grab a plate. It's hot!

Robert Michie, poet
from "Cooking on the Dixie Range," 1981

able. People who make the effort to partake of these treasures from the past are apt to gain more than a taste of history; they can also look forward to the pleasure of preparing and sharing some wonderful things to eat.

On July 1, 1985, as the summer garden season was reaching its peak in the South, we sat down at home to a dinner of pan-fried chicken, fresh buttered beets, green beans cooked with a chunk of seasoning bacon, fried corn (some call it stewed or creamed), new potatoes, sliced tomatoes, cucumbers and onions, freshly made apple sauce, cornmeal griddle cakes, iced tea with mint, and peach cobbler. It was the best meal I had eaten in months, or so it seemed—everything in its prime, fresh from a Tennessee farm or garden and hot off the stove. As good as many of our restaurant meals were, I can think of only a few places that consistently offer the variety and quality of dinners like that one.

Later, Thanksgiving dinner at the same table delivered a different kind of feast: roast turkey and cornbread dressing, country ham and beaten biscuits, ambrosia, cranberry sauce, sweet potato casserole, oyster casserole, baby lima beans, mashed potatoes and gravy, yeast rolls, pickled peaches, coffee, coconut cake, chess pie, and boiled custard. Dinners such as this are not everyday occasions, but neither are they unattainable pleasures from the distant past. Recipes for about twenty of the dishes served at these two meals are included below. They are not family heirlooms, more to be admired as works of art than reproduced and enjoyed; they are little pieces of Southern history, inviting you to partake. Just as the best way to learn about Southern restaurant food is to get out on the road and try it, so the best exposure to home cooking is to get into the kitchen with some appealing recipes. One of the strengths of this collection is that it invites such experimentation and discovery. Taken as a whole, these recipes cover a broad range of foods in Southern history that both master cooks and novices can happily embrace.

In the organization and presentation of the recipes, I have tried to follow a simple and logical method that will help readers to find, easily and quickly, whatever foods they seek. The arrangement is thus both alphabetical and progressive, from accompaniments at the beginning of a meal to sweets at the end.

Accompaniments takes in foods that precede or complement a good dinner: jellies, jams, and preserves; pickles and relishes; sauces, gravies, and dressings; snacks, spreads, and nibblings. Not only are the categories alphabetical, but the listings within each category are too. The order thus serves as an internal index, and the same is true in the other five groupings of recipes.

Beverages covers everything from water and milk to soft drinks and whiskey in the general discussion, but the recipes are divided into two sections: everyday drinks (coffee, iced tea, lemonade) and holiday/party/dessert drinks (boiled custard, café brûlot, eggnog, mint julep, sangria, syllabub, and such).

My mother loved to cook, and fed everyone who came to her door. If anyone passed the house near mealtime, she would ask them to come in and eat with her. She often said she hoped no one had passed her house hungry.

They had a large family, so the table was extra long. My mother always had this big long table filled with bowls and platters of food, more than enough for her own family.

My sister told me of one time when seven men stopped in out of a rain storm. They were on their way from Carr [Kentucky], going to Wayland to work in the coal mines. When the men came into the house, my mother had dinner on the table. She asked the men to eat with them. All she added extra on the table were the seven plates and seven knives and forks. Yet everyone had all they wanted to eat.

Verna Mae Slone
What My Heart Wants to Tell, 1979

Breads ranges over the entire spectrum of cornmeal and flour creations, with about two dozen recipes in four classifications: biscuits and rolls, breakfast breads, cornbreads, and loaf breads. The focus throughout is on the Southern penchant for hot breads.

Main Dishes, next in the alphabetical list as well as on the dinner table, is divided into six sections, under each of which are four or more recipes. The six are beef, chicken, game, pork, seafood and freshwater fish, and a selection of soups and stews.

Side Dishes is made up of more than thirty recipes in four units: cheese and egg dishes, fruit dishes, salads, and vegetables (including rice dishes). There are at least five recipes in each section, with by far the most—about twenty— under vegetables and rice.

Sweets concludes the categories and the meal with about thirty recipes in five groupings: cakes; candies and cookies; pies, cobblers, and dumplings; puddings; and specialty desserts. As with the other five main groupings, the list of sweets is in no sense comprehensive, but it is generally representative of the best-known and most appreciated of Southern desserts.

In all our sampling of Southern recipes, we naturally experienced some frustrations and failures along with the many pleasures. When Ann was doing the cooking, the gastronomical benefits were usually substantial; on the occasions when I was in charge, the results were far less predictable. But my mistakes— even my disasters—were at least instructive, and all of them were valuable learning experiences. Whether I was cooking or simply taking notes, I gained a deeper respect and appreciation for the women and men of earlier times in the South who overcame great obstacles to produce culinary wonders of superior quality.

Accompaniments

JELLIES, JAMS, PRESERVES

Southerners have been preserving food at home for centuries, and from the early 1800s until the post–World War II era, a major portion of all the food they ate was "put up" in some manner for later consumption. Glass containers with sealed lids first came into limited use in this country about 1820, and within fifty years they had become commonplace among home canners generally. For decades after the Civil War, Southerners dried, salted, pickled, potted, canned, jelled, or otherwise preserved almost every kind of food. The advancement of refrigeration and freezing in the twentieth century has made most foods commercially available the year around, and of course these newer methods are also at the service of the housekeeper. Home canning and freezing are no longer as common as they once were, in the South or anywhere else, but there are still many people who carry on the ancient practice of preserving foods in one way or another. Whether or not it is an economical alternative to grocery shopping, it does yield products that are usually superior in appearance, taste, and nutritive value.

It takes experience to master the art. With jellies, jams, and preserves, a good place to start is simply to learn the terminology—to distinguish, for example, between jelly (made from fruit juice), jam (from fruit pulp), preserves (whole or chunk fruit), butter (puréed fruit), marmalade (fruit pulp and rinds), and conserve (fruits mixed with nuts and raisins). It is also helpful to have some understanding of the relative levels of natural pectin, sugar, and acid in certain fruits, and when these should be supplemented to assure jelling or to enhance flavor. The cook must also acquire the skill of judging—by time, temperature, color, or consistency—when a fruit has cooked long enough. The sterilizing of jars, the use of rubber-lined lids or paraffin as sealers, and the special cooking and packaging requirements for freezing foods are among the other aspects of home canning and preserving that should be studied. (These general rules should be followed: Jars, whether new or used, should be sterilized. Paraffin can be used to seal jams and jellies, but almost all other canned products require sterilized vacuum-seal dome lids. These lids should be new, the better to assure tight seals; the screw-on portion of two-piece lids does not have to be new, but should be sterilized.)

But the process is not as complicated as it may seem. Detailed instructions on all these matters are readily available in many cookbooks and in special publications of the U.S. Department of Agriculture and the state and county representatives of agricultural extension programs; the companies that sell food

See that your table is set with neatness, and every thing on it well ordered, then there will be no danger of being frustrated by unexpected company. Never strive to have a great variety of made dishes on your table when you have but few to eat with you: perhaps half of them would not be tasted; it of course would only be a superfluous waste. Just try to learn what your company is fondest of, and have their favorites. A few things well ordered will never fail to give a greater appetite, and pleasure to your guest, than a crowded table badly prepared; and as there is a time for all things, there will be a time to crowd your table with delicacies. We should not only consult economy, but daily practice it; which is nothing more than a saving knowledge, carried into action. Such a course will bind up a lasting treasure for the rich, and secure a plentiful living to the poor.

Mrs. Lettice Bryan
The Kentucky Housewife, 1839

preservation equipment and supplies also publish materials on canning and freezing. It's easy to find out how much sugar should be added to a given fruit, or when lemon juice is needed to increase acidity, or what the optimum degree of ripeness is for making the best jam or jelly. There are charts that show jell-causing pectin to be high in some fruits (apples, barely ripe blackberries, grapes, plums) and low in others (peaches, strawberries, cherries), and there are commercial fruit pectins that greatly simplify jam and jelly making and assure a more uniformly favorable result.

Like any handmade product, a good jelly takes time, skill, and energy, and with so many commercial varieties in the groceries, it may seem hardly worth the effort to make it at home. But then, how many stores can offer such exotic flavors as muscadine jam, sumac-berry jelly, wild apricot preserves, or mango butter, and how could either the flavor or the history of something like quince jelly ever be captured in a store-bought jar? Molasses and honey also come from the supermarket, but they are no match for the sorghum and sourwood that country people put up at home, and the same is true of such homemade specialties as apple butter and cranberry sauce.

When Ben Hutcherson was growing up in a tenant-farming family around Jingo, Tennessee, in the 1920s, he watched and learned as his mother made jams and jellies from the fruits and berries that grew wild around them. Jingo has become Fairview in the modern age, and Hutcherson's jelly making also includes a modern touch with the addition of packaged fruit pectin. "It's quicker," he says, "and it takes the guesswork out of cooking the fruit." But he still uses the same methods and the same fruits and berries that his mother favored, and he also gets the same good results. From sumac bushes, for example, he gathers deep red berries that stand up in a tightly bunched cone (another variety, of gray metallic color and drooping, are said to be poisonous) and boils them to extract a sour liquid. Mixed with sugar, lime juice, and pectin, it makes a tart and distinctively flavored jelly. "Sumac—or shoemake, as we always called it—is an old, old jelly," says Hutcherson. "The Indians used to make it."

The Indians of Florida and the Caribbean also had guavas, a pear-shaped sweet fruit from which jelly is made, and the Europeans who came to the East Coast in the seventeenth century brought quince, a similar-looking but very tart fruit. The earliest of cookbooks used in this country contained recipes for quince jelly, and jams and preserves made from cherries, strawberries, and plums were also common in the colonial period. The quince tree is rarely seen in the United States now, but a low ornamental shrub known as japonica, or Japanese quince, bears a hard, tart, quincelike fruit that some Southern traditionalists use to make jelly. Clearly, the making of jams and jellies still holds an attraction for cooks who, like Ben Hutcherson, enjoy the search for food in history—and for history in food.

From the many jellies, jams, and preserves that are closely identified with the South (albeit enjoyed elsewhere too, of course), we have chosen six to present here.

Blackberry Jam

The first English settlers found blackberries growing in Virginia 380 years ago. The Indians ate them both raw and cooked. Only the very ripest of blackberries have a natural sweetness; before they reach that stage they're firm and tart, even sour—but still delectable when sprinkled with sugar (a staple brought to the New World by Columbus). Given the affinity between berries and sugar, it was probably inevitable that they would find their way into the same stewpot. Something very much like blackberry jam must have been cooking over colonial fires long before the American Revolution—and if so, the method used then could not have differed very much from this dependable recipe.

Wash 1 quart (4 cups) of firm, tart, barely ripe blackberries in a colander and put them in a large enamel or stainless-steel cooking pot. (It's best to make preserves of all kinds in small quantities—1 quart or so at a time is ideal—but a 3- or 4-quart pan should be used to allow ample room for rapid cooking.) Stir and mash the berries over low heat and then add ⅔ cup to 1 scant cup of sugar for each cup of berries, tasting to get the right balance of tartness and sweetness. When the sugar has dissolved and the mixture is a lumpy mass of juice and pulp, bring it to a boil and cook, stirring frequently, for about 20 minutes. (There will be lots of foam at first; skim it off and discard it.)

Judging when the jam has cooked long enough may be difficult. The total cooking time might vary from 15 to 30 minutes; the liquid should be thick enough to drip slowly from the spoon, and a small quantity of it dropped on a cold plate should stay in place and not be runny. (A more certain method is to use commercial pectin, following the directions on the package.) Remove from heat and pour into sterilized half-pint or pint jars. Seal when cool with melted paraffin or new lids and wait for a winter morning and a pan of hot biscuits. Four cups of berries will make about 2 pints (4 cups) of jam.

"Honey," said Mother Mayberry with a pleased laugh as she seated the minister's wife in a large rocker under the honeysuckle vine, "don't you know that nothing in the world compliments a woman like the asking her for one of her cooking rules? I never took much notice to my 'Riz' biscuits until Ellinory got to making me famous for 'em, but this is the recipe that both me and my cousin Selina Sue down to the Bluff brought with us from our old home in Warren County [Tennessee]. You mix a teaspoonful of soda and one of salt in a quart of sifted flour and then rub in a lump of lard the size of a big hen egg. After it's all rubbed fine, mix it with good buttermilk into as light a dough as you can handle, cut thin and bake in a quick oven. Served with blackberry jam, or ham gravy, they are mighty apt to put men folks in a good humor with the world."

Maria Thompson Daviess, quoted by Mrs. W. C. Cleveland, in Some Favorite Recipes, 1911

Damson Jam

The sour little purple damson plums that ripen in the mid-South in August and September are descendants of a fruit the British have enjoyed for centuries. The plums have to be very ripe in order to taste good raw, but firm and tart ones cooked with sugar make wonderful preserves—skins included. There are freestone damsons now, and it's easy to split them and remove the single large seed. Under the purple skin, the fruit stays greenish yellow in color until it becomes fully ripe, or until you cook it; then it turns a deep crimson. The recipe is similar to the blackberry jam formula:

> Start with 1 quart (4 cups) of split and seeded plums, skins on. Put fruit in a large pot with ¼ to ½ cup of water and cook over low heat, stirring and mashing, for about 10 minutes, or until plums are tender and mushy. Add 1 cup of sugar per cup of fruit (more or less, depending on tartness). Blend together and bring to a rolling boil. Reduce heat and, stirring frequently, continue boiling for about 10 more minutes, or until liquid pours in a sheet from spoon and a small amount dropped on a cold plate stays together in a soft ring. Remove from heat, stir well, and pour or spoon into sterilized jars. Seal with paraffin or new lids. A quart of damsons will make about 2 pints (4 cups) of preserves.

Guava Jelly

Guavas are native to tropical America; the trees were reported growing in the Caribbean by Columbus. In south Florida today, guavas still flourish, yielding a sweet-tasting pear-shaped fruit with a reddish color and a pungent odor. They can be eaten raw, but the most common way to use them is to cook the fruit, strain the juice, and make jelly from it. This recipe has been a standard in Florida for many years:

> Select firm, tart guavas, not overripe. Wash the fruit, cut off the blossom end, and slice the rest into a large heavy pot. Barely cover with water and cook with a lid on over low heat until the fruit is soft. Stir and mash to release all the liquid. When the fruit is fully cooked, put the mixture in a jelly bag or clean pillowcase and hang over a large bowl to drip overnight.
>
> To make the jelly, put 2 cups of guava juice, 2 cups of sugar, and 2 tablespoons of lemon or lime juice into a large saucepan, stir it to a boil over high heat, and continue boiling for 8 to 10 minutes. As soon as it

A cruet of sorghum or 'lasses was standard equipment on tables from early fall to late spring. . . . Sorghum is still made but the supply is limited. It appears in neighborhood grocery stores and at farmers' markets packed in fruit jars or jugs in late October or early November. Most of the sorghum will turn to sugar or will ferment with the warm spring weather. But with a family which loves to "sop" the supply is gone long before warm weather arrives, and they begin looking forward to a new batch in the fall. Soppin' sorghum is rather an art— one based on the individual. Some folks begin by slicing off a big hunk of soft butter. Sorghum is poured over the butter and the two are stirred together. Big flecks of yellow butter mingle with the golden syrup. A hot biscuit is pushed around and around in this mixture until it is coated. Those who are dainty push the biscuit with a fork, but most often, the biscuit is hand pushed.

Elizabeth Hedgecock Sparks
North Carolina and Old Salem Cookery, 1955

begins to lose its liquid form and show signs of jelling, pour into sterilized jars and cover when cool with paraffin or two-piece lids. Two cups of juice should make a pint of jelly.

It's much better to make small amounts of jelly one after the other than to attempt one large batch; larger amounts must be cooked longer, are harder to regulate, and produce uneven quality.

Muscadine Jam

Muscadines, also called scuppernongs, are a variety of wild or fox grapes that flourished along the Eastern Seaboard long before the Europeans arrived, and they still can be found growing uncultivated in many parts of the South. There are both deep purple and yellow-white types of these thick-skinned grapes, and their musky odor may explain the origin of their most common name. Muscadines have been used since the seventeenth century to make jams and wines. They are now grown commercially in some Southern states; the Carolina Blueberry Co-op Association in Burgaw, North Carolina, is one source. We purchased a quantity of white muscadines from co-op member Clayton Chestnut of Tabor City and subsequently made jam by the following fairly standard method.

Squeeze the pulp from the skins, separate the seeds from the pulp, and discard the seeds. Cook the skins until they are tender, then recombine them with the pulp and juice. For each cupful, add ¾ cup of sugar and boil the mixture, stirring frequently, for 10 to 20 minutes, or until the juice becomes noticeably thicker. Put up in half-pint jars and seal when cool with paraffin or two-piece lids. Each cup of the fruit should make a half-pint (1 cup) of jam. Muscadine jam has a flavor as distinctive as the raw grapes.

Peach Preserves

From the time the Spaniards first brought peaches to this continent, they were an immediate success, "spreading through Indian America faster than the white man did," according to food historian Waverley Root. Recipes for peach preserves are among the oldest in our cookbooks, and the Southern states have always been the primary source of the fruit. This method of cooking preserves is remarkably similar to many others:

Measure 4 cups of peeled and sliced fresh peaches. Put them in a glass or crockery bowl, sprinkle on 3 cups of sugar, and let the mixture stand overnight, covered but unrefrigerated. Next day, transfer to a large saucepan and boil for 15 to 30 minutes, stirring frequently to keep them from sticking. When the preserves begin to thicken, stir in a pinch or two of salt and 2 tablespoons of lemon juice. Remove from heat, pour into sterilized jars, and seal when cool with paraffin or two-piece lids. Four cups of peaches will make 2 pints of preserves.

Pepper Jelly

Slowly over the past three or four decades, pepper jelly has gained wide popularity in the South and a certain mystique beyond the region. It's a sweet-hot concoction, often used as a topping for cream cheese on crackers. It seems to have originated after World War II; the earliest recipe we could find is in *Charleston Receipts*, published in 1950. Recipes for pepper jelly vary considerably, some calling for two or three times more sugar or more peppers than others. Having tried several, Ann finally came up with this version.

Remove core and seeds from 6 medium-sized red bell peppers and 6 to 12 jalapeños (mild or hot, as you like), mince the peppers, and combine them in a large saucepan with 6 cups of sugar, 1 cup of white vinegar (5% acidity), and ½ cup of fresh lemon juice. (The jalapeños are best handled with rubber gloves, for their fiery quality lingers on the fingers.) Simmer for about 10 minutes, or until the peppers are nearly tender. Mash the mixture through a strainer to obtain all the juice, discard the peppers, and return the juice to the pot. Bring to a rolling boil, add 6 ounces of liquid commercial pectin, and let the mixture boil hard again for 1 minute. Remove from heat immediately, skim off foam (if any), and pour into sterilized half-pint jars. When the jelly has cooled and become firm, cover it with paraffin or a two-piece lid. This recipe makes 6 to 8 jars of red-orange jelly—a delicate balance of pepper-hot and sugar-sweet flavors.

PICKLES, RELISHES

The use of salt water (brine) or vinegar to preserve foods is called pickling, and it was employed extensively before refrigeration to prolong the edible life of all sorts of foods—fish, meat, vegetables, fruits. (Salt in dry form has also been used for centuries to preserve and cure meats.) Since vinegar has its own distinctive flavor and can also act as a carrier of other strong flavors such as herbs and spices, pickling had become a versatile tool of European cooks by the time American colonization began. The earliest cookbooks used in this country thus reveal a multiplicity of foods preserved and flavored by pickling.

In its modern usage, "pickle" is more often a noun than a verb, and it is applied primarily to cucumbers that have been preserved by some variation or other of the ancient process. But pickling remained a vital home-kitchen technique until refrigeration and freezing came along, and like home canning, it is still done by people who appreciate the end result. Southerners have long prided themselves on their pickled foods, as their old and new cookbooks clearly show. Many kinds of vegetables—beets, beans, peppers, corn, onions, and of course cucumbers, to name some of the most common—are still put up in vinegar and spices or chopped and combined to make relish; fruits, too (peaches especially), are favorites for pickling.

The practical necessity of getting maximum benefit from the harvest and minimizing spoilage led generations of early farmers and homemakers to invent numerous ways of serving and preserving foods. Peaches are an illustrative example. Without benefit of a refrigerator or freezer, Southerners at the turn of the century made the most of the peach crop by eating them raw; making peach butter, jam, and preserves; baking pies, cakes, and dumplings; using the fruit in bread and ice cream; making peach leather (a sugared purée dried in the sun); drying peach slices; making peach brandy; and pickling whole peaches in a vinegary spice.

Pickled peaches are one of a small sample of pickles and relishes for which we have provided recipes here. As condiments adding spice and color to a variety of meat and vegetable dishes, these five have been popular mainstays on Southern tables for many decades.

Chowchow

John F. Mariani, in his *Dictionary of American Food & Drink,* says "chowchow" may be derived from the Mandarin Chinese word *cha,* meaning "mixed," and goes back to the 1840s and the coming of Chinese laborers as immigrant workers to California. Whatever the origin of the word, the vegetable relish it is applied to has been known in the South and elsewhere in this country for well over two hundred years. Also called piccalilli (another word of uncertain origin) and Indian pickle, this spicy mixture of chopped and pickled vegetables was

"Good old Brother Bethune," somebody was murmuring out in the crowd, "he's warming up now."

"No corn in our cribs, no meal in our barrel, no feed and no shoes and no clothing—tra la la la!" he sang. . . . "Pigs is eating on the watermelons. All you people without any watermelons come on over to my house. Too cheap to haul from the field this year! And yet! It'd be a mighty hard stunt to starve a bunch like us. . . . We got hay made and in the barn, we'll soon have some fresh meat, the good ladies has stocked the closet shelf with what garden we saved by hauling water. We got milk and butter and eggs, and maybe even after today's slaughter there'll be a few chickens left. . . ."

"Tell us some more!" the men cried, their voices aching with laughter the same as his, while Miss Beulah behind Jack's shoulder cried, "Ready for your next plateful? Here's the sausage I saved you from last year's hog! Here's some more home-cured ham, make room for more chicken. Elvie! Buttermilk! This time bring him the whole pitcher!"

Eudora Welty
Losing Battles, 1970

included in many early American recipe collections, including the 1770 receipt book of Harriott Pinckney Horry of South Carolina. (She called it Ats Jaar, or Pucholilla, but didn't say where those terms came from.)

Modern recipes for chowchow vary somewhat, but most contain green tomatoes, onions, hot peppers, sweet peppers, and cabbage (cucumbers, celery, and cauliflower are used optionally). The vegetables are chopped fine, mixed with vinegar and sugar, seasoned with various spices, cooked, and then put up in jars. Here is a typical recipe.

Begin with a peck (¼ bushel) of hard green tomatoes (about 4 dozen of medium size), 6 medium-sized onions, 12 bell peppers (6 red, 6 green), a medium-sized bunch of crisp celery, and about half of a medium-sized head of cabbage. Chop them coarse. (This is slow work by hand, a little faster with a food chopper, and a quick job with a food processor, but the last way tends to extract too much liquid from the vegetables, making the mixture runny. Hand chopping may make for the best texture, consistency, and taste.) Mix everything in a large heavy pot and add 4 cups of cider vinegar (5% acidity), 4 cups of sugar, and salt to suit your taste (about 1 tablespoon to start). Mix well, bring to a boil, and then lower the heat and simmer uncovered for 1½ hours, stirring occasionally to prevent sticking. Midway through the cooking process, tie 4 tablespoons of pickling spices (a commercial product) in a cloth and add to the pot. When the relish is tender and well-seasoned, remove and discard the spice bag. Ladle the piping hot mixture into sterilized pint jars and seal them with new two-piece lids. The recipe makes about 12 pints.

Cucumber Pickles

Mary Randolph had a recipe for cucumber pickles in *The Virginia House-Wife* in 1824, and she was not the first—and certainly not the last—to discover the highest destiny of a vegetable that archaeologists say was being cultivated in Southeast Asia ten thousand years ago. The cucumber seems made to be a pickle; nothing else makes a better one, and its other uses in cooking are rather limited. This recipe for Old South Cucumber Lime Pickles comes from antiquity in Tupelo, Mississippi, and has been widely circulated.

Dissolve 2 cups of pickling lime (available in groceries) in 2 gallons of water. Wash 7 pounds of cucumbers, slice them crosswise about ¼ inch thick, and soak 12 hours or more in the lime and water mixture (a crockery or enamel container is best for this). Rinse cucumbers 3 times in clean water, then soak 3 more hours in ice water and drain in a colander. Make a syrup of 10 cups of white vinegar (5% acidity), 10 cups of sugar, 1 tablespoon of non-iodized salt, and 2 teaspoons of pickling spices (a commercial product). Bring to a low boil, stir until the sugar is dissolved, and remove from heat. Return the cucumbers to the crockery or enamel vessel, pour the syrup over them, and let stand 5 hours or more. Next, boil the cucumbers in the syrup for 35 minutes and then, using a teacup and a wide-mouth funnel, pour them into sterilized pint jars, making sure that the pickles are completely covered with syrup. Seal the jars with new two-piece lids and store them for several weeks, by which time they should be tart, crisp, crunchy, and full of spicy flavor. This recipe should produce about 12 pints. Keep each jar refrigerated after it has been opened.

Pickled Okra

Like pepper jelly, pickled okra seems to have surfaced about forty years ago and rocketed to prominence as a favorite condiment of the "Old South." If it pre-dated World War II, it was surely one of the best-kept secrets of its time. The oldest recipe we could find for it is, like the one for pepper jelly, in *Charleston Receipts* (1950). Most recipes for pickled okra are similar.

Wash and stem 3 pounds of fresh okra pods no longer than 4 inches and place them in sterilized pint jars, alternating stem ends and points to get a snug fit. Along with the okra, put into each jar a small clove of garlic, two small slices of onion, one small red pepper pod, ½ teaspoon of celery seed, and ½ teaspoon of dill seed (or a sprig of fresh dill). In a saucepan, boil 1 quart of white vinegar (5% acidity), 1 cup of water, and ½ cup of non-iodized salt, simmer 5 minutes, and then fill the jars with it, completely covering the okra. Seal the jars with new lids and store them at least 6 weeks for best flavor. Serve chilled as an appetizer or accompaniment. Three pounds of okra will make about 8 pints.

Pickled Peaches

South Carolina and Georgia are the leading peach producers in the South, and cookbooks from those states are filled with recipes for this versatile fruit.

Pickled peaches have been a dinner-table treat in many parts of the South since colonial times, and they still are a popular accompaniment prized for their distinctive flavor. This recipe is typical of most.

Select about 12 small, firm clingstone peaches (5 or 6 of the right size can be wedged into a pint jar). Dip them in boiling water for 1 minute, slip the skins off, and stick about 5 whole cloves into each peach. In a saucepan, combine 2 cups of cider vinegar (5% acidity), 2 cups of sugar, 1 cup of water, and 2 cinnamon sticks. Bring to a boil, stirring well, and continue boiling for 20 minutes. Put the peaches into the syrup, cover the pot, reduce heat, and simmer 5 minutes or a little longer. Then pack the peaches into sterilized jars, cover completely with syrup, and seal with new lids. Store for at least 6 weeks before using. Serve chilled. This recipe yields 2 pints.

Watermelon Rind Pickles

Virginia is the home of this pickle; the earliest cookbooks there feature it, and it shows up now on menus in most "old Virginia" restaurants. It is made from the white portion between the green rind and the pink flesh of the watermelon, and the most tedious task in making the pickles is extracting this firm flesh and cutting it into thin wafers about 1 inch square.

Soak 8 cups of rind chips overnight in a bowl of water containing ¼ cup of coarse non-iodized salt. Drain and rinse chips, then cover with fresh water in a large pot. Bring to a boil, reduce heat, cover, and cook at a low boil for 5 minutes, leaving chips firm and crisp. Remove from heat. In another pot, combine 4 cups of sugar, 2 cups of cider vinegar (5% acidity), 2 cups of water, 1 lemon, sliced thin, 1 tablespoon of whole cloves, and 2 cinnamon sticks. Bring to a boil, simmer uncovered for 20 minutes, remove spices and lemon slices, put rind chips in the pot, and simmer for 5 to 10 minutes. Then ladle pickles into sterilized jars, cover well with syrup, seal with new lids and store. Makes 4 pints.

SAUCES, GRAVIES, DRESSINGS

At the first mention of rich and savory sauces, it is almost impossible not to think of New Orleans and south Louisiana, for that is the region where fine

My aunt puts a Southern dinner on the table: pork chops and cream gravy, a platter of fried chicken, a vast square pan of dressing with the giblets in it, green beans simmered all day with onions and a piece of salt meat, a dish of fried okra, which I especially love, sliced tomatoes so solid and delectable as to suffice for dinner all by themselves, home-made relishes and pickles, white beans and ham hock, field peas cooked for an eternity and served with hot peppers on the side, fresh biscuits and cornbread—fine-textured, sour, flat, white cornbread made from stone-ground meal and buttermilk. There are a few things missing: the brick of fresh-churned butter, the bowl of clabber, the pitcher of warm buttermilk with the yellow flecks still swimming in it— they don't keep a cow these days.

We eat this feast in shifts around an enormous oak table set with ten plates at a time. . . . I fill my plate twice over, and Cecil tells me I'll fade away if I can't do better than

sauces have highlighted the cuisine for more than two centuries. The French influence is principally responsible; both New Orleans Creole and Louisiana Cajun, city and country cousins of international culinary renown, are prime beneficiaries of the great and venerable traditions of French cooking. Drawing heavily on their Franco-Southern heritage, Creole and Cajun cooks have created dozens of memorable sauces, gravies, and dressings, including the basic brown roux (see page 194), white and cream sauces, vinaigrette, béarnaise, remoulade (see page 293), and hot-pepper sauces that are bottled and sold around the world.

Mayonnaise and hollandaise and meunière sauce seem to belong as much to Louisiana as to France, and old and new cookbooks alike feature hundred-year-old recipes for all these exceptional taste enhancers. In both quantity and quality, none of the books is more impressive than *The Picayune Creole Cook Book,* first published in 1900. It contains recipes for sixty-seven sauces, including many still being used at such long-established New Orleans restaurants as Antoine's and Arnaud's. The *Picayune's* white and cream sauces are the same basic combinations of butter, flour, and water or milk that are the standard tools for legions of good cooks. The roux, a disarmingly simple combination of fat and flour—and at the same time a complex mixture to execute with precision—is the foundation of many a famous Creole and Cajun dish, and the proper way to make it has not changed since it was described in the *Picayune.*

As impressive as the Louisiana sauces are, however, they are not the only good Southern sauces and gravies by any means. Homemade catsups and vinegars, for example, have been specialities in Virginia and the Carolinas since the seventeenth century. Virginia, North Carolina, Kentucky, and Tennessee are celebrated for their essence of country ham known as red-eye gravy. Florida and the coastal South have long been prime sources of outstanding seafood sauces, and every Southern state has countless cooks who excel at chicken gravy (a sort of upcountry roux), sawmill gravy (a tasty reminder of lean times), and barbecue sauce. The mystique of barbecue seasonings (variously called sauces, bastes, and dips) easily rivals the arcane wonders of the Louisiana roux or any other "secret" of Southern cookery.

And for sheer originality, nothing can match chocolate gravy, a breakfast treat of long standing in the Arkansas Ozarks. Made in a saucepan with butter, flour, sugar, cocoa, and milk, it is customarily poured over hot biscuits. A 1976 recipe collection of the United Methodist Church women of Conway, Arkansas, resurrects this remarkable dish, the origin of which is lost in history.

Our sampling of about a dozen sauces, gravies, and dressings from the Southern kitchen is taken from among the oldest and best the region has to offer.

that. *"You're pore as a snake," he says, "skinny as a fence railing."* . . . It is a ritual banquet, of course, almost as exceptional to them as to me. For half of what is on the table has come from the supermarket, not the garden or the smokehouse or the cellar. No one, least of all Arkansas farm families, eats like this any more.

Shirley Abbott
Womenfolks, 1983

All honor then to that turbaned mistress of the Kentucky kitchen—the Kentucky cook. . . . Is there a Southerner who does not hold her, in spite of her faults, in loving remembrance? As far as I know she has never got her just due. She is gone, and there are good ones today who fill her place, but none who are full worthy. Publicly I acknowledge an everlasting debt, and to that turbaned mistress of the Kentucky kitchen gratefully this Southerner takes off his hat.

John Fox, Jr.,
in his introduction to
The Blue Grass Cook Book, 1904

Barbecue Sauce I

This exceedingly popular concoction was developed in the University of Kentucky Poultry Department in the 1940s as a basting sauce for chicken. It has many virtues, one of which is that it contains no tomato ingredients, and thus is far less likely than most sauces to produce burned and charred meat. Not just chicken but pork ribs and other barbecued meats are greatly enriched by generous applications of this spicy-hot sauce.

Combine in a large saucepan the following ingredients: 2½ cups water, 1 tablespoon sugar, 2½ teaspoons black pepper, 2 tablespoons vegetable oil, ¼ cup cider vinegar, 2½ teaspoons salt, 2 tablespoons Worcestershire sauce, 1 small onion minced fine, 1 teaspoon powdered mustard, ½ teaspoon hot-pepper sauce, 1 clove of garlic minced fine, ½ teaspoon red pepper, and 2 teaspoons chili powder. Stir and simmer for a few minutes until the flavors blend. Apply the warm sauce liberally to meat as it cooks.

Barbecue Sauce II

Scott Wakefield's barbecue sauce was conceived in Georgia and refined in Tennessee. He uses it principally as a rib dip (page 254), basting the ribs thoroughly about thirty minutes or so before they finish cooking and again when they are removed from the grill. If you're cooking on a "fast" (hot) fire, more frequent basting will be necessary.

Combine the following ingredients in a large saucepan: 2 cups cider vinegar (5% acidity), 2 cups thick catsup, 6 tablespoons Worcestershire sauce, 1½ teaspoons Tabasco sauce, 2 teaspoons salt, 1 teaspoon black pepper, 1½ teaspoons cayenne pepper, 2 teaspoons brown sugar, and 4 tablespoons butter. Place over low heat for about 1 hour, stirring often. Never let the sauce boil; it should be hot enough for the flavors to blend, but boiling reduces their sharpness. The recipe makes a little over 1 quart. Bottle and refrigerate any leftover sauce—it improves with age.

If you taste a spoonful of this sauce straight from the stove, it may seem too strong or peppery-hot, but when applied to the meat it produces a pleasantly hot and spicy taste—not burning, and not overwhelming. You can, of course, adjust the peppers up or down to suit your taste. The sauce should be warm when applied to the meat, both on the grill and at the table. (One of its many virtues is that it is both a basting and a table sauce.)

Barbecue Sauce III

In eastern North Carolina, pork barbecue and its sauces have a very distinctive character. For one thing, folks around Raleigh and points east favor whole-hog cooking. For another, they like to mince and shred the meat, not slice or pull it. And for a third, their choice in sauce leans to vinegar and red pepper.

Fred Powledge, a native of that region now living in self-imposed exile in the North, has spent years attempting to capture and duplicate the sauce he was weaned on in and around Raleigh years ago. It was, as he remembers it, more of a cooking and basting sauce than a table dressing, but it usually ended up on the table as well as beside the pit. Now, Powledge's research and experimentation have borne impressive fruit; with this sauce, he has effectively transplanted the eastern North Carolina barbecue sauce tradition to New York. (For an explanation of his application of it in the kitchen, see page 254.)

In a large saucepan, combine the following: 2 cups cider vinegar (5% acidity), 1 tablespoon peppercorns, 1 teaspoon celery seed, 1 teaspoon salt, 1 tablespoon hot pepper flakes, 1 onion chopped fine, and 1 cup water. Bring combined ingredients almost to a boil, reduce heat, and simmer uncovered for about 1 hour. Then strain the sauce, if you like, to remove the peppercorns, and apply it generously to your meat—before, during, and, if you prefer, after its cooking.

Chicken Gravy

There may be no better gravy in the Western world than that made in a black skillet recently vacated by crisp pieces of fried chicken. Southerners of every class and station can identify with it. Like a good roux, it begins with fat and flour; a little water and some salt and pepper to taste, and suddenly a miracle is born. This is a widely followed method.

Leave 2 or 3 tablespoons of grease and the dregs or sediment in the skillet in which the chicken was fried. Over very low heat, slowly sprinkle in 2 or 3 tablespoons of flour, stirring constantly until the mixture is a rich, deep shade of brown. Then slowly pour in a cup of lukewarm water, continuing to stir to avoid lumpy gravy. Bring the mixture to a simmering bubble and cook it for a minute or two, still stirring, until the gravy thickens. Season to taste and serve warm in a separate bowl.

An alternative method, to prevent lumpiness, is to place the flour in a

The South is legend—legend begetting legend. Never doubt it. . . . As in all myth, truth holds fast at the center: We are hospitable, our women are beautiful, and our men are gallant and brave. And a whole lot of other things, all wildly improbable and richly contradictory. Whatever else the world has thought of the fabulous land below the Mason-Dixon line, it has granted us one supreme achievement— Southern cooking, which, like the South herself, is not one but many. The number of cookbooks on the market purporting to be Southern is astounding. In fact, cookbooks [in the South] outsell everything but the Holy Bible.

Jack and Olivia Solomon
Cracklin Bread and Asfidity, 1979

shaker with the water, shake well, pour over the dregs, and proceed as above. Also, milk can be used instead of water, making a cream gravy; some people prefer it, but to my taste, water makes a richer, tastier gravy.

French Dressing

In a beautifully written but almost unknown book called *Dishes and Beverages of the Old South* (1913), Martha McCulloch-Williams of Montgomery County, Tennessee, accomplished the rare feat of uniting history and culture with cookery. These are her instructions—in her own words—for "a sweet French dressing" to be poured on a fresh fruit salad.

> "Mix well a scant teaspoonful of granulated sugar, the same of dry mustard, half a teaspoonful salt, as much black pepper and paprika mixed, put in the bottom of a deep small bowl, and stir for two minutes. Wet with claret vinegar, adding it gradually, and stirring smooth. Make as thick as cream. Add twenty drops Tabasco, twenty drops onion juice, the strained juice of half a lemon, and half a teaspoonful of brandy, rum or whiskey. Mix well, then add, tablespoonful at a time, a gill [½ cup] of salad oil, stirring hard between spoonfuls. Put in more vinegar, more oil—the seasoning suffices for half a pint of dressing. Stir till it thickens—it should be like an emulsion when poured upon the salad. Keep on ice. The oil and vinegar will separate, but the dressing can be brought back by stirring hard."

This is an all-purpose French salad dressing with a nice balance of sweet and spicy flavors. The recipe is a bit involved, but it's well worth the trouble, both for the taste and for the historical context from which it comes.

Lemon-Butter Sauce

The most basic principles of French sauce making are embodied in this simple New Orleans garnish for baked or broiled fish and meat dishes. The combination of butter and lemon juice is the foundation on which many sauces are built. In *The Picayune Creole Cook Book,* recipes for drawn butter sauce and brown butter sauce contain only slight variations on this standard union; in Lafcadio Hearn's *La Cuisine Creole* (1885), essentially the same blend is called parsley and butter sauce; in still other recipe collections, it becomes meunière

A few miles north of Bon Secour [Alabama] is an old locality, not a town, called Vernant Park. Most of the people of this area are people of Latin descent, both French and Spanish. Their ancestors, the first residents, lived nearby on Magnolia River, Weeks Bay, and Bon Secour Bay. Long before 1800 there was a little group of devout Roman Catholics that gathered in one of the larger homes whenever a priest could come from Mobile to say mass. About 1840 this group of people formally organized a mission with the name of St. John the Baptist. . . .

Early in its history this congregation started the custom of a fete day in the month of May centering about the Dinner on the Grounds. . . . Many a famous dish of gourmet quality is served there too. In fact, that dinner has become so well known all over Baldwin County that people come from miles away to enjoy the fine meal with its French and Spanish dishes, many of which are made from treasured family recipes.

Charley and Meme Wakeford
Food, Fun, and Fable, 1965

sauce, or amandine (with slivered almonds), or hollandaise (with egg yolks). Relative amounts of butter and lemon juice vary from recipe to recipe, depending on individual tastes. This is our preferred version of basic lemon-butter sauce.

Melt 1 stick of butter in a saucepan. Stir in 3 tablespoons of fresh lemon juice, 2 tablespoons of finely chopped fresh parsley, and as much salt, black pepper, and paprika as you like. When well-blended, pour the warm sauce over the prepared fish or meat. The recipe makes ½ to ⅔ cup.

Mayonnaise

As far back as 1847—in *The Carolina Housewife*, by Sarah Rutledge—Southerners had instructions for preparing homemade mayonnaise, and the contents were about the same then as they are today: egg yolk, oil, vinegar or lemon juice, and seasonings. Made popular by Mrs. Rutledge and others, it has held favor as a salad dressing and sandwich spread for 140 years. Now, with the aid of a blender or food processor, it's quick and easy to make. This is one way.

Break 1 whole egg into your blender or food processor and add ½ teaspoon of salt, 3 tablespoons of fresh lemon juice, and 2 or 3 shakes of cayenne pepper. Give them a brief whirl and then, with the motor running, add 1½ cups of salad oil in the slowest possible drizzle. The mayonnaise will take shape right before your eyes. Before you remove it from the mixer, you may want to adjust the flavor with more salt or cayenne, or with paprika or dry mustard. In any case, you'll have a pint of rich and creamy dressing that store-bought mayonnaise only faintly resembles.

Red-Eye Gravy

The cookbooks are strangely muted on this divine elixir; it is only the fortunate consumers of it who wax eloquent. One reason for the lack of recipes may be its utter simplicity: a little water (or black coffee) in a skillet where ham has been cooked. Another could be that the kind of cured and aged country ham that yields this rich gravy has simply become too rare.

There is a tale of dubious authenticity that credits Andrew Jackson with the naming of this liquid. He reportedly instructed a whiskey-drinking cook of

The most nourishing liquid in this world is the gravy that fried ham gives up. It is made by pouring a little cold water into the hot skillet after the ham has been forked out onto the platter. . . . There is abundant life in ham gravy. It will put hair on the hairless chest of a man, or bloom into the pale cheeks of a woman. Breast-fed babies whose mothers eat ham gravy are destined to develop sturdy bodies and sound minds. Biscuits sopped in ham gravy will satisfy the gnawing appetite of a growing boy quicker than any combination of patented foods we hear praised on the radio. . . . But ham and gravy is a lopsided combination. The gravy always gives out before the ham. Nine times out of ten, the platter will be half full of ham when the last drop of gravy has been soaked up by the bread on some eager diner's plate. I have seen a bowl of gravy emptied on the first round, but enough ham left for the second table.

That, sir, is why we cannot bottle ham gravy to sell to gravy lovers. A surplus of ham gravy cannot be attained.

Allan M. Trout,
in the Louisville *Courier-Journal*,
circa 1948

his to bring him some ham with gravy "as red as your eyes." More likely, the rich red color of natural country ham juice suggested the name.

Into a black skillet in which slices of salt-cured, hickory-smoked, properly aged country ham have been fried, pour ½ cup of tap water. (Some people insist on using black coffee or a combination of coffee and water, more for color than flavor, but if the ham is *real* ham, the coffee won't be necessary.) Turn up the heat, scrape the ham leavings from the bottom and side of the skillet, and stir constantly as the liquid boils. After a minute or two, pour the brothlike gravy over the ham, or into a separate pitcher to moisten biscuits, grits, and eggs.

Roux

Some cookbooks specify unclarified salted butter as the base for a good roux; others call for various alternative kinds of shortening, including margarine, lard, vegetable oil, or even bacon drippings. Whatever is used, the ratio of shortening to flour is usually the same: 1 to 1. It may take a half-hour or so (depending on your stove, the temperature and humidity, and other mysterious factors) to make a roux, so be patient. You can make more than you need—say, ½ cup each of flour and shortening—and store the excess in the refrigerator.

Put the shortening in a black skillet over very low heat. When it is warm and fluid, gradually sprinkle in the flour and begin stirring. The mixture will brown very slowly. Stir it constantly. The art of roux making is to achieve a rich, brown, nutlike color without burning it in the slightest. (If it does burn, it's ruined; throw it out and start over.) A little practice will help you to know when the color, consistency, and flavor are at their proper point; that is when the roux must either be removed immediately from the heat or augmented with additional ingredients (meat or fish stock, herbs and spices, vegetables, or whatever the recipe calls for). Recipes that call for roux will specify the amount you need to make.

Sawmill Gravy

It is rare to find in any cookbook a recipe for this quite common and popular companion to hot biscuits. The reasons probably have more to do with social

I remember sitting by the sideboard, still waking up, and watching the first step in the preparation of my grillades—the making of a roux. The roux is the basis of all Creole and Acadian cooking and yet more than that: it is the embodiment of a tradition. It was in the roux that the great French sauces became great Creole gravies, cooked with the food rather than apart. Any South Louisiana cook will tell you that if you can't make a good roux, you had better not cook at all. Yet a roux is little more than a heated mixture of flour and fat, often with stock added. Its color is the acid test. Ideally, a roux should have something like the color of deep honey, brown but not quite brown, a color that comes into being in a moment and lasts for only a few seconds before it turns too dark and must be thrown out.

Peter S. Feibleman
American Cooking:
Creole and Acadian, 1971

and economic class than anything else; sawmill gravy is commonly thought of as a subsistence food of the poor, and cookbooks seldom focus on such fare. That's too bad, since breakfast lovers regardless of income would probably find it a tasty and satisfying dish. The barest scraps of meat and a little milk are enough to make a delicious gravy, and in lean times, many a family has gotten by on a combination of meat grease, flour, and water.

Even the name suggests poverty. By some accounts, it derives from the fact that backwoods sawmill crews often subsisted on little more than coffee, biscuits, and gravy. In some parts of Kentucky, the dish was called poor-do—a little something on which the poor made do. Native Kentuckian Jane Brock Woodall recalls that her grandmother in Casey County made the gravy from sausage or chicken dregs, and when there was not enough food to go around, the men ate first and got whatever meat there was and the women and children got by on the poor-do. Elsewhere, people who would have shunned anything called poor-do or even sawmill gravy ate essentially the same thing and called it white gravy or cream gravy. By whatever name, it was and is a flavorful and familiar dish on many Southern tables. This is how Charles F. Bryan, Jr., learned to make sawmill gravy from his elders when he was growing up near McMinnville, Tennessee.

> After cooking sausage in a black skillet, leave behind the sediment or dregs and about 2 or 3 tablespoons of grease. Over medium heat, slowly sift in 3 tablespoons of flour, stirring constantly until the mixture is well-browned. Then pour in a cup of sweet milk, add salt and pepper to taste, and continue stirring as the gravy cooks and thickens. (As an alternate method, the milk and flour can be blended in a shaker and poured into the skillet.) A piece or two of cooked sausage crumbled into the gravy adds substance as well as flavor. After it has simmered and blended for 2 or 3 minutes, pour the gravy into a separate bowl and serve it with biscuits, potatoes, or whatever. This recipe makes about 1½ cups.

Seafood Cocktail Sauce

For some reason, cold seafood—shrimp in particular—seems to cry out for a pungent, savory sauce to give its delicate flavor a lift. A quick and simple mixture of catsup, horseradish, and lemon or lime juice works wonders. For a more elaborate treatment, this pungent and spicy dunk sauce, from *Florida Seafood Cookery,* a 1956 publication of that state's department of agriculture, is exemplary.

Rural Alabama, 1936: The biscuits are large and shapeless, not cut round, and are pale, not tanned, and are dusty with flour. They taste of flour and soda and damp salt. . . . They are better with butter, and still better with butter and jam. . . . Field peas are olive-brown, the shape of lentils, about twice the size. Their taste is a cross between lentils and boiled beans; their broth is bright with seasoning of pork, and of this also they taste. The broth is soaked up in bread. The meat is a bacon, granular with salt, soaked in the grease of its frying: there is very little lean meat in it. What there is is nearly as tough as rind; the rest is pure salted stringy fat. The eggs taste of pork too. They are fried in it on both sides until none of the broken yolk runs, and heavily salted and peppered while they fry. . . . There is even in so clean a household as this an odor of pork, of sweat, so subtle it seems to get into the very metal of the cooking-pans. . . . yet this is the odor and consistency and temper and these are true tastes of home; I know this even of myself; and much as my reflexes are twitching in refusal of each mouthful, a true homesick and simple fondness for it has so strong hold of me that in fact there is no fight to speak of and no faking of enjoyment at all.

James Agee
Let Us Now Praise Famous Men, 1939

Blend together the following ingredients: ½ cup chili sauce, ¼ cup horse-radish (well-drained), 1 teaspoon Worcestershire sauce, 1 teaspoon minced onion, ½ teaspoon salt, ¼ teaspoon garlic salt, ⅛ teaspoon black pepper, 2 dashes hot-pepper sauce, 1 tablespoon vinegar, 1 teaspoon celery seed, 1 teaspoon celery salt, 2 tablespoons sugar. Refrigerate the sauce for a day or two, giving its flavors time to blend, and then serve it cold.

SNACKS, SPREADS, NIBBLINGS

"When I was growing up, everything in a Southern meal was put on the table at the same time," wrote Nathalie Dupree in *Cooking of the South*. Rarely, and if you were very lucky, you might find "some toasted pecans and maybe some peanuts put out in the living room before dinner—or even some cheese straws." Even those tidbits apparently were not part of the experience of Eula Mae Strat-ton, who recalled in her *Pioneer Cookbook* that her Arkansas great-grandmother, Delilah Baldwin, "did not hold with something to nibble on before coming to the table to enjoy a good meal."

A few pecans or peanuts, maybe some cheese straws, and that was it; you just didn't ruin a big dinner with finger food. But the South has gone modern now, and its new cookbooks reflect the trend with page after page of appetizers, snacks, hors d'oeuvre, canapés, dips, sandwiches, and assorted nibblings that would make Delilah Baldwin wonder. In this age of stand-up eating at fast-food shops, brunches, buffets, cocktail parties, patio cookouts, and the like, it some-times seems that finger foods have almost replaced the more substantial meals that require knives and forks and spoons.

But lest we conclude that this is an altogether new development, it is worth recalling the snack foods that were enjoyed by young and old alike in the South of the early twentieth century. In country general stores and groceries and ser-vice stations, working people on the move and children out of school dined on bologna (a.k.a. baloney) and crackers, little tins of sardines, round and stubby Vienna sausages, pickled pigs' feet, pickled boiled eggs, beef jerky, and a wide array of Southern-made soft drinks. At home, there might be leftover biscuits and even some bacon or sausage in the warmer on top of the woodstove, and in mid-afternoon the remains of dinner lay waiting for the supper bell under a cloth on the table, and in the tin-sided pie safe there might be something sweet and inviting. There was bread and jam, too, and peanut butter, and fruit, always a popular between-meals nourishment—citrus from Florida, apples from Vir-ginia and other highland areas, peaches from Georgia and South Carolina and elsewhere, summer pears, figs, plums, grapes, watermelons, and cantaloupes grown locally in many parts of the region. There were even such exotic fruits as coconuts and pineapples on occasion, and lots of bananas from the tropics. Fulton, Kentucky, situated at a major junction of railroad freight lines, became the banana capital of the United States, and the town still holds an annual festival to spotlight its unique role. In winter months, dried peaches, apples, and apricots were commonly found in many kitchens, and these were destined to be munched on or encased in spicy half-moon pies. In all but the very poorest households you could usually get a snack, all right, just not the dainty ones passed around on trays before dinner; it simply wasn't done.

Sandwiches as light lunches were gaining a toehold in the South before World War I. Jennie Benedict, a noted Louisville caterer and tearoom operator, featured a club sandwich (mayonnaise, lettuce, bacon, and cold chicken on bread) in her *Blue Ribbon Cook Book* in 1904, and her Benedictine spread, for which a recipe appears below, brought her a measure of wider recognition. In Nashville, Betty Lyles Wilson published a cookbook in 1914 that included directions for making such sandwiches as pimento cheese, egg salad, olive, and deviled ham.

Other kinds of snacks gradually found their way into Southern homes. Florida avocados took kindly to a Mexican paste called guacamole (essentially lime juice, hot peppers, and other seasonings mixed with mashed avocado into a spicy purée). In south Florida, the *Key West Cook Book* (1949) had a recipe for bollos (sometimes called bollitos), a Caribbean blend of black-eyed peas, bird peppers, garlic, and salt made into a paste, rolled into little balls, and deep-fried in hot fat. Along the Mississippi River in delta towns such as Greenville, Mississippi, Mexican hot tamales became an established specialty, and in some of those communities even now, there are people who make them with consummate skill and market them daily. Where deep-fried dill pickles, another specialty featured in some Mississippi and Arkansas restaurants, came from, no one seems to know.

From before the cocktail party era, here are a few favored old recipes for Southern snacks, spreads, and nibblings.

If you like dishes made out of a piece of lettuce and ground-up peanuts and a maraschino cherry and marshmallow whip and a banana
You will not get them in Savannah,
But if you seek something headier than nectar and tastier than ambrosia and more palatable than manna,
Set your teeth, I beg you, in one of these spécialités de Savannah.
Everybody has the right to think whose food is the most gorgeous,
And I nominate Georgia's.

Ogden Nash, in his introduction to
The Savannah Cook Book, 1933

Benedictine Spread

Between 1893 and 1925, Jennie Benedict was a celebrated caterer and restaurant hostess in Louisville—so beloved, in fact, that when a St. Louis group tried to lure her away from her old Kentucky home, a crowd of anguished patrons rose up en masse and pleaded publicly with her to stay (she did). In her tearoom and soda-fountain shop, her extensive catering business, and her cookbooks, she was a harbinger of a style of cooking that was ahead of its time—the lighter and more delicate luncheon style that is widely favored now. Benedictine spread is a perfect example.

Peel, seed, and grate or mince 1 medium-sized cucumber and press the pulp in a paper towel to remove as much moisture as possible. Combine with 8 ounces of softened cream cheese. Add 1 tablespoon of finely grated onion. Next add a dash of hot-pepper sauce and about ¼ teaspoon of salt, or as much of each as you prefer. Finally, a tablespoon or more of mayonnaise will give the proper consistency. Stir the mixture thoroughly until it is smooth, then refrigerate (the flavors will blend and taste best after a day or so). Spread on crackers, bread rounds, finger sandwiches—or, if you want to use it as a dip, thin it with a little milk or sour cream.

Cheese Straws

It's hard to say how, when, or where these favorites came to prominence in the South, but noted cooks as widely scattered as Henrietta Dull, the Atlanta author of *Southern Cooking*, and Pauline Goddard Dedman, hostess of the Beaumont Inn in Harrodsburg, Kentucky, were making them forty years or more ago.

So was Matalie Grant. She moved to Washington, D.C., from her native Alabama in the early 1940s after her husband, George M. Grant, was elected to Congress. One of the recipes Mimi Grant took with her—and one of her treasured specialties still—is this prescription for cheese straws or wafers.

Bring 2 pounds of sharp Cheddar cheese and ½ pound (2 sticks) of salted butter to room temperature. Grate the cheese and blend with the butter in a large mixing bowl. Sift and measure 4 cups of all-purpose flour, then sift it again with 4 teaspoons of baking powder, ½ teaspoon of salt, and 2 or 3 teaspoons of cayenne pepper (as you like it). Blend these dry ingredients into the cheese and butter until the dough is smooth and stiff. A cookie press is almost essential for forming the dough into long thin strips, or straws. (An alternative method is to divide the dough into 4 or 5 cucumber-shaped rolls, wrap each separately in wax paper, and refrigerate for easier handling. When thoroughly chilled, remove one roll at a time and slice it into thin rounds.) Place in narrowly spaced rows on ungreased cookie sheets and bake on the middle or lower shelf of a preheated 300° oven for 20

I've failed in a long effort to trace the origins of pimento cheese, but it was the peanut butter of my childhood—homemade by Mother. I suspect it's a Southern invention (I've seldom met a non-Southerner who knew what it was, though they take to it on contact); in any case, prepared versions can be bought to this day in Southern supermarkets—

minutes, or until a delicate golden brown. Cool on cookie racks and store in tightly covered tins between layers of wax paper. Thus protected from dampness, they will keep for several weeks. They also freeze well.

The quantities of ingredients given here will produce a very large pile of cheese straws or rounds. A half-recipe will make enough to fill a large cookie tin.

Crab Puffs

It's a tedious job to pick all the sweet white meat from a crab shell, but lovers of the crustacean don't seem to mind. All along the Atlantic and Gulf coasts there are millions of devoted crab eaters, and over the years they have come up with a multiplicity of ways to prepare this tender delicacy for the table. One of those notable recipes is this appetizer from a Virginia coastal kitchen.

Beat 2 egg whites with a pinch of salt until stiff. Season 1 cup of crab meat to taste with salt, cayenne pepper, lemon juice, and paprika, and then mix lightly with ½ cup of mayonnaise. Fold the egg whites into the crab mixture. Spread on triangles of bread that have been toasted on one side (or cracker rounds, or pastry puffs) and run under the broiler for 3 minutes or until hot and puffy. Serve immediately. Makes 4 to 6 dozen, depending on size of triangles.

Pecans (Roasted)

Pecans are the premier nut of the South. No other country likes pecans the way this country does, and no other region grows or eats as many as the South. Pecan pie (see page 334) could make a strong claim to be the best-known and most popular of all Southern desserts. But that's just one way to eat them. Here's another, favored on holiday tables and before meals too.

Melt 1 stick of butter in a saucepan. Add 1 pound (3 to 4 cups) of shelled pecan halves and swirl them in the butter until they're well coated. Spread out on a baking sheet and bake at 250° for 30 minutes, or until the nuts begin to toast through and turn a darker shade of brown. Drain on paper towels. When they have cooled a bit, sprinkle with salt to taste, and when thoroughly cooled store in tightly covered jars or tins.

most of them made apparently from congealed insecticides. Last year, once I'd acquired a Cuisinart, I rebelled and tried to reconstruct Mother's recipe. I've made a change or two, in the interest of midlife zest; but I think any child of the thirties and forties (from, say, Baltimore down) will recall the glory and bless my name.

Grate a pound or more of extra sharp Cheddar cheese. Chop coarsely one jar of pimentoes (four ounces, more if you like) with one or two cloves of garlic. Mix into the grated cheese with plenty of freshly ground pepper and a minimum of salt; then gradually add enough homemade mayonnaise (maybe three tablespoons) to form a stiff chunky paste. Sometimes I add a little lemon juice or a very little wine vinegar or Tabasco—nothing to disguise the bare cheese and peppers and good mayonnaise. I've been caught eating a pound in two days (though it keeps well), especially if life is hard. On rough brown bread, it's a sovereign nerve-salve.

*Reynolds Price,
in The Great American Writers' Cookbook,
1981*

Sausage Pinwheels

Sometime after World War II, when brunches and buffet luncheons began to come into their own, an anonymous Southerner who loved sausage and biscuits came up with this way of combining them in a single recipe. It's a trendy treat in party circles, but that doesn't keep it from being good—so good, in fact, that it seems certain to remain a favorite of Southern cooks and eaters from now on. Sausage pinwheels are especially handy on holidays or when company is around, because they can be made ahead of time and kept refrigerated or frozen until needed.

Sift together these dry ingredients: 2 cups plain flour, 2 tablespoons sugar, 1 teaspoon salt, 2 tablespoons plain cornmeal, and 2 teaspoons baking powder. With a pastry cutter, work in ¼ cup of shortening, then add ½ cup of sweet milk. Mix together and knead into a dough. Divide into 2 balls of equal size and chill for easier handling. Then roll each ball into a thin rectangle about 8 by 12 inches. Next, divide 1 pound of hot or mild sausage meat in half and spread it evenly over the dough rectangles. Roll up each strip like a jelly roll and pinch the dough together on the ends. You should wind up with 2 rolls about 2 or 3 inches in diameter and 8 inches long. Wrap them in wax paper and chill for easier slicing. To cook, cut off slices about ½ inch thick and lay them on a cookie sheet. Bake in a preheated 375° oven for about 20 minutes, or until the sausage is thoroughly cooked and the bread is golden brown. Drain on a paper towel. Each roll will give 12 to 15 slices that taste like just what they are: crusty and delicious sausage biscuits.

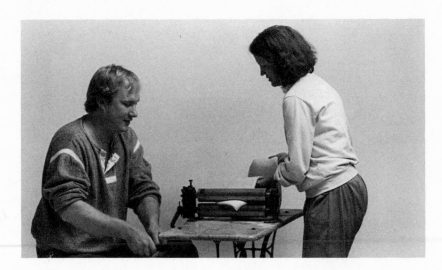

Beverages

The liquids that people consume are so numerous and often so intermingled that it is difficult to classify them. Hot and cold, sweet and sour, soft and hard, weak and strong, plain and fancy, fresh and fermented and distilled—the possibilities seem practically endless, and new combinations keep coming along with steady regularity.

There was variety even in the early days of the Virginia colony. Water was a precious substance on the Atlantic voyages, but it was not the only potable; beer, ale, wine, brandy, and rum were brought too, and with cows and goats there was also milk. Once established on the Eastern Seaboard, the English settlers and other Europeans quickly began their own brewing and wine-making projects. They made mead with fermented honey water, beer with molasses and spruce needles and other substances, wine and brandy with all sorts of fruits and vegetables. Apple cider became a common drink for all ages in all stages of colonial life. Scotch and Irish whiskeys may not have been consumed in huge quantities in pre-Revolutionary America, but rum certainly was; whether imported from Europe or the West Indies or manufactured domestically with sugarcane byproducts, it flowed freely in the colonies.

But water was vital and elementary, and it is thus the logical opening subject for a short treatise on Southern beverages. The spring waters the weary voyagers found to slake their ship-bound thirst must have been unforgettably satisfying—cold, sweet, refreshing, and abundant. When the newcomers moved to higher altitudes inland, the broad, silent rivers of the coast became tumbling, rushing torrents, even colder and clearer and sweeter than the lowland waters. These mountain rivers and creeks were like lifelines running down to the sea, and the exploring colonists, in imitation of their Indian kinsmen, used the streams for transportation, for finding their way in the wilderness, for watering their patches of corn, and of course for their own refreshment and good health. In time, they also used them for grinding corn and making whiskey.

Water was the only safe drink. Milk was more nourishing, but it spoiled quickly; wine and beer had their attractions, but also their bad side effects. The settlers eventually proceeded to dig wells and cisterns, drawing water from the depths of the earth and catching it as it fell from the sky. Like the Indians before them, they found foul-smelling sulphur springs that they believed were invested with mystical healing powers, and hot-water-belching mineral springs that also were thought to be curative. Ponce de León, the Spanish explorer who landed on the east coast of Florida in 1513, is remembered in history and legend as a man in search of a spring whose waters had the power of restoring youth. (That he never found it is attested to by the fact that he died in 1521, still in his early sixties.) A little later, in 1541, Hernando de Soto led an expedition all the way to the present site of Hot Springs, Arkansas, to see and sample the miraculous mineral waters that the Indians held in such reverence. Those springs have been an attraction ever since, and water from their perpetual fountains is bottled and sold with as much authority—if not as much profit—as French Perrier.

Milk was not known on the North American continent until the Europeans came bringing the first cows and goats. By the mid-1600s, most landholders had fresh milk, butter, and cheese, but milk was so perishable that only the cow-owning few could benefit from its wholesome and nutritious qualities. More than 200 years passed before condensed milk was developed and pasteurization was applied to make dairy products safe and accessible to the general population. Long before that, though, Southerners and other Americans had adapted old English recipes and created some of their own to produce a variety of milk-based drinks, among them syllabub and eggnog.

The process by which sweet milk and cream were turned to butter began with the formation of a semisolid sour milk called clabber. Butter was separated from this thick mass by beating and churning, and the leftover liquid was known as buttermilk. Clabber has been a treat for some Southerners since the seventeenth century. It is especially savored with cornbread crumbled in it; Louisiana Cajuns still enjoy such a dish, which they call coush-coush. As for buttermilk, it has long had a special status in the South, not only as a drink but as a vital ingredient in the making of some kinds of biscuit, cornbread, cake, and pie. Those who drink it with regularity—and a good many Southerners do—tend to praise it highly as a nutritious and delicious beverage with a thick, lumpy, buttery texture of its own.

Early Americans home-brewed or fermented most of their own intoxicating liquids—cider, beer, wines, brandies, and other liqueurs—and drank astonishing quantities of them. No social or religious prohibitions were applied to alcoholic drinks in any general way until well into the nineteenth century. Baptists and Methodists, Episcopalians and Catholics, Presbyterians and Shakers and Quakers imbibed freely and frequently—at barn raisings, sheep shearings, horse races, weddings, even funerals. If Southerners were not the pacesetters in that practice, they certainly kept pace with the rest. Almost all of the cookbooks from the region prior to the Civil War—and many of them after that time— contained alcoholic drinks: punches, toddies, shrubs, orgeats, ratifias, bounces, flips, fools. Mary Randolph's 1824 classic, *The Virginia House-Wife*, contained a dozen such recipes, and the Louisiana and South Carolina hostesses of that time were, if anything, even more disposed to strong drink.

In Kentucky, to which Pennsylvania whiskey makers fled in the 1790s

SOME NAME-BRAND BEVERAGES THAT ORIGINATED IN THE SOUTH

- *Old Crow Kentucky Bourbon Whiskey, distilled by James C. Crow, Woodford County, Kentucky, 1835*

- *Jack Daniel's Tennessee Sour Mash Whiskey, distilled by Jack Daniel, Lynchburg, Tennessee, 1866*

- *Mountain Valley Mineral Water, bottled by Peter Greene near Hot Springs, Arkansas, 1871*

to escape a federal excise tax on their product, hundreds of home distillers were making clear grain alcohol from corn by the turn of the century. They were Scotch or Irish or Scotch-Irish, for the most part, inheritors of an ancient whiskey-making tradition, and by 1820 they had made "Kentucky whiskey" an established commercial product in the East as well as the South. The early stuff was all the same: corn liquor imbibed straight from the still, without benefit of aging or other mellowing refinements. The names it later acquired—moonshine and white lightning—were quite descriptive of its mystical and explosive powers.

It remained for a Scottish immigrant, Dr. James C. Crow, a physician and chemist, to introduce scientific methodology and quality control (and, incidentally, the sour-mash distilling process) to Kentucky whiskey making in the 1820s. Within a decade or so, the product had acquired a more or less standard formula. Distilled from a mixture of corn and rye and barley, combined with pure limestone spring water, aged for several years in new white-oak barrels (charred to add color and perhaps some taste), the whiskey of Crow and other skilled Kentucky producers was a distinctive and potent libation. It also took on a name—bourbon—that applied to all similarly produced whiskey in that region of central Kentucky. Now, 150 years later, the method and the name are unchanged.

Before the refinement of corn liquor into bourbon took place, the only distinction to be made among Kentucky whiskey distillers was between those who paid the federal excise tax and those who did not; their product was essentially the same. Today, bourbon and other domestic whiskey, where they can be legally manufactured and consumed, differ greatly from illicit whiskey, which spans the scale in quality but generally tends to resemble the unrefined moonshine and white lightning of old. At its best, homemade whiskey is held in high regard by masters of the distilling art; at its worst, it is recognized as dangerous, even life-threatening. And good or bad, it is illegal, since federal law prohibits the private manufacture of distilled spirits, even for personal use.

But tradition and heritage and pride of craft are powerful motivating forces. They compel at least one former Kentuckian, now a resident of Tennessee and a man of means, to go on practicing the art, and no doubt there are others. At considerable expense to himself—and at some risk—he has constructed a modern home distillery capable of producing superior whiskey. His four-gallon, double-run copper still, designed by a veteran of the craft and constructed by a master plumber, produces a small quantity of clear, smooth, 90-proof corn whiskey for home consumption.

The making of beer, wine, and whiskey moved from the home and farm to the commercial arena in the nineteenth century, and it has remained there. But another kind of Southern liquid refreshment—soft drinks—was never much of

- Dr Pepper, created by Charles Alderton, Waco, Texas, 1885 (named for Dr. Charles Pepper, Rural Retreat, Virginia)

- Coca-Cola, created by John S. Pemberton, Atlanta, Georgia, 1886

- Maxwell House Coffee, roasted and blended by Joel O. Cheek, Nashville, Tennessee, 1892

- Pepsi Cola, created by Caleb D. Bradham, New Bern, North Carolina, 1896

- Barq's Root Beer, developed by Edward A. Barq, Biloxi, Mississippi, 1898

- RC Cola, successor to Royal Crown, a ginger ale created by Claud A. Hatcher, Columbus, Georgia, 1902

- Dixie Beer, brewed by Valentine Merz, New Orleans, Louisiana, 1907

- Gatorade, developed by Dr. Robert Cade, Gainesville, Florida, 1965

a homemade product at all. The development of carbonated water and glass bottles and the coincidental rise of opposition to alcohol abuse set the stage in the late 1800s for a surge of new or newly popular drinks, including ginger ale, root beer, and colas. Many of them originated in the South, where relief from summer heat and humidity was a constant concern. The big-league drinks from that lineup—Coca-Cola and Pepsi, Dr Pepper and RC—have been competing in a national and even global marketplace since the 1950s (as witness the worldwide alarm when Coca-Cola announced a change in its formula in 1985), but many small and relatively unknown soft drink companies still operate successfully in the region. Among them are Blenheim Ginger Ale (South Carolina), Buffalo Rock Ginger Ale (Alabama), Pop Rouge (Louisiana), Dr. Enuf (Tennessee), and Ale 81 (Kentucky).

Just as soft drinks have always been thought of as commercial products, some refreshing liquids long associated with food in the South are generally considered domestic, even though all of them are available in the marketplace. Sweet milk and buttermilk, iced tea and coffee, orange juice and lemonade are the leading drinks on this list, but there are others as well. From this array of home-front beverages, we offer a little history and a few recipes.

EVERYDAY DRINKS

Coffee and tea are the most universal of all drinks, and in the United States they are probably enjoyed by more people than any other liquid refreshments. Ironically, though, neither of the plants from which they come is grown in this country. Coffee is generally thought to have been discovered growing in Ethiopia more than a thousand years ago, and comes now mainly from the higher elevations of Latin America, Africa, and Asia; it has been extremely popular in this country almost from the time it was first brought here by Dutch traders in about 1670. Tea has been an American favorite almost as long—since about 1700—and it was also the Dutch who first brought it from Asia (where much of it is still grown) to the Western Hemisphere.

Thus, for more than three hundred years, Americans have maintained an undying devotion—some would say a general addiction—to these two stimulants. With great care and attention, we roast, grind, and blend coffee beans from afar and then boil, drip, and percolate them to produce an aromatic brew. In the modern age, we also have frozen, dried, crystallized, and powdered coffee to make "instant" drinks mixed with hot water. Our tea comes loose, in bags, and in instant forms to be consumed hot or cold with sugar, honey, lemon, spices, milk, or simply plain. Per capita annual consumption of coffee and tea in the United States exceeds eleven pounds—enough to make more than a thousand cups or glasses for each and every one of us.

The South's share of those astonishing quantities must surely exceed its proportion of the population. With iced tea especially, there is a distinct Southern accent; people in the region drink it the year around, whenever and wherever food is served, and have done so with increasing regularity since ice became generally available in the late nineteenth century.

It was at about the same time that grocers in this country began to market coffee in ready-to-perk form, and it was a Southerner, Joel Owsley Cheek of Nashville, who led the way. Cheek was a twenty-year-old drummer—a traveling salesman—for a Nashville wholesale grocery company in 1872, and in his regular journeys through the Tennessee and Kentucky mountains he sold a lot of coffee beans. In those days it was customary for people to buy green coffee beans that had to be dried (roasted) and ground by hand at home. The combining of different types of beans into a pleasing blend was considered an art, and Cheek, learning from his customers, became very proficient at it. In about 1892, after his experiments with roasting, grinding, and blending coffee beans had produced a formula that won consistent praise, he persuaded the owner of Nashville's leading hotel, the Maxwell House, to adopt it as the house coffee. Maxwell House Blend thus surged to the head of the American coffee parade, helped along by President Theodore Roosevelt, who stayed at the hotel in 1907 and reportedly praised the coffee as "good to the last drop," a phrase the company's advertising executives have since made a part of the language.

Cheek's coffee—not only roasted, ground, and blended, but also packaged in small quantities especially for the consumer—was a marketing sensation. One food historian, John F. Mariani, has asserted that the contemporary American taste in coffee is largely due to Cheek and his Maxwell House Blend. Perhaps the most impressive measure of that achievement is the fact that Cheek sold his coffee business to Postum (later General Foods) in 1928 for $42 million.

Elsewhere in the South, New Orleans has long maintained a solid reputation for its coffee. The traditional coffee of Louisiana is a very dark and strong blend of coffee beans and chicory root; the brew is taken straight and black by the hardiest drinkers and laced with hot milk (café au lait) by the rest. It is customarily made in one of two ways: by pouring boiling water over the coffee grounds in a Neapolitan or drip pot or some other kind of appliance that filters the brew, or by a cold-water filtration method that extracts the essence of the coffee in a concentrated liqueur. Lafcadio Hearn called drip coffee "the French mode" in 1885. It is also the basis for some potent concoctions of coffee and spirits, among them café brûlot, a dramatic climax to a grand New Orleans dinner.

Coffee is, perhaps, more nutritious, and certainly more permanent in its stimulating effects, than tea. But its influences, on the whole, are less genial. Taken in large quantities, at once, it not only produces morbid vigilance, but affects the brain, so as to occasion vertigo, and a sort of altered consciousness, or confusion of ideas, not amounting to delirium; which I can compare to nothing so well as the feeling when one is lost amid familiar objects, which look strange, and seem to have their positions, in reference to the points of the compass, changed. I have experienced these feelings myself, after a cup of cafe à la Français, early in the morning, in New Orleans; and the late Professor Brown, of Transylvania University [in Lexington, Kentucky], informed me that, when traveling in North Alabama, he was thrown into the same condition, which lasted for nearly half a day, by drinking a large quantity of strong coffee, on an empty stomach, in the morning. He afterward died of apoplexy.

Daniel Drake, M.D.
Principal Diseases of the
Interior Valley of North America, 1850

After coffee and tea, the next most common homemade drinks in the South are probably lemonade and orange juice. Ever since Hernando de Soto brought oranges to Florida from Spain in 1539, citrus fruits have thrived there, prevailing against all kinds of threats—war, pestilence, frigid blasts of arctic air, even invasions of manufactured drinks. Today as always, Florida produces virtually all of the subtropical and tropical fruits that grow east of the Mississippi. Orange and grapefruit juices have been canned and marketed since about 1915, and concentrated and frozen since the 1930s, but fresh juice is still the best. There is nothing more distinctive and delicious than a morning glass of orange or grapefruit juice that has just been squeezed from tree-ripened fruit, and there is nothing that can be added to it to make it better. Not soda water, mineral water, seltzer water, tonic, or spirits. Nothing. Fresh orange juice is an original masterpiece that can't be improved upon.

From these everyday drinks—coffee, tea, citrus—we offer three old and respected Southern classics.

Boiled Coffee

Back when Joel Cheek's empire was still just a gleam in a country drummer's eye, all coffee was boiled, there being no other way to extract the brew from the beans until fancy percolators and drip pots came along. All the old cookbooks, South and North, offered one or more versions of boiled coffee. No one makes it like that much anymore, but it's still a superior method. If you have ever tasted an expertly made brew from an enamel pot that has been suspended over a campfire, you have known the essence, the highest form of this marvelous liquid. The pleasure can be approximated on a kitchen stove in the following manner.

Scrub an old-fashioned enamel coffeepot and rinse it with boiling water. Drop into the pot 8 tablespoons (½ cup) of freshly ground coffee (coarse grind). Break an egg over the grounds, crush the eggshell and add it with a pinch of salt and ½ cup of cold water, then stir everything together well. Set the pot over medium heat, pour in 6 measuring cups of boiling water, stuff the pot spout with a paper towel to trap the fragrant aroma inside, and bring the coffee to a boil. When it reaches that point, reduce the heat and simmer for about 3 minutes; then take the pot off the stove and wait 3 minutes more for the coffee to steep and clear. The egg, the shell, and the coffee grounds will coagulate in a lump in the bottom of the pot, leaving 8 serving cups of aromatic, crystal clear, intensely flavorful coffee that should

I've ground many a coffee bean. Started grinding when I was about six years old. . . . Back then, you couldn't buy roasted coffee around here. It come green, in the bean . . . in 100-pound burlap sacks. My mother would take the green coffee and parch it in a big bread pan. She usually parched three or four pounds at a time. Enough to last us a week or two. There's nothing that smells so tantalizing as coffee parching. . . . Mother knew how to do it. She never let it burn. When it come off the fire it was brown like a chestnut. . . . We kept our parched coffee beans in a glass jar that sat on a shelf in the kitchen. We only ground enough for a pot at a time. That way you always got fresh coffee. . . . To me, no storebought coffee ever tasted as good as the coffee we parched and ground at home. It was the pure stuff, unadulterated.

75-year-old Frank Sutton,
of Barker's Creek, North Carolina,
quoted by John Parris,
in Mountain Cooking, 1978

pour without straining. To keep the remainder hot after you've poured a round, set the pot in a pan of very hot water. Do not boil again.

Some people call this egg coffee. By whatever name, I share Mrs. W. T. Hayes' enthusiasm for the brew. In her *Kentucky Cook Book,* published in 1912, she said that her egg coffee would "make any man glad he has left his mother."

Iced Tea

Considering how much iced tea is consumed in the South, it is surprising how many brewers of the leaves botch the job. Part of the problem is in the tea itself; instead of just loose-leaf orange pekoe, the standard in this country for generations, the grocery shelves now sag with a seeming infinity of choices, from herb teas to "flow-through" bags to decaffeinated leaves, and some of them don't make good iced tea. Another obstacle could be the water—no longer clear and pure as a mountain stream, but laced with minerals, chemicals, purifying agents, and who knows what else. Even with loose pekoe and pretty decent water, though, some tea makers miss the mark, turning out pitchers full of weak, bitter, cloudy, and/or tasteless brew. Making good tea is a simple process that ought to be easy for anyone to master. Here is the method we have used without modification for years.

Put 3 cups of fresh water in a non-aluminum saucepan and bring it to a rapid boil. Reduce heat to low, put 3 heaping teaspoons of fresh orange pekoe bulk tea into the water, cover the pan, and let the tea steep and simmer for 5 to 10 minutes. Strain into a large pitcher, add 4 cups of cold water, and the job is finished. The yield is a cup less than a half-gallon. Serve in ice-filled glasses with sugar, lemon or lime, and mint sprigs, if available, for flavoring.

Lemonade

Among citrus fruits, lemons and limes are in a class by themselves. Too strong to be eaten like oranges and grapefruit, they are useful mainly for their seasoning and flavoring qualities. The juice must be diluted with water and sweetened with sugar to be drinkable—and that, in fact, is practically a recipe for lemonade, a Southern refreshment of the first order since colonial times. All three of the nineteenth-century Southern "Housewife" cookbooks—from Virginia,

Kentucky, and South Carolina—had recipes for lemonade. Some early recipe collections called for tinting the drink with raspberry or cherry juice, and this so-called pink lemonade was a favorite at parties and other special occasions throughout the region.

In *The Taste of Country Cooking*, Edna Lewis recalls hot summer afternoons at her family's home in rural Virginia, "when a stone crock of tangy lemonade was brought out with a big, free-form piece of ice and thin slices of lemon floating on it. It would be ladled out in tall glasses and the cool drink always fitted the occasion." It still does. This is one way to make it.

Prepare a simple syrup by boiling together 2 cups of sugar, 2 cups of water, and a small handful (about 10 sprigs) of fresh mint. As soon as the syrup is clear and smooth, set it aside to cool. Squeeze 12 large lemons or limes and put the juice (about 2 cups) in a bowl or pitcher large enough to hold a gallon of liquid. Add cold water in a ratio of 5 or 6 to 1 (10 to 12 cups or 2½ to 3 quarts of water to 2 cups of juice). Add 1 cup of the syrup (including the mint sprigs) to the mixture, stir and taste, and add more water and/or syrup if needed. (Leftover syrup can be kept in the refrigerator to sweeten other drinks.) A few thin slices of lemon or lime will add color and zip to the drink. A gallon of lemonade, served over ice, should be enough for 8 to 10 people. A sprig of mint in each glass adds a final touch of color.

HOLIDAY, PARTY, AND DESSERT DRINKS

Rich and creamy dessert drinks such as boiled custard, eggnog, and syllabub are surviving remnants of the English heritage in America, and especially in the South; in fact, custard and eggnog are as much a part of winter holiday dining in the region now as they were in the seventeenth century. Milk, cream, sugar, and eggs are the foundations on which these deliciously filling liquids are based, and some of them also include wine, whiskey, brandy, or rum—all of which suggests that judicious sipping is advised to regulate both the calories and the alcohol.

The combination of wine and spirits with such foods as sugar, cream, eggs, and fruit goes back to Europe, well before the beginning of colonial settlement in the New World, and these concoctions showed up in the very earliest American recipe collections. Harriott Horry's 1770 receipt book from South Carolina included Shrub, a mixture of 1 gallon of old rum, 5 pints of citrus juice, and 3½ pounds of sugar. "Shake the Shrub every day for two Months," she wrote.

"She won't cook." That was the worst thing my mother could ever say about another woman—worse, I'm sure, than adultery, which, after all, merely involved a change of loyalties. But a woman's refusing to cook implied, for her, a fundamental renunciation of her duty. . . . The motives for such a renunciation may have been many and complex; but

"The vessel should be kept close cork'd during the whole process." Mrs. Horry also offered The Duke of Norfolk Punch, made with 12 gallons of water, 12 pounds of sugar, the whites of 30 eggs, 5½ quarts of orange juice, 3½ quarts of lemon juice, the peels of 30 oranges and 30 lemons, and 5 gallons of rum. Clearly, colonial Southerners had wide-ranging tastes in alcohol. Irvin S. Cobb, a noted Kentucky writer and tippler early in this century, identified a hot drink known as a flip as "the earliest chronicled American potation." It was, he said, made of home-brewed beer, molasses, and rum, and was heated with a red-hot poker from the fire.

From a variety of early American sources, we selected a few holiday, party, and dessert drinks that have had a long and happy identification with the South. Recipes for these alcoholic and non-alcoholic concoctions follow.

Boiled Custard

As a rich liquid dessert, nothing is older or better than boiled custard, a delicious combination of milk, eggs, and sugar that varies only slightly from recipe to recipe. English in origin, custard came early to this country, and it has stayed to brighten many a holiday, especially in the South. Some recipes use whole eggs, others just the yolks; beyond that, most differ only in the amounts of milk, sugar, and vanilla flavoring they call for. Here is a typical formula from long ago in rural Kentucky, updated slightly for modern cooks.

Beat 8 whole eggs with a wire whisk. Add 1 cup of sugar and a pinch or two of salt, beating all the while. Into a large heavy pot or double boiler, pour ½ gallon of whole milk and warm it to a very hot stage without boiling or scalding. Slowly combine small amounts of the milk and egg mixtures back and forth between the two containers until the two are completely blended in one pot (rapid blending of the yolks and hot milk may cause curdling). Return the pot to the stove, stirring constantly, and gradually increase the heat until the custard is thick enough to form a thin coat on a silver or stainless-steel spoon. The trick here, learned only from experience, is to know exactly when the right thickness has been reached, for if it stays too long over the heat, the milk and eggs will separate; if this happens, it may help to set the pan in a container of cold water and beat the custard vigorously. When the mixture has cooled, stir in 1 or 2 teaspoons of vanilla extract to suit your taste and store in jars in the refrigerator. It will thicken a bit when it is cold. The right consistency is thin enough to pour and thick enough to either drink or eat with a spoon. Served with whipped cream on

I'm sure that, for my mother, there was only one explanation—laziness, which was another cardinal sin in her book. Because it all went back to her fundamental belief about good cooking—or good anything else: it was trouble, and there was just no getting away from that. . . .

There were no short cuts, of course, in good cooking; the idea of "instant" anything was abhorrent to her. . . . For her memorable coconut cakes in the winter and particularly at Christmas, there had to be fresh coconut, grated so fine it would almost make your fingers bleed in the process, and of course the coconut milk for the icing. . . . Boiled custard, its usual accompaniment, had to be just the right consistency too: boiled too little it was too thin, boiled too much it was too thick. And everything was all done by eye and smell and taste (no clinical detachment on the part of the cook) on a big coal range in winter, a smaller coal oil stove in summer.

Robert Drake, in
Southern Partisan, Fall 1983

top and a companion slice of coconut cake, boiled custard is a classic holiday dinner climax in many parts of the South.

Café Brûlot

THE MINT JULEP RECIPE OF JUDGE SOULE SMITH OF LEXINGTON, KENTUCKY, CIRCA 1890 . . .

Take from the cold spring some water, pure as angels are; mix with it sugar until it seems like oil. Then take a glass and crush your mint within it with a spoon—crush it around the borders of the glass and leave no place untouched. Then throw the mint away—it is a sacrifice. Fill with cracked ice the glass; pour in the quantity of Bourbon which you want. It trickles slowly through the ice. Let it have time to cool, then pour your sugared water over it. No spoon is needed, no stirring is allowed—just let it stand a moment. Then around the brim place sprigs of mint, so that the one who drinks may find a taste and odor at one drought. When it is made, sip it slowly. August suns are shining, the breath of the south wind is upon you.

The literal French name of this hundred-year-old New Orleans ceremonial drink, the crowning touch to a Creole dinner, is "coffee and burnt brandy." In the most elegant homes and restaurants, specially made silver brûlot bowls and ladles were used, and this spectacular flaming beverage was prepared at the table and served with a dramatic flair in dimly lit rooms. It's hardly as impressive or as romantic, but the same result can be obtained with a chafing dish—or even a saucepan. Recipes for the drink are quite similar.

Brew 4 cups of fresh coffee and keep it hot on the stove (dark roast Creole drip coffee is the authentic requisite, but alternatives can be used). Put into a chafing dish or other container the peel of ½ orange, cut into thin slivers, and 6 to 8 thin lemon slices. Add 1 cinnamon stick, 6 whole cloves, 6 whole allspice, and 4 lumps or 2 teaspoons of sugar. Next add 2 ounces of curaçao (orange liqueur) and 4 ounces of brandy. Over low heat, stir to dissolve the sugar. When the mixture is near to simmering, take up a half-filled ladle and light it. Returned to the container, the ladle will spread its flames over the entire surface. Then, stirring gently, pour the hot coffee in a slow, steady stream into the brandy, and keep stirring until the flames go out. Ladle the brûlot into demitasse cups and serve immediately. There should be enough for at least 8 3-ounce cups.

Eggnog

Eggnog is a rich English cousin of boiled custard, at least as old and just as simple and straightforward. It's another milk-egg-sugar combination—with spirits added. Originally made with a strong ale (a "nog" to the British), it has been Americanized and Southernized with the substitution of bourbon (rum and brandy may also be used). Recipes for the drink are a bit more varied than those for boiled custard, but the ingredients (except for the liquor) are very much the same, the main difference being that most eggnogs are not cooked. This old Southern recipe is typical of many.

Separate a dozen eggs and put the 12 egg yolks and 1 cup of sugar in a large bowl. Beat until the mixture is light and smooth. Slowly add up to 4 cups of bourbon (to suit your taste), beating vigorously all the while, and continue whipping (an electric mixer is virtually essential for this) while adding 3 ounces of white rum and 1 quart of light cream or half-and-half. In a separate bowl, beat 1 quart of heavy whipping cream to soft peaks and fold it into the egg mixture, then beat the 12 reserved egg whites stiff and fold them in too. The result: almost a gallon of eggnog. Left to stand in the refrigerator for two or three days, it will mellow and ripen to a velvet-smooth finish. Serve cold with a sprinkle of grated nutmeg, and it's a venerable cup of cheer—25 or 30 cups, in fact.

Mint Julep

Of all the libations identified with the South, the most celebrated and romanticized is surely the mint julep, a disarmingly simple (and potent) refreshment for which claims have been voiced from Virginia to Louisiana. Richard Barksdale Harwell gave an engaging and inevitably controversial account of the drink's history in a little book called *The Mint Julep* in 1975. In it he asserted: "Clearly the mint julep originated in the northern Virginia tidewater, spread soon to Maryland, and eventually all along the seaboard and even to transmontane Kentucky." The words stung like a whip in the Bluegrass state, where bourbon was invented and the very notion of a Virginia julep is a blasphemous heresy. Kentucky's julep heritage reaches at least as far back as the early years of the nineteenth century, when Henry Clay was a young congressman, and virtually every Kentucky politician of note since that time has waxed eloquent on the subject.

The formulas, the secrets, the mystical and romantic descriptions of julep making are endless—there must be silver goblets as frosty as an October morn, unbruised mint leaves picked in the dewy dawn, mellow bourbon aged in the wood no less than a decade, and so on. But keep this in mind: There are two aromas—bourbon and mint—and three flavors—bourbon, mint, and sugar—that must be present in a julep that has found its equilibrium, and none must dominate or overwhelm. Any method of achieving this balance will suffice, even if it is accomplished in a paper cup. Here are two well-tested methods to that end.

Put 1 level teaspoon of sugar, 1 teaspoon of water, and 5 or 6 large fresh mint leaves in the bottom of your drink container (silver cup, jelly glass, or

. . . AND THE JULEP RECIPE OF HENRY WATTERSON, RENOWNED LOUISVILLE NEWSPAPER EDITOR, CIRCA 1910:

Pluck the mint gently from its bed, just as the dew of the evening is about to form upon it. Select the choicer sprigs only, but do not rinse them. Prepare the simple syrup and measure out a half-tumbler of whiskey. Pour the whiskey into a well-frosted silver cup, throw the other ingredients away and drink the whiskey.

whatever). Stir and mash with a spoon or wooden muddler to dissolve the sugar and extract the minty essence of the leaves. Fill the vessel with finely crushed ice. As soon as frost forms on the outside, pour in 2 ounces of aged Kentucky bourbon or Tennessee sour mash and let it trickle slowly through the ice. Stir again to blend the mint and sugar with the whiskey, add a sprig of mint for garnish, and serve.

The alternative is to boil and steep a fistful of mint sprigs in a saucepan of simple syrup (see lemonade, page 207), let it cool thoroughly, and use 1 teaspoon of this mixture in place of mint leaves and sugar. Either way, you'll be taste-testing Kentucky's pride.

Planter's Punch

Several famous punch drinks have persisted in the South for generations, true to their names if not to the formulas by which they were created. Mrs. Horry's Duke of Norfolk punch is one example, and then there are the British regimental punches such as Chatham Artillery. From the coast of North Carolina, Marion Brown obtained a recipe for the "original" Cape Fear punch—"for generations a guarded secret"—and published it in her *Southern Cook Book* in 1951. It included, in addition to sugar and lemon juice, 1 quart of tea, 4 quarts of rye or bourbon, 1 quart of rum, and 1 quart of brandy. The mixture was aged for 30 to 90 days, and then sparkling water, champagne, and fresh oranges and lemons were added before serving. The potency of that concoction is enough to suggest that the Fear in its name may have had less to do with geography than with a state of mind. The recipe is an ironically sobering reminder of how heavily our ancestors imbibed the spirits of the day.

Less excessively overpowering but almost as old a Southern rum drink is planter's punch, for which there are dozens of recipes dating back to the early nineteenth century. All have in common the union of rum, lime or lemon juice, and sugar; beyond that they sport a multitude of distinctive touches. This recipe for Mississippi planter's punch takes its inspiration from several planter classics of the past half-century.

Dissolve 1 tablespoon of sugar with 2 ounces of water in a cocktail shaker or mixing glass. Add 2 ounces of fresh lime juice, ½ jigger of rum, ½ jigger of bourbon, and ½ jigger of brandy. Add plenty of finely crushed or shaved ice, cover, and shake vigorously until outside of shaker is heavily frosted. Pour into a tall glass.

RAMOS GIN FIZZ

The saloons of Henry C. Ramos were famous for the gin fizzes shaken up by a busy bevy of shaker boys. Visitors, not to mention home folk, flocked in droves to the Ramos dispensary to down the frothy draft that Ramos alone knew how to make to perfection. One poetical sipper eulogized it thus: "It's like drinking a flower!" . . . Ramos came to New Orleans from Baton Rouge [in 1888]. . . . He purchased Tom Anderson's Stag saloon [in 1907]. . . . At times the Stag became so crowded that customers were forced to wait an hour or more (or so it seemed) to be served. The corps of busy shaker boys behind the bar was one of the sights of the town during Carnival, and in the 1915 Mardi Gras, 35 shaker boys nearly shook their arms off, but were still unable to keep up with the demand. . . . The recipe given is the original formula.

Sangaree (Sangria)

A light punch with French and Spanish roots is sangaree, popularly known in the South and elsewhere as sangria. The translation suggests the blood-red color of wine, which is its base. It's a mild and pleasantly refreshing cooler, a combination of wine, sugar, fruit, and ice. Sangria is especially popular in the Spanish restaurants of Florida, where variations on the basic formula are jealously protected secrets. Here is one version created by Tom Stovall, a native Tennessean who probed the mysteries of sangria making while living in Florida years ago.

> Slice 2 oranges, 3 lemons, and 1 lime (unpeeled) as thin as possible, place in a large bowl, cover with 1 cup of sugar, and let stand for about 1 hour. Pour a 1½-liter bottle of dry red wine over the fruit and refrigerate for another hour or so. Just before serving, add two 25-ounce bottles of sparkling catawba grape juice, stir lightly, and pour over cracked ice in tall glasses. Garnish with a slice or two of the marinated fruit in each glass. These amounts will make close to 1 gallon of sangria—enough for about 15 servings of 8 ounces each.

1 tablespoon powdered sugar
3–4 drops orange flower water
½ lime—juice only
½ lemon—juice only
1 jigger dry gin
1 white of egg
1 jigger rich milk or cream
1 squirt seltzer water
2 drops extract vanilla (optional)

Mix in a tall barglass in the order given; add crushed ice, not too fine as lumps are needed to whip up the froth of the egg white and cream. Use a long metal shaker and remember this is one drink which needs a long, steady shaking. Keep at it until the mixture gets body—"ropy" as some experienced barkeepers express it. When thoroughly shaken, strain into a tall thin glass for serving.

Stanley Clisby Arthur
Famous New Orleans Drinks, 1937

Sazerac Cocktail

New Orleans is the birthplace of several mixed drinks, including one that gave a name to them all: the cocktail. Antoine Amedée Peychaud, an apothecary, is credited with its creation. Peychaud moved to New Orleans in 1793. In his drug shop he sold a liquid tonic called bitters, a compound to settle the stomach or to relieve other maladies, much like a patent medicine. Sometimes he poured it up with a dram of brandy, the better to ease its passage to the stomach. The ritual caught on and spread; soon other local watering holes, imitating Peychaud, were serving brandy and bitters in little china egg cups called *coquetiers*. In the New Orleans pronunciation, the word became "cocktail"—and the egg cup became the model for the liquid measurer now known as a jigger.

After Peychaud's original, the two most famous New Orleans cocktails are the Sazerac and the Ramos gin fizz, both of which are now more historical curiosities than popular libations. Saloonkeeper Henry C. Ramos invented his gin fizz in about 1888 and never gave up the formula—but a half-century later, in 1937, a local writer, Stanley Clisby Arthur, published what he claimed was the original recipe in a little book called *Famous New Orleans Drinks*.

The Sazerac was developed as a brandy cocktail by John B. Schiller in the 1850s. It was named for Schiller's French Quarter coffeehouse, which in turn was named for the French manufacturer of a popular brand of cognac later used in the drink. Rye or bourbon was eventually substituted for brandy, and absinthe, a liquor distilled from a herb known as wormwood, was added, but absinthe was eventually declared an addictive and destructive substance, and its sale was banned in this country in 1912. In time, substitutes came on the market—Pernod, Ojen, Herbsaint, Anisette—all with the same absinthe-like flavor of anise or licorice. Modern versions, such as the one below, are still served in some New Orleans bars and elsewhere. In addition to the absinthe substitute, the recipes still call for bitters like the tonic compounded by Antoine Peychaud in his apothecary almost two hundred years ago; the spicy red syrup and its companion, Angostura bitters, can be found in some drugstores, liquor stores, and supermarkets. The Sazerac cocktail, after 130 years, is still a sweet sip of New Orleans history.

Fill a 4-ounce barglass with cracked ice and set it in the freezer. In another glass, combine 1 jigger of bourbon or rye whiskey, a drop or two of simple syrup (see page 208), and up to ¼ teaspoon of bitters (Peychaud, Angostura, or a combination of the two). Mix well with a spoon. Fill the glass with ice from the glass in the freezer, and coat the bottom and sides of the now empty glass with 1 teaspoon of Anisette or other absinthe substitute, pouring out any excess. Return the mixed drink and ice to the coated glass, rub the rim with a lemon peel, and serve.

Spiced Tea

Tea was strictly a hot drink in the United States until sometime after 1850, when an unsung hero discovered how good it tasted with ice. It was in that precooled era that various combinations of hot tea and spices became popular, and many of them have survived to the present as both hot and cold drinks. For some reason, the name Russian tea attached itself to these refreshments, and recipes under that name can be found in many old cookbooks, South and North. The kitchen files in the governor's mansion in Raleigh, North Carolina, contain a formula for Russian tea that predates the Cold War by a good many years. Here is a similar version.

Squeeze the juice from 6 large oranges and 6 lemons and set aside. Combine 7 cups of water, 2 cups of sugar, the used orange and lemon rinds, 1 teaspoon of whole cloves, 1 teaspoon of whole allspice, and 1 cinnamon stick in a large non-aluminum saucepan and boil for 15 minutes. Reduce heat to simmer, put in 3 heaping tablespoons of loose tea, and let it steep for 5 to 10 minutes. Strain and dilute with 3 quarts of water. Stir in the lemon and orange juice and serve the spiced tea hot or cold. These ingredients will make nearly 1½ gallons of tea—enough to fill 6-ounce cups for 25 to 30 people.

Sunday School Punch

The addition of spirits to fruit juices gives them punch—in fact, the name punch itself may have originated as a description of the effect. But there are punches without spirits too, of course—Sunday school punches, in the vernacular—and many of the combinations, such as this grape juice refresher, have been Southern favorites for many years.

Combine the juice of 12 lemons and 6 oranges in a container that will hold 3 or more gallons. Add 1 quart of water, the contents of a 46-ounce can of pineapple juice, and 4 quarts of grape juice. Sweeten to taste with sugar syrup (see lemonade, page 208). Add 3 quarts of ginger ale just before serving, and pour over crushed ice. This recipe will make 2½ gallons of punch, or enough to fill forty 8-ounce glasses.

Syllabub

One final ancient sippage from England: syllabub, a frothy blend of milk or cream and wine, a sort of light eggnog that women and children enjoyed while the men were more heavily engaged. The name is derived from Sillery, in the Champagne region of France, and "bub," an early English slang word for a bubbling drink. Long ago, so legend has it, syllabub was made by milking a cow directly into a bowl of wine, thus creating a thick and frothy head of foam. More conventional recipes were in all the old cookbooks, and the drink has retained a certain seasonal popularity, especially in some parts of the South.

Combine 2 cups of dry white wine, ½ cup of powdered sugar, ¼ cup of strained fresh lemon juice, and 2 cups of light cream or half-and-half in a bowl and beat with a mixer until frothy. To serve 6, spoon into six 6-ounce cups and sprinkle nutmeg or other spice on top.

To make a solid syllabub, a nice dessert 1 pint of cream ½ pint of wine, the juice of one lemon sweetened to your taste. Put it in a wide mouthed bottle—a quart bottle will answer. Shake it for ten minutes. Pour it into your glasses. It must be made the evening before it is to be used.

from Harriott Pinckney Horry's notebook of receipts, Charleston, South Carolina, circa 1770

Breads

In any discussion of the eating habits of a nation or region, one question that arises early is: What kind of bread do they eat? Next to water, bread is the most fundamental and symbolic form of nourishment. It is made primarily from corn, one of the oldest and most essential of all plant foods, or from wheat, the universal staff of life, and almost every society on the globe has one or more kinds of bread with which it is identified.

It would be hard to overstate the importance of bread in the food history of the South. In every age, Southern bread has been a front-line weapon against poverty, hunger, and malnutrition; a litmus test for accomplished practitioners of the culinary arts; and a repeated gastronomic delight for people of every race, sex, age, and income level.

Southern bread is everywhere. There are breads for early morning, midday, and evening, for breakfast, dinner, and supper: beignets and pain perdu and buttermilk biscuits, yeast rolls and battercakes and corn sticks, dodgers and cracklin bread and hush puppies. There are breads hot and cold, light and heavy, simple and complex, plain as pone and pretty as Sally Lunn. Nothing is as soft as Southern spoonbread—or as hard as a puck of Pensacola hardtack. The quick breads and slow breads, the light breads and shortbreads, the pancakes and fruit-nut loaves, the multiple forms of cornmeal and flour products, all are part of an extensive showcase of baked and fried delights. Some Southerners also make bread from rice, sweet potatoes, hominy, and other foods, usually as a supplement to flour or cornmeal.

Leftover breads are also a source of good recipes. Bread pudding (see page 337), a favorite dessert of New Orleans, is made from stale bread, as is pain perdu, or French toast (see page 225). Leftover biscuits, split and toasted, make a delightful next-morning breakfast bread. Mary Baxter Cook of Charlotte, Tennessee, recalls that in her early-twentieth-century youth, her mother mixed crumbled cold biscuits with hot water, a beaten egg, soda, baking powder, flour, bacon drippings, and buttermilk to make something called biscuit batter-bread—little patties of hot bread baked on a griddle like pancakes.

With such notable exceptions as the French bakeries of New Orleans and the Moravian bake shops around Winston-Salem, North Carolina, the South has not been as renowned for its commercial breads as the North. In times past and present, there have been and are more good German, French, and Scandinavian bakeries above the Ohio River than below it. But the South has always claimed to have the best homemade breads (not to mention pies, cakes, cob-

It is better to be plump than to live on baker's bread. We call it "light bread" at the Creek, and a friend from the Big Scrub goes an intelligent step farther and calls it "wasp-nest" bread. It's an old tale that the South is known as the land of the hot biscuit and the cold check. Yet a part of the placidity of the South comes from the sense of well-being that follows the heart-and-body-warming consumption of breads fresh from the oven. We serve cold baker's bread only to our enemies, trusting that they will never impose on our hospitality again.

Marjorie Kinnan Rawlings
Cross Creek Cookery, 1942

blers, and cookies), and the best restaurant breads may also be found in this region. These assertions are debatable, of course, and unprovable in any case. Still, for historical interest, creative originality, variety, and beauty as well as taste, it is hard to imagine any community of bakers having more to offer than the breadmakers of the South.

One of the most readily identifiable characteristics of Southern bread eaters is their distinct preference for hot breads—straight-from-the-oven biscuits and cornbread, pancakes and waffles billowing steam, spoonbread and hush puppies hot enough to burn the roof of your mouth, rolls and loaves of yeasty, butter-melting goodness. The region-wide instruction that comes automatically with a pan of biscuits has become an overworked cliché: "Take two and butter them while they're hot."

The recipes in this section come directly from this hot-bread tradition. They are divided into four main groupings: biscuits and rolls, breakfast breads, cornbread, and loaf breads. The selections are not comprehensive, of course, but they are broadly representative of the types and kinds of Southern breads that have held favor in the region for generations. Many of them have also been adopted by bread lovers in other parts of the country.

Old Southern cookbooks used to make a distinction between "quick" breads (those, such as biscuits, that can be made from scratch and brought to the table in about thirty minutes), and "slow" breads, the more complex yeast breads that need time to rise. Now, all homemade breads are considered "slow," and the only "quick" breads are those that come in plastic bags or cardboard tubes from the supermarket. What follows here is a sampling of old and delicious slow breads from the home kitchens of the South.

BISCUITS AND ROLLS

Angel Biscuits

Far back in the American past, cooks and bakers devised natural leavening agents to aerate and lift and lighten their breads. Some early Indian societies had these yeastlike substances. Pearl ash from the fireplace was used for this purpose in the late 1700s. Commercial baking soda was available by about 1840, and baking powder was introduced in 1856. These were the so-called quick agents; yeast took longer, but made a lighter bread with a distinctively superior taste. Commercial yeast has been on the market in this country since 1868. In both cake and dry or granular form, it has survived such later innovations as self-rising flour, ready-mixed dry ingredients, and canned and packaged baked goods of every description. Yeast has escaped extinction simply because it makes peerless breads. These biscuits are a case in point.

Sift together 5½ cups of plain all-purpose flour, 4 tablespoons of sugar, 3 teaspoons of baking powder, 1 teaspoon of soda, and 1 teaspoon of salt. With a pastry cutter, blend 1 cup of solid shortening into the dry mixture.

Thoroughly dissolve 1 package of dry yeast in 2 tablespoons of warm water, and add this with 2 cups of buttermilk to the dry ingredients, stirring with a fork to mix. As soon as a cohesive dough ball can be formed, turn it out on a floured surface and knead it for about 5 minutes, adding more flour if necessary to reduce its stickiness.

This ball of dough will make at least 6 dozen 2-inch biscuits. You can make them all at once or pull off a portion of the dough and keep the rest refrigerated in a tightly covered bowl. (It actually seems to make tastier biscuits the second or third day.)

To bake, roll out dough to about ½-inch thickness, cut and place biscuits close together on a baking sheet, cover with a tea towel and let stand a half-hour or so in a warm place to rise, and bake in a preheated 400° oven for 10 to 15 minutes, or until nicely browned.

Two general reminders may be helpful at this point. First, ovens are like people in that no two are exactly alike, so you must adjust all baking instructions to your own conditions and circumstances. Second, the standard method we use for baking bread and pastries is to start out on the bottom shelf for one fourth to one third of the baking time, and then to move up to mid-oven. This permits even browning, top and bottom.

Beaten Biscuits

There is something mysterious and intriguing about beaten biscuits. Where did they come from? England? The British had unleavened breads, of course, but nothing quite like this. Africa? John and Karen Hess suggest that possibility in their book *The Taste of America*—but again, there is no clear evidence. The Indians? Mary Randolph, in her *Virginia House-Wife* (1824) had an unleavened biscuit recipe that called for beating the dough with a pestle, and she gave it an Indian name: Apoquiniminc cakes. No connection has been found, though, between recipes for beaten biscuits and any breads baked by the Indians.

The only flour biscuit in Harriott Horry's 1770 collection of South Carolina recipes is very much like a beaten biscuit, except that it calls for kneading the dough for an hour instead of beating it. Long before soda and baking powder

Don't get me started on biscuits. That is one subject on which I can hold forth tirelessly, and more than once I've cleared the room with a passionate defense of the crusty-all-over school or a thoughtful discourse on the merits of vegetable shortening. Just for the record, you're not talking to any armchair biscuit-head here. My opinions are backed up by years of solid experience in the field. To be blunt, I have eaten more biscuits than you have. By "biscuits" I do not mean muffins,

and yeast transformed the American biscuit into a soft and puffy bread, these queer little unleavened hard biscuits had somehow found their way from parts unknown to the kitchens of the colonial South. Now, just as mysteriously, beaten biscuits have all but disappeared. We found practically no trace of them in restaurants, and only a handful of bakeries and cottage-industry outlets still sell them over the counter or by mail. Even in Southern home kitchens, the delicacy is rare.

One obvious reason for their demise is that they require considerable time and effort to make. The old method was to make a firm dough of flour, lard, and milk, and to beat it vigorously with a heavy mallet, a skillet or other flat object, or even the side of an ax, continuously folding and flattening the dough until it became soft and smooth. This layering and pounding process introduced air into the dough and gave the biscuits a lift in the oven; it also gave them their name.

In 1877, when the labor involved in making beaten biscuits (a labor usually performed by black cooks) had come to be viewed as too burdensome and time-consuming, Evelyn L. Edwards of Vineland, New Jersey, received a patent for a dough-kneading machine she had invented to do the job. It utilized a hand crank to turn two rollers, between which the dough could be passed repeatedly until it reached the desired smoothness. Like the cotton gin, this Yankee invention swept through the South, and for another half-century or more, it not only saved beaten biscuits from extinction but actually made them smoother, prettier, and more popular than before.

Mary Stuart Smith wrote in her *Virginia Cookery-Book* in 1885 that beaten biscuits had become a rarity because of the difficulties involved in making them. "A machine may be obtained that answers the purpose admirably, but it is rare," she noted. "We have only seen one specimen in use." Within a few years, however, several different types were on the market. One especially popular model, called a beaten biscuit brake, was manufactured by J. A. DeMuth of St. Joseph, Missouri. It consisted of two nickel-plated rollers mounted one above the other on a marble slab, which in turn was attached to a cast-iron base similar to that of a sewing machine.

It was in the upper South that beaten biscuits remained popular midway through the twentieth century, and it was no mere coincidence that the same territory also was known as the country ham belt, for the combination of country ham and beaten biscuits was a culinary delight that many people considered without peer in Southern gastronomy. Southerners who could resist paper-thin slices of prime country ham piled high between halves of a beaten biscuit were few and far between. They still are.

Maryland beaten biscuits can still be found (one octogenarian Marylander, Ruth Orrell of Wye Mills, has been making and selling them for a half-century),

rolls, popovers, or scones. I do not mean any product of the National Biscuit Company (which sensibly changed its name to Nabisco, perhaps after realizing that it manufactured cookies and crackers, not biscuits). I do not mean refrigerated tubes of dough that you open by whacking on the side of a kitchen table, or truck-stop hardtack whose age can be determined only by carbon-14 dating. By "biscuits" I mean *biscuits*. Within the haziest reaches of my conscious mind, lodged there as a kind of dream-memory, is the tantalizing awareness of a biscuit I ate circa 1955 at my grandmother's house in Tennessee. That was where it all started, I now believe; that was the beginning of the obsession that would one day grow to consume me and haunt my dreams. . . . My grandmother died before I had the sense to ask her for the recipe, and so for these many years I have trod the earth, looking for a biscuit that could recapture for me that primal moment.

Stephen Harrigan,
in Texas Monthly, 1984

and now and again a Virginia or North Carolina maker is heard from, but the strongest tradition survives in a narrow band stretching from the Kentucky bluegrass to the low hills of northern Alabama. That's where the most biscuit brakes can be found, at any rate, and they're not all museum pieces, either; some have even been motorized to ease the process of turning out this classic old-fashioned bread.

When we were boys, my brother and I turned the crank for many a batch of our grandmother's beaten biscuits, and as the inheritor of that machine, I have continued the ritual of making the biscuits in the winter holiday season or whenever a good country ham is available to go with them. Now, the marvels of the food processor make a reasonable facsimile of the silky-smooth original more widely accessible (they won't look as pretty or have the same texture, but the flavor will be reasonably close). Here are two recipes, the first my grandmother's and the second a modification adapted to contemporary equipment.

Combine 7 cups of all-purpose flour, 1 teaspoon of salt, 1 teaspoon of baking powder, and 4 tablespoons of sugar, and sift together 3 times. With a pastry cutter, blend in 1 cup of lard (solid vegetable shortening will suffice, but it's a poor substitute), continuing until the mixture is grainy, like coarse cornmeal. Then pour in 1½ cups of icy cold milk or half-and-half and begin kneading the dough, adding another ¼ to ½ cup of liquid if it seems too dry but taking care not to get it too moist (if you do, add a little flour). When a firm, cohesive dough ball results, flatten it out and begin running it between the rollers of the brake (someone else must turn the crank for you) or pounding it with a blunt instrument. Press and fold the dough continuously until it becomes smooth and glossy, forming air bubbles between the layers. Depending on the method used, this process will take 30 minutes to an hour, possibly longer.

When the dough seems smooth enough, roll it to a thickness of about ¼ inch, cut out the biscuits and place them close together (but not touching) on ungreased baking sheets, and pierce each one clear through with a fork two or three times (this to allow air to escape during baking). In a preheated 325° oven, bake the biscuits for about 30 minutes, or until they are slightly browned on the bottom and a smooth, pale tan on top. Leave them in the oven with the heat off for a few more minutes, if necessary, to make sure they are firm and dry on the inside. Cool on racks and then store in tins with tight-fitting lids; thus protected from moisture, they will keep well unrefrigerated for a month or more. This recipe will make 7 or 8 dozen 2-inch biscuits—firm, smooth, tender, flaky, intricately layered pastries, utterly unique biscuits out of Southern antiquity.

The same basic recipe also serves the food-processor variety, but the amounts are reduced to about one fourth the original to make the dough easier to handle.

Combine 2 cups of flour, ¼ teaspoon of salt, ¼ teaspoon of baking powder, and 1 tablespoon of sugar and sift together 3 times. Cut in ¼ cup of lard with a pastry cutter and then pour in ⅓ cup of cold milk or half-and-half and knead into a firm ball. If more liquid is needed, add it a teaspoonful at a time, taking care not to get the dough too moist. Break up the dough ball and put all of it in the food processor to spin with the dough blade for 2 minutes. Remove and knead a few minutes. Roll and fold the dough by hand several times. When it becomes smooth, roll it out to a thickness of about ¼ inch, cut the biscuits, pierce each one with a fork, and bake as described above. An ancient wonder of Southern cookery is hereby resurrected.

Buttermilk Biscuits

The basic, standard, regular biscuit of the South has variously been called a soda, baking powder, or buttermilk biscuit, because it contains all three of those ingredients. It is the original quick bread, and recipes for it are usually quite similar. Experienced cooks can throw this dough together in a wink, without bothering to measure the ingredients. This recipe, which has been widely used in many parts of the South for at least fifty years, is a little more precise; it differs only slightly from methods much older than that.

Sift together 2 cups of all-purpose flour, 3 teaspoons of baking powder, ½ teaspoon of baking soda, and ½ teaspoon of salt. With a pastry cutter, blend in 6 tablespoons of solid shortening, and when thoroughly mixed, add ⅔ cup of fresh buttermilk. Stir the mixture with a fork, then knead it quickly (about ½ minute) and roll it out on a floured surface to a thickness of ¼- to ½-inch. Cut round biscuits 2 inches in diameter, place them close together on a baking sheet, and bake in a preheated 450° oven for about 8 to 10 minutes, or until golden-brown and puffy. This recipe makes 30 or more biscuits.

ON BEATEN BISCUITS

This is the most laborious of cakes, and also the most unwholesome, even when made in the best manner. We do not recommend it; but there is no accounting for tastes. Children should not eat these biscuits—nor grown persons either, if they can get any other sort of bread.

When living in a town where there are bakers, there is no excuse for making Maryland biscuit. Believe nobody that says they are not unwholesome. Yet we have heard of families, in country places, where neither the mistress nor the cook knew any other preparation of wheat bread. Better to live on indian cakes.

Eliza Leslie
Directions for Cookery in its Various Branches, 1837

Potato Icebox Rolls

For well over a century, this variation on the basic Southern dinner roll has been popular in some parts of the South. Mashed potatoes may seem like a curious addition, since they give no clearly detectable taste to an already delicious bread. Their presence may relate to the fact that yeast was made from potatoes in the 1800s—although potatoes are used in addition to yeast in these rolls, not in place of it. The texture may also be affected by the potatoes. In any case, this is an outstanding hot bread with a sterling reputation. Opal McCauley of Lexington, Kentucky, has been the guardian of this particular recipe since the 1940s, but it goes back much further than that.

Peel and boil 2 medium-sized potatoes until tender, mash them well, and set them aside to cool. (Leftovers won't do, since the need is for plain, unseasoned potatoes.) In a separate bowl, dissolve 1 package of dry yeast (or 1 cake, if you prefer) in ¼ cup of lukewarm water and set aside. Then bring 1 cup of milk to the boiling point and pour it over ½ cup of lard (or shortening) in another bowl, stirring until the lard is completely melted. Add the potatoes to the milk and lard mixture and blend until smooth. Next add 3 hand-beaten eggs, ½ cup of sugar, and 2 teaspoons of salt to the mixture, and stir until well-blended. Sift and then measure 5 cups of all-purpose flour. Stir 4 cups of it into the batter, followed by the yeast and then the other cup of flour, mixing thoroughly. Now the dough is complete. Put it into a large greased bowl, brush melted butter on top, cover and refrigerate for several hours (overnight is best), so the dough can rest and chill.

When ready to use, pull off a portion (one fourth of the dough will make about a dozen rolls) and drop it onto a well-floured surface. The dough may be quite sticky, so have flour handy. Roll out to a thickness of ¼ to ½ inch, cut out and shape rolls as you wish (e.g., cloverleaf, envelope, biscuit), and place in greased roll pans or on greased baking sheets. Let rise for about 1 hour in a warm place and then bake in a preheated 400° oven for about 15 minutes, or until golden brown on top. Served hot, the rolls will be light, spongy, and delicious.

Yeast Rolls

Another yeast bread of a somewhat different composition is this old recipe calling for buttermilk. We trace it to rural western Kentucky and the kitchen of

---

LEGACIES

her grandmother called her from the playground
  "yes, ma'am"
  "i want chu to learn how to make rolls"
said the old woman proudly
but the little girl didn't want
to learn how because she knew
even if she couldn't say it that
that would mean when the old one died
she would be less dependent on her spirit so
she said
  "i don't want to know how to make no rolls"
with her lips poked out
and the old woman wiped her hands on
her apron saying, "lord
these children"
and neither of them ever
said what they meant
and i guess nobody ever does

                              Nikki Giovanni
                              My House, 1972

Della Lane Bleidt, who was winning praise for these rolls more than a half-century ago.

Measure 4 cups of unsifted all-purpose flour into a large bowl and mix with it 1½ cups of buttermilk. Add, in order, 3 tablespoons of melted lard, 1 teaspoon of baking powder, 1 scant teaspoon of baking soda, 1 teaspoon of salt, and ⅓ cup of sugar. Dissolve 1 package of dry yeast in ½ cup of warm water and add it to the dough mixture, stirring well. When thoroughly combined, turn it out on a well-floured surface and knead, using more flour (sifted) as necessary to obtain a dough smooth and easy to handle. Put it in a greased bowl, cover, and refrigerate overnight.

When ready to bake, pull off small bits of the dough, shape into cloverleaf or envelope rolls, place in greased pans, and brush with melted butter or shortening. Let rise in a warm place for about 1 hour. When the rolls have risen to about double their size, bake them in a preheated 400° oven for 10 to 12 minutes, or until golden brown. The recipe makes about 3 dozen small rolls.

BREAKFAST BREADS

Beignets

The 1901 *Picayune Creole Cook Book* probably did more to spread the good word on New Orleans food than any other volume in the first half of this century. In it are more than a thousand Creole recipes and a mother lode of background information on Louisiana foodways and kitchen customs. There is, for example, a chapter on Sweet Entremets—fruit dishes, crepes, doughnuts, pancakes, and fritters. Beignets, the French Market doughnuts for which New Orleans is now famous, are presented in the chapter primarily as a batter for making deep-fried fruit fritters. "The ancient French colonists brought the custom" to New Orleans, said the *Picayune*, and when the cook was preparing to make fritters and hungry children were underfoot, she often responded "by handing a beautiful golden beignet, piled with snowy sugar, to the expectant little ones."

Here, with modern adjustments, is the *Picayune*'s basic beignet recipe. There are more elaborate formulas, but the old way is very satisfying—and certainly better than the commercial beignet mixes.

Beat 2 large eggs with an electric mixer in a large mixing bowl. With the mixer still running, add ½ cup of milk, 1 cup of flour, ¼ teaspoon of salt,

We picked up one excellent word—a word worth traveling to New Orleans to get; a nice, limber, expressive, handy word—"Lagniappe." They pronounce it lanny-yap. It is Spanish—so they said. We discovered it at the head of a column of odds and ends in the *Picayune* the first day; heard twenty people use it the second; inquired what it meant the third; adopted it and got facility in swinging it the fourth. It is the equivalent of the thirteenth roll in a "baker's dozen." It is sometimes thrown in, gratis, for good measure. When a child or a servant buys something in a shop—or even the mayor or the governor, for aught I know—he finishes the operation by saying: "Give me something for lagniappe." The shopman always responds; gives the child a bit of licorice-root, gives the servant a cheap cigar or a spool of thread, gives the governor—I don't know what he gives the governor; support, likely.

Mark Twain
Life on the Mississippi, 1883

2 tablespoons of sugar, 2 teaspoons of baking powder, 1 tablespoon of melted butter, and 1 teaspoon of vanilla extract. When thoroughly blended, fold 2 stiffly beaten egg whites into the batter. The dough will be quite sticky. You can either put it on a heavily floured surface, press it to a thickness of about ½ inch, and cut off 1- to 2-inch squares to be deep-fried in hot shortening, or simply drop teaspoonfuls of it directly into the fat. Square or round, the dough will make about 3 dozen deliciously hot, puffy doughnuts. Sprinkle them with powdered sugar and a little cinnamon, if you like, and serve them quickly with hot coffee.

Buttermilk Pancakes

Pancakes, like most of the other breakfast breads, are too much of an all-American favorite to be claimed exclusively by the South or any other region. They belong to us all, the same as waffles do, and they have been standard fare in one form or another since English and Dutch colonists brought the recipes in the seventeenth century. The Indians already had cornmeal versions of essentially the same thing. If there is anything particularly Southern about pancakes, it may be the prevalent use of buttermilk in the batter. This is a typical recipe.

Sift together 2 cups of all-purpose flour, 2 tablespoons of sugar, 1 teaspoon of salt, and 1 teaspoon of baking soda. Add 2 cups of buttermilk, stirring lightly but leaving the batter a bit lumpy. Add 2 tablespoons of vegetable oil, mix well, then fold in 2 well-beaten eggs. Don't overstir the batter. Ladle onto a hot griddle, forming cakes as big around as you wish—from silver dollars to 6-inch discs. Cook completely on one side and then the other, turning only once. This recipe makes 10 to 12 puffy 5-inch pancakes.

Serve with melted butter and a topping of your choice, such as BROWN SUGAR SAUCE, which Marion Flexner, in *Out of Kentucky Kitchens* (1949), said "many old-time, dyed-in-the-wool Kentuckians prefer . . . to any other for their waffles and pancakes." Mix 1 cup of firmly packed dark brown sugar in a saucepan with 4 tablespoons of water and 1 tablespoon of butter. Boil until the sugar melts, stirring to prevent sticking. Serve warm.

STRAWBERRY HONEY, another syrup good for pancakes (or ice cream), is a Southern summer treat, the formula for which is attributed to novelist Katherine Anne Porter. Bring 1 cup of clear honey to a boil in a saucepan and add about 15 small fresh strawberries, washed and hulled. Leave over low heat about 2 or 3 minutes. When the two flavors have blended, pour up the sauce in a pitcher and serve warm.

Cornmeal Waffles

Marion Flexner is the source for this recipe, which she said came from an old Virginia cookbook. The ingredients are similar to many oven-baked cornbreads. Butter and syrup go well with these light, crisp, crunchy waffles, but they make a better meal with a hot and spicy hash made of venison, turkey, chicken, or beef. For a classic and traditional Southern breakfast—or supper—try these.

Put ¾ cup of unsifted white cornmeal in a large mixing bowl. Sift together 2 tablespoons of flour, ⅓ teaspoon of salt, ¼ teaspoon of baking soda, ½ teaspoon of baking powder, and 1 teaspoon of sugar, and add this mixture to the cornmeal. Beat 1 egg with a whisk and blend it with the dry mixture. Slowly add 1 cup of buttermilk, beating to prevent lumping, then add ¼ cup of melted butter. When the batter is thoroughly mixed, spoon it onto a slightly greased and smoking-hot waffle iron. This much batter will make 8 to 10 small, 4-inch waffles.

French Toast

In *La Cuisine Creole*, Lafcadio Hearn's anonymously written 1885 collection of New Orleans recipes, there is a short instruction on Pain Perdu, or "lost bread." The basic recipe has lingered on now for a century, and it still ranks as one of Louisiana's and the South's favorite breakfast dishes. The idea is very simple: Stale bread almost lost to any useful purpose is soaked in a custard of milk, egg, and sugar and fried in a hot skillet. Virtually every Louisiana cookbook since Hearn's has offered some fine points in the advanced art of making pain perdu. Here is our version.

Slice 6 pieces of day-old French bread about ½ inch thick. In a large mixing bowl, beat 3 eggs well. Add 1 cup of milk, 1 tablespoon of sugar, ½ teaspoon of vanilla extract, ¼ teaspoon of flour, and whip together into a froth. In a heavy skillet or on a griddle, melt 2 tablespoons of butter and mix together with 2 tablespoons of vegetable oil. When the fat is quite hot, dip the bread slices in the custard until they are thoroughly soaked and transfer them with a spatula to the skillet. Cook quickly at high temperature, and turn only once, like pancakes. Cooked pieces can be kept warm on a platter in a 150° oven until ready to serve. At the table, sprinkle the slices with a mix of powdered sugar and cinnamon, or try one of the syrups given with the pancake recipe above. Six slices of bread will soak up all the custard.

Biscuit for breakfast is a social and economic self-measurement among croppers and hands. Those who always have biscuit for breakfast regard themselves as successful persons of dignity. They pity and look down on the unfortunate who have to go back to corn pone during hard times. The first breakfast at which corn pone is eaten is a sad ceremonial at which the partaking family, by partaking, admit they have been deserted by their Cap'ns and have sunk to the lowest level of human subsistence. A Garth Negro or white cropper would relish corn pone for dinner or supper, but to have had to eat it for breakfast would have broken his spirit and made him feel that he had been cast into the outer darkness by the Cap'n. Corn pone for breakfast among croppers is like a patch on the seat of the britches for a man, or drawers made of flour sacks for a woman among the landowning whites.

William Bradford Huie
Mud on the Stars, 1942

CORNBREAD

We return once again to the ultimate American grain, Indian corn, and to its versatile wonders, this time focusing upon the panoply of hot breads that Southerners and many other Americans make from cornmeal. For hundreds of years before Europeans reached the shores of North America, the native Indian populations from Canada to Mexico apparently were making bread in a variety of ways from ground corn. Among the names they used for these breads were suppone and appone—and pone has remained the most basic form of cornmeal bread throughout four centuries of the European presence on the continent.

Although corn is a primary vegetable in all parts of the United States and is grown much more extensively in the Midwest than in the South, cornbread remains closely identified with the Southern states. The reasons for that are not at all clear; some say the explanation is simply that cooks in the South consistently make a superior bread. In any case, many people North and South concede the greater qualities of Southern cornbread, and have been doing so for a long time. In *Dr. Chase's Third, Last & Complete Receipt Book*, published in Detroit in 1887, A. W. Chase offered several recipes for "Corn Bread, Southern, Far-Famed," and observed: "The Southern people raise the white corn only, or, at least, almost wholly so; and some people, even in the North, think it makes the best bread. It would be well, then, to give it a thorough trial in the North, and if it proves more valuable than the yellow, let it be raised especially for cooking purposes." Almost a hundred years later, in *Southern Voices* magazine, Redding S. Sugg, Jr., noted that Yankee cornbread has always been characterized by yellow meal and significant amounts of sugar and flour, whereas Southerners tend to favor white meal and to use sugar and flour sparingly, if at all. Without attacking the Northern product directly, Sugg proceeded to assert, citing numerous recipes in evidence, that the Southern breads are still superior.

The wilderness settlers who moved west and south out of Virginia centuries ago took their Indian bread wisdom with them. Throughout the Southern region, says Richard J. Hooker in *Food and Drink in America*, "corn breads were eaten without thought that there existed other kinds," and all of the pone-type breads that still remain in our cookbooks—ashcake, hoecake, dodgers—were widely known even then. All were essentially combinations of meal, salt, and water. Corn dodgers were cooked in boiling water, according to Hooker, and "the name, which probably came from the lively motion given the morsel by the boiling water, was retained even when the same pieces were baked." Harriette Simpson Arnow, in *Seedtime on the Cumberland*, wrote that the hoecake "was said to have been so named from the custom of the slaves in Virginia, who, given only meal, mixed it with water and baked it on their hoes." Another pone, johnnycake, is probably either a corruption of journey cake (a durable pocket

To try to cook without cornmeal in the South is a lost cause. Aside from cornbread which many Southerners make at least once a day, we need "meal" to fry fish or squirrel. . . . We use meal in chess pie and most "dressings" or stuffings. We use cornmeal dumplings for turnip greens and poke salad . . . and many will tell you that fried chicken must be dipped in cornmeal.

Sallie F. Hill
*The Progressive Farmer's
Southern Cookbook,* 1961

bread that travels well) or of Shawnee cake (giving credit to a particular tribe that made it).

As the frontier receded and living standards improved, Southern cornbread also moved up the scale. To the basic mix of meal, water, salt, and grease were added eggs, milk (sweet and sour), baking powder, baking soda, and the afore-mentioned sugar and flour. Cracklings—crispy morsels left over when pork fat has been rendered into lard—were a common byproduct of hog killing on the farm, and they too found their way into cornbread. In time there were such further refinements as corn light bread, cornbread dressing, griddle cakes of various kinds, muffins and corn sticks baked in specially made irons, hush puppies and corn cakes cooked in hot fat, and finally what Redding Sugg called "the apotheosis of cornbread," the ultimate, glorified ideal: spoonbread, a steaming hot, feather-light dish of cornmeal mixed with butter, eggs, milk, and seasonings and lifted by the heat of the oven to a soufflé of airiness.

Tracing the evolution of cornbread from suppone to spoonbread is in some ways similar to studying history through an examination of fossils and other artifacts. There is a rough parallel in these recipes with the social and cultural movement of people through history. A properly prepared dish of spoonbread can be taken as testimony to the perfectability of humankind; a crisp cornbread dodger or hoecake, on the other hand, demonstrates another kind of perfection, an enduring strength that has not been improved upon in four centuries of service to hungry people.

As a representative sampling of cornbread dishes straight out of Southern history, we offer six recipes here. A seventh, for cornmeal waffles, was given earlier with Breakfast Breads (see page 225); an eighth, for cornbread dressing, is presented under Side Dishes (see page 282).

Cornbread Muffins

Muffins and corn sticks are baked in heavy black irons—some with round, fluted molds, others semicircular, still others shaped like little ears of corn. The Shaker Society at Pleasant Hill, Kentucky, an active community from 1805 to 1910, adopted a recipe very similar to this from their Kentucky neighbors. Unlike many of the South's cornbread recipes, it contains both sugar and flour.

Mix together 1 cup of plain white cornmeal, ½ cup of flour, ½ teaspoon of salt, ½ teaspoon of baking soda, ½ teaspoon of baking powder, and 1 tea-spoon of sugar. Add 2 tablespoons of vegetable oil, 1 cup of buttermilk, and 1 egg, and blend the mixture well. Grease the muffin irons with bacon drip-

TENNESSEE MUFFINS

Sift three pints of yellow Indian meal, and put one-half into a pan and scald it. Then set it away to get cold. Beat six eggs, whites and yolks separately. The yolks must be beaten till they become very thick and smooth, and the whites until they are a stiff froth that stands alone. When the scalded meal is cold, mix it into a batter with the beaten yolk of egg, the remainder of the meal, a salt-spoonful of salt, and, if necessary, a little water. The batter must be quite thick. At the last, stir in, lightly and slowly, the beaten white of egg. Grease your muffin rings, and set them in an oven of the proper heat; put in the batter immediately, as standing will injure it. Send them to table hot; pull them open, and eat them with butter.

Eliza Leslie
Directions for Cookery in its Various Branches, 1837

pings, get them sizzling hot in a 450° oven, then fill each mold half full with batter and bake in the preheated oven for about 10 minutes, or until well-browned. The recipe makes 10 to 12 muffins.

Cornbread (Pan or Skillet)

This is a standard family recipe from Kentucky that has not changed in at least three generations, and it could as easily be claimed in any of the Southern states. The batter can be cooked in a black iron skillet or a square cake pan. (We prefer the skillet.) In our oven, preheated to 425°, the bread is baked for about 5 minutes on the bottom rack and 12 to 15 minutes more on the middle rack, by which time it is a crispy golden brown.

In a mixing bowl, whip 1 egg with a wire whisk. Add 1 teaspoon of salt and ½ teaspoon of baking soda, mixing thoroughly. Sprinkle in 1 cup of plain white cornmeal. Still stirring, slowly add about 1 cup of fresh buttermilk—just enough to make a medium-thick batter, neither thin and runny nor heavy and stiff. Meanwhile, put 2 tablespoons of bacon grease in a 9- or 10-inch skillet or pan and get it smoking hot on a burner of the stove. Stir half the hot grease into the batter, mix well, and then quickly pour the batter into the skillet and put it in the oven. Bake as noted above. The yield will be 10 to 12 pie-shaped wedges (or squares, if pan-baked). With the possible addition of a teaspoon of baking powder, this cornbread recipe can be found in all parts of the South.

Corn Cakes

In the treatment of pone that follows, hoecake is presented as a stovetop cornbread; so are corn cakes, but theirs is a more complex mixture. Variously called batter cakes, griddle cakes, eggbread, or corn cakes, this is "second-generation" hoecake with several enriching ingredients. The particular recipe offered here is from Redding Sugg's "Treatise Upon Cornbread" in a 1974 issue of *Southern Voices* magazine. It might just as easily have come from an early twentieth-century collection of Mississippi or Georgia or Virginia recipes.

Sift together 1 cup of plain white cornmeal, 2 tablespoons of flour, 1 teaspoon of baking powder, 1 teaspoon of salt, and ½ teaspoon of baking soda.

Rooster set about preparing our supper. Here is what he brought along for "grub": a sack of salt and a sack of red pepper and a sack of taffy—all this in his jacket pockets—and then some ground coffee beans and a big slab of salt pork and one hundred and seventy corn dodgers. I could scarcely credit it. The "corn dodgers" were balls of what I would call hot-water cornbread. Rooster said the woman who prepared them thought the order was for a wagon party of marshals.

"Well," said he, "when they get too hard to eat plain we can make mush from them and what we have left we can give to the stock."

He made some coffee in a can and fried some pork. Then he sliced up some of the dodgers and fried the pieces in grease. Fried bread! That was a new dish to me. He and LaBoeuf made fast work of about a pound of pork and a dozen dodgers.

Charles Portis
True Grit, 1968

Drop in 1 whole egg with 1 cup of buttermilk and 1 tablespoon of bacon grease and mix together (but do not beat the mixture smooth). Then, on a hot griddle, spoon puddles of batter to make cakes of the size you want. When bubbles form on top, turn the cakes and cook the other side. Serve them hot with butter. Corn cakes go well with almost any meal.

Cornpone

The ancient and original cornbread of Indian and colonial societies is here in these simple breads. The first pones were a batter made of coarsely ground cornmeal, water, perhaps a little salt, and bear grease. Cooked on flat rocks or metal surfaces, they were hoecakes; boiled in water or baked in makeshift ovens, they were cornbread dodgers; wrapped in cabbage leaves or cornshucks and baked in the coals of the fire, they were ashcakes. Pone was an easy bread to make, and it was good—as it still is. Here's how.

Put 2 cups of plain white cornmeal in a mixing bowl, add 1 teaspoon of salt and 1 tablespoon of bacon grease, and then slowly stir in enough boiling water to make a mush that is thick and wet and substantial—neither stiff nor runny. For hoecakes cooked in a skillet or on a griddle, spoon the batter in round shapes like small pancakes onto a hot, greased surface; cook one side until lightly browned, then turn, pat down, and cook the other side the same way. For dodgers baked in the oven, grease a cookie sheet lightly, shape the pones into small patties, and bake them on the middle oven rack at 425° for 20 to 30 minutes, or until they are light brown, crisp, crunchy, and hard. About 10 or 12 hoecakes or dodgers will be produced by this recipe.

Hush Puppies

Most people around St. Marks, Florida, an old fishing village on the Gulf Coast south of Tallahassee, will tell you that the late T. J. Posey's seafood restaurant there is the home of the hush puppy, a deep-fried ball of cornmeal batter and seasonings that has become an all-parts companion of fried fish. It's a dubious claim, in light of the fact that hush puppies have been written about since the World War I era and Posey's restaurant is of more recent vintage. Nevertheless, there are other accounts that say hush puppies originated in the general vicinity of St. Marks (the term being what camp cooks supposedly shouted to the barking hounds when they tossed them batter-ball scraps from the fish skillets), and it may be that somehow T. J. Posey was truly present at the creation. Wherever the truth lies, hush puppies have entered the national cuisine so completely that people from coast to coast call for them wherever fried fish is served.

Like barbecue sauce and chili, hush puppies have inspired endless "secret" formulas, each one said to be "the first" or "the best." When Kentucky novelist James Still disclosed his own recipe for the morsels during an interview on National Public Radio's *All Things Considered* program a few years ago, the network was deluged with calls and letters asking for the directions.

There's nothing secret or original about the recipe below; it's just good. Slight variations of it are in the Kentucky files of Carrie Wallace and Lucille Wilson, and in the South Carolina notes of Pres Lane.

In a mixing bowl, combine 1 cup of self-rising white cornmeal, ½ cup of self-rising flour, ½ teaspoon of salt, and 1 teaspoon of sugar (or use regular meal and flour with the salt and sugar and add ½ teaspoon each of baking powder and baking soda). Blend in 1 egg and add enough buttermilk (up to 1 cup) to produce a thick batter that will drop slowly but easily from a teaspoon. (Finely minced green onion and garlic, black or red pepper, or a few drops of hot-pepper sauce may be added to suit your taste.) To make golf-ball-sized pups, drop teaspoonfuls of the batter into fat that is hot enough and deep enough for the morsels to float (about 375° and 3 inches, respectively). Fry to a golden brown and drain on absorbent paper, keeping the cooked ones warm in a 150° oven until ready to serve with a platter of fish. The recipe makes about 2 dozen or more hush puppies.

Spoonbread

Far back into the Virginia past, almost as far as Mary Randolph in 1824, there were dishes that came close to this rich, light delicacy. In fact, the Indian porridge called suppone or suppawn is considered by some food historians to be the true ancestral source of spoonbread. But the butter, milk, and eggs that make spoonbread such a special dish came later, much later—probably after the Civil War. John F. Mariani, in *The Dictionary of American Food & Drink*, says the term was not used in print until 1906. Whether it belonged first to Virginia, Maryland, the Carolinas, Kentucky, or Tennessee (those are the most likely candidates, with Virginia having the edge), it is claimed now by those states and others as a highly prized and appreciated dinner-table specialty.

Grits is the first truly American food. On a day in the spring of 1607 when sea-weary members of the London Company came ashore at Jamestown, Va., they were greeted by a band of friendly Indians offering bowls of a steaming hot substance consisting of softened maize seasoned with salt and some kind of animal fat, probably bear grease. The welcomers called it "rockahominie." The settlers liked it so much they adopted it as a part of their own diet. They anglicized the name to "hominy" and set about devising a milling process by which the large corn grains could be ground into smaller particles without losing any nutriments. The experiment was a success, and grits became a gastronomic mainstay of the South and symbol of Southern culinary pride.

*Turner Catledge,
in The New York Times,
January 31, 1982*

The ingredients in spoonbread are very much the same from one recipe to the next, the major difference being that about half use baking powder and/or sugar and the rest use neither. The following recipe can be considered fairly typical. It was a specialty in the country kitchen of Elizabeth Carpenter Wilson in western Kentucky more than fifty years ago.

In a large saucepan, combine 1 cup of white cornmeal with 2 cups of water and then add 1 teaspoon of salt. Bring to a boil, then lower the heat and cook for 5 minutes, stirring constantly. (The mixture will be very stiff at first, but the proportions are right, so keep stirring and don't add more water.) Remove from heat and very gradually stir in 1 cup of cold sweet milk, followed by 2 well-beaten eggs and 2 tablespoons of melted butter. Pour the thoroughly mixed batter into a hot, greased baking dish and bake it in a preheated 400° oven for about 40 minutes, or until firm in the middle and well-browned over the top. Serve it hot, straight from the dish. This quantity provides 4 to 6 small servings; for more, double the recipe.

Spoonbread is the lightest, richest, most delicious of all cornmeal dishes, a veritable cornbread soufflé. It is an excellent companion to country ham and red-eye gravy—to any meat and gravy, for that matter—and it is also well-matched with seafood, fresh garden vegetables, hot fruit dishes, and salads. Like very few dishes, it is a welcome and suitable menu item for any meal—breakfast, lunch, or dinner.

LOAF BREADS

The breads people ate in colonial America, whether made from flour or cornmeal or other foundation foods such as rice, were typically homemade. From simple cornpone, the way led to soda biscuits and on to more complex cornbreads and wheat breads. Finally, in the late 1800s, the widespread availability of commercial yeast, baking powder, baking soda, sweet milk, and buttermilk turned bread making into a rather sophisticated art. Some breads were sold in bakeries and other shops; of course, but the common practice in most households was to bake bread on a regular, even daily, basis. That pattern continued, especially in the South, until World War II and even beyond. Surveys made as late as the 1950s showed that many rural Southerners still ate far more homemade than store-bought bread.

Commercially baked white bread, sliced for sandwich making, first began to

The question is often asked, "What is the most important branch of culinary knowledge? What the chief requisite in supplying the table well and healthfully?"

The experienced housewife cannot hesitate as to the reply: Beyond doubt, the ability to make good bread. No one need rise hungry from a table on which is plenty of light, sweet bread, white or brown, and good butter. . . . [The housewife] is culpable if she fails to see that her board furnishes three times a day a bountiful allowance of what I hope none of my friends in council will ever call "healthy bread."

Marion Harland's Cookbook, 1907

appear in bakeries and groceries in the 1920s, and in less than a half-century it had almost completely replaced homemade loaves. Hot breads have remained popular in many Southern homes—cornbread and biscuits are not exactly forgotten foods of the past, even though they may no longer be made regularly. But loaf bread is more threatened. As good as it is, the light bread that used to come daily from so many kitchens is now an endangered art form. It is slow bread, yeast-risen and time-consuming, and rare is the cook who still bakes it week in and week out. By whatever name—yeast bread, light bread, white bread—it is gone from the home kitchen, and it won't be back, except occasionally as a specialty or nostalgia item.

Still, a warm, yeasty loaf of freshly baked home bread is delicious enough to justify whatever trouble it takes, at least once in a while. And not surprisingly, people who venture back into this abandoned activity often make at least three happy discoveries: It's easier than they thought it would be, and quicker, and it's a lot of fun.

Egg Bread

Barnie Higgs, a native Virginian who has also lived for extended periods in Africa and Tennessee, has drawn from all those places to develop a high level of skill as a home baker. His staple loaf, which he makes regularly, is called Country Fair Egg Bread. Beginners won't master this light and fragrant loaf the first time, but they should find, as we have, that even the failures make good toast.

Into a large mixing bowl, put ¼ cup of vegetable oil, 4 tablespoons of softened butter, ½ cup of sugar, and 2 teaspoons of salt and stir them together. Pour in 1½ cups of scalded milk, stir well, and set the bowl aside to cool. Dissolve 2 yeast cakes or 2 packages of dry yeast in ½ cup of lukewarm water, adding ½ teaspoon of salt and ½ teaspoon of sugar to hasten the bubbling action of the yeast. Wait a few minutes, then pour the yeast into the cooled milk mixture and add 2 lightly beaten eggs. When all these ingredients are thoroughly blended, gradually stir in 5 cups of sifted bread flour (or all-purpose flour if this is not available). When the dough ball has taken shape in the bowl, cover it with a tea towel, set it in a warm place, and let the dough rise to double its size, usually within 1 hour or less. (If you can't find a warm spot, turn oven to 400° for 1 minute, then turn it off and set dough bowl inside.) Then knead 4 more cups of sifted bread flour into the dough, working it vigorously until it becomes smooth and elastic. Next shape into 2 loaves of equal size and place them in greased 9-inch loaf pans (or 4 loaves can be made in pans about half that size). Let the bread rise again before baking in a preheated 425° oven (bottom rack) for 10 minutes. Reduce heat to 325° and bake about 40 more minutes on the middle rack, taking care not to let the top crust get too brown. (Butter brushed over the tops of the loaves or a sheet of aluminum foil laid across them will help prevent that.) When done, turn out on a rack to cool.

Light Bread

A somewhat simpler loaf with a different taste and texture is this traditional recipe from Lexington, Kentucky. Eva and Sella Leach, sisters who rented rooms to college boys there in the 1940s and '50s, called it "just an everyday loaf of light bread," but the boys held it in higher esteem. The aroma of it coming out of the oven was overpoweringly inviting, and the taste lived up to the smell. By today's standards, it's still a superior loaf.

Sift 4 cups of all-purpose flour (or bread flour). In a saucepan, combine 1½ cups of sweet milk, 1 teaspoon of salt, 2 tablespoons of sugar, and 6 table-spoons of solid shortening and stir over low heat until the shortening melts. Let the mixture cool to lukewarm, then add 2 crumbled cakes of fresh yeast (or 2 packages of dry yeast) and stir until dissolved. Add the milk mixture to the sifted flour a little at a time, stirring continuously to get a smooth and thoroughly blended dough ball. Transfer it to a greased bowl, cover with a damp cloth, and let rise in a warm place to double its size. When dough has risen, turn it out on a floured surface and knead it for several minutes to get a smooth and elastic texture. Shape to fit into a greased 9-inch loaf pan, let it rise again in the pan to double its size, bake on the bottom shelf of a preheated 425° oven for 8 to 10 minutes, then reduce heat to 350° and leave on bottom shelf for 30 more minutes, or until nicely browned and firm on top. If the loaf seems to be browning too quickly, brush top with butter and lay a sheet of aluminum foil loosely over it.

Sally Lunn

There are some who claim that Sally Lunn, a rich and tasty bun/cake/loaf bread, was among the first recipes (along with syllabub) the Jamestown colonists prepared to remind them of England. Was Sally Lunn a woman who sold cakes on the street in Bath, England, in the eighteenth century? Or was there once a French girl who sold buns with tops as gold as the sun (*soleil*) and bottoms as white as the moon (*lune*), leading Americans eventually to call the bread Sally Lunn? No one knows. What *is* known is that there were recipes for loaves like this in early colonial America, and that there was a quick and lasting fondness for the bread in the Southern states especially, whether it was made into loaves, cakes, or buns. Sally Lunn recipes once graced virtually every Southern cookbook, and cooks from Virginia in particular sang its praises. It is seldom seen now, but the occasional modern recipes for it bear a close resemblance to the old, most containing butter, eggs, milk, sugar, flour, salt, and yeast. It is more likely to be served as a cake or dessert loaf than a dinner bread. In whatever shape or mode, it's delicious, especially when warm and fresh from the oven. This recipe is typical.

Heat 1 cup of sweet milk to the boiling point, cool to lukewarm, and dissolve in it 1 yeast cake or package of dry yeast. In a mixing bowl, combine 1 stick of softened butter with ½ cup of sugar and beat together until creamy. Add 3 whole eggs to the butter and sugar, beating hard (a mixer helps) to make a smooth paste. In another bowl, sift together 4 cups of all-purpose flour and add 1 teaspoon of salt. Alternately add small amounts of the flour and the milk to the butter-and-egg mixture, blending thoroughly after each addition. Put the resulting dough ball in a large bowl, cover it with a tea towel, and set it in a warm place to rise. When it has about doubled in size (probably within an hour), punch it down and beat it vigorously with a wooden spoon. Pour it into a well-greased funnel cake pan or tube pan and let it rise again to double its size. Bake in a preheated 350° oven (bottom rack) for 45 to 50 minutes, or until it is nicely browned on top and well-baked clear through. Cool in the pan for about 10 minutes before turning it out onto a rack.

Sally Lunn can be sliced while it's still warm enough to melt butter, and to eat it thus with a dish of fresh fruit and a cup of coffee or a glass of cold milk is a singular experience, one that calls to mind all of the delightfully varied hot breads that have distinguished Southern cooking for upward of four centuries. The best of these breads may rarely be seen in the South today, but they're still as close as a good cookbook.

[At my Aunt Ida's house in Macon, North Carolina, in the 1930s and '40s, we] seldom sat down to a meal that was not splendid, and splendidly prepared. The cooks were Ida herself and her long-time black helper, Mary Lee Parker. So I began life as the recipient of great cooking . . . by two master chefs.

The genius of North Carolina country cooking before the advent of packaged foods lay precisely in its loving respect for the raw materials. . . . the aim of Ida and Mary Lee was the enhancement—not the disguise or tarting up—of superb fresh vegetables, chickens killed only two hours before cooking, pork aged and smoked by men with centuries of practice behind them, berries picked that day from the garden or the roadside and baked in a pastry as exquisite as any Parisian pâtissière's. . . .

But the secret ennobling ingredient was time—time and pride and family

Main Dishes

Southern literature and history give us countless glimpses of plain and fancy home cooking laid out before kin and company. In every era, in every state and county, in every social and economic stratum, loving cooks have needed hardly any excuse at all to bring their best to the table, and many a writer has strived to capture the spirit, if not the flavor, of ordinary occasions being transformed into memorable meals.

Meat and fish and fowl have come in for special attention. In *Dishes and Beverages of the Old South* (1913), Martha McCulloch-Williams recalled the splendor of "a dining" in her parents' nineteenth-century Tennessee home, with the table anchored by "a stuffed ham at one end, a chicken or partridge pie at the other, side dishes of smothered rabbit, or broiled chicken." Marshall Fishwick, in *The American Heritage Cookbook* (1964), used the same descriptive technique to cover a festive plantation banquet board: "At the head, in the customary pride of place, was a goodly ham, rich in its own perfections. . . . Opposite was a huge roasted saddle of mutton. . . . In between was an enticing diversity of poultry." Novelists Frances Parkinson Keyes (*Dinner at Antoine's*) and Alfred Leland Crabb (*Supper at the Maxwell House*) made the dining table a dramatic focal point where delectable pork and fish creations were served along with the dialogue. Others, writing in the Atlantic and Gulf coast states or in the Southern interior, have glowingly catalogued such exotic and familiar viands as coon and possum, venison and lamb fries, pork chops and country fried steak, deviled crab and baked red snapper.

And so it has gone, through generations of reality and imagination. An almost ceaseless parade of main dishes has returned time and time again to grace the Southern table, and the menu has expanded to embrace scores of specialties of local, regional, or universal renown: country ham, fried chicken, barbecue, catfish, shrimp, oysters, crawfish, gumbo, jambalaya, Brunswick stew, burgoo, boudin, bolichi, spiced round, country captain, and on and on. Throughout their history, Southerners have paid particular attention to the meats and other entrees at either end of the table, beginning with the game and fish they subsisted on centuries ago and continuing to the beef, pork, poultry, and seafood they consume now. There are many breads, vegetables, and sweets that distinguish Southern cooking, of course, but the notable array of main dishes is equally celebrated—and deserving of fame.

The historic emphasis on meat is grounded in persuasive logic. The abundance of wild game and fish spelled the difference between survival and extinc-

affection. If either of the women once regretted the stewing-hot hours spent daily at the stove, the endless dishes washed in hand-drawn pails of well water, they flew no visible signal. . . . Like the proud artists they were, they knew their worth, and they took their reward from . . . an endless succession of gratified guests. I'm aware that I speak as a man and am therefore in danger of sentimentalizing an enforced female drudgery. But children are never fooled, and the child I was still affirms the fact, still thanks their ghosts.

Reynolds Price,
in *Southern Living*,
February 1986

tion for the first generation of Europeans who explored America; indeed, three hundred years after the first voyage of Columbus, interior territories such as Kentucky and Arkansas were still mostly wilderness and the hunt was the main method of procuring meat. Most Indian tribes depended on game and fish, and it was their methods of catching and cooking that the newcomers adopted.

As time went on, game was not only killed for food but to protect corn crops and other cultivated or settled areas. So abundant were some animals and birds—passenger pigeons, for example—that they were considered a nuisance. Billions of passenger pigeons once flocked over the continent, but wholesale slaughter made them totally extinct by 1900. Wild turkeys were so plentiful in Benjamin Franklin's time that he favored the turkey as our national bird. However, though they were once cheaper than chickens in the marketplace, they survive now only in protected areas. Likewise bear, buffalo, beaver, terrapin, canvasback duck, and other coveted forms of wildlife: Though they still exist, they have been so diminished that most people have long since ceased to think of them as a source of food.

Pork was the first domesticated meat in America, and until 1900 it was the meat most eaten by people in all parts of the country. Beef then became the preferred meat of the nation as a whole, but pork kept its dominance in the South, and in some parts of the region it is still eaten more than any other meat. (It is interesting to note in passing that Americans ate more meat per capita in 1830 than they do now.)

There are numerous reasons for the popularity of pork. As the early settlers demonstrated, hogs are the cheapest, quickest, easiest farm animals to raise. A pig can increase its weight 150-fold in its first eight months of life. In colonial times, hogs roamed free, feeding themselves on street scraps and foraging in the woods, and they were so abundant that householders and farmers didn't even bother to count them in stock inventories. (Cows, on the other hand, required considerable tending.) More of the pig was edible, too, and pork meat could be preserved more readily, yielding hams and sausage and even pickled delicacies, not to mention lard and cracklings. The smokehouse, the larder, the pork barrel—these were a useful measure of family fortune. It is easy to see how political perquisites came to be nicknamed pork barrel projects.

And on top of all its utilitarian assets, pork was also good; people liked to eat it. Salt pork, wrote Evan Jones in *American Food*, "could be cooked with skill and undoubtedly love, could be served three times a day in such variety that it did not pall." Everybody liked it at first, and then Southerners most of all—and still. As far back as the early 1800s, the North had a reputation for good beef and bad pork, but in the South it was the other way around. So dominant was pork for so long in the region that consumption remained high even when production plummeted during and after the Civil War. Food habits are very durable; Southerners who could not raise enough pork to feed themselves bought huge quantities of salt pork and lard from packing houses in the Midwest for decades, and traces of that pattern can still be found. Kentucky novelist James Still remembers a graphic bit of evidence. His household's daily ration of fatback came from packing houses in Cincinnati; it was used in a variety of standard ways, but on special occasions it was dipped in egg, rolled in cornmeal or flour, and fried to a crisp and delicious golden brown. "That was a fancier dish," Still says. "We called it Cincinnati chicken."

Another Kentuckian, Bige Hensley of Clay County, remembered hard times in his neighborhood when a "community sinker"—a large piece of fatback or perhaps a ham bone—was tied on a string and passed from house to house, hanging for a while in each family's pot of soup beans or cabbage. Pork was, without a doubt, a vital commodity. It was the meat of survival.

In the South today, pork barbecue still ranks near the top of many people's preference list, but other forms of pork may be taking a back seat to beef, chicken, and fish. Beef production has risen substantially in the region in the past three or four decades; Georgia, Arkansas, and Alabama are in the top five of poultry-producing states nationwide; and Mississippi produces more pond-raised catfish than all the other states combined. Louisiana is the crawfish capital of the universe, and the coastal states from Louisiana to Virginia are the leading harvesters of shrimp, oysters, crabs, and other seafoods. All in all, the South is the point of origin for a substantial proportion of the foods that end up as main dishes on American tables. This is certainly not to say that it raises more beef than the West, or more pork than the Midwest, but when all of the meats, poultry, and fish are combined, the South probably produces more than any other region—and certainly far more than its proportional share.

In the following pages, we have assembled a few recipes for and some historical background on Southern beef, chicken, game, pork, seafood and freshwater fish, and soups and stews (the last grouping being treated as main dishes because most of them are meat or fish based and all are hearty enough to serve as primary foods). Having eaten a multiplicity of entrees in restaurants and reported on some of them in the Eating Out section, we turn now to a consideration of the home style of preparing a select number of essentially Southern main dishes.

places in the stores were the lard barrels and the meat boxes. Literally millions of pounds of meat were shipped south every month. Broad thick sides of Iowa, Illinois, Ohio, and Indiana salt pork were sliced into five- and ten-pound orders on Saturdays for hungry families of cotton farmers. . . . Saturday night at the stores, greasy and exhausted clerks stood between meat boxes and scales slicing off pieces of fat back. . . . At home wives sliced off thick pieces of Iowa meat and fried it for breakfast, boiled hunks of it for dinner, and fried more of it for supper. They thickened the gravy with flour and served it and molasses as sop for corn bread and biscuit.

Thomas D. Clark
*Pills, Petticoats and Plows:
The Southern Country Store,* 1944

BEEF

The rapid rise of restaurants and fast-food chains in contemporary American culture has had a dramatic effect on beef consumption in the South. As recently as fifty years ago, both the general availability and the quality of beef in the region—and in the nation at large—were rather limited; now, everything from hamburger to prime rib to chateaubriand can readily be found in choice and prime grades, and diners in the South eat as much of it as anyone else. They may consume relatively little mutton or lamb, goat or game, or even veal, but they have learned to love mature beef in all its cuts and culinary styles.

Steak has gradually gained a more prominent place in the regional and national diet since it began showing up on menus in the nineteenth century, and it has always been more common as a restaurant entree than as a main dish at home. Curiously, not just high-quality steak but all of the more expensive cuts of beef, such as prime rib and sirloin roast, seem to have received less attention in Southern cookbooks than the more proletarian recipes—hamburger, country fried steak, meat loaf, pot roast, liver, stuffed peppers, and the like. That is a paradox, considering the upper-class bias of cookbooks in general, but beef itself—almost any cut of beef—has tended to hold something of a class advantage over most cuts of pork and other meats.

Nevertheless, there are some excellent and long-appreciated Southern recipes that are cherished both at regular meals and on special occasions. In our small sample we include two dishes made from "the people's cuts" of everyday beef—country fried steak and pot roast—and two renowned subregional specialties of a somewhat fancier character—bolichi and spiced round.

Bolichi

In Tampa, Miami, Key West, and other Florida communities, generations of cooks have drawn upon their Spanish heritage and their immediate surroundings to create a varied and distinctive indigenous cuisine. High on any list of main dishes from this venerable branch of Southern cookery is bolichi, an eye-of-the-round beef roast stuffed with sausage, ham, and spicy seasonings. Served with black beans and rice—another Spanish and Cuban specialty—bolichi makes a memorable meal that is savored by natives and newcomers alike. The stuffing can be tailored to the individual cook's taste; this recipe evolved from just such experimentation.

Begin with a 3-to-4-pound eye-of-the-round, a long, cylindrical cut of beef roast. Working from both ends with a sharp knife, hollow out a pocket or tunnel 1 to 2 inches in diameter clear through the center. Grind the meat thus removed (about 1 cup, when finely ground) and mix with it ½ cup each of finely ground sausage and ham. (Spanish chorizo sausage is recommended, but smoked country sausage or any kind of spicy sausage can be substituted; the ham, too, can be spicy or mild, as you prefer.) Mince 1 clove of garlic, 1 medium-sized sweet onion, and half a green bell pepper and combine thoroughly with the ground meat. Stuff the mixture into the hollowed roast and close both ends with toothpicks. Next, rub the roast with salt, pepper, and paprika. Put 2 or 3 tablespoons of bacon drippings in a large skillet or heavy roaster and brown the meat in the grease over medium heat, turning frequently to ensure even browning. Then add ¾ cup of hot water, 1 bay leaf, and 4 or 5 whole cloves, and lay 1 or 2 strips of raw bacon lengthwise across the roast. Cover and cook, with occasional basting, in a preheated 325° oven for about 3 hours, or until the roast is very tender. Let it cool a bit, so it can be sliced in thin rounds without falling apart. Keep the gravy hot and serve it separately to be spooned or poured over the meat. This much bolichi will make a feast for 8 to 10 people.

Country Fried Steak

It may be called chicken fried steak by some people and smothered steak by others—or, as in this case, country fried steak—but the differences in this standard Southern beef dish are slight. A relatively inexpensive cut such as round steak forms the usual foundation, and gravy gives it spice and style. To oversimplify a little bit, you can think of smothered steak as being simmered in gravy, chicken fried steak as being dipped in an egg batter and dredged in flour, and country fried steak as being dredged in flour without the egg coating; beyond those distinctions, the recipes are very much the same. This is a standard procedure for preparing country fried steak.

Cut up 1 pound or so of good-quality round steak into 3 or 4 serving-sized pieces. Pound well with a wooden mallet to tenderize the meat, sprinkling on a little salt and pepper in the process. Heat 2 or 3 tablespoons of shortening in a heavy skillet over medium heat. Meanwhile dredge each piece of meat in flour, coating it completely, and put in the skillet. When the steak is well cooked and browned on both sides, remove and drain it on a paper towel. Pour off the grease, leaving the dregs in the skillet. Reduce the heat a bit and either sprinkle in 2 or 3 tablespoons of flour, stirring well and adding 1 cup of water; or blend the flour and water in a shaker and pour into the skillet. Either method will make a rich gravy. Cook and stir over low heat for 3 to 5 minutes, seasoning to taste. When the gravy has browned and thickened, pour it over the steak pieces and serve hot.

One hot August I spent a week visiting a Tennessee camp meeting, the Taylor family's kinsfolk revival held near Brownsville, sixty miles north of Memphis. This meeting has been a family tradition for over one hundred years. Here the good eats came next to godliness.

. . . . .

There was the clatter of dishes. Came the good eating smells, all fittin' to stir the hunger of a stone man. Southern ham was frying, buttermilk biscuits were baking; rich simmerings gave off their varying scents as cooks lifted pot lids.

. . . . .

Pan-fried steak for supper, and green beans, whipped potatoes, steak gravy. Of course, hot biscuits to make one more background for good gravy. Sliced tomatoes, big thick slices, the color of Christmas, a spaghetti dish as an extra filler, and Dick's candied apples, corn on the cob, chess pie for dessert.

Clementine Paddleford
How America Cooks, 1960

Pot Roast

We associate pot roast with England, from whence the dish came—but here in the United States, and especially in the South, it has picked up seasonings and spices that give it special character. A pot roast cooked with fresh garden vegetables can make a meal as satisfying and delicious as any standard Southern entree. This recipe has given yeoman service in Kentucky, Tennessee, and Florida for more than thirty years.

Select the best available cut of chuck roast weighing at least 2 pounds. Rub with salt, pepper, minced garlic, and paprika, put in a deep black iron skillet or other heavy roaster, and cook uncovered on the bottom rack of a preheated 325° oven. Roast 2 hours or more (or until well done), basting occasionally with its own juices, and adding a little hot water to the skillet if necessary to assure an adequate amount of gravy. Meanwhile, on top of the stove, combine several cut-up carrots, potatoes, and onions and cook them in a small amount of water just long enough to be tender but firm—not mushy. Drain off the water, place the vegetables around the roast in the pot, spoon gravy over them, and return to the oven long enough for the meat and vegetables and gravy to form a hot, juicy union of separate but interdependent equals. With cornbread and sliced tomatoes and perhaps a green vegetable, this celebrated middle-class offering makes a first-class meal for at least 4 people.

Spiced Round

Since about 1865, meat-packing companies in Nashville that were founded by Swiss and German immigrants have been marketing a traditional Christmas holiday meat called spiced round, and in the Tidewater region of Virginia a similar delicacy is produced. Originated before refrigeration as a way of preserving beef, spiced round was made by rolling strips of hog fat in spices and threading them through thick cuts of round roast. The rounds were then soaked in brine like corned beef and stored in cool cellars. As it aged, the beef took on the sweet and pungent flavors of brine, pork fat, and spices. Every packing house had its own well-guarded formula for seasoning spiced round, and still does; several Nashville meat companies ship it at Christmas now to every state in the union as well as overseas. This is one widely tested method of cooking a commercially cured spiced round.

For weeks before the old-time Christmas [in the early 1800s] the ladies of the house were preparing for the Christmas dinner: penning up the turkeys to fatten, preparing mince-meat for pies, and making all kinds of pickles, and saving eggs and butter for cakes, making spice rounds, and such things. . . . At nine o'clock they would have a big breakfast consisting of boiled spareribs, sausages, birds, hominy, light bread, biscuits, corn muffins, coffee, chocolate, and milk. . . . A big dinner was always prepared for Christmas. A nice stuffed ham, a big fat turkey nicely roasted, spice round, and pickles and jellies of every kind, and every winter vegetable, and always a plum pudding with rich wine sauce, boiled custard, with whipped cream on it, fruit-cake, pound-cake, spongecake, apples, raisins and nuts, and wine, or cordial, and sweet cider, composed a part of most of the dinner. They had such dinners all Christmas week.

Jane H. Thomas
Old Days in Nashville, 1897

Immerse the spiced round in cold water for 1 hour or more and then rinse in fresh water. Wrap the roast tightly in heavy foil (a tightly sewn cloth sack was once used to serve the same purpose of maintaining the roast's firm and compact shape). Place a trivet or rack in a large, deep kettle and dissolve 1 cup of sugar or 1 cup of sorghum molasses in cold water deep enough to cover the roast completely. Add the roast to the kettle, bring to the boiling stage, and then simmer for 15 minutes per pound. Leave it to cool in the water, then refrigerate in fresh foil wrapping. When chilled, slice paper thin and serve with biscuits.

You can also cure your own spiced round; this dry-cure method from an old Nashville cookbook takes about two weeks.

Mix 1 cup of salt, 1 cup of firmly packed dark brown sugar, and ½ teaspoon of powdered saltpeter in a large deep dish or pan. Set a compact beef round roast, about 4 inches thick and weighing 5 or 6 pounds, into the mixture and rub thoroughly on all sides. Cover tightly and refrigerate overnight. Next, combine 1 tablespoon of ground allspice, 1 tablespoon of cinnamon, 1 tablespoon of ginger, 1 tablespoon of nutmeg, 1 tablespoon of freshly ground black pepper, and 1 teaspoon of cayenne pepper and rub this mixture into the roast. Cover again and refrigerate for two weeks, turning the meat daily and basting it with the liquid that will accumulate in the dish. Lay 10 to 12 strips of pork fat or beef suet (each about 5 inches long and ½ inch square) into this marinade early in the curing process and let them absorb its spiciness. At the end of the two-week period, poke holes through the roast with a sharp skewer or larding needle and thread the strips of fat through the holes. The remaining marinade can be poured into the water in which the spiced round is cooked. Then wrap and cook roast as directed above.

CHICKEN

Chickens already had a 3500-year history as domesticated animals when Columbus brought them to America nearly five centuries ago, and they have been perpetually conspicuous in this nation's cookery ever since. Before it became commonplace in the fast-food age, chicken was a festive dish, a universal entree of celebration for people of all classes. Even now, there is something timeless and nostalgic about a heaping platter of crisp fried chicken. It is faintly reminis-

Sunday was a day of difference—
"Welcome, sweet day of rest." It was
a rest day at least for the big black
mule, who was sometimes allowed
to rest while the folks walked to
church. As for Uncle John, it was
the brightest of the seven days.
Sleeping a little later, reminiscent of
"everlasting rest," clean clothes,
shaving, if not indeed already Saturday night, trimming of the long
mustache. Grandchildren of any age
coming in, ready for preaching, and
always dinner in abundance, home-
produced: chicken pie and dumplings, fried chicken and gravy, hot
biscuits, string beans and cornbread, pies and cakes, that the "old
lady" had prepared for on Saturday
and the womenfolks had cooked together on Sunday. Kinsfolk were in
to spend the day, children and
grandchildren, brothers and sisters,
and the picture was in great contrast
to the earlier days after the war,
when wheat bread was rarity of rarities, and coffee was made from
parched corn with "long sweeten-
ing"—meaning molasses—instead
of sugar.

Howard W. Odum
The Way of the South, 1947

cent of Sunday dinner and family picnics and all manner of ritual feasts. In the hard-times election of 1932, the Republican Party's campaign slogan was "a chicken in every pot." Centuries earlier, in 1589, King Henry IV made a similar promise to the peasants of France. The fact that neither the party nor the king could deliver on the promise may have diminished their popularity, but not that of the chicken; now as always, the bird enjoys universal favor.

It would be overstating the case to suggest that the South has a special proprietary claim on this celebrated fowl, but there are several chicken dishes that have been closely identified with the region for generations, and the foremost of these, fried chicken, is generally recognized as the South's gift to the world of food. The late Harland Sanders and his Kentucky Fried Chicken chain may have had a lot to do with that in recent times, but cookbooks in the region have featured Southern fried chicken for more than 150 years, and the enormous popularity of the dish in and out of the South could be said to have assured the success that Sanders and his fast-food companions and competitors have enjoyed.

There are other chicken dishes with interesting histories in the region, including chicken and dumplings, chicken pilau, and country captain. These three and the classic fried chicken of history and legend are the four dishes we offer as examples of Southern cooking at its best.

Chicken and Dumplings

Dumplings are often associated with Pennsylvania Dutch cooking, and it may be that they found their way to the South from that region. Whether or not that is so, there is no doubt that Southerners took a special liking to both flour and cornmeal dumplings a long time ago, and in some parts of the region there is still a deep fondness for them. Cornmeal dumplings seem to go best with vegetables; one favorite way of cooking them is in the pot likker (the juicy residue) from a large kettle of greens. Flour dumplings are more often made with meat dishes, especially chicken and squirrel. Here is a typical recipe:

> Put a 2½- to 3-pound chicken in a large stew pot with 3 quarts of water and add 1 bay leaf, 1 onion, quartered, 1 rib of celery, cut up, and a few shakes of salt and pepper. Bring to a boil and simmer until the chicken is tender and easily penetrated with a fork—about 30 minutes. Let it cool in the broth, then remove and cut up, throwing away the skin, gristle, and bones. Strain the broth (about 2 quarts) and return it to the pot, adding 1 stick of butter to melt in the warm liquid.

To make the dumplings, sift together 2 cups of all-purpose flour, 1 teaspoon of salt, and 1 teaspoon of baking powder. Add 1 cup of broth to the dry mixture, blending and kneading to make a stiff dough. Roll out on a well-floured surface to a thickness of about ⅛ inch and cut in strips about 1 inch wide and 3 inches long. Spread the strips on wax paper to dry for 1 hour or more. Thicken the remaining broth by blending 1 cup of it with 3 tablespoons of flour and returning the mixture to the pot. Bring to a boil and drop the dumpling strips in slowly, one at a time. Cover pot and let dumplings simmer for about 15 minutes; they should retain their shape and look somewhat like pasta. Return the cut-up chicken to the pot for reheating, and then ladle meat, dumplings, and broth into bowls. The recipe should serve 4 to 6 people generously.

Chicken Pilau

What's in a name? Usually, a good story. We found sixteen alternative spellings of pilau: pilaf, pilaff, pillaux, pilav, pilaw, pillo, pilloe, pelos, perleau, perlew, perloo, plaw, pullao, purlo, purloo, purlow. We found it traced to Turkey, India, Iran, Iraq, Spain, Minorca, Greece, Poland, and the Orient. We found it claimed in this country by South Carolina (especially Charleston), Louisiana (especially New Orleans), and Florida (especially St. Augustine). We found related dishes called chicken mull, chicken bog, chicken and yellow rice (*arroz con pollo*), and paella, a Spanish dish that seems both lexically and gastronomically kin to pilau. And finally, we found an abundance of Southern recipes not only for chicken pilau but also for shrimp, squab, okra, and tomato pilaus.

That such an exotic dish should end up in so many Southern kitchens is intriguing. The most plausible explanation for its arrival seems to be that the recipe came by ship to the port of Charleston shortly after rice arrived in that South Carolina harbor in about 1680. Whatever its true history in America, pilau in all its many forms and flavors has been a favorite in much of the South for upward of three centuries. Southern cooks repeatedly changed the pronunciation and spelling of the word, and modified the content of the dish too—it is, says one cookbook, "a dish of amazing variations"—and the result is an infinite variety of rice-based dishes combined with meat, seafood, or vegetables. Chicken pilau is among the most prominent. This version draws inspiration from several South Carolina cookbooks.

Stew a 2½- to 3-pound chicken in 3 quarts of water until tender, about 30 minutes. When cool enough to handle, strip the lean meat and cut into

Pilau, a blend of rice with chicken, or shrimp, or other ingredients varying from locality to locality, has been a standard dish in the South since the introduction of the grain [in the late 1600s]. Its pronunciation also varies all the way from Charleston to New Orleans. Generally spelled pilau or pilaf(f), it is spoken "perloo," or "perlowe." It is thought to be of Oriental origin, perhaps Persian or Turkish. As early as 1612 the word was used in England. But because the dish is commonest in this country in regions influenced by French and Spanish cookery, it was probably brought to America by the French or Spanish.

Kathleen Ann Smallzried
The Everlasting Pleasure, 1956

bite-sized pieces. Reserve the broth. In a skillet, melt 3 tablespoons of butter and sauté in it 1 cup of diced green onions and 1 cup of diced celery. When the vegetables are tender, combine them and the chicken in a large baking dish. Spread 1 cup of raw rice over the mixture, pour in 2 cups of strained chicken broth, and season with salt and pepper. Don't stir. Cover and bake in a preheated 375° oven for 30 minutes. Remove and stir, mixing the chicken through the rice. Adjust the seasonings and return to the oven for about 10 more minutes, or until the rice is tender and has absorbed all the liquid. With salad and bread, this makes a hearty meal for 4 people.

The two Spanish dishes mentioned above, *arroz con pollo* and paella, are contemporary favorites in many of the fine Spanish and Cuban restaurants of Florida. The former includes green peas and pimentos and a touch of saffron in the rice; the latter is a richer and more complex blend of chicken, ham, and seafood with rice and seasonings.

Country Captain

What pilau is to South Carolina and Florida, country captain is to neighboring Georgia. Eliza Leslie, in her mid-nineteenth-century *New Cookery Book*, claimed that British colonials brought the dish to the West from India, and this is probably true, although Georgians like to dispute the claim; they say a sea captain in the spice trade told the recipe to friends in the port of Savannah, and their enthusiasm for it made the dish a fixture in the city and country kitchens of Georgia. In any case, country captain was given a big boost by Mrs. W. L. Bullard of Warm Springs, Georgia, in the 1940s when she served it to President Franklin D. Roosevelt and General George Patton, among others, and their praise rekindled a colonial flame. As it has come down to the present, country captain has retained a dominance of Indian spices in the seasonings, but Southern touches are also apparent. This version closely resembles several others that have found a permanent place in the region's cookbooks.

Cover ½ cup of currants with boiling water (or chicken broth, if available), set aside, and let stand to become plump and soft. Fry 4 strips of bacon crisp in a black skillet, drain on paper towels, crumble, and set aside. Cut up a frying-sized chicken into serving pieces (or use 4 chicken breasts, if you prefer only white meat) and put in the skillet with 2 or 3 tablespoons of hot bacon grease (more if necessary). Cook until tender, turning the pieces frequently to assure uniform browning. Remove and sprinkle with salt and

FRICASSEE OF SMALL CHICKENS

Take off the legs and wings of four chickens, separate the breasts from the backs, cut off the necks and divide the backs across, clean the gizzards nicely, put them with the livers and other parts of the chicken, after being washed clean, into a sauce pan, add pepper, salt, and a little mace, cover them with water, and stew them 'till tender, then take them out, thicken half a pint of the water with two table spoonsful of flour rubbed into four ounces of butter, add half a pint of new milk, boil all together a few minutes, then add a gill [4 ounces] of white wine, stirring it in carefully that it may not curdle, put the chickens in and continue to shake the pan until they are sufficiently hot and serve them up.

Mary Randolph
The Virginia House-Wife, 1824

pepper. Mince 2 ribs of celery, 2 medium-sized onions, 1 medium-sized green bell pepper, and 2 cloves of garlic, and sauté these in the skillet in 2 or 3 tablespoons of bacon grease. Then add 2 cups of fresh or canned tomatoes (peeled, cored, and chopped), 1 tablespoon of curry powder (more or less, as you like it), ½ teaspoon of mace, ¼ teaspoon of white pepper, ½ teaspoon of thyme, ½ teaspoon of salt, and ½ teaspoon of black pepper. Stir well, bring the mixture to a boil, reduce heat to low, cover skillet, and let it simmer for about 10 minutes. Then, in a large baking dish, arrange the chicken pieces and cover with the skillet mixture and broth from the currants. Cover the dish and bake at 325° for 30 minutes. Add the currants, 1 teaspoon of chopped fresh parsley, ½ cup of slivered almonds, and the crumbled bacon, and return to the oven for 10 to 15 more minutes. Serve hot, with freshly boiled rice. Mango chutney is an excellent accompaniment. These proportions will serve 4 people generously.

Fried Chicken

In 1828, Mary Randolph put in the third edition of her *Virginia House-Wife* practically everything that needs to be said about the fine art of frying chickens: Cut them up, dredge them in flour, sprinkle with a little salt, put the pieces in a skillet with hot fat, fry them a golden brown, and then make gravy in the leavings. Millions of words have been written since then in a vain attempt to improve upon her method. There are all sorts of little refinements and special touches and personal tricks of the trade that make good pan-fried or skillet-fried chicken a topic for endless discussion (we gladly leave the deep-frying method to the fast-food chains), but in the end they are simply minor variations on Mrs. Randolph's original theme. Southern fried chicken in all its manifestations derives from that base.

Following are some of the variations, tips, modifications, suggestions, and special twists that keep the conversations going. James Villas, in *American Taste* (1982), soaks his chicken pieces overnight in milk and lemon juice, and cooks them in vegetable shortening fortified with 4 tablespoons of bacon grease. Beatrice Mize, in *Four Great Southern Cooks* (1980), dips the pieces in a beaten egg and water mixture and then dredges them in flour mixed with a little baking powder. Some insist on frying only in lard; others say the pan or skillet must be covered; still others use only young chickens weighing 2 pounds or less—and for each of these firm instructions, there are equally firm counterinstructions: Use only shortening, never cover the skillet, select fat chickens.

We like our chicken very crisp and dry on the outside, tender and moist on

When it comes to fried chicken, let's not beat around the bush for one second. To know about fried chicken you have to have been weaned and reared on it in the South. Period. The French know absolutely nothing about it, and Yankees very little. Craig Claiborne knows plenty. He's from Mississippi. . . . Now, I don't know exactly why we Southerners love and eat at least ten times more fried chicken than anyone else, but . . . we take our fried chicken very seriously. . . . Once you've eaten real chicken fried by an expert chicken fryer in the South . . . there are simply no grounds for contest.

James Villas
American Taste, 1982

the inside; we like our gravy made with water, not milk (see page 191), and we prefer it served on the side, not poured over. With those biases confessed, here is a simple restatement, with minor adjustments, of Mary Randolph's wisdom.

Whether you buy whole chickens and cut them up yourself or choose special cuts (breasts, thighs), select the leanest, smallest bird(s) you can find. (There are no more "barnyard" chickens to be fried the same day they are killed, but just remember that young and lean is better than old and fat, and do the best you can.) Soak the pieces in lightly salted cold water for an hour or more to extract the blood. Drain and pat dry, then rub with salt and pepper. In a deep, heavy black skillet, melt enough shortening to reach a depth of ½ inch or so and add 3 or 4 tablespoons of bacon grease to it. Put a cup or more of flour and ½ teaspoon each of salt and pepper in a paper sack and shake each piece of chicken individually in the sack until it is well coated. Then lay the pieces gently into the medium-hot grease (sizzling but not smoking). Don't crowd the pieces. When golden brown and crispy-looking on one side, turn with tongs and cook to the same state on the other side. Depending on the size of the chicken and the heat of the grease, the total cooking time should be 20 to 30 minutes. An uncovered skillet will make drier, crispier chicken. When done, lay the pieces out on absorbent paper to soak up excess grease. Then put them on a platter in a warm oven to wait for the gravy, rice or mashed potatoes, hot biscuits, and other companion dishes.

Virtually every Southern cookbook since Mrs. Randolph's has featured fried chicken as a primary meat for all seasons. Colonel Sanders and his secret recipe of herbs and spices took the finger-lickin' good news from the back end of a service station in Corbin, Kentucky, to almost every nook and cranny around the globe, but that simply made Southern fried chicken famous; legions of Southern cooks before him had already made it a peerless main dish for everybody's dinner table—and far better as a pan-fried delight than the colonel could ever hope to make it in a vat of hot grease.

GAME

From the founding of Jamestown to the Civil War, a period of more than 250 years, game was a significant and substantial part of the daily diet of Americans. This was especially so for those who, like the great majority of Southerners,

I've heard my neighbor Johnson say
His choice was chicken pie;
And Perkins 'lows he likes to stay
His stomach with a fry;
And Jones, he says, says he, "I think
Good old Kentucky rye
Suits me the best; give me a drink,
Whenever I am dry."
But I have never tasted meat,
Nor cabbage, corn nor beans,
Nor fluid food one half as sweet
As that first mess of greens.

Cotton Noe
The Loom of Life, 1912

spent their lives in rural areas and small towns. It is no accident that the United States has been known historically as a nation of meat eaters; for several generations after its colonial beginnings, its people ate more game than almost anything else. Game and fish were not only abundant and accessible, but also tasty and nourishing. Even after pork, beef, mutton, and chicken had made farm-raised meats a commonplace feature of American cookery, wild animals and birds still retained visibility and importance at the table.

Game meat is not available commercially, as a rule, meat inspection regulations being what they are, but hunting enthusiasts do bring in a surprisingly large quantity of wild food for private consumption or for traditional public rituals. Throughout the South (and elsewhere in the country too), these periodic "critter suppers" feature venison, rabbit, squirrel, coon, possum, duck, goose, quail, and other forms of wildlife. A typical example is the Sure Shot Rabbit Hunters Association's annual supper in Nashville. Twelve hunters started the affair in 1954; now, more than five thousand people pay ten dollars apiece to dine on the bounty of several hundred local hunters.

Game is so central to the history of Southern food that no book of this kind could be complete without some reference to it. As a small sample of wildlife history and cookery, we have chosen four meats that were savored by native Americans before Jamestown and still show up on some Southern tables today: venison, wild turkey, duck, and squirrel. The recipes may be somewhat modernized, but they are not noticeably different from the ones used by pioneer cooks to roast, stew, and fry these meats three centuries ago.

Duck

Wild ducks by the millions flocked across America in the 1600s, and they were still abundant more than two centuries later. Of them all, the canvasback was the most coveted, a gourmet's delight. There are still a few canvasbacks around, but they are no longer plentiful, nor are they the most prized. That superlative belongs now to the mallard, the grain-eating, chicken-sized king of the Mississippi flyway. From hatching areas in Canada, mallards fly south through the heart of the country each fall, searching for warmer waters and feeding grounds. In the marshy flatlands of west Mississippi and eastern Arkansas, the ducks have been stopping to eat for decades, and legions of hunters have gone there to meet them. The rice fields of Arkansas are especially attractive to the birds, and the grain diet makes them singularly appealing to both hunters and camp cooks. The green-headed male mallard is the principal quarry. Cleaned and dressed, it

There was a little hommock or islet containing a few acres of high ground, at some distance from the shore, in the drowned savanna, almost every tree of which was loaded with nests of various tribes of water fowl. . . . We visited this bird isle, and some of our people taking sticks or poles with them, soon beat down and loaded themselves with these squabs, and returned to camp; they were almost a lump of fat, and made us a rich supper; some we roasted, and made others into a pilloe with rice.

William Bartram
Travels Through North and South Carolina, Georgia, East & West Florida, etc., 1773–1778

can be cooked several ways, but the most common method is roasting. Thanks to the generosity of Tennessee duck hunters Flash Gregory, Claude Banister, and Bill Hackett—and to a self-described "duck widow," Elizabeth Hackett—we were able to focus on mallards in a variety of ways, and finally to settle on this recipe from Bee Lane of Bluffton, South Carolina:

> Rinse and pat dry a dressed mallard weighing 2 to 3 pounds. Rub inside and out with salt, pepper, and butter. Stuff the cavity with pieces of potato, onion, celery, carrot, or other vegetables. Cover the bottom of a roaster with ½ cup of vegetable oil and stir into it ½ teaspoon of salt, ½ teaspoon of thyme, and ¼ teaspoon of black pepper. (A clove of garlic, chopped, and ½ cup of dry red wine may also be added if you like.) Blend the mixture and put it in a preheated 350° oven to get hot. Then put in the duck, turning it to coat the skin with oil, and cook, breast up, for about 1½ hours, or until tender, basting with the pan juice several times. (The roaster should be covered for the first hour and then uncovered for the last half-hour or so to let the duck brown.) The pan sauce makes a very rich gravy. One duck is ample for 2 people.

Squirrel

Of all the denizens of the Southern woods, none is more common than the squirrel, and the bushy-tailed rodents have been there in great numbers since long before Columbus. Indians roasted them over the open fire or stewed them in clay pots; later, new Americans from Europe and Africa fried them in skillets. Thomas Jefferson and many another Southerner after him—if not before—considered squirrel an essential ingredient of Brunswick stew; Kentucky burgoo makers (see page 276) have always felt the same way.

According to most contemporary preferences, the favored way to cook squirrel is smothered in a rich gravy made from pan liquids and flour. The same basic recipe is also used with other small game, such as rabbit and quail—and, for that matter, it's an excellent way to cook chicken. We followed these directions to prepare two squirrels given to us by Tennessee hunter Bart Stephenson of the Hermitage Sportsmen's Club. (Stephenson also supplied the venison for our recipe on page 250.)

> Fresh squirrel, dressed and quartered, should be washed in cold water, patted dry, rubbed with salt, and refrigerated (covered) overnight. Next day, drain any liquid and transfer pieces to a large heavy pot or dutch oven in

We went at half past four, and I must say that in spite of all my experience of the strange arrangements of American dinners I confess this style did astonish me, and what any of you who have never seen such would have thought I cannot say. There was a huge party invited to meet us, all gentlemen with the exception of four ladies belonging to the house. . . . There was the same

which 2 or 3 tablespoons of vegetable oil or shortening are heating. Over medium heat, brown the squirrel pieces on all sides. Remove and add 2 tablespoons of flour to the pot, stirring well. Next add 1 cup of water or chicken broth, bring to a boil, and cook until the gravy thickens. Add more liquid if necessary to assure enough gravy. Return squirrel to the pot, cover tightly, and cook in a preheated 275° oven for about 2 hours, basting and turning the meat occasionally. When quite tender, serve smothered in gravy, accompanied by rice or potatoes and hot biscuits. Two squirrels should be enough to serve 4 average eaters.

Turkey (Wild)

Wild turkey is native to this country. The birds grew large in the early days, weighing perhaps thirty pounds on the platter, and whether boiled in water or roasted on a spit, they were universally enjoyed. They were also plentiful throughout the colonial period and well into the nineteenth century. Now, domestic turkeys have almost entirely replaced the wild birds, but several Southern states and others around the country allow some carefully regulated hunting of them. Expert hunter and birdcaller Harold Knight of Cadiz, Kentucky, supplied us with a twenty-two-pound gobbler for the recipe below.

Wild turkeys are lankier and not as plump as the commercial birds, and the meat is somewhat darker, but it is just as tender, and it has a richer flavor and a finer texture. Backyard smokers offer a new and excellent way to cook the bird, but Louise Littlejohn Birdsong of Cadiz prefers an old and traditional way; she boils it in water until tender, strips the meat from the bones, and bakes it with its own gravy and a pan of cornbread dressing. (Turkey of any kind fairly cries out for dressing, either stuffed in the bird or baked separately; for a recipe, see page 282.) Roasting offers a third method, and the most common.

Wash the dressed bird in cold water, pat it dry, and rub it inside and out with butter and salt. Fill the cavity with cut-up carrots, onions, and celery. Truss the turkey tightly and lay it breast up in a large roaster. Put 3 or 4 strips of bacon across the breast and cover with a square of cheesecloth that has been soaked in bacon grease. Cover turkey very loosely with aluminum foil and roast in a preheated 325° oven for about 20 minutes per pound. Baste frequently with pan drippings. Cook to well-done, removing foil, cheesecloth, and bacon for the last hour to let the bird brown. Make gravy with the pan drippings and serve as a side dish with the turkey and dressing. A 12-pound turkey should easily feed 10 to 12 people.

fuss before dinner of calling the mistress of the house out of the room and so on, and finally she and another elderly, female relation disappeared altogether and we found them standing ready placed at the upper end of the table, and then with one consent the gentlemen fell to carving the dishes nearest to them with a degree of dispatch and eagerness that I never saw equalled anywhere out of a steamboat. The top dish was a ham which Mrs. Taylor herself showed her power of carving upon by beginning to cut it in pieces from the knuckle upwards. The rest of the entertainment consisted of turkeys, roast and broiled, chickens, roast ducks, corned beef, and fish, together with various dishes of sweet potatoes, Irish potatoes, cabbage, rice, and beetroot, to demolish which we were furnished with two pronged forks, and if you were troublesome enough to call for a second knife you were furnished with one merely half wiped.

Mrs. Basil Hall of Canada, describing dinner with an "aristocratic family" in Columbia, South Carolina, in 1827

Venison

The whitetail deer is an ancient inhabitant of North America, predating the arrival of white colonists by thousands of years. There was a time about a century ago when the graceful animal seemed on the way to becoming an endangered species, but conservation and the deer's own prolific nature have increased the population significantly. In the Southern states, deer hunters have always been active, and venison roasts can be found in many a country freezer. This recipe for a marinated roast combines elements from the instructions of cooks in Georgia, Tennessee, and Arkansas. We cooked a 3- to 4-pound shoulder roast and found it dark, rich, flavorful, and tender.

In a large pan or bowl, chop and combine 1 rib of celery, 1 large onion, 1 large carrot, and 2 cloves of garlic. Add 2 crushed bay leaves, 1 teaspoon of peppercorns, 1 tablespoon of Worcestershire sauce, 1 teaspoon of salt, ½ teaspoon of thyme, ½ teaspoon of basil, the juice of 1 lemon, ½ cup of vegetable oil, and 1 quart of dry red wine. Blend well, add roast to the marinade, cover tightly, and refrigerate overnight (turning meat once or twice). Remove roast and bring to room temperature, saving the marinade. Heat ¼ cup of vegetable oil in a frying pan and brown roast on all sides. Transfer to a roaster, sprinkle with salt and pepper, pour 1 cup of marinade around the base, put in 1 onion, freshly sliced, cover tightly, and roast in a preheated 300° oven for 2 to 3 hours, or until tender, basting occasionally. Served with vegetables and hot bread, a venison roast of this size is ample for 4 to 6 people.

PORK

We have returned time and again in these pages to the noble pig, sustainer of the South through four centuries of grief and glory. We have looked at hogs in history, followed them from the fields and forests to the smokehouse and the dinner table, and sampled the wonders of barbecued shoulders, ribs, and whole hogs in almost every Southern state. Now it is time to conclude this intermittent treatise with a few observations about cooking pork at home. Bacon and sausage, country ham, and barbecue are the main topics, and there is also a recipe for jambalaya, a ham-based rice dish from Louisiana that bears a resemblance to the pilaus of South Carolina and elsewhere.

Whether PORK IS HEALTH, as a fence-post sign in Chilton County, Alabama, proclaims, or unclean and diabolical, as the Biblical wise man Leviticus and

If you live in the South or have visited there lately, you know that the old White Trash tradition of cooking is still very much alive, especially in the country. This tradition of cooking is different from "Soul Food." White Trash food is not as highly seasoned, except in the coastal areas of South Carolina, Georgia, and North Florida, and along the Gulf coasts of Alabama, Mississippi, Louisiana, and Texas. It's also not as greasy and you don't cook it as long. Of course, there's no denying that Soul Food is a kissin' cousin. All the ingredients are just about the same. But White Trash food . . . has a great deal more variety.

    . . . . .

I know you'll lay down and scream when you taste Loretta's Chicken Delight. And Tutti's Fruited Porkettes are fit for the table of a queen. Just how can you miss with a dessert that calls for twenty-three Ritz crackers? And then, there are recipes for coon, possum, and alligator. . . .

many since him have asserted, or "angelic meat," as the nineteenth-century French poet Charles Monselet rhapsodized, it is indisputably the leading meat of the earth. Even though two of the world's largest religious faiths, Judaism and Islam, forbid their adherents to eat it, pork is still more widely consumed and loved than any other meat, and has been since time immemorial. In *Food*, Waverley Root's 1980 authoritative dictionary of world edibles, the pig is identified as man's second oldest domesticated animal, after the dog. "The origin of the common pig is mysterious," Root declares, adding that it "seems to have been an invention of man," since humans "apparently domesticated the presumed ancestor of the pig, the wild boar, and evolved a recognizably different family of animals."

As it has come down to Southern barnyards and kitchens through the centuries, the hog is a celebrated and beloved symbol of gastronomic excellence. Southerners make no extravagant claims of discovery or ownership with respect to pork, nor do they claim to have created any of the many ways of cooking it. But even as they acknowledge that others preceded them in developing the fine arts of butchering, curing, seasoning, and cooking hog meat, the culinary artists of the South bow to no one in their mastery of these skills. Whoever else has done it or still does it, no one can outperform a gifted Southerner when it comes to such activities as curing hams and barbecuing shoulders.

These jewels of the porcine art are less plentiful than they once were—and even when they can be found, they often seem less authentically delicious than before. All the more reason, then, to include here a few recipes and stories reminiscent of the pork of the past. It is still possible, with some effort, to recapture a bit of that old-time flavor, and thereby contribute to an ongoing appreciation and enjoyment of the goodly pig.

You'll be the talk of your social club or sewing circle when you prepare a Resurrection Cake that's guaranteed to resurrect when you pour on the whiskey sauce. . . . It's not hard to catch on to our ways. Even an awful cook will soon sop them up and become deathly accurate with the sweet potato pones and Miss Bill's Bucket Dumplins.

Ernest Matthew Mickler
White Trash Cooking, 1986

Bacon and Sausage

The ready availability of bacon and sausage in supermarkets has all but blotted out the memory of times not so long ago when most bacon was salt-cured and hickory-smoked on the farm, and sausage was made at hog-killing time and either eaten fresh or sacked, smoked, and aged in those same country smokehouses. The differences between old and new methods are substantial. Today's bacon and sausage are not cured and aged but packaged fresh at the slaughterhouse—hermetically sealed in plastic and fortified with sodium nitrate and nitrite for taste and color enhancement and protection from bacteria.

There are some commercial meat-packing firms, especially in the South, that market slab bacon and sack sausage that has been cured and smoked.

These products are often pleasantly suggestive of the old-fashioned meats, even though the methods used to prepare them are usually accelerated. The slow, natural way of curing, smoking, and aging pork has been almost entirely replaced in the commercial arena by methods predicated on speed and high-volume output. The old ways are too time-consuming; they are fading out, and a lot of great taste in pork is disappearing with them.

But all is not lost. Bacon grease—or drippings, as some prefer to say—remains a primary seasoning ingredient in Southern cooking, and slices of the jowl and the side meat of the hog still have an important role to fulfill in many a pot of greens, beans, or cabbage. Side meat has as many names as uses. In one form or another, it may be referred to as fatback, salt pork, sowbelly, middlings, white meat, streak-of-lean, bacon, white bacon, seasoning bacon, seasoning meat, or simply meat. In those places where salt-cured, hickory-smoked, properly aged slab bacon and other kinds of side meat can't be obtained, there is still store-bought bacon—and the grease saved for seasoning is as vital as butter or sugar or cream in traditional Southern cookery.

Sausage offers more options to the home cook. It can be bought in links or in packages for slicing into patties, and there are various kinds of cured sausages on the market too. And, for those who want to reconstruct a bit of the past, fresh sausage can also be made at home. Few cookbooks give recipes for it (*Out of Kentucky Kitchens* and *The Foxfire Book of Appalachian Cookery* are notable exceptions), but the method is surprisingly quick and easy. A 1938 circular issued by the University of Kentucky College of Agriculture explained a way of making sausage at hog-killing time, and the recipe has been widely used in the state ever since. It provides the basis for this contemporary sausage-making method.

Get from the butcher 2¼ pounds of lean fresh pork (tenderloin is best) and ¾ pound of pork fat (backbone fat is best). Either have the butcher grind the lean and fat together or grind at home, first with a coarse, then with a fine blade in a meat chopper. Add to the mixture 1 tablespoon of salt, 2 teaspoons of black pepper, 1½ teaspoons of powdered sage, and ½ teaspoon of cayenne pepper. Blend well by kneading. Cook a small patty for taste-testing and adjust seasonings if necessary. Wrap in wax paper and keep refrigerated. When cooking, make into round, flat patties like small hamburgers and cook over low heat, turning once or twice, until meat is well done. This recipe makes 3 pounds of sausage.

A HOG KILLING

Look, over there, beneath the carshed, to the tables, to the women, busy with knives and grinders and spoons and forks; the greasy tables littered with salts and peppers and spices, hunks of meats, bloody and in pans, meats to be made into sausages, and pans of cooked liver to be ground into pudding . . . can you smell the odor of cooking meats and spices, so thick, so heady? Can you hear the women talking? . . . Their jabber is constant and unchecked, rising and falling, recollection and gossip, observation and complaint, in and out, out and in, round and round, the rhythm, the chant, a chaotic symphony . . .

"Getting a early start?" asks a woman who is mixing the ground liver with meal and sage and pepper and salt in a tub, her arms into the stuff up to her elbows.

"Well, girl," says Ruth, "you know I don't like no long ride in nobody's

Barbecue

Parts of North and South Carolina, Kentucky and Tennessee, Georgia, Alabama, and Arkansas make up the heart of the Southern barbecue belt (Texas, keep in mind, is beyond the purview of this book), and it is in these states that the fine art of pit cooking is pursued with all the zealous fervor of a religious calling. Elsewhere in these pages we have reported on some of the restaurants and roadside stands where good barbecue is sold commercially (Eating Out, page 147), and we have also offered some recipes for barbecue sauce (pages 190–1). Here is a look at some methods of home-style barbecue cooking, for a handful of eaters or a multitude.

If barbecue is a big business in the South, it is an equally big pleasure. Completely apart from the people who cook it for a living, there are thousands of others who cook it for charity, for entertainment, and for personal satisfaction. Barbecue means a method of cooking, a cooked meat, a public event. It is at once serious and high-spirited, complex and simple. For some, it has a spiritual dimension, making the pit-bound pig the modern equivalent of the Biblical fatted calf. In all of the barbecue states and elsewhere as well, a public or private "pig pickin" or whole-hog roast is a signal occasion, and each presiding conductor brings to the task a personal flair or a quiet touch of genius. Cooking tips from some of these home-fire tenders provide valuable lessons in the venerable art of barbecue making.

Marshall Maben of Ripley, Tennessee, nearing eighty years of age, is a shoulder man—pork shoulder, that is, in the ten- to fourteen-pound range. He cooks it patiently over hickory and other hardwood coals in a makeshift oil-drum pit behind his house. Maben is a legendary pit cooker in west Tennessee, an old-school artist who shifted from a real pit in the ground to an oil drum only when his advanced age made stooping difficult. His method is disarmingly simple: a good cut of meat, a very slow fire, a minimum of turning, and no basting at all until the cooking is almost done.

"I put the shoulder on in the early morning and take it off that evening," he explained. "It's got to cook real slow. Then I mop it with my own secret dip just before I take it off the pit." His dip is a catsup- and vinegar-based hot sauce that is "thick enough that it'll hold on to the sandwich."

Maben has done plenty of commercial cooking in his time, but his backyard pit and grill experience makes him an ideal adviser to neophytes. That is not a new role for him; he has taught lots of people how to barbecue.

The South's great barbecue tradition is in large measure a cultural gift from black men like Marshall Maben. In the early decades of the nineteenth century, when accounts of huge barbecue feasts in the region first appeared in print, it was almost always black men who were described as tenders of the fires and

car. So I'm just as happy to get this trip over and done with as I pleases to be."

"Know what you mean, Sister Ruth," says a woman grinding meat for a sausage link. This meat is raw and red and at the end of the grinder another woman fits on several casings, smaller guts that slid over the spout at the end of the grinder like a prophylactic. The woman begins to stuff meat and grind; like a worm emerging from a hole, the ground meat fills the empty casing, creating sausage after new, pink sausage.

Randall Kenan
A Visitation of Spirits
(unpublished manuscript)

cookers of the meat and makers of the sauce. Over the years, black cooks mastered the ancient art, adapted it to their time and place in Southern history, and then passed the wisdom on to others, black and white. Today, the region's proud reputation for pit cooking is shared by men and women of both races.

In the Flint Hill community near Manchester, Georgia, Andy Lipscomb and his neighbors turned a mid-1970s backyard cookout into a ten-year tradition of pig roasting. Each September, they devoted a weekend to the affair, cooking a hundred-pound pig carcass over a slow hardwood fire from midnight one evening to mid-afternoon the next day. "It's got to cook slow," Lipscomb said. "If you can hear it sizzling on the pit, your fire's too hot." When their crowd of eaters grew to four hundred, the Georgia pit crew was forced to discontinue the party. "We just couldn't meet the demand for barbecue," Lipscomb explained.

Fall is also the time for an annual barbecue on Big East Fork in Williamson County, Tennessee. On a picturesque farm there, Luther King and his sons from Backbone Ridge cook a whole hog over a fire so slowly that the 160-pound dressed animal needs eighteen hours to reach the desired state of doneness. "If you want to do it right, you've got to cook it slow," said King. "You get a sweeter-tasting meat that way."

Fred Powledge, an expatriate North Carolinian living in New York, can approximate eastern Carolina shredded pork shoulder in his oven. With a Boston butt weighing about five pounds, he utilizes slow cooking (40 minutes per pound at 300°) and heavy doses of his vinegar sauce (see page 191) to achieve a falling-apart tenderness that makes mincing in the Carolina style an easy task.

Another inheritor of the pork barbecue tradition is Scott Wakefield, who lives near Crossville, Tennessee. His mentor was a black cook in the Athens, Georgia, area. "I live outside the Southern barbecue belt," Wakefield said, "but I was lucky enough to learn about ribs and sauce from a master of the art."

Wakefield is now a rib specialist in his own right. He knows pork, having raised hogs, and he has settled on ribs as the cut of meat he most prefers to cook. (His sauce is on page 190) These are some of his tips and pointers on rib cooking:

❖ Use only whole racks or slabs of ribs weighing 3 pounds or under (so-called 3-and-down ribs). These come from young pigs weighing about 180 pounds; they're small boned and tender and have the right ratio of lean meat to fat. A whole slab will be 18 to 24 inches long, tapering to a point on one end. Don't buy slabs that have been sawed or cut down; cut pieces will lose their juices and dry out as they cook.

❖ Before cooking, sprinkle salt, pepper, and hot-pepper sauce on the meat and rub in well.

A lot of things have changed in barbecue lately. While the dish itself seems more popular than ever, Health Department regulations and the scarcity of hardwood have altered many of the traditional approaches to cooking and marketing. Most troublesome is the difficulty in finding men willing to perform the hot, strenuous and lonely work of running the pits all night. Pitmen are usually older blacks, who often tend farms in addition to their restaurant jobs. More and more restaurateurs are turning to gas or electric heat as a way out of the labor predicament. Besides being less trouble, it is a faster and cheaper method.

Others, thank the Lord, have their principles.

"People say you can't tell the difference," one manager of 15 years sniffs indignantly. "But I tell you, it's like night and day. . . . If we have to give up pit cooking, we'll close. That's all there is to it."

*Kathleen Zobel,
in Southern Exposure
(Summer 1977)*

+ Cook the ribs as slowly as possible, and as far above the fire as possible; the slower they cook, the tenderer they will be. If circumstances permit, it is ideal to have the grill 30 inches above the fire, and to cook the meat for 5 or 6 hours.

+ A 3-pound rack of ribs will feed 2 average eaters or 1 with big appetites. You can cook as many as 6 or 8 racks at a time, even on a standard-sized kettle grill, simply by stacking them in a heap. Stacking actually helps; it slows the cooking, holds in the juices, and serves as a heat regulator. Rotate the slabs occasionally, using tongs to pick them up.

+ The fire can best be regulated by having an auxiliary source of burned-down coals that can be added to the cooker as needed. It shouldn't be necessary to baste the meat, but you may need to control the fire with a sprinkler bottle filled with water and vinegar (a good ratio is 7 parts of water to 1 of vinegar, with black pepper added optionally to help season the meat).

Wakefield applies his sauce to the cooking ribs only once—in the last half-hour or so before they come off the grill. A second basting follows immediately after their removal, and then they are served.

The similarity between Wakefield's methods and those of Maben and the others mentioned here is noteworthy. For all the cooks, the key factor is a slow fire that allows the meat to cook gradually for an extended time. Whether hardwoods or charcoals are used, the same principle applies. Good barbecue is the ultimate slow food; there is no way to speed up the process and retain top quality.

The sauces of these cooks are significantly different from each other, but most of the cooks agree that the application should come toward the end of the barbecuing process. In fact, the considered opinion of many experts is that properly cooked barbecue shoulders or ribs fresh off the pit often cannot be improved upon with the application of any sauce. The meat will be at its peak the moment it is removed from the pit, and no amount of careful handling, warming, or even sauce application is apt to enhance its pinnacle flavor—or restore it once it has passed. As Marshall Maben put it, "When it's right, it's right—and there ain't no way to make it better."

Here at home, I have put a twelve-pound pork shoulder in an outdoor smoker and left it for twelve hours without removing the top. The result was not world-class barbecue, but it was close enough to make me think I might be able to perfect the system. Here is another backyard method that draws from all the experts above.

Bring a 5-pound Boston butt to room temperature and rub it with salt, black pepper, and a half-and-half mixture of vinegar and hot-pepper sauce. Build a charcoal fire in a kettle grill and let it burn down to low heat. Have a separate bed of warm coals nearby to replenish the main fire. Add some water-soaked hickory chips to the main fire to create heavy smoke. Put the shoulder meat on to cook, turning every 30 minutes to assure uniform cooking. Damp the fire and meat with a water-vinegar solution (7 to 1) if it gets too hot. Strive for a slow, steady fire. After about 3 hours, the meat should be getting tender. Cook it between 3 and 4 hours, basting once in the last hour with your choice of sauce. Have more warm sauce available for individual application at the table. This much meat should make 6 to 8 big sandwiches.

Country Ham

There is no finer ham than the Smithfield ham. Those who have tested it can testify to its superior qualities. It is as different from the ordinary ham perpetrated by pork packers as beer is different from champagne. As a matter of fact the average market ham is not fit for a man to eat. The Smithfield ham commands a higher price than any other ham, but as good hams are produced in some parts of Georgia, Alabama and Tennessee. With the average modern farmer, however, curing meat seems to be a lost art.

The Knoxville Cook Book, 1907

Given the documentary evidence that pigs were raised for food in China, Egypt, Greece, and Rome more than two thousand years ago, it is not surprising to find that many countries, including Italy, Poland, and Denmark, have long and proud ham traditions. So does the United States, and especially the southeastern region. Around Smithfield, Virginia, not far from Jamestown, they claim that English hogs fattened on African peanuts and cured by Indian methods of salting and smoking were the source, as early as 1650, of the first Smithfield hams, now a product known around the world.

Although pork has never been solely a Southern commodity in this country, the passion of Southerners for the meat has always had a special quality. As early as 1737, William Byrd complained in his *Natural History of Virginia* that the people of that colony ate so much pork that they were becoming "extremely hoggish in their temper . . . and prone to grunt rather than to speak."

By the end of the eighteenth century, cured ham was widely praised as a coveted Southern delicacy. The earliest manuscript collections of recipes from the Southern colonies contained instructions for salting, smoking, and aging hams, as well as for cooking them. Practically every farm family from the Tidewater to the Ozarks came to include the tribal ritual of hog killing in its seasonal activities, and most of the meat they ate consisted of hams, bacon, side meat, and sausage from their smokehouses.

Smithfield is the undisputed birthplace of Southern-style country ham. Ever since Mallory Todd made a name for himself as an exporter of Smithfield hams in the late 1700s, that little Tidewater village of fewer than five thousand people has been shipping hams to the world (England's Queen Victoria received them regularly during the last half of the nineteenth century). In the post–Civil War era, P. D. Gwaltney, Jr., first with his father and then with his sons, turned from tobacco and peanut farming to meat packing, and the Gwaltney name is still prominent in the industry. By 1907, Smithfield ham producers were shipping forty thousand hams a year. (Now, the annual output is an astronomical 10 million, which figures out to around 40,000 a *day*.)

The hams that made Smithfield famous—both those from the commercial packers and those from the farms in the area—were said to be distinguished by two features: what the hogs ate, and how the meat was cured. *The Smithfield Cookbook* (1978), a locally produced collection of recipes and history, explains that "after a spring and summer of foraging in the woods for acorns and other wild nuts, hogs on the farms around Smithfield are turned into the fields to root for the peanuts that have been left behind by the harvesters." Such a diet is said to make the meat redder, the fat yellow, and the taste slightly oily—all considered positive qualities of Smithfield distinction. After slaughtering, the hams are properly salted, coated with black pepper, smoked with hardwoods, and hung up to age through a full summer or longer. That, at least, was the ham-producing method of Smithfield-area farmers in times past.

The end result became the standard by which country hams were measured. As farmers and others elsewhere in the South began to produce and market hams of their own, the Virginia legislature decided in 1926 to guard the traditions (and, critics say, to protect the Gwaltneys) by writing into law a formal definition of "genuine Smithfield hams." They were, said the statute, hams "cut from the carcasses of peanut-fed hogs, raised in the peanut-belt of the State of Virginia, or the State of North Carolina, and which are cured, treated, smoked, and processed in the town of Smithfield, in the State of Virginia."

The law was later amended to exclude the references to what the hogs ate and where they were raised; it now defines Smithfields as "hams processed, treated, smoked, aged, cured by the long-cure, dry-salt method of cure and aged for a minimum period of six months," with all these steps to be followed inside the town limits of Smithfield and nowhere else. The penalty for violation of the statute is set at "not less than $25 nor more than $300."

But if the Smithfield name is thus protected, there is no such restriction on the generic term "country ham," which is generally taken to mean any ham that has been cured or preserved by the dry-salt method and aged for at least six months. It is still possible to find such hams in rural sections of Virginia and a half-dozen other Southern states, but they are far less common than they used to be, and their quality is uneven and unpredictable. The best of these hams usually weigh between twelve and twenty-four pounds and have a distinctive smoky aroma and a rich reddish brown color. They have been cured in a bed of dry salt for about five weeks, usually smoked with green hickory or other

The smokehouse at Berry Hill Farm [near Smithfield, Virginia] is one of the area's oldest and most interesting. Built more than two hundred years ago and continuously used as a smokehouse, it is constructed almost entirely of brick. Its wood shingled roof vents the smoke and its terraced brick floor is used for salting meats, as a base for the fires and to catch drippings. . . . Nancy Bell Dashiell, who grew up at Berry Hill, recalls, "My mother was responsible for the smokehouse, the only building at Berry Hill that was always locked, and the big wrought iron key was never out of her possession. The last thing she did before going to bed at night was to put the key on the mantle in her room. If the key was missing, nobody went to sleep until it was located and safely in place."

The Smithfield Cookbook
Smithfield, Virginia, 1978

smoldering hardwoods for anywhere from two weeks to two months, and then hung up to age through the spring and summer. An "old ham" customarily means one that has aged a year or more. In the common understanding of people who know this meat, any ham that has been taken from the slaughterhouse to the table in fewer than eight or nine months is thought of as deficient. In most cases, country hams are taken green (that is, fresh from slaughtering) in December or January and are not considered ready to eat until mid-September at the earliest.

Since the U.S. Congress passed the Wholesome Meat Act in 1967, the U.S. Department of Agriculture has been involved in the regulation of meat processing within the states. In the same period, as the commercial ham industry has grown, agricultural research in several Southern universities has developed various ways of shortening the production time for salt-cured hams. Out of all this have come many changes and much confusion. Hams are called country-style or country-cured or sugar-cured, but these terms have no real meaning. (Sugar-cured is actually a misnomer, since sugar is not a curing agent.) Most commercial firms now use some or many of the modern shortcut methods: immersion in brine or injections of brine instead of dry-salt curing; liquid smoke or no smoke at all; and a combination of refrigeration and heating rather than natural temperatures for aging. Instead of hams produced in nine months, many companies are now turning out "90-day wonders," and further "refinements" may soon reduce the process to about forty days.

The U.S.D.A. regulations assure sanitary slaughterhouse procedures, proper salting of hams, minimum weight loss, and sufficient heating to eliminate any disease-causing bacteria or insects, but they assure nothing with respect to the taste, texture, and appearance of the hams. Thus, ironically, big-volume commercial producers in total compliance with the regulations may in fact be marketing tough, salty, and unappealing "country hams," while farmers who follow traditional methods and produce superlative hams that have not been approved by an inspector could technically be considered "bootleggers" of impure and inferior products.

To put the best possible face on these confusing and discouraging developments, it can be said that the combination of government regulation, university research, and modern corporate marketing has turned a small backyard farming trade into a multi-million-dollar industry in several Southern states. Without any question, more meat labeled country ham is now sold in all parts of the country than ever before, and it might even be argued that it is better protected by quality-control and health standards than the traditional product.

But it is not genuine country ham—not what the Virginia lawmakers defined for Smithfield, and not what more than three hundred years of history have defined for generations of Southern farmers. At best, it is a passable facsim-

Few aspects of southern life have undergone such fundamental changes as dietary habits have. . . . An appreciable number of homes either own or have ready access to quick frozen-food facilities. Refrigeration has all but made salt meat a thing of the past. No longer does a southern farmer have to get the almanac, a drove of hogs, and the weatherman into agreement in order to butcher. The unpredictable changes of southern weather have no influence on the preparation of most meat today. No sudden warm spells destroy thousands of tons of it. In the face of all this progress a really good country ham becomes a true museum piece.

Thomas D. Clark
The Emerging South, 1961

ile; at worst, it is virtually inedible. But the new generation of consumers, never having tasted the real delicacy that graced Southern tables for so many years, now have nothing with which to compare the modern product. They will either acquire a taste for the new ham with the old label or leave it out of their choice of foods entirely. Meanwhile, the remnant of Southerners and others who have known the unique flavor and the sentient pleasures of bona fide country ham will continue to seek it out whenever and wherever they can, and to glory in it until it is gone for good.

In order to appreciate fully the contrast between "old" and "new" ham, "country" and "city" ham, farm-cured and commercially cured ham, it may be helpful to look at a couple of places where tradition and modernism exist side by side: first, Cadiz, Kentucky, six hundred miles due west from Smithfield, and then back to the starting point, to Smithfield itself.

There are numerous communities in Kentucky—or in Tennessee, North Carolina, Georgia, Alabama, or Arkansas—that could be cited as worthy examples of "non-Virginia" country ham production; Cadiz is one of these. Its ham traditions are probably as old as the town itself, which was founded in about 1820—and both the founders and the traditions came into the area directly from Virginia. There are, in fact, some close similarities between Cadiz and Smithfield. Both are small towns in agricultural regions near the same latitude, both have produced substantial amounts of tobacco and corn, neither has been "thrust into the forefront of history," as a Smithfield writer once put it— and both are widely noted for their hams.

Trigg County hams, as the ones from around Cadiz are called, differ from Smithfields in some important particulars, but they are certainly close relatives. In the days when most farmers killed their own hogs, Trigg County farmers customarily fattened theirs on corn, not peanuts; now, most all pork comes from packinghouse hogs that are fed pretty much the same scientifically balanced diet the country over. Around Cadiz, the green hams are usually put down in pure salt or in a mixture of three parts salt and one part sugar, with a tiny amount of saltpeter (potassium nitrate) added, the formula having been devised at the University of Kentucky College of Agriculture almost fifty years ago.

Time in the salt depends on the size of the ham and the temperature, and the guidelines are about the same as Smithfield's (about five weeks for a twenty-pound ham when the weather stays at or just above freezing). The Trigg farmers tend to smoke their hams a good bit longer—a matter of weeks rather than days—but they prefer less dense smoke. The heavy coat of black pepper applied to a Smithfield ham has seldom been used in Cadiz. And finally, the aging time is roughly the same—from early spring to early fall at a minimum. Farmers in both places speak of the "summer sweats"—the hot July and August weather— as an essential rite of passage for all good hams.

The United States of America might properly be called the great Hog-eating Confederacy, or the Republic of Porkdom. . . . [In the South] it is fat bacon and pork, fat bacon and pork only, and that continually morning, noon, and night, for all classes, sexes, ages, and conditions; and, except the boiled bacon and collards at dinner, the meat is generally fried, and thus supersaturated with grease in the form of hogs' lard. But the frying is not confined to the meat alone: for we have fried vegetables of all kinds, fried fritters and pancakes . . . fried bread not infrequently, and indeed fried everything that is fryable, or that will stick together long enough to undergo the delightful process. . . . Hogs' lard is the very oil that moves the machinery of life, and they would as soon think of dispensing with tea, coffee, or tobacco . . . as with the essence of hog.

John S. Wilson, M.D.
Godey's Lady's Book, 1860

There are about seventy-five farmers in Trigg County who produce country hams each year, some for their own use and some for sale. A few still kill their own hogs, but most buy green hams already butchered. At the Trigg County Ham Festival each October, many of these small producers enter a judging competition to determine the year's grand champion ham. As Billy and Bayless Sumner, Douglas Freeman, Pink Guier, Robert Flood, Boyce Braboy, and Plomer Wilson, all winners of the coveted prize, can freely attest, the recognition is very satisfying. Few of the Trigg farmers produce as many as a hundred hams a year. It is strictly a sideline with them, a generations-old tradition they are trying to keep alive; they pride themselves on making good hams the way their parents and grandparents made them, and they are not interested in shortcutting the process.

One of the sponsors of the ham-judging contest is Broadbent's B&B Food Products, a Trigg County "country gourmet" food store and mail-order business. Smith Broadbent III and his twin brother, Robert, drawing on three generations of ham-curing experience and a record string of state-champion hams (including one that brought over $35,000 at a charity auction), have developed a successful commercial operation that ships hams, bacon, sausage, and other products into all fifty states and several foreign countries.

Broadbent hams are not entered in the judging. Technically speaking, they are ineligible; the contest is strictly for traditionalists whose hams are dry-cured on the farm, hardwood-smoked and aged in farm smokehouses, and taken through the entire process of nine months or more in natural temperature and weather conditions. The Broadbents do much of that—more than most commercial producers—but theirs is a year-round commercial operation that must rely on regulated cooling and heating.

Positioned as they are between the traditionalists and the modern businesses that produce and market "90-day wonders," the Broadbent brothers are pulled in both directions. They know and appreciate the genuine article, the hand-crafted year-old ham, and they take pride in helping to keep the tradition alive through sponsorship of the Trigg County ham contest. But at the same time, their commercial competitors continue to shorten the quick-cure process, to make more hams in less time, and to sell them at ever-cheaper prices that producers who don't take shortcuts can't match.

"It's getting harder and harder to hold the line," said Smith Broadbent III. "There's no way the traditional method could work in a high-volume operation. We just want to stay as close to the old way as we can and still be competitive. We're doing okay now, but the movement is definitely away from tradition."

Back in Virginia, where the tradition began, pride of craft still invigorates the natives. One of them, Marshall Fishwick, writing in *The American Heritage Cookbook* in 1964, delivered the Virginia point of view with unabashed chau-

Trigg County, in western Kentucky, is a small county of moderate wealth. And yet it is the most ham-conscious county in two states. About 7,000 hams are sold each year in Cadiz, the county seat. . . . The dealers in Cadiz do not cure the hams they sell. They depend on the Trigg County farmers for those, but the

vinism: "Let those who prefer Tennessee country ham backed with pickled peaches, Texas ham with corn-meal coating, Georgia country ham, glazed sugar-coated ham with champagne sauce, fried Kentucky ham with red gravy, Alabama ham loaf with mustard sauce, or Florida ham with cayenne pepper argue their cases. All one has to do to be completely won over to Virginia ham is to *eat* it."

Well, not exactly. The truth of the matter is that the traditional country hams of Virginia, North Carolina, Kentucky, Tennessee, and parts of three or four other states are quite similar in taste. The farmers around Smithfield who still cure and smoke and age hams follow processes that differ only in minor details from those followed in Trigg County and most other places.

"Nobody fattens hogs on peanuts around here anymore," said Tommy Darden, a Smithfield-area producer of traditional country hams. "I never cared for that taste anyway—too soft, too oily. And that business about hogs being turned into the peanut fields to fatten, that was always more of a fairytale than the truth, even in the old days. Very few farmers raise and slaughter their own hogs anymore. Just about all the hog meat comes from the packinghouse, and the hogs come from all over—most of them, I suppose, from the Midwest."

What Darden does with the green hams to make them into genuine country hams is pretty much what Doug Freeman and Pink Guier and the Trigg County farmers do: He salts them according to a standard formula, smokes them over smoldering hardwoods, and hangs them to sweat through the summer. They will lose 25 to 30 percent of their weight in that time (a twenty-two-pound ham will end up weighing about fifteen pounds), and that is more than the minimum required under the U.S.D.A. regulations. They will also take on at least the minimum amount of salt required by the U.S.D.A., and they will get hot enough in the smokehouse in July and August to exceed the government's temperature standard for killing disease-carrying bacteria.

In short, the traditionalists will accomplish through natural methods all that the U.S.D.A. requires—but since no inspectors will come to examine their hams periodically, as they do at the commercial enterprises, the farmers will have no certified proof of compliance with government standards. If the U.S.D.A. chose to apply a narrow technical interpretation of its regulations, the hams could be declared uninspected and unapproved products, and their sale could be prohibited.

Fortunately, no such rigid judgment has yet been made, nor is one likely; in fact, the U.S.D.A. has expressly approved the over-the-counter sale of farm-produced hams cured and aged the traditional way, requiring only that the fresh meat must come from hogs slaughtered under government inspection. The dwindling number of Southern farmers who still put up hams in the smokehouse every year thus can continue the practice for as long as they and their

dealers maintain smokehouses in which they give further treatment to the hams needing it. In the course of time a fine morale has been developed among the county's farmers. They trim a ham very carefully; they are most exacting in their salting and smoking. There is one small item which is unique to the county: to each batch of hickory wood a tobacco stalk is added. This, the curers maintain, offers two advantages. One is the richer color in the product; the ham is apparently refinished in mahogany. The other is the acute allergy that skipper flies have for anything hinting of tobacco. Vice-President [Alben] Barkley was a great partisan of the Trigg County ham. He had about twenty sent to him in Washington for use on special occasions. Trigg County ham has been served on the White House table during the occupancy of at least three Presidents.

Alfred Leland Crabb,
in the Tennessee Historical Quarterly, 1966

customers value the end result. "They'll never stop us from doing it right," said one Trigg County farmer. "If they did, the U.S.D.A. inspectors wouldn't have anywhere left to buy a real ham."

But the real hams may die out anyway, simply because fewer and fewer people will be willing to spend the time it takes to cure, smoke, and age them. "Hardly anybody does it like this anymore," observed Tommy Darden of Smithfield. "It's about to become a lost art."

At Gwaltney of Smithfield and the other major commercial packinghouses inside the town limits, the Virginia law that sets penalties for using the Smithfield name on ersatz country hams is technically obeyed—not by following the old production methods, but simply by calling most of their products something other than Smithfield hams. More than 99 percent of the hams they produce are "quick-fix" meats processed in decidedly untraditional ways, and though they trade heavily on the rich tradition of Virginia hams, they subtly avoid the label Smithfield. The relative handful of hams that are dry-salted, hickory-smoked, and aged for at least six months—and called Smithfields—still hang in artificially heated and cooled aging rooms, never experiencing the summer sweats. Real country ham, as Tommy Darden said, is almost a lost art.

But as long as the smell of fried ham in the skillet or the taste of boiled ham on a biscuit survives in memory, there will be traditionalists at work in country smokehouses, carefully crafting this gem of Southern foods. Whenever a genuine country ham can be found, it is a cause in itself for joyful celebration. Here are two of the classic and primary ways to prepare it for the table.

In the North man may not be able to live by bread alone; but in the South, and particularly in Charleston, he comes mighty near to it, provided the bread is hot.

Helen Woodward,
in her introduction to
*Two Hundred Years
of Charleston Cooking*, 1930

With the assistance of a butcher, or using a handsaw yourself, start at the narrow hock end and saw off the hock in rounds about 1 inch thick. (On short-hock hams, you may get only 2 or 3 of these; on a long-neck Smithfield ham, you may get 6 or 8.) Wrap separately and freeze. One or two hock rounds in a pot of turnip greens, white beans, black-eyed peas, or other garden-fresh vegetables will add zest, seasoning, and overall distinction.

The next step is best taken by a butcher, but it is still possible to accomplish it at home. At the point where the ham begins to flare out from the hock, cut off several ¼-inch slices, the number depending upon how much you like fried ham. (I generally take 8 to 10 slices; that leaves about half of a 15- to 20-pound ham for boiling.) Trim away the rind or skin and some of the fat from each slice, scrape clean with a knife blade, and wrap separately in wax paper and then aluminum foil. Ham will keep well in the refrigerator for about 2 or 3 weeks; for longer storage it is best to freeze the slices, but not for more than about 3 months.

To fry, place slices in a cold iron skillet. Over low heat, the ham will slowly begin to sizzle and turn a deeper shade of red. Cook first on one side and then the other (about 5 minutes each), heating it thoroughly but taking care not to overcook or burn it. If the ham is moist and juicy, as it should be, it will make a rich red gravy of its own, and only a little water need be added to make red-eye gravy (see page 193). If it is dry, add ¼ to ½ cup of water and cover the skillet. Served hot with eggs, grits, fried apples, biscuits, and coffee, fried country ham makes a memorable breakfast.

The remainder of a ham after the hock and frying pieces have been removed reaches its zenith when boiled, then topped with a special mixture of spicy seasonings, and served cold in paper-thin slices. As a buffet highlight piled high between halves of beaten biscuits (see page 220), as a featured entree with vegetables, or as a companion dinner meat with fried chicken or sliced turkey, boiled country ham (or baked, as some prefer it) is an ancient and inimitable treasure, the highest form of the Southern gastronomic art.

To prepare a boiled ham, first soak it overnight in a large kettle of cold water to which 1 cup of cider vinegar has been added. Then scrub with a stiff brush to remove any remaining mold or other encrustations. (Mold on an old ham is a harmless but telling sign of age; simply scrub it off.) Put fresh water in the cooking pot to cover the ham, bring to a simmer (not a boil), and let cook at that level for 1 hour. Remove and rinse ham again, refill the pot with fresh water, stir into it 2 cups of apple juice and 1 cup of sugar, submerge the ham again, and cook at just below the boiling point for 15 to 20 minutes per pound. When tender, remove from the heat and leave ham in the water until it is cool enough to handle (about 1 hour). Remove to a platter or paper-lined tray, trim off the hard skin and some of the fat, remove any bones that come out easily, and while the meat is still quite warm, pat on a mixture made of equal parts dark brown sugar and fine breadcrumbs (about 1 cup of each) and 2 teaspoons of black pepper (more or less to suit your taste). As the ham cools, the topping will harden a bit and form a crust. Later, when the meat is cold, each thin slice will combine a layer of the spicy-sweet topping, a ribbon of white fat, and a morsel of the tender, red, delicious ham. This is the South's oldest, richest, and most delectable dinner-table treat.

A boiled or baked country ham needs no refrigeration; just cover the platter with a cloth and leave it sitting on a table or sideboard—next to a tin of beaten biscuits, if possible. That sterling combination would remain fresh and delicious for two weeks or more, if by some miraculous exercise of restraint the diners should allow it to last that long.

Jambalaya

There are countless versions of jambalaya, all of them hearty one-dish meals in the manner of gumbo and shrimp creole and many of the pilaus. Though it could be categorized in several places—with soups and stews, rice dishes, seafood—we have chosen to put it here with pork primarily because of its name, the first two syllables of which trace to both the French and the Spanish words for ham. Cajun and Creole cooks have thrown just about everything into jambalaya for at least one hundred years, but ham has always been a prime ingredient. In Gonzales, Louisiana, the self-styled Jambalaya Capital of the World, you can find about as many recipes for this dish as there are households. In the spirit of that diversity, our recipe is an eclectic dish that draws inspiration from many others. Made with chopped morsels of country ham, it's a wonderfully rich and flavorful dish.

Chop 1 cup of lean ham into small pieces (country ham if possible, some other kind if necessary) and set it aside. In a large saucepan, bring 1½ quarts of salted water to a boil, put in 1 pound of fresh shrimp, and boil uncovered for 3 to 5 minutes. Empty the firm, pink shrimp into a colander to cool, then peel and set them aside. In a large heavy pot, heat 4 or 5 tablespoons of bacon grease or vegetable oil. Prepare 1 cup of minced onions, ½ cup of minced green bell pepper, ½ cup of minced celery, and 2 minced garlic cloves and sauté in the pot until soft. Add the drained contents of a 1-pound can of tomatoes (cored and chopped), saving the juice. Stir in 1 tablespoon of chopped fresh parsley, ½ teaspoon of thyme, ½ teaspoon of salt, ½ teaspoon of black pepper, and ⅛ teaspoon of cayenne pepper. Mix well together and simmer uncovered until the combination is thick and thoroughly blended. Combine the left-over tomato juice with 1 tablespoon of Worcestershire sauce and enough chicken broth or hot water to make 2 cups of liquid, and add it to the pot. Then put in 1 cup of uncooked rice and, without stirring, cover the pot and cook at the lowest heat for 20 minutes. Remove the cover, stir well, and add the ham and shrimp, blending them in. Cover again and let the flavors mingle for 10 minutes or so. Adjust seasonings if necessary and serve the jambalaya hot with bread and salad. The recipe provides generously for 4 people.

SEAFOOD AND FRESHWATER FISH

No meat, not even pork or game, goes back as far in the recorded history of America as fish. De Soto, Ponce de Leon, and other early Spanish explorers

The Key Manhattan [an offshore oil rig] operates in the blue-gray waters of the Gulf of Mexico. . . . [Faye] Cleckler, 57, the food manager, finds cooking more rewarding aboard the rig than it is back home in Brooklyn, Miss. . . .

"Lunch is ready now," Cleckler announced with motherly firmness.

recorded the abundant diversity of finned and shelled sea creatures around them before they ever stepped ashore in the New World, and Columbus did likewise. The story is told that the Spaniards who landed at Port Royal on the coast of present-day South Carolina in 1566 met Indians who offered them roasted oysters; now, more than four centuries later, the identical dish—freshly harvested oysters steamed over an open fire until their shells pop open—is still a popular favorite along the same stretch of Carolina coast.

Throughout the history of this region, along its hundreds of miles of sea-shore and its latticelike network of rivers and streams and lakes, entire communities and societies have grown up and prospered around the perpetual harvest of the waters. The Cajun and Creole cuisines of Louisiana are firmly and inseparably anchored in aquatic foods. The Gulf Coast regions of Mississippi and Alabama, though small in terms of miles, are substantial in tradition and influence in the culinary profiles of those states. The Florida peninsula, with its two thousand miles of exposure to the sea, has always taken a major portion of its sustenance from the water. The sea islands and low country of Georgia and South Carolina give a strong aquatic flavor to the preferred foods in those states. North Carolina and Virginia, colonized as they were by people from the sea almost four centuries ago, still retain a special fondness for fish and shellfish. In all of these coastal states, the legacy of the Indian populations included a love of seafood, and the attraction has never waned.

Only three Southern states—Kentucky, Tennessee, and Arkansas—lack a coastal tradition, and they have compensated by harvesting catfish, crappie, bream, trout, bass, and scores of other freshwater fish from their many lakes and rivers. Catfish, as we have seen, is now a major agricultural product of Mississippi, and both Arkansas and Tennessee have begun to move into that market too. This shift to aquaculture in the old-time Land of Cotton represents a figurative and literal sea change of enormous proportions.

Many deep-rooted gastronomic traditions have developed around seafood in the South. The combination of grits with any number of small pan fish—a dish commonly called grits and grunts—is a breakfast favorite in the Florida Keys and elsewhere along the coast as far north as the sea islands of Georgia and South Carolina. On the Gulf Coast, mullet is also called Biloxi bacon, or lisa, the latter apparently intended to give a more romantic image to a good fish that suffers low esteem because of its unmelodic common name. (Smoked mullet is an excellent specialty that deserves a wider reputation.)

Fish fries and oyster roasts and shrimp festivals are celebrated year in and year out from the Virginia Tidewater to the Louisiana bayous. Pan-fried rainbow trout, fresh from the cold, clear streams of the Southern mountains, are the pride of fishing enthusiasts and cooks alike. Oysters moved from the coasts to the interior as soon as steamboats and railroads arrived to transport them

After a dreamlike helicopter trip through the hot haze of sea and sky . . . the big-city food critic was more than ready for a restorative meal. What she was not ready for was the dazzling variety of Cajun and Southern specialties, impeccably garnished and laid out cafeteria-style. . . . Justifiably renowned black-eyed-pea jambalaya . . . Gumbo enriched with a coffee-colored roux . . . fried chicken, shrimp, oysters, catfish and corn-meal hush puppies . . . catfish court bouillon . . . red beans . . . with sausage and snowy mounds of steamed rice. Okra mellowed in a gentle tomato sauce . . . Southern-style potato salad gilded with mustard. . . . The dessert table suggested a church-supper cake sale with the centerpiece being red velvet cake. . . . It was a meal that would have been remarkable even on shore and, in a place where weekly supplies must be replenished by boat, was absolutely astonishing.

Mimi Sheraton,
in Time, April 14, 1986

there, and their popularity has remained high throughout the region from that time to this. Shrimp, more perishable than oysters, took much longer to arrive in the landlocked cities from the coast, but refrigeration changed that picture dramatically, and now, of course, they are everywhere.

It is this same ready availability that makes seafood and freshwater fish important as a main-dish food in all parts of the South, especially along the coasts. This small sample of nine recipes offers just a taste of food from the waters that people in the South have been eating with pleasure and sharing with others for generations. The most common and widely enjoyed seafoods are represented: shrimp and oysters, crabs and crawfish, catfish and flounder and red snapper. There are also a couple of less common dishes: frog legs and shad. The list is anything but comprehensive, yet it does at least suggest how broad and diverse the South's water-borne foods truly are.

AT A FISH LODGE
NEAR ATHENS, GEORGIA

Inside, wherever an oddity or natural phenomenon could hang, one hung: stuffed rump of a deer, snowshoe, flintlock, hornet's nest. The place looked as if a Boy Scout troop had decorated it. Thirty or so people, black and white, sat around tables almost foundering under piled platters of food. . . .

I was watching everyone else and didn't see the waitress standing quietly by. Her voice was deep and soft like water moving in a cavern. I ordered the $4.50 special. In a few minutes she wheeled up a cart and began off-loading dinner: ham and eggs, fried catfish, fried perch fingerlings, fried shrimp, chunks of barbecued beef, fried chicken, French fries, hush puppies, a broad bowl of cole slaw, another of lemon, a quart of ice tea, a quart of ice, and an entire loaf of factory-wrapped white bread. The table was covered.

"Call me if y'all want any more." She wasn't joking.

> William Least Heat Moon
> Blue Highways, 1982

Catfish (Pan-Fried)

Like chicken, catfish is generally deep-fried in restaurants and pan-fried at home; also like chicken, there are almost as many minor variations on the basic cooking method as there are cooks to prepare this Southern favorite among all freshwater fish. Our method is probably the oldest and simplest, with no tricks or secrets.

Select fresh catfish, whole or fillets; wash well in cold water and pat completely dry with paper towels. (This recipe is for fillets, preferred because they are easier to clean, fry, and eat; allow about ½ pound per person.) In a heavy iron skillet, melt enough lard or shortening to reach a depth of ½ to 1 inch. Rub the fish with salt and black pepper and coat with white cornmeal, shaking off any excess. When the fat in the skillet is hot (but not smoking), lay the pieces of fish in gently (spaced so as not to touch) and fry for about 4 minutes, or until they are crisp and well browned on the bottom side. Turn carefully and fry to the same crispness on the other side. Then lift the pieces out carefully and drain on a platter covered with absorbent paper. An ample supply of lemon wedges will provide ideal seasoning, though some people prefer tartar, hot-pepper, or catsup-based sauces.

Hush puppies (see page 229) are among the favorite companion dishes for fried catfish. Other freshwater fish, such as bass, crappie, and bream, are also delicious fried. For us, though, nothing beats pond-raised catfish—not even the native cats of the South's lakes and rivers.

Crabs (Deviled)

From the Maryland, Delaware, and Virginia shores of Chesapeake Bay to the Gulf Coast waters off Alabama, Mississippi, and Louisiana, crabs are a highly regarded shellfish. Hard-shell and soft-shell crabs offer a wide range of culinary options, from boiled and deep-fried in the shell to combination baked dishes such as crab cakes and deviled crab. The late, legendary Mary Branch of Coden, Alabama, used milk-soaked bread and raw eggs with onion, pepper, celery, and spices to fortify her deviled crab recipe, and people came to her restaurant from miles around just for the pleasure of that dish. Elsewhere along the Gulf and Atlantic coasts, deviled crabs may get their primary flavor and texture (in addition to what the crab provides) from a sautéed blend of onions and other vegetables, or from mayonnaise, or from hard-boiled eggs combined with milk or cream. Many minor variations also show up from one recipe to the next. The recipe below contains elements of many from the upper Chesapeake to the mouth of the Mississippi.

Pick over 1 pound of lump crab meat to remove any remaining shell fragments. (Fresh crab meat makes a superior dish, but canned or frozen may be substituted.) Add ¾ cup of mayonnaise, 1 tablespoon of prepared mustard, 2 tablespoons of finely chopped green onions, ¼ teaspoon of coarsely ground black pepper, and 2 teaspoons of fresh lemon juice, blending well. The mixture should hold together easily. Add 1 or 2 tablespoons of breadcrumbs if you wish, and then divide into 8 crab shells or individual ovenproof dishes. Sprinkle breadcrumbs lightly over the tops, dot with butter, and bake in a preheated 375° oven for 20 minutes, or until bubbly hot and crusty brown on top.

Crawfish Étouffée

Crawfish are hard to come by outside of Louisiana. We happened upon a good source at a place called Big D's Crawfish Shack just off the interstate highway near Oakland in north Mississippi. Denman "Big D" Reed and his wife, Nell, former Louisianans, had perfected a weekly shuttle system to keep fresh supplies of seafood from the bayou country on hand. Among other things, they sold crawfish three ways: live, boiled in the shells, and frozen in one-pound packages of tail meat. We iced down an ample supply, hoping to make an étouffée and a crawfish bisque—a peppery stew served with rice and a rich and complex soup, respectively—but we never got past the étouffée, a dish that Peter Feibleman,

"There is now quickening of tempo in the flow of life by river and sea. The languorous Southerner seems to find energy in the dynamo of summer's sun; this is the climate of his being. . . . Fishermen are stirred to frenzy . . . if that measured and contemplative sport can be so described. Even crabbers are relentlessly active. No one is safe from the young of that persuasion. We see them coming across the lawn, their faces ambivalent with pride and anxiety. Pride in the gift they are bearing; anxiety lest some of the fighting, clawing catch escape and nip bare toes. . . .

Shrimpers are out. On the blue creek's edge their nets are an intermittent flutter of descending white. Beaufort County June shrimp by their tiny size are not easy to peel; but they are worth the trouble. Deep sea shrimp are fine. But the small June ones are for the epicurean . . . and who does not so fancy himself?"

Edith Ingelsby
A Corner at Carolina, 1968

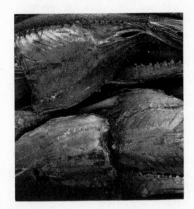

in *American Cooking: Creole and Acadian,* called "possibly the best of all Acadian crawfish foods." As most Cajun specialties tend to do, this dish varies greatly from cook to cook. We tried several recipes, and thoroughly enjoyed them all. In the spirit of Cajun creativity, our version is partly inspired by others and partly invented by us.

Prepare and set aside 2 cups of crawfish tail meat, including some of the yellow fat from the crawfish body. You will also need 4 tablespoons of brown roux (see page 194) and 2 cups of fish stock.

To make the stock, melt 3 tablespoons of butter in a large saucepan and sauté ½ cup each of coarsely chopped onion and celery and ¼ cup of coarsely chopped carrots. Add peppercorns and cloves (about 6 of each), ½ cup of white wine, 2 bay leaves, ½ teaspoon of thyme (or 1 sprig fresh), the rind of ½ lemon, 2 cups of cold water, and 2 cups of fish pieces (crawfish shells, fish heads, bones, tails, etc.). Bring to near boiling and cook uncovered for 15 minutes. This liquid, when strained, is the stock; discard everything else. Put 2 cups of the stock in a covered saucepan and keep it warm.

In a large, heavy casserole, warm the 4 tablespoons of roux over low heat, stirring constantly. Have these finely chopped ingredients ready to add as soon as the roux is hot: 1 cup of white onions, 1 cup of green onions, ½ cup of celery, ½ cup of green bell pepper, and 3 cloves of garlic. Combine with the roux, stirring frequently over moderate heat until the vegetables are soft, about 5 minutes. Next, add the hot fish stock in a slow, steady stream, stirring all the while, and bring the mixture to a boil. As soon as it begins to thicken, add the contents of a 16-ounce can of tomatoes (cored and chopped—save the juice), 1 tablespoon of Worcestershire sauce, and 2 teaspoons of lemon juice. If the étouffée seems too thick, add some of the leftover tomato juice. Season to taste with salt, black pepper, and cayenne pepper, and simmer, stirring frequently, for 15 to 20 minutes. Stir in the crawfish and continue simmering for 10 to 15 more minutes. As soon as the crawfish are tender and the flavors and seasonings are well-blended, ladle the étouffée over mounds of freshly cooked hot rice and serve. With salad and bread, this is a hearty one-dish meal for 4.

Flounder (Broiled)

One of the great catches of the Southern seas is flounder, a delicate, mild-flavored fish with thin skin and fine-textured flesh. Like all seafoods, it can be prepared according to many recipes of varying degrees of complexity, but no one has ever improved on the simplest and most uncomplicated method of all: broiling. This monument to simplicity has been served all along the Southern coast for generations.

Prepare a lemon-butter sauce (see page 192). Clean and rinse 1 whole fresh flounder (remove the head but leave the tail) and pat it dry with paper towels. Score one side of the fish with X-shaped slits. Rub thoroughly on both sides with a small amount of salt and pepper, baste with sauce (about 2 or 3 tablespoons), and lay in a broiling pan, scored side up. Preheat the oven to broil, and broil fish for 5 minutes on top rack, about 4 inches from the heat. Remove and check for doneness (if it flakes easily with a fork, it's ready; if not, broil for 1 minute more). The intense heat from the broiler will cook the fish through, making it unnecessary to turn it. Remove to a warm platter, pour as much of the remaining warm lemon-butter sauce as you like over the flounder, and serve immediately. One fresh flounder weighing a pound or so makes an excellent dinner for 2 when served with bread, slaw, and perhaps a green vegetable.

Frog Legs

Neither fish nor fowl nor game, frogs are hard to classify—but frog legs, the only edible part of the animal, have an appealing and faintly familiar taste and texture much like chicken. The abundance of frogs in freshwater ponds and rivers all over the South has made frog legs a popular delicacy in some restaurants for decades, often as an entree companion to catfish. Well-stocked meat and fish markets should have on hand or be able to obtain frog legs ready to cook (hind legs already cleaned and skinned). Allowing 2 large legs or about 1/2 pound per person, fry according to this old and simple recipe.

In a heavy iron skillet, heat enough shortening to reach a depth of 1/2 to 1 inch and add 3 to 4 tablespoons of bacon grease to it. Rub frog legs with salt and black pepper. Beat 2 eggs with 2 tablespoons of lemon juice and 2 tablespoons of water. Put 1 cup of white cornmeal, flour, or fine bread-crumbs—or any combination of these—on a large plate and mix in 1/2 teaspoon of salt and 1/4 teaspoon of pepper. When the shortening is hot (but not smoking), dip the frog legs into the egg mixture, roll to coat them completely in the dry mixture, and lay gently in the skillet. Fry on one side and then the other—about 5 minutes on each—and place on absorbent paper to drain. Serve hot, like fried chicken.

[Florida] crackers are especially partial to fish as a food and may frequently be heard to say, "I done et so free of fish my stomach rises and falls with the tide." The old-fashioned fish-fry—where folks get together for a day's fishing and then gather on the shore to fry their catch—is one of the Palmetto Country's most typical folkways. Until prohibited by law—and even yet on dark nights—the crackers have had their own ways of obtaining abundant supplies of fresh-water fish— by dynamiting, seining, and toxic stupefaction with sawdust or berries. Their ancestors learned the berry trick from the Indians.

Stetson Kennedy
Palmetto Country, 1942

Oysters Bienville

In 1899, Jules Alciatore, son of the founder of Antoine's Restaurant in New Orleans, created a dish of baked oysters topped with a rich-as-Rockefeller sauce and named it for the tycoon himself, John D. Rockefeller. All of the great Creole restaurants of New Orleans subsequently flattered Antoine's with imitations, but no one ever got the original recipe, which remains a closely guarded secret.

More than twenty years after oysters Rockefeller made their debut, a Frenchman named Arnaud Cazeneuve—Count Arnaud to his friends—started a restaurant in the French Quarter of New Orleans that soon became famous for its creative cuisine. Now, nearly three quarters of a century later, Arnaud's Restaurant is still there, and so are its most celebrated culinary specialties, foremost among them being oysters Bienville, once described as "by all odds the most priceless gem" ever imagined by the count or prepared by his chefs.

Down through the years, gourmets have debated incessantly and without resolution the relative virtues of oysters Rockefeller and oysters Bienville. Both specialties can still be enjoyed in the two restaurants, but only oysters Bienville can be prepared at home in close resemblance to the original, its recipe having been published in *The New Orleans Restaurant Cookbook* by Deirdre Stanforth in 1967. Here is an oysters Bienville recipe similar to Count Arnaud's inspired creation.

You will need 3 dozen oysters on the half shell, with oyster liquor; 1 bunch of green onions with tops or 1 large yellow onion, chopped fine; 1 stick of butter; 2 heaping tablespoons of flour; 2 cups of hot chicken or fish broth (see page 268); 1½ pounds of fresh shrimp, boiled, peeled, and chopped fine; 4 fresh mushrooms, chopped fine; 3 egg yolks; ½ cup of light cream; 3 ounces of white wine (sauterne or other sweet); salt, black pepper, cayenne pepper, and Tabasco sauce to taste; ¼ cup of fine breadcrumbs; ½ cup grated fresh Parmesan cheese; and ⅛ teaspoon of paprika.

Half fill 6 piepans with rock salt, place 6 half-shell oysters in each pan, and bake in a preheated 375° oven for about 10 minutes, or until oysters curl around the edges. Remove and set aside; when cool enough to handle, drain and reserve liquor from oysters. Brown onions in butter, stirring constantly, until they become soft. Add flour slowly, stirring over low heat until smooth and brown. Slowly add hot broth, which has been heated to the scalding point (but not boiled). Add shrimp and mushrooms, simmering until mixture begins to thicken, then set aside to cool slightly.

Beat the egg yolks well with the cream and blend the wine with them. Slowly pour the warm broth mixture into the egg-cream-wine sauce, stirring constantly to keep smooth and avoid curdling. Next add the strained oyster liquor. Season the mixture to taste with salt, black pepper, and cayenne pepper or Tabasco sauce. Return to stove and cook over low heat for 10 to 15 minutes, stirring constantly to prevent lumping or scorching. When the sauce is quite thick, spoon carefully over each oyster in its half-shell. Then combine the breadcrumbs, Parmesan, and paprika and sprinkle a fairly thick covering of the mixture over each oyster. Bake in a preheated 400° oven until the tops become golden brown, and serve at once. Each piepan can be served as an individual offering of 6 oysters, straight from the oven.

Red Snapper (Stuffed)

As a Southern seafood *pièce de résistance*, we could hardly do better than stuffed and baked red snapper, another of the famed Creole specialties of Louisiana. For more than a century, Gulf Coast cooks from Texas to Key West have prized snapper. A tender, spicy, exquisitely blended snapper and sauce combination such as the one below deserves the highest praise.

Begin with a whole 2-pound dressed red snapper or 2 fillets weighing a total of 1½ to 2 pounds. Wash and pat dry with paper towels. Rub well with salt, pepper, a sprinkle of powdered thyme, and softened butter. Lay the fish in a large casserole, drip 1 tablespoon of lemon or lime juice over it, and let stand. Peel and wash ½ pound of uncooked shrimp and drain ½ pint of oysters; mince together in a bowl and set aside.

Mince ½ small green bell pepper, ½ rib of celery, 6 green onions (tops included), 2 cloves of garlic, and 4 sprigs of fresh parsley; combine these with 2 bay leaves and sauté in a black skillet with 2 tablespoons of butter until soft, about 5 minutes. Remove half the mixture and reserve to make a sauce. In a separate pan, crumble 2 slices of white bread (without crusts). Add 1 egg beaten with 1 tablespoon of cream. Blend to a paste and set aside.

To the sautéed mixture remaining in the skillet, add the minced shrimp and oysters; simmer, stirring, for 5 minutes. Then add the egg and bread mixture, a sprinkle each of mace and thyme, and salt and pepper to taste. Stir and simmer 10 more minutes and then either stuff the snapper with it or distribute evenly over one fillet and put the other on top.

Heat the reserved sautéed mixture in a saucepan. Add to it 1 tablespoon of flour, blending well. Then add 1 cup of fresh or canned tomatoes (drained, peeled, cored, and finely chopped) and a sprinkle of thyme. Stir and simmer for 1 minute, and pour the sauce over the stuffed fish. Bake at 400° for 20 minutes, covered loosely with a sheet of aluminum foil. Baste

TO FRY OYSTERS

Beat Eggs, with a little salt, grated Nutmeg, and thicken it like thick Batter, with grated white Bread and fine Flour; then dip the Oysters in it, and fry them brown with Beef-dripping.

E. Smith, The Compleat Housewife: or, Accomplish'd Gentlewoman's Companion, 1742

271

several times with pan juices. This recipe makes a spectacular main dish for 4 people.

Shad (Planked)

For reasons that are difficult to interpret, certain fish at various times in history have drifted mysteriously in and out of public favor. Mullet along the Gulf Coast and carp in the Southern interior are two examples; they may be the people's choice in one age, and a common trash fish in another.

Shad has known the same rising and falling fortunes. Time was when the fish was so plentiful along the Atlantic Seaboard as to be considered too common to eat—but in other times, the spring spawning season was greeted with joy by shad lovers from the St. Johns River in north Florida to the Virginia coast and beyond. The Indians were said to use shad for fertilizer, but they also ate it, and ate shad roe (eggs) as well. One method of cooking the fish attributed to some East Coast tribes was to lay it out on a plank and roast it over hot coals. Whether or not this is a historically accurate story of the origin of planked shad, it is a fact that the recipe appears in a good many old Southern cookbooks— and not so many years ago, there were hardware stores in the region that sold oak planks for the specific purpose of cooking shad. With a few modifications, the experience can be reconstructed. Here is one method.

Rub a smoothly planed but unfinished oak plank (about 8 by 12 inches) with bacon grease and heat it in a preheated 400° oven for about 5 minutes. Rub 4 shad fillets with salt and pepper, place them skin side down on the plank, and baste them with lemon-butter sauce (see page 192). Top each fillet with 1 strip of raw bacon. Return to oven and bake 15 minutes. (Put a pan on a lower shelf to catch any drippings.) Remove again and line the edge of the plank with mashed potatoes. Place in the oven once more for 5 to 10 minutes, or until potatoes are browned and shad is flaky and well-done. The end result should be 4 servings of a very unusual dish out of Southern history.

Shrimp Creole

What the rest of the South knows as shrimp Creole, the veteran cooks of Louisiana are more inclined to call shrimp sauce piquante. In New Orleans and in Cajun country, sauce piquante is a rich and highly spiced reddish brown gravy

Presently a murmur arose among the watchers. Out at the harbor mouth, against the thin greenish-blue of the horizon, appeared the "Mosquito Fleet." Driven by a steady breeze, the boats swept toward the city [Charleston] with astonishing rapidity.

.   .   .   .   .

A cheer went up from the crowd. Never had there been such a catch. The boat seemed floored with silver which rose almost to the thwarts. . . . Indeed the catch was so heavy that as boat after boat docked, it became evident that the market was glutted, and the fishermen vied with each other in giving away their surplus cargo, so that they would not have to throw it overboard.

De Bose Heyward
Porgy, 1925

used to smother almost any meat, from chicken and veal to frog legs and alligator tail, but nothing goes better with it than shrimp. As befits the individual creativity of Louisiana cooks, the dish varies substantially from one recipe to another, and at the annual Sauce Piquante Festival in Raceland, diversity is much more of a rule than an exception. From a multiplicity of sources comes this version of shrimp sauce piquante (or shrimp Creole), Louisiana style. By whatever name, it's delicious.

Peel and wash 2 pounds of fresh shrimp. Mash the shells in a saucepan with 2 cups of water and boil, covered, to make a stock. In a large heavy cooking pot, heat 4 tablespoons of bacon grease. Mince 2 large onions, 1 small green or red bell pepper, 3 cloves of garlic, and ½ rib of celery and sauté over medium heat until soft. Add ⅛ teaspoon of powdered thyme, 2 bay leaves, 1 teaspoon of salt, ½ teaspoon of black pepper, ½ teaspoon of cayenne pepper, and 1 teaspoon of sugar, continuing to stir and cook. Slowly sprinkle in 1 tablespoon of flour, stirring carefully to keep it from lumping. With the mixture simmering, add 2 cups of fresh or canned tomatoes (peeled, cored, and finely chopped). Then add 1 tablespoon of Worcestershire sauce, 1 tablespoon of minced parsley, ¼ teaspoon of ground allspice, and 1 tablespoon of fresh lemon juice, and stir in 1 cup or more of the strained shrimp-shell stock—just enough to give the mixture the consistency of a thick gravy. Finally, add the raw whole shrimp and simmer partly covered for about 20 minutes, or until the flavors are well-blended and the shrimp are pink and firm. Serve shrimp Creole/sauce piquante steaming hot with rice. This amount should be ample for 4 to 6 people.

SOUPS AND STEWS

There is no need trying to settle here the eternal argument about the difference between soup and stew; for our purposes they are close kin, and they fit together compatibly as dishes best eaten with a spoon. A harder distinction is to separate soup, stew, chowder, consommé, bisque, and the like from such combination dishes as chicken pilau, country captain, jambalaya, shrimp Creole, and various hashes, mulls, and bogs. In another direction, there are numerous rice and vegetable dishes that present a similar classification problem, and the dividing line there, too, is fuzzy. (For those combinations, see Rice Dishes, pages 307–8)

Since the spoon test, with all its imperfections, is the only one we could find to apply, it dictates what follows here: a selection of soups and stews that Southerners have customarily eaten with spoons out of bowls. The list is not long, but it is old and distinguished. Soups and stews in the South have long been characterized as hearty, substantial, and filling, often taking the place of meat and fish as the main dish of the day. We offer a representative few to illustrate their importance in the history of Southern cookery.

But first, a few words of appreciation for some of the "spoon specialties" that aren't on this short list of recipes. Crawfish bisque, for example: For well over a century, it has been the pride of New Orleans and south Louisiana. The recipes are complex and involved, featuring, among other things, floating craw-fish heads stuffed with a spicy breadcrumb mixture. Food writers Rima and Richard Collin once declared bisque to be "the highest test of a great Louisiana cook." It is that, and more—a pure example of the supremacy of Louisiana cookery.

There are many other sterling soups and stews to be found in the region: conch chowder in south Florida; oyster stew all along the Atlantic and Gulf coasts; bouillabaisse in New Orleans; pot likker wherever greens have been cooking; all manner of cucumber and broccoli and asparagus soups, hot and cold, in virtually every state; terrapin stew and clam chowder drifting down from neighboring Maryland; chili easing over the border from Texas. All of these have long been loved in the South. Some, of course, are loved everywhere.

And then there is U.S. Senate bean soup. Is it Southern? Nothing in the record of that august body hints at such an origin. By one account, it was a fixture on the menu in the Senate restaurant as far back as the administration of Grover Cleveland in the 1890s; Senator Fred T. Dubois of Idaho is said to have pushed through a resolution requiring that the soup be served every day. Another version attributes the bean soup mandate to Senator Knute Nelson of Minnesota in 1903. The official recipe now printed on the back of the Senate restaurant menu calls for Michigan navy beans; Craig Claiborne once wrote that the best bean for the soup was reportedly a pea bean from California.

But look closely at the official recipe. It calls for 1½ pounds of smoked ham hocks, boiled slowly in a covered pot for three hours with the beans. Does that sound like Michigan? California? Minnesota? Idaho? Of course not. It sounds like North Carolina or Alabama or Arkansas, like every Southern state where cooking with pork is a 375-year-old tradition. Any fair and honest person seeking the creators of U.S. Senate bean soup would ask not who the *senators* were at the time the soup was given official status, but who the *cooks* were.

When Senators Dubois and Nelson gained a measure of immortality with their bean soup mandates nearly a century ago, the cooks in the Senate kitchen were mostly black Southerners. There ought to be a plaque somewhere in the capitol to honor those skillful citizens, their names now forgotten, who cooked bean soup in the Southern style with such a masterful touch that even the

As granddaughters, nieces, and cousins of morticians, we have attended our share of funerals and surprisingly have found that some of the best Southern cooking is to be had during these times of sorrow. The custom of caring for the bereaved in this manner stems back to ancient Africa, where the family of the deceased was given not only food but items of value, including

solons of the North and West came to realize that they simply could not do without it.

Returning to Louisiana, we note another stewlike dish: dirty rice, a highly seasoned combination of chopped meats (principally chicken livers and gizzards) with rice. In South Carolina, something very similar to that is called hash, or sometimes rice and hash. It is usually made with pork liver or other cuts of pork, and is a standard feature of many barbecue pits. And that brings up another stew that is often associated with the barbecue trade: Brunswick stew, known and loved for generations in many parts of the South—and, according to food writer Raymond Sokolov, "the most famous dish to emerge from the campfires and cabins of pioneer America."

The story related by Sokolov in *Fading Feast,* a collection of essays on disappearing American regional foods, is that a black cook named Jimmy Matthews concocted a squirrel stew for his master, Creed Haskins, in Brunswick County, Virginia, in 1828, and that became the standard from which Brunswick stew evolved. In Brunswick County, North Carolina, and in the city of Brunswick on the coast of Georgia, disclaimers can be heard against the Virginia story. In cookery, proof of origin is always a difficult task, at best. It seems safe to say that Indians were making stews with wild game long before any Europeans arrived, and in that sense there was Brunswick stew before there was a Brunswick.

What survives today in all of the Brunswick locales and in many other places, mostly in the South, is a thick and highly spiced stew to which many vegetables have been added and squirrel has been displaced in favor of chicken, pork, veal, or other meats. The exact ingredients differ from place to place and cook to cook, but chicken is far and away the most common meat base, and the vegetables almost always include onions, potatoes, tomatoes, butter beans, and corn. There's plenty of red and black pepper, too.

At Lawrenceville, the seat of Brunswick County, Virginia, the heritage and tradition associated with Brunswick stew are a serious matter, and big public cookings of the hearty hash take place frequently. We stopped at Lawrenceville on a Sunday afternoon in the spring of 1985, hoping to find such a pot simmering, but at Mitch's Mini-Market we were told that the local volunteer fire department's fund-raiser the day before had exhausted a two-hundred-gallon supply. The clerk sent us to Darrell Spence's nearby service station and store, saying we might find some left there. Spence was unable to help, but while we were talking to him, in walked Ronnie Mayton, a volunteer fireman.

"You the guy looking for the Brunswick stew?" he asked. "They told me at Mitch's I'd find you here. I just happen to have a quart on ice out in my truck." Mayton, a third-generation Brunswick Countian and stew maker, insisted on giving us the quart. We nursed it in a cooler all the way to Baltimore, where it became our contribution to a dinner for four. It was a delightful evening. We

wardrobes, by the entire community in an effort to offset the loss in a practical manner. This was particularly important if the deceased was the head of a household and the continuation of family stability was a concern. In the antebellum South, churches, fraternal orders, and burial societies took over a similar function, and to a significant extent this continues today. Friends and neighbors also play an important role, each preparing and donating food to those who are grieving so that they need not have the burden of cooking for themselves or the many guests who will be visiting the home. Those closest to the bereaved family take up vigil in the home from morning till night to clean and prepare for visitors and to receive their gifts of food. Tables are arranged and the food tastefully displayed for the dinner following the funeral, when family and friends will come together to mourn, to comfort, and to share their feelings with one another.

Norma Jean and Carole Darden
Spoonbread and Strawberry Wine, 1978

all loved the Brunswick stew, and we lifted a toast to Ronnie Mayton and Jimmy Matthews and the cooks of past and present who gave us such a bowl of cheer.

A little farther west across the country and a little later on in history, Brunswick stew spawned an imitator, and it soon took on a character and identity of its own. Its name, burgoo, has been variously attributed to seventeenth-century Arabs, eighteenth-century Turks, and nineteenth-century Americans, red, black, and white. Was it at first *burgout*, a French word similar to ragout, itself a stew of highly seasoned meats and vegetables? Was it simply a mispronunciation of bird stew, or perhaps of barbecue? No one knows. But this much is clear: For well over a century, this delectable, pepper-hot blend of various meats and up to a dozen vegetables, similar in most ways to Brunswick stew, has been a fixture at public gatherings in Kentucky, so much so that wherever it is known today, it is generally known as Kentucky burgoo.

In Owensboro, an Ohio River city west of Louisville, Catholic parishes and other religious and secular institutions claim a barbecue heritage that goes back to the 1830s, and burgoo has been associated with it for so long that no one can say when it started. Mutton is the primary barbecue meat around Owensboro, and it shows up as well in the burgoo, giving it a distinctive flavor that seems closer to the gamy quality of earlier times.

To the east of and upriver from Louisville, at the tiny hamlet of Ghent, a Kentucky newspaper columnist named James Tandy Ellis was almost as well-known for his burgoo recipe as for his syndicated column, *Tang of the South*. Ellis, a witty storyteller, claimed to have learned the secrets of burgoo from a Frenchman named Gus Jaubert, a famed chef in Lexington, Kentucky, who, according to legend, made the stew for General John Hunt Morgan and his Confederate raiders—and lived on long enough to serve six thousand gallons of it at a Louisville reunion of the Grand Army of the Republic in 1895. Tandy Ellis claimed that he "trailed with Gus Jaubert on one occasion when he went to Ohio and served 10,000 people." Another pretender to the burgoo master's crown was J. T. Looney, a Lexington chef whose services were in demand among the well-heeled followers of horse racing. Colonel E. R. Bradley of Idle Hour Farm once named one of his thoroughbreds Burgoo King in honor of Looney, and the horse won the 1932 Kentucky Derby. (It is not recorded whether burgoo was included in the horse's diet.)

Burgoo

Most recipes for burgoo are based on mind-boggling quantities such as Jaubert and Looney used when they were cooking in enormous kettles (six hundred pounds of meat, two hundred pounds of potatoes, etc.). One virtue of Tandy Ellis' recipe is that it makes a more manageable amount of stew—about 1½ gallons, enough to ladle out hearty servings to fifteen or twenty people. Ellis gave the recipe to Kentucky cookbook writer Marion Flexner in the 1940s, and it has since appeared in print enough times to be thought of as a public trust and a standard by which modern burgoo is made. We used it as the basic formula for a splendid pot of the historic stew, modifying little except to increase the spiciness and tang with small amounts of cayenne pepper, vinegar, and lemon juice. A squirrel or two would have added much in the way of both flavor and history, but a very good burgoo can be made without any game meat at all, as witness this version.

In a large, heavy kettle (2-gallon capacity or more), put 2 pounds of lean beef (cubed), ½ pound of lamb or mutton, and 1 medium-sized chicken (cut up). Add 4 quarts of water, bring to a hard boil, reduce heat, and simmer the meat for about 2 hours with the pot covered. Remove chicken, discard bones and skin, cut up the meat, and return it to the pot. Continuing to simmer, add these ingredients one at a time, stirring them in well: 2 cups of diced potatoes, 2 cups of diced onions, 2 cups of small green butter beans or baby limas, 2 green bell peppers, diced, 3 carrots, diced, and 2 cups of fresh corn kernels (canned or frozen yellow kernel corn can be substituted). Keep simmering for about 3 hours, stirring occasionally, and add more water from time to time if the stew seems too thick. For seasoning, put in 1 or more red pepper pods, 1 teaspoon of cayenne pepper, and as much salt and black pepper as your taste dictates. After the burgoo has been on the stove for about 6 hours, add 2 cups of cut-up okra (fresh is best, but frozen will do), 1 dozen fresh tomatoes (peeled, cored, and cut up) or the contents of a 1-quart can of tomatoes, 2 cloves of garlic, minced, ¼ cup of cider vinegar, and ¼ cup of fresh lemon juice, and keep simmering for at least 3 hours more, stirring and tasting occasionally and adjusting the seasonings and adding water if necessary. The Ellis recipe suggests 7 hours of cooking, by which time the burgoo should be beginning to take shape—or rather to lose shape—and become a real stew. Seven hours is a minimum; 10 or 12 seems much more appropriate, the better to blend the flavors and give the stew a rich and hearty character. Like many great soups and stews, it improves with age, both on the stove and in the refrigerator or freezer. Served hot with a barbecue sandwich or with homemade light bread or cornbread, burgoo is a genuine Kentucky wonder, the gastronomical equivalent of a superlative Louisiana gumbo.

RESPECTING THE POOR

I promised a few hints, to enable every family to assist the poor of their neighborhood. . . . Into a deep coarse pan put half a pound of rice, four ounces of coarse sugar, or treacle, two quarts of milk, and two ounces of dripping; set it cold in the oven. It will take a good while, but will be an excellent solid food.

A very good meal may be bestowed in a thing called Brewis, which is thus made: cut a very thin crust of bread and put it into the pot where salt beef is boiling and nearly ready; it will attract some of the fat, and when swelled out, will be no unpalatable dish to those who rarely taste meat. . . .

In every family there is some superfluity, and if it is prepared with cleanliness and care, the benefit will be very great to the receiver and the satisfaction no less to the giver. I found in times of scarcity, ten or fifteen gallons of soup could be dealt out weekly, at an expense not worth mentioning. . . . If in the United States abounding with opulent families, the quantity of ten gallons were made in ten gentlemen's houses, there would be a hundred gallons of wholesome agreeable food given weekly for the support of forty poor families, at the rate of two gallons and a half each.

S. Thomas Bivins
The Southern Cookbook, 1912

Corn Soup

Many a Southern cookbook, from Lettice Bryan's *Kentucky Housewife* (1839) to Jesse Willis Lewis' *Creole and Deep South Recipes* (1954) and on to the present, offers an excellent use for corn in a variety of soups and chowders. The recipes tend to be quick and simple, the soups light and delicate, the flavors appealingly fresh and appropriately close to that of corn itself. Here is one time-honored version.

In a large pan, make a cream sauce with 2 tablespoons of butter, 2 tablespoons of flour, and 2 cups of milk or half-and-half. Add 2 cups of chicken broth and blend the mixture well over medium heat. Then add 2 cups of corn—freshly cut from the cob is best, but canned or frozen will work. Season to taste with salt and pepper and simmer gently for 5 to 10 minutes, stirring as it thickens.

Gumbo, of all other products of the New Orleans cuisine, represents a most distinctive type of the evolution of good cookery under the hands of the famous Creole cuisinières of old New Orleans. Indeed, the word "evolution" fails to apply when speaking of Gumbo, for it is an original conception, a something sui generis in cooking, peculiar to this ancient Creole city alone, and to the manner born. With unequalled ability Creole cooks saw the possibilities of exquisite and delicious combinations in making Gumbo, and hence we have many varieties, till the occult science of making a good "Gumbo à la Creole" seems too fine an inheritance of gastronomic lore to remain forever hidden away in the cuisine of this old Southern metropolis.

The Picayune Creole Cook Book, 1901

Gumbo

So many recipes for gumbo appear in so many Southern (especially Cajun and Creole) cookbooks that putting one here seems both essential and superfluous. Lafcadio Hearn's *La Cuisine Creole* (1885) and *The Picayune Creole Cook Book* (1901) and all the other venerable and respected Louisiana collections go on for pages about the mysteries of gumbo making, the "occult science" that draws upon Indian and African and Franco-Spanish resources. The word gumbo comes from an African term for okra, the base upon which the first such stews were made in New Orleans early in the nineteenth century. Within twenty years, filé powder also came into use, the source being ground sassafras leaves from the Choctaw Indians of Louisiana and Mississippi. Filé gumbos usually do not have okra in them. Okra gumbo and filé gumbo are still the two basic kinds, each with an infinite number of variations. Our version of this very individualistic dish draws primarily from recipes in the two old books cited above, with a few additional ideas from elsewhere.

Prepare 1½ cups of fresh crab meat. In a large pot boil 3 quarts of water with 2 bay leaves, 2 slices of lemon, 2 slices of onion, and judicious amounts of salt, black pepper, red pepper pods, and parsley. Wash 2 pounds of fresh shrimp and put them into the pot to boil for 2 minutes. Peel the shrimp, returning the shells to the stock for later use, and set the shrimp and crab meat aside. Next, wash and cut up 2 pounds of okra and sauté it in 3 tablespoons of bacon grease in a large black skillet. The okra will start out gummy and bright green, turning darker and losing some of its stickiness as it cooks. When it is soft and mushy, transfer it to a large stew pot and add 4 fresh medium-sized tomatoes (peeled and cut up) or the contents of an 8-ounce can of tomatoes, drained. Stir and mix together well. Clean the skillet, heat 3 tablespoons of bacon grease in it, and sauté 2 onions, 2 green bell peppers, and 2 red pepper pods, all finely chopped. When soft, add these ingredients to the stew pot.

In a saucepan, warm 4 tablespoons of brown roux (see page 194); strain and stir in 2 cups of the warm shrimp stock. When well-blended, add this mixture to the large stew pot with the other ingredients. Bring to a boil and simmer for 2 hours, adding more strained stock as needed to maintain the consistency of a thick soup. Adjust seasonings with salt, pepper, thyme, and parsley. When the gumbo has simmered for at least 3 or 4 hours and the flavors have begun to blend nicely, add the shrimp and crab meat and continue cooking for about 15 more minutes—long enough for the seafood flavors to be introduced, but not so long that the shrimp become flabby.

Serve gumbo hot with freshly boiled rice in large, shallow soup bowls. A good gumbo improves with age in the refrigerator and can be reheated without harm to the flavor. This recipe provides generous servings for 6 to 8 people.

The wonderful thing about gumbo is that it welcomes and assimilates so many diverse flavors. You can use duck, oysters, chicken, smoked sausage, or other meats and seafoods. Hot peppers, garlic, and numerous spices are favored by some cooks. Every good Louisiana cook seems almost honor-bound to have a distinctive "signature" gumbo, with its formula a closely guarded secret.

Peanut Soup

George Washington Carver, in his pathfinding agricultural research at Tuskegee Institute in Alabama early in this century, presented peanut soup as one of the many nourishing dishes to be derived from the versatile peanut. A savory soup usually made with peanut butter and chicken stock, it is much better than it sounds. In Georgia, one of the South's two leading peanut-producing states, the soup has never gained an avid following, but in Virginia, the other leading state, it is found on menus in many places and is a prized house specialty in some. It was Carver, though, who first gave visibility to the soup, and in some places it is called Tuskegee soup in his honor. This recipe is typical of many.

Sauté ½ cup of finely chopped celery and ½ cup of finely chopped green onions (tops included) in 4 tablespoons of butter in a large heavy pot. When the vegetables are soft, slowly sprinkle in 2 tablespoons of flour, stirring until smooth. Gradually add 3 cups of warm chicken broth and bring the mixture to a boil. Blend in ¾ cup of creamy peanut butter, reduce heat, and simmer for about 15 minutes, stirring frequently to achieve a smooth and thorough union of ingredients. Season to taste with salt and pepper. Just before serving, stir in 1½ cups of light cream or half-and-half and reheat to just below boiling. A small dish of ground peanuts on the table makes a nice garnish to be sprinkled on the soup by each diner. The recipe will serve 4 to 6 people.

Pine Bark Stew

In the Carolinas and Georgia, where this spicy fish stew is best known, there are almost as many explanations for the name as there are ways to make it. One account says that the small, tender roots of the pine tree were used as a seasoning back in the eighteenth century. Another says the stew's color is like that of pine bark. Still another claims that pine bark was the principal wood in the fires over which the stew was cooked. The most improbable of all is that early backwoodsmen who got the dish from the Indians made it thick enough to be served on slabs of pine bark. Regardless of its origin, pine bark stew deserves to be more widely known and appreciated.

Cut 6 strips of bacon into small pieces and fry crisp over low heat in a large heavy pot. Drain bacon on paper towels and pour off all but about 3 tablespoons of the grease. Sauté 2 cups of diced potatoes in the pot and add 1 cup of minced onions when the potatoes are beginning to soften. Continue cooking and stirring until the onions are soft. Season to taste with salt, black pepper, cayenne pepper, and thyme. Place 2 pounds of seasoned freshwater fish fillets (bass, perch, trout, bream, or whatever) on top of the onion-potato mixture and cover with 4 to 5 cups of boiling water. Simmer for 30 minutes. Then add 1½ cups of peeled, cored, and chopped tomatoes (fresh or canned) and continue simmering for about 10 minutes more. Stir carefully, trying not to break the fish into small flakes. When the fish is tender, add the bacon bits and serve. There should be enough for 4 to 6 helpings.

She-Crab Soup

Along the low-country coast of South Carolina and Georgia, and especially in Charleston and Savannah, she-crab soup has long been considered a "home dish," belonging to this area the way burgoo belongs to Kentucky or gumbo to Louisiana. In its authentic and original form, she-crab soup gets its distinctive flavor from crab roe (eggs). When these are not available, cooks usually substitute crumbled hard-boiled egg yolks. This version draws upon several old and representative she-crab soup recipes from the Carolina-Georgia coastal region.

Crumble and set aside about ¼ cup of cooked crab roe (or the yolks of 3 hard-boiled eggs). In a heavy saucepan, melt 2 tablespoons of butter over low heat. Stir in 2 tablespoons of flour, blending until smooth. Gradually add 2 cups of milk and 2 cups of half-and-half or light cream, stirring constantly. Add 1 teaspoon of finely grated lemon rind, ⅛ teaspoon of mace, ⅛ teaspoon of black pepper, a dash of cayenne pepper, 5 or 6 drops of onion juice, ½ teaspoon of salt, and ½ teaspoon Worcestershire sauce. Cook over low heat, stirring occasionally, for about 20 minutes (don't let it boil). Stir in 2 cups of lump crab meat and bring to near boiling.

   To serve: Place a tablespoon of warmed sherry and some of the roe or crumbled yolk in each individual bowl and ladle soup over. Garnish with finely chopped fresh parsley and a sprinkle of paprika. Serves 6.

Spanish Bean Soup

The ancient and ubiquitous chick-pea or garbanzo bean, a tan, wrinkled, rock-hard pellet in dried form, swells and softens in water to make a tasty soup bean widely used in Hispanic cultures. Its most prevalent use in this country is in the Spanish-speaking communities of south Florida, where garbanzo- or Spanish-bean soup has been a staple for more than a century. This recipe is typical.

Cover ½ pound of garbanzos with salted water and soak overnight. Drain and wash beans and put them in a large pot with 2 quarts of water, a beef bone, and a ham bone. (A few small cubes of salt pork will add additional flavor.) Simmer over low heat, covered, for about 2 hours, or until beans begin to soften. Add 1 onion, chopped and sautéed, 2 cups of diced potatoes, a pinch of paprika, and a pinch of saffron. Season to taste with salt and continue simmering until potatoes and beans are quite soft. Serve in bowls with slices of Spanish chorizo sausage or pepperoni on top. Serves 4 to 6 people.

True southerners hold historical and cultural bonds to the heart, above geography; they remain southern wherever they are—New York, Chicago, Paris, London—and their food is part of their cultural identity. . . . In the South the history of the region is all pervasive and embraces the cuisine. Southern food is not just food cooked south of the Mason-Dixon line. It is a product of time and people as well as place. From 1607 to 1860, European, African, and native American cultures accepted and modified each other's agricultural, dietary, and social customs and molded them into a distinct regional cuisine. The cooking, like the society it reflected, was never homogeneous, but it was a synthesis of the major forces behind it. . . . Southern cooking is born of these three parents—European, African, and native American.

Bill Neal's Southern Cooking, 1985

Side Dishes

In 1931, the Florida Department of Agriculture issued a catalogue of more than fifty vegetables and an even greater number of fruits growing in that state. Some were tropical, of course, and thus could be found nowhere else in the South, but many others—probably a majority—were typically and pervasively Southern.

Now as then, Southerners grow practically every vegetable and fruit to be found anywhere in this country; in fact, hardly an example comes to mind of a food plant produced in the continental United States that does not grow somewhere in the South. California aside, the South is the nation's primary and perennial orchard grove and truck garden. (There have been times when the region failed to produce enough foodstuffs to feed its own people, but the failure was not due to geography or climate.)

The side dishes of the American table spill forth from this cornucopia of foods harvested from the earth. In Southern cooking, such support dishes have always been supremely important, adding variety and contrast to the primary offerings of meat and bread and easing the way to the multitude of sweets that follow and climax the meal. There is so much diversity, both in the raw materials and in the infinite ways of preparing them, that repetition need never become a problem.

To illustrate a little bit of this plentitude, we have chosen a small number of typically Southern side dishes to present in four categories: cheese and egg recipes, fruits, salads, and vegetables (including rice). In each group are only a relative handful of all the traditional dishes that could have been presented, but most of them are deeply rooted in Southern culinary history.

There is one side dish of special importance that defies categorization. It is cornbread dressing, an indispensable accompaniment to holiday turkey. Neither a fish nor a fowl nor a vegetable—nor even a bread, though its name implies it—this dressing is a singular dish, truly in a class by itself. To give it the prominence it deserves, we will begin with it.

Cornbread Dressing

There are many names for this venerable companion dish with roast turkey and chicken: turkey stuffing, onion dressing, cornmeal stuffing, bread dressing. It

Ruby came in the front door of the apartment building and lowered the paper sack with the four cans of number three beans in it onto the hall table. She was too tired to take her arms from around it or to straighten up and she hung there collapsed from the hips, her head balanced like a big florid vegetable at the top of the sack. She gazed with stony unrecognition at the face that confronted her in the dark yellow-spotted mirror over the table. Against her right cheek was a gritty collard leaf that had been stuck there half the way home. She gave it a vicious swipe with her arm

appears in a multitude of Southern cookbooks under Meat, Poultry, or Bread, but it is none of these. It is a highly seasoned mixture of crumbled cornbread (often with biscuits or light bread added), fortified with onions and a rich poultry broth, then either stuffed into the cavity of the bird or baked separately. (We prefer it as a separate dish, shaped into patties the size of eggs and baked to a crusty brown on a cookie sheet.) Lettice Bryan gave directions for making a turkey stuffing in her *Kentucky Housewife* in 1839. This particular recipe is not that old, but it does have a documented history of almost a century in Kentucky and Tennessee.

Mix together 1 cup of white cornmeal, 1 cup of flour, ³⁄₄ teaspoon of baking soda, 2 teaspoons of baking powder, 1¹⁄₂ teaspoons of salt, and ³⁄₄ teaspoon of black pepper. Stir in 1 beaten egg and add up to 1¹⁄₂ cups of buttermilk— just enough to give the mixture a thick, pouring consistency. Heat 2 table-spoons of bacon grease in a large black skillet; when smoking hot, pour the batter in and set on the bottom rack of a preheated 350° oven. Bake 5 minutes there, then move up to the middle rack for 15 or 20 minutes more, or until crispy brown. Turn out on a cake rack. When cold, crumble thoroughly in a large pan or bowl. Next, mince 1 medium-sized onion and 1 rib of celery and sauté in 2 tablespoons of bacon grease. When the vegetables are soft, add them to the cornbread crumbs and sprinkle in 1 teaspoon of poultry seasoning or sage (or more, to suit your taste). Moisten the mixture with broth (from the roaster or the giblets), making it just sticky enough to shape into patties. Taste and adjust seasonings if necessary. Spoon the dressing into the turkey's cavity to cook along with the bird, or shape it into about 20 small patties and bake at 350° until rich brown and crusty (20 to 30 minutes). Serve hot with the turkey and giblet gravy. For 4 or more holiday diners, a double recipe may be advisable.

and straightened, muttering, "Collards, collards," in a voice of sultry subdued wrath. . . . "Collard greens!" she said, spitting the word from her mouth this time as if it were a poisonous seed.

She and Bill Hill hadn't eaten collard greens for five years and she wasn't going to start cooking them now. She had bought these on account of Rufus but she wasn't going to buy them but once. You would have thought that after two years in the armed forces Rufus would have come back ready to eat like somebody from somewhere; but no. When she asked him what he would like to have special, he had not had the gumption to think of one civilized dish—he had said collard greens. She had expected Rufus to have turned out into somebody with some get in him. Well, he had about as much get as a floor mop.

Flannery O'Connor
"A Stroke of Good Fortune," 1949

CHEESE AND EGG DISHES

For as long as cows and chickens have belonged to the American farm animal population—which is to say virtually from the beginning of the colonial period—there have been cheese and egg dishes on the table. In many casseroles, soufflés, and sauces, both cheese and eggs are combined with other ingredients to make rich and creamy ensembles; at other times, either cheese or eggs are used singly to add color, flavor, or texture—or all three—to a diversity of meat, vegetable, and seafood dishes. Many of these combinations have appeared in

Southern cookbooks for well over a century. Cheese and other milk products were an uncommon luxury, particularly in the warmer climate of the South, until safe methods of preserving them were developed in the nineteenth century. Eggs, though, have enjoyed great and universal popularity, particularly at breakfast, since the 1600s. Lettice Bryan had sixteen egg recipes in her Kentucky cookbook a century and a half ago, and about half of them were omelets, soufflés, and fricassees.

A small sample of five recipes can only suggest the range of possibilities with these two basic foodstuffs. Our selections have both longevity and wide recognition in Southern kitchens.

Brains and Eggs

For generations, farm cooks considered it routine procedure to utilize virtually all parts of the animals they butchered for food. Not just livers and kidneys but hearts, lungs, and even intestines (chitterlings) were prized by many eaters as great delicacies, and it is not uncommon even now to find country kitchens in which these foods are greatly appreciated. In the South, one of the favorite historic and contemporary dishes of this sort is brains, especially when they are stewed and then scrambled with eggs. Recipes for cooking calf, pig, and lamb brains can be found in many old manuscript cookbooks and in some modern volumes as well. The combination of brains and eggs produces a rich, delicate flavor that is subtle and distinctive.

In the South . . . one of the delicacies especially regarded by the working classes (as well as the leisured classes) is scrambled brains and eggs. Hog brains are used, not calf brains. Fresh hog brains. They are not always easy to come by. They spoil quickly. One had to buy them at the slaughterhouse each morning early, and not every day was a day for slaughtering hogs. This fact was

Put ½ pound of brains in water to which 1 tablespoon of vinegar and 1 teaspoon of salt have been added, and refrigerate for 1 hour or more. Rinse in fresh water and carefully remove the membrane encasing each lobe. Put brains in a saucepan, barely cover with fresh water, and add ½ teaspoon of salt. Bring to a boil, lower heat, cover pan, and simmer for about 15 minutes. When the brains have taken on a creamy gray-white color and formed a soft mass, remove to drain in a colander. Then pour brains into a skillet containing 2 or 3 tablespoons of hot bacon grease, mash with a fork or spoon, and cook briefly before adding 4 large, lightly beaten eggs. Stir and scramble until cooked to your liking (soft and creamy or a little firmer), and serve on a heated platter with bacon slices. These proportions should serve 4 for breakfast. Salt, pepper, Worcestershire sauce, hot-pepper sauce, and other seasonings can be added during cooking.

Cheese Grits

Marjorie Kinnan Rawlings was eating cheese grits with regularity and pleasure when she wrote *Cross Creek Cookery* in 1942. Whoever first came up with the idea of adding sharp Cheddar cheese to this staple of Southern cookery got too little credit for the achievement, and now the cook's name is lost in history. The time probably was not long before Mrs. Rawlings first prepared the dish in Florida, though, because we could find no earlier recipe for it than hers. There is more about grits and hominy later (see page 302), but here the emphasis is on cheese and its transforming qualities. Over the past thirty years or so, cheese grits have become a breakfast and brunch favorite all over the South, even among many diners who profess not to like them plain. The standard recipe is widely published, and quite simple.

Stir 1 cup of quick (not instant) grits into 4 cups of briskly boiling water; reduce heat to simmer and cook for 3 or 4 minutes, stirring occasionally. When the mixture is no longer watery and is quite thick, remove from heat and add 1 stick of butter, 1 cup of grated Cheddar cheese, and, if you like, 2 cloves of garlic, minced fine. When the butter and cheese have melted and the mixture has cooled a bit, add 2 beaten eggs. Mix well. Pour into an oven-proof casserole and bake at 350° for about 30 minutes, or until firm and golden brown. This should be enough for 6 people.

Cheese Pudding

In practically every corner of the South, there are locally popular casseroles, puddings, and soufflés of long standing that have occasionally found a broader spotlight. The Wimsett family of Hodgenville, Kentucky, had one such recipe, an especially pleasing dish called cheese pudding, which they featured on the menu at the Lynn Hotel there in the 1920s and '30s. The hotel had closed when President Dwight D. Eisenhower came to visit Abraham Lincoln's nearby boyhood home in 1954, but cheese pudding was still a local favorite. It was served to Eisenhower at a luncheon in his honor, and he liked it so much that he asked for seconds—and the recipe. His pleasure was duly recorded in the press and thus in history, assuring Hodgenville cheese pudding a certain well-deserved permanence.

Prepare and set aside the following: 4 hard-boiled eggs, chopped or grated; 1 cup of crumbled soda crackers; 2 cups of grated Cheddar cheese; ¾ cup

not borne in mind by the brakemen, firemen, engineers and conductors who . . . constituted the bulk of the morning's patronage in the short-order restaurant over which my father presided. They wanted brains and eggs every morning. Some intuition flashed into my father's mind, one morning when he had an order for brains and eggs and there were no brains in the icebox, that boiled oatmeal (the same ordinarily used as a cereal) tasted, when properly salted and peppered, very much like scrambled hogs' brains. He scrambled his eggs, plopped in a saucer-ful of cooked oatmeal, mixed the two hurriedly, browning the latter slightly, and dished it out. His customer thought it was the best dish of brains and eggs he had ever eaten and promptly ordered another. Thereafter my father did not bother to go down to the slaughterhouse at five o'clock in the morning to get a day's mess of hog brains.

Burton Rascoe
Before I Forget, 1937

pimentos, diced and drained. Next, make 2 cups of a basic white sauce by melting 4 tablespoons of butter in a saucepan and blending in 4 tablespoons of flour, stirring over low heat until the mixture becomes a smooth paste; add 2 cups of milk or cream and 1/2 teaspoon of salt, and continue stirring until the sauce thickens. Then, into a greased casserole, put about 1/4 cup of sauce, a sprinkling of crumbled crackers, and successive layers of eggs, cheese, and pimentos. Repeat the sequence until all the ingredients are used, ending with a layer of cracker crumbs on top. Dot with bits of butter and bake at 350° for 30 minutes. Serve bubbling hot as a side dish at dinner or as the main attraction at a light supper. There should be enough for 4 people.

Hot Brown

A chef named Fred K. Schmidt is credited with the creation of the Hot Brown Sandwich at the Brown Hotel in Louisville in the 1930s. (He made a cold Brown too, but it never soared.) The hot Brown was so well-liked that it spread to other restaurants across Kentucky and beyond. It even outlasted the hotel itself (the Brown is now staging a comeback after being closed for a number of years). The hot Brown has long since become a fixture in many cookbooks and restaurants in the upper South. This variation includes elements from Chef Schmidt's original and numerous others we have enjoyed.

Make a basic white sauce as described in the preceding cheese pudding recipe and add to it 1/2 cup of grated Cheddar cheese. Season it with sprinklings of black and cayenne peppers. Toast 4 to 8 slices of commercial or homemade white bread—1 or 2 for each person to be served. Lay the toast pieces in a large, shallow baking dish or other suitable container. Top each piece with a thin slice of turkey or chicken, a generous spreading of sauce, a slice of country ham or pieces of cooked bacon, a large slice of fresh tomato, more cheese sauce to cover it all, and a sprinkling of Parmesan cheese or paprika (or both). Bake in a 350° oven for 20 minutes, then turn up to broil just long enough to make the sandwiches bubbling hot and golden brown on top. Serve straight from the oven with a salad and something cold to drink. One hot Brown per person makes a satisfying supper; two make a heavy meal.

It's hard to know how to classify a hot Brown in a collection of recipes. It's a sandwich, but not the handholding kind; with turkey and ham, it's also quite definitely a meat dish; and it's a casserole of sorts. We finally chose to put it here with cheese dishes because of the Cheddar and the Parmesan, both of which give the crowning touch to a flavorful and distinctive combination.

FRUIT DISHES

Apples from the highlands of northern Virginia, citrus from the southernmost reaches of Florida, and all manner of melons, berries, and tree-ripened flavors in between—these are the featured fruits of the South, and have been for centuries. A major share of the nation's leading commercial fruits, including oranges, grapefruit, peaches, and watermelons, comes from the region; so do several less common kinds of cultivated and wild-growing fruits, among them persimmons, guavas, mangoes, muscadines, and papayas. A few varieties of figs, plums, and cherries are considered backyard treasures by some Southerners, but like persimmons, virtually no one in the region produces them commercially. (A larger variety of cultivated persimmons can sometimes be found in supermarkets.)

The first Europeans to explore the southern part of North America found the Indians to be fond of persimmons, a peculiar little walnut-sized tree fruit that stays bitter right up to the time it fully ripens in the fall sun and turns suddenly soft and sweet. Figs were brought in by the Spanish over four hundred years ago. California is the only state to cultivate and market them in large quantities, but there are people in the coastal areas of South Carolina, Georgia, and Florida who insist that nothing is tastier than a bowl of freshly peeled figs with cream.

Virtually all of the fruits that Southerners and other Americans enjoy, with the exception of bananas and pineapples, can be found growing somewhere in the region. For various reasons, fruits don't lend themselves to cooking as readily as vegetables do (probably more of them are served in salads than as side dishes), but there are a few favorites of long standing that often appear on Southern tables along with the meats and seafoods and vegetables. Five familiar recipes make up our short but representative sample of fruit side dishes.

Ambrosia

For well over a century, Southerners have reveled in this delicious dish featuring oranges and coconut. The name is from Greek and Roman mythology and means "food of the gods." Far from being celestial, though, ambrosia is a down-to-earth dish of great simplicity. It makes a nice light dessert after a heavy holiday dinner, but more often is served as a side dish with the dinner itself. Some recipes call for sliced bananas or pineapple or such colorful fruits as strawberries, blackberries, or cherries, but the oldest and simplest combination is still the best and most common.

Remove the skin and membranes from 6 large seedless oranges and either grate enough fresh coconut to make 2 cups or substitute that amount of frozen, packaged, or canned coconut. Place a layer of orange pieces in the bottom of a glass bowl, add a layer of coconut, and repeat the process until all the fruit and coconut have been used. (If the oranges are not especially sweet, a light sprinkling of powdered sugar on each layer will help.) Cover the bowl tightly and refrigerate it for an hour or more before serving. This amount should make ample servings for 6 people.

Apples (Fried)

Cooked apples have long been a popular dish in many parts of the United States, and Southerners seem to like them at any meal. A Shaker recipe from Pleasant Hill, Kentucky, makes a dinner-table side dish of tart apples peeled and cut into wedges and cooked in a skillet with butter, sugar, a dash of cinnamon, and a squeeze of lemon juice. A somewhat different dish is fried apples, a long-time favorite at the Southern breakfast table.

Core 6 to 8 firm, tart, green apples and slice them into bite-sized pieces, skins on. Heat 2 or 3 tablespoons of bacon grease in a skillet and add the apples. Cook uncovered, stirring frequently and sprinkling in enough white or brown sugar to suit your taste. When the apples are done (some like them mushy and shapeless, others prefer them firm), serve hot with bacon or sausage, biscuits, and coffee.

Melon Fruit Bowl

It would be hard to imagine a prettier showcase of Southern fruits than this: a scooped-out watermelon filled with cut-up peaches, cantaloupe, honeydew melon, apples, strawberries, blackberries, blueberries, cherries, figs, mangoes, and the watermelon itself. Oranges and bananas and grapes can go into it too—in fact, practically any fruit is a welcome addition. Flossie Morris called it a watermelon fruit basket in her *Unusual Cookbook*, and it's perfect for an outdoor picnic or dinner party. A striped melon about 18 inches long is a worthy symbol of the best in Southern fruits; it's also big enough to provide abundantly for a dozen or more people.

Slice off the upper third of the melon and scallop the edges of the larger piece with a knife. Carefully scoop it out with a melon baller or a spoon, discarding the seeds and putting the red fruit in another bowl. Assemble all the other fruits you plan to use. When everything is properly peeled, seeded, and cut up, mix thoroughly and refill the empty melon shell. Cover and refrigerate until serving time. On a large oval platter or serving dish, the overflowing melon, garnished with sprigs of mint, presents a feast of flavors and a kaleidoscope of colors.

Peach Compote

On many a Southern country dinner table, hot fruit compote has long been a familiar side dish. Never mind that it closely resembles fruit dumplings and cobblers, and could easily serve as dessert; when it comes to the table with the beans and peas and potatoes, you can be sure that it's no mistake—and there will be pies or other sweets later. The venerable peach, a distinctive Southern fruit if there ever was one, makes a better hot side dish than most people realize. Many Southern cookbooks, including *The Peach Sampler*, by Eliza Mears Horton of Lexington, South Carolina, contain a variety of compote recipes. This version is representative of the multitude.

Peel, halve, and remove seeds from 4 large freestone peaches (or use canned peaches if fresh aren't available). Slice 1 or 2 peeled oranges into rounds about ¼ inch thick, cut these in half, and place them like fan-shaped partitions between the peaches. Mix ½ cup of orange juice, ¼ cup of firmly packed brown sugar, and ½ teaspoon of grated lemon rind, and pour this mixture over the fruit. Cut up 2 tablespoons of butter and dot it over the peaches. (The addition of ½ cup of shredded coconut sprinkled over the whole is optional.) Bake in a preheated 425° oven for 15 to 20 minutes, or until the dish juices are bubbling hot. Serves 4.

It takes four ingredients—the right seed, the right soil, the right climate, and the know-how. If you've got all that—and then if you grow it right around Hope, Arkansas—you've got yourself a devil of a big watermelon. We're accused a lot of times of talking big about these melons, but it's the truth, more or less. This year it rained a whole lot, and the vines started growing too fast, and the only way to protect those big melons was to put a roller skate under them to keep the vine from dragging them to death. I'm telling you, boy, they're big—100 pounds apiece, or even bigger. We've shipped these seeds all over the country, but I've never heard of anyone to produce really big melons from them anywhere else but here. What we've got here is the Hope diamond of watermelons.

C. M. "Pod" Rogers,
Hope, Arkansas, 1974

. . . . . .

Ten-year-old Jason Bright established a new world record in 1985 when he grew a 260-pound watermelon on his grandfather's farm near Hope. The melon was 46 inches long.

SALADS

Mary Randolph was a woman ahead of her time; along with the many other innovations she brought to Southern (and American) cookery through *The Virginia House-Wife* in 1824, she gave us a lucid treatise on garden salad. Not until a century later did salads like hers finally become a regular element of the American diet. Now, of course, salads are an important and highly visible part of what we eat. If Mary Randolph were around today, she probably would feel right at home with the restaurant salad bars that have swept the nation in the past decade or so.

Our salads come from everywhere. We can thank the Germans for potato salad and the Italians for popularizing tomatoes as a salad headliner. The Greeks brought us a wonderful combination salad of greens with feta cheese and anchovies, the Scandinavians introduced us to the smorgasbord with its open-face sandwiches and cold meat and vegetable salads, and from Mexico we have received such exotic salad ingredients as avocados and mangoes. Closer to home, a maître d' at the Waldorf-Astoria in New York nearly a hundred years ago gave us the combination of apples, celery, and mayonnaise we call Waldorf salad. (The nuts and raisins came later.)

Congealed or molded salads, usually made with gelatin, have been popular for most of this century, with fruit as a common addition, and the South often has led the way in developing new combinations. Meat, vegetable, and fruit salads abound in the South now, embracing seafood and poultry, the entire run of garden harvests, and the fruits and nuts of every season. Indeed, a modern cookbook from the region without twenty or thirty pages of salads and salad dressings is not keeping up with the times. In the next few pages, we present a handful of traditional and representative Southern salads, some of the basic cold side dishes from which today's great variety flows.

Cole Slaw

Lettice Bryan, an aptly named pioneer of American cookery, deserves more credit than she has yet received for her many contributions to the style and content of modern food service in this country. Among the many features of her *Kentucky Housewife*, published in 1839, were her recipes for "cold slaugh" and "warm slaugh," which were her interpretations of a dish of Dutch origin (*kool sla*, or cabbage salad). *Cole* is the old English word for cabbage, and that is the spelling we use today. The dish itself is still frequently made the same way Lettice Bryan did it: with crisp shavings of raw cabbage, salt and pepper, and

The ridge [near Campbellsville, Kentucky] has provided me with some very good dishes indeed. Dry land creases, for instance . . . a small, flat plant growing close to the ground, with leaves very similar to our water cress. Creases? Cress, of course. . . . They are the first greens to appear in the spring. . . . We have dry land creases sometimes when there is still snow on the north side of the house.

You know about poke sallet of course. . . . Poke is one of my favorite greens. . . . I usually mix it with wild mustard, lamb's-quarters, or dandelions. I avoid dock, for it has a coarse, rough texture, and I don't like to spoil the delicacy of poke with it.

We also have dry land fish. Mushrooms to you. But they are not the familiar mushroom of the city market. They are a big, oval, porous

lots of cider vinegar. Creamy cole slaw is quite different, but also very popular in the South, especially as a side dish with fried fish and hush puppies. The old-fashioned Southern way of making it requires a cooked or boiled dressing such as this tangy-sweet one.

Combine 2 scant tablespoons of sugar, ½ teaspoon of dry mustard, ½ teaspoon of salt, ⅛ teaspoon of cayenne pepper, and ½ teaspoon of celery seed in the top of a double boiler and mix with it 6 tablespoons of cider vinegar. Add ½ cup of sour cream, 1 teaspoon of onion juice, and 1 tablespoon of melted butter. Beat 1 egg lightly and mix it well with the other ingredients. Cook over gently boiling water, stirring frequently, for 10 to 15 minutes, or until dressing thickens. Chill in refrigerator.

Meanwhile, prepare 4 cups of finely grated raw cabbage (or, if you prefer, 3½ cups of cabbage and ½ cup of grated carrot, onion, and green bell pepper). Pour the dressing over the slaw, toss with a spoon to combine thoroughly, and serve cold. This amount should be enough for 4 people.

Congealed Fruit Salad

Southerners have come up with some unusual combinations in the fruit salad department—grapefruit and avocado, for example, and peanut butter on bananas, or a dressing of mayonnaise and chopped pecans on bananas. At Allen's Cafe in Auburndale, Florida, one of the featured dishes is Green's salad, named for its long-ago originator; the ingredients are grapes and avocado chunks coated with a mixture of mayonnaise, sour cream, and chopped pecans.

One of the most popular of Southern salads is congealed fruit. Natural gelatins made from calves' feet and other animal and fish parts have been around for a long time, but it took electricity and refrigeration in the early decades of this century to create the demand that resulted in quick and easy powdered commercial gelatin. This fifty-year-old recipe from Florida combines gelatin, lime juice, and pieces of fruit to produce an intense and delightful taste.

Empty a 1-tablespoon packet of unflavored gelatin into a bowl, soften with 3 tablespoons of cold water, and dissolve in 1 cup of boiling water. Add ½ cup of fresh lime juice, ½ cup of sugar, and ¼ teaspoon of salt. Stir well and place in refrigerator.

Meanwhile, chill a 3- or 4-cup ring mold. Prepare 2 or 3 cups of fresh fruit balls or chunks (seeded grapes, melons, papayas, or whatever). Mix the fruit with the partially firm gelatin. Rinse the mold with cold water (to help

plant, brown on top and pearly pink beneath. Henry tells me their botanical name is the common morel. . . . They do have a slightly fishy taste. I think it is actually more of a fish texture than a taste. The crisp, brown outside may be flaked off, leaving a mealy white meat, but if you're wise you'll pop the whole thing in your mouth, chew twice, and then reach for another one!

Janice Holt Giles
40 Acres and No Mule, 1952

prevent sticking) and then pour the gelatin and fruit mixture into the mold. Chill until completely firm (2 to 4 hours). Serve on lettuce with a topping of homemade mayonnaise.

Gazpacho Salad

Columbus introduced lettuce to the New World, and Thomas Jefferson considered it one of the prize vegetables in his great garden, but not until well into this century did Americans generally take a liking to it. Now, lettuce and all the other garden vegetables so prominent in salads—celery, carrots, cucumbers, tomatoes, radishes, onions, green peppers—are consumed in huge quantities; annual consumption of lettuce in the nation exceeds twenty-five pounds per person. There are several varieties of leaf and head lettuce that make up what is commonly called garden lettuce in the South. One variety, Bibb lettuce, was developed in Frankfort, Kentucky, well over a century ago by an amateur horticulturist named John Bibb.

Long before lettuce was common in Southern gardens, people in the region enjoyed a salad of Spanish origin called gaspacha (or gaspachee, or gazpacho), a tomato-onion-cucumber combination. (There is also a popular cold soup called gazpacho, and the ingredients are similar.) Around Pensacola, Florida, and Mobile, Alabama, where Spanish influences are four centuries old, the salad is commonly called gaspachee, and it is made with hardtack (sea biscuit). The Premier Bakery in Pensacola must surely be one of the few establishments still baking hardtack anywhere in the world—and the sole reason is to supply gaspachee makers. This is an old Pensacola recipe for the salad.

Soak 2 hardtack biscuits in cold water for 6 hours and drain the gooey mass in a colander and squeeze the water out. Spread a ½-inch layer of the softened bread in the bottom of a large bowl. (Toasted cubes of bread or breadcrumbs can be substituted.) Cover with a thin layer of mayonnaise and a little salt. Then add a layer of peeled tomato slices. Repeat the sequence, substituting peeled cucumber slices and minced onion for the tomato. Add hardtack, mayonnaise, and salt once more, garnish with green bell pepper rings and paprika, and refrigerate the salad for several hours to let the flavors blend. Serve it chilled to 4 diners.

Hearts of Palm Salad

The sabal or cabbage palm is the state tree of Florida. Centuries ago, the Seminole Indians discovered that the bud or new growth in the top of a young sabal palm was tender and delicious, and they made it a part of their diet. The white settlers who later came to the area also learned to like the delicacy. They called it swamp cabbage or hearts of palm, and they devoured it with such relish that the sabal palm itself finally had to be declared a protected species. Only under certain tightly restricted conditions can swamp cabbage be harvested in Florida now, but the memory of its goodness is so durable that the people of LaBelle in the south-central region still celebrate it at the annual Swamp Cabbage Festival, and gourmet stores do a brisk business in canned hearts of palm imported from South America.

The flavor of hearts of palm is somewhat reminiscent of asparagus. It can be cooked and served as a side dish, presented cold as an appetizer, or combined with other ingredients to make a salad. A 14-ounce can, drained of its juice, will make 2 large salads, and with the addition of other vegetables may be adequate for 4.

On a bed of lettuce, arrange hearts of palm with sliced tomatoes, green bell pepper rings, pitted black olives, and hard-boiled egg slices. Top with mayonnaise or a vinaigrette dressing. Season to taste with salt and pepper and serve chilled.

Shrimp Remoulade

Seafood salads are considered by many Southerners to be the top of the line in cold dishes, with shrimp and crab being the prime favorites. In Mobile, Alabama, restaurant owner William Bayley, a one-time seaman and port steward, introduced a specialty called West Indies salad back in the 1940s, and it has long since become a regular feature on menus all over the Mobile area. In essence, West Indies salad is fresh lump crab meat marinated in oil and vinegar and served chilled on a bed of lettuce.

In Louisiana, perhaps the most popular of all seafood salads is shrimp remoulade. Practically every New Orleans cookbook has at least one recipe for this spicy treat—and like most Louisiana dishes, the versions are all different, and all delicious. One of our favorites is Pleasant Hill Remoulade; it was first printed in the *Melrose Plantation Cookbook*, by François Mignon and Clemen-

TO DRESS SALAD

Boil two fresh eggs ten minutes, put them in water to cool, then take the yolks in a soup plate, pour on them a table spoonful of cold water, rub them with a wooden spoon until they are perfectly dissolved, then add two table spoonfuls of oil; when well mixed, put in a teaspoonful of salt, one of powdered sugar, and one of made mustard; when all these are united and quite smooth, stir in two table spoonfuls of common, and two of tarragon vinegar; put it over the salad, and garnish the top with the whites of the eggs cut into rings, and lay around the edge of the bowl young scallions, they being the most delicate of the onion tribe.

Mary Randolph
The Virginia House-Wife, 1824

tine Hunter, published in Natchitoches, Louisiana, in 1956. Mignon, a Frenchman, was a more or less permanent guest at Melrose, and Mrs. Hunter, the resident cook, was a skillful artist at both the cookstove and the canvas. Her primitive paintings were featured in *Look* magazine in 1954 and at the Delgado Museum in New Orleans the following year; her recipes, a distinctive blend of French and Creole, soul and Southern, were gathered by Mignon in their charming little book. This recipe, inspired by Mrs. Hunter's remoulade creation, is our addition to the scores of others for shrimp remoulade.

> Boil, peel, and chill 1 pound of fresh shrimp. Boil 4 eggs until hard. Mash the yolks into a smooth paste with 1 teaspoon of prepared French or Creole mustard. Add 1 teaspoon of finely minced onion, 1 teaspoon of finely minced celery, 1 teaspoon of fresh lemon juice, 1/4 teaspoon of white pepper, 1/8 teaspoon of cayenne pepper, 4 tablespoons of heavy cream, and salt to taste. Stir well until all ingredients are smoothly blended. Add just enough wine vinegar (1 or 2 teaspoons should do) to leave the sauce thick and creamy, not runny. Let it stand at room temperature for an hour or so. When the flavors are well-united, divide the cold shrimp among 4 salad plates lined with lettuce and spoon the sauce over each.

VEGETABLES AND RICE DISHES

Some of the most positive impressions of Southern cooking—and at the same time, some of the most negative—come into sharp focus on vegetables. Green beans cooked with ham hock or salt pork, for example, are either the tenderest, tastiest, most satisfying of all garden vegetables, as any pole-bean lover will tell you, or the flabbiest, greasiest, and most overcooked, in the opinion of unappreciative critics.

Without question, the traditional Southern way of cooking most vegetables leans to the heavy; bacon grease and chunks of seasoning meat have been used extensively, and so have some other ingredients now thought to be unhealthy, such as salt, sugar, butter, and cream. In the contemporary trend to lighter foods, the tendency is to reduce these seasonings drastically, or even to eliminate them altogether. But there are sound reasons of taste and nourishment, as well as history, for retaining some of the old culinary ways. It should be possible for most people who so desire to reduce the amount of heavy seasonings and to cook less and eat less in the old style without resorting to the total elimination of Southern-cooked vegetables from the diet. It is worth remembering that

Nashville is the turnip-greens and hog-jowl center of the universe. These two were used in fitting combination in Nashville by 1810, and the townspeople's appetite for them has not waned. It is likely that at first they were boiled too long, wasting some of their better parts. Then a home-economics fad for semi-rawness came in and took some of

the culinary winds of change blow constantly, but not always in the same direction.

Living as they have so close to the gardens and fields, Southerners have maintained a fondness for vegetables through good times and bad. Beans and peas, cabbage and corn, grits and greens, potatoes and tomatoes and onions have often been as basic as bread and water and more important than meat to the survival and well-being of people in the region. Pots of white beans or cabbage or turnip greens or collards or Irish potatoes have been known to provide many a poor family with its main source of nutrition for days and weeks on end—and multitudes of the less desperate have devoured them too, not simply because they were available and nutritious, but because they were also tasty and filling. More often than not, it has been good taste rather than hard necessity that has compelled the people of the region to eat large quantities of Southern-style vegetables.

To underscore the importance of vegetables in the Southern diet down through the years, we have gathered a sample of about twenty familiar old recipes. (The list includes rice and grits, which are sometimes classified as grains or cereals.) Our emphasis, as it has been throughout the book, is on the traditional and historical dimensions of Southern cooking.

BEANS AND PEAS

There are at least a dozen varieties of beans and peas common to the South, and it is often difficult to keep them sorted out, or even to separate the beans from the peas. We won't attempt such a division here; our beans and peas are together in the same pod. The names are far more numerous than the ways of cooking them. There are pole beans and string beans and green beans, field beans and shucky beans and leather britches, red and black and white beans, navy beans and great northerns, lima beans and butter beans, October beans and cornfield beans and horticulture beans—and some of these are different names for the same basic vegetable. There are also June peas and English peas and sweet peas, cowpeas and stock peas and black-eyed peas, field peas and pigeon peas and lady peas, crowder peas and chick-peas and purple-hull peas, and no doubt others. Beans and peas are not only various but abundant and accessible; most of them can be purchased frozen, dried, canned, or fresh (in season), or grown in the garden. They have been a cheap, nourishing, filling staple on the Southern table for generations, but rarely have they worn out their welcome. Southerners seem to love beans now as much as ever.

our cooks captive. But we got over that. Now we are cooking the greens just about right. Turnip greens, well selected and cooked with carefully chosen hog jowl, served with corn bread and liberal portions of butter and ample glasses of buttermilk, will leave the average citizen of Nashville in a state of uplift. Nowhere are pole beans, cooked with ham hock, better done or held in higher esteem than right here. The beans preferably should be of the Kentucky Wonder variety. The ham hock will take longer to cook, so it is to be boiled awhile before the beans are dropped into the pot. But the beans, no less than the turnip greens, must be thoroughly cooked. One who prefers the other kind would do well to move across the rivers, and so escape the tempest in beans-and-greens pots stirred up by home economists who got their training north of the rivers.

Alfred Leland Crabb
Nashville: Personality of a City, 1960

Early June peas cooked in water with small new potatoes make a rare and delicious side dish to welcome summer, and cowpeas or black-eyed peas cooked with a piece of ham hock or a chunk of cured bacon are a traditional New Year's Day good-luck dish. In the months between, all of the varieties of beans and peas make their appearance, and one or more of them can be counted on to show up daily on many Southern tables. Recipes for two classic dishes of beans and peas are presented below.

Green Beans

Anyone who has lived within driving distance of a garden row of Kentucky Wonder pole beans knows that they have no peer; by virtually unanimous acclamation, this variety has exceeded all others in popularity for decades. For maximum taste, there is only one basic way to cook them: very slowly, in a black pot or skillet, with a ration of cured pork or bacon grease added to enhance the flavor. Beans picked early in the morning, snapped and stringed, and washed in cold water will bring the best results. One pound of beans off the vine (or from the grocery) will yield about three cups in the pot. There are two variations on the primary cooking method.

The first method is to simmer a 2-inch cube of salt pork or a small piece of country ham hock in a deep, covered pot or skillet with 4 cups of water for 1 hour or more. Put in 1 pound of beans, snapped and stringed, and cook them covered over low heat for 3 to 4 hours. Stir occasionally, and add water if the beans become dry. Add 1 teaspoon of salt, or more if needed (though the pork may provide enough).

The other method is to put 2 tablespoons of bacon grease in a heavy iron skillet over medium heat. When the grease is hot, put in the beans, stirring until the grease is well distributed. Reduce heat to simmer, put a tight-fitting lid on the skillet, and cook the beans slowly for 3 hours or so. They must be stirred frequently at first to keep them from sticking, and it may be necessary to add a little water now and then, but condensation in the closed pot should provide most of the moisture needed. Add salt if necessary.

One pound of beans will produce 4 ample servings.

Some cooks add a little sugar or a pod of red pepper or an onion to the pot when cooking green beans, but none of these is essential; the basic beans, with pork seasoning and salt, require nothing else. Whatever the additions, if any, this dish is known throughout the South as a mess of beans. Properly cooked, they are generally considered to be the most popular dinner-table side dish in the region.

Black-Eyed Peas

Ranking close behind green beans in popularity are black-eyed peas, also known as cowpeas. African in origin, they have been a staple in the Southern diet for more than three centuries. Sometimes served with rice (see hoppin John, page 308), black-eyes are often associated with a mystical and mythical power to bring good luck, and many a Southern New Year's Day menu features the dish in one form or another. Two pounds of peas in the pod will yield about one pound, or two cups, when shelled; 1 pound of dried peas also equals about two cups (uncooked). Dried peas should be soaked in water overnight, after which they are cooked the same as fresh ones. Crowder peas, field peas, and most other fresh peas are best cooked in this same basic way.

In a large pot, cover 2 cups of peas with cold water, put in a small piece of seasoning meat (hog jowl, ham hock, salt pork), and bring the pot to a boil. Reduce heat to simmer and cook covered for about 2 hours, stirring occasionally. (Fresh peas require much less cooking time than dried peas—30 to 45 minutes—but the method is the same. Season to taste with salt, pepper, quartered onion pieces, and a pod of red pepper—any or all of these. The aim of slow cooking is tenderness, not disintegration; be sure the peas keep their shape and do not become a mushy puree. If they seem too dry, add a little hot water. Whether served as a side dish or in individual bowls, black-eyed peas call for some kind of cornbread. Two cups of peas should produce 4 large servings.

Cabbage (Scalloped)

Cabbage is another primary Southern staple, as common in many parts of the region as beans, peas, potatoes, and corn. The basic cooking methods are essentially two: shredded and fried in a skillet with bacon grease or a piece of salt pork; or cut into wedges and boiled in a pot of water. (The latter method produces a fine pot likker, especially if the cabbage has been seasoned with salt and pepper and a piece of pork.)

Whenever a staple is taken out of its everyday role and given a richer appearance and taste, it becomes a sort of Cinderella vegetable. Cabbage, thus elevated, becomes "company" cabbage, or scalloped cabbage, a golden, bubbling-hot casserole transformed by milk and cheese and breadcrumbs.

Chop ½ of a medium-sized cabbage into small chunks, put in a pan with just enough water to cover the bottom, and boil with lid on for about 5 minutes. As soon as the leaves are barely limp, drain and distribute in an oven-proof casserole. Make a standard white sauce by melting 2 tablespoons of butter in a pan and sprinkling in 2 tablespoons of flour, stirring constantly. Slowly add 1 cup of sweet milk to the pan and continue stirring over medium heat until the sauce is creamy and somewhat thickened. Remove from heat and add 1 cup of grated Cheddar cheese, blending thoroughly until the cheese is melted. Pour the sauce over the cabbage, sprinkle ½ cup of breadcrumbs on top, dot with butter, and bake in a preheated 350° oven for 20 minutes, or until the casserole is lightly browned and bubbly. The recipe provides 4 to 6 servings.

CORN

Here is our final tribute to the mighty giant of the Southern garden, the grain that sustained our ancestors. It has continued to carry far more than its share of the gastronomic load, providing bread, drinks, and sweets, as well as side dishes—and even meat, in an indirect way, since it is also a primary feed for cattle, hogs, and poultry. Nothing is as versatile as corn, or as valuable; if it disappeared tomorrow, every dimension of the Southern diet would be adversely affected.

As a side dish, corn can be fried, boiled, stewed, or roasted; made into crisp fritters; or baked in a creamy pudding. It can also be combined well with other vegetables, notably tomatoes and okra. The oldest cooking method, roasting, was the standard way of the Indians all along the Atlantic Seaboard four hundred years ago. Boiling has almost completely replaced roasting now, but Southerners still call corn on the cob by its ancient name: roasting ears.

The proper way to boil corn on the cob is to bring a large pot of water to a rolling boil, reduce the heat to simmer, and cook the corn for about 10 minutes. If the ears are placed in the bottom of the pot and boiling water is poured over them, they will stay submerged and cook more evenly, but it may be more practical to drop the ears into the boiling pot. Either way, 10 minutes should be enough to make green corn tender. (Green corn is the common term for young ears with soft, juicy kernels; when these harden, the grain is called mature.)

Someone once referred to fresh corn as the most immediate of all vegetables, meaning that its peak of flavor is reached the instant it is pulled from the stalk, and the quality diminishes steadily from that moment on. People who know and understand the chemistry of corn assert that about 90 percent of its natural sugar turns to starch within an hour or two of picking. True or not, there are corn purists who swear that they don't even like to gather it until someone hollers from the kitchen that the water is boiling. Others find it acceptable (though barely) to pull the ears early in the morning, remove the shucks and silks, and refrigerate them until they can be boiled for a midday meal.

Silver Queen, a relatively new hybrid, is now the preferred variety of a majority of Southerners. A sweet and tender white corn, it matures in the mid-South around the first of July, and if the weather cooperates and the patch is big enough, it may remain in season for almost a month. The early American Indians and colonists surely would have found it to be a superlative grain.

In addition to corn on the cob, we offer recipes for corn fritters (light, puffy, deep-fried); fried corn (some call it creamed); and the historic roasting ears.

Corn Fritters

Cut 1½ cups of fresh corn from the cob (or use an equal measure of whole-kernel canned corn, drained). Sift together 1 cup of flour, 1 scant teaspoon of salt, and 1 teaspoon of baking powder. Beat 1 egg with ½ cup of milk. Combine the milk and egg with the dry ingredients, mixing just enough to moisten. Lightly stir in the corn. (Too much mixing and stirring flattens the batter). Drop tablespoons of the batter into deep fat heated to medium hot or sizzling, about 375°, and cook like hush puppies for about 3 minutes, or until golden brown. Drain on absorbent paper and keep warm in 150° oven until ready to serve. This recipe should make 18 to 20 fritters.

Fried Corn

Cut the grains from 6 fresh ears with a sharp knife and scrape the cobs to get all the milky liquid. Heat 2 tablespoons of bacon grease or butter in a black

It's roastin'-ear time in the hills. And for folks who like their corn on the cob, these are mouth-watering days. . . . Out in the country there's the sweet perfume of corn in the early August air. . . . The Cherokee Indians knew August as the month of the Greencorn Moon. They celebrated the ripening of corn in dance and festival. To mountain folks, August is roastin'-ear time, albeit corn is seldom roasted any more. As Fannie Hensley observed . . . it's common to hear folks talk about having a mess of roastin' ears. "But they don't roast 'em," Mrs. Hensley said. "They boil 'em. Now, way back yonder, we roasted 'em. Roasted 'em in the shuck in the fireplace."

. . . . . .

There's nothing quite like the fresh sweet smell of roastin' ears. To know this is to step into the kitchen when a pot of sweet corn is finishing its six minutes of boiling. . . . Corn-on-the-cob loses its sweetness if it isn't cooked right after it's picked. The fresher it is the better. And it must be eaten steaming hot with a lavish of butter.

John Parris
Mountain Cooking, 1978

iron skillet, and when it is moderately hot, add the corn. Simmer until tender, stirring frequently. (A small amount of hot water may be needed to keep the corn from sticking.) Season to taste with salt and pepper. Total cooking time should be 10 to 15 minutes, depending on the freshness of the corn. This amount should make 4 to 6 servings.

Roasting Ears

Pull the shucks back from each ear of green corn and remove the silks. Close the shucks again over the grain and secure them firmly with a wire twist-tie. Immerse the ears in cold water for several minutes, letting the shucks get thoroughly soaked. Shake off excess water and then bury the corn in the hot ashes and coals of a fireplace or charcoal grill or campfire and leave for about 1 hour, rotating 3 or 4 times to assure an even distribution of heat. Remove and test one ear for doneness. When the grains are tender, remove the shucks, apply butter and salt, and enjoy a historic roasting ear the likes of which Powhatan may have shared with Captain John Smith.

Eggplant

Thomas Jefferson grew eggplant experimentally in his Virginia garden, and others before (in Asia and Europe) and since (in the Middle East) have prized it, but it has never been a leading vegetable in this country. Even so, cooks in several Southern states have taken a liking to the peculiar-looking purple fruit of the vine. Many eggplant lovers prefer it dredged in cornmeal or flour and fried, but the dish that has won more renown is an eggplant casserole. In a dish with cheese, eggs, onions, and spicy seasonings, it is a Creole and Southern delight. This recipe is fairly typical of numerous others.

Peel and cut up 2 medium-sized eggplants and drop the pieces into a pot of cold water. Drain water from the pot and add ½ cup of fresh water, ½ teaspoon of salt, and 1 bay leaf. Cover and cook over medium heat for about 15 minutes, or until the eggplant is tender. Fry 3 slices of bacon and set aside. Sauté ½ cup of minced green onions in 2 tablespoons of the bacon grease.

Drain the cooked eggplant in a colander and discard the bay leaf. In a greased casserole, combine eggplant, onions, and crumbled bacon. Season

I hated turnip greens when I was a child, but they were a staple for the family. My grandfather grew them in his garden and used to make me help pick them, which was like making the guest of honor at a hanging help build the gallows. . . . Now that I'm older and forced to eat modern foods, however, I enjoy the

to taste with salt and pepper, and stir in 1 teaspoon of freshly minced parsley. Top the casserole with 2 or 3 tablespoons of freshly grated Parmesan cheese, ¼ to ½ cup of breadcrumbs, and about 2 tablespoons of butter cut into small pieces. Bake in a preheated 350° oven for 30 to 40 minutes. Serve when crispy brown and hot. This casserole will provide 4 servings.

Greens

There are more varieties of wild and cultivated greens in the South than most people realize—turnip and collard greens, mustard and dandelion greens, poke sallet, spinach, kale, lamb's quarters, dock, rape, chard, beet greens, watercress, creases, crow's toes, and no doubt others. In the Appalachian and Ozark mountain regions, the early spring harvesting of wild greens is a ritual that goes back to the beginning of white settlement, and probably to the Indians who preceded the Europeans.

Turnip greens (not the same as turnip tops, which many people also eat) are the most common of these leafy vegetables in the upper South, while collard greens are more prevalent in the lower tier of states. For both—in fact, for all greens—the traditional cooking method is essentially the same, the only real difference being how long they are boiled. This is the most common way to prepare a mess of turnip greens.

Thoroughly wash 2 pounds of fresh greens, trim off the stalks, and immerse the leaves a few at a time in one and a half gallons of boiling water, to which has been added a quarter-pound piece of seasoning meat (ham hock or salt pork). Stir in 1 tablespoon of salt (more if needed). Cover the pot and simmer for 1 hour or more, or until the greens are tender. As with cabbage or beans, additional seasonings such as onions and red pepper pods may be put into the pot. This amount of greens will boil down from a large mass to a more manageable amount—about enough to serve 4 people.

Some of the more exotic greens, such as crow's toes or creases (also spelled creeces), a tender upland shoot similar to watercress, are known only to experienced gatherers of edible wild plants. More familiar is poke sallet, a tall, leafy green plant about which songs have been written. Now, a vegetable canning company in Arkansas is trying to gather enough wild poke to add it to its line of products. The young, tender leaves of the poke weed have a mild flavor similar to spinach, but the more mature leaves are strong and unappealing, and the berries and roots of the plant are poisonous. No one has yet discovered how to

occasional turnip greens that I get. My Aunt Jessie makes them for me when I visit her. Recently, Aunt Jessie had a sort of family reunion at her house, and she cooked a huge pot of turnip greens. As I was saying how tasty they were, Aunt Jessie's daughter, cousin Glenda, spoke up and said turnip greens are sort of how she came to meet her new husband. I enjoy a good love story, so I asked her to explain.

"Well," she said, "I was working at a Hardee's and Owen was working at a gas station next door. One day, I stopped to fill up my tank and he came out to wait on me.

"While the gas was pumping, we started talking and I casually asked him how he was getting along. He said everything was fine, except that somebody had given him a mess of turnip greens and he didn't have a pot to cook them in.

"I said, 'Well, I've got a pot if you've got the greens,' and next thing you know, we got married."

You'll never find that moving a love story in True Romance.

Lewis Grizzard
Elvis Is Dead and I Don't Feel So Good Myself, 1984

cultivate poke, but it is easily spread along fencerows and roadside ditches by birds whose digestive system makes the seeds permeable to water. Polk stalk is also edible, both batter-fried and pickled.

Pot likker from greens is a delicacy enjoyed by most greens lovers, and even by some who don't care for the vegetables themselves. At Mary Mac's, a sprawling Southern-style dining room in Atlanta, pot likker is served daily as an appetizer or hot soup, and it is extremely popular and quite delicious. We could find no other restaurants that serve this tasty broth.

GRITS AND HOMINY

Our farewell to corn was a bit premature; we still have grits and hominy, which are corn products. How much longer we will have them is another question. The U.S. Department of Agriculture's barometer of grits consumption has been falling slowly but steadily over the past twenty years or so, and now, for the first time, annual per capita consumption has dropped below three pounds. (Hominy hardly registers on the scale at all.) Even in the South, where most of the grits and hominy are eaten and where many a restaurant breakfast automatically includes grits, these traditional dishes are definitely on the wane.

The late Turner Catledge, a Southerner who was for many years an editor of *The New York Times,* observed a few years ago that grits eating attained the status of a cult around Washington during the administration of President Jimmy Carter. (Catledge also noted that "the word grits has a grammar of its own and can be used with a singular or plural verb at the option of the speaker.") After Carter returned in defeat to his native Georgia, however, grits and many other distinctively Southern dishes fell into disfavor—and if the U.S.D.A. statistics can be believed, they have not recovered.

Before these historically important and delicious foodstuffs are added to the endangered species list, let us say a few words in their behalf, beginning with a simple explanation of what they are.

Hominy and grits are products made from mature (hard) corn kernels. Whole kernels soaked in a solution of water and lye to remove the outer hulls or husks become hominy; when hominy is dried and coarsely ground, it becomes grits. Old-fashioned stone-ground cornmeal and grits, still available in some areas, are made by grinding mature corn kernels (coarse is grits, fine is meal). The products are bolted (sifted) to remove the husks.

Store-bought grits generally come in two forms: quick (cooked in 5 minutes) and instant (mixed with boiling water and served). The direct and un-

SONG TO GRITS

When my mind's unsettled,
When I don't feel spruce,
When my nerves get frazzled,
When my flesh gets loose—

What knits
Me back together's grits.

Grits with gravy,
Grits with cheese,
Grits with bacon,
Grits with peas.
Grits with a minimum
Of two over-medium eggs mixed in
'em: um!

Grits, grits, it's
Grits I sing—
Grits fits
In with anything.

Rich and poor, black and white,
Lutheran and Campbellite,

adorned dish so common to Southern breakfast tables is usually the quick variety, simply cooked in boiling water and served hot. Consistency is important; grits should spoon from the pot as thick as a heavy porridge—not runny enough to spread across the plate, and not firm enough to hold shape. Unseasoned grits are rather bland and tasteless; they need butter and salt or gravy to attain excellence. More refined recipes such as cheese grits (see page 285) are also very popular in the region.

Fried Grits

Here is a recipe that finds favor, made from leftovers.

Leftover grits, when cold, are firm enough to slice easily with a knife. Dip ½-inch-thick slices in a batter made with 1 egg and ½ cup of sweet milk and fry them in 1 tablespoon of butter or bacon grease in a medium-hot skillet. (Even without the egg and milk batter, cold grits fry nicely and make a tasty breakfast dish.) Allow 2 or 3 slices per person.

Hominy

Hominy is sold principally as a canned vegetable (when it is sold at all), and is simply heated and served, sometimes with a piece of side meat added to the pot for flavor. It is rare to find anyone who still makes hominy the traditional way. Alma Rowsey of Montezuma, Tennessee, is one of the few. This is her recipe.

Place 2½ gallons of dried white corn kernels and 2 tablespoons of lye in a large pot. Cover with 2½ gallons of water and stir well. Bring to a boil and cook rapidly for 30 to 40 minutes to loosen the hulls. Drain, discarding the lye water, and rinse several times with fresh water, removing the hulls as they separate from the kernels. Return kernels to the large pot, cover with water, and boil 2 to 3 hours, or until soft and tender. Add more water as needed during the boiling to keep the hominy covered. Put up in sterilized jars or freezer containers.

Alma Rowsey's formula makes a huge quantity of hominy—40 pints or more. To make a much smaller amount—say, 1 quart—start with 1 pint of dried corn and use 2 teaspoons of lye dissolved in about 3 quarts of water.

Jews and Southern Jesuits,
All acknowledge buttered grits.

Give me two hands, give me my wits,
Give me forty pounds of grits.

Grits at taps, grits at reveille.
I am into grits real heavily.

True grits,
More grits,
Fish, grits, and collards.
Life is good where grits are swallered.

Grits
Sits
Right.

Roy Blount, Jr.
One Fell Soup, 1982

Okra (Fried)

There is little doubt that okra originated in Africa and reached this country with the slave trade about three centuries ago. We have met it earlier in these pages as a base for gumbo. It is also used in a Carolina pilau called limping Susan, and in various combination dishes with tomatoes and other vegetables. As a separate stewed vegetable, it has a slick and gummy quality that many people dislike, but when okra slices are rolled in cornmeal and fried in hot fat, something miraculous happens. Everything about the vegetable that is unattractive disappears, and a crisp, crunchy, dainty, and delicious morsel takes its place.

Slice off the thick stem ends of 1 pound of okra pods, cut into ¼-inch rounds, place them in a large bowl, sprinkle liberally with salt, cover with ice water, and refrigerate until quite cold. Drain well. Roll slices in cornmeal seasoned with salt and pepper, and when well-coated fry them in hot fat about ½ inch deep in a black skillet. When brown and crisp, drain on paper towels and serve hot. One pound should make 2 to 4 servings.

Onions (Baked)

In the mountains of Tennessee and North Carolina, festivals are held annually to celebrate the ramp, a small and odoriferous cousin of the little green onion (and perhaps of garlic) that admiring and undaunted eaters call Tennessee truffles. Ramps get not so much as a single line in Waverley Root's comprehensive dictionary of the world's great foods, but they get plenty of attention from people in the Southern mountains.

Southerners seem to like onions as much as anybody, and a lot better than most. There are numerous varieties that grow in the region, but by far the most famous is the Vidalia, a large, sweet, yellow onion grown in and around Vidalia, Georgia, population 10,000. The story goes that onion plants brought into the area from Texas after World War II produced an especially mild and sweet vegetable when grown in the sandy loam around Vidalia. (Like Hope watermelons from Arkansas, it's not the variety but the soil that makes them distinctive.) Another story has it that a Toombs County farmer named Moses Coleman ordered some Bermuda onions from a seed catalogue in 1930, and when he harvested them on his farm, they were "as sweet as Coca-Cola."

However they got to south Georgia, they are now a coveted item and a major agricultural product for area farmers. The Vidalia Chamber of Commerce

Northern people are funny about food. There is a documented case in a Little Rock household of a transplanted New Yorker who declined a serving of fried okra on the ground that he was a vegetarian. The man seemed to be under the impression that each segment was a tiny crustacean scraped from the bottom of an Arkansas River towboat. It should be noted in fairness, however, that the chances of the man's partaking of that Southern delicacy could not have been helped by the sight of his host spitting in the grease to make sure it was hot enough.

Mike Trimble,
in the Arkansas Gazette,
April 15, 1979

certifies and safeguards the real thing under a registered trademark (Yumion), and pains are taken—not always successfully—to prevent others from peddling lesser onions under the Vidalia name.

Vidalias and other sweet onions make excellent deep-fried onion rings, dipped first in a sticky batter. Stale beer and flour is one such mixture that is commonly used; another popular recipe calls for soaking the rings in milk and then dipping them in a batter made of 1 cup of flour, ½ teaspoon of salt, ⅔ cup of water, 2 tablespoons of salad oil, and 1 stiffly beaten egg white. A quite different onion dish enjoyed by many Southerners is baked onions.

Select 4 onions about as large as tennis balls, peel them, and remove a small slice from each top. Drop the onions into a pot of boiling water to cook for about 10 minutes, leaving them firm but not crunchy. Drain and dry, and place in a deep casserole, flat tops up. Pour 1 cup of rich beef boullion or beef broth over the onions. Mix ¼ cup of breadcrumbs with sprinklings of salt, minced garlic, black pepper, grated Parmesan cheese, and paprika, and put 1 tablespoon of the mixture on each onion top. Add a pat of butter to each. Bake at 350° for about 30 minutes, or until the onions are tender, basting periodically with the beef broth. If the topping becomes too brown before the onions are done, cover the dish loosely with foil.

Potatoes (White)

Next to wheat, potatoes are the largest food crop in the world. They didn't reach North America for fully a century after Jamestown was settled, and didn't become a staple here for more than a century after that, but since the late 1800s they have tended to dominate the American vegetable parade fully as much as corn and beans.

Along with white beans and cabbage and yams, garden potatoes were a symbol of survival in the Depression-era South. Starchy, filling, and relatively inexpensive, they seemed always to be cooking on the kitchen stove. Better times brought more than just salted water to cook them in; butter, milk, and prepared sauces came along to enrich their flavor and elevate their status. Creamy mounds of mashed potatoes showed up on the Sunday dinner table with rich gravies filling dipped-out craters like volcanic lava. Then came huge Idaho baking potatoes from the West—a new and different dining treat for isolated Southerners. French fries were included in some early American cookbooks, but it was not until the fast food revolution began after World War II that they swept the country.

A vidalia onion is absolutely the most exquisite, delicate, succulent, scrumptious onion known to man. . . . Grown in the vicinity of Vidalia, a small town in southeast Georgia, [this onion] . . . is mild. Actually, the word is sweet. You can eat it like an apple. It will not make your eyes water, your heart burn, or your sweetheart gag. . . . In the last four or five years, people all over the nation have begun to find out about vidalias and want some. It started in 1977 when we Georgians descended on Washington, and were overheard whispering about suppliers, shipments, and prospects for this year's crop. This naturally attracted the attention of gossip columnists and other riffraff. Soon, vidalias were appearing on the shelves of the Georgetown Safeway—the Washington supermarket of the elite. . . . The Wall Street Journal featured vidalias in a front-page story. That did it. . . . There just aren't enough to go around. The predictable result is onion fraud—unscrupulous dealers . . . trying to sell their onions as vidalias. . . . How tacky can you get?

Jody Powell,
in a syndicated column,
May 1983

Today, processed potatoes are consumed in far greater quantities than fresh ones, and the difference between the two is striking. Frozen, dehydrated, and even reconstituted potatoes flood the markets and restaurants; in fact, it is rare to find freshly peeled and cooked potatoes on plate-lunch menus. The odds may be a little better at home—but there, too, cooks have many quicker options to choose from. Homemade mashed potatoes with a rich brown gravy were never an exclusively Southern dish, but generations of diners in the region have deemed it an essential companion to fried chicken and pork chops and country ham.

Peel and cut up 6 medium-sized potatoes and put them in a pot with just enough water to cover. Put a lid on the pot, bring to a boil, reduce heat, and cook for 15 to 20 minutes, or until the potatoes are tender. Drain well and mash in the pot with an electric mixer, adding salt, pepper, and softened butter to taste. Then, with the mixer running, add ½ cup or more of warm milk—just enough to get the desired consistency. Cover the pan and leave it on the stove to stay warm until time to serve the meal. This amount, with gravy on the side, should satisfy 4 hungry eaters.

Potatoes (Sweet) and Yams

Practically no one can tell the difference between sweet potatoes and yams (though they are botanically distinct), and as far as cooking is concerned, there *is* no difference—the two are absolutely and completely interchangeable. Between 1898 and 1943, George Washington Carver issued nearly four dozen bulletins on his research and experimentation with sweet potatoes at Tuskegee Institute in Alabama, and much of the vegetable's popularity in the South (as well as some fine recipes) can be credited to those reports. (Carver's work also increased the popularity of peanuts, black-eyed peas, and tomatoes.)

Southerners like sweet potatoes baked, boiled, steamed, mashed, candied, made into croquettes, and baked in pies (see page 335). The candied variety, for which recipes abound in Southern cookbooks, involves boiling, peeling, and slicing potatoes, laying the rounds in a baking dish, and seasoning them with brown sugar, butter, spices, and perhaps oranges or lemons. Sweet potato puddings and casseroles in which the potatoes are cooked and mashed and then mixed with spices yield a different taste, also delicious. Two accomplished Tennessee cooks, Lorena Owens of Adams and Wilma Parker of Gallatin, prepare an almost identical sweet potato soufflé highlighted by a crusty baked topping of brown sugar, crushed cornflakes, chopped pecans, and butter.

As a food for human consumption, the sweet potato has been, and always will be, held in very high esteem, and its popularity will increase as we learn more about its many possibilities.

There is an idea prevalent that anybody can cook sweet potatoes. This is a very great mistake, and the many, many dishes of illy cooked potatoes that are placed before me as I travel over the South, prompt me to believe that these recipes will be of value. . . .

•

*No. 18, A SOUTHERN DISH
Cut cold baked sweet potatoes into slices and put into an earthen dish; add sugar and butter to each layer and bake until slightly brown.*

*No. 19, CROQUETTES
Take two cupfuls of mashed, boiled, steamed or baked sweet potatoes; add the beaten yolks of two eggs and season to taste; stir over the fire until the mass parts from the sides of the pan. When cold, form into small croquettes, roll in egg and bread crumbs, and fry in hot lard to amber color.*

*George Washington Carver,
Bulletin No. 38, Tuskegee Institute, 1922*

Yet another distinctive flavor results when finely grated raw potatoes are blended with milk, spices, and other seasonings and baked in a pudding. Recipes such as the one below have a long history in the South.

Grate 2 large sweet potatoes or yams to a pulp in a blender or food processor, adding ½ cup of milk. Mix the mushy pulp in a large casserole with 2 more cups of milk. Beat 3 eggs well in a separate bowl, gradually adding 1 firmly packed cup of light brown sugar, 2 teaspoons of cinnamon, 1 teaspoon of cloves, and 2 teaspoons of lemon juice. When well-blended, stir the mixture into the potatoes. Also stir in ½ cup of finely chopped pecans, sprinkle another ¼ cup of the nuts over the top, and dot with butter. Bake the dish in a preheated 300° oven for 2 hours. The pudding makes 6 to 8 generous servings.

RICE DISHES

Considering its long and interesting history in the South, both as a crop and as a generator of recipes, rice deserves more detailed treatment than it gets here. First grown in South Carolina in the seventeenth century, it shifted to Louisiana and Arkansas more than a hundred years ago, and thus has been continuously produced in the region since early colonial times. South Carolinians no longer grow rice, but love to eat it; Arkansans, on the other hand, grow a lot but eat very little. We have already used several recipes that call for rice—Carolina pilaus, Louisiana gumbos, country captain, jambalaya, and the like. In this section, we offer a few rice and vegetable combinations.

First, though, the basic recipe for boiled rice should be recorded, since it is preliminary to so many combination dishes, and also a side dish that stands nicely on its own, with a little seasoning. This simple, fail-safe method satisfies all recipes that call for cooked rice.

Boiled Rice

Put 2 cups of cold water in a large saucepan with a tight-fitting top, add a pinch or two of salt, and bring to a rolling boil. Lift the lid and pour in 1 cup of good quality long-grain rice. Reduce heat to the lowest possible level and replace the top. Set the stove timer for 20 minutes and leave the pot alone—don't stir it, and don't even lift the lid. When the buzzer goes off,

It was by a romantic accident that rice was first successfully grown in South Carolina. In 1694 a vessel set out from Madagascar, then as remote in the thought of America as Mars might seem today. She was bound for Liverpool but was blown so far off her course that she put into Charleston for repairs. Landgrave Thomas Smith boarded the ship, whether for duty or pleasure it is not stated. The captain presented him with a small package of rough rice for seed. The Landgrave planted it in the proper marshy soil and there sprang up a crop so large that he was able to supply the whole colony. Thus from a storm-tossed ship grew the enormous rice wealth of South Carolina.

Blanche Salley Rhett,
in Two Hundred Years of
Charleston Cooking, 1930

the rice should be dry, fluffy, and tender. Turn off the heat and leave the covered pot sitting on the stove until time to serve dinner.

Rice can be combined with a number of vegetables—tomatoes, okra, peas—but the best combinations are with beans. Black beans and rice (Moors and Christians) is a dish straight out of the Spanish heritage in Florida, and in Louisiana the recipe is almost the same but the beans are red.

Still another famous rice-and-beans combination similar to these two is hoppin John, the toast of the Carolina coast. Cowpeas, or black-eyed peas, are the base. Nobody is certain how the name came to be, but it was in use as early as 1838, and the dish itself is even older. Black populations all along the Southern coast and throughout the Caribbean have eaten rice and beans for more than two centuries, and the three dishes noted here have long since become an integral part of Southern cookery.

Hoppin John and the other beans-and-rice dishes share the legend of New Year's Day good luck. From Charleston clear around the coast of Florida to Mobile and New Orleans, black and white Southerners by the thousands welcome the arrival of every new calendar with hearty bowls of hoppin John, or Moors and Christians, or red beans and rice, repeating a ritual that has survived the centuries. The recipes are very much alike. This one is typical.

Now hopping-john was F. Jasmine's very favorite food. She had always warned them to wave a plate of rice and peas before her nose when she was in her coffin, to make certain there was no mistake; for if a breath of life was left in her, she would sit up and eat, but if she smelled the hopping-john, and did not stir, then they could just nail down the coffin and be certain she was truly dead.

Carson McCullers
The Member of the Wedding, 1946

Hoppin John

Begin with 2 cups (1 pound) of dried black-eyed peas. Soak in cold water overnight, then rinse well and set aside. Boil about ¼ pound of seasoning meat (salt pork or ham hock) in a large pot with 1 quart or more of water for about 1 hour, then add the peas to the pot, reduce heat to simmer, and cook covered for about 1 hour and 30 minutes, or until tender. Sauté 1 cup of finely chopped onions in 2 tablespoons of bacon grease for about 3 minutes and add to the peas.

In a separate large pan, cook 2 cups of raw rice in 4 cups of water as described in the preceding recipe. Finally, combine the cooked rice and the beans and simmer together for about 30 minutes. Season with salt, pepper, and hotter spices of your choosing, add a small amount of hot water if necessary to assure moistness, and serve steaming hot in bowls. This amount should serve 10 to 12 people.

Red Rice

One more rice recipe before we move on. It is called red rice in South Carolina, Creole rice in Louisiana, and Spanish rice in the interior of the South, to which it somehow found its way in the 1930s. In *The Savannah Cook Book* (1933), it is called tomato pilau; in the *Georgia Sampler Cookbook* (1983), it is called Savannah rice. By whatever name, it's a very tasty and delightful dish, an all-souls casserole that goes well with many other foods.

Fry 4 or 5 strips of bacon until crisp; drain on paper towels, crumble, and set aside. Leave about 3 tablespoons of grease in the skillet. Chop 1 medium-sized onion and sauté it in the fat for about 3 minutes. Then pour in 1 cup of raw long-grained rice, 2 cups of peeled and cut-up tomatoes (or the contents of a 1-pound can, drained), and these seasonings: ½ teaspoon of salt, ¼ teaspoon of black pepper, ⅛ teaspoon of cayenne pepper, and 1 tablespoon of Worcestershire sauce. Stir the mixture well and cook over low heat for about 10 minutes. Then pour it into a 1-quart casserole, add the crumbled bacon, stir well, cover the dish, and bake for about 45 minutes in a preheated 350° oven. Once or twice during that time, lift the lid and stir the rice with a fork. As soon as the rice is tender, the dish is ready to be served. Take care not to let it get dry and hard on the bottom or around the edges. The dish should provide 6 servings.

Squash

Squash and pumpkins were found growing in North America by the first Europeans who ventured here in the fifteenth century. Numerous varieties of squash have flourished on the continent ever since, and several of them are prominent in the South. Stewed squash is a fairly common side dish, especially when summer gardens are thriving, and so is fried squash; another popular dinner-table specialty is baked squash casserole. This recipe is similar to many that have long been featured in cookbooks of the region.

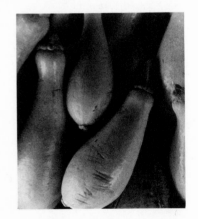

Wash and cut up 2 pounds of yellow squash in a large saucepan. Stir in 1 medium-sized onion, minced, 1 clove of garlic, minced, and 1 teaspoon of salt. Add ¼ cup of water, bring to a boil, reduce heat, cover pot, and cook about 20 minutes, or until squash is tender. Drain well and mash thoroughly in the pan. Add ¼ to ⅓ cup of evaporated milk, 1 tablespoon of butter, 1 cup of grated Cheddar cheese, 2 well-beaten eggs, and ⅛ teaspoon of black pepper, stirring well. If the mixture is too soupy, add enough cracker crumbs to thicken it. Transfer to a greased casserole. Cover the top with a mixture of ¼ cup of cracker crumbs, 2 tablespoons of melted butter, and 3 tablespoons of grated Cheddar. Bake at 350° for 30 minutes. The golden brown and bubbling hot casserole should yield about 6 generous servings.

In 1970 while I was in London . . . a Kenyan invited me to an "African" dinner. He served deep-fried goat (because goat was cheaper than chicken), sweet potatoes, black-eyed peas, corn on the cob, corn bread, and a salad of bell peppers, tomatoes, and little green onions. The meal made me as homesick for the Delta as it made that Kenyan for his part of Africa, and it also cleared some of the cobwebs from my thinking about the old problem of the provenance of Southern distinctiveness. As far as cuisine was concerned, an answer seemed possible: Southerners eat what they do because so many of them have an African heritage. . . . I mean the style of cooking that had some vogue in the 1960s as "soul food," but which Southerners, black and white, rich and poor, grow up eating because it is the food of the country. . . . This was [the Afro-American's] native food and the traditional ways of cooking came with it.

Margaret Jones Bolsterli,
in the *Southern Humanities Review*, 1982

TOMATOES

Last but not least in the pantheon of Southern vegetables (although it is technically a fruit), we come to the tomato—the bright red, home-grown, juicy, acid, vine-ripened siren of summer. No hothouse can duplicate these classics. They are a summer blessing to be savored with homemade mayonnaise and cottage cheese, on bacon, lettuce, and tomato sandwiches, or simply sliced and eaten raw as a side dish with almost anything. Cooked tomatoes are less common than raw ones at the table, but there are at least two ways in which Southerners cook the vegetable (or fruit) and serve it as a hot dish. We offer recipes for both specialties.

Fried Tomatoes

Like grits and fried apples, fried tomatoes make a splendid breakfast companion for sausage or bacon and eggs. Whether green or ripe or in between, they are always welcome at the morning table.

Fry 4 or more slices of bacon in a large heavy skillet. Remove and drain, leaving the hot grease. Slice several garden-fresh tomatoes, picked anywhere from gourd-green to ripe but firm, depending on your preference; make the slices about ½ inch thick, and allow at least 3 or 4 per person. Coat each slice in cornmeal seasoned with salt and pepper. Lift them gently with a fork or spatula into the hot grease and fry until the meal is brown and crusty, then turn and cook the other side. Additional grease may be needed. When the tomatoes are fried to a toasty crispness, drain on paper towels and serve.

Stewed Tomatoes

This tomato side dish doesn't require fresh tomatoes; home-canned or even store-bought ones will do quite well.

Sauté 1 medium-sized onion, minced, in 2 tablespoons of butter in a saucepan. Peel and core 4 cups of fresh tomatoes (or substitute canned ones), and put them in the pan. Season with 1 teaspoon of salt, 1 teaspoon of sugar, and black pepper to taste. Bring the mixture to a boil, lower the heat, cover the pan, and simmer for about 20 minutes. Adjust seasonings. If too thin and watery, add several small cubes of white bread and stir until the right consistency is reached. Serve in individual bowls. This amount should be enough for 4 persons.

Former restaurant owner Hap Townes was famed for his stewed tomatoes, among other things, when he operated a diner in Nashville (see page 67). After his retirement, his recipe was published in a syndicated newspaper column, bringing letters of appreciation from all over the country. The recipe is a monument to simplicity: the contents of a 28-ounce can of tomatoes, 6 pieces of toasted white bread, 1 stick of butter, and 1 cup of sugar, all combined and simmered together slowly, with salt and pepper added to taste. These amounts were meant to make 6 to 8 servings, but Hap made it up in much larger quantities than that.

The difference between these two recipes, both delicious, illustrates how versatile and impressive stewed tomatoes are in the lineup of Southern side dishes and dinner-table specialties.

Sweets

Ask any group of mature Southerners to recall some of the specific foods they enjoyed at home in the years of their youth, and the responsive litany is almost certain to accentuate sweets. They may mention cornbread and hot biscuits, of course, or ham and chicken, or beans and greens and corn, but the cakes and pies and puddings will quickly edge to the center and finally dominate the list.

There are some good reasons for this. One is the celebrated Southern sweet tooth, part and parcel with the all-American fondness for sugary things but going beyond that to a devotion with its own distinctive character. Before they ever got to dessert, Southerners in the past encountered sweets at every course along the way, from molasses and honey and preserves to sweetened drinks, fruit compotes, and sweet breads. Cookies and candy found a place for themselves too, both after and between meals. Southerners remember sweets in part simply because they have always eaten lots of them.

Another reason they remember is that eating has been a leading form of entertainment as well as a necessity in the South, and sweets lend themselves well to ceremonies of fellowship and social interchange. Throughout the decades when big dinners were one of the few social outlets open to people, Southerners took with great seriousness their roles as hostesses, cooks, providers, and presiders. It mattered very much to them what they served and who was there to enjoy it and whether or not everyone got plenty and had a good time. The tradition of Southern hospitality is at root a tradition of laying before family and friends an impressive array of carefully prepared food and drink, and sweets are the crowning glory of such a presentation. For showmanship and flair, nothing is more spectacular than a big four-layer cake or a specialty dessert of some kind.

Another reason is that even in lean times (of which the South has known more than its share), a sweet conclusion to a meal was like a happy ending to a book or a fairytale: a way of delaying or denying harsh reality. Sweets are akin to pleasure, to optimism, to a romantic view of life—and such an outlook has often seemed in keeping with the regional character. When they had precious little from which to draw hope, Southern cooks could at least bring smiles and expressions of delight with such simple and unpretentious creations as peach ice cream or sweet potato pie.

Finally, Southerners remember the sweets of their younger years because so many women (and some men) were expert bakers and pastry makers, and their creations often left deep and lasting impressions. A strawberry shortcake or a

In the hills of southwest Virginia I was invited one day to a "'lasses boilin'." To the tune of a fiddle, against the scent of wood smoke and the blue mist of the evaporating juice, we danced our square dances, dominated by the thick, sticky sweet

black bottom pie or a multilayered coconut cake with rich filling and frosting was quite literally memorable—too outstandingly impressive to be forgotten.

Now, the advent of such "quick and easy" substitutes as cake mixes and frozen pies and ready-to-bake cookies has lowered the quality and quantity of homemade sweets, decimated the ranks of skilled dessert makers, and all but reduced the mighty showcase of sugary Southern confections to a museum collection of fading memories. Few people make cakes from scratch anymore, and even pies and puddings are apt to be bought frozen or made from commercial mixes. Modern admonitions against excessive use of sugar, cream, and butter are further hastening the decline of baking, pastry making, and other such kitchen skills.

Before we lose forever this fine art of our grandmothers, a trip through the pantry of Southern history may be in order. In these final pages of thoughts on home cooking, we have assembled about thirty recipes for sweets that cooks and diners in the region have held in high esteem through many decades and generations. The recipes are arranged in five categories: cakes; candies and cookies; pies, cobblers, and dumplings; puddings; and specialty desserts. The list of recipes could easily have been two or three times as long without sacrificing either quality or historical interest. As it is, it contains a fairly representative cross-section of the confections for which Southern cooks have long been famous.

In times past, it was not at all unusual for cookbooks in the South to devote half or more of their pages to sweets. On the surface, that would seem to indicate that the region's cooks prepared an inordinate and excessive number of confections. But another explanation may be closer to the truth. The authors of these kitchen collections may have assumed that everybody knew how to cook vegetables, make salads, and even prepare certain commonly enjoyed meats and breads, but desserts were another matter. Cakes and pies and most other sweets called for skill and experience that not every cook possessed, and detailed, precise instructions were necessary in order to assure success.

Today, it may be truer than ever that the preparation of fine cakes, candies, cookies, pies, and the like requires a good bit of experience, if not special skills—and certainly takes more time and effort than most people are willing to devote to the task. Nevertheless, there is much pleasure and satisfaction to be derived from preparing a time-honored confection in the traditional way— and often, the process turns out to be more fun and less work than the reluctant baker might expect. And there is a bonus: Through trial and error and retrial, a willing cook gains deeper knowledge of the techniques and keener appreciation of the bakers of old who operated without benefit of electric mixers, food processors, and the whole range of utensils and kitchen aids that modern cooks take for granted.

smell of sorghum. . . . But the high point of the ceremony approached. Like participants at a sacrament, we drew near. This year's sorghum, essence of sun and rain and light and earth, was poured, hot still from the evaporators, upon biscuits. We ate, and tongues were burned by the heated syrup. But over everything, man and woman and child, and stretching black shadow, hung this sacramental feeling, like a mist of holiness. For deep in the heart of man, though he may live in an age of civilization that can build cities like New York and Chicago, deep within him lies the need to celebrate and to worship, uncurbed and undestroyed by the machine. Here in the mountains of Virginia, with biscuit and sorghum, we held our little saturnalia; but simple though it might be, with a squeaky fiddle for music and smoke from evaporating syrup for incense, it held within this cup of the hills the spirit of all celebration and all earth worship. In the mountains of Virginia, on a night of October, sanity reigned unconquered.

Clare Leighton
Southern Harvest, 1942

CAKES

The prevalence of so many fine cakes in Southern cookery forces a hard choice. In selecting seven recipes to include, we have had to leave out twice as many more of sterling reputation, including some that we know from firsthand experience to be truly outstanding.

Fruitcake, for example: Nelly Custis Lewis had a recipe for black cake in the housekeeping journal she kept in Virginia in the 1830s, and it was, for all intents and purposes, a fruitcake. Fifty years later, in her *Housekeeping in Old Virginia* (1879), Marion Cabell Tyree included no fewer than fourteen fruitcake and black cake recipes. Elsewhere in the South, in such widely scattered places as Claxton, Georgia, and the Acadian towns of south Louisiana, fruitcake has long enjoyed high visibility and renown. The pecan bourbon cake we offer here is perhaps a cousin of the fruitcake, having as it does some of the requisite nuts, raisins, and spices.

Caramel cake—or more precisely, a white cake with caramel icing—is another of the South's old favorites. It is rare indeed to find the old-fashioned burnt sugar icing made the way Annie Smith of Adams, Tennessee, and other fine Southern bakers of her generation made it not so long ago—by caramelizing white sugar in a heavy iron skillet. The recipes are there to be followed, though, in such classic volumes as *Marion Brown's Southern Cook Book* and *Southern Cooking*, by Mrs. S. R. Dull.

Cooks for General Robert E. Lee made a sponge layer cake with citrus juice and rind tartly dominant in the filling and frosting. The Confederate commander loved it dearly, and the cake has borne his name ever since. Marion Tyree's Virginia volume noted above was one of the first to include the recipe, and there is also a version in *The American Heritage Cookbook*. Patsy Curtis, a superlative professional cook and baker who directs food service operations for a Nashville-based corporation, shared her rendition of the *American Heritage* recipe for Robert E. Lee cake with us, and it was delicious.

Another great Southern layer cake is coconut; in many homes, it's as much a fixture on the holiday dinner table as ambrosia and boiled custard. The coconut cake with lemon filling that Eugene Walter included in *American Cooking: Southern Style* is a memorable confection. We can attest to that, having sampled one made by George Anne Egerton of Elizabethtown, Kentucky, a cake baker of exceptional ability.

The list of classic Southern confections could go on and on—angel food, devil's food, yellow cake, orange cake, and an array of icings and fillings and frostings to encase them. In the days when homemakers had ready access to fresh cream and eggs, cakes were the pride and joy of many a cook, and at times

The black stove, stoked with coal and firewood, glows like a lighted pumpkin. Eggbeaters whirl, spoons spin round in bowls of butter and sugar, vanilla sweetens the air, ginger spices it; melting, nose-tingling odors saturate the kitchen, suffuse the house, drift out to the world on puffs of chimney smoke. In four days our work is done. Thirty-one cakes, dampened with whiskey, bask on window sills and shelves.

Truman Capote
"A Christmas Memory," 1956

almost an insignia of status. Everyone in the neighborhood knew who made the best caramel or coconut or chocolate cake, and at community dinners those prized creations were the first to disappear.

In the seven recipes we have chosen to include here, there is no "best of the best" ranking. These are simply a few fine old Southern cakes, each quite different from the rest, and all belonging to the rich tradition of regional cookery and history.

Chocolate Cake

There are many varieties of chocolate cake, none of them uniquely Southern, but chocolate has been a favorite confection in the region for many decades, showing up in cakes, pies, cookies, and candy in every state. We picked up a chocolate cake recipe in the 1960s that has proved to be perennially popular. The combination of ingredients is rather unorthodox, but they go together easily and always yield a flawless result. We lost the source of the recipe somehow, remembering only that it was clipped from a Southern newspaper. Now, a virtually identical version has made its way to us from a 1938 cookbook of the Women's Club of Munfordville, Kentucky. It's a chocolate pan cake with chocolate icing.

Sift together 2 cups of sugar, 2 cups of all-purpose flour, and ¼ teaspoon of salt in a large mixing bowl. In a saucepan, combine 2 sticks of butter, 4 tablespoons of unsweetened cocoa, and 1 cup of water. Bring slowly to a boil, stirring, and when well-combined, pour the mixture over the dry ingredients, blending thoroughly. Dissolve 1 teaspoon of baking soda in ½ cup of buttermilk and add it to the batter. Then add 2 lightly beaten eggs and 1 teaspoon of vanilla extract. When well-mixed, pour into a greased 6- by 12-inch cake pan and bake in a preheated 350° oven for about 30 minutes, or until the middle is firm and spongy.

Meanwhile, make a frosting by combining 1 stick of butter, 4 tablespoons of cocoa, and 6 tablespoons of sweet milk in a saucepan, stirring over medium heat until it boils. Sift a 16-ounce box of powdered sugar into a bowl, add the chocolate mixture and 1 teaspoon of vanilla extract, and beat with a spoon or mixer until smooth. Spread the warm frosting over the warm cake in the pan, let cool, and then cut and serve from the pan.

My grandmother's milk-house, by an ingenious amateur engineering arrangement, had a constant slow stream of cool well water washing under its pan of milk, with the golden cream on top thick enough, as an uncle of mine puts it, "to be folded back like a saddle-blanket." Here were shelves laden with glass jars filled with butter tied in muslin bags and put away in brine against some possible unhappy time when all the cows might go dry. . . . They entertained on the grand scale—to have forty extras for dinner on the Sundays of "big meetin'" and the Christmas season or fourteen guests over the week-ends was a joyous commonplace. A bounteous larder was a bare necessity.

Eleanore Ott
Plantation Cookery of Old Louisiana, 1938

Jam Cake with Caramel Icing

There are jam cake recipes in the cookbooks of practically every Southern state, going back for many years, but for some reason, Tennessee and Kentucky seem always to have been the center of the jam cake universe. Recipes for the rich, spicy confection abound in those states, and they differ more in proportions than in the basic ingredients. This version is similar to the methods of several renowned Southern cookbook writers, including Marion Brown of North Carolina, Cissy Gregg of Kentucky, Kathryn Tucker Windham of Alabama, and Phila Hach of Tennessee.

Cream together 2 sticks of softened butter and 1 cup of light brown sugar (firmly packed). Separate 5 eggs, beat the yolks well, and add them to the butter-sugar mixture, stirring until smooth. Dissolve 1 teaspoon of baking soda in 1 cup of buttermilk. Sift together 3 cups of all-purpose flour and 1 teaspoon each of cinnamon, nutmeg, cloves, and allspice. Alternately add the buttermilk and flour mixtures to the sugar and egg mixture a little at a time, stirring to blend thoroughly. Next, add 1½ cups of blackberry jam (with or without seeds, as you prefer), 1 cup of chopped pecans, and 1 cup of raisins. Finally, beat the 5 egg whites until stiff and fold them into the batter. Grease three 9-inch cake pans (round or square) with shortening, line the bottom of each pan with wax paper, and divide the batter among the three. Bake in a preheated 325° oven for 25 minutes, or longer as needed, removing as soon as a toothpick inserted in the center comes out clean. Cool on racks for about 10 minutes and then turn the cakes out of the pans, remove the wax paper, and dribble 2 or 3 tablespoons of bourbon over each layer.

To make the caramel icing the way Sue Smith of Nashville makes it, combine 3¾ cups of white sugar with 1½ cups of milk and a pinch or two of baking soda in a deep and heavy pot and bring slowly to a boil over medium heat. While it is heating, put ¾ cup of white sugar in a black iron skillet and stir it constantly over low heat for 10 minutes or so; the granular sugar will slowly liquefy and caramelize. Pour this rich brown sauce into the boiling milk and sugar mixture. It will pop and spatter, and then settle into a rolling boil. Add 2 tablespoons of butter and continue cooking over medium heat, stirring frequently, until the mixture reaches soft-ball stage (238° on a candy thermometer). Remove it from the heat, stir in 2 teaspoons of vanilla extract, and let the icing cool for 5 minutes. Then beat it vigorously by hand for about 3 minutes, and when it is satiny and still soft enough to pour very slowly from the stirring spoon, spread it around the sides and top of each layer, stacking them and frosting the finished cake.

Jam cake will age and mellow and ripen for a week or more, seeming to taste better and better as the days pass. Keep it well covered to avoid having it become dry and crumbly.

Lady Baltimore Cake

"Each year at Christmas time hundreds of white boxes go out of Charleston to all parts of the country bearing the round, the tall, the light, the fragile, the ineffable Lady Baltimore cakes," wrote Alicia Rhett Mayberry in *Two Hundred Years of Charleston Cooking* in 1930. She had created and named the original herself many years before that (not in Baltimore, ironically, but in her South Carolina home city), and novelist Owen Wister had given the cake a certain immortality when he described it in a romantic novel, *Lady Baltimore*, in 1906. A thriving cottage industry in baking and a tearoom called the Lady Baltimore were two of the spin-off benefits accruing to Charleston from the Wister book. For her part, Mrs. Mayberry got the pleasure of knowing that her confection was famous all over the country.

It might have achieved renown even without the publicity, so rich and delicious is it. A white cake covered with an egg-white frosting full of nuts and raisins, the Lady Baltimore remains an all-time classic in South Carolina and other parts of the region, and different versions of it can be found in dozens of Southern cookbooks. The one below borrows elements from several old recipes.

Combine 2 cups of sifted all-purpose flour with 2 teaspoons of baking powder and ¼ teaspoon of salt and sift three more times. In a separate bowl, cream 1 stick of softened butter and gradually add to it 1¼ cups of sugar, stirring until well-combined. Alternately add the flour and ¾ cup of milk to the butter and sugar, blending thoroughly, and stir in 1 teaspoon of vanilla extract. Separate 3 eggs, beat the whites to moist peaks, and fold them into the batter. Grease two 9-inch round cake pans with shortening, line the bottoms with wax paper, and divide the batter between the two. Bake in a preheated 325° oven for about 25 minutes, removing as soon as it tests done in the center. (Be sure not to overcook, since the cake dries out quickly.) Set on racks to cool for about 10 minutes, then turn out of the pans and remove the wax paper from each layer.

To make the frosting: Combine 1 cup of chopped raisins and 1 cup of chopped pecans or walnuts in a small bowl, add ½ cup of sherry, brandy, rum, or water, whichever you prefer, and let the mixture soak for about an hour. (It will save time to do this first, while the cake is being assembled and

This happy story of love ends with a wedding, and begins in the Women's Exchange, which the ladies of Kings Port [Charleston, South Carolina] have established. . . .

"I should like a slice, if you please, of Lady Baltimore," I said with extreme formality. . . . She brought me the cake, and I had my first felicitous meeting with Lady Baltimore. Oh, my goodness! Did you ever taste it? It's all soft, and it's in layers, and it has nuts—but I can't write any more about it; my mouth waters too much.

Delighted surprise caused me once more to speak aloud, and with my mouth full. "But, dear me, this is delicious!"

A choking ripple of laughter came from the counter. "It's I who make them," said the girl. "I thank you for the unintentional compliment."

Owen Wister
Lady Baltimore, 1906

baked.) In a saucepan, boil 1 cup of sugar and ½ cup of water over medium heat until a syrup forms that makes a long thread when poured from a spoon. Separate 2 eggs; beat the whites in a large bowl with ¼ teaspoon of cream of tartar, and when stiff peaks form, add the hot syrup slowly, beating all the while. Stir in 1 teaspoon of vanilla extract and 1 teaspoon of lemon juice, add the moistened nuts and raisins, and continue beating until the icing begins to thicken and glaze. Spread it quickly over the sides and top of each layer, stack one on top of the other, and cover the entire cake with the rest of the icing. Store the cake in an airtight container to keep it moist.

Lane Cake

Plenty of Southern cooks have a version of the Lane cake in their repertoire, and some even claim to have originated it, but the true creator was Emma Rylander Lane of Clayton, Alabama. She published the recipe in her hometown cookbook, *Some Good Things to Eat,* in 1898. The Lane cake, she wrote modestly, is "my prize cake, and named not from my own conceit, but through the courtesy of Mrs. Janie McDowell Pruett, of Eufaula, Ala." The original recipe called for raisins and "one wine-glass of good whiskey or brandy" in the filling; many later versions have added pecans and coconut.

When I made a Lane cake for the first time, using a recipe similar to Mrs. Lane's original, my three hours of painstaking labor were richly rewarded with a beautiful and delicious confection that left me with a warm feeling for Emma Lane and all the patient bakers of the South who once performed these labors for the benefit and pleasure of others.

Combine 3½ cups of sifted all-purpose flour with 3 teaspoons of baking powder and ¼ teaspoon of salt, and sift three more times. Put 2 sticks of softened butter into a large mixing bowl, gradually add 2 cups of sugar, and blend thoroughly to a light, creamy consistency. Add alternately small amounts of the sifted flour and 1 cup of milk to the butter-sugar mixture and continue blending until the batter is smooth. Separate 8 large eggs and beat the whites until they form firm peaks. Stir in 1½ teaspoons of vanilla extract and then fold the whites gently into the batter. Grease three 9-inch cake pans (round or square) with shortening and cover the bottoms with wax paper. Divide the batter into the pans and bake them in a preheated 325° oven for about 25 minutes, or until the centers are spongy and firm. Set on racks to cool for a few minutes, then turn the cakes out of the pans and remove the wax paper.

The Lane cake recipe is an old one, named for a south Alabama family where it originated. The recipe calls for bourbon or brandy in the filling and although Muv's town is dry and her church and her immediate circle of friends frown on spirits in any form, she feels so strongly about the

To make the filling, beat the 8 egg yolks to a smooth, lemony color and blend in 1 cup of sugar. In a double boiler melt 1 stick of butter, add the egg and sugar mixture, and stir constantly over boiling water for 15 or 20 minutes, or until it thickens a bit and drips slowly from the spoon. Remove from heat and stir in 1 teaspoon of vanilla extract, ½ cup of bourbon, and 1 cup each of chopped pecans, chopped raisins, and shredded coconut. Beat until the filling is well-blended and thick enough to hold its shape, then quickly spread it over the sides and top of each layer, stack the layers, and cover the entire cake with the remainder of the icing. (An alternative favored by some Lane cake bakers—not including Mrs. Lane herself—is to make a separate white frosting for the outside of the cake.)

Like so many rich and elaborate layer cakes, Emma Lane's creation begs for a special occasion. It is truly a ceremonial confection, one to be remembered—as it has been since 1898.

Pecan Bourbon Cake

The combination of nuts, raisins, spices, and whiskey can be found in many a Southern cake recipe, going back a half-century or more. The nuts are usually pecans, but they may be walnuts or hickory nuts (hickernuts, in the vernacular); the most common spice is nutmeg, and the preferred whiskey is bourbon. Baked in a tube pan, this cake comes out rich and heavy, somewhat reminiscent of a fruitcake. Marion Flexner, in *Out of Kentucky Kitchens* (1949), credited her favorite recipe for the confection to Peggy Gaines, who, she said, had made the cake professionally for years. Whatever its origin, it is popular in Kentucky and elsewhere, especially in the Christmas holiday season. Our version has Kentucky roots—and branches from Tennessee and Georgia.

Coarsely chop 3 cups of pecan halves (or break them by hand) and combine with 1 cup of raisins. Mix with ½ cup of sifted all-purpose flour and set aside. Combine 1 cup of sifted all-purpose flour with 1 teaspoon of baking powder and sift twice more. Dissolve 2 teaspoons of nutmeg (freshly grated is more flavorful, but prepared is fine) in ½ cup of bourbon and let stand several minutes. Cream 1 stick of butter with 1¼ cups of sugar, beating well. Separate 3 eggs and add the yolks one at a time to the butter and sugar, blending to a smooth, lemon-light finish. Alternately add the whiskey and the flour to this mixture a little at a time, stirring well. Fold in the floured nuts and raisins, then add 1 teaspoon of vanilla extract, and finally

Lane cake that she will go to almost any length to get the proper seasoning for it. Once this resulted in a harrowing experience in a Panama City bistro. Muv rode down to the coast after church one day with one of her friends and while the friend was on another errand she slipped into the first place she saw with a neon sign blinking "Bar."

"It was a nice sunny day," Muv reported to us, "but dark as the inside of a cow in that place. I had on my good church clothes, hat and gloves and all, and this creature came slithering up to me wearing . . . I don't know what."

"Probably a cocktail dress, Muv," one of the children suggested.

"Maybe so," said Muv. "Anyway she looked half naked and she was downright impudent. She said, 'Madam, this is a cocktail lounge.' So I just drew myself up and said, 'My dear, I didn't think *it was the Methodist parsonage! I'll have half a pint of Early Times please.'"*

Celestine Sibley
A Place Called Sweet Apple, 1967

beat the 3 egg whites with a pinch of salt until stiff and fold them into the batter.

Grease a 10-inch tube cake pan with shortening, cut out a piece of brown paper to line the bottom (grease the paper on both sides), and pour the batter into the pan, letting it sit a few minutes to settle. Decorate the top with pecan halves and (optionally) candied cherries. Bake in a preheated 325° oven for 1 hour and 10 minutes and then test for doneness with a toothpick or straw. (Overbaking will make the cake dry and crumbly.) Set pan to cool on a rack for 30 minutes or so, and then carefully turn it out onto a plate and turn it right side up back onto the rack. When cool, store in a cake tin, draped with a bourbon-soaked cloth. The first slice, topped with whipped cream, is delicious—and it improves with age.

Pound Cake

By most accounts the pound cake is of British origin, getting its name from the weight of its principal ingredients: a pound each of butter, flour, sugar, and eggs. The cake was eaten in Virginia before the Revolution, and some Virginians have claimed that it was they who exported it to England, not the other way around. Wherever the truth lies, the cake has been gracing Southern sideboards for more than two centuries. There are numerous versions, and every state seems to include one or more in its gallery of prized confections. We have acquired several outstanding pound cake recipes over the years, the one below prominent among them. You might call it a half-pound cake.

The most special of occasions was a dining. . . . The hour was two o'clock, but guests came around eleven or twelve—and spent the day. They sat down to tables that well might have groaned, even howled, such was the weight they carried. . . . a stuffed ham at one end, a chicken or partridge pie at the other, side dishes of smothered rabbit or broiled chicken, at least four kinds of sweet pickle, and . . .

In a mixing bowl, cream together 2 sticks of softened butter and 3 cups of sugar. Add 6 eggs, one at a time, blending them in well. Then add alternately 3 cups of sifted all-purpose flour and 1 cup of heavy cream a little at a time, mixing thoroughly with each addition until the batter is well-blended. Finally, stir in 2 teaspoons of vanilla extract. Pour the batter into a well-greased and -floured 10-inch tube pan and bake it in a preheated 325° oven for about 1 hour and 15 minutes, or until a toothpick inserted near the center comes out clean. Set it on a rack to cool in the pan for about 10 minutes and then turn it out. A warm slice is special, but the cake keeps well for several days. Fresh strawberries or peaches and whipped cream make it a memorable dessert.

Stack Cake

In the mountains of southern Appalachia—parts of Virginia and West Virginia, Kentucky and Tennessee, North Carolina and Georgia—dried apple stack cake is among the oldest and most favored of desserts. Dried apples are a mountain staple, preserved in great quantities from the summer and fall crops, and the cake has long been a natural consequence of their availability. (Fresh or canned apples can be used, but dried ones are best.) Sidney Saylor Farr, in a contemporary collection of mountain recipes called *More Than Moonshine*, remembered her mother's dried apple stack cake as a highlight of fall in the kitchen. Versions are similar; this is one.

Put 1 pound of dried apples in a heavy pan, cover with water, and cook with the lid on for 15 minutes, adding a little water if necessary to keep the apples from sticking. Remove from heat, mash with a fork, and stir in 1 cup of brown sugar, 1 teaspoon of cinnamon, 1/2 teaspoon of allspice, 1/4 teaspoon of nutmeg, and 1/4 teaspoon of cloves. Return to the stove, stirring and simmering until the fruit is soft, thick, and spicy. Turn off the heat and leave the pot covered.

Cream together 2 cups of sugar and 1 cup of solid shortening. Combine 1 teaspoon of salt and 1 teaspoon of ginger with 4 cups of sifted all-purpose flour and sift twice more. Dissolve 2 teaspoons of baking soda in 1 cup of buttermilk. Alternately add the flour and buttermilk mixtures to the sugar and shortening a little at a time, stirring well. Beat 3 whole eggs and add them to the batter slowly. Grease and flour three or four 9-inch cake pans and, using half the batter, divide it among them. Bake in a preheated 350° oven for 15 minutes, or until done in the center. Turn the cakes out onto racks to cool, wash the pans, grease and flour them again, and distribute the rest of the batter in the same way. The final result will be 6 to 8 thin layers of cake. Let them cool to room temperature.

To assemble the stack cake, put the first layer on a large platter, spoon a generous portion of the cooked apples over it, top it with another layer, add more fruit, and continue until all the layers are stacked and the apples are divided among the layers and on top. Sprinkle 1 tablespoon or more of powdered sugar on top and let the cake stand, covered, in a cool place for a day or two before cutting. By then the cake layers and apples will have blended and mellowed, and the stack will be a firm pillar that slices well.

all the vegetables in season. I have seen corn pudding, candied sweet potatoes, Irish potatoes, mashed and baked, black-eyed peas, baked peaches, apples baked in sugar and cloves, cabbage boiled with bacon, okra, stewed tomatoes, sliced raw tomatoes, cucumbers cut up with onions, beets boiled and buttered, and string beans, otherwise snaps, all at one spread. There was water to drink, also cider in season, also milk, sweet and sour, and the very best of homemade wine. . . . Dessert was likewise an embarrassment of riches. Cakes in variety, two sorts of pie, with ice cream and sherbet, or fresh fruit. . . . In cold weather, coffee in big cups, with cream and sugar, often went with the main dinner. Hot apple toddies preceded it at such times. In hot weather the precursor was mint julep, ice cold. Yet we were not a company of dyspeptics nor drunkards—by the free and full use of earth's abounding mercies we learned not to abuse them.

Martha McCulloch-Williams
Dishes and Beverages of the Old South, 1913

CANDIES AND COOKIES

Between lighter-than-air sugar cookies that melt in your mouth and sconelike teacakes that sometimes attain the hardness of jawbreakers, a vast array of cookies and candies claim shelf space in the Southern pantry. This short list includes a few classic old confections. If they are not all originally Southern, their long tenure in the region qualifies them as residents.

Benne Seed Wafers

Nowhere else in the United States except in the South Carolina low country are you apt to hear sesame seeds referred to as benne seeds. That name is associated with the African origin of the seeds, which were first brought to this country by slaves in the seventeenth century. From that time to this, South Carolina cooks, black and white alike, have made bread, cookies, and candy with benne seeds as a central ingredient. Here is an old recipe, typical of many.

Toast ⅔ cup of benne (sesame) seeds in a heavy pan in a preheated 400° oven for about 10 minutes, or until they take on a light brown color, and let cool. Cream together 1 stick of butter and 1 cup of light brown sugar. Add to the mixture 1 egg (beaten), ¾ cup of all-purpose flour (sifted), and ¼ teaspoon of baking powder, blending thoroughly. Next, add 1 teaspoon of vanilla extract and the ⅔ cup of toasted benne seeds. When the dough is well mixed, drop it by teaspoonfuls onto a buttered cookie sheet and bake in a preheated 325° oven for 10 minutes. Let cookies cool for one minute and then remove to racks. They will harden and stick on sheet if left longer. When completely cooled, store in tins with tight-fitting lids. The recipe will make about 5 dozen cookies.

Bourbon Balls

Among the confections closely identified with the South since World War II is bourbon balls, a holiday favorite in Kentucky, Tennessee, and a few other states. They may predate the war years, but not by much. Whatever the time and place of their origin, bourbon balls are simple (no cooking) and flavorful. The basic recipe varies only slightly from one cookbook to the next. Here is the standard method.

Dinner on my last evening in Savannah was an experience—an eating place almost totally unknown, except to a few local cognoscenti, who refer to it in whispers as "Mrs. Wilkes's Boarding House." . . . We entered the basement by the kitchen door into a large, sweet-smelling, spotlessly white room. In the center were five long tables, each seating about eight, plates turned upside down and cutlery wrapped in white napkins. . . . Through the archway, one could see five white-coated ladies laboring around the stove. The aromas on the air were those of a fine home kitchen. On the stroke of five-thirty, Mrs. Wilkes sounded a gong. We stood up simultaneously, walked forward and took positions behind the chairs. We all held hands and a white-haired old gentleman, the senior boarder of the house, said grace. . . .

One could hardly praise the food too highly. It was the exact equivalent, in regional, Savannah terms, of the food in a first-class pension in a French provincial city.

Roy Andries de Groot,
in Esquire, 1971

Thoroughly combine 1 cup of finely crushed vanilla wafer crumbs, 1 cup of finely chopped pecans, 1 cup of powdered sugar, and 2 tablespoons of unsweetened cocoa. In a separate bowl, blend 2 ounces of bourbon and 1½ tablespoons of light corn syrup. Stir this liquid into the dry mixture, and when well blended, cover and chill in the refrigerator for 1 hour or more. Sift ½ cup or more of powdered sugar on a cookie sheet. Shape small bits of the dough into balls and roll them in the powdered sugar. Store the balls in tins with tight-fitting lids. They keep well refrigerated, and can be frozen. The recipe makes about 3 dozen.

Divinity

Like ambrosia and angel food, divinity belongs to the gods. Who knows where it came from or how it got here? It's a timeless holiday candy, too rich for everyday living, too sweet for regular consumption—and too delicious for words. Recipes for it (and there is one in almost every Southern cookbook) tend to be very much alike, most of them containing only sugar, water, corn syrup, egg whites, and vanilla. This is the common method.

In a mixing bowl, beat 1 large egg white until it will stand in stiff peaks on the end of the beater. In a heavy 2-quart saucepan, combine 2 cups of sugar, ½ cup of light corn syrup, and ½ cup of water. Bring them quickly to a boil, stirring until the sugar dissolves. Lower heat and continue cooking uncovered until a drop of the syrup forms a compact ball in a cup of ice water, or until the mixture reaches 255° on a candy thermometer. Remove from the heat immediately and pour in a slow, steady stream into the bowl of beaten egg white, beating all the while. (Don't scrape the sides of the saucepan; use only the syrupy liquid, not the hard crystals.) Add 1 teaspoon of vanilla extract and continue to beat the candy until it begins to thicken and hold its shape. Then quickly drop spoonfuls of it onto a sheet of wax paper. (Note: If the candy becomes too stiff to handle, stir 1 or 2 tablespoons of boiling water into it.) Top each mound with a pecan half before it becomes firmly set. The recipe should make about 2 dozen bite-sized morsels.

Southern cooking is still an eclectic mix of down-home and elegant, of ordinary and exotic. . . . If there are masters of this uncommon fare, they are the old-time, live-in professional cooks. . . . They served up the best food the South had to offer, whether a simple lunch for two or a six-course party for 20. . . . Their cooking, and the cooking of many like them, is one of the South's proud legacies.

Four Great Southern Cooks, 1980

Moravian Cookies

Elsewhere in these pages we have taken note of the Moravians, a pious sect of Protestants from Eastern Europe who migrated by way of Pennsylvania into

North Carolina before the American Revolution. At the Winkler Bakery in the restored village of Old Salem, at the Moravian Sugar Crisp Company in Clemmons, and elsewhere in the vicinity of Winston-Salem, North Carolina, a culinary tradition more than two centuries old still survives in the daily production of Moravian cookies and cakes. Like the Pennsylvania Dutch, their theological and gastronomical kin, the Moravians have long been noted for their baking. Some of the recipes that Evva and Travis Hanes use at their Moravian Sugar Crisp Company bakery have been in active service for longer than the Moravians have been in North Carolina. They don't publish their recipes, but numerous formulas for Moravian Christmas cookies are available, including one in *The American Heritage Cookbook* and another in *Marion Brown's Southern Cook Book*. The thin spicy cookies are essentially a blend of shortening, molasses, flour, sugar, and spices. Our recipe sticks close to the Moravian tradition.

Cream together ½ cup of firmly packed light brown sugar and ½ cup of softened shortening. Stir in 1 cup of good-quality sorghum molasses or cane syrup. Sift together 4 cups of all-purpose flour, 1 teaspoon of cinnamon, 1 teaspoon of ground cloves, ½ teaspoon of ground ginger, ½ teaspoon of mace, ½ teaspoon of allspice, and 1 teaspoon of baking soda and slowly add this dry mixture to the sugar-shortening-syrup combination. Stir in 1 teaspoon of finely grated lemon rind and 1 tablespoon of brandy. The dough should be very stiff. Refrigerate until it is thoroughly chilled. Then roll it out quite thin (⅛ inch or thinner), and using a variety of cookie cutters make many different shapes. Bake the cookies in a preheated 350° oven for 8 to 10 minutes, or until lightly browned. Take care not to overcook. The recipe will make several dozen thin and crispy spice cookies. They keep well stored in tins.

Peanut Brittle

The late Lillian Carter, mother of former President Jimmy Carter, understood well the social dimension of food, and her graceful blending of cookery and conversation is clearly displayed in *Miss Lillian and Friends*, a 1977 book by Beth Tartan and Rudy Hayes. Among the many excellent recipes included there is one for President Carter's favorite peanut brittle. It happens to be very similar to our own favorite, and since the confection has been around for almost a century in the South, a recipe for it is in order here.

"North Carolina food," says an authority, "is substantial, but does not soar." That is true, by and large, but Tar Heel cuisine covers quite a wide range from chitterlings to syllabub, from the broiled bluefish of Kitty Hawk to the corn-beans-and-acorn bread of the Cherokee Reservation, from a Halifax rockfish muddle to a Moravian cookie, and from immature but precociously vigorous corn

Boil together 3 cups of sugar, ½ cup of water, and 1 cup of light corn syrup until it spins a slender thread (about 230° on a candy thermometer). Add 3 cups of salted peanuts and stir constantly until the syrup turns golden brown and reaches the hard-crack stage (300°). Remove from the heat and add 2 teaspoons of baking soda, 4 tablespoons of butter, and 1 teaspoon of vanilla extract. Stir until the butter melts, then pour the candy out quickly onto a large buttered cookie sheet with sides. Spread it thin and let cool. When the candy has hardened, break it into pieces and store in a tin with a tight-fitting lid.

Pralines

Two classic New Orleans cookbooks published in 1885, *The Creole Cookery Book* and *La Cuisine Creole*, made no mention of pralines, but *The Picayune Creole Cook Book* (1901) gloried in these "dainty and delightful confections that have, for upwards of 150 years, delighted the younger generations of New Orleans, and the older ones, too." That would put the candy's Louisiana origin back to about 1750, which would be in line with John F. Mariani's explanation in *The Dictionary of American Food & Drink* that a French diplomat named Cesar du Plessis-Praslin gave his name to a caramelized almond and sugar confection in the late seventeenth century. Happily, Creole cooks got rid of the almonds in favor of pecans—and, since the *Picayune* was published, other refinements have given the candy a creamier texture. Our recipe draws upon the wisdom of numerous others that have appeared in Southern cookbooks during the past eighty-five years.

Combine 2 cups of white sugar, 1 cup of light brown sugar (firmly packed), and ¾ cup of half-and-half in a heavy pot or deep iron skillet and bring to a boil over medium heat, stirring only enough to prevent sticking. Do not scrape down the sides. As soon as the candy is boiling rapidly, add 2 cups of coarsely chopped pecans, 2 tablespoons of butter, and a pinch of salt. When the temperature reaches 230° as measured on a candy thermometer, remove pot from the heat and stir in 1 tablespoon of vanilla, beating vigorously by hand for about 2 minutes (but again, take care not to scrape the hard crystals from the sides). When the candy begins to cool and thicken ever so slightly, spoon it very quickly in little 2-inch pools on greased wax paper and leave to cool completely before wrapping individually and storing in tight-sealing tins. (Pralines can also be frozen.) The recipe will make 3 to

liquor in a half-gallon fruit jar to "Mrs. Durham's Pink Rose Petal Wine."

. . . . .

Tar Heels have always been great pork eaters, and in some parts of the coastal plain they have developed its preparation . . . into something closely resembling a fine art. . . . The eastern North Carolina ham, when properly cured and aged for two or three years, is accounted by Tar Heel connoisseurs to be the best meat in the country, if not in the world. . . . The curing could not be forced, the aging took a lot of time and shrank a lot of ham, but the result was frequently a masterpiece. It is almost impossible to find a great vintage ham nowadays; the art is becoming a lost one in a too-hurried age.

The North Carolina Guide, 1955

At New Emanuel Baptist Church in
Chattanooga, the finest traditions of
black southern cooking are upheld.
To walk in to the church luncheon
on Women's Days, when the project
is to raise funds for the church, is to
smell chicken frying. Women are ar-
ranging one tall cake after another
on the dessert table and another
line of women is filling plates with
ham, chicken, sweet potatoes,
green beans, pickled beets, new potatoes, cheese noodle casserole, tomato and lettuce salad, fresh
cornbread and hot homemade rolls
just from the oven. For dessert,
there is sweet potato pie, apple pie,
and pound cake. Friends of the
church order plates ahead of time,
come to the church, pay for them,
and take away some of the finest
Tennessee southern cooking in the
world.

Helen McDonald Exum,
in her introduction to
The Original Tennessee
Homecoming Cookbook, 1985

4 dozen pralines—sweet and creamy disks that are firm enough to hold and soft enough to melt in your mouth. The most important factor in making good pralines is knowing precisely when to spoon the hot candy onto the wax paper. There is no way to learn this except by trial, error, and eventual triumph.

PIES, COBBLERS, AND DUMPLINGS

The idea of pie—of meat, fish, vegetables, or fruits baked in a crust of pastry— goes back a very long way, probably to the Roman era. Europeans ate meat and fish pies and fruit tarts long before America was colonized. Mincemeat and pumpkin pies are associated with the New England Puritans, and the early colonists in Virginia probably were making pies with apples, lemons, plums, sweet potatoes, and a variety of custards before the seventeenth century was over.

Nothing, we are told, is as American as apple pie—and nobody is as fond of pie as Americans. In every region of the country, there is a pie tradition of long standing. In the South, the tradition is not only old but encompassing. We found delicious restaurant pies in every state of the region, and the same could not be said of any other type of food. The South certainly doesn't have a monopoly on outstanding pies, but it does generate a major share of the pie-making energy.

"We have eaten Key lime pies in Florida and wild blackberry pies in Oregon, blueberry pies in Maine, and sour cream raisin pies in Iowa," wrote Jane and Michael Stern in *Goodfood,* a guide to outstanding regional restaurants, "but the place we like eating pies best is the South, where love of sweets [is] a regional obsession."

In spite of the general decline in home cooking and baking, private pie making is still a fine and widely practiced art. On our list are eight representative Southern pies (plus one cobbler recipe and another for dumplings). In arriving at this roster, we had to pass over more than a dozen classic examples of pie making at its best, including apple, peach, cherry, rhubarb, and plum pies in the all-pastry class, butterscotch and coconut and caramel pies in the meringue class, and such legendary local favorites as Sister Lizzie's Shaker sugar pie from South Union, Kentucky, brown sugar pie from Lynchburg, Virginia, Kentucky Derby pie from Louisville, and cushaw pie from north Georgia. But the ones we have included all deserve to be classed among the region's best and most popular pies, and all are deeply rooted in Southern gastronomic history.

As a prelude to the pies, we begin with a dumpling dessert and a cobbler.

Apple Dumplings

The firm, tart apples of fall that appear in colorful abundance from northern Virginia to north Georgia and beyond are the ideal base for apple dumplings, which have been around in one form or another for almost as long as the apples themselves. This recipe is similar in most ways to the generality of dumpling dishes found in scores of Southern cookbooks for well over a century.

Peel 2 large apples and cut them up in bite-sized chunks, dropping the pieces into a pan of cold water to stay fresh until needed. Make a dough by sifting together 2 cups of flour, ½ teaspoon of baking powder, and ¼ teaspoon of salt. Cut in ¾ cup of shortening and then add ice water a tablespoon at a time (3 or 4 tablespoons total) until the dough makes a cohesive ball. Wrap in wax paper and refrigerate for about 30 minutes. Meanwhile, combine in a saucepan 1 cup of sugar, ½ teaspoon of cinnamon, ½ teaspoon of nutmeg, and ½ teaspoon of allspice; add 2 cups of water and 4 tablespoons of butter. Bring the mixture close to the boiling point, stirring until the sugar dissolves, and then turn off the heat and leave the pan covered to stay warm. In a small bowl, mix ½ cup of sugar and 2 teaspoons of cinnamon and set aside.

Roll the dough as thin as pie crust and cut it into 6-inch squares. Drain the apple pieces in a colander. Put several pieces on each square, sprinkle on 1 teaspoon of cinnamon and sugar, add a small pat of butter, and pull up the corners of the square to surround the apples and spices in a dough pouch. Set these side by side in a large buttered baking dish, pour the warm syrup over them, and bake the dumplings at 375° for 30 to 40 minutes, by which time the apples should be bubbling hot and the pastry well-cooked. Baste the spicy mounds once or twice with sauce during the baking process. The recipe should make about 8 dumplings.

Apples were scarce one year. Real scarce. My grandmother had a half bushel of apples. She canned the apples, and then she taken the peelings and canned those. Washed 'em real clean and canned 'em.

My mother said at the time, "I'll never eat those." But then later on, she was down in the hayfield, and when she came in, my grandmother had baked two wonderful pies from those peelings. And my mother ate three pieces.

They used so many things that we throw away. I remember Grandmother peeled the potatoes real deep and planted the peelings. Raised our potatoes that way!

77-year-old Winnie Biggerstaff, quoted by Patsy Moore Ginns, in Snowbird Gravy and Dishpan Pie: Mountain People Recall, *1982*

Blackberry Cobbler

The arrival of ripe blackberries in midsummer in the rural South used to be a signal occasion eagerly awaited by multitudes of country folks. They found them growing wild in the fencerows and in weed-choked backlot gullies, an enticing repository of deep purple sweetness buried in tangled thickets of briar-spiked canes. The price paid in briar scratches and chigger bites for a gallon bucket of berries was frightfully high, but they were well worth it. Eaten fresh with cream and sugar or cooked into jam or baked into pies and cobblers, black-berries were a great delight—and they still are, of course, wherever they can be found. The wonders of modern agriculture have produced domesticated black-berry vines with big, juicy berries and no briars, and the fruit can also be bought canned or frozen. An old-fashioned homemade cobbler thus can still be had. Here is one method of preparation.

Make a pastry by sifting together 2 cups of flour and ¼ teaspoon of salt. Cut in ½ cup of shortening and then add ice water, a tablespoon at a time, mixing until the dough forms a cohesive ball. Refrigerate until well chilled, then roll out about two thirds of the dough on a floured surface to the thickness of pie pastry and press it against the bottom and sides of a lightly greased 9-inch baking dish or cake pan.

In a large saucepan, cover 2 cups of fresh berries with 2 cups of water (or use canned or frozen berries and their juice), and carefully stir in ½ cup of sugar and 2 tablespoons of cornstarch. Cook over low heat until the mixture starts to thicken, then pour it into the pastry-lined dish. Roll out the remainder of the pastry and cut ½-inch strips to lay criss-crossed over the top of the cobbler. Bake it at 350° for 45 minutes to 1 hour, or un-til the pastry is well-browned and the berries are bubbling.

Black Bottom Pie

"I think this is the most delicious pie I have ever eaten," exclaimed Marjorie Kinnan Rawlings in her 1942 kitchen narrative, *Cross Creek Cookery.* She had combined two recipes, one from "an old hotel in Louisiana" and the other of uncertain origin, and the result was "a pie so delicate, so luscious, that I hope to be propped up on my dying bed and fed a generous portion. Then I think that I should refuse outright to die, for life would be too good to relinquish."

Duncan Hines, the wandering hotel and restaurant scout from Kentucky, published an almost identical black bottom pie recipe in his *Adventures in Good Cooking* in the early 1940s, having found the dessert in a restaurant in Oklahoma City, but it isn't clear whether his discovery preceded Mrs. Rawlings' or drew its inspiration from hers. James Beard, in his *American Cookery,* said black bottom pie "began appearing in cookbooks around the turn of the cen-tury," but he cited none; it wasn't in Fannie Farmer's magnum opus or *Joy of Cooking* until after Rawlings and Hines published it. But if the story of its origin has been lost, the basic formula for its unique combination of flavors is safe—and certain to remain with us. Let it suffice to say that black bottom is a South-

I spent some days at a plantation a few miles from Montgomery [Ala-bama]. . . . It was now the middle of April. In the kitchen-garden the peas were ripening, and the straw-berries turning red, though the spring of 1835 was very backward. We had salads, young asparagus, and radishes.

The following may be considered a pretty fair account of the provision for a planter's table at this season; and except with regard to vege-tables, I believe it does not vary

ern pie that has been spreading joy in and out of the region for close to fifty years or more. The formula is time-consuming, but the end result is spectacular.

To make the crust: Reduce about 2 dozen gingersnaps or graham crackers to fine crumbs, moisten with 6 tablespoons of melted butter, and press firmly against the bottom and sides of a 9-inch deep-dish pie plate or pan. When the surface is completely covered, bake for 10 minutes at 325° to set the crust. Put aside on rack to cool.

To make the filling: Soak 1 tablespoon of gelatin in 4 tablespoons of cold water. In a separate bowl, mix together ½ cup of sugar, a pinch of salt, and 1 tablespoon of cornstarch. Separate 4 eggs, set the whites aside, and beat the yolks well. Melt 2 squares of unsweetened chocolate in a saucepan over very low heat, stir in 1 teaspoon of vanilla extract, and set aside. In another saucepan scald 2 cups of milk, add the sugar and cornstarch mixture to it, let cool slightly, pour in the egg yolks very slowly, and transfer the well-blended custard to a double boiler, stirring constantly as it cooks and thickens over boiling water for about 10 minutes. Then stir in the gelatin. Pour about half of the custard—a cup or so—into the melted chocolate, mix, and set the other half aside to cool. Beat the 4 egg whites with ⅛ teaspoon of cream of tartar and ½ cup of sugar to a stiff meringue and fold it into the cooled plain custard. Slowly stir in 2 tablespoons of rum.

To assemble the pie: Pour the chocolate custard into the crust and smooth it out to the edges. Pour the rum custard on top and level it. Chill thoroughly in the refrigerator (overnight if possible). Beat 1 cup of whipping cream to stiff peaks, adding 2 tablespoons of powdered sugar in the process (optional) and spread on top of the pie. Garnish with a little bit of finely grated unsweetened chocolate. The well-defined layers of whipped cream, rum custard, chocolate custard, and crumb crust make a spectacular pie—to look at, and to taste.

Buttermilk Pie

Custard pies made with buttermilk were appearing in Southern cookbooks more than a century ago. A recipe in an 1882 issue of *Farm & Home Magazine* was very similar to the one we enjoy now. We got it from Jettie Lawrence, a Kentucky lady who has turned this old standard into a modern work of art.

First, to make a pastry: Sift together 1½ cups of all-purpose flour and ¼ teaspoon of salt, then sift again. Cut in ½ cup of lard or shortening, or a

much throughout the year. Breakfast at seven; hot wheat bread, generally sour; corn bread, biscuits, waffles, hominy, dozens of eggs, broiled ham, beef-steak or broiled fowl, tea and coffee. Lunch at eleven; cake and wine, or liqueur. Dinner at two; now and then soup (not good), always roast turkey and ham; a boiled fowl here, a tongue there; a small piece of nondescript meat, which generally turns out to be pork disguised; hominy, rice, hot cornbread, sweet potatoes; potatoes mashed with spice, very hot; salad and radishes, and an extraordinary variety of pickles. . . . Then succeed pies of apple, squash, and pumpkin; custard, and a variety of preserves. . . . Dispersed about the table are shell almonds, raisins, hickory, and other nuts; and, to crown the whole, large blocks of ice-cream. Champagne is abundant, and cider frequent. Ale and porter may now and then be seen; but claret is the most common drink.

Harriet Martineau
Society in America, 1837

Close to noon on Christmas Day we saw them coming down the road: forty-eight men in stripes, with their guards. They came up the hill and headed for the house, a few laughing, talking, others grim and suspicious. All had come, white and Negro. We had helped Mother make two caramel cakes and twelve sweet potato pies and a wonderful backbone-and-rice dish (which Mother, born on the coast, called pilau); and there were hot rolls and Brunswick stew, and a washtub full of apples which our father had polished in front of the fire on Christmas Eve. It would be a splendid dinner. . . . The day was warm and sunny and the forty-eight men and their guards were sitting on the grass. . . . Eight of the men were lifers; six of them, in pairs, had their inside legs locked together; ten were killers. . . . They were our guests, and our father moved among them with grace and ease. . . . When Mother said she was ready, our father asked "Son," who was one of the killers, to go help "my wife, won't you, with the heavy things." And the young man said he'd be mighty glad to. The one in for raping and another for rob-

mixture of shortening and margarine, using a pastry cutter. Add ice water a tablespoon at a time (about 3 tablespoons in all), stirring the dough around the bowl with a fork. As soon as it is moist enough to gather into a cohesive ball, wrap it in wax paper and refrigerate for about 30 minutes. Handle the dough as little as possible. Roll it out on a floured surface to a thickness of ⅛ inch or less. This much dough should make a double crust for a 9- or 10-inch pie, or two single crusts. Some pies go to the oven in an unbaked crust, but the buttermilk pie calls for a prebaked one. Prick the shell with a fork, bake in a preheated 350° oven for about 3 minutes, then remove and prick some more if it is puffing up. Return to the oven for 5 additional minutes before setting it on a rack to cool.

Then, to make the filling: Beat 3 egg yolks in a mixing bowl with 1 cup of sugar, 2 tablespoons of cornstarch, and a pinch of salt. Add to the mixture 4 tablespoons of melted butter, 1 tablespoon of lemon juice, and 1 cup of buttermilk. Stir well and pour into the prebaked pastry. Bake at 350° for about 20 minutes, or until the custard is almost set in the center.

In the meantime, make a meringue with the 3 egg whites. Beat until frothy with an electric mixer, adding ¼ teaspoon of cream of tartar. Then gradually add ⅓ to ½ cup of sugar and continue beating until the meringue makes peaks that stand straight up.

Remove the partially baked pie from the oven, cover it with meringue (spread to the edges and make sure it is touching the crust all around), and return to the oven. Bake about 10 more minutes, or until the top is golden brown.

Chess Pie

Here is a mystery: Where did this thoroughly Southern pie get its name? The British had a cheese pie that was somewhat similar, but not the same. Chess pie by that name doesn't show up in American cookbooks until the twentieth century, at least not with any regularity, not even in the South. There was transparent pie and jelly pie and Jefferson Davis pie, all of which seem to be variations of what we now call chess, but the modern version of chess pie is rarely found in old recipe books.

For the past forty or fifty years, though, it has appeared throughout the region (and hardly anywhere else), and it is now so thoroughly identified with Southern cookery that most people assume it has been here forever. As for its name, there are two stories among the many that seem to ring true. The first has to do with an old piece of Southern furniture called a pie safe or pie chest.

It's a cupboard with perforated tin panels, and its name is derived from the fact that pies and other confections were put there for storage and safekeeping. Chess pie may have been called a chest pie at first, meaning that it held up well in the pie chest.

The other story is even simpler and more appealing. It is that a creative Southern housewife came up with this concoction and tried it out on her husband. He loved it. "What kind of pie is this?" he is said to have exclaimed. His wife shrugged and smiled. "I don't know," she said; "it's ches' pie."

There are many recipes for Southern chess pie. This thoroughly tested and proved one is fairly typical.

Beat 3 eggs with a wire whisk. Add 1½ cups of sugar, 3 tablespoons of melted butter, 1 tablespoon of plain white cornmeal, ⅓ cup of buttermilk, ½ teaspoon of salt, and 1½ teaspoons of vanilla extract. Mix the ingredients well and pour into an unbaked 9-inch pie shell (for pastry, see the buttermilk pie recipe above). Bake in a preheated 375° oven on the bottom rack for 15 minutes, then reduce heat to 350° and bake 20 minutes more.

Half-Moon Pies

Before the days of packaged snack foods, dried fruit—peaches, apples, and apricots in particular—was a very common and nutritious between-meals nibbler. Stewed peaches and apples were also popular dinner-table side dishes. Because they were so convenient and economical, as well as delicious, dried fruits were a winter staple in the rural South. The most favored use of all for this leathery, wrinkled treat was in fried pies—fruit-filled pastry pouches folded like half-moons and fried in hot fat.

There are a few places around the South where delicious fried pies can still be found for sale. Mary Thomas' Family Pie Shop in De Valls Bluff, Arkansas, and Sprayberry's, a barbecue restaurant in Newnan, Georgia, are two sources that come quickly to mind.

And then there is Vernie Stephens of Portland, Tennessee, who sold 3,442 fried pies out of her kitchen in 1984. Using her own dried fruits and a secret combination of spices, she made 3½ dozen every morning and marketed them through a Portland restaurant and to local churches, private groups, and individuals. "People say they can't make them like I do," she reported. "There's more to it than just the recipe. You've got to practice it." Vernie Stephens has been practicing for a long time. She is over ninety years old.

Half-moon pies can be baked in the oven as well as fried in a heavy skillet,

bing a bank said they'd be pleased to help, too, and they went in. . . . They came back in a few minutes bearing great pots and pans to a serving table we had set up on the porch. My sister and I served the plates.

Lillian Smith
Memory of a Large Christmas, 1961

and cooks who don't have home-dried fruit can find it in the supermarket. This recipe is similar to many traditional ones.

Cover 2 cups or a 12-ounce package of dried fruit with water, bring to a boil and simmer, covered, for 15 minutes, by which time a soft puree should result. Mash with a fork and stir into it ½ cup of sugar and a combination of spices—cinnamon, nutmeg, allspice, ginger, cloves—to achieve a tart and savory flavor that suits your taste. Leave the mixture simmering, stirring occasionally, and let it cook down to a thick, saucy stew. Then set it off the stove to cool.

Meanwhile, make a pastry by sifting together 2 cups of all-purpose flour and ½ teaspoon of salt, cutting in ½ cup of shortening, and adding just enough ice water (3 or 4 tablespoons) to make a cohesive dough ball. Chill it for easier handling, then roll out very thin and cut into rounds about 4 or 5 inches in diameter (an empty 46-ounce juice can makes an ideal cutter). Spoon a heaping tablespoon of the cooled fruit onto each round and fold the dough over to envelop the fruit. Crimp the edges tightly with a fork or your fingers. Fry in about 1 inch of hot shortening in a heavy skillet, turning once, or in deep fat, not turning at all. If you prefer to bake the pies, 30 minutes in a preheated 400° oven should be about right. A 12-ounce package of dried fruit will make about a dozen pies.

Key Lime Pie

The thin-skinned, juicy, extremely sour Key lime (also known as the Mexican, West Indian, or golden lime) originated in Southeast Asia many centuries ago, and it is thought that Columbus brought seeds to Haiti in 1493 and established the thorny little trees there. The limes were thriving on the southern tip of Florida well before the Civil War, and the name by which they are best known comes from their association with the Florida Keys. Key limes were a thriving commercial crop there until 1926, when a hurricane wiped out the groves. Now only a scattered few Key lime trees are left, and it is exceedingly rare to get a piece of restaurant pie anywhere that has been made with real Key lime juice. (The larger, greener, less tangy, seedless Persian lime is the only type available commercially.)

When condensed milk was readily available after the Civil War, many Southern cooks used it in place of perishable dairy products. In the Keys as far back as the 1890s, a simple pie combining egg yolks, condensed milk, and lime juice in a graham-cracker crumb crust was a well-established local favorite. It is essentially that same pie that persists in cookbooks and restaurants today, though it is generally made with Persian lime juice and sometimes is baked in a regular crust with meringue on top or egg whites folded into the custard. Green food coloring is also commonly used to boost the rather bland and colorless natural appearance, and some recipes call for gelatin to make the custard stand up. Key West Conchs (natives) are disdainful of these modern "improvements," insisting that the simple old way is still the best.

Separate 3 large eggs and beat the yolks with an electric mixer until they thicken and become lemon-colored. Empty a 14-ounce can of sweetened condensed milk into the bowl and blend thoroughly with the yolks. Slowly add ½ cup of fresh lime juice and continue beating until the mixture is very thick. Then, either pour it into a regular 9-inch pie plate lined with the baked crumb crust described below and refrigerate it (for at least 6 hours), later to be topped with whipped cream and grated lime rind, or pour it into a standard prebaked pastry crust, make a meringue with the reserved egg whites (see page 330), and brown it for 8 to 10 minutes in a preheated 350° oven. (Another option is to make individual pie tarts.) The custard will be runny if sliced hot, but sets up well when cool.

To make a crumb crust, reduce a quantity of graham crackers to 1½ cups of fine crumbs, add ¼ cup of sugar and ¼ cup of melted butter, and press the sticky mixture firmly against the bottom and sides of a 9-inch pie plate. Bake for 8 to 10 minutes at 350°. Vanilla wafers or ginger snaps may be substituted for graham crackers, and finely grated pecans may also be added. Baked crumb crusts should be cooled before filling, and finished pies should be refrigerated.

Lemon Meringue Pie

Lemons and other citrus fruits from Spanish Florida and the Caribbean found their way to plantation kitchens along the Atlantic Seaboard very early in the colonial period. Nobody ever figured out a good way to cook a lemon, or even to eat one raw, but its juice was discovered to be delightfully flavorful when combined with sugar in both confections and drinks. Lemonades and rum punches probably were established drinks in America three hundred years ago, and lemon puddings and custards, some of them baked in pastries, must have come along at about the same time. Meringue came later, and then all the necessary elements were at hand to make lemon meringue pie, which surely must rank with chocolate as the oldest and most popular meringue pies in the

I drove down from Miami . . . impelled by a lifelong desire to taste an authentic Key lime pie. As I crossed the last bridge, from Stock Island onto Key West, I assumed I was only minutes from enjoying a rich slice of Florida's most famous regional specialty. But after a week of stuffing down piece after piece of one so-called Key lime pie after another . . . I came to realize that probably none of these pies . . . contained a single drop of freshly squeezed Key lime juice.

Indeed, after some serious inquiry among local experts, I am now morally certain that virtually all "Key lime" pies [sold commercially] are actually made with the juice of the Tahiti (or Persian or Bearss) lime, which is not a true lime at all. This hybrid of mysterious origin is the "lime" sold in supermarkets all over the country. . . . It is a satisfactory fruit, but it is not at all the equal of its cousin Citrus aurantifolia (a.k.a. Key lime, Mexican lime, or West Indian lime).

Raymond Sokolov
Fading Feast, 1981

country. In the South, at least, these two are tops in longevity and popularity. The buttermilk pie recipe on page 329 gives directions for making the pastry and meringue called for here. Lemon pie fillings are quite common in Southern cookbooks, from the oldest to the most recent. This is a typical and traditional example.

Mix 1 cup of sugar, 5 tablespoons of cornstarch, and ¼ teaspoon of salt in the top of a double boiler. Set it over boiling water and slowly add 2 cups of sweet milk, stirring well. Continue stirring over moderate heat until the mixture thickens and clings to the spoon. Remove top of double boiler and let the pan cool slightly. Then add the following ingredients separately, mixing in each one well: 1 tablespoon of butter, 3 lightly beaten egg yolks, 6 tablespoons of fresh lemon juice, and 1 teaspoon of finely grated lemon rind. Return the pan to the double boiler and cook the mixture for a few more minutes, stirring constantly. When the custard is hot and quite thick—beyond pouring, but still easily shaped with a spoon or spatula—set the pan in cold water to cool for 5 minutes or so. Then spoon the mixture into a prebaked 9-inch pie shell, spread it out evenly, top with meringue, and bake at 350° for 8 to 10 minutes, or until nicely browned. This is not a refrigerator pie, and it slices poorly (but tastes wonderful) when hot; it is best served at room temperature.

Pecan Pie

The pecan—named by the Indians—is a variety of native American hickory nut, and the trees from which it comes thrive especially well in the Southern states. Thomas Jefferson raised pecan trees at Monticello, and he helped George Washington get them started at Mount Vernon, but it is in the Deep South, from Georgia to Louisiana and Texas, that the tall, shady trees and their tender nuts do best. We have heard the claim that Louisianans were eating pecan candies before 1800, and with the sugar and syrup produced from cane at that time, it is conceivable that they were eating pecan pies too, but there are no recipes or other bits of evidence to prove it.

Probably no other dessert is more closely identified with the South today than pecan pie—and yet, surprisingly, recipes for it were not commonly found in the region's cookbooks until about fifty years ago. Molasses pie, which is essentially pecan pie without pecans, was a Southern favorite early in the nineteenth century and perhaps even before that, but not even the comprehensive *Picayune Creole Cook Book* (1901) added pecans to the molasses recipe. No one seems to know when and where the combination was first tried. Once it did appear, though, it spread quickly. Fannie Farmer and *Joy of Cooking* and other nationally famed cookbooks added recipes for pecan pie in the 1940s, and now it is considered a national dessert.

The basic recipe tends to be very much the same from one place to the next. Butter, sugar, eggs, syrup, and plenty of pecans are the primary ingredients, with variations supplied by such flavor-altering additions as vanilla, bourbon, and chocolate. We have tasted some wonderful pecan pies in restaurants and private homes around the region, from Delpha Rhoades in Kentucky and Melba Tolleson's in Tennessee to Anne Griffin's in Georgia and Jocelyn Mayfield's in Mississippi and Emily Chase's in Louisiana. Rising to the challenge, we have come up with a good one of our own, as follows.

Set aside an unbaked 9-inch pie crust (see recipe, page 329). Combine 4 tablespoons of softened butter with ¾ cup of firmly packed light brown sugar and cream together until smooth. In a separate bowl, whip 3 whole eggs with a fork or wire whisk and blend them into the sugar and butter. Then sift 1 tablespoon of cornstarch and ⅛ teaspoon of salt into the mixture, and stir in 2 teaspoons of vanilla extract. Next, blend in ¾ cup of good-quality dark cane or corn syrup, followed by 1 cup of broken pecan pieces. When all the ingredients are thoroughly mixed, pour into the pie crust and bake at 325° for 30 minutes, then at 300° for 30 more minutes, or until the center is firm. Served warm with whipped cream or vanilla ice cream on top, pecan pie is a rich and delicious dessert in the finest Southern tradition.

Sweet Potato Pie

Well-traveled sweet potatoes and yams went from Central and South America to Europe with the Spaniards and back to North America in the seventeenth century. Southerners have eaten them in many forms since about 1650, and it may be that sweet potato pie was an English delicacy long before that. George Washington Carver's extensive research on the sweet potato at Tuskegee Institute helped to popularize the vegetable and also to put more recipes using it into circulation. Carver's pie recipe, published in a Tuskegee bulletin early in this century, was a prototype of modern versions, combining potatoes, milk, eggs, sugar, and spices. Many a Southern cookbook features one or more sweet potato pie recipes, and the principal variation among them is in the combination of spices. Our recipe borrows from several others. We arrived at it by combining spices in the filling until we got a taste that suited us best.

The first settlers on the southern reach of the Atlantic shores found the Indians eating sweet potatoes and followed suit. . . . When it first reached Europe, imported at the beginning of the sixteenth century by the Spaniards, who named it batata, *it was endowed, quite gratuitously, with the reputation of being aphrodisiac. For this and other reasons, it appealed to Henry VIII, who imported sweet potatoes from Spain and ate them in the form of pies, very sweet and heavily spiced.*

Waverley Root and Richard de Rochemont
Eating in America, 1976

Prepare a 9-inch deep-dish or 10-inch regular pie crust (see recipe, page 329). Boil 3 medium-to-large sweet potatoes until tender, cool them, and then peel and mash enough to make 3 cups. Cream 1 stick of softened butter with 1 cup of firmly packed brown sugar (light or dark), then beat 3 eggs and combine with the butter and sugar mixture. Add ¼ teaspoon of salt, ½ teaspoon of vanilla extract, and a combination of spices (cinnamon, cloves, ginger, nutmeg, allspice, mace) totaling 1½ teaspoons. Stir in the mashed sweet potatoes. Add 1 cup of sweet or evaporated milk or half-and-half, beat the mixture well with an electric mixer and pour into the pie shell. Bake at 350° for 50 minutes to 1 hour, or until the center is firm.

PUDDINGS

The British colonists who came to America brought with them a devotion to puddings, especially sweet ones, and they were the forerunners of the abundance and variety of pies and puddings in modern cookbooks. Some were baked in a crust, others baked without a crust, still others boiled or steamed. To these English recipes were added in time some distinctly American ones, the first and most popular of which was Indian pudding, so called because it was made with Indian cornmeal. Among the Indians themselves the dish was called sagamite, and some colonists, particularly in New England, called it hasty pudding. North and South, it was a very common and well-liked dish for generations, and it also served as a standard sweet pudding all along the westward-moving frontier. Amelia Simmons had three recipes for it in *American Cookery* (1796), the first truly American cookbook, and Mary Randolph's *Virginia House-Wife* (1824) included both baked and boiled versions. The basic ingredients—milk, cornmeal, butter, eggs, sugar, and spices—were more or less standard, creating a soft pudding with a flavor very similar to gingerbread. Today, Indian pudding is rarely found in the South.

Another old Southern dish with an interesting history but not much current favor is rice pudding. Sarah Rutledge included recipes for it in *The Carolina Housewife* (1847), but Elizabeth Verner Hamilton, in her foreword to a 1976 reprint of *Two Hundred Years of Charleston Cooking* (first published in 1930), declared, "The very idea of sweets with rice upsets Charlestonians who take rice very seriously." (Carolina's serious rice devotees thus must have been disturbed to find, on page 247 of the original cookbook, a recipe for rice pudding.)

More contemporary, but equally as rare, is Ozark pudding, a dish which apparently originated in the mountains of northwest Arkansas and southwest Missouri. It is essentially an apple and nut mixture combined with sugar, eggs,

For a lot longer than I can remember, the Sedberry Hotel was famous for its food and hospitality. There was a hotel on that corner of the square in McMinnville from early in the 1800s. The last one was built in about 1870, and Mrs. Oceana Tucker Sedberry, an attractive widow from west Tennessee, came to operate it

and a little flour. Curiously, Ozark pudding is seldom found in Arkansas cookbooks, even old ones, but it does show up occasionally in other Southern recipe collections.

Our abbreviated list of pudding recipes includes banana pudding and bread pudding, both widely enjoyed in the region, and a local favorite, Woodford pudding, which originated in Kentucky more than a century ago.

Banana Pudding

Since virtually all the bananas eaten in the United States are imported, this dessert can't be claimed as a native Southern dish. It has been known and loved in the region for many decades, though, and this particular version has been handed down through four generations of a Kentucky family (mine) with all the care and attention properly reserved for an heirloom.

Separate 6 eggs. Beat egg yolks until smooth and then carefully and slowly add 1 tablespoon of flour, a pinch of salt, ¾ cup of sugar, and 1½ cups of milk. Pour the mixture into a double boiler and stir constantly over boiling water until it thickens (in about 5 to 10 minutes); set the pan off the heat and let it cool a little. Beat 6 egg whites with ½ teaspoon of cream of tartar until frothy and then add ½ cup of sugar very slowly and beat until stiff.

Cover the bottom of an 8- by 12-inch baking dish with about 2 dozen vanilla wafers in a single layer, and then place 4 large, firm bananas split in half on top of the wafers. Spread the cooled custard pudding evenly over the cookies and bananas, cover with the thick layer of meringue, and bake at 350° until the dish is bubbling all around and the meringue is a landscape of golden brown peaks (12 to 15 minutes should do it). Served warm with a cold glass of milk, banana pudding is exemplary. This recipe should make at least 8 large servings.

Bread Pudding

No self-respecting New Orleans restaurant remotely associated with the traditional ways of cooking would be without a bread pudding recipe on its menu, or so it seems from the proliferation of such dishes in the city's dining places and cookbooks. The New Orleans Junior League's *Plantation Cookbook* features a very popular version with cognac sauce, and we have delighted in it

in 1913. She bought it in 1920, and she or her daughters, Connie and Erbye, ran it in high style until it closed in 1954.

The Sedberry was a grand place. The dining room seated about one hundred people, and it was Victorian fancy—crystal chandeliers, red velvet draperies, deep rose china, pink linens, thumb-pressed goblets. Miss Erbye was the hostess from about 1925 on, and people came from all over the country to dine there—Babe Ruth, Huey Long, even Al Capone. In 1927, the American Automobile Association called it "the best little hotel on the North American continent."

The Sedberry women were all good cooks, and they hired excellent local cooks, too. I remember three black women in particular who worked there for a long time: India Hill and Viola Lowe and Marian Ryan. The food they turned out was legendary, from the cornsticks and fried chicken and stuffed squash to the most delectable pies and cakes and homemade ice cream you ever tasted. When I think of Southern food at its very best, I think of the old Sedberry Hotel.

a reminiscence by Edith Hillis Bryan, McMinnville, Tennessee, 1985

many times. Our personal favorite, though, is a recipe created by a lady named Ruth Puckette Carter, who divided her years between the rural Alabama town of Mt. Meigs and the cities of Chicago and Nashville. The late Mrs. Carter was what cookbook writer Flossie Morris called "a natural-born cook." Her bread pudding recipe is a model of elegant simplicity.

Toast 8 slices of white bread and cut off the crusts. Cut the bread into small cubes and spread half of them evenly over the bottom of a 9-inch round cake pan. Scatter ½ cup of raisins over the bread, then add the rest of the bread cubes. Melt 4 tablespoons of butter and pour it over the bread and raisins. In a mixing bowl, beat 4 whole eggs well, add ½ cup of sugar, 2 cups of milk, and 1 teaspoon of vanilla extract. When thoroughly blended, pour into the cake pan, making sure that all the toast and raisins are soaked. Bake in a preheated 350° oven for 1 hour, then test the center to see if it is firmly set; continue baking for up to 15 more minutes if necessary, taking care not to let it overcook and begin to dry out. Remove to a cooling rack and then turn the pudding onto a large plate to slice and serve.

To make 1 cup of sauce, mix ½ cup of sugar and 1 tablespoon of cornstarch well, stir in 1 cup of water, and cook the mixture, stirring frequently, until it thickens and clears. Remove from heat, cool a few minutes, and stir in ¼ cup of fresh lemon juice and ½ teaspoon of vanilla extract. Mix a small amount of the sauce with ¼ teaspoon of nutmeg to dissolve the spice thoroughly, then combine with the larger portion. The pudding and sauce will make 8 servings.

Woodford Pudding

In Woodford County, Kentucky, near Lexington, cooks have been making a dish called Woodford pudding for well over a century; a recipe for it appeared in *Housekeeping in the Bluegrass* in 1875, and it probably was not the first. A creamy pudding spiced with cinnamon and nutmeg, it originally had a sauce topping; some cooks later substituted a meringue. Marion Flexner, in *Out of Kentucky Kitchens* (1949), passed on a whiskey sauce she credited to Judge H. H. Tye of Williamsburg, Kentucky, a noted dinner-table host of some years earlier. We made the spongy, spicy pudding according to *Housekeeping in the Bluegrass* and topped it with a sauce similar to Judge Tye's.

Cream together 1 cup of sugar and 1 stick of softened butter. Sift together ½ cup of flour, ½ teaspoon of cinnamon, and ½ teaspoon of nutmeg. Dis-

The idea that any living creature, without regard to race or color, should go hungry through lack of funds with which to buy provender was foreign to the imaginations of the community. Excepting at the hotel, food was to be given away, not to be sold. You might be frugal with your dollars but to hoard food was stinginess and stinginess was contemptible; it was "common," which was even worse. Let a gentleman— almost any gentleman from almost anywhere—be quartered at the hotel and some local gentleman presently would be calling to introduce

solve 1 teaspoon of baking soda in 1 tablespoon of buttermilk. Add 3 whole eggs to the butter and sugar, one at a time, and blend thoroughly. Add the flour and spices to this mixture, followed by the buttermilk and soda. Blend in 1 cup of blackberry jam (with or without seeds). Grease a 9-inch square cake pan and then pour in the pudding and bake it in a preheated 325° oven for 40 minutes, or until spongy in the center. Cool on a rack and then cut into 9 squares to serve.

To make the sauce, cream together 4 tablespoons of softened butter and ½ cup of sugar. Blend in 1 well-beaten egg. Put the mixture in the top of a double boiler over gently boiling water and stir until it thickens. Remove from heat and stir in 1 or 2 ounces of whiskey or brandy, to suit your taste. Spoon the hot sauce over the Woodford pudding and serve.

SPECIALTY DESSERTS

A few of the South's most cherished desserts don't classify as cakes, pies, or puddings. We will close out this section on sweets with brief mention of several colonial and early American specialties, and with recipes for egg kisses, flan, peach ice cream, and strawberry shortcake. And, for good measure, there is one final confection, also strawberry and more of a pie than a cake.

Many of the desserts of colonial America were British or French creations with names that now sound quaint and unfamiliar to most of us: charlotte russe, blanc mange, jumbals, slips, fools, flummery, rusks, trifles, floating islands. Syllabub and boiled custard were discussed earlier among the dessert drinks; here, we have a list of custards and puddings and sweet breads that have largely disappeared from the cookbooks. In fact, of all the desserts named here, only boiled custard is still an active favorite in Southern kitchens. Only rarely, on special occasions, do we encounter the likes of Carolina trifle.

But once—and for a long time—these were all considered standard sweets in Southern cookery, and elsewhere in the country too. Mary Randolph had recipes for them in her *Virginia House-Wife*. Her charlotte, originally a French creation, was followed by multiple versions, and by the time of the Civil War, charlotte russe was in most Southern recipe collections. It stayed around for a long time, and even now can occasionally be found on holiday tables. As it evolved in the South, charlotte russe was usually a molded and chilled pudding made with ladyfingers; Mrs. Randolph's version sounds more like a fruit cobbler.

More familiar to contemporary Southern eaters are the sweet dishes below, all of them regional favorites of long standing (though none is indigenous to the South, unless strawberry shortcake can make such a claim).

himself and to proffer the hospitalities of his home.

. . . . .

To Gilmartin it seemed they had practically everything for dinner. He soon found out though how far short his estimate of the Kentuckian's capacity for loading a dinner table had fallen. . . . The food came on in caravans; it came in flotillas; it came in argosies. There were only two courses—first the meats, the hot breads, the vegetables—almost countless shoals of vegetables—the pickles and the preserves and the spicy home-made condiments; and at the last, the desserts consisting of two kinds of pie and watermelon and sliced peaches with cream and cookies and fat slices of layer cake. The coffee was served—in big cups—with the meal.

Irvin S. Cobb
Red Likker, 1929

Flan

Spanish custard, the Floridians call it: a cool, shimmering mass of molded custard swimming in a tangy caramel sauce. Wherever Spanish cuisine can be found, there will be flan. We first encountered it in Tampa, Florida, in 1960, when our neighbor Mary Speziale served it after a delicious dinner, and we have prized the dessert ever since. Flan has been a fixture on Florida restaurant menus for almost as long as the oldest city restaurants there have been in business. Columbia Restaurant in Tampa, for example, served flan when it opened in 1905. Alba Payas reinforced the tradition when she brought this recipe to Tampa from her native Cuba in the early 1960s.

Beat 6 whole eggs with a mixer and add, in order, the contents of a 12-ounce can of evaporated milk, 1½ cups of water, 6 tablespoons of sugar, 2 teaspoons of vanilla extract, and a pinch of salt. Blend and set aside.

Next, set a heavy iron skillet over very low heat, grease lightly with margarine or shortening, add ¾ cup of white sugar, and stir constantly for 8 to 10 minutes, by which time the sugar should be melted and darkening to a straw-colored hue. Remove from heat and slowly stir in ¾ cup of very hot water. (If the water is added too fast or isn't hot enough, the syrup will spurt and spatter and lack smoothness.) When the sugar and water have been thoroughly combined, return the skillet to low heat and continue cooking and stirring for another 8 to 10 minutes, or until the syrup becomes as thick and dark as maple syrup. (Take care not to burn.)

Divide the hot syrup among 10 small (4-ounce) ovenproof custard cups. Pour the custard mixture on top of the syrup. Set the cups in a large cake pan and pour lukewarm water around them to a depth of about 2 inches. Place the pan on the bottom shelf of a preheated 300° oven for about 1 hour, or until the custards are firmly set. Transfer the cups to a rack to cool, then refrigerate. When chilled, invert each one onto a dessert dish. With a little bit of coaxing around the edges, out will drop a shimmering, caramel-crested mini-mountain of custard, swimming in its own sauce.

My grandmother [and] my grandfather . . . had been bride and groom in a Kentucky wedding somewhere around 1850. . . . The wedding cake was tall as the flower girl and of astonishing circumference, festooned all over with white sugar roses and green leaves, actual live rose leaves. . . . All the children had their own table in a small parlor, and ate just what the grownups had: Kentucky ham, roast turkey, partridges in wine jelly, fried chicken, dove pie, half a dozen sweet and hot sauces, peach pickle, watermelon pickle and spiced mangoes. A dozen different fruits, four kinds of cake and at last a chilled custard in tall glasses with whipped cream capped by a brandied cherry. . . .

In my childhood we ate, my father remarked, "as if there were no God." By then my grandmother . . . had become such a famous cook it was mentioned in her funeral eulogies. . . . Several venerable old gentlemen, lifelong friends of my grandmother, sat down, pen in hand, after her death and out of their grateful recollection of her bountiful hospitality—their very words—wrote long accounts of her life and works . . . and each declared that at one time or another he had eaten the best dinner of his life at her table.

Katherine Anne Porter
"Portrait: Old South," 1944

Peach Ice Cream

A few determined fanciers of cold sweets made ice cream in this country before the Revolution, and our early presidents from Virginia—Washington, Jefferson, Madison—all loved it. Dolley Madison made strawberries and ice cream a very familiar and popular dish in the early 1800s, and by then the frosty treat was available daily in New Orleans and some other cities. By 1850, a hand-cranked ice cream freezer had been patented.

It is that same basic device—now turned, more likely than not, by electricity—that produces this Southern and universal delight, homemade peach ice cream. Other fruits work just as well, of course, but there is something special about fresh peaches in combination with cream and vanilla. Traditional regional cookbooks as old as Mary Edgeworth's *Southern Gardener and Receipt-Book* (1859) and as new as Norma Jean and Carole Darden's *Spoonbread and Strawberry Wine* (1978) have paid homage to this queen of Southern ice creams. Here is a typical recipe.

Peel, seed, and cut up 5 or 6 large and fully ripe freestone peaches, add ¾ cup of sugar, stir until the sugar dissolves, and then cover the bowl tightly and refrigerate overnight. Next day, whip 3 eggs by hand in a large saucepan and add 2 cups of light cream or half-and-half. Make a dry mixture of ½ cup of sugar, ⅛ teaspoon of salt, and 2 tablespoons of cornstarch and blend this gradually into the egg and cream mixture. Set the saucepan over low heat and cook the custard, stirring constantly, until it thickens a little and drips heavily from the spoon. Remove from the heat for about 15 minutes; then cover and chill in the refrigerator for about 2 hours. Next, puree 1 cup of the sugared peaches and stir them into the custard, followed by 2 cups of heavy cream and 3 tablespoons of vanilla extract. Place this mixture— about 1½ to 2 quarts in volume—in the metal canister of the ice cream maker and process it. When the ice cream is finished, remove the dasher, add the remaining 3 or 4 cups of peach chunks and juice, stir well, pack with a spoon, and put the canister back in the ice bucket or in the freezer section of the refrigerator to age and "cure" for about 2 hours. As soon as it has hardened enough to suit your preference, it's ready to serve. There should be enough for 10 or 12 servings.

*S*trawberry *S*hortcake

In late February and early March, the strawberries begin to ripen in south Florida, and for the next six months the season migrates slowly northward to the Great Lakes area. In the mid-South, the peak period is the last two or three weeks of May, and berry lovers rush to indulge in their goodness for as long as they last. Strawberries from Tennessee and Kentucky seem to have just the right blend of tart acidity and juicy sweetness. They're equally good sliced over cereal or ice cream, processed in ice cream, made into jams and preserves, dipped in sour cream and brown sugar, or made into pies.

But without a doubt, the oldest and best-loved strawberry dessert of all is strawberry shortcake, which may be a Southern original and certainly is a national treasure. All sorts of cakelike stuff gets put under a pile of berries and called shortcake, but the real thing, the genuine article, is what the old-time cooks called a paste, and what we know as pastry, an unleavened combination of flour, shortening, and a little water. The first shortcake to support a mound of strawberries may have been a flat, somewhat puffy, flaky disk of pastry, about 4 or 5 inches in diameter. Here is an old recipe for the dessert.

Wash and hull 1 quart or more of fresh strawberries; cut them up if large, sprinkle with sugar to taste, cover tightly, and refrigerate.

Make a pastry by sifting together 2 cups of flour, 6 tablespoons of powdered sugar, and 2 tablespoons of cornstarch, sifting again twice, and working in ⅔ cup of softened butter or shortening. If the dough is too crumbly, add 1 teaspoon of ice water. Refrigerate the dough ball to chill it. Then divide into 6 or 8 pieces and roll or pat each one into a thin disk. This can be done on a floured surface or between pieces of wax paper. Prick the pastries with a fork, brush with melted butter, and bake them at 350° for about 15 minutes, or until light brown and flaky. When done, spoon on the cold berries, top with whipped cream, and serve.

For one last variation on the strawberry theme—and for a final encore in this exploration of Eating In, Southern style—consider this dish. It's a pie, if you think of it as glazed berries in a refrigerated crust—but it's very much like a shortcake if you consider how similar the pastry is to traditional pastes and shortcakes. Call it what you like—a pie, a refrigerated shortcake. By whatever name, it's a classic touch of timeless Southern hospitality. This version was given to us more than twenty-five years ago by Virginia Stovall, then a Floridian, later a Kentuckian, now a Tennessean, and always a Southern cook of the first rank.

Prepare and bake a 9- or 10-inch pie pastry (see page 329). Wash and drain 6 cups of fresh strawberries, set aside a few perfect ones for garnish and hull the rest. Crush 2 cups of the berries in a bowl. In a saucepan, mix ½ cup of water, 1 cup of sugar, and 3 tablespoons of cornstarch, then add the crushed berries, bring the mixture to a boil, and cook until it clears and thickens (3 to 5 minutes). Add 1 tablespoon of butter and stir until it is melted and well-blended, then press through a strainer to get a smooth sauce or glaze. Place the remaining 4 cups of whole berries in the pie shell, mounding in the center, and spoon the warm glaze on top, completely covering the fruit. Refrigerate the dessert until it is firm and well-chilled. Slice and serve with a dollop of whipped cream and an uncapped strawberry atop each piece.

CONCLUSION:

"An Elegant Sufficiency"

In 1856, a merchant named Robert Orr began trading in dried beans from a waterfront store on the Cumberland River in downtown Nashville, Tennessee. Buying and selling from riverboats and mule-drawn wagons, he and two of his brothers established a thriving food marketing business that four generations of Orrs had prospered from by the end of World War II. At that time, after ninety years of service, the company was handling about five hundred food items.

Now part of a Texas-based international food service conglomerate, the Robert Orr Company is headquartered in a sprawling warehouse complex a few miles from its original location. Sophisticated computers keep track of the fresh, frozen, and processed foods that come and go constantly via air, rail, and refrigerated truck. In these modern facilities, the Orr inventory has been expanded to include more than ten thousand food items, among them Spanish artichokes, Belgian salsify, Norwegian salmon, Nova Scotia lox, New Zealand lamb, Russian caviar—and, of course, Tennessee dried beans.

The explosive growth in size and diversity of Robert Orr's bean business is hardly an isolated phenomenon; throughout the South and the nation, many more examples of the postwar revolution in the food industry (and consequently in people's eating habits) can readily be found. In supermarkets and convenience stores, in fast-food chains and fancy restaurants, in scores of food service corporations like Robert Orr and in home kitchens everywhere, a swift and accelerating wave of change is transforming the eating habits of Southerners and other Americans.

Much about these changes is positive and encouraging. Increased interest in health and nutrition has made more popular a wide range of fresh and natural foods unadulterated by chemical additives. New books, magazines, and instructional programs are making the art and science of cooking more accessible. Modern tools such as the food processor and the microwave oven have eased and quickened the cook's task. Even the variety of new restaurants and food products can be seen as a plus, broadening as it does the experiences and the horizons of cooks and eaters everywhere.

But in the shift from traditional to contemporary and from provincial to

The Southern cook has always welcomed new dishes and with ingenious skill has adapted them to his or her own requirements. Since the first noticeable amalgamations of Southern cookery took place, the evolution has moved on. Now in almost any modern Southern home or restaurant one is likely to find on the menu dishes from practically every section of the country and from almost every foreign country that has traditional good food. The result of all this is that the Southern "meal" can no longer be rigidly defined. There still are sections in the South where neither the atmosphere nor the "table" has changed; the same rich ingredients like "loads" of butter, cream, and eggs are used to make original dishes. Cakes and breads are baked from scratch with infinite care, vegetables are still boiled with salt pork or ham hock, and smoke houses hang heavy with meats. But progress is being made in every other field. It is only natural that cookery, too, should be on the move.

Marion Brown's Southern Cook Book, 1968

cosmopolitan, there is a real danger that both the methods of delivery and the food itself—the so-called new American cuisine—are only hastening the decline and disappearance of Southern cookery and other distinctive regional foods of high quality and historical importance. In the new age of sophisticated packaging, of celebrity chefs and food gurus and kitchen personalities, form is becoming more important than substance, and virtually anything old may be dismissed as banal and worthless.

Speed and style are now what matter most in the arty, trendy, chic world of nouvelle cuisine. The movement's chefs, like fashion designers, strive constantly for novelty and originality in producing complex creations that are meant to inspire awe, not imitation; in fact, many of the dishes are almost impossible to duplicate. The result is a continuous parade of discordant and often outlandish combinations, putative works of culinary art that may be impressive to look at but seldom are remembered as wonderful things to eat. At its best, this cult of novel variety may be dramatic and entertaining; at its worst, it is haughtily pretentious, snobbish, and outrageously expensive. But for all its excesses of addition, the most harmful aspect of the new American cuisine may be the sin of subtraction—the disdain for almost everything old that is indiscriminately driving out the best and the worst regional fare. Southern food and other traditional forms of American cookery are struggling to survive in competition with the fast and fancy new styles of cooking—and now as always, it appears that the race is going to the swift.

In defending the Southern food heritage and advocating its perpetuation as an element of American cookery, I am mindful that change is both inevitable and essential to growth. It is not the addition of new foods but the disappearance of old ones that I resist. The best of Southern food, as it has evolved through the centuries, has been passed down and modified and expanded from one generation to the next. It has become a cultural treasure, a showcase of history and quality and taste. Like our language, our food is a living asset, not a dead artifact; it should be nourished and cultivated and extended, not casually discarded as if it were just another perishable commodity.

Southern food at its most appealing is surprisingly simple, relatively inexpensive, and inclusive rather than exclusive. It is suffused with history and continuity. It is integrated food—black and white, soul and country, Creole and Cajun, mountain and coastal, plain and fancy. More than any other remnant of the region's past, it reflects the reality of good and bad times and the social values of Southerners of all races and classes in every generation. I am convinced that the best Southern food is well worth defending and preserving, not only as one of the few active and continuing examples of the South at its best, but also for the multitude of simple joys and pleasures it still delivers.

(That it may also be more nourishing and less harmful than its critics have

"How your papa did relish good food!" Mama said. "Whether it was the first strawberries of the season, or a big pan of hot baked sweet potatoes with yellow butter melting in them, or a glass of fresh-churned buttermilk still cool from the springhouse."

Ivy nodded. "I remember how he'd send Frone and me back to the

charged is suggested by chemical analyses of my blood before and after I ate more than two thousand typically Southern dishes—certainly an abnormally high number—in restaurants and homes across the region in a period of just twenty months. A battery of blood tests known in medical parlance as a SMAC profile—Sequential Multiple Analyzer, C-Model—measured the levels of cholesterol, triglycerides, salt, sugar, and about twenty other elements in my system. By almost every measure, I was closer to the middle of the normal reference range in the tests conducted after I did my extraordinary eating than in the analyses made before I started. My cholesterol and triglycerides levels actually went down from the high end of the normal range to the middle. My blood pressure also went down a little (to a very healthy 120/75), and my metabolism remained at a low-normal level. My weight increased by a mere three pounds, and I lost them back when I resumed a more normal manner of eating. None of this proves that cream, butter, eggs, sugar, salt, and lots of pork are the secrets to good health, of course—but it does raise some interesting questions about the effect of these and other foods on individual health.)

In all our encounters with cooks in homes and restaurants, with waiters and waitresses, cashiers and caterers, regular customers and private dinner guests and strangers passing through, we met almost no one who was unwilling to explore the fascinating subject of Southern food with us. True to their long-standing and well-deserved reputation for enjoying both food and talk, the Southerners we met regaled us with good stories and strong opinions about the past, present, and future of Southern food. We dined with them early, late, and often, lingered over tables and counters to talk, took their recipes home with us—and almost always, we found that the food, like the conversation, was honest and unaffected and immensely satisfying. Some of it made me think of a phrase that Lenda DuBose of Nashville recalled hearing her grandmother Ruby Gollithan Bates use to describe lean times: "There was a lot of shuffling of the dishes for the fewness of the vittles." And some of it reminded me of what Lee Anderson of Athens, Georgia, was taught to say in the house of her grandmother Jessie Read when she wanted to be excused from the table: "I've had an elegant sufficiency."

Whatever else they may have to offer, many Southerners can still set a fine table and surround it with conversation and laughter and love. On such occasions, special things can happen, and nothing—not even the fewness of the vittles—can keep those present from receiving and enjoying an elegant sufficiency. It's an old Southern skill, a habit, a custom, a tradition, and it deserves to last as long as the corn grows tall.

kitchen for hot biscuits after the bread plate had been passed once. He wanted biscuits so steaming the butter melted before it had even left the knife and touched them."

"And creamed corn and fried apples for breakfast, you remember that, don't you, Ivy?"

She remembered. . . . And as Papa took that first bite of fresh nut-flavored corn and popped a whole buttered biscuit in his mouth, he always said, "No Astor or Vanderbilt has better eating than this. You young'uns just remember, the richest man living on Park Avenue in New York City can't eat what we've got set before us right here this morning. His corn's stale, his eggs have been shipped in from someplace, his milk's all treated some way—I tell you, we're lucky folks!" And before he had finished, Ivy and the other children were sorry for millionaires who had only money and could not enjoy the fruits of the earth at the peak of their season.

Wilma Dykeman
The Far Family, 1966

SOURCES
AND RESOURCES:
The Keys to the Kitchen

In cookery as in virtually every realm of creative endeavor, the margin of excellence that lifts truly great artists above the ranks of the merely good ones may have more to do with resourceful imagination than anything else. Great cooks stand out among their contemporaries and live on in the memory of appreciative eaters primarily because they seem blessed with the ability to improvise, to transform little or nothing into something wonderful.

Every great Southern cook since colonial times has known instinctively where to find the resources from which memorable meals are made. It is not having everything or even knowing everything that makes a great cook; rather, it is knowing where to turn for the ingredients, the recipes, the ideas, and the expertise that can transform a routine dish into an extraordinary offering.

In times past, cooks kept stock of what was available in the pantry, the cellar, the larder, the springhouse, and the smokehouse. Now as then, it is this same confident grasp of sources and resources that sets Southern cooks apart.

Like a good cook, a good book on food ought to have its own pantry, its own storehouse of sources and resources, so that readers can quickly and easily find their way around in it. To that end, I have assembled here five kinds of information: a list of people who provided vital helping hands in the development of the book; an annotated bibliography of the published materials I drew upon; a roster of the restaurants we visited for the Eating Out section; a listing by category of the recipes included in the Eating In section; and a general index, which will also include the recipes.

Among the people who provided a graphic and visible resource in the making of the book are those who appear in Al Clayton's photographs. We are unable to name all of them, but we take pleasure in identifying the ones listed below, and in expressing thanks to them: Annie Lou Bonner (page 71); Jimmy and Mary Bowen with John Sanka (page 346); Willie Brown at Wintzell's (page 136); Lucille "Mama" Cole (page 75); Wentworth Caldwell at Sylvan Park (page 80); David Hopkins and Mary Ann Clayton (page 200); Jack Landry (page 117); maitre d' Biff Mason, standing, and waiter M. Guillot at Galatoire's (page 120); Margaret Lupo and the cooks at Mary Mac's (page 6); Doug Mahan at Bowen's (top pages 50–1); Jocelyn Mayfield (page 8); C. T. Roberson (page 9); Louis "Hawk" Rogers (page 109); John Sanka (page 142); "Hap" Townes (page 67); Ruskee Williams, Donnell Bond, Robert Bond at the Sunny Side Oyster Bar (page 178); James Willis at Leonard's (page 147); Charlie Wrape (page 49).

It might be of interest to know some of the places in the photographs as well. They are: Hopkins Boarding House in Pensacola, Florida (page 89); a church dinner at the Shiloh-Marion Baptist Church in Buena Vista, Georgia (page 55); the International Barbecue Cooking Contest at Memphis, Tennessee (page 167); and the Sauce Piquante Festival at Raceland, Louisiana (page 311).

APPRECIATION

Writing may be a solitary pursuit, but books are never one-person projects. That is especially so in the case of a book about food, because there probably is not a more plural activity in our society than the preparing, serving, and eating of food. As I have worked along on this extended endeavor, I have tried to keep a list of the people who helped in large ways and small. A few of them have been so indispensable that the book simply would not have come to full flower without them. I think especially and continually of Ann Egerton, whose contributions were too numerous to count; of Al and Mary Ann Clayton, who freely gave a rich abundance of professional and personal support; and of Ann Close, who brought to the book not only her great skill as an editor but also her firsthand knowledge of the South and its food. Several other Southerners also gave me extraordinary assistance: Joe Gray Taylor and Richard Collin, who read portions of the manuscript and suggested vital changes; Will Campbell, who supplied criticism, counseling, encouragement, and even some foodstuffs; Betty Anderson and Marysarah Quinn, who designed the book; and three superlative Tennessee cooks—Sue Smith, Virginia Stovall, and Evelyn Wakefield. To all of these I express again my gratitude and appreciation.

To the others whose help sustained me, I am also deeply grateful. The recording of their names in alphabetical order below is a token but sincere expression of my thanks. Inevitably, there will be some I overlooked. For whatever omissions, mistakes, or other shortcomings the list may have, I apologize. It is worth risking such faults to be able to express public appreciation to more than four hundred people who helped to make *Southern Food* a reality.

Finally, beyond the ones whose names appear here, there are countless others identified in the text, the marginalia, and the bibliography, and still more—cooks, caterers, librarians, collectors, appreciative eaters—whose knowledge of and enthusiasm for the traditional foods of the South they generously shared with me. To one and all, I lift my cup in praise.

Roger Abramson, Frank and Margaret Adams, Harriett Aldridge, Dick Allison, Nan Allison, Bob and Lee Anderson, Bernie Arnold, Bev and Vicky Asbury, H. Brandt Ayers, William F. Baltz, Claude and Sue Banister, Emma Jane Barnes, Jack Bass, Jim and Harriette and Andrew Bateman, Mary and John and Gillian Beach, Ursula Beach, Kay Beasley, Julia Bennett, Terry Birdwhistell, Dallas Blanchard, Roy Blount, Anna Bodine, Julian Bond, Bill and Carol Boozer, Bobby Braddock, Clayton and Jowain Braddock, Pat Braden, Max Brantley, David and Mary Britt, Bebe Broadbent, George and Connie Brosi, Jack and Jean Brown, Charles and Cammy Bryan, Edith Hillis Bryan.

Wentworth Caldwell, Marcelle Cameron, Anne Campbell, Robert F. Campbell, Brenda Campbell, Libby Campbell, Roane Carey, Gena Carter, Jeffrey Caruth, W. T. Caruth, Steve and Nancy Channing, Jacky Christian, Granville Clark, Reese and Cheree Cleghorn, Paul Clements, Alice Cobb, Jim Collins, John and Edythe Connelly, Mary Baxter Cook, Samuel DuBois Cook, Dorothea Cooper, Eleanor Cooper, Ed and Jean Crawford, Carol Crowe-Carraco, Hayden Cunningham, Patsy Curtis, Pete Daniel, Gene Davenport, Louise Davis, Harris Dean, Lane Denson and Caroline Stark, Greg Dent and Susan Peterson, Mark and Dee Dickson, Linda Dorland, Evalin Douglas, Robert Drake, Lenda and Lucius DuBose, Betty Duggan, Les and Peggy Dunbar, Tony and Patty Dunbar, Georgianna Hines Duncan, Charles Durant, Wilma Dykeman.

Celia Eckhardt, Linda West Eckhardt, Clyde Edgerton, Bob Edwards, Brooks Egerton, Doug and Rhonda Egerton, George Anne Egerton, Graham and Anne Egerton, Hardin and Patty Egerton, Hugh and Hoyt Egerton, John G. Egerton, Judy Egerton and Mike Overstreet, March Egerton, Rowland and Donna Egerton, Harry E. Ellis, Dan and Zita Elrod, Bill Emerson, Allison Engel, Margaret Engel, William Ferris, Rubye Fitzsimmons, Harold and Ginna Fleming, Midge and John Folger, Douglas and Euneda Freeman, Frye Gaillard, Dovie Gentry, Mary Ann Gentry, James E. Gillenwater, Rose Gladney, Ann Golovin, Margaret Gooch, Matalie Grant, Carol Gray, Winifred Green, Flash Gregory, John and Anne Griffin, Alice Griffith, Kitty Griffith, Mary Grinter, Greg and Bubbles Guirard, Tootie Guirard.

Annette Hale, Bob Hall, Tom T. Hall, Wade Hall, Ed Hamlett and Linda Wilson, Travis and Evva Hanes, Clive Hardy, Kathleen and John Harkey, Caroline Harkleroad, Betty Bryan Haslam, Bill and Sylvia Havard, Leland Hawes, David Hawpe, Leonard Haynes, Mary Glenn Hearne, Billy and Patsy Heaton, Will Hendricks and Susan Gordon, Roy Herron and Nancy Carol Miller, Robin Hess, David Higgs and Marietta Lovell, Graham Higgs and Lou Horner, Janet Higgs, Skip and Barnie Higgs, Fred Hobson, David Hopkins, Eliza M. Horton, Charles and Nora House, Charlesetta Hughes, Andy Hughes, Bob and Nancy Hull, Burt Hummell, Burn and James Locke Humphries, Ben and Jean Hutcherson, Stanley Idzerda, Joe and Becca Ingle, Nancy Jarrell, Audrey Jefferson, Jackie Jefferson, Eddie Jones, Carolyn Karhu, Sarah Kennedy, Gisela Knight, Harold Knight, Mary Lynn Kotz, Pres and Bee Lane, Jettie Lawrence, Paul Leeper, Jim Leeson, Helen Lewis, John Lewis, Andy and Jane Lipscomb, Dennis Longwell.

Janie Macey, Jody Macey and Sheryl Walton, Sally McArthur, J. A. and Opal McCauley, Laura McCray, Anne and Jim McDaniel, John and Barbara McDaniel, Isaac McDaniel, Bill McDonald, Sharon Macpherson, Betsy and Gayle Malone, Betty Mastin, Cliff Meador, Robert Michie, Jim Wayne Miller, Connie Mills, Margaret Minich, Hayes Mizell, Rick Montague, Lynwood Montell, Herman

Moore, Jane Morningstar, Flossie Morris, Bill Moyers, Paul Murphy, Jack Murrah, Julia Neal, Roy and Suzanne Neel, John Netherton and Martha Weesner, La Una Gay Nielsen, Gurney Norman, Loyd and Velva Northington, John Norton, Paul Ogilvie, Carol Orr, Steve Otto, Lorena Owens, Anne Paine, Grace and Tom Paine, Ophelia Paine, John Ed Pearce, Joe Pennel, Lucy Massie Phenix, Bob and Jeanne Pitner, Sara Pitzer, Johnny and Frances Popham, Fred and Tammy Powledge, Reynolds Price.

John Shelton Reed, Roy and Norma Reed, Delpha Lane Rhoades, Louise Black Richards, Carolyn and Frank Richardson, Dee Dee Risher, Reita Rivers, Betty Roberts, Charlie and Carol Robins, C. M. "Pod" Rogers, Dennis Rogers, Gamble Rogers, Louis "Hawk" Rogers, Newman and May Rogers, Sally Rogers, Anne Romaine, Martha Ross, Camille Rucker, Jim and Julia May Rush, Carter Russell.

John S. Sanders, Patricia Brady Schmit, Bill Schrader, Bernie and Adele Schweid, Richard Schweid and Ornella Zoia, Walter and Joyce Searcy, Skip Shaw, Bill Shelton, Ann Allen Shockley, Bland Simpson, Ward Sinclair and Cass Peterson, Claude Sitton, Mollie Slabosky, Al Smith, Annie Smith, Herbie Smith, Lee Smith, Mildred Ann Smith, Randy and LeaAnn Smith, Sam Smith, Stephen A. Smith, Stephen B. Smith, W. O. and Kitty Smith, Dixie Snell, Nancy Solley, Jean Haskell Speer, Mary Speziale, Dot and Dorris Stephenson, B. J. Stiles, James Still, George Stoney, Katherine Stoney, Howard Stovall and Analy Scorsoni, Jeff Stovall and Adria Bernardi, Molly and Tess Stovall, Thomas F. Stovall, Tom Stovall and Marsha Luie, Georgiana Strickland, Reginald Stuart, Steve Suitts, Alice Swanson, David and Barbara Swift.

Mary Teloh, Fredrika Teute and Clyde Haulman, Dick Thomas, Gertie Thomas, Charles B. Thorne, Sue Thrasher, M. Naige Todhunter, Melba and Morris Tolleson, Hap Townes, Calvin Trillin, Allen Tullos, Bob Tune, Larry Van Dyne, Don Wakefield, Scott Wakefield, Carrie Lane Wallace, Peggy and Tom Ward, Terry Warth, Ron Watson, Pat and Glenda Watters, Dick and T Weesner, Ada Whisenhunt, Abner T. White, Mary Grinter White, Walden and Hallie White, Bob and Ruby Wickersham, Eliot Wigginton, Teri Wildt, Charles D. Williams, Daniel T. Williams, Shirley Williams, Eleanor Willis, Charles R. Wilson, Lucille Wilson, Geneva Winningham, Wendy Wolf, Marice Wolfe, Jane Brock Woodall, Harmon Wray and Judy Parks, Jack Wright and Sharon Hatfield, Larry and Roberta Wright.

BIBLIOGRAPHY

Of all the subjects that have inspired books, surely none has sparked such an outpouring of volumes as food. In every library and bookstore, collections on American cookery fill shelf after shelf, and no one knows how numerous and extensive are the private libraries on the subject. From tattered notebooks filled with handwritten recipes to lavish coffee-table volumes printed in full color, books about food in this nation alone probably would number in the hundreds of thousands.

Southern food has more than held its own in the book derby; hardly a town or church or service club can be found in the region that has never produced a collection of favorite recipes. With so many books to choose from, any bibliography is bound to be incomplete and arbitrarily selective; this one is no exception. It catalogues close to three hundred books devoted exclusively or partially to the subject of food in the South. They are a mix of old and new, rare and commonplace, and they are local and regional and national in focus. They were chosen for inclusion here because they are, taken together, broadly indicative of the diversity and importance of food throughout more than four centuries of Southern history.

The bibliography is divided into three major sections: *The States,* which contains entries related to each of the eleven states here identified as Southern; *The Region,* which includes not only general books about Southern food but also books on subregions such as the mountains and the coasts and on distinctive cooking styles such as Cajun and Creole; and *Beyond the Region,* which lists a variety of nationally focused volumes that either include Southern material or otherwise add substantially to an understanding of the major place food has held in the life of the South.

Within each division of the bibliography, entries are presented alphabetically by title, followed by the names of authors, editors, or compilers; the names and locations of publishers and dates of publication are given in parentheses. The brief annotations following each entry contain descriptive information and subjective assessments of the books. The annotations also call attention to a number of books we found to be particularly interesting, informative, and important. If there is a single characteristic that makes these volumes stand out from the others, it is their narrative content; far more than simply collections of recipes, they are carefully researched, effectively organized, and skillfully written and edited works of social and cultural history.

One further note: Some of the antiquarian books in the bibliography may be impossible to locate, even in major libraries. They have been included here because they seemed especially fascinating and revealing artifacts of the culture from which they came. They may also encourage and inspire an ongoing search for them and for more books of the same rare quality in dusty repositories everywhere.

THE STATES

ALABAMA

The *Alabama Heritage Cookbook,* by Katherine Durham and Susan Rush (Heritage Publications, Birmingham, Ala., 1984). Old Alabama elegance is the focus in this attractive combination of historic residences with menus and recipes.

Around the Spiral Staircase, from the Alabama Legislative Wives Club, 1975–79 (Strode Publishers, Inc., Huntsville, Ala., 1979). A good combination of recipes and history, this book includes thumbnail sketches of each of Alabama's sixty-seven counties and an array of dishes from those jurisdictions.

Cracklin Bread and Asfidity, compiled by Jack and Olivia Solomon (University of Alabama Press, Tuscaloosa, Ala., 1979). Folk recipes and home remedies from rural Alabama and elsewhere in the South are the main ingredients of this oral history collection. The recipes give valuable historical background on many regional foods.

Eating Out in Alabama, by Herman Moore (Title Books, Inc., Birmingham, Ala., 1984). A well-known Alabama traveler whose friends call him Hungry Herman drew upon thirty years of road knowledge to seek out and describe more than two hundred of his favorite eating places in the state. Every state needs a guide like this.

Food, Fun, and Fable, by Charley and Meme Wakeford (Paragon Press, Montgomery, Ala., 1965). From Meme's, a remote but renowned seafood restaurant on the Alabama Gulf Coast, came this entertaining and taste-filled collection. Meme's is closed now, but the book at least preserves some memorable dishes, including deep-fried crab fingers that are simply peerless. There's also an ample serving of local history.

From Gaineswood and Other Whitfield Kitchens, by Mary Augusta Whitfield (A Little Publishing House, Inc., Dauphin Island, Ala., 1977). Gaineswood, a Greek-revival plantation house built in the 1840s in Demopolis, is the source and inspiration for this collection of extended family recipes with an Old South flavor.

Gulf City Cook Book, compiled by the Ladies of the St. Francis Street Methodist Episcopal Church, South, of Mobile (United Brethren Publishing House, Dayton, Ohio, 1892). Classic old Southern cuisine from eighty-two churchwomen. There were both earlier and later editions than this one, indicating how popular the book was in its time. The reputation was well-deserved.

Huntsville Heritage Cookbook, compiled and published by the Grace Club Auxiliary, Inc. (Huntsville, Ala., 1967). This women's volunteer service organization's collection makes a brief bow to heritage in the introduction and then gets directly into a wide range of interesting recipes, old and new.

Mrs. Kirtland's New Cook Book, by Mrs. A. E. Kirtland (Holt & Crawford, Montgomery, Ala., 1883). A fascinating glimpse of the nineteenth-century Southern kitchen and dining room, including tips on cooking on a wood stove. Sweets in one form or another take up half the book.

The Linly Heflin Cook Book, compiled and published by the Linly Heflin Unit, a women's service organization founded during World War I. The group's original cookbook, *Oven Magic,* was published in Birmingham in 1940; this one followed in 1962. It contains mostly old Southern favorites.

Purefoy Hotel Cook Book, by Eva B. Purefoy and Louise P. McClung (privately published, Talladega, Ala., 1941). This rare treasure was revised and reprinted several times before the hotel closed in 1961. The popular dining room featured such dishes as sweet potato pudding and cheese spoonbread. Duncan Hines slept here—and loved it.

Recipe Jubilee!, compiled and published by the Junior League of Mobile (Mobile, Ala., 1964). A compendium of great Southern dishes, with the accent on seafood and sweets. A successor volume, *One of a Kind,* was published by the league in 1981.

Some Good Things to Eat, by Emma Rylander Lane (privately published in Clayton, Ala., 1898). The most noted recipe in this little book is not the one Mrs. Lane calls "my favorite" (that's a brown fruitcake) but the one she calls "my prize cake"—the now-famous Lane cake—"named not from my own conceit, but through the courtesy of Mrs. Janie McDowell Pruett, of Eufaula, Ala."

Southern Recipes, compiled and published by the Junior League of Montgomery (Montgomery, Ala., 1941). A handwritten and illustrated collection of recipes—a forerunner of the more polished Junior League cookbooks of the postwar era. There are contemporary Junior League cookbooks in Birmingham, Montgomery, and several other Alabama cities that offer a more extensive array of recipes.

Treasured Recipes, compiled by the Montrose Garden Club (Montrose, Ala., 1958). Handwritten gems from a little town on the east side of Mobile Bay offer a glimpse at south Alabama foodways a quarter of a century ago. An interesting companion volume from nearby Point Clear is *The Black Kettle,* a 1981 book of recipes and history by Susan Pacey Harvison.

Tried and True Recipes, compiled by Elizabeth B. Bashinsky (Paragon Press, Montgomery, Ala., third edition, 1937). With her sister members of the Alabama United Daughters of the Confederacy, Mrs. Bashinsky of Troy produced an extensive and popular collection of Southern recipes, among them multiple versions of pecan and chess and lemon pies. The book is dedicated to Martha Dismukes, a black cook and housekeeper, for "a faithful service of thirty-five years" in the Bashinsky household.

Wiregrass Cooking Through the Years, compiled and published by the Henry County Historical Society (Abbeville, Ala., 1981). Local history in a ten-county area of southeast Alabama known as the Wiregrass—once the domain of the Creek Indians—is thoroughly blended with these "white settler" recipes.

ARKANSAS

Billy Joe Tatum's Wild Foods Cookbook and Field Guide, by Billy Joe Tatum (Workman Publishing Co., New York, 1976). An Ozark Mountain woman noted for her foraging and cooking here presents a readable and informative description of foods from the woods—how to find them and fix them.

Border City Cook Book, by "various Fort Smith housekeepers," members of the Central Methodist Church (Fort Smith, Ark., circa 1907). This book from early in the twentieth century is the oldest Arkansas cookbook we could find. It contains no catfish or trout or barbecue recipes, no game, no Ozark pudding; there are plenty of corn and wheat breads, though, and beef, chicken, and vegetables. Sweets are about half the book.

Dixie Cookbook, compiled and published by the women of the First Presbyterian Church (Fort Smith, Ark.; fifth edition, 1972). First published in 1920, this collection has been revised several times. Its current edition contains recipes from all of the predecessor volumes. The sweets stand out, but Ozark pudding is still not among them.

From My Ozark Cupboard, by Cora Pinkley-Call (Allan Publications, Kansas City, Mo., 1950). Pork and poultry lead the way in this collection of old and new recipes from the Arkansas-Missouri mountains. Some brief but interesting glimpses of Ozark folklife are served up with the food.

In Good Taste, compiled and published by members of the El Dorado Service League (El Dorado, Ark., 1980). Numerous duck and rice recipes are included in this collection from the south-central Arkansas city, but no explanation of the rice-growing and duck-hunting traditions of the area is given.

Kitchen Dividends, compiled and published by Women of Worthen, an organization of women bank employees (Little Rock, Ark., 1973). Included are some interesting recipes and a smidgen of background material about their origins.

Little Rock Cooks, compiled and published by the Junior League of Little Rock (Little Rock, Ark., 1972). It was reprinted several times and then succeeded by a new title, *Traditions,* in 1983. North Little Rock has its own Junior League volume, *Rave Reviews,* published in 1982. Neither city's efforts include background material on the food or the social-cultural history of the region.

Old South Cook Book, compiled and published by the St. Luke's Episcopal Church Auxiliary (Hot Springs, Ark.; second edition, 1946). There are "a thousand Southern ways to please, to serve, to save," but not much seems indigenous to Arkansas. The seafood and shellfish dishes smack of Louisiana, and several other states get more credit than the home one. There's a notable bourbon-and-rum eggnog recipe that calls for "one new-laid egg per person," and it's anything but a Sunday-school punch. The book was first published in 1938.

The Ozark Folk Center Cook Book, by Ruth Moore Malone and Bess Malone Lankford (Ozark Folk Center, Harrison, Ark., 1975). A popular and respected resource center located in an Arkansas state park produced this compilation of folklore and recipes.

Ozark "Vittles," by Maria M. Melton (privately printed; third edition, 1958). These "original hillfolk recipes collected by word of mouth" include much that has a pioneer flavor—biscuits and cornbread, pork and squirrel and venison, cabbage and tomatoes, cakes and pies, a yeast muffin/roll called featherbeds, and a dried tomato recipe called antebellum tomato figs.

Pioneer Cookbook, by Eula Mae Stratton (The Ozarks Mountaineer, Branson, Mo., 1969). This descriptive narrative is a cook's mixture of recipes, kitchen culture, and mountain recollections. It has been revised and reprinted several times.

Suggin Cookbook, by Josephine Hutson Graham (Suggin Productions, Newport, Ark., 1974). The author's Scotch-Irish ancestors in northeast Arkansas were the source of much that is in this unusual little book of handwritten recipes and pen-and-ink drawings.

Tasted Treasures, compiled and published by the Sisterhood of B'Nai Israel (Little Rock, Ark., 1963). A blend of Jewish and Southern culinary traditions can be detected here, but faintly; the blintzes, matzo balls, borscht, and chicken gumbo are more or less universal.

Where to Eat in the Ozarks, by Ruth Moore Malone (Pioneer Press, Little Rock, Ark., 1961). Though out of date now (and ably replaced by a statewide magazine called *Arkansas*

Times), this guide to Ozark foods and restaurants provides an interesting and revealing look at the area twenty-five years ago.

FLORIDA

Canopy Roads, compiled by the Tallahassee Junior Women's Club (Tallahassee, Fla., 1979). A blend of regional and ethnic dishes and seafood specialties, with a little bit of historical background and a strong Southern flavor throughout.

Cracker Cookin', by B. J. Altschul (LaFray Publishing Co., St. Petersburg, Fla., 1984). This companion volume to *Famous Florida Underground Gourmet* offers more examples of recipes and restaurants in the "real" Florida that still exists in the backcountry beyond the tourist attractions.

Cross Creek Cookery, by Marjorie Kinnan Rawlings (Charles Scribner's Sons, New York, 1942). The personal charm and liveliness of the novelist-author make a delightful running story of this collection of favorite recipes from her Florida country home. Here is a rare and unbeatable combination: great Southern dishes, superbly told.

Famous Florida Underground Gourmet, by Barbie Baldwin (LaFray Publishing Co., St. Petersburg, Fla., 1982). A guide to about three dozen of the state's down-home restaurants featuring native foods, with recipes for some of their specialties, including chicken and yellow rice, swamp cabbage salad, conch fritters, and Key lime pie.

Florida Food Fare, compiled and published by the Entre Nous Club (Bradenton, Fla., 1953). A curious hodgepodge of handwritten recipes and advertisements for Florida commercial enterprises, many of them food-related.

Florida Heritage Cook Book, compiled and published by the Women's Committee of the Florida Symphony Society (Orlando, Fla., 1967). An interesting collection of Florida recipes—including swamp cabbage, a palm-heart delicacy—and a little food history too.

Food Favorites of St. Augustine, by Joan Adams Wickham (C. F. Hamblen, Inc., St. Augustine, Fla., 1973). More than four centuries after its founding, the oldest continuously inhabited European settlement in America reveals in its foodways the strong and continuing influences of Spain, Minorca, England, and of course the United States.

The Gasparilla Cookbook, compiled and published by the Junior League of Tampa (Tampa, Fla., 1961). Gasparilla is Tampa's answer to Mardi Gras, and this book is a showcase of the city's cuisine, which is not as great as that of New Orleans, but excellent nonetheless. Southern, Spanish, Cuban, white and black and brown, inland and seaside come together to produce such specialties as guacamole, Spanish bean soup, bolichi, chicken and yellow rice, and flan.

Gulfshore Delights, compiled and published by the Junior Welfare League of Fort Myers. (Fort Myers, Fla., 1984). Greek and Spanish dishes, seafood, and traditional Southern cuisine are featured in this collection.

Jacksonville and Company, compiled and published by the Junior League of Jacksonville (Jacksonville, Fla., 1982). Like most of the other cookbooks in the Junior League family, this one is long on recipes and short on background.

Jane Nickerson's Florida Cookbook, by Jane Nickerson (University Presses of Florida,

Gainesville, 1973). Before she moved to Florida, Jane Nickerson was Craig Claiborne's predecessor as food editor of *The New York Times.* Her two-hundred-page collection of Florida and Southern recipes has such features as a glossary of lesser-known native fruits and vegetables.

Key West Cook Book, by the members of the Key West Woman's Club (Farrar, Straus & Co., New York, 1949). A charming book done with pen and ink in the handwriting of the contributors—and with drawings by some of them—this volume has recently been re-printed by the club. From its mood-setting foreword ("It is morning . . . the patio is still shady . . . let me bring you some chilled papaya, your morning coffee. . . .") to the spiced bread pudding recipe three hundred pages later, this is a distinctive book, very personal and inviting.

North Hill Cookbook, compiled and published by the North Hill Preservation Association (Pensacola, Fla., 1981). A local group formed to protect the architectural integrity and historical environment of a Pensacola neighborhood produced this book as a fund raiser. It contains some interesting local history as well as such historic old recipes as smoked mullet and gazpacho ("Spanish summer soup").

Palm Beach Entertains Then and Now, compiled by the Junior League of the Palm Beaches (Coward, McCann & Geoghegan, Inc., New York, 1976). Lots of history—about a third of the entire book—describing the fabled (and not necessarily Southern) "good life" at the clubs and in the private homes in the boom years of the late nineteenth and early twentieth centuries. What the wealthy transplants and winter residents ate, however, included a great many local and regional foods.

GEORGIA

Atlanta Cooknotes, compiled and published by the Junior League of Atlanta (Atlanta, Ga., 1982). A few historic footnotes accompany this collection of more than seven hundred recipes, but the book leans decidedly toward modern rather than traditional Southern cooking. Even so, it offers more social-cultural background than most of the newer Junior League cookbooks of Georgia and other Southern states.

Atlanta Cooks for Company, compiled and published by the Junior Associates of the Atlanta Music Club (Atlanta, Ga., 1968). Some brief historical notes on the city, together with three hundred pages of recipes for festive occasions—brunches, teas, luncheons, dinners, and holidays at home.

The Atlanta Exposition Cookbook, compiled by Mrs. Henry Lumpkin Wilson and published in 1895 under the title of *Tested Recipe Cook Book* (facsimile reprint by University of Georgia Press, Athens, 1984). Something of a forerunner of the women's club cookbook phenomenon of the past quarter-century or so, this book was well-received when it appeared at the great Southern exposition ninety years ago.

Atlanta Woman's Club Cook Book, edited and published by the home economics department of the club (Atlanta, Ga., 1921). Interspersed with lots of good recipes are some photographs and drawings and several amusing essays, among them a list of "secrets to kitchen happiness" and a paean to "Queen Sweet Potato."

Betty Talmadge's Lovejoy Plantation Cookbook, by Betty Talmadge (Peachtree Publishing

Co., Atlanta, Ga., 1983). The ex-wife of former Georgia senator Herman E. Talmadge serves up a tasty and entertaining collection of stories and recipes from the old Southern estate where she has lived since 1946. Like her earlier book, *How to Cook a Pig and Other Back-to-the-Farm Recipes* (Simon & Schuster, New York, 1977), this one is chatty, humorous, and helpful.

Coastal Cookery, compiled and published by the Cassina Garden Club (St. Simons Island, Ga., 1937). Though it is devoid of any historical context, this 264-page, handwritten and spiral-bound volume does contain scores of excellent recipes from the sea island region.

Georgia Sampler Cookbook, by Margaret Wayt DeBolt (Donning Publishers, Norfolk, Va., 1983). The author of *Savannah Sampler Cookbook,* with help from Carter Olive and Emma Rylander Law (a granddaughter of the noted Alabama cake maker Emma Rylander Lane), put together this collection of old and new Georgia recipes to commemorate the state's 250th anniversary.

Macon Cook Book, a collection of recipes tested principally by the Macon Wesleyan College alumnae, and published by them (Macon, Ga., 1909). The fare here includes beaten biscuit "kneaded with a machine made for that purpose" and many other high-cuisine offerings. Among the more unusual dishes are breadcrumb griddle cakes and pompey's head, a baked ground beef concoction.

Miss Lillian and Friends: The Plains, Georgia, Family Philosophy and Recipe Book, as told to Beth Tartan and Rudy Hayes (A&W Publishers, Inc., New York, 1977). This was among the many books spawned by Jimmy Carter's meteoric rise to the White House. It includes almost one hundred pages of favorite recipes from the Carters and their neighbors around Plains. Pork, hot bread, fresh vegetables, and a host of cakes and pies lead the way. The three P's are also prominent: peaches, peanuts, pecans.

A Place Called Sweet Apple, by Celestine Sibley (Doubleday & Co., Garden City, N.Y., 1967). Atlanta *Constitution* columnist Sibley reclaimed an old north Georgia cabin from near-ruin and infused it with her own delightful touches. The rescue is entertainingly recounted here with sparkle, taste, and humor, and so are nearly a hundred of her favorite recipes.

Recipes and Reminiscence, edited by Miriam S. Peifer and published by the Oconee Center for Senior Citizens (Watkinsville, Ga., 1980). Here is impressive proof that good books on food and history can be put together by small organizations with limited resources. In addition to an abundance of fine old Southern recipes, this book captures the flavor of a place and time: a rural Georgia county in the late nineteenth and early twentieth centuries. Like a handmade patchwork quilt, the book blends many pieces into a charming whole.

The Savannah Cook Book, collected and edited by Harriet Ross Colquitt (Walker, Evans & Cogswell Co., Charleston, S.C., 1933). Old-fashioned receipts and background stories from the Georgia coastal city are told with entertaining charm by a lifelong resident. There is also a whimsical poetic introduction by Ogden Nash.

Somethin's Cookin' in the Mountains, edited by John E. LaRowe et al. (Soque Publishers, Clarkesville, Ga., 1982). A combination cookbook and tourist guide, this collection of mountain traditions and modern foodways draws from dozens of commercial establishments and individuals to construct a usable and informative portrait of the northeast Georgia high country.

Tea Time at the Masters, compiled and published by the Junior League of Augusta (Augusta, Ga., 1977). Another strictly-business recipe book from the women's organization that has mastered the art of recording local and regional cookery.

Tullie's Receipts, compiled and edited by the Kitchen Guild of the Tullie Smith House Restoration (Atlanta Historical Society, Atlanta, Ga., 1976). Plain-style Southern cooking and living mark this documentation of life on a yeoman farmer's eight-hundred-acre north Georgia farm in the 1840s.

KENTUCKY

The Blue Grass Cook Book, by Minnie C. Fox (Fox, Duffield & Co., New York, 1904). Mrs. Fox, having migrated from southwest Virginia and eastern Kentucky to the bluegrass region of Kentucky, gathered recipes from about fifty of her friends to augment her own. Her novelist son, John Fox, Jr., wrote the introduction, praising in it the black cook, without whom, he said, the food of the South would not have gained distinction. "She has never got her just due," he concluded. The book is illustrated with photographs of black cooks and servants.

The Blue Ribbon Cook Book, by Jennie C. Benedict (John P. Morton & Co., Louisville, Ky., 1904). A renowned Louisville caterer and cafe owner from 1893 to 1925, Miss Benedict pioneered in gas-stove cooking and was a creator as well as a replicator of classic dishes. Benedictine spread was one of her contributions. The recipes in this collector's dream of a cookbook are a blend of Southern and cosmopolitan, from spoonbread and sugar pie to lamb chops.

Cissy Gregg's Cook Book, two collections of recipes and columns by the Louisville *Courier-Journal*'s long-time "home consultant" (Louisville Courier-Journal, Louisville, Ky., 1953 and 1959; reissued by Foodwork of Louisville, 1981). The gospel according to Cissy is still invoked around Kentucky—a tribute not only to her chatty and highly readable style but also to her expert touch with the food Kentuckians have loved for generations. Lillian Marshall, Cissy Gregg's successor, edited a 1971 cookbook published by the newspaper; about a third of it is made up of Gregg classics—hot Browns, burgoo, bourbon pecan cake, and beaten biscuits, among others.

The Cooking Book, compiled and published by the Junior League of Louisville (Louisville, Ky., 1978). As a later example of the cookbook tradition of both the Junior League and Kentucky, the Louisville book blends old recipes and a little history with modern design and contemporary dishes.

Famous Kentucky Recipes, compiled and published by the women of the Cabbage Patch Circle (Louisville, Ky., 1952). A highly regarded collection of recipes and menus, from Derby breakfast to dessert, put together by volunteers at an urban settlement house.

Housekeeping in the Bluegrass, compiled and published by the ladies of the Presbyterian Church of Paris (Paris, Ky., 1874; reissued by Kentucke Imprints, Berea, 1975). An airtight case is made here for the legendary Kentucky sweet tooth: Fully a third of the book's 190 pages are devoted to sugared treats.

Mrs. John G. Carlisle's Kentucky Cook Book, by Mrs. John G. Carlisle and others (F. Tennyson Neely, Chicago, Ill., 1893). Another volume of evidence in support of Kentucky's early and continuing renown in the art of cookery.

Kentucky Cook Book, "by a Colored Woman"—Mrs. W. T. Hayes (J. H. Tompkins Printing Co., St. Louis, Mo., 1912). Emma Allen Hayes, "a colored cook of many years' experience," called her recipes "easy and simple for any cook." She and S. Thomas Bivins, who wrote *The Southern Cookbook* in 1912, apparently were the first blacks to have cookbooks published under their names.

The Kentucky Cookery Book, by Mrs. Peter A. White (Belford-Clarke Co., Chicago, Ill., 1891). The Kentucky connections are not made clear, but the food is clearly Southern: pounded (beaten) biscuit, cornmeal muffins and batter cakes, gumbo, salt-cured Kentucky ham, fried okra, sweet potato pudding and pie, egg kisses, and much more.

Kentucky DAR Cookbook, selected from favorite recipes of members and published by the Kentucky Chapters of the Daughters of the American Revolution (Lexington, Ky., 1970). Brief histories of old Kentucky inns are interspersed with an impressive collection of traditional Kentucky and Southern dishes, from spoonbread (12 versions!) to transparent pie.

The Kentucky Housewife, by Mrs. Lettice Bryan (Shepard & Stearns, Cincinnati, Ohio, 1839). A contemporary reproduction by Collector Books of Paducah has made this great old cookbook available, and it's a gem: nearly 1300 recipes, many of them painstakingly detailed, embrace the heart and soul of Southern cooking in the decades before the Civil War. Here are such modern favorites as "cold slaugh," barbecued shoat, fried pies, Moravian and coconut cakes, biscuits, hoecakes, and many more. Even the reprint is now out of print.

Kentucky Hospitality, edited by Dorothea C. Cooper (Kentucky Federation of Women's Clubs, Louisville, Ky., 1976). Anchored by seven essays on food in the history and culture of Kentucky and topped off by more than five hundred of the state's prized recipes, this book celebrates a two-hundred-year tradition of fine food and hospitality. Corn fritters, burgoo, Woodford pudding, jam cake, fried pies, and bourbon balls are among the specialties. Few food books are as well-conceived as this one—or as well-executed.

Kentucky Receipt Book, by Mary Harris Frazer (Bradley & Gilbert Co., Louisville, Ky., 1903). Having lived as a girl in Louisiana and as a woman in Virginia and Kentucky, Mary Frazer made bold to claim that "a more comprehensive cook book has never been issued in the South." In point of fact, there were several bigger and better ones before it, but hers is still worth noting.

Kentucky's Capital City Cookbook, by Pat Layton (Roberts Printing Co., Frankfort, Ky., 1982). Small doses of commentary and local history are served up with recipes that lean more toward the contemporary than the traditional.

The New Kentucky Home Cook Book, compiled by the Ladies of the Methodist Episcopal Church, South, Maysville (Southern Methodist Publishing House, Nashville, Tenn., 1884). Considering the time and place—a small Kentucky town after the Civil War— this is a surprisingly broad and elegant assortment of culinary creations. More than two hundred women from Kentucky and beyond contributed recipes.

Out of Kentucky Kitchens, by Marion Flexner (Franklin Watts, Inc., New York, 1949). In a state noted for its cuisine and its cooks, this little volume holds a place of honor. The author, a well-known cook and food writer in Louisville in the midcentury years, also wrote *Dixie Dishes* (1940). Her recipes are mostly Southern, and the Kentucky accent is pronounced: mint juleps, burgoo, barbecue, country ham, and many more. Bramhall House, a New York reprint publisher, issued a later edition.

The Somerset Cook Book, compiled and published by the Ladies' Society of the Presbyterian Church (Somerset, Ky., 1912). From a small-town church group in southeastern Kentucky came a surprising variety of "mainstream" dishes of the day: charlotte russe, pineapple sherbet, oyster soup, and such. There is also an interesting disclaimer concerning spirits: "The committee took the liberty of substituting *grape juice* for whiskey and wine."

Stay For Tea . . . and More, compiled and published by the University of Kentucky Woman's Club, (Lexington, Ky., 1983). Following *Stay For Tea* (1948) and *Stay For Tea . . . Again* (1975), the club issued this third volume of contemporary and traditional Kentucky recipes.

We Make You Kindly Welcome, by Elizabeth C. Kremer (Pleasant Hill Press, Harrodsburg, Ky., 1970). In the two-hundred-year-old tradition of the religious community of Shakers in America, this collection of recipes from the Shaker village at Pleasant Hill—a thriving society for nearly one hundred years, beginning in 1814—shows how Southern-style pork, corn, and sweet dishes influenced the tastes of New England Shakers. Pleasant Hill is now a restored village with inn and dining accommodations.

What's Cooking in Kentucky, by Irene Hayes (Hayes Publishing Co., Hueysville, Ky., 1970). From its roots in eastern Kentucky, this book has grown through reprints and revisions into an all-Kentucky favorite. There are hundreds of down-home recipes from all over the state.

What to Cook and How to Cook It, by Nannie Talbot Johnson (first published in Louisville, Ky., in 1899, revised and enlarged in 1923; reissued several times after that by the Franklin Press, Louisville). The cookbook of Nannie Johnson, a noted innkeeper and cook in Kentucky, was billed as "a Bible of the kitchen to householders of the South."

LOUISIANA

American Cooking: Creole and Acadian, by Peter S. Feibleman (Time-Life Books, New York, 1971). The Time-Life series of books on regional cooking is a splendid union of recipes, photographs, and narrative writing. The Creole and Cajun volume is every bit the measure of the others—a compact store of knowledge and a delight to look at and read.

Antoine's Restaurant Cookbook, by Roy F. Guste, Jr. (Carberty-Guste, New Orleans, La., 1979). The oldest (since 1840) and most famous restaurant in New Orleans, and one of the most noted in America, is celebrated in this collection of original recipes compiled by a great-great-grandson of the founder.

Bayou Cook Book, by Thomas J. Holmes, Jr. (Bayou Books, Franklin, La., 1967). In this handwritten volume, bayou means Creole. and Creole means an amalgam of French, Spanish, Indian, and Afro-American cookery. An interesting and unusual presentation of food in Louisiana history.

La Bouche Creole, by Leon E. Soniat, Jr. (Pelican Publishing Co., Gretna, La., 1981). A celebration and interpretation of Creole taste by a native son who learned the mysterious ways from his mother and grandmother. Like so much Creole and Cajun, this is a perfect blend of food and talk.

Brennan's New Orleans Cookbook, by Hermann B. Deutsch (Robert L. Crager & Co., New Orleans, La., 1961). The history of the Brennan family and their now-famous New Orleans French Creole restaurant serves here as the introduction to many of their prize recipes, including eggs Benedict, grilled grapefruit, and bananas Foster—all on the menu for the celebrated breakfast at Brennan's.

Chef Paul Prudhomme's Louisiana Kitchen, by Paul Prudhomme (William Morrow & Co., New York, 1984). An entertaining and taste-tempting treatment of Louisiana's renowned cookery by the latest star in the Cajun-Creole sky.

The Creole Cookery Book, edited by the Christian Woman's Exchange of New Orleans (T. H. Thomason, New Orleans, La., 1885). Along with Lafcadio Hearn's famous cookbook published the same year, this is a primary classic of nineteenth-century New Orleans cuisine. The "occult science of the gumbo" is here revealed, along with recipes for "jumballaya" and sauce piquante; there are also some interesting advertisements, including one from the Midwest for butter shipped by express straight to the city's waiting cooks.

Creole Feast, by Nathaniel Burton and Rudy Lombard (Random House, New York, 1978). Fifteen master chefs of New Orleans reveal their culinary secrets. Profiles of the cooks and 320 of their prize recipes make up this fitting and fascinating tribute to black chefs in America's premier food city.

La Cuisine Creole, written anonymously by Lafcadio Hearn (Will H. Coleman, New York, 1885). Hearn, a prolific and troubled nineteenth-century writer who lived in New Orleans for ten years, was devoted to the city's cosmopolitan mixture of people and to their equally distinctive food. He claimed that this book was "the only one in print containing dishes peculiar to 'la Cuisine Creole.'" Included were recipes for "filé gombo, bouille-abaisse, jambolaya, crayfish bisque, café brûlé, Brûlot." A reprint edition with an introduction by Hodding Carter was issued by Pelican Publishing House in 1967; it too is now out of print.

Favorite New Orleans Recipes, by Suzanne Ormond, Mary E. Irvine, and Denyse Cantin (Pelican Publishing Co., Gretna, La., 1979). A 260-year-old culinary heritage presented the authors with thousands of foods and food combinations. From them, they chose 119 recipes representative of New Orleans home cooking and put them in this basic primer.

Gourmet's Guide to New Orleans, by Natalie V. Scott and Caroline Merrick Jones (Pelican Publishing Co., Gretna, La., 1975). This is a facsimile reprint of a popular New Orleans cookbook first published in 1931 and prized for its breadth and clarity.

The Justin Wilson Cook Book, by Justin Wilson (Pelican Publishing Co., Gretna, La., 1979). A popular television cook and Cajun storyteller transfers his rambling oral offerings to paper in this collection of traditional Cajun recipes. First you make a roux . . . and then follow such dishes as chicken jambalaya, shrimp and oyster gumbo with filé, dirty rice, mustard greens *au vin,* many crawfish dishes, and others. Naturally, there's a sequel.

Louisiana Cookery, by Mary Land (Louisiana State University Press, Baton Rouge, 1954; reprinted by Claitor's Publishing Division, Baton Rouge, 1965). An especially useful collection of recipes, menus, and fundamentals of Louisiana cookery, including lists of herbs and spices and a glossary of commonly used terms in Creole and Acadian kitchens.

Melrose Plantation Cookbook, by François Mignon and Clementine Hunter (privately printed in Natchitoches, La., 1956). A fascinating little book of history and cookery from a Louisiana plantation by one of its white residents and its black cook. Mrs. Hunter's recipes are as original and inviting as the murals and paintings for which she is also justly noted.

The New Orleans Cookbook, by Rima Collin and Richard Collin (Alfred A. Knopf, New York, 1975). After ten years in print, this is still a very popular and widely used book. The reasons are obvious: It's an excellent combination of history, culture, cookery, and good writing. Rima Collin is a scholar of modern literature and a food consultant; her husband, Richard, is a food critic and historian. In a constellation of glittering Louisiana cookbooks, this one shines as bright as any.

New Orleans Cook Book, by Lena Richard (Houghton Mifflin Co., Boston, Mass., 1939). Lena Richard was one of the first black cooks in New Orleans to get some credit for culinary mastery. She was an accomplished cateress who opened a cooking school in 1937 to prepare black men and women to cook and serve food and to "be in a position to demand higher wages." With encouragement from a variety of admirers, she decided to "compile my life's work in book form," and this wonderful collection of recipes is the result.

New Orleans Creole Recipes, by Mary Moore Bremer (published by Dorothea Thompson, New Orleans, La., 1932). A ninety-page gem of a book, full of wonderful dishes described in an expansive, conversational style—yet another example of the superlative cookbooks (and cuisine) of New Orleans and Louisiana.

The New Orleans Restaurant Cookbook, by Deirdre Stanforth (Doubleday & Co., Garden City, New York, 1967). The culinary quality of Louisiana and a handful of New Orleans' most noted restaurants is the subject here. You'll find all the masterpieces, from oysters Rockefeller to café brûlot.

The New Orleans Underground Gourmet, by Richard H. Collin (Simon & Schuster, New York, 1970). The New Orleans historian and restaurant critic serves as a guide to more than 250 restaurants in the city with the most distinctive cuisine in America.

The Picayune Creole Cook Book, compiled by the editors of the New Orleans *Picayune* (Picayune Publishing Co., New Orleans, La., 1900). For all its old-South immersion in divisions of race and class, this must surely be the definitive Creole cookery volume, having kept its popularity for more than eighty years. It is descriptive, voluminous (446 pages of small type), entertaining, comprehensive, and crammed with wonderful recipes. The "enlarged and amended" second edition (1901) has been reprinted many times. The book's post–World War II editions have put back in the wine and liquor recipes that were outlawed during Prohibition.

The Plantation Cookbook, compiled and written by members of the Junior League of New Orleans (Doubleday & Co., Garden City, N.Y., 1972). Unlike most of the Junior League cookbooks, this one contains a lot more than recipes: historical sketches of Louisiana plantation houses and some historical background on a delectable assortment of foods.

River Road Recipes, compiled and published by the Junior League of Baton Rouge (Baton Rouge, La., 1959). Since it first appeared, *River Road* has not only been reprinted virtually every year but also has given birth to a new volume, *River Road II.* The popularity is well-deserved. Like so many Louisiana cookbooks, this is an indispensable collection of Cajun, Creole, and Southern specialties.

Talk About Good!, compiled and published by the Junior League of Lafayette (Lafayette, La., 1969). This volume and its sequel—*Talk About Good II* (1979)—are big, popular, typically flavorful Cajun country collections.

200 Years of New Orleans Cooking, by Natalie V. Scott (Jonathan Cape and Harrison Smith, New York, 1931). This fascinating Depression-era recipe book includes a good many dishes that weren't in the New Orleans culinary showcase fifty years earlier, but have become standards in the fifty years since: pain perdu, crayfish bisque, grillades, pecan pralines, trout marguery, red beans and rice.

MISSISSIPPI

Bayou Cuisine, compiled and published by the women of St. Stephen's Episcopal Church (Indianola, Miss., 1970). Delta history and cookery are combined in this volume, and everybody from the Indians and de Soto to "space age cooks" gets some credit—except the blacks who did most of the cooking.

Cherished Cookery, "for and by the men of Oxford and Ole Miss" (Rebel Press, Oxford, Miss., 1966). What is most interesting about this companion volume to a local book by the town's women is that it precedes by almost twenty years an assertion (and subsequent cookbook title) by Mississippi agriculture commissioner Jim Buck Ross: "Down here, men don't cook."

Cooking Up a Storm, by Katy Caire (Lafayette Publishers, Pass Christian, Miss., 1971). A native of Biloxi and lifelong resident of the Mississippi-Louisiana coastal area exhibits both cooking and writing skills in this interesting narrative on regional cuisine.

A Cook's Tour of Mississippi, edited by Angela Meyers (Mississippi Publishers Corp., Jackson, 1980). A cleverly done combination of restaurant profiles, recipes, interviews, and stories on such Southern fare as catfish, molasses, and cushaw (a melon squash).

Court Square Recipes, by Eva Davis (Clarksdale Printing Co., Clarksdale, Miss., undated but probably circa 1950). "Southern cooking at its delicious best" by a Vicksburg promoter and amateur historian; included is a 140-year-old recipe for buttermilk pie.

Dinner at the Mansion, by Elise Winter with Frank Smith (Yoknapatawpha Press, Oxford, Miss., 1982). The wife of Mississippi Governor William Winter tells who came to dinner at the official residence—and what they had to eat. A similar book, *Dinner with Dot,* by Dorothy Power Johnson, was published by the University and College Press of Mississippi in 1973 when the author's husband, Paul Johnson, was governor.

How We Cook in Columbus, compiled and published by the Columbus Auxiliary of the Old Ladies' Home Association (Columbus, Miss., undated but probably circa 1900). An interesting picture of a time and place, and some appealing recipes for such Southern fare as chess pie, jam cake, salt rising bread, Sally Lunn, beaten biscuits, blackberry cordial, chowchow, peach pickle, and "cabbage cooked so a baby can eat it with impunity."

The Laurel Cook Book, compiled and edited by the women of St. John's Guild (Laurel, Miss., 1949). This is the fifth edition of a cookbook first edited by Mrs. George Gardiner in 1900. Close to half of the one thousand recipes are aimed at the Southern sweet tooth.

The Mississippi Cookbook, compiled and edited by the Home Economics Division of the Mississippi Cooperative Extension Service (University Press of Mississippi, Jackson, 1972). From more than seven thousand recipes submitted by cooks all over the state, the editors chose 1200 to include in this 475-page volume.

Monuments and Menus, compiled by the Pilgrimage Garden Club (Natchez, Miss., 1972). Recipes and historical sketches from the antebellum homes of Natchez, including a good many sweets and liquor-based recipes.

Natchez Recipes, selected by Anne Young White and edited by Nola Nance Oliver (privately published, Natchez, Miss., circa 1940). A collection of old Southern recipes, some of them said to be previously unpublished, from the pantries of antebellum Natchez.

Old Trace Cooking, by Gladiola Branscome Harris (Riverside Press, Memphis, Tenn., 1981). Native American and pioneer recipes from the Natchez Trace are presented here by a retired Mississippi extension home economist. Choctaw, Chickasaw, and Natchez Indian cookery and foods prepared by pioneer families are placed in the historical context of early times on the trace—1780 to 1840.

Poor Folks Cook Book, compiled by Mrs. W. R. Waites (published privately, Lucedale, Miss., 1972). An account of "the ways we cooked, how we made do, and made meals that filled up lots of hungry people," by a sharecropper's daughter who helped to raise a large family in rural Mississippi. A model of bare-bones self-sufficiency, the book includes recipes for cracklin bread, scratch gravy (bacon grease and flour), field peas, greens, fish, and game.

Southern Sideboards, compiled and published by the Junior League of Jackson (Jackson, Miss., 1978). The Jackson club's volume with its introductory essay on food and fellowship by the late Wyatt Cooper has more than 200,000 copies in print.

Standing Room Only, compiled and published by New Stage Theater (Jackson, Miss., 1983). This "cookbook for entertaining" begins with introductory words from playwright Beth Henley and author Eudora Welty and follows with more than three hundred pages of modern Southern hospitality.

NORTH CAROLINA

Betty Feezor's Carolina Recipes, by Betty Feezor (Dowd Press, Charlotte, N.C., 1957). A popular television cook puts her best material—a blend of traditional and modern—into print. Revisions and new editions appeared regularly for several years.

Capital City Recipes, by the ladies of the Raleigh Presbyterian Church (Capital Printing Co., Raleigh, N.C., 1900). This is an interesting period piece from a bygone day. Not to be outdone, the ladies of Raleigh's First Baptist Church issued a similar volume in 1907. Both are filled with basic Southern cuisine.

The Carol Dare Cookbook, by Carol Dare (*The State* magazine, Raleigh, N.C., 1972). A widely read food columnist in North Carolina sifted through thirty-five years of her magazine's back issues and pulled out these "favorite recipes of yesterday and today," most of them long familiar to eastern North Carolina cooks.

The Henderson Cook Book, compiled and published by the Ladies' Aid Society of the First Baptist Church (Henderson, N.C.; second edition, 1914). Sweets and yeast breads are here in abundance, but the most surprising inclusions are several recipes for homemade wines and cordials.

High Hampton Hospitality, compiled and illustrated by Lily Byrd McKee (Creative Printers, Inc., Chapel Hill, N.C., 1970). Recipes and history from High Hampton Inn, where Southerners have escaped the summer heat in the mountains of western North Carolina for 150 years.

Mountain Cooking, by John Parris (Asheville Citizen-Times Publishing Co., Asheville, N.C., 1978). A veteran newspaper columnist and author in western North Carolina brings mountain cookery to life in this fine blend of traditional recipes, oral history interviews, and descriptive prose.

North Carolina and Old Salem Cookery, written and published by Elizabeth Hedgecock Sparks (Kernersville, N.C., 1955). The eighteenth-century Moravian settlement of Salem is the springboard for this informal history of the evolution of food in North Carolina. The old-fashioned recipes and the history are ably presented.

North Carolina's Historic Restaurants and Their Recipes, by Dawn O'Brien (John F. Blair, Publisher, Winston-Salem, N.C., 1983). A short profile and two or three recipes from each of forty-five noted dining places in the state make up this book. The author has continued the pattern with books from South Carolina and Virginia.

Old North State Cook Book, compiled and published by the Junior League of Charlotte (Charlotte, N.C., 1942). This was one of the first of the Junior League cookbooks, and it's a good one, with interesting stories to preface many of the recipes. The Charlotte organization later published *Cooking Mother's Goose* (1964), *The Charlotte Cookbook* (1971), and *Charlotte Cooks Again* (1981).

The Original Calabash Cookbook, compiled and edited by Banks Shepherd (Calabash Publishing Co., Calabash, N.C., 1977). This tiny coastal community has become widely known for its lightly breaded fried seafood. Tips on buying, seasoning, and cooking shellfish are featured in the book.

Southern Appalachian Mountain Cookbook, edited by Ferne Shelton (Hutcraft, High Point, N.C., 1964). A short collection of basic recipes from the pioneer past.

A Taste of History, compiled and published by the North Carolina Museum of History Associates, Inc. (Raleigh, N.C., 1982). A large and attractive collection of old and contemporary Southern recipes—but inexplicably, not a line of history.

A Tryon Palace Trifle, edited and published by the Tryon Palace Commission (New Bern, N.C., 1960). English cookery in North Carolina before the Revolution is extolled in this collection of eighteenth-century recipes and snippets of history.

The Webster Cookbook, edited by Joe P. Rhinehart (Edwards & Broughton Co., Raleigh, N.C., 1974). A "book of good and plain food" from Webster, a century-old North Carolina mountain community.

Woman's Club Cook Book of Southern Recipes, compiled by members of the Woman's Club of Charlotte (Ray Printing Co., Charlotte, N.C., 1908). Succinct directions for hundreds of regional favorites of the time, including Robert E. Lee cake, jam cake, and strawberry shortcake.

SOUTH CAROLINA

Carolina Cuisine, compiled by the Junior Assembly of Anderson, S.C. (Hallux, Inc., Anderson, S.C., 1969). The recipes and menus of this fifty-year-old civic and charitable organization include many "heirloom" dishes.

The Carolina Housewife, by Sarah Rutledge (University of South Carolina Press, Columbia, S.C., 1979). This facsimile of the classic 1847 volume includes an introductory essay by Anna Wells Rutledge and a list of South Carolina cookbooks published before 1935. Both the new and old material are rich with history, good writing, and wonderful things to eat.

Charleston Receipts, collected by the Junior League of Charleston (Charleston, S.C., 1950). Now, twenty-five printings and more than a half-million copies later, it has attained the stature of a classic. The black mammy motif and verses in dialect are ridiculously out of date, but the recipes are timeless—three hundred pages of Southern treasures, from hoppin John to syllabub.

Clemson House Cook Book, by Russie H. Paget (Heritage House, Charlotte, N.C., 1955). Upcountry South Carolina and the village of Clemson are the focus in this big (475-page) book of "heirloom" and contemporary recipes.

Coastal Carolina Cooking, gathered and published by the women's auxiliary of the Ocean View Memorial Hospital (Myrtle Beach, S.C., 1958). More than three hundred pages of handwritten recipes introduced by South Carolina poet and author Archibald Rutledge. The low-country cuisine includes lots of seafood, game, and sweets.

A Colonial Plantation Cookbook: The Receipt Book of Harriott Pinckney Horry, 1770, edited and introduced by Richard J. Hooker (University of South Carolina Press, Columbia, 1984). Thanks to the resurrection of an old and previously unpublished manuscript and the historical interpretation of Richard Hooker, a vivid picture of colonial plantation life emerges.

Recipes from Pawleys Island, compiled by the women of All Saints Waccamaw Episcopal Church (Walker, Evans & Cogswell, Charleston, S.C., 1955). From Pawleys Island, a favorite coastal retreat of generations of Southerners, comes this excellent little collection of low-country recipes—creek shrimp, red rice, and lots of pilaus among them. Two other cookbooks from inns on the island—*Potluck from Pawleys* (Cassena Inn, 1974) and Tip Top Recipes (Tip Top Inn, 1974)—also contain personal and regional treasures.

Rect. Book No. 2, by Eliza Lucas Pinckney, 1756. The mistress of Belmont Plantation near Charleston compiled at least two handwritten books of recipes and home remedies, and this one survives as a museum piece. It is a fascinating glimpse at Southern food in colonial times. Among the foods described are bread pudding, yam pudding, quince wine, currant wine, egg pies, boiled rice, oyster soup, and boiled ham. There are also instructions for curing, smoking, and aging hams.

The Sandlapper Cook Book, compiled by Catha W. Reid and Joseph T. Bruce, Jr. (Sandlapper Press, Orangeburg, S.C., 1973). A collection of the editors' favorite South Carolina and Southern recipes from *The Sandlapper,* a popular state magazine.

Sea Island Seasons, edited by a committee of Beaufort countians (Beaufort County Open Land Trust, Beaufort, S.C., 1980). The South Carolina low country's distinctive cuisine is impressively displayed in this collection of shrimp, rice, okra, sweets, and much more.

The South Carolina Cook Book, collected by the South Carolina Council of Farm Women and edited in the State Home Demonstration Department (University of South Carolina Press, Columbia, 1954; revised and reissued, 1969). Quoting Samuel Pepys ("Strange to see how a good dinner and feasting reconciles everybody"), the ladies pursue reconciliation with more than four hundred pages of carefully chosen and tested state and regional recipes, from grits and greens to puddings and pies. The recipes were chosen from hundreds sent in from all over South Carolina.

A Taste of Carolina, compiled by the Palmetto Cabinet (R. L. Bryan & Co., Columbia, S.C., 1983). The Palmetto Cabinet—wives of South Carolina legislators—assembled these old and new recipes and combined them with thumbnail histories of every county in the state and many of its old buildings. Some of the recipes are historic treasures too.

Two Hundred Years of Charleston Cooking, gathered by Blanche S. Rhett and edited by Lettie Gay (first published in 1930; subsequently revised, and replicated by the University of South Carolina Press, Columbia, 1976). A new introduction by Elizabeth Verner Hamilton sets the scene and mood for this period piece of race- and class-conscious Charleston. The recipes include shrimp pie, baked shad, pine bark stew, chicken pilau, and Carolina trifle.

Three Hundred Years of Carolina Cooking, compiled and published by the Junior League of Greenville (Greenville, S.C., 1972). South Carolina's tricentennial celebration prompted the publication of this volume, which includes, among other interesting features, thirty-five pages on cooking wild game.

TENNESSEE

Anne Foster Caldwell's Book of Southern and Creole Home Cooking, by Anne Foster Caldwell (privately printed, Nashville, Tenn., 1929). A noted hostess and food specialist of her time, Anne Caldwell was a pillar of Nashville's Centennial Club, then and now a celebrated venue of private luncheons in the old Southern style. Among her most-loved recipes: divinity candy, Lady Washington cake, and beaten biscuits—the dough pounded "with a club made of hickory." The same venerable women's club also inspired *Recipes and Party Plans* (1958), by another of its able hostesses, Sadie LeSueur.

The Cumberland Cook Book, compiled and published by the ladies of the Cumberland Presbyterian Churches of Nashville (Nashville, Tenn., 1895). A 1980 reprint of this period piece makes its interesting contents accessible again. Included in one hundred pages of recipes are forty pages of sweets, as well as thirteen oyster dishes and nine kinds of chowchow relish.

Flossie Morris' Unusual Cookbook and Household Hints, by Flossie Morris (privately printed, Nashville, Tenn., 1967). Unusual indeed are a good many of the recipes in this little book by an enterprising and creative lady who cooked for many years in the household of the late Hank Williams of country music fame. Among the unconventional dishes: stuffed oranges, sausage and rice croquettes, and fried bananas.

Good Things to Eat, by Mrs. W. H. Wilson and Miss Mollie Huggins (Methodist Publishing House, Nashville, Tenn., 1909). Turn-of-the century *haute cuisine* in Tennessee and the mid-South gets loving treatment here.

Helen Exum's Chattanooga Cook Book, by Helen McDonald Exum (privately published, Chattanooga, Tenn., 1970). A folksy mélange of recipes and stories, most of them local or Southern, by a food columnist of the Chattanooga *News-Free Press.*

Hermitage Hospitality, edited by Ginger Helton and Susan Van Riper (Aurora Publishers, Inc., Nashville, Tenn., 1970). Recipes from the Andrew Jackson era in Tennessee (roughly 1800–1840), with some descriptive commentary on early Tennessee cooking.

The Housekeeper's Manual, compiled by the ladies of Moore Memorial Presbyterian Church of Nashville (Methodist Publishing House, Nashville, Tenn., 1875). Having "recourse to the private Receipts of the best housewives of Virginia and Tennessee," the ladies selected more than five hundred to publish—including a large number of alcoholic concoctions. The dessert recipes are also extensive.

How We Cook in Tennessee, compiled and published by the Silver Thimble Society of the First Baptist Church (Jackson, Tenn., no date). This third edition, while undated, appears to be an early-twentieth-century collection of mid-South recipes.

The Knoxville Cook Book, compiled and edited by the directors of the Knoxville Woman's Building Association (Bean, Warters & Co., Knoxville, Tenn., 1901). Calling east Tennessee "the asparagus bed in the Tennessee garden-spot," the women proceeded to put forth a diverse and interesting collection of recipes—and described them with an entertaining flair.

The Memphis Cook Book, compiled and published by the Junior League of Memphis (Memphis, Tenn., 1952). It was the first to follow the example of the phenomenal *Charleston Receipts* and seek a broader commercial market. There have been subsequent volumes, including *Party Potpourri* (1970).

Minnie Pearl Cooks, by Minnie Pearl, a.k.a. Sarah Ophelia Cannon (Aurora Publishers, Inc., Nashville, 1970). The country music comedienne draws on her rural Tennessee upbringing for this collection of down-home stories and Southern recipes. Especially appealing are the breads and sweets.

Miss Mary's Down-Home Cooking, by Diana Dalsass (New American Library, New York, 1984). Until she died in 1983 at the age of 102, Mrs. Mary Bobo was the first lady of Lynchburg, Tennessee. Her fame, which reached far beyond the state, derived from the incomparably delicious boardinghouse dinners she served for seventy-five years. Inexplicably, it took a New Jersey woman to see the cookbook potential in such a culinary treasury. The best of Miss Mary's country food recipes are preserved in this well-written little volume.

Mrs. Black's Choice Recipes, by Mrs. Tennessee W. Black (J. T. Camp, Printer, Nashville, Tenn., 1907). Cakes were Mrs. Black's specialty, but she was a noted cook of diverse dishes and a perennial prize winner at fairs, and her cookbook enjoyed great popularity in the Nashville area.

The Nashville Cookbook, compiled by the Nashville Area Home Economics Association. (McQuiddy Printing Co., Nashville, Tenn., 1976). In addition to some excellent local and regional recipes, this bicentennial-year volume contains an informative essay on old cookbooks and historical sketches of such local landmarks as the Maxwell House Hotel, where President Theodore Roosevelt called the house coffee "good to the last drop."

Nashville Seasons Cook Book, compiled and published by the Junior League of Nashville

(Nashville, Tenn., 1964), and *Nashville Seasons Encore,* the league's 1977 volume, contain a wealth of old and valuable recipes, as all Junior League cookbooks do—but like most, they lack a social-cultural-historical dimension.

Nashville: 200 Years of Hospitality, compiled and published by the Tennessee Federation of Women's Clubs, Nashville division (Nashville, Tenn., 1979). On the occasion of the city's bicentennial, this organization combined profiles of noted Nashville women in history with an impressive selection of recipes, menus, and notes of food history.

Old Time Tennessee Recipes, compiled and edited by the women of First Presbyterian Church (Nashville, Tenn., 1943). Three hundred pages of handwritten recipes from midtwentieth-century Tennessee kitchens.

The Original Tennessee Homecoming Cookbook, edited by Daisy King (Rutledge Hill Press, Nashville, Tenn., 1985). A solicited collection of all-time favorite Tennessee recipes, edited by a well-known Nashville tearoom hostess and cook.

Our Food Heritage, a community study series compiled and published by the Nashville Public Schools (Nashville, Tenn., 1958). This mimeographed mixture of recipes and social-cultural history contains a wealth of little-known information about food served in a variety of old Nashville restaurants, hotels, clubs, and homes.

Rugby Recipes, compiled and published by the Rugby Restoration Association (Rugby, Tenn., 1971). A small group of English idealists and others founded a utopian community in the Tennessee mountains in 1880; this is a collection of recipes from original colonists and some who followed.

The Sewanee Cook Book, compiled and edited by Queenie Woods Washington (Baird-Ward Printing Co., Nashville, Tenn., 1926). Called "a collection of autographed recipes from Southern homes and plantations," this volume is filled with time-tested recipes, special-occasion menus, household remedies, and advertisements from the period. The names and addresses of more than one hundred contributors are listed. Sewanee—The University of the South—is an Episcopal college in Tennessee.

VIRGINIA

Aunt Caroline's Dixieland Recipes, by Emma and William McKinney (Land & Lee, Inc., Chicago, Ill., 1922). A collection of celebrated dishes "drawn from the treasured memories of Aunt Caroline Pickett, a famous old Virginia cook." Among the jewels are spoonbread, beaten biscuits, Brunswick stew, chess pie, and an array of sweet potato dishes.

Colonial Virginia Cookery, by Jane Carson (Colonial Williamsburg, Williamsburg, Va., 1968). One in a series of research studies sponsored by Colonial Williamsburg, this book focuses on food supplies, popular menus and dishes, cooking methods, and preserving methods in the seventeenth and eighteenth centuries.

The Housekeeper of Staunton, Virginia, by Mrs. A. M. Fauntleroy (Stoneburner & Prufer, Staunton, Va., 1891). This collection of nineteenth-century recipes and menus comes from west of the Blue Ridge. Curiously, there's much more veal, beef, lamb, venison, and fish than pork.

Housekeeping in Old Virginia, edited by Marion Cabell Tyree (John P. Morton & Co., Louisville, Ky., 1879; reprinted by Favorite Recipes Press, Louisville, 1965). A granddaughter of Patrick Henry compiled this post–Civil War guide to food preparation and household management. It harks back to the "good old days" of early Virginia and contains recipes from "two hundred and fifty of Virginia's noted housewives" whose names and home-towns are listed.

Nelly Custis Lewis's Housekeeping Book, edited by Patricia Brady Schmit (Historic New Orleans Collection, New Orleans, La., 1982). George Washington's adopted daughter compiled this handwritten recipe and remedy book when she was mistress of a large Virginia plantation in the 1830s, and Patricia Brady Schmit has enriched it with an illuminating introduction and historical notes. Nelly Custis Lewis also had an eighteenth-century household manuscript that had belonged to her grand-mother, Martha Washington; in 1981, Columbia University Press in New York published it, transcribed and annotated by Karen Hess.

Norfolk Cookery Book, by Sandra Kytle Woodward (Donning Co., Norfolk/Virginia Beach, Va., 1981). This attractive book of recipes from a three-hundred-year-old Virginia sea-port city is an interesting combination of old and new recipes and local history.

Recipes from Old Virginia, compiled by the Virginia Federation of Home Demonstration Clubs (Dietz Press, Richmond, Va., 1961). This is not, as claimed, "a complete collection of old and new Virginia recipes," but it is nonetheless a diverse assemblage of well-received dishes. Almost half its pages are devoted to sweets.

The Smithfield Cookbook, edited by Caroline Darden Hurt and Joan Hundley Powell (Jun-ior Woman's Club of Smithfield, Va., 1978). Three and a half centuries of cooking and dining traditions are wonderfully united here with the larger history of Smithfield and its generations of residents. This is a model of what a good local cookbook should be: a blend of careful research, oral history, kitchen wisdom, and unerring good taste. The famed Smithfield hams get center stage, but they're joined by hundreds of other fine dishes and by the interesting people who have raised, cooked, served, and eaten them.

Two Centuries of Virginia Cooking, by Gibson Jefferson McConnaughey (Mid-South Pub-lishing Co., Amelia, Va., 1977). From the Haw Branch Plantation near Petersburg comes this serving of food and history by an eighth-generation descendant of the founders. The introduction is revealing of the kitchens and households of upper-class planters before the Revolution. They enjoyed, among other things, such exotica as coconuts, lemons, and pineapples.

Virginia Cookery Book, published by the League of Women Voters of Richmond (Richmond, Va., circa 1922). Though not dated, the book is known to have been produced around 1922, when the league was a young organization. The recipes and advertisements help to bring a bygone era to life.

Virginia Cookery-Book, by Mary Stuart Smith (Harper & Bros., New York, 1885). The in-troduction says "two Virginia ladies . . . herein lay before their sisters a collection of recipes," but the other lady is not identified. In the style of many post–Civil War house-keeping guides, this volume offers detailed instructions to a surviving class of inexperi-enced white women. "Old domestic institutions [i.e., slavery] having been done away with," says the writer, "there is danger that the composition of many an excellent dish may become forgotten lore."

Virginia Cookery Past and Present, compiled and published by the Woman's Auxiliary of

Olivet Episcopal Church (Franconia, Va., 1957). This old church with a long and active history offers many great recipes, including some that are said to be previously unpublished dishes from the Lee and Washington families.

Virginia Country Life and Cooking, by Frances Darlington Simpson (privately printed, Fairfax County, Va., 1963). A reminiscence of country life in Fairfax County before World War II, and a tribute to a superlative black cook named Belle.

The Virginia House-Wife, by Mrs. Mary Randolph (Plaskitt & Cugle, Baltimore, Md., 1824). "Method is the soul of management," the author proclaimed in this fascinating collection, one of the very first that could properly be called a Southern cookbook. Mrs. Randolph compiled these recipes "for the young inexperienced housekeeper" and for women with servants. Notwithstanding the occasional quaint phrasing, the book's contents bear a striking resemblance to traditional Southern cookbooks of the past 160 years: "ochra" soup, catfish, beef steaks, salt-cured and hickory-smoked hams, fried oysters, roast turkey, fried chicken, creamed cabbage, potatoes mashed and fried, stewed tomatoes, beets, carrots, turnip greens, lima beans, sweet potatoes, field peas, all manner of puddings, apple fritters, biscuits, gazpacho salad, cornmeal batter cakes, ice cream, strawberry jam, cucumber pickles, and much more. A 1984 facsimile reprint of the Randolph classic by the University of South Carolina Press contains excellent historical notes and commentaries by Karen Hess.

The Williamsburg Art of Cookery, by Mrs. Helen Bullock (Dietz Press, Richmond, Va., 1938). Colonial Williamsburg fashioned this olde English volume and subtitled it "Accomplish'd Gentlewoman's Companion," just as Eliza Smith's *Compleat Housewife* was called in 1742 when it was reprinted in Williamsburg from the original English edition and thus became the first cookbook to be published in colonial America. The two-hundredth anniversary edition draws extensively upon its ancestor and from several nineteenth-century American cookbooks to present "upwards of five hundred of the most ancient and approv'd recipes in Virginia cookery." The quaint lettering is somewhat distracting, but the recipes offer a fascinating glimpse of foodways in the colonies.

The Williamsburg Cookbook, compiled and adapted by Letha Booth and the staff of Colonial Williamsburg (Colonial Williamsburg, Williamsburg, Va., 1971). A blend of traditional and contemporary recipes from Virginia, this volume contains formulas for and some history of such Southern favorites as eggnog, ice creams, and sherbets (first reported in Maryland in the 1740s), Sally Lunn bread, roasting ears (described by Robert Beverley of Virginia in 1705), and peanut soup.

THE REGION

American Cooking: Southern Style, by Eugene Walter (Time-Life Books, New York, N.Y., 1971). More than twenty years after he left his native Mobile to live in Europe, Eugene Walter returned to write with grace and style about the food traditions of the South. This is a superlative treatment of Southern cooking in its social-cultural-historical context. A more recent but lesser-known Walter book focuses on Mobile: *Delectable Dishes from Termite Hall* (Madaloni Press, Mobile, Ala., 1982).

Bill Neal's Southern Cooking, by Bill Neal (University of North Carolina Press, Chapel Hill, N.C., 1985). A young Southern chef and restaurant owner (Crook's Corner, Chapel Hill) writes with style and feeling about the food of his native culture.

The Centennial Receipt Book, by "A Southern Lady" (Mary J. Waring), presumably published in Charleston, but noted only as having been "written in 1876." Mary Waring, who lived in Charleston from 1851 to 1947, is known to have authored this collection of about three hundred recipes that were popular in the South in the nineteenth century. Many of them still are.

Confederate Receipt Book, compiled by "A Confederate Lady" (West & Johnston, Richmond, Va., 1862; reissued with an introduction by E. Merton Coulter, University of Georgia Press, Athens, 1960). The only known recipe book to be published in the South during the Civil War, this little volume was aimed at helping Southern housekeepers plagued by shortages of foodstuffs.

Cooking Across the South, by Lillian B. Marshall (Oxmoor House, Birmingham, Ala., 1980). A veteran food editor's collections and recollections include some interesting and informative historical perspectives on Southern food.

Cooking of the South, by Nathalie Dupree (Irena Chalmers Cookbooks, Inc., New York, 1982). A short course (eighty-three pages) on the food of the South by an Atlanta writer and cooking school director. Many of the classic dishes and a little of the history are combined in an easy-to-read format.

Culinary Echoes from Dixie, by Kate Brew Vaughn (McDonald Press, Cincinnati, Ohio, 1914). Such dishes as Woodford pudding, pecan pralines, and Lady Baltimore cake demonstrate the author's acquaintance with cooking in various parts of the South.

Damnyankee in a Southern Kitchen, by Helen Worth (Westover Publishing Co., Richmond, Va., 1973). A New York cooking school director and food writer ventures into the South to sample the food, and comes away with an entertaining and informative interpretation of the region's culinary ways.

Dishes and Beverages of the Old South, by Martha McCulloch-Williams (McBride, Nast & Co., New York, 1913). A three-hundred-page narrative by a Tennessee woman who not only knew her way around the kitchen but was handy with a pen as well. Definitely a period piece ("it was through being the best fed people in the world," she wrote, that "we of the South Country were able to put up the best fight in history"), the book is nonetheless an interesting blend of usefulness and charm—and filled with mouthwatering recipes.

The Dixie Cook-Book, compiled anonymously by Estelle Woods Wilcox (L. A. Clarkson & Co., Atlanta, Ga., 1883; revised and enlarged as *The New Dixie Cook-Book,* 1889). Estelle Wilcox was an entrepreneurial wizard who preferred to take no personal credit for her impact on American cookery. The *Dixie* was just one of five cookbooks she produced in Ohio, Minnesota, Colorado, and Georgia between 1876 and 1894; many of the recipes were used in more than one book. The first *Dixie* was credited to "well-known ladies of the South"; the second to "well-known ladies, North and South." They were dedicated "to the mothers, wives, and daughters of the 'Sunny South,' who have so bravely faced the difficulties which new social conditions have imposed upon them." Detailed instructions for preparing hundreds of common dishes were spelled out for the benefit of white women who knew how to direct others in the kitchen, but not how to cook. The second *Dixie* was an especially imposing 1288-page volume.

Eating, Drinking, and Visiting in the South, by Joe Gray Taylor (Louisiana State University Press, Baton Rouge, 1982). A personal, informal, and exceedingly well-informed history of food in the social and cultural development of the South, written by a native Tennessean and long-time professor of history in Louisiana. A basic and indispensable book on a long-neglected subject.

Fish House Cook Book, by Mary Arthur Henderson (privately printed, Little River, S.C., 1982). This sixty-eight-page collection of recipes, drawings, and explanatory background deserves a wider audience. It effectively evokes the sea-oriented way of living and eating that has characterized the people of coastal North and South Carolina for generations. The food is as inviting as the book itself.

The Flavor of the South, by Jeanne A. Voltz (Doubleday & Co., Garden City, N.Y., 1977; new edition by Gramercy Publishing Co., New York, 1983). A native Southerner who became food editor for a major national magazine drew upon her memories and her modern experiences to assemble a collection of Southern dishes suited to contemporary methods and tastes.

Four Great Southern Cooks, edited and published by DuBose Publishing (Atlanta, Ga., 1980). Daisy Redman, Ruth Jenkins, Beatrice Mize, and William Mann, Jr.—four Georgians who are "among the last of the old-time cooks"—are featured in this tribute to the plain and fancy creations of live-in professional cooks whose mastery of Southern cuisine is almost absolute. The recipes range from collard greens to caviar pie.

The Foxfire Book of Appalachian Cookery, edited by Linda Garland Page and Eliot Wigginton (Foxfire Press/E. P. Dutton, Inc., New York, 1984). Following up its phenomenal success with the now-famous series of folklore books from the north Georgia mountains, the Foxfire aggregation here presents a comprehensive volume of regional recipes, supplemented by oral history, lots of black-and-white photographs, and instructions on how to produce, preserve, and prepare the foods that have nourished mountain people for generations. This is a wonderful way to make a book about food.

From Mother with Love, by Rebecca Stewart Wight and Selma Wight Beard (Peachtree Publishing Co., Atlanta, Ga., 1984). Collected letters of a mother to her daughter, a Southern war bride of the early 1940s. This unusual and absorbing book is full of recipes, advice, wisdom—and love. The daughter, Selma Beard, calls the letters "a crash course in cooking—and living."

Grace Hartley's Southern Cookbook, compiled by Grace Hartley (Doubleday & Co., Garden City, N.Y., 1976). The long-time food editor of the Atlanta *Journal* chose these recipes from the thousands published in the paper during her tenure; they came from homes and restaurants all over the South.

The Hand-Me-Down Cookbook, by Cherry Parker and Frances Bradsher (Moore Publishing Co., Durham, N.C., 1969). A Kentucky-born mother-daughter team, from their homes in Tennessee and North Carolina, combined their skills in restaurant management, writing, and cooking to produce this collection of old-time Southern recipes and stories.

The Heritage of Southern Cooking, by Camille Glenn (Workman Publishing Co., New York, 1986). Camille Glenn was raised in the kitchen of her parents' Kentucky country inn and has herself been a noted cook and teacher of cooks for 50 years. This is her magnum opus.

Hog Meat and Hoecake, by Sam Bowers Hilliard (Southern Illinois University Press, Carbondale, 1972). A fascinating and revealing scholarly study of the production, consumption, and distribution of foodstuffs in the South prior to the Civil War, this volume helps to explain how and why Southern food habits began.

Holland's Southern Cookbook, compiled and edited by Charleen McClain (Tupper and Love, Inc., Atlanta, Ga., 1952). This collection, being mostly "old favorites, handed down in Southern families for generations," comes from the pages of *Holland's Magazine,* which featured cooking with a Southern accent.

Jesse's Book of Creole and Deep South Recipes, by Edith Ballard Watts with John Watts (Viking Press, New York, 1954). The kitchen genius of Jesse Willis Lewis, private cook for more than forty years for the family of New Orleans newspaper editor Marshall Ballard, is proudly celebrated in this book by one of the Ballard children.

Mammy Lou's Cook Book, by Betty Benton Patterson (Robert M. McBride Co., New York, 1931). This book is typical of many that were published during the late 1800s and the early decades of this century; lamentations for the vanishing black "mammy" whose cooking and home- and child-management skills kept many a Southern white woman in genteel leisure. Mammy Lou, in this case, is "a composite characterization of all the negro mammies we have known, loved, and lost." Along with her words of wisdom (rendered, as always, in obtrusive dialect) are some excellent recipes.

Marion Brown's Southern Cook Book, by Marion Brown (University of North Carolina Press, Chapel Hill, 1951; revised edition, 1968). One of the many strengths of this volume is its self-conscious effort to show Southern cooking as a dynamic, evolving cuisine with a firm foothold in history. African, French, Hispanic, and other influences meet here with yams, pork, corn—and the rest is history. A very comprehensive, five-hundred-page treatment of Southern cookery, the Brown volume is valuable as history as well as cookery.

Mary Lyles Wilson's New Cook Book, by Mary Lyles Wilson (The Southwestern Co., Nashville, Tenn., eleventh edition, 1937). The author's mother, Betty Lyles Wilson, published the first version of this book in 1914; it remained a popular favorite for more than forty years, with numerous reprintings and revisions. Mother and daughter gained a measure of recognition for baking "the official White House Christmas cake" during seven presidential administrations, and their books featured a great variety of cakes in a broad spectrum of Southern foods.

More Than Moonshine, by Sidney Saylor Farr (University of Pittsburgh Press, Pittsburgh, Pa., 1983). Combining recipes with narrative, the author, a native of eastern Kentucky, describes a pervasive way of life in southern Appalachia over the past forty years. The recipes include persimmon pudding, rhubarb conserve, apple stackcake, honey butter, shuck beans, sallet greens, squirrel and gravy, cracklin bread, and birch beer.

Mountain Makin's in the Smokies, compiled and published by the Great Smoky Mountains Natural History Association (Gatlinburg, Tenn., 1957). Good instructions accompany these traditional recipes, which include pot likker dumplings, corn light bread, scrapple, dried apple fruitcake, stack cake, molasses muffins, and persimmon pudding.

Mrs. Hill's New Cook Book, by Mrs. A. P. Hill (Carleton, Publisher, New York, 1873). A Georgia gentleman's widow dedicated this fascinating volume to "inexperienced Southern housekeepers," and offered four hundred pages of very detailed instructions to the thousands of young white women who until the Civil War had depended on slaves to do their cooking.

Mrs. Porter's New Southern Cookery Book, by Mrs. M. E. Porter (Philadelphia, Pa., 1871; reprinted by Promontory Press, New York, 1973). One in a series of reissued volumes on American cookery, this post–Civil War cookbook by a Virginia lady seems self-consciously aimed at Americanizing the foodways and recipes of the South. The introduction to the new edition by Louis Szathmary is an interesting and insightful look at regional cookery and history.

The New York Times Southern Heritage Cookbook, by Jean Hewitt (G. P. Putnam's Sons, New York, 1976). A collection of traditional Southern recipes, with an introduction by the author extolling the variety of the region's cuisine.

Old Southern Receipts, by Mary D. Pretlow (Robert M. McBride Co., New York, 1930). The author resurrected a large number of Norfolk, Virginia, family heirlooms from people "who keep good tables and use only Southern cooking—*good* Southern cooking."

Plantation Recipes, by Lessie Bowers (Robert Speller & Sons, New York, 1959). Lessie Bowers, granddaughter of slaves, went north from South Carolina in the Depression and gained fame, if not fortune, as the founder and chief cook of The Virginia Restaurant in Bronxville, New York. This is a collection of the basic and classic Southern dishes that were her favorites.

The Progressive Farmer's Southern Cook Book, by Sallie F. Hill (The Progressive Farmer Co., Birmingham, Ala., and G. P. Putnam's Sons, New York, 1961). More than 2500 recipes fill the book to overflowing with Southern dishes and some of the stories behind them. The postwar advance of food and kitchen technology is acknowledged, but there is still praise for "old time and new dishes started from scratch."

Secrets of Southern Cooking, by Ethel Farmer Hunter (Tudor Publishing Co., New York, 1948). A daughter of the South here surrenders some family jewels from the kitchen. The collection is broad and basic, and of high quality.

The Southern Cookbook, by S. Thomas Bivins (Press of the Hampton Institute, Hampton, Va., 1912). "Recipes used by noted colored cooks and prominent caterers" are the highlight of this manual of domestic service compiled by a Pennsylvania-based training-school principal. Bivins and Mrs. W. T. Hayes, whose *Kentucky Cook Book* was also published in 1912, may have been the first black authors to write and publish volumes on food.

Southern Cooking, by Mrs. S. R. Dull (Grosset & Dunlap, New York, 1968). Before and after she first published this book in 1928, Henrietta Stanley Dull was a renowned Georgia editor, teacher, and cook. After her death at the age of 100 the book was reissued by a New York publisher, but it had been in print for forty years by then. It remains a classic of Southern cookery, called by its publisher "a complete cookbook" and "the standard by which regional cooks are measured." Included are more than 1300 recipes.

Southern Cooking to Remember, by Kathryn Tucker Windham (Strode Publishers, Inc.,

Huntsville, Ala., 1978). The author of three other cookbooks—traditional collections from Alabama, Georgia, and Tennessee—writes with deep feeling for the history and the foods of the South.

Southern Country Cookbook, by Lena Sturges and the editors of *Progressive Farmer* magazine (Progressive Farmer Books, Birmingham, Ala., 1972). More than four hundred pages of staple foodstuffs of the South, prepared in traditional ways.

The Southern Gardener and Receipt-Book, by Mary L. Edgeworth (J. B. Lippincott & Co., Philadelphia, Pa., 1859). There are few clues here to the identity of Mrs. Edgeworth, other than that the foreword to the third edition was written by her at Fort Valley, Georgia. The 175 pages of recipes offer some valuable glimpses at antebellum cookery. Included are "purlow" (rice with "a piece of bacon, or sound salt pork, and one or two fowls"), snap beans with pork, "barbacue shoat," sweet potato pie, bread pudding, syllabub, blanc mange, quince preserves, many kinds of corn and wheat breads, and beers made with ginger, persimmons, spruce, and hops.

The Southern Hospitality Cookbook, by Winifred Green Cheney (Oxmoor House, Birmingham, Ala., 1976). A preface by Eudora Welty and informed commentary throughout bolster this extensive and well-organized compilation of recipes Southerners have put before company for generations.

The Southern Junior League Cookbook, edited by Ann Seranne (David McKay Co., New York, 1977). Here are more than seven hundred time-honored recipes—the inevitable "best of the best" from twenty-nine Junior Leagues in the South. Junior League cookbooks have gained wide popularity in the nation's cities since they were first published in the South in the early 1940s. Like other women's service organizations before them, the league has found cookbooks to be excellent fund-raising instruments. Montgomery, Alabama, and Charlotte, North Carolina, apparently started the Junior League cookbook trend; now, more than 125 American cities (over one third of them in the South) have published one or more collections. A representative few are included in this bibliography.

Spoonbread and Strawberry Wine, by Norma Jean and Carole Darden (Doubleday & Co., Garden City, N.Y., 1978). Two sisters on a pilgrimage in search of their Southern roots came up with this wonderful gastronomic portrait of an extended black family skilled at cooking and table talk.

The Taste of Country Cooking, by Edna Lewis (Alfred A. Knopf, New York, 1976). Here are recipes and reminiscences of a master cook and storyteller who grew up in Freetown, Virginia, a community of black farming families, and kept its strengths in her mind and heart when she moved away. Organized around the morning, noon, and evening meals in the four seasons of the year, the book conveys not only a wealth of information about Southern food but a vivid sense of the setting in which it was prepared and consumed.

Treasured Southern Family Recipes, by Geddings deM. Cushman and Ora Lou O'Hara Cushman (Hastings House, New York, 1966). Selected favorite recipes from five generations of three families in Augusta, Georgia, and Aiken, South Carolina.

White Trash Cooking, by Ernest Matthew Mickler (The Jargon Society, Winston-Salem, N.C. 1986). "The victuals of white, Southern, rural peasants" are celebrated here in "snapbean prose style" by an itinerant cook and certified good ole boy whose offerings include cold collard sandwiches, drop biscuits, and soda cracker pie.

BEYOND THE REGION

The African Heritage Cookbook, by Helen Mendes (Macmillan, New York, 1971). A native of New York whose mother grew up in a South Carolina tenant-farming family here delivers an absorbing and informative account of the passage through history, from ancient Africa to modern America, of soul food. Among the more than two hundred recipes are scores of country dishes that black and white Southerners have eaten for generations.

American Cookery, by Amelia Simmons (Hudson & Goodwin, Hartford, Conn., 1796; facsimile edition by Oxford University Press, New York, 1958). The first cookbook to be written by an American for American readers was, like the English reprints before it and many others to come, devoted solely to the interests of upper-class women whose "proper place" was in the home. The forty-three pages of recipes contained such Southern favorites as rice pudding, Indian pudding, hoecake, Indian slapjacks, syllabub, fruit preserves, and mention of more than a dozen kinds of field peas and beans. Amelia Simmons and Eliza Leslie, whose *Directions for Cookery in its Various Branches* appeared in 1837, are perhaps the best known early American cookbook writers, but there were others whose work was more substantial: Mary Randolph and her *Virginia House-Wife* (1824) and Lettice Bryan and her *Kentucky Housewife* (1839), to name two.

American Cooking, by Dale Brown (Time-Life Books, Alexandria, Va., 1968). The gastronomic diversity of the United States is celebrated in this thoughtfully designed and illustrated volume, one of the early entries in what has become a groundswell of voices proclaiming a new American cuisine. The Southern contribution here is substantial.

American Food: The Gastronomic Story, by Evan Jones (E. P. Dutton & Co., New York, 1975; second edition, Random House, New York, 1981). First in a narrative on the place of food in our history and then, collaborating with Judith B. Jones, in a collection of representative recipes, Evan Jones defines and describes the ethnic and regional elements that make up American cookery-cum-cuisine. An especially useful volume.

American Fried, by Calvin Trillin (Doubleday & Co., Garden City, N.Y., 1974). In almost twenty years of crisscrossing the country to write his *U.S. Journal* articles for *The New Yorker,* Trillin—Kansas City native, New York resident, one-time sojourner in Georgia—has earned an enviable reputation as the funniest and most entertaining food writer around. The South gets generous attention in this and the other two volumes in Trillin's "Tummy Trilogy"—*Alice, Let's Eat* (Random House, New York, 1978) and *Third Helpings* (Ticknor & Fields, Boston, Mass., 1983).

The American Heritage Cookbook, compiled by the editors of *American Heritage* magazine (American Heritage Publishing Co., New York, 1964). The ambitious goal of the editors—to present "recipes for the most delectable and historically interesting dishes prepared in America from the time of its discovery to the beginning of this century"—is admirably approached, if not fully reached. Background, history, and culture are served along with more than five hundred recipes that have been "modernized"—adapted to the latest kitchen equipment and methods and technology. More than a fifth of the dishes are either Southern originals or long-time favorites in the region.

American Home Cooking, by Nika Hazelton (Viking Press, New York, 1980). The South's culinary niche vis-à-vis the rest of the country is clearly shown in this well-prepared collection.

American Taste, by James Villas (Arbor House, New York, 1982). The regional virtues of American food are celebrated here by a native North Carolinian who lingers lovingly over such distinctively Southern specialties as fried chicken, barbecue, bourbon, and the famed foods of New Orleans.

Barbecued Ribs and Other Great Feeds, by Jeanne Voltz (Alfred A. Knopf, New York, 1985). The author, a native of Alabama and former food editor of *Woman's Day* magazine, explores the barbecue mystique in this useful and entertaining guidebook/cookbook.

The Buckeye Cook Book, compiled anonymously by Estelle Woods Wilcox (Buckeye Publishing Co., Dayton, Ohio, and Minneapolis, Minn., 1887; reprinted by Dover Publications, New York, 1975). An omnibus collection of traditional recipes ostensibly from the Midwest, this book has a distinct Southern flavor: vegetables cooked with pork fat, cornbread dodgers, chowchow relish, pan-fried chicken, boiled custard, even chess pie. For a partial explanation of this curious turn, see *The Dixie Cook-Book.*

Common Sense in the Household, by Marion Harland (C. Scribner & Co., New York, 1872). Novelist Mary Virginia Hawes Terhune labored in obscurity, but when she wrote cookbooks under the name of Marion Harland, she enjoyed enormous success. This one by the Virginia-born writer stayed in print for more than fifty years and was called a worthy successor to Mary Randolph's *Virginia House-Wife.* It's deliberately national—but distinctly Southern.

Consuming Passions, by Peter Farb and George Armelagos (Houghton Mifflin Co., Boston, Mass., 1980). Subtitled *The Anthropology of Eating,* this absorbing study of people's relationships to food is crammed with information on all sorts of serious and whimsical eating patterns. There's also a good bibliography.

A Date with a Dish, by Freda De Knight (Hermitage Press, New York, 1948). Coming as it did right after the end of World War II, this "cook book of American Negro recipes" sponsored by *Ebony* magazine could be thought of as an early forerunner of the soul food cookbooks that came along twenty years later. Freda De Knight, who grew up in South Dakota, took pains to show that black cooks are not all Southern; nevertheless, the food of the South dominates the collection. Along with the recipes are some short profiles of and quotes from many of the cooks who contributed to the volume.

The Dictionary of American Food & Drink, by John F. Mariani (Ticknor & Fields, New Haven, Conn., 1983). An excellent and indispensable encyclopedia of hundreds of American food terms and their origins. The South's contributions to the nation's gastronomy are well covered.

Directions for Cookery in its Various Branches, by Miss Leslie (Carey & Hart, Philadelphia, Pa., 1837). One of the most popular of early American cookbooks, Eliza Leslie's readable and informative volume had reached its seventeenth printing by 1843. Interestingly, it contains a number of dishes long popular in the South, such as "ochra and tomata" gumbo ("a favourite New Orleans dish"), corn muffins, Sally Lunn bread, and boiled country ham; its directions for curing and aging ham are quite similar to the time-honored methods of the South.

The Early American Cookbook, by Hyla O'Connor (Prentice-Hall, Inc., Englewood Cliffs, N.J., 1974). Old recipes (and a generous salting of history) adapted for the modern cook from original colonial sources. It's especially good on soups, stews, chowders, and hot breads.

Eating in America, by Waverley Root and Richard de Rochemont (William Morrow & Co., New York, 1976). An absorbing and highly informative history of what people in America have been eating and drinking for the past four hundred years. A masterful synthesis of a sweeping subject. The South's place in the larger social-cultural picture is substantial.

Ethnic and Regional Foodways in the United States, edited by Linda Keller Brown and Kay Mussell (University of Tennessee Press, Knoxville, 1984). A collection of essays on food as a vital factor in the self-identity and survival of subcultural groups in American society. The essay on Cajuns by Paige Gutierrez is of particular interest and pertinence to the South.

The Everlasting Pleasure, by Kathleen Ann Smallzried (Appleton-Century-Crofts, Inc., New York, 1956). Starting with Spanish chick-peas—garbanzos—in sixteenth-century Florida, the author follows and records influences on America's kitchens, cooks, and cookery through the post–World War II introduction of new electrical appliances.

Fading Feast, by Raymond Sokolov (Farrar, Straus & Giroux, Inc., New York, 1982). On assignment for *Natural History* magazine, food writer and social critic Raymond Sokolov produced these finely crafted essays on some of America's best—and most endangered—regional foods. Among the Southern delicacies he traces and extols are Brunswick stew, burgoo, Key limes, country hams, and hot Cajun sausages.

The Favorite Cookbook, edited by Mrs. Grace Townsend (W. B. Conkey Co., Chicago, Ill., 1894). Called "a complete culinary encyclopaedia," this old volume contains recipes for such Southern favorites as baked stuffed tomatoes, fried green tomatoes, gumbo filé, Sally Lunn bread ("formerly used on Southern tables only"), beaten biscuits, and Southern cornbread.

Food, by Waverley Root (Simon & Schuster, New York, 1980). From aardvark to zulu nuts, the foods of the world are presented in dictionary style, delightfully and authoritatively written by an incomparable food critic and historian. The Southern entries, from apples to yams, are excellent.

Food and Drink in America, by Richard J. Hooker (Bobbs-Merrill Co., Indianapolis, Ind., 1981). A concise, well-written history of American eating and how it has shaped us—physically, psychologically, socially.

Food Finds, by Allison Engel and Margaret Engel (Harper & Row, New York, 1984). This large-format paperback is a combination mail-order catalogue and visitor's guide to "America's best local foods and the people who produce them." Of the 340 small businesses and cottage industries included, forty-six are in the South; they offer such delicacies as poke sallet greens, country ham, grits, gumbo roux, and she-crab soup.

Food Odyssey, by Duncan Hines (Thomas Y. Crowell Co., New York, 1955). Twenty years after his pathfinding *Adventures in Good Eating* launched him on a phenomenal career as a food and lodging expert, Hines, a native of Bowling Green, Kentucky, took a reflective trip back across the country, stopping at his favorite inns and restaurants and sampling their specialties. The guidebooks, food products, cooking institutes, and other ventures of the resourceful Hines and his colleagues made his name a household word. A cosmopolitan diner, he nonetheless retained a Southerner's sense of the pleasures of good food and drink and table conversation.

The Frances Parkinson Keyes Cookbook, by Frances Parkinson Keyes (Doubleday & Co., Garden City, N.Y., 1955). The "culinary memoir" of a prolific writer, world traveler, and hostess who lived for a number of years in New Orleans and south Louisiana. A 120-page section of the book called "The Southern Writer" is her Louisiana remembrance, with recipes and commentary.

Good Home Cooking Across the U.S.A., by Nell B. Nichols (Iowa State College Press, Ames, 1953). A brief history of foods in each of the major regions of the country accompanies these recipes. The Atlantic and Gulf coasts and the South all receive ample and loving treatment from this Midwestern visitor.

Goodfood, by Jane and Michael Stern (Alfred A. Knopf, New York, 1983). Billed as "the adventurous eater's guide to restaurants serving America's best regional specialties," the book entertainingly describes 384 eating places in forty-three states; 114 of them are in the South. As in their earlier book, *Roadfood,* the Sterns display a genuine fondness for Southern cooking.

How America Eats, by Clementine Paddleford (Charles Scribner's Sons, New York, 1960). One of America's favorite food writers interviewed more than two thousand top cooks for this entertaining book, and the South provided about a fourth of them.

The Integrated Cookbook, by Mary Jackson and Lelia Wishart (Johnson Publishing Co., Chicago, Ill, 1971). In the spirit of the times, here is "The Soul of Good Cooking" by two black women who grew up on farms, one in North Carolina, the other in New York. The pork dishes use everything but the squeal.

James Beard's American Cookery, by James Beard (Little, Brown & Co., Boston, Mass., 1972). From a lifetime of preparing, eating, and writing about American food, the late James Beard here assembles the voluminous sum and substance of his experience. He calls the book "a record of good eating in this country with some of its lore." Among the more than 1500 recipes are a representative number of Southern ones.

The New York Times Cook Book, edited by Craig Claiborne (Harper & Bros., New York, 1961). This book and its 1979 sequel contain about 2500 recipes—but surprisingly, Southern-born editor Claiborne (a native of Indianola, Mississippi) has included very little from his native turf. A cake or two, a couple of pies, spoonbread and buttermilk biscuits (but hardly any cornbread), a few meat and vegetable recipes, and that's about it. The aim is "making the American palate more sophisticated." Collards and fatback don't fit.

Official Cookbook of the 1982 World's Fair, compiled and edited by Phila Hach (privately published at Clarksville, Tennessee, 1981). A popular Tennessee restaurant owner and cook included here, in her fifth cookbook, about six hundred Southern, Appalachian, and international recipes in conjunction with the 1982 World's Fair in Knoxville.

Pearl's Kitchen, by Pearl Bailey (Harcourt Brace Jovanovich, New York, 1973). A breezy and entertaining narrative of the famous entertainer's growing-up years in her mother's kitchen in Philadelphia. The roots, though buried deep, are unmistakably Southern.

Soul Food Cookbook, compiled by the editors of *Tuesday* magazine (Bantam Books, New York, 1969). Soul food made a big splash in the North and West in the late 1960s, adding yet another dimension to the diverse foods emanating from the South. Like Cajun, Creole, coastal, and mountain foods, the soul food of black Americans is part and parcel of the historic diet of Southerners, black and white. Here are ham hock and peas, meat loaf, fried salt pork, stuffed peppers, fried chicken, sweet potatoes, cornbread, pecan pie, pralines, and many other familiar items. *Mahalia Jackson Cooks Soul* (Aurora Publishers, Inc., Nashville, Tenn., 1970) is another of the books of this period.

The Taste of America, by John L. Hess and Karen Hess (Grossman Publishers, New York, 1977). Firing first at historian Daniel Boorstin and continuing the cannonade at such lofty food figures as James Beard, Craig Claiborne, M. F. K. Fisher, and Julia Child, the Hesses carry out an all-fronts attack on a legion of food writers, packagers, processors, and palate killers who they say have Americanized our food into a tasteless puree. Not specifically Southern, but pertinent.

The Thirteen Colonies Cookbook, by Mary Donovan, Amy Hatrak, Frances Mills, and Elizabeth Shull (Praeger Publishers, New York, 1975). The Southern colonies (Georgia, the Carolinas, Virginia, Maryland) get their share of the space in this interesting blend of history and food. Spoonbread, sweet potato pie, red rice, and corn pudding are among the recipes.

Vibration Cooking, by Vertamae Grosvenor (Doubleday & Co., Garden City, N.Y., 1970). Subtitled *The Travel Notes of a Geechee Girl,* this is a breezy, colloquial, entertaining book, a wonderful combination of stories and recipes from the portable kitchen of a woman whose soul food odyssey reaches from Allendale County, South Carolina, to Harlem and Africa and many other places.

ROSTER OF RESTAURANTS

In the course of our travels to gather information for *Southern Food,* we visited 335 restaurants in eleven states. Of those, a total of 225 are mentioned in this narrative. They are listed below in alphabetical order by state, and page numbers indicate the places at which each one is most prominently mentioned. At about a dozen of these restaurants, we were unable for various reasons to order and sample the fare, but we did interview owners, managers, servers, and/or patrons.

Also mentioned in the text (but not listed below) are approximately 50 restaurants that were not on our 1984–85 itinerary. Some are now closed, others were visited by us before this project began, and the rest—about a dozen—are high on our list of places to visit in the future.

ALABAMA

Archibald's, Northport, pages 151–2
Bob Sykes, Bessemer, page 152
The Bright Star, Bessemer, pages 95–6
Cromwell's Bar-B-Que, Phenix City, page 151
David Gibson's Bar-B-Q #2, Huntsville, pages 152–3
Dreamland Drive-Inn, Tuscaloosa, pages 151–2
The Elite Cafe, Montgomery, page 95
John's Restaurant, Birmingham, page 95
Old Plantation Bar-B-Q, Birmingham, page 152
Twix 'n' Tween, Centerville, page 74
The Waysider, Tuscaloosa, page 63
Walt's Seafood, Opelika, page 137
Wintzell's Oyster House, Mobile, pages 135–6
Wolf Bay Lodge, Miflin, pages 136–7

ARKANSAS

B.J.'s Restaurant, Benton, page 60
Bryce's Cafeteria, Texarkana, pages 81–2
Catfish 'N, Dardanelle, page 144
Club Cafe, Hot Springs, pages 74–5
Couch's Bar-B-Q, Jonesboro, page 154
Dixie Pig, Blytheville, page 154
Earl's Hot Biscuits Restaurant, West Memphis, pages 74–5
Family Pie Shop, DeValls Bluff, page 169
Jones Cafe, Noble Lake, pages 62–3, 74
Lindsey's Barbecue, North Little Rock, page 154
McClard's Barbecue, Hot Springs, page 153
Mexico Chiquito, North Little Rock, page 169
Murry's Cafe, DeValls Bluff, page 146
Sam-Ann's, Hollis, page 102
Sims Barbecue, Little Rock, page 154
Stubby's Bar-B-Q, Hot Springs, page 153

FLORIDA

Allen's Cafe, Auburndale, page 97
The Coffee Cup, Pensacola, pages 59–60
Columbia Restaurant, Tampa, page 96
Flora & Ella's Restaurant, LaBelle, pages 97–8
Hopkins Boarding House, Pensacola, pages 86–7
Latam, Tampa, page 96
Mama Cole's, Panama City, page 75
Mama Lo's, Gainesville, pages 75–6
Maxine's, Pahokee, page 59
The Oaks Motel and Restaurant, Panacea, page 137

VIRGINIA

CHAIN RESTAURANTS

INDEX OF RECIPES

All of the recipes included in the Eating Out section are listed below in the order of their appearance (which, for ease of locating, is also in alphabetical order). Page numbers are given following each entry.

INDEX